MEASUREMENT IN ECONOMICS

A HANDBOOK

MEASUREMENT IN ECONOMICS

A HANDBOOK

Edited by

Marcel Boumans

University of Amsterdam, The Netherlands

Emerald

United Kingdom – North America – Japan –
India – Malaysia – China

Emerald Group Publishing Limited
Howard House, Wagon Lane, Bingley BD16 1WA, UK

First edition 2007

Published by Emerald Group Publishing Limited in 2008

First published by Elsevier in 2007

Reprints and permission service
Contact: books@emeraldinsight.com

British Library Cataloguing in Publication Data
A catalogue record for this book is available from the British Library

ISBN: 978-0-1237-0489-4

Printed and bound in Great Britain by
CPI Antony Rowe, Chippenham and Eastbourne

Awarded in recognition of Emerald's production department's adherence to quality systems and processes when preparing scholarly journals for print

Preface

This volume owes its existence to a brave initiative of J. Scott Bentley, Executive Editor of Elsevier Inc. Based upon my article 'Economics, Strategies in Social Sciences' in the *Encyclopedia of Social Measurement* (Elsevier 2004), Bentley expressed in August 2004 his interest in publishing a handbook on measurement in economics, and asked me whether I would be interested to serve as the editor-in-chief. I did not need much time to think about this challenging invitation. The Amsterdam Research Group in History and Methodology of Economics had just concluded a project on Measurement in Economics, directed by Mary Morgan. Morgan had successfully linked this Amsterdam project to a project 'Measurement in Physics and Economics', at the Centre for Philosophy of Natural and Social Science of the London School of Economics and Political Science, which ran from 1996 to 2001, and was co-directed by Nancy Cartwright, Hasok Chang, and Carl Hoefer. Another event that had an important influence on the ultimate structure of this book was the 10th IMEKO TC7 International Symposium on Advances of Measurement Science, held in St. Petersburg, Russia, June 30–July 2, 2004. There, a number of different perspectives on measurement employed in sciences other than engineering were examined. For that reason, Joel Michell was invited to give his account on measurement in psychology, Luca Mari to discuss the logical and philosophical aspects of measurement in measurement science, and I was invited to give my account on measurement in economics. Together with Ludwik Finkelstein and Roman Z. Morawski, this multi-disciplinary exchange was very fruitful for developing the framework that has shaped this volume.

A volume on Measurement in Economics with contributions from all the people I had met when developing my own ideas about Measurement Outside the Laboratory would be a perfect way to conclude this research project. In fact, this volume is a very nice representation of the achievements of the many people that were involved. From the beginning we attached importance to the aim of having contributions from a broad range of backgrounds. We welcomed contributions from practitioners as well as scholars, from various disciplines ranging from economics, econometrics, history of science, metrology, and philosophy of science, with the expectation that an intensive exchange among these different backgrounds would in the end provide a deeper understanding of measurement in economics. Thanks to all contributors I do think we attained this goal.

An important step towards the completion of this volume was an Author Review Workshop that took place in April 2006, in Amsterdam, through the generous financial support of Netherlands Organisation for Scientific Research (NWO), Tinbergen Institute and Elsevier. At this workshop, the contributors presented their work to each other, which, together with the subsequent profound discussions, improved the coherence of the volume considerably.

There are many scholars who made a significant contribution to the project but whose work is not represented in the volume: Bert M. Balk, Hasok Chang, Francesco Guala, Michael Heidelberger, Kevin D. Hoover, Harro Maas, and Peter Rodenburg.

I would also thank the Elsevier's anonymous referees who helped me improve the structure of the volume and the editors at Elsevier: J. Scott Bentley (Executive Editor), Kristi Anderson (Editorial Coordinator), Valerie Teng-Broug (Publishing Editor), Mark Newson and Shamus O'Reilly (Development Editors), and Betsy Lightfoot (Production Editor), and Tomas Martišius of VTEX who saw the book through production.

Marcel Boumans
May 2007, Amsterdam

List of Contributors

Numbers in parentheses indicate the pages where the authors' contributions can be found.

Roger E. Backhouse (135) University of Birmingham and London School of Economics, UK. E-mail: R.E.Backhouse@bham.ac.uk.

Marcel Boumans (3, 231) Department of Economics, University of Amsterdam, Roetersstraat 11, Amsterdam 1018 WB, The Netherlands. E-mail: m.j.boumans@uva.nl.

Hsiang-Ke Chao (271) Department of Economics, National Tsing Hua University, 101, Section 2, Kuang Fu Road, Hsinchu 300, Taiwan. E-mail: hkchao@mx.nthu.edu.tw.

Frank A.G. den Butter (189) Vrije Universiteit, Department of Economics, De Boelelaan 1105, NL-1081 HV Amsterdam, The Netherlands. E-mail: fbutter@feweb.vu.nl.

Dennis Fixler (413) Bureau of Economic Analysis, 1441 L Street NW, Washington, DC 20230, USA. E-mail: dennis.fixler@bea.gov.

Christopher L. Gilbert (251) Dipartimento di Economia, Università degli Studi di Trento, Italy. E-mail: cgilbert@economia.unitn.it.

Glenn W. Harrison (79) Department of Economics, College of Business Administration, University of Central Florida, Orlando FL 32816-1400, USA. E-mail: gharrison@research.bus.ucf.edu.

Eric Johnson (79) Department of Economics, Kent State University, Kent, Ohio 44242, USA. E-mail: ejohnson@bsa3.kent.edu.

Alessandra Luati (377) Dip. Scienze Statistiche, University of Bologna, Italy. E-mail: luati@stat.unibo.it.

Jan R. Magnus (295) Department of Econometrics and Operations Research, Tilburg University, The Netherlands. E-mail: magnus@uvt.nl.

Luca Mari (41) Università Cattaneo – Liuc – Italy. E-mail: lmari@liuc.it.

Thomas Mayer (321) University of California, Davis, CA 94708, USA. E-mail: tommayer@lmi.net.

Melayne M. McInnes (79) Department of Economics, Moore School of Business University of South Carolina, USA. E-mail: mcinnes@moore.sc.edu.

Joel Michell (19) School of Psychology, University of Sydney, Sydney NSW 2006, Australia. E-mail: joelm@psych.usyd.edu.au.

Peter G. Moffatt (357) School of Economics, University of East Anglia, Norwich NR4 7TJ, United Kingdom. E-mail: p.moffatt@uea.ac.uk.

Mary S. Morgan (105) London School of Economics, London, UK and University of Amsterdam, The Netherlands. E-mail: m.morgan@lse.ac.uk.

Marshall B. Reinsdorf (153) US Bureau of Economic Analysis, USA. E-mail: Marshall.Reinsdorf@bea.gov.

E. Elisabet Rutström (79) Department of Economics, College of Business Administration, University of Central Florida, USA. E-mail: erutstrom@bus.ucf.edu.

Theodore M. Porter (343) Department of History, UCLA, Los Angeles, CA, USA. E-mail: tporter@history.ucla.edu.

Tommaso Proietti (377) S.E.F. e ME. Q., University of Rome "Tor Vergata", Italy. E-mail: Tommaso.proietti@uniroma2.it.

Duo Qin (251) Department of Economics, Queen Mary, University of London, UK. E-mail: d.qin@qmul.ac.uk.

Contents

Preface v

List of Contributors vii

Part I: General 1

Chapter 1. Introduction 3
Marcel Boumans

Chapter 2. Representational Theory of Measurement 19
Joel Michell

Chapter 3. Measurability 41
Luca Mari

Chapter 4. Measurement With Experimental Controls 79
Glenn W. Harrison, Eric Johnson, Melayne M. McInnes and E. Elisabet Rutström

Chapter 5. An Analytical History of Measuring Practices: The Case of Velocities of Money 105
Mary S. Morgan

Part II: Representation in Economics 133

Chapter 6. Representation in Economics 135
Roger E. Backhouse

Chapter 7. Axiomatic Price Index Theory 153
Marshall B. Reinsdorf

Chapter 8. National Accounts and Indicators 189
Frank A.G. den Butter

Chapter 9. Invariance and Calibration 231
Marcel Boumans

Part III: Representation in Econometrics 249

Chapter 10. Representation in Econometrics: A Historical Perspective 251
Christopher L. Gilbert and Duo Qin

Chapter 11. Structure 271
Hsiang-Ke Chao

Chapter 12. Local Sensitivity in Econometrics 295
Jan R. Magnus

Chapter 13. The Empirical Significance of Econometric Models 321
Thomas Mayer

Part IV: Precision 341

Chapter 14. Precision 343
Theodore M. Porter

Chapter 15. Optimal Experimental Design in Models of Decision and Choice 357
Peter G. Moffatt

Chapter 16. Least Squares Regression: Graduation and Filters 377
Tommaso Proietti and Alessandra Luati

Chapter 17. Timeliness and Accuracy 413
Dennis Fixler

Author Index 429

Subject Index 439

PART I

General

CHAPTER 1

Introduction

Marcel Boumans

Department of Economics, University of Amsterdam, Amsterdam, The Netherlands
E-mail address: m.j.boumans@uva.nl

Abstract

Measurement in Economics: a Handbook aims to serve as a source, reference, and teaching supplement for quantitative empirical economics, inside and outside the laboratory. Covering an extensive range of fields in economics: econometrics, actuarial science, experimental economics, and economic forecasting, it is the first book that takes measurement in economics as its central focus. It shows how different and sometimes distinct fields share the same kind of measurement problems and so how the treatment of these problems in one field can function as a guidance in other fields. This volume provides comprehensive and up-to-date surveys of recent developments in economic measurement, written at a level intended for professional use by economists, econometricians, statisticians and social scientists.

The organization of this Handbook follows the framework that is given in this introductory chapter. It consists of four major parts: General, Representation in Economics, Representation in Econometrics, and Precision.

1.1. Introduction

Measurement in economics is the assignment of numerals to a property of objects or events – 'measurand' – according to a rule with the aim of generating reliable information about these objects or events. The central measurement problem is the design of rules so that the information is as reliable as possible. To arrive at reliable numbers for events or objects, the rules have to meet specific requirements. The nature of these requirements depends on the nature of the event or object to be measured and on the circumstances in which the measurements will be made.

Measurement in economics is not a unified field of research, but fragmented in various separate fields with their own methodology and history, for instance econometrics, index theory, and national accounts. This volume will discuss these various fields of studies, which have developed their own specific requirements for measurement, often independently of each other. Despite this fragmentation it appears that these separate fields share similar problems and have developed similar methods of solution to these problems. This volume is a first attempt to bring these approaches together within one framework to facilitate exchange of methods and strategies.

To make comparisons of these – at first sight, quite different – strategies possible and transparent, the scope of the strategies is strongly simplified to a common aim of finding a 'true' value of a system variable, denoted by x.[1] The reliability of measurement results can so be characterized by three features: 'invariance', 'accuracy' and 'precision'. 'Invariance' refers to the stability of the relationship between measurand, measuring system and environment. 'Accuracy' is defined as the "closeness of the agreement between the result of a measurement and a true value of the measurand" (VIM, 1993, p. 24), and 'precision' is defined as "closeness of agreement between quantity values obtained by replicate measurements of a quantity, under specified conditions" (VIM, 2004, p. 23). The difference between invariance, accuracy and precision can be illustrated by an analogy of measurement with rifle shooting, where the bull's eye represents the true value x. A group of shots is precise when the shots lie close together. A group of shots is accurate when it has its mean in the bull's eye. When during the shooting the target remains stable this is a matter of invariance.

To explore these three requirements and to show how different strategies deal with them, a more formal, though simplified, framework will be developed. For all strategies, it is assumed that x is not directly measurable. In general, the value of x is inferred from a set of available observations y_i $(i = 1, \ldots, n)$, which inevitably involve noise ε_i:

$$y_i = F(x) + \varepsilon_i. \tag{1.1}$$

This equation will be referred to as the observation equation.

To clarify the requirement of invariance, and of accuracy and precision when control is possible, it is useful to rewrite Eq. (1.1) as a relationship between the observations y, the system variable x, and background conditions B:

$$y = f(x, B) = f(x, 0) + \varepsilon. \tag{1.2}$$

The observed quantity y can only provide information about the system variable, x, when this variable does influence the behavior of y. In general, however, it will be the case that not only x will influence y, but also there will be many other influences, B, too. To express more explicitly how x and other possible

[1] 'True value' is an idealized concept, and is unknowable. Even according to the Classical Approach, as expressed in VIM (1993), it is admitted that 'true values are by nature indeterminate' (p. 16). In current evaluations of measurement results this term is avoided. The in metrology influential *Guide to the Expression of Uncertainty in Measurement* (GUM, 1993) recommends to express the quality of measurement results in terms of 'uncertainty', see section Precision below and Mari in this volume.

factors (B) influence the behavior of the observed quantities, the relationship is transformed into the following equation:

$$\Delta y = \Delta f(x, B) = \frac{\partial f}{\partial x}\Delta x + \frac{\partial f}{\partial B}\Delta B \tag{1.3}$$

where $\partial f/\partial x$ and $\partial f/\partial B$ denote how much y will change proportionally due to changes in x and B, respectively.

To achieve reliable measurement results, the following problems have to be dealt with:

1. Invariance problem: $\partial f/\partial x$ is the element of Eq. (1.3) that expresses the relation between the observed quantity y and the measurand x. This element should be, as much as possible, invariant – that is to say, it has to remain stable or unchanged for, and to be independent of, two kinds of changes: variations over a wide range of the system variable, Δx, and variations over a wide range of background conditions, ΔB.
2. Noise reduction: Taking care that the observations are as informative as possible, or in other words, are as accurate and precise as possible, we have to reduce the influences of the other factors B. In a laboratory, where we can control the environment, this can be achieved by imposing *ceteris paribus* conditions: $\Delta B = 0$. For example, by designing experiments as optimally as possible (discussed by Moffatt in Chapter 15) one can gain precision.
3. Outside the laboratory, where we cannot control the environment, accuracy and precision have to be obtained by modeling in a specific way. To measure x, a model, denoted by M, has to be specified, for which the observations y_i function as input and $\hat{x}$, the estimation of x, functions as output:

$$\hat{x} = M[y_i; \alpha] \tag{1.4}$$

where α denotes the parameters of the model. The term 'model' is used here in a very general sense; it includes econometric models, filters, and index numbers (see also Chapter 6 in which Backhouse discusses other representations than those usually understood to be useful as models in economics).

Substitution of the observation equation (1.1) into model M (Eq. (1.4)) shows what should be modeled (assuming that M is a linear operator):

$$\hat{x} = M\big[f(x) + \varepsilon_i; \alpha\big] = M_x[x; \alpha] + M_\varepsilon[\varepsilon; \alpha]. \tag{1.5}$$

A necessary condition for $\hat{x}$ to be a measurement of x is that model M must be a representation of the observation equation (1.1), in the sense that it must specify how the observations are related to the measurand. Therefore we first need a representation of the measurand, M_x. This specification should be completed with a specification of the error term, that is, a representation of the environment of the measurand, M_ε. As a result, accuracy and precision will be dealt with in different ways. To see this, we split the measurement error $\hat{\varepsilon}$ in two parts:

$$\hat{\varepsilon} = \hat{x} - x = M_\varepsilon[\varepsilon, \alpha] + \big(M_x[x, \alpha] - x\big). \tag{1.6}$$

To explore how this measurement error is dealt with, it may be helpful to compare this with the 'mean-squared error' of an estimator as defined in statistics:

$$E\big[\hat{\varepsilon}^2\big] = E\big[(\hat{x} - x)^2\big] = \operatorname{Var}\hat{\varepsilon} + (x - E\hat{x})^2. \tag{1.7}$$

The first term of the right-hand side of Eq. (1.7) is a measure of precision and the second term is called the bias of the estimator (see also Proietti and Luati's Section 5.1 in this volume). Comparing expression (1.6) with expression (1.7), one can see that the error term $M_\varepsilon[\varepsilon, \alpha]$ is reduced, as much as possible, by reducing the spread of the errors, that is by aiming at precision. The second error term $(M_x[x, \alpha] - x)$ is reduced by finding an as accurate as possible representation of x.

This splitting of the error term into two and the strategies developed to deal with each part explains the partitioning of this volume. After a General Part in which general and introductory issues with respect to measurement in economics are discussed, there will be two parts in which the problem of obtaining accurate representations in economics and in econometrics are looked at in turn. The division between economics and econometrics is made because of the differences between strategies for obtaining accuracy developed in the two disciplines. While there is an obviously stronger influence from economic theory in economics, one can see that econometrics is more deeply influenced by statistical theories. The last part of this volume deals with the first error term, namely Precision.

1.2. General

The dominant measurement theory of today is the Representational Theory of Measurement. The core of this theory is that measurement is a process of assigning numbers to attributes or characteristics of entities or events in such a way that the relevant qualitative empirical relations among these attributes or characteristics are represented by these numbers as well as by important properties of the number system.

This characterization of contemporary measurement theory is heavily influenced by the formalist, representationalist approach presented in Krantz et al. (1971, 1989, 1990). This formalist approach defines measurement set-theoretically as: Given a set of empirical relations $R = \{R_1, \ldots, R_m\}$ on a set of extra-mathematical entities X and a set of numerical relations $P = \{P_1, \ldots, P_m\}$ on the set of numbers N, a function ϕ from X into N takes each R_i into P_i, $i = 1, \ldots, m$, provided that the elements $x, y, \ldots$ in X stand in relation R_i if and only if the corresponding numbers $\phi(x), \phi(y), \ldots$ stand in relation P_i. In other words, measurement is conceived of as establishing homomorphisms from empirical relational structures $\langle X, R \rangle$ into numerical relational structures $\langle N, P \rangle$ (Finkelstein, 1975). Typically for this formalist approach is the requirement of axioms characterizing the empirical relational structure. Then a 'representation theorem' asserts that "if a given relational structure satisfies certain axioms, then a homomorphism into a certain numerical relational structure can be constructed" (Krantz et al., 1971, p. 9).

In Chapter 2, Michell gives the historical background from which this approach arose. The development of the Representational Theory of Measurement can be best understood in respect of developments in the philosophy of science in the 20th century, in particular Patrick Suppes own specific view on theories, the so-called Semantic View.[2] According to the logical positivist (or empiricist) account of theories, also referred to as the Syntactic View or Received View, the proper characterization of a scientific theory consists of an axiomatization in first-order logic. The axioms are formulations of laws that specify relationships between theoretical terms. The language of the theory is divided into two parts, the observation terms that describe observable objects or processes and theoretical terms whose meaning is given in terms of their observational consequences. Any theoretical term for which there are no corresponding observational consequences is considered meaningless. The theoretical terms are identified with their observational counterparts by means of correspondence rules, rules that specify admissible experimental procedures for applying theories to phenomena.

A difficulty with this method is that one can usually specify more that one procedure or operation for attributing meaning to a theoretical term. Moreover, in some cases the meanings cannot be fully captured by correspondence rules; hence the rules are considered only partial interpretations for these terms. The Semantic View solution to these problems is to provide a semantics for a theory by specifying a model for the theory, that is, an interpretation on which all the axioms of the theory are true. To characterize a theory, instead of formalizing the theory in first-order logic, one defines the intended class of models for a particular theory. This view still requires axiomatization, but the difference is that it is the models (rather than correspondence rules) that provide the interpretation for the axioms (or theory). In short, a theory is in the Semantic View a family of a finite number of axioms. A model is an interpretation of the undefined terms of a theory that renders all the axioms of the theory simultaneously true.

Both the Semantic View and its related Representational Theory of Measurement made one believe that modeling and measurement are only possible in those fields that allow for axiomatization. At the same time, however, in various fields in economics all kinds of numerical representations, sometimes also called models, were developed with the aim of measurement without any onset

[2] See also Chao in this volume. For surveys of model accounts, see Morgan (1998) and Morrison and Morgan (1999).

of axiomatization.[3] Particularly, the practice of modeling in econometrics was an answer to the question of how to find laws outside the laboratory (Morgan, 1990). Schlimm (2005) distinguishes between relation-rich and object-rich domains. He observes that relation-rich domains, that are domains with few objects and a rich relational structure, do not lend themselves to axiomatization, but for object-rich domains, domains with many elements but with only few relevant relations between them, axiomatization seems to be most appropriate. Some structures simply do not lend themselves to axiomatization while this doesn't mean that modeling and measurement are impossible.

Michell (Chapter 2) shows that the development of the Representational Theory of Measurement was in particular a response to doubts about the possibilities of measurement in psychology, which were induced by the above epistemological discussions. Independent of these discussions, a science of measurement, called metrology, arose. Contributions to this field come mainly from engineers and deal with measurement in relation to instrumentation. Key concepts of this engineering approach to measurement are explicated by Mari (Chapter 3). According to this approach a formal characterization of measurement is not complete, and therefore should be completed with a description of the structure of the measurement process. A measurement process is a mutual measurand-related interaction of three components: the object or event under measurement, a measuring system and an environment. This approach emphasizes that measurement as a homomorphic evaluation results from an experimental comparison to a reference. In other words to characterize measurement the Representational Theory of Measurement is not sufficient and should be completed with information about the measuring system and environment, usually obtained by calibration. The result of this approach is a shift from a truth-based view, which only reports directly about the state of the measurand, to a model-based view, where a model includes the available relevant knowledge on the measurand, the measuring system and the environment, see also Boumans in this volume.

To explore the various possible strategies to achieve accuracy and precision, one should notice that there is a whole spectrum over which we have to discuss this issue of reliability. At one end of this spectrum we are in the position of full control of the measuring system and environment – the ideal laboratory experiment – and at the opposite end, where we lack any possibility of control, accuracy is obtained by careful modeling the measurand, measuring system and environment.[4]

An ideal laboratory experiment assumes full control of background conditions and full control of the 'stressor', x. Full control of background conditions is usually understood as arranging a 'sterile', 'clean' or 'pristine' environment: $\Delta B = 0$ (*ceteris paribus* conditions) or $B = 0$ (*ceteris absentibus* conditions),

[3] See for examples Morgan's history of the measurement of the velocity of money in Chapter 5, Backhouse's chapter on Representation in Economics, and den Butter's chapter on national accounts and indicators.

[4] See Boumans and Morgan (2001) for a detailed discussion of this spectrum.

cf. Eq. (1.3). In such noiseless environment, we attempt to obtain knowledge about the relationship between x and y (whether it is invariant and significant) by varying systematically the stressor x:

$$\frac{\partial f}{\partial x} = \frac{\Delta y}{\Delta x}. \tag{1.8}$$

At the opposite end of this spectrum of experiments are the so-called 'natural experiments', where one has no control at all, and one is fully dependent on observations only passively obtained:

$$\Delta y = \frac{\partial f}{\partial x}\Delta x + \frac{\partial f}{\partial z_1}\Delta z_1 + \frac{\partial f}{\partial z_2}\Delta z_2 + \frac{\partial f}{\partial z_3}\Delta z_3 + \cdots \tag{1.9}$$

where the z_i's represent all kinds of known, inexactly known and even unknown influencing factors.

To discuss these latter kinds of experiment and to chart the kind of knowledge gained from them, it is helpful to use a distinction between 'potential influences' and 'factual influences', introduced by Haavelmo in his important 1944 paper 'The probability approach in econometrics'. A factor z has potential influence when $\partial f/\partial z$ is significantly[5] different from zero. Factor z has factual influence when $\partial f/\partial z \cdot \Delta z$ is significantly different from zero. In practice, most of all possible factors will have no or only negligible potential influence: $\partial f/\partial z_i \approx 0$, for $i > n$. So change of y is determined by a finite number (n) of non-negligible potential influencing factors which are not all known yet:

$$\Delta y = \frac{\partial f}{\partial x}\Delta x + \frac{\partial f}{\partial z_1}\Delta z_1 + \frac{\partial f}{\partial z_2}\Delta z_2 + \cdots + \frac{\partial f}{\partial z_n}\Delta z_n. \tag{1.10}$$

To find out which factors have potential influence, when one can only passively observe the economic system, we depend on their revealed factual influence. Whether they display factual influence ($\partial f/\partial z \cdot \Delta z$), however, depends not only on their potential influence ($\partial f/\partial z$) but also on whether they have varied sufficiently for the data set at hand (Δz). When a factor hasn't varied enough ($\Delta z \approx 0$), it will not reveal its potential influence. This is the so-called problem of passive observation. This problem is tackled by taking as many as possible different data sets into account, or by modeling as many as possible factors as suggested by theory.

Generally, to obtain empirical knowledge about which factor has potential influence without being able to control, econometric techniques (e.g. regression analysis) are applied to find information about their variations:

$$\Delta z_j = g_x \Delta x + g_y \Delta y + g_1 \Delta z_1 + \cdots + g_n \Delta z_n \quad (j = 1, \ldots, n). \tag{1.11}$$

---

[5] Whenever this term is used in this chapter, it refers to passing a statistical test of significance. Which statistical test is applied depends on the case under consideration.

On the spectrum of experiments, 'field experiments' are considered to cover the broad range between laboratory experiments and natural experiments: "Field experiments provide a meeting ground between these two broad approaches to empirical economic science" (Harrison and List, 2004, p. 1009). It is an experiment in the field: outside the laboratory, however not in the wild, but on a piece of cultivated land. So, similar to natural experiments, changes of y are determined by a finite number of non-negligible influencing factors which are not all known. But now we have control of some of the influencing factors:

$$\Delta y = \frac{\partial f}{\partial x}\Delta x + \frac{\partial f}{\partial c_1}\Delta c_1 + \cdots + \frac{\partial f}{\partial c_m}\Delta c_m + \frac{\partial f}{\partial z_1}\Delta z_1 + \cdots + \frac{\partial f}{\partial z_k}\Delta z_k \tag{1.12}$$

where beside the stressor x, the c_i's indicate the influencing factors which are also controlled by the experimenter. The experimenter intervenes by varying these control factors in a specific way, according to certain instructions or tasks, $\Delta c_i = I_i$, where I_i represents a specific institutional rule assumed to exits in the real world or a rule which is correlated with naturally occurring behavior. Knowledge about these rules is achieved by other experiments or econometric studies. Harrison et al. (Chapter 4) investigate how knowledge about one of these experimental controls might influence the measurement results. This knowledge depends on previous experiments or is based on theoretical assumptions. Misspecification of these controls may lead to inaccurate measurement results.

Each economic measuring instrument can be understood as involving three elements, namely, of principle, of technique and of judgment. A particular strategy constrains the choices and the combinations of the three elements, and these elements in turn shape the way individual measuring instruments are constructed and so the measurements that are made (see also Morgan, 2001). Morgan (Chapter 5) provides examples of different measurement strategies; these different strategies all have the common aim to measure the 'velocity of money'. Interestingly she observes in her history of the measurement of the velocity of money a trajectory that may be a general feature of the history of economic measurement: a trajectory of measuring some economic quantity by direct means (measurement of observables), to indirect measurement (measurement of unobservables) to model-based measurement (measurement of idealized entities).[6] The latter kind of measurement involves a model that mediates between theory and observations and which defines the measurand.

---

[6] A similar study has been carried out by Peter Rodenburg (2006), which compares different strategies of measuring unemployment.

1.3. Representation in Economics

Finding an accurate representation of an economic phenomenon is a complex process; representations are not simply derived from theory. Much background knowledge is involved. Backhouse (Chapter 6) distinguish five different types of knowledge that are involved with modeling: statistics, history and experience, metaphysical assumptions, empirical representations and theoretical representations. Other studies of practices of model building in empirical economics and econometrics (Morgan, 1988; Boumans, 1999) show that models have to meet implicit criteria of adequacy, such as satisfying theoretical, mathematical and statistical requirements, and be useful for policy. So in order to be adequate, models have to integrate enough items to satisfy such criteria. These items include theoretical notions, policy views, mathematical concepts and techniques, analogies and metaphors, empirical facts and data.

As we have seen above, in the Representational theory of Measurement, representations of economic phenomena should be homomorphic to an empirical relational structure. To be considered homomorphic to an empirical structure, models have to meet specific criteria. In economics there are two different approaches: an axiomatic and an empirical approach. The axiomatic approach is supported by the formal representational approach of Krantz et al. (1971). This axiomatic approach has been most influential where (behavioral) economics and (cognitive) psychology overlap, namely fields where decision, choice and game theory flourish. Key example is von Neumann and Morgenstern's (1956) *Theory of Games and Economic Behavior*. Beside this often-referred application, the axiomatic approach was also successful in index theory. Reinsdorf (Chapter 7) shows that in axiomatic price index theory, axioms specify mathematical properties that are essential or desirable for a price index formula. One of the main problems of axiomatic index theory is the impossibility of simultaneously satisfying *all* axioms. In practice, however, a universal applicable solution to this problem is not necessary. The specifics of the problem at hand, including the purpose of the index and the characteristics of the data, determine the relative merits of the possible attributes of the index formula.

National accounts, discussed by den Butter (Chapter 8), are examples of representations that fulfill criteria of the empirical approach. This doesn't mean that these representations only fulfill empirical criteria, see Chapter 6. Other criteria are: (1) consistency, (2) flexibility, (3) invariance, and (4) standardization. Consistency of the data in the accounting scheme is crucial for its use in economic analysis and policy. This consistency is guaranteed by using definitional equations and identities, which relate the various statistical sources to each other. A consistent structure of interdependent definitions enables a uniform analysis and comparison of various economic phenomena. Between these criteria there are inevitably tensions, also between the requirements of accuracy and timeliness of the estimates, which are extensively discussed by Fixler (Chapter 17).

Another important criterion for achieving reliable measurement results is that the empirical relational structure is an invariant structure, see also Chao's discussion of structure (Chapter 11). In the axiomatic approach this invariance is secured by the axioms. In the empirical approach, however, invariance has to be verified empirically, which is hard outside the laboratory. Boumans (Chapter 9) distinguishes two strategies to achieve this kind of invariance. One is by building models that not only represent the measurand but also the measuring system and its environment, see also the metrological criteria discussed by Mari (Chapter 3). The other strategy is calibration: the model parameters should represent stable facts about the system under investigation.

1.4. Representation in Econometrics

Generally, the system under investigation is a dynamic system, $x_{t+1} = Fx_t$, where t denotes time, and other lower case letters are vectors. Often it is assumed that the system is a linear system, so a matrix, $A = (\alpha_{ij})$, can represent it: $x_{t+1} = Ax_t$. As a result, accuracy, that is the reduction of $(M_x[x, A] - x)$, cf. Eq. (1.6), is obtained by finding an as accurate as possible representation – structure – of the economic system: $\|Ax_t - Fx_t\| \approx 0$, where $\|\cdot\|$ is a statistically defined norm.

Standard textbook accounts of econometrics, assume that these structures are provided by economic theory. It is then the task of econometrics to put empirical flesh and blood on these theoretical structures. This involves three steps of specification. First, the theory must be specified in explicit functional – often linear – form. Second, the econometrician should decide on the appropriate data definitions and assemble the relevant data series for the variables that enter the model. The third step is to bridge theory and data by means of statistical methods. The bridge consists of various sets of statistics, which cast light on the validity of the theoretical model that has been specified. The most important set consists of the numerical estimates of the model parameters, A. Further statistics enable assessment of the precision with which these parameters have been estimated. There are still further statistics and diagnostic test that help in assessing the performance of the model and in deciding whether to proceed sequentially by modifying the specification in certain directions and testing out the new variant of the model against data.

Gilbert and Qin (Chapter 10) take this standard account as starting point to survey the developments and concerns that resulted from it. One of these concerns was that more sophisticated estimation methods did not automatically lead to an improvement of the validity of models. Another concern was whether the three-steps way – specification, identification and estimation – was the golden route to invariant structures. These concerns established doubt about whether theory was such a good guide with respect to model specification. Gilbert and Qin observe a shift in methodology: from a competitive strategy to an adaptive strategy. This distinction is from Hoover (1995), who labels the standard econometric textbook account as a competitive strategy: "theory proposes, estimation and testing disposes" (p. 29). The adaptive strategy begins with an idealized and simplified product of the core theory. "It sees how much mileage it can get out of that model. Only then does it add any complicating and more realistic feature" (p. 29). Mayer (Chapter 13) discusses a similar 'disagreement' between these two strategies.

Structure is one of the key concepts of measurement theory, including econometrics. Surveying the literature on this subject, Chao (Chapter 11) observes that structure has two connotations: one is that it refers to a system of invariant relations and the other to a deeper layer of reality than its observed surface. They are, however, connected. The latter connotation implies that we can only assess that layer indirectly, we need theory to connect surface with the layers below. The connection between the observations y_i and the measurand x, denoted by F in Eq. (1.1) is made by theory. As we have seen, in order to let the observations y be informative about x, this relation must be stable across a broad range of variations in both x and background conditions.

Magnus (Chapter 12) shows that one should not only use diagnostic tests to assess the validity of the model specification, but also sensitivity analysis. Morgan (Chapter 5) raises the issue that observations and measurements are always taken from a certain position – observation post. This implies that the view of the nearest environment of this position is quite sharp, detailed and complete, but the view of the environment farther away becomes more vague, less detailed, incomplete, and even incorrect. The question is whether this is a problem. Is it necessary for reliable measurement results to have an accurate representation of the whole measuring system plus environment? No, not necessarily, as Magnus argues, but a reliability report should include an account of the scope of the measurement: a sensitivity report.

Models contain two sets of parameters: focus parameters (α) and nuisance parameters (θ). The unrestricted estimator $\hat{\alpha}(\tilde{\theta})$ is based on the full model, denoted by $\tilde{\theta}$, and the restricted estimator $\hat{\alpha}(0)$ is estimated under the restriction $\theta = 0$. Magnus shows that the first order approximation of their difference can be expressed as:

$$\hat{\alpha}(\tilde{\theta}) - \hat{\alpha}(0) \approx \left.\frac{\partial \hat{\alpha}(\theta)}{\partial \theta}\right|_{\theta=0} \tilde{\theta} \equiv S\tilde{\theta} \tag{1.13}$$

where S denotes the sensitivity coefficient. In metrology, see Chapter 3, a similar sensitivity coefficient is being used where it expresses the propagation of uncertainty. In econometrics the choice between both estimators is based on whether $\tilde{\theta}$ is large or small (t- or F-statistics). However, it might be that the model parameter is insensitive to this misspecification, that is, when S is small.

The empirical assessment of representations in economics and econometrics is not simply a matter of statistical significance. As Mayer (Chapter 13) shows, for achieving accuracy one has to deal with the reliability of data, the theory-data correspondence, and the possibilities of testing outside the laboratory. Besides these problems, which appears to be central to a lot of measurement problems, as witnessed by the several chapters in this volume, Mayer discusses the problem of data mining: the repetition of operations until the desired results are obtained. The problem is to validate the accuracy of these results. An important way to assess the results' accuracy is to see whether these results can be reproduced. Reproduction is the opposite of data mining. In VIM (1993) reproducibility is defined as: "closeness of the agreement between the results of measurement of the same measurand carried out under changed conditions of measurement" (p. 24). The changed conditions might include: principle of measurement, method of measurement, observer, measuring instrument, reference standard, location, conditions of use, and time. A similar strategy in non-laboratory sciences is 'triangulation', see also Chapter 6. The term 'triangulation' is often used to indicate that more than one method is used in a study with a view to multiple checking results. The idea is that we can be more confident about the accuracy of a result if different methods lead to the same result (see e.g. Jick, 1979).

1.5. Precision

Precision is not defined in the 1993 edition of the *International Vocabulary of Basic and General Terms in Metrology*, only closely related concepts as 'reproducibility', see above, and 'repeatability', that is "closeness of the agreement between the results of successive measurements of the same measurand carried out under the same conditions of measurement" (VIM, 1993, p. 24). However, comparing this 1993 version of the Vocabulary with the draft of the 3rd edition (VIM, 2004), one will find a remarkable change of vocabulary. 'Accuracy' has disappeared, and 'precision' is now introduced into the Vocabulary, see Introduction above.

The reason for the disappearance of accuracy in the proposed 3rd edition is a change of approach in metrology, from a Classical (Error) Approach to an Uncertainty Approach; see also Mari in this volume for a more elaborate discussion of this change of approach. The Classical Approach took it for granted that a measurand can ultimately be described by a single true value, but that instruments and measurements do not yield this value due to additive 'errors', systematic and random. In the new Uncertainty Approach, the notion of error no longer plays a role, there is finally only one uncertainty of measurement. It characterizes the extent to which the unknown value of the measurand is known after measurement (VIM, 2004, p. 2). So, instead of evaluating measurement results in terms of errors, it is now preferred to discuss measurement in terms of uncertainty. Uncertainty is defined as the "parameter that characterizes the dispersion of the quantity values that are being attributed to a measurand, based on information used" (VIM, 2004, p. 16).

For the evaluation of uncertainty two types are distinguished. Type A evaluation: by a statistical analysis of quantity values obtained by measurements under repeatability conditions; and Type B evaluation: by means other than a statistical analysis of quantity values obtained by measurement. Precision is often equated with Type A uncertainty. Discussions about how to achieve accuracy are rather similar to the discussions about assessing Type B uncertainty.

Precision or Type A uncertainty can be objectively established for any chosen metric, they are considered to be quantitative concepts. However, accuracy or Type B uncertainty depends much more on qualitative knowledge of the measurand itself and cannot be assessed in the same objective way. That objective standards are not enough for evaluating measurement results is admitted in the *Guide to the Expression of Uncertainty in Measurement*:

> Although this *Guide* provides a framework for assessing uncertainty, it cannot substitute for critical thinking, intellectual honesty, and professional skill. The evaluation of uncertainty is neither a routine task nor a purely mathematical one; it depends on detailed knowledge of the nature of the measurand and of the measurement. The quality and utility of the uncertainty quoted for the result of a measurement therefore ultimately depend on the understanding, critical analysis, and integrity of those who contribute to the assignment of its value (GUM, 1993, p. 8).

This is a remarkable position, which reinforces a longer existing assumed connection between 'intellectual honesty and professional skill' and 'precision'. As Porter (Chapter 14) shows, precision creates trust: trust in the results, in the measuring instrument, in the scientist, or who or what else is considered to be responsible for the results. Because we do not know the true value – otherwise we wouldn't need to measure – accuracy is a highly problematic criterion to validate the trustworthiness of a result. Precision, on the other hand, is a feature that can be 'objectively' evaluated without knowing truth. Results that lie close together gives trust in the measuring system, laboratory, or model. A drawback, however, is that we indeed are not informed about the results' accuracy. That means that the aim for Precision does not preserve us from arriving at spurious results, artifacts.

Precision is a quality of the measuring instrument, measurement system or experiment. Optimal precision can be achieved by optimal design. Moffatt (Chapter 15) unravels strategies for optimal experimental design.

A very old and simple method to reduce ('filter') noise is taking the arithmetic mean of the observations (cf. observation equation (1.1)):

$$\frac{1}{n}\sum_{i=1}^{n} y_i = F(x) + \frac{1}{n}\sum_{i=1}^{n} \varepsilon_i = F(x). \tag{1.14}$$

This method is, of course, based on the assumption that the errors are symmetrically distributed around zero. Nonetheless, it is an early example of a model of the errors, M_ε.

Taking the arithmetic mean to reduce noise also implicitly assumes that the observations are taken under the same conditions, the assumption of repeatability. Repeatability, however, is a quality of a laboratory. Economic observations are rarely made under these conditions. For example, times series are sequential observations without any assurance that the background conditions haven't changed. To discuss noise reduction outside the laboratory and at the same time to keep the discussion as simple as possible, we now take as observation equation:

$$y_t = x_t + \varepsilon_t. \tag{1.15}$$

A broadly applied model taking account of changing conditions in economics – indices, barometers, filters and graduation – is a weighted average of the observations:

$$\hat{x}_t = \sum_{s=-n}^{n} \alpha_s y_{t+s} = \sum_{s=-n}^{n} \alpha_s x_{t+s} + \sum_{s=-n}^{n} \alpha_s \varepsilon_{t+s}. \tag{1.16}$$

To turn the observations y_t into a measurement result $\hat{x}_t$, one has to decide on the values of the weighting system α_s. In other words, the weights have to be chosen such that they represent the dynamics of the phenomenon (cf. Eq. (1.5)):

$$M_x[x; \alpha] = \sum_{s=-n}^{n} \alpha_s x_{t+s} \tag{1.17}$$

and at the same time reduce the error term:

$$M_\varepsilon[\varepsilon; \alpha] = \sum_{s=-n}^{n} \alpha_s \varepsilon_{t+s}. \tag{1.18}$$

Usually a least squares method is used to reduce this latter error term. Proietti and Luati (Chapter 16) give an overview and comparison of the various models that are used for this purpose.

Fixler (Chapter 17) discusses the tension between the requirement of precision and of timeliness. Equation (1.4) seems to assume immediate availability of all needed data for a reliable estimate. In practice, however, this is often not the case. Collecting data takes time; economic estimates are produce in vintages, with later vintages incorporating data that were not previously available. This affects the precision of early estimates.

1.6. Conclusions

Measurement theories have been mainly developed from the laboratory. In economics, however, many if not most measurement practices are performed outside the laboratory: econometrics, national accounts, index numbers, etc. Taking these theories as starting point, this volume aims at extending them to include these outdoor measurement practices. The partitioning of this volume is based on an expression (1.6) that represents the key problems of measurement:

$$\hat{\varepsilon} = \hat{x} - x = M_\varepsilon[\varepsilon, \alpha] + \big(M_x[x, \alpha] - x\big).$$

Measurement is the achievement of providing reliable numerical facts about an economic phenomenon. The reliability of the measurement depends on two qualities: accuracy (minimizing second term) and precision (minimizing first term). The aim for accuracy requires modeling of the phenomenon, that is, developing accurate representations of the measurand. The achievement of this aim for accuracy is neither a mechanical task nor a purely formalistic statistical one; beside detailed knowledge and understanding of the measurand, it also requires consistency and standardization.

Knowledge of the measurand includes knowledge about its invariant characteristics, which is hard to find outside the laboratory. It involves a lot of theory and expertise: "it is not a problem of pure logic, but a problem of actually *knowing something* about real phenomena, and of making realistic assumptions about them" (Haavelmo, 1944, p. 29).

Models have two faces. On the one hand they represent the phenomena, on the other hand they operationalize the measurand, that is, models define the measurand in observable terms. Accuracy concerns the ability of the model to measure what we want it to measure. As den Butter (Chapter 8) and Fixler (Chapter 17) both argue, it is therefore essential that the model definitions are consistent with accounting schemes, or any other classification scheme. Accuracy, however, not only depends on consistency with these schemes, but also on institutional acceptance of these schemes: standardization (see also Chapter 14 and Porter, 1994).

Precision has more to do with knowledge of the measuring system than knowledge of the measurand. The improvement of precision can be achieved by improvement of technique, model or experiment. Because it can be evaluated by formal procedures it is sometimes confused with rigor, as has been shown in a work with a nicely provoking title 'Truth versus Precision in Economics' (Mayer, 1993). Precision is one of the two legs on which the reliability of the measurement stands; not only do we need expertise of the economic phenomena but also expertise of the measuring systems being applied. This volume gives a survey of current expertise in economics of both fields.

Acknowledgements

I am grateful to Harro Maas, Luca Mari, Thomas Mayer and Marshall Reinsdorf for their valuable comments.

References

Boumans, M. (1999). Built-in justification. In: Morgan, M.S., Morrison, M. (Eds.), *Models as Mediators*. Cambridge Univ. Press, Cambridge, pp. 66–96.

Boumans, M., Morgan, M.S. (2001). Ceteris paribus conditions: Materiality and the application of economic theories. *Journal of Economic Methodology* **8** (1), 11–26.

Finkelstein, L. (1975). Fundamental concepts of measurement: definitions and scales. *Measurement and Control* **8**, 105–110.

GUM (1993). *Guide to the Expression of Uncertainty in Measurement*. ISO, Geneva.

Haavelmo, T. (1944). The probability approach in econometrics. *Econometrica (Supplement)* **12**.

Harrison, G.W., List, J.A. (2004). Field experiments. *Journal of Economic Literature* **42**, 1009–1055.

Hoover, K.D. (1995). Facts and artifacts: Calibration and the empirical assessment of real-business-cycle models. *Oxford Economic Papers* **47**, 24–44.

Jick, T.D. (1979). Mixing qualitative and quantitative methods: Triangulation in action. *Administrative Science Quarterly* **24** (4), 602–611.

Krantz, D.H., Luce, R.D., Suppes, P., Tversky, A. (1971, 1989, 1990). *Foundations of Measurement, 3 volumes*. Academic Press, New York and London.

Mayer, T. (1993). *Truth versus Precision in Economics*. Edward Elgar, Aldershot.

Morgan, M.S. (1988). Finding a satisfactory empirical model. In: de Marchi, N. (Ed.), *The Popperian Legacy in Economics*. Cambridge Univ. Press, Cambridge, pp. 199–211.

Morgan, M.S. (1990). *The History of Econometric Ideas*. Cambridge Univ. Press, Cambridge.

Morgan, M.S. (1998). Models. In: Davis, J.B., Hands, D.W., Mäki, U. (Eds.), *The Handbook of Economic Methodology*. Edward Elgar, Cheltenham, UK and Northampton, USA, pp. 316–321.

Morgan, M.S. (2001). Making measuring instruments. In: Klein, J.L., Morgan, M.S. (Eds.), *The Age of Economic Measurement*. Duke Univ. Press, Durham and London, pp.235–251.

Morrison, M., Morgan, M.S. (1999). Introduction. In: Morgan, M.S., Morrison, M. (Eds.), *Models as Mediators*. Cambridge Univ. Press, Cambridge, pp. 1–9.

Porter, T.M. (1994). Making things quantitative. *Science in Context* **7** (3), 389–408.

Rodenburg, P. (2006). *The Construction of Instruments for Measuring Unemployment*. Thela Thesis, Tinbergen Institute Research Series. Amsterdam.

Schlimm, D. (2005). Towards a more comprehensive understanding of analogies. Working paper.

VIM (1993). *International Vocabulary of Basic and General Terms in Metrology*, second ed. ISO, Geneva.

VIM (2004). *International Vocabulary of Basic and General Terms in Metrology*. Revision of the 1993 edition (Draft Guide 99999). ISO, Geneva.

Von Neumann, J., Morgenstern, O. (1956). *Theory of Games and Economic Behavior*. Princeton Univ. Press, Princeton. (Original edition 1944.)

CHAPTER 2

Representational Theory of Measurement

Joel Michell

School of Psychology, University of Sydney, Sydney, NSW 2006, Australia
E-mail address: joelm@psych.usyd.edu.au

The representational theory of measurement expands on the idea that measurement is '... the correlation, with numbers, of entities which are not numbers' (Russell, 1903, p. 158). It came with the twentieth century as part of Bertrand Russell's logicism. Then N.R. Campbell tailored it to quantitative physics and used it to denounce measurement in psychology, which, in his turn, the psychologist, S.S. Stevens, defended, blending the representational idea with positivism and operationalism. The theory was completely reconstructed by Patrick Suppes and Duncan Luce, who argued that measurement in physics could be understood as homomorphisms from empirical systems to numerical systems and considered the possibility that measurement in psychology could be likewise construed. Despite its shortcomings, their version provides an invaluable resource for those who believe that claims to be able to measure always require evidential support.

2.1. Introduction

Measurement has characterised science since antiquity, and many have written on its philosophy, but during the twentieth century an unprecedented number of attempts were made to uncover its foundations. Such attempts generally emphasised one or more of three aspects: first, the processes of measuring (e.g., Dingle, 1950); second, the structure of measured attributes (e.g., Hölder, 1901 and Mundy, 1987); and, third, evidence that putative measurement processes actually *measure*. It is to this third aspect that the representational theory of measurement is most directly relevant.

Initially, the representational theory emerged from the philosophy of mathematics, specifically, from changes in the understanding of what numbers are. In the nineteenth century, increasingly abstract and formal theories made it difficult to think of numbers as features of the real-world situations to which processes of measurement apply. This raised the issue of why, if they are not real-world features, they appear indispensable in measurement? One proposal was that while numbers are not, themselves, features of the real world, they might serve to *represent* or model such features. On its own, this idea could never have energised the flourishing sub-discipline that representational measurement theory became. The energy derived from a controversy over psychological measurement. Critics used the representational idea to question the credentials of psychological procedures and, in response, psychologists attempted to find space for these procedures within the representational paradigm.

Attempts at measurement in psychology were a product of *scientism*, the view that new sciences should mimic the methods of physics. Opposing scientism was *empiricism*, the view that knowledge claims are sanctioned only by observational evidence, which implies that measurement requires such evidence of measurability. During the hegemony of logical empiricism, with its doctrine that mathematics is devoid of empirical content, this empiricism found its clearest voice in the version of the representational theory of measurement that was developed in the second half of the twentieth century.

2.2. The Traditional Theory and the Emergence of the Representational Idea

The first to define measurement in representational terms (Michell, 1993) was Bertrand Russell, who wrote that,

> [m]easurement of magnitudes is, in its most general sense, any method by which a unique and reciprocal correspondence is established between all or some of the magnitudes of a kind and all or some of the numbers, integral, rational, or real, as the case may be (1993, p. 176).

By 'magnitudes' he meant the class of measurable attributes, that is, *properties* (such as mass or length) and *relations* (such as distance or velocity). He proposed this definition after abandoning the traditional, *ratio* concept of number and embracing *logicism*, the idea that the truths and concepts of mathematics derive exclusively from logic. The traditional concept was a development of the Euclidean idea (see Book V of Euclid's *Elements* (Heath, 1908)) that measurement concerns ratios of magnitudes, where a *ratio* is understood as the relation of 'relative greatness' (De Morgan, 1836, p. 29) between them. This concept in turn sustained the ratio concept of number, expressed by Isaac Newton as the idea that *number* is 'the abstracted Ratio of any Quantity to another Quantity of the same kind, which we take for Unity' (1967, p. 2). The concept of *ratio* tied those of *magnitude* and *number* together and meant that measurement was defined as the estimation of the ratio between any magnitude and unit.

Otto Hölder (1901) grounded this understanding by defining the concept of an *unbounded, continuous quantitative attribute* (i.e., the kind figuring in the laws of physics) and proving that ratios of its magnitudes possess the structure of the positive real numbers. Let any attribute of this sort be symbolised as Q; specific magnitudes of Q be designated by $a, b, c, \dots$, etc.; let it be the case that for any three magnitudes, a, b, and c, of Q, $a + b = c$ if and only if c is entirely composed of discrete parts a and b; then Hölder's axioms of quantity are as follows:

1. Given any magnitudes, a and b, of Q, one and only one of the following is true:
   (i) a is identical to b (i.e., $a = b$ and $b = a$);
   (ii) a is greater than b and b is less than a (i.e., $a > b$ and $b < a$); or
   (iii) b is greater than a and a is less than b (i.e., $b > a$ and $a < b$).
2. For every magnitude, a, of Q, there exists a b in Q such that $b < a$.
3. For every pair of magnitudes, a and b, in Q, there exists a magnitude, c, in Q such that $a + b = c$.
4. For every pair of magnitudes, a and b, in Q, $a + b > a$ and $a + b > b$.
5. For every pair of magnitudes, a and b, in Q, if $a < b$, then there exists magnitudes, c and d, in Q such that $a + c = b$ and $d + a = b$.
6. For every triple of magnitudes, a, b, and c, in Q, $(a + b) + c = a + (b + c)$.
7. For every pair of classes, ϕ and ψ, of magnitudes of Q, such that
   (i) each magnitude of Q belongs to one and only one of ϕ and ψ;
   (ii) neither ϕ nor ψ is empty; and
   (iii) every magnitude in ϕ is less than each magnitude in ψ,
   there exists a magnitude x in Q such that for every other magnitude, x', in Q, if $x' < x$, then $x' \in \phi$ and if $x' > x$, then $x' \in \psi$ (depending on the particular case, x may belong to either class).

For example, for length, these axioms mean: 1, that any two lengths are the same or different and if different, one is less than the other; 2, that there is no least length; 3, that the additive composition of any two lengths exists; 4, that all lengths are positive; 5, that the difference between any pair of lengths constitutes another; 6, that the additive composition of lengths is associative; and 7, that the ordered series of lengths is continuous (i.e., any set of lengths having an upper bound (i.e., a length not less than any in the set) has a least upper bound (i.e., a length not greater than any of the upper bounds)). This is what it is for length to be an *unbounded continuous quantity*.

Because magnitudes were understood as attributes of things, the traditional view entailed that numbers are intrinsic features of the situations to which the procedures of measurement apply. Consequently, the conceptual thread binding *number*, *magnitude* and *ratio* would seem to unravel if either, (i) magnitudes were denied a structure capable of sustaining ratios or, (ii) if numbers were not thought of as located spatiotemporally. It was the first of these that applied in Russell's case. He stipulated that magnitudes are merely ordered (one magnitude always being greater or less than another of the same kind) and denied that they are additive (i.e., denied that one magnitude is ever a sum of others) and thus, by implication, denied that magnitudes stand in relations of ratio, thereby severing the thread sustaining the traditional theory. His reasons were idiosyncratic (Michell, 1997) and not accepted by his fellow logicists, Gottlob Frege (1903) or A.N. Whitehead (see Whitehead and Russell, 1913), who treated logicism as compatible with the ratio theory of number. Nonetheless, Russell, for his own reasons, gave flesh to the representational idea, and it proved attractive.

2.3. Early Representational Theory and Criticism of Psychological Measurement

One of its first advocates was Campbell (1920 and 1928), who, applying it to a distinction of Hermann von Helmholtz (1887), produced the concepts of *fundamental* and *derived* measurement. He distinguished measured *quantities*, such as length, from measured *qualities*, as he called them, like density. Quantities, he claimed, are like numbers in possessing additive structure, which is only identifiable, he thought, via specification of a suitable concatenation procedure. For example, when a rigid straight rod is extended linearly by another adjoined end to end with it, the length of these concatenated rods stands in a relation to the lengths of the rods concatenated that has the form of numerical addition, in the sense that it conforms to *associative* ($a+[b+c]=[a+b]+c$) and *commutative* ($a+b=b+a$) laws, a *positivity* law ($a+b>a$), and *the Euclidean law* that equals plus equals gives equals (i.e., if $a=a'$ and $b=b'$, then $a+b=a'+b'$) (Campbell, 1928, p. 15). Evidence that these laws are true of lengths could be gained by observation. Therefore, thought Campbell, the hypothesis that any attribute is a quantity raises empirical issues and must be considered in relation to available evidence.

If, for any attribute, such laws obtain, then, said Campbell, numerals may be assigned to its specific magnitudes. Magnitudes are measured *fundamentally* by constructing a 'standard series' (1920, p. 280). This is a series of objects manifesting multiples of a unit. If u is a unit, then a standard series displays a set of nu, for $n=1,2,3,\ldots$, etc., for some humanly manageable values of n. If an object is compared appropriately to a standard series, a measure of its degree of the relevant quantity can be estimated and this estimate is taken to represent the additive relation between that degree and the unit. The sense in which measurements are thought to represent empirical relations is therefore clear.

Campbell recognised that not all magnitudes are fundamentally measurable. There is also *derived* measurement of qualities, which is achieved by discovering constants in laws relating attributes already measured. He believed that the discovery of such laws is a result of scientific research and must be sustained by relevant evidence. An example is density. For each different substance, the ratio of mass to volume is a specific constant, different say for gold as compared to silver. The numerical order of these constants is the same as the order of degrees of density ordered by other methods. Thus, said Campbell, these constants are *derived* measurements of density, but the sense in which they represent anything beyond mere order is not entirely clear from his exposition.

However, that the ratio of mass to volume is correlated with the kind of substance involved suggests that each different substance possesses a degree of a general property accounting for its associated constant ratio. Because the effect being accounted for (the constant) is quantitative, the property hypothesised to account for it (viz., density) must likewise be quantitative, otherwise the complexity of the property would not match the complexity of the effect. Although

Campbell did not reason like this and never explained how derived measurement instantiated the representational idea, it seems that it can.

When the British Association for the Advancement of Science established the Ferguson Committee to assess the status of psychophysical measurement, Campbell's empiricism confronted psychologists' scientism head-on: he insisted that their claims to measure intensities of sensations be justified via either fundamental or derived measurement. Instead of doing this, he argued, 'having found that individual sensations have an order, they assume that they are measurable' (Ferguson et al., 1940, p. 347), but 'measurement is possible only in virtue of facts that have to be proved and not assumed' (Ferguson et al., 1940, p. 342).

While the failure of psychologists to produce evidence for more than order in the attributes they aspired to measure was the basis for Campbell's critique, there is nothing in the representational idea *per se* that restricts measurement to fundamental and derived varieties. Campbell had simply tried to translate the traditional concept of measurement into representational terms and because the former concept is confined by the role it gives to the concept of ratio, representational theory is thereby needlessly narrowed. Morris Cohen and Ernest Nagel served the latter better when they wrote that numbers

> have at least three distinct uses: (1) as tags, or identification marks; (2) as signs to indicate the *position* of the degree of a quality in a *series* of degrees; and (3) as signs indicating the quantitative relations between qualities (Cohen and Nagel, 1934, p. 294).

Use (1) is not something that Russell or Campbell would have called measurement, but the representational idea does not exclude it. Use (2) is the assignment of numbers to an ordered series of degrees to represent a relation of *greater than*. For this, Cohen and Nagel required that the represented order relation be shown by observational methods to match the ordinal properties of the number series, such as transitivity and asymmetry. They called this use measurement of 'intensive qualities.' Use (3) covered fundamental and derived measurement and their treatment of these added little to Campbell's, but the popularity of their textbook meant that the representational idea was well broadcast.

However, inclusion of ordinal structures within representational theory only highlighted psychology's dilemma. If no more than ordinal structure is identified for psychological attributes, then the fact that psychological measurement does not match the physical ideal is displayed explicitly, a point laboured by critically minded psychologists (e.g., Johnson, 1936). By then, practices called 'psychological measurement' occupied an important place, especially attempts to measure intellectual abilities (Michell, 1999). Psychologists had devoted considerable energy to constructing numerical assignment procedures (such as intelligence tests), which they marketed as measurement instruments, but without any observational evidence that the relevant attributes possessed the sort of structure thought necessary for physical measurement.

A key concept within the representational paradigm, and one that future developments traded upon is the concept of *structure* (see Chao, 2007). The sorts of phenomena investigated in science do not consist of isolated properties or objects. Crucial to scientific investigation is the concept of *relation*. That a thing possesses a *property* is a matter involving it alone. For example, that Socrates is male is a situation involving, in and of itself, no one but Socrates. However, that a thing stands in a *relation* to something else involves not just that thing but the thing that the relation is to, as well. For example, that Socrates is shorter than Aristotle is a situation involving, in itself, both Socrates and Aristotle. To see structure in things is to see how they are related. A house, for example, is not a mere collection of bricks; it is the bricks in a definite spatial arrangement. That is, a house is a relational structure. More generally, *a structure is a class of things together with one or more relations holding between the things in the class*. For example, an ordered structure is a class of things together with a transitive and asymmetric relation holding between pairs of things within the class.

Such an understanding of the concept of structure gives a prominent place to the concept of relation, but this concept is not unproblematic. For example, in the relational situation of *a book's being upon a desk*, we know what it is for something to be a book and what it is for something to be a desk, but in what does the *uponness* consist? A relation is not a third *thing* present in the situation, so what is it? There is tradition within British empiricism of treating relations as 'having no other reality but what they have in the minds of men' (Locke, 1959, p. 499). Since all scientific laws deal with relations of one sort or another, this so-called 'empiricist' view has the unfortunate consequence of making science a subjective construction of the human mind rather than an attempt to identify the structure of independently existing systems (the realist view). Scientific realism is better served by interpretations, such as Armstrong's, which try to understand relations objectively as 'ways things are' (1987, p. 97) independently of human minds or practices. Nonetheless, the issue of the objective character of structure was the fulcrum upon which the next development of the representational theory turned.

The representational idea seemed to lack the flexibility psychologists wanted: the represented attribute was understood to possess a definite, intrinsic structure (e.g., ordinal or additive) and it was this that was represented numerically. Different possible structures could be explored theoretically and, in principle, there is no end of these. However, considering these only threw the onus onto psychologists to find evidence that the relevant attributes possessed structures of the sort contemplated, thereby raising questions, not securing existing claims. Russell, Campbell, and Cohen and Nagel saw the structure of the represented attribute in an *empirical realist* way, in that natural structures were supposed to exist independently of scientists and while scientists could possibly discover the character of such structures, they had no room to postulate the existence of desirable structures in the absence of relevant evidence. Russell thought that the 'method of "postulating" what we want has many advantages; they are the same as the advantages of theft over honest toil' (1919, p. 71). In contrast, Stevens (1946 and 1951) adapted representational theory to the demands of scientism by allowing the structure of attributes to be thought of as constituted via operations used to make numerical assignments.

2.4. Representational Theory Operationalised

Stevens had developed the *sone* scale to measure sensations of loudness (Stevens and Davis, 1938), an achievement the Ferguson Committee disputed (Ferguson et al., 1940). However, he saw Percy Bridgman's (1927) operationalism and Rudolf Carnap's (1937) logical positivism as philosophical tools for deflecting Campbell's objections. Carnap thought that logic and mathematics are systems of symbols, each with a syntax (i.e., rules for constructing formulas and deductions) consisting of conventions, not empirical truths. Stevens agreed, holding that 'mathematics is a human invention, like language, or like chess, and men not only play the game, they also make the rules' (1951, p. 2). How come then that successful applications of arithmetic are so ubiquitous? He responded that

> the rules for much of mathematics (but by no means all of it) have been deliberately rigged to make the game isomorphic with common worldly experience, so that ten beans put with ten other beans to make a pile is mirrored in the symbolics: $10 + 10 = 20$ (1951, p. 2).

However, if these rules are *isomorphic* with 'common worldly experience', then they are not mere conventions lacking empirical content. But the mood of the times was with him; the 'received view' being that arithmetic reduces to set theory and the concept of the empty set. From this point of view, the number system is a formal, axiomatic system devoid of empirical content, and numbers, being sets, are thought of as 'abstract entities.' Any remaining vestiges of the traditional theory were thereby exorcised.

Cohen and Nagel (1934) had noted that not all numerical representations are the same. Stevens made this explicit, distinguishing four kinds of scales, *nominal*, *ordinal*, *interval*, and *ratio*. He believed that kind of scale could be determined by asking how the numerical assignments could be altered without altering the scale's purpose. Numerical assignments are always arbitrary to some extent, but the degree of arbitrariness varies. Stevens held that in any case where scale values might be altered, the purpose of making numerical assignments on a *ratio scale* is unaltered (or invariant) only if all scale values are multiplied by a (positive) constant (a *positive similarity transformation*); the purpose of making numerical assignments on an *interval scale* is unaltered only if all scale values are multiplied by a (positive) constant and a (positive or negative) constant is added (a *positive linear transformation*); the purpose of making numerical assignments on an *ordinal scale* is unaltered if all scale values are altered by an order-preserving function (an *increasing monotonic transformation*); and the purpose of making numerical assignments on a *nominal scale* is unaltered if all scale values are altered by a one-to-one substitution (a *one-to-one transformation*). These distinctions have merit, but scientism has no use for ordinal scales. Stevens needed a licence to claim measurement on interval or ratio scales.

He believed (Stevens, 1939) he found it in Bridgman's tenet that the meaning of a concept is defined by the operations used to measure it, which implies that the meaning of quantitative concepts, such as length, derives from measurement operations and not from the attribute's intrinsic character. Thus, he concluded that for a ratio scale, operations used to 'determine' equal ratios 'define' equal ratios. The procedures used to construct his sone scale involved instructing subjects to judge loudness ratios directly. Stevens took the resulting scale 'at its face value' (1936, p. 407) as a ratio scale and, cocking his snoot at Russell's scruples announced that if this 'is thievery, it is certainly no petty larceny' (1951, p. 41), thereby deriding the issue of whether loudness intensities stand in ratios independently of the operations supposed to identify them.

This delivered the sort of conceptual pliability needed to claim measurement without having to interrogate established methods in the way that realist interpretations of representational theory required. It allowed psychologists to claim that they were measuring psychological attributes on scales like those used in physics (Michell, 2002). For the majority of procedures used in psychology there is no independent evidence that hypothesised attributes possess even ordinal structure, but the received wisdom since Stevens is that 'the vast majority of psychological tests measuring intelligence, ability, personality and motivation ... are interval scales' (Kline, 2000, p. 18).

2.5. The Logical Empiricist Version of Representational Theory

From an empirical realist point of view, if the only defence of psychological measurement is to allow scale structure to be operationally defined via numerical assignment procedures, then whatever its popularity, this manoeuvre is an admission of the correctness of Campbell's critique, for from the realist perspective, science attempts to investigate things as they are and not merely as reconstructed by our procedures. Inevitably some psychologists rejected operationalism and reshaped representational theory to see if a genuine, empirical defence of psychological measurement was possible (see Krantz et al. (1971), Suppes et al. (1989) and Luce et al. (1990)). However, like Stevens, they retained the logical positivist (now called 'logical empiricist') premise that number systems are man-made constructions of abstract entities devoid of empirical content.

According to this version of representationalism, establishing a measurement scale involves five steps:

1. An empirical system is specified as a relational structure, that is, as a non-empty set of empirical objects of some kind together with a finite number of empirical relations between them, where the issue of whether these objects stand in these relations is empirically decidable.
2. A set of, preferably, empirically testable axioms is stated characterising this empirical system.
3. A numerical system is identified such that a set of homomorphisms between the empirical system and this numerical system can be proved to exist. This is called a *representation theorem*.
4. A specification of how the elements of this set of homomorphisms relate to one another is given. This is called a *uniqueness theorem*.

5. If the weight of evidence supports the set of axioms, at least one of the homomorphisms between the empirical and numerical systems is selected as a scale of measurement for the relevant attribute.

The following examples illustrate these ideas, but hardly scratch the surface, given the range of possible empirical systems elaborated by proponents of this version. (See also Reinsdorf, 2007, for an example from economics.)

2.5.1. An empirical weak order

Consider a set, A, of rigid, straight rods of various lengths and the relation, *a spans b*, holding between any pair of rods whenever the length of a at least matches that of b (symbolised as $b \leqslant a$). For any pair of rods, whether this relation holds can be decided empirically by, say, laying them side-by-side. This set of rods and the spanning relation constitute an empirical system, $\mathbf{A} = \langle A, \leqslant \rangle$. Consider the following two axioms in relation to this system: for any rods, a, b, and c in A,

1. If $a \leqslant b$ and $b \leqslant c$, then $a \leqslant c$ (transitivity);
2. Either $a \leqslant b$ or $b \leqslant a$ (connexity).

A system having this character is a *weak order* and any weak order is homomorphic to a numerical structure, $\mathbf{N} = \langle N, \leqslant \rangle$ (where N is a subset of positive real numbers and $\leqslant$ is the familiar relation of one number being less than or equal to another). That is, it can be proved (Krantz et al., 1971) that a many-to-one, real-valued function, ϕ, exists such that for any rods, a and b, in A,

$$a \leqslant b \quad \text{if and only if} \quad \phi(a) \leqslant \phi(b).$$

That is, positive real numbers may be assigned to the rods where the magnitude of the numbers reflects the order relations between the rods' lengths. Furthermore, if ψ is any other function mapping $\mathbf{A}$ into $\mathbf{N}$, such that

$$a \leqslant b \quad \text{if and only if} \quad \psi(a) \leqslant \psi(b),$$

then ϕ and ψ are related by an increasing monotonic transformation. Given that axioms 1 and 2 above are true, ϕ is an ordinal scale of length.

It should be noted that the mapping from $\mathbf{A}$ to $\mathbf{N}$ is *partial* in the sense that it is into only a subsystem of the positive real numbers. $\mathbf{N}$ is a subsystem of the positive real numbers in two respects: first, N is typically only a proper subset of the positive real numbers; and, second, the numerical relation, $\leqslant$, is just one of the relations characterizing the complete system of positive real numbers. Clearly, then, representational theory does not preclude partial mappings. Indeed, the following examples are also of partial mappings because the empirical systems described lack the continuity of the real numbers (see, for example, Hölder's 7th axiom). Instead, they are merely Archimedean systems.

2.5.2. An empirical extensive system

Suppose that A, above, is augmented by including a ternary relation, Γ, which holds between any three rods, a, b, and c whenever $a * b \leqslant c$, where $a * b$ signifies the rod formed by concatenating rods a and b end to end linearly. Consider the following axioms for $\boldsymbol{A}' = \langle A, \leqslant, \Gamma \rangle$, for any a, b and c in A (Suppes and Zinnes, 1963):

1. If $a \leqslant b$ and $b \leqslant c$, then $a \leqslant c$;
2. $(a * b) * c \leqslant a * (b * c)$;
3. If $a \leqslant b$, then $a * c \leqslant c * b$;
4. If not $a \leqslant b$, then there is a c in A such that $a \leqslant b * c$ and $b * c \leqslant a$;
5. Not $a * b \leqslant a$;
6. If $a \leqslant b$, then there is a number n such that $b \leqslant na$ (where the notation na is defined recursively as follows: $1a = a$ and $na = (n-1)a * a$).

Such a system is an empirical extensive system. Axiom 1 is just transitivity; axiom 2 is that $*$ is associative; 3 is a combined monotonicity (if two rods are each concatenated with rods equal in length, any equality or inequality is preserved) and commutativity (order of concatenation is unimportant) condition; 4 is that concatenating some other rod with the shorter of any two can compensate for any difference between them; 5 is that all rods' lengths must be positive; and 6 is an Archimedean condition (any rod, no matter how short, extended by a finite number of replicas will span any other rod).

Suppes and Zinnes (1963) proved that a homomorphic mapping from any extensive structure, $\langle A, \leqslant, \Gamma \rangle$, into a subsystem of the positive real numbers, $\langle N, \leqslant, P \rangle$ exists, where P is a ternary relation holding between any three positive real numbers, x, y, and z, whenever $x + y \leqslant z$. Furthermore, they proved that any two such mappings are related by a positive similarity transformation. Given that these axioms are adjudged true, any such mapping is taken to be a ratio scale for length.

2.5.3. An empirical conjoint system

A conjoint system involves three attributes where increase in one is a function of increase in the other two, as for example, mass increases with increases in volume and/or density. Consider a set, B, of objects composed of various kinds of homogeneous solid stuff, which differ in volume, such as lumps of various minerals. Further, allow that if B contains a volume, x, of any such solid, say volume x of pure gold, then B contains volume x of each other different kind of stuff as well. Note that this does not require measurement of volume, only classification of sameness or difference in volume, which could be made via sameness or difference of volumes of liquid displaced when the solids are completely immersed. Hence, there exists a relation of equality of volume between some elements of B. Likewise, since sameness of density is correlated with sameness of stuff, there is also a relation of equality of density between some elements of B. This means that the equivalence class of volume and of density that it belongs to identifies each element of B. Let the set of volumes be V and the set of densities, D, then B may be thought of as the Cartesian product of D and V, that is, $B = D \times V$. Finally, one further relation on the elements of B is required: a weak order with respect to mass. This could be assessed using an equal-arm pan balance such that when volume x of stuff a is placed on the first pan and volume y of stuff b on the second, if the first pan does not drop, then the mass of x of a does not exceed that of y of b (symbolised as $\langle a, x\rangle \leqslant \langle b, y\rangle$). For convenience, let $\langle a, x\rangle = \langle b, y\rangle$ if and only if $\langle a, x\rangle \leqslant \langle b, y\rangle$ and $\langle b, y\rangle \leqslant \langle a, x\rangle$; $\langle a, x\rangle < \langle b, y\rangle$ if and only if $\langle a, x\rangle \leqslant \langle b, y\rangle$ and not $(\langle b, y\rangle \leqslant \langle a, x\rangle)$; $a < b$ if and only if for all x in V, $\langle a, x\rangle < \langle b, x\rangle$; and $x < y$ if and only if for all a in D, $\langle a, x\rangle < \langle a, y\rangle$. Consider the following axioms for $\boldsymbol{B} = \langle D \times V, \leqslant\rangle$ (Krantz et al., 1971, p. 257):

1. For any a, b, and c in D and x, y, and z in V, if $\langle a, y\rangle \leqslant \langle b, x\rangle$ and $\langle b, z\rangle \leqslant \langle c, y\rangle$, then $\langle a, z\rangle \leqslant \langle c, x\rangle$ (double cancellation).
2. Given any three of a and b in D and x and y in V, the fourth exists such that $\langle a, x\rangle = \langle b, y\rangle$ (solvability).
3. Every strictly bounded standard series of elements of D and of V is finite (Archimedean condition)

(where a *strictly bounded standard series* of elements of D is a series of equally spaced elements of D, $a_1, a_2, a_3, \ldots, a_n$ (for some natural number, n) (that is, for any x and y in V, where $x < y$, and any b in D, where $a_1 < b$, (i) $\langle a_{i+1}, x\rangle = \langle a_i, y\rangle$ (for all $i = 1, \ldots, (n-1)$) and (ii) $\langle a_{n-1}, x\rangle < \langle b, y\rangle \leqslant \langle a_n, x\rangle$); and a *strictly bounded series* of elements of V is analogously defined).

The relation, $\langle a, y\rangle \leqslant \langle b, x\rangle$, may be interpreted as saying that the shift from x to y in volume has at least as much effect upon mass as the shift from a to b in density. Looked at this way, axiom 1 says that if the shift from x to y in volume has at least as much effect upon mass as the shift from a to b in density and the shift from y to z in volume has at least as much effect upon mass as the shift from b to c, then (if these effects upon mass are additive) the shift from x to z must have at least as much of an impact upon mass as the shift from a to c. That is, it can be interpreted as a kind of additivity condition. Axiom 2 means that the effect upon mass of any difference in volume can always be matched by a difference in density, anywhere within the density attribute; and the effect upon mass of any density difference can be similarly matched by a difference in volume. That is, either degrees of both density and volume are equally finely spaced or both are order dense in the same sense as the rational numbers. Finally, axiom 3 says that the effect upon mass of a difference in volume, no matter how great, can always be spanned by the sum of the effects of a finite number of consecutive and equal density differences, no matter how small separately; and vice versa. That is, relative to their effects upon mass, differences between densities or between volumes are never infinitesimally small or infinitely large relative to one another.

Krantz et al. (1971) proved that if a conjoint structure satisfies these axioms then there exist functions, ϕ and ψ, into the positive real numbers, such that for any a and b in D and x and y in V,

$$\langle a, x\rangle \leqslant \langle b, y\rangle \quad \text{if and only if} \quad \phi(a) + \psi(x) \leqslant \phi(b) + \psi(y).$$

Furthermore, they proved that if λ and θ are any other functions satisfying this condition for a given conjoint structure, then λ and ϕ are related by a positive linear transformation, as are θ and ψ also. That is, θ and ψ are interval scales of density and volume. They are, in fact, logarithmic transformations of the scales normally used in physics because, of course, if $mass = density \times volume$ then $\log(mass) = \log(density) + \log(volume)$. So, equally, the above conjoint structure also admits of a multiplicative numerical representation, in accordance with conventional practice in physics.

These examples illustrate the fact that the concept of scale-type derives from the empirical system's intrinsic structure (Narens, 1981) and not, as Stevens thought, from the measurer's purposes in making numerical assignments. Recognising this has allowed for progress to be made with respect to two problems.

The first is the problem of 'meaningfulness' (Luce et al., 1990). This problem arises whenever the structure of the system represented falls short of the structure of the real number system itself. Then numerically valid inferences from assigned numbers may not correspond to logically valid deductions from empirical relations between objects in the system represented (Michell, 1986).

Following the lead of Stevens (1946) and Suppes and Zinnes (1963), Luce et al. (1990) and Narens (2002) have attempted to characterise the *meaningfulness* of conclusions derived from measurements in terms of invariance under admissible scale transformations. Non-invariant conclusions are generally held to be not meaningful. For example, consider the question of which of two arithmetic means of ordinal scale measures is the greater? The answer does not necessarily remain invariant under admissible changes of scale (in this case, any increasing monotonic transformation). Hence, such conclusions are said not to be meaningful relative to ordinal scale measures.

In so far as this issue has affected the practice of social scientists it relates to qualms about whether the measures used qualify as interval scales or are only ordinal, and, thus, to the meaningfulness of conclusions derived from parametric statistics (such as t and F tests) with ordinal scale measures. Since many social scientists believe that the existence of order in an attribute is a sign that the attribute is really quantitative, recent thinking on the issue of meaningfulness has considered the extent to which interval scale invariance may be captured by conclusions derived from ordinal scale measures (Davison and Sharma, 1988 and 1990). For example, even though the concept of an arithmetic mean has, itself, no analogue within a purely ordinal structure, calculation of means with ordinal data may still be informative if it is assumed that the attribute measured possesses an underlying, albeit presently unknown, interval scale structure.

The second problem in relation to which this new understanding of scale-type has facilitated progress is that of specifying the structural unity underlying each type of scale. This will be exemplified here only for the case of ratio scales. Quite different kinds of empirical systems are representable by ratio scales, for example, extensive and conjoint systems, and indefinitely many others. However, all such systems share an underlying structural unity, a point hinted at by the fact that proofs of the relevant representation theorems all employ the same result, known in the literature as *Hölder's theorem* (the proposition that any Archimedean ordered group is isomorphic to a positive subgroup of the real numbers). This theorem applies because when any empirical system admitting a ratio scale representation is repeatedly mapped (or translated) into itself in distinct but structure preserving ways, the resulting set of *translations* has the structure of an Archimedean ordered group (Luce, 1987). For example, take an extensive system, such as that described above. Suppose each rod in A is mapped into a rod twice as long. Such a translation preserves both the ordinal and the additive structure of the system, as does any other translation of A into A, where each rod is mapped into one r-times as long (where r is any positive real number). The full set of all such translations constitutes an Archimedean ordered group and because of this A is representable as a ratio scale. So without going beyond the empirical system, the structural feature common to all systems admitting ratio scale representations is specified. The significance of this is that it demonstrates the way in which ratio scalability is an intrinsic feature of the empirical system represented.

2.6. Implications of the Logical Empiricist Version of Representational Theory

Beginning with Ernest Adam's (1966) paper, the logical empiricist version has been subjected to numerous critiques. Many of these are based upon misunderstandings. For example, one common criticism concerns error. If data were collected using objects and relations of the kinds specified in any of the above examples, with the aim of testing the axioms involved, then as exact descriptions of data, the axioms would more than likely be false. However, this is not a problem for the representational theory because the axioms were never intended as exact descriptions of data. From Krantz et al. (1971) to Luce (2005), it has been repeatedly stressed that the axioms are intended as idealisations. That is, they are intended to describe the form that data *would have* in various situations, *were they completely free of error*. In this respect, as putative empirical laws, the axioms are no different to other laws in science. (On this issue see also Boumans, 2007.)

It also goes without saying that its proponents are not claiming that such axiom systems played a role in the historical development of physical measurement. In so far as physics is concerned, as Suppes (1954) said at the outset, such systems are mainly intended to display how 'to bridge the gap between qualitative observations ("This rod is longer than that one") ... and the quantitative assertions demanded in developed scientific theories ("The length of this rod is 5.6 cm")' (p. 246). Even if no physicist ever subscribed to the representational idea, the point of identifying axioms for empirical systems would not be lost. Representationalism is a philosophical theory about how numbers get involved in measurement and to have any plausibility, it must display a *possible* representational role for numbers in all instances of physical measurement. That the three volumes of the *Foundations of Measurement* do this is an outstanding triumph.

However, for the social sciences, its point is different. If, as its proponents maintain, this theory is the best available account of the role of numbers in measurement (i.e., of the *logic* of measurement), and if it does not cover 'measurement' in the social sciences, then the best available account of the logic of measurement provides no justification for regarding these practices as instances of measurement. While Luce (2005) thinks that some psychological practices come close to meeting the requirements of representational theory, most, and, significantly, psychometric testing, do not. As one psychometrician, reviewing the *Foundations of Measurement*, noted, 'It would be a good thing, in my opinion, if we could restrain our use of terms such as "measurement" ... in the context of fields such as mental testing' (Ramsay, 1991, p. 357). The argument leading to such a recommendation rests on the premise that the logic of measurement is representational, which in turn rests upon the claim that axiom systems, like those for extensive and conjoint systems, obtain for all attributes measured in physics. However, if no one in the history of physics has ever carried out the relevant sets of observations (e.g., checking the behaviour of rigid straight rods *vis à vis* the axioms of an extensive system), is it reasonable to dismiss the entire class of psychometric practices from the category of measurement on the grounds of what it is thought ideal observations *would* amount to? And is it not strange that an empirical tradition pushes a seemingly non-empirical argument so far?

However, commitment to empiricism does not preclude argument as a means of confirming or falsifying hypotheses. Generally, in science, hypotheses are confirmed or falsified in two ways. The first is the directly empirical method of evaluating hypotheses in the light of relevant observational data. The second is the less directly empirical method of judging hypotheses in the light of propositions already accepted as true. In the clearest cases, a hypothesis (or its contradictory) can be deduced (Philip Catton, 2004 provides some interesting examples). Logical empiricists have tended to put the emphasis on the first way, but as the present discussion shows, they rely upon the second also. So while no one in the history of physics may ever have made observations relating directly to the axiom systems for extensive or conjoint measurement, the relevant question is, *Are there any good reasons to believe that were such observations to be made, the data would support the axioms*?

And there are: viz., our theories of the attributes involved. Take the case of length. If we come to the above example of an empirical extensive system armed with a concept of length as an unbounded continuous quantity, in the spirit of Hölder's axioms, then, knowing what we do about rigid, straight rods and their behaviour in standard circumstances, we have no trouble inferring that the six axioms given above are true. Also, in part, it is because we hold this theory that we know that even if data failed to fit the axioms perfectly, the most plausible explanation would be error in the data, not falsity of the axioms. We accept the six axioms as true of the situation described and this is an inference from a theory of length already endorsed. Of course, in accord with the values of science, this theory is ultimately based upon observational evidence, but it is not based upon direct tests of these six axioms or of any others.

The theory of length as a quantitative attribute takes length to be a relational structure. However, the domain of the theory is not a set of objects, but a set of attributes, viz., the set of all possible lengths. As captured, say, in Hölder's axioms, this set is understood as ordered by a *greater than* relation, this order is thought of as continuous, and various lengths are taken to stand in additive relations to others. As such, this relational structure is better suited, conceptually, to account for measurement than the extensive structure proposed earlier, if only because no actual set of rigid, straight rods could ever instantiate all possible lengths. So, a more satisfactory version of the representational theory would be one that shifted its focus from systems of directly observable *objects* to systems of *attributes*, not all of which need be directly observable. Brent Mundy (1987 and 1994) and Chris Swoyer (1987) advocate this kind of shift, that is, replacing the logical empiricist version of the representational theory by a *realist version* ('realist' in the sense that it takes attributes to be real and makes them its centrepiece).

The fact that measurement of physical attributes occurs at all implies that there must be something about the character of the relevant attributes that makes it possible. While various kinds of relationships between objects may inform us about the structure of attributes, it is that structure itself, which should be central to measurement theory because in the final analysis, it is attributes that are measured. We might loosely say that we measure a rod, but in fact it is the rod's *length* or *weight* or *temperature*, etc. that we measure. If, in measurement, numbers represent, then it is attributes that they represent, not objects. (See also Mari's, 2007, treatment of 'measured properties'.) When the logical empiricist version is thought through, the realist version results.

With this shift, representational theory shifts towards the traditional theory, to which Russell at first opposed it, the major remaining difference being a thesis about numbers. The realist version of representational theory tries to retain the doctrine that numbers are abstract entities, 'existing', if at all, only outside space and time. The traditional theory accepts numbers as relations between magnitudes of unbounded continuous quantities and, so, as located wherever such magnitudes are found. To the quantitative scientist, this difference might seem irrelevant. Yet, if scientists use any philosophy it is *naturalism*, the view that in attempting to understand nature's ways of working, the realm of space and time is world enough. Combining naturalism with the view that the system of real numbers is defined by its structure (i.e., any system isomorphic to the real numbers is an instance of them), Hölder's result that the structure of ratios of magnitudes of unbounded, continuous quantities is isomorphic to the system of positive real numbers entails that such ratios instantiate real numbers (for a more detailed defence see Armstrong, 1997 and Michell, 1994).

There is another reason for moving from the realist version of representational theory to the traditional theory of measurement and this is that the former entails the latter. Simply because representational theory is premised upon the possibility of real-world systems being similar in structure to mathematical systems, it follows that there is no sharp divide between natural and mathematical structures. Recognition of this has occasionally surfaced: Cohen believed that mathematical systems 'apply to nature because they describe the invariant relations which are found in it' (1931, p. 204); Nagel wrote that 'if mathematics is applicable to the natural world, the formal properties of the symbolic operations of mathematics must also be predicable of many segments of the world' (1932, p. 314); and Narens and Luce noted that 'in many empirical situations considered in science ... there is a good deal of mathematical structure already present' (1990, p. 133); but none acknowledged that if a theory requires a this-worldly location for mathematical structures, then denying numbers a real-world existence is hardly being consistent. When representational measurement theory is worked-out consistently, the traditional theory follows.

This is not to deny that proponents of the representational theory have made contributions to measurement theory of fundamental importance. The logical empiricist version, with its emphasis upon characterising empirical systems via sets of testable axioms has advanced our understanding of possible forms of empirical evidence for the hypothesis that attributes are quantitative. Measurement always starts with the hypothesis that an attribute is quantitative. This hypothesis is always empirical in the sense that its truth is never logically necessary. Thus, from a scientific perspective, its truth must always be assessed relative to available evidence. To the extent that this evidence depends upon direct observation, the logical empiricist version has identified in detail, relevant, albeit idealised, possible data structures, such as the above extensive and conjoint systems.

However, as noted, direct, observational evidence is not the only possible kind. Sometimes hypotheses are tested relative to things already taken to be true. Thus, while the hypothesis that, for example, density is quantitative could be tested via conjoint measurement theory, this has never been done and centuries before the theory of conjoint measurement was proposed, density was already accepted as quantitative. Similarly, social scientists have long thought that they have good reason to believe that their attributes are quantitative. For example, psychologists typically reason (Michell, 2006) that if an attribute is ordered, then it must be quantitative, although its quantitative structure may be presently unknown. F.H. Bradley (1895) fleshed-out their argument as follows: if degrees of an attribute admit of order, whenever one degree is greater than another, the two must differ by some amount, with the greater degree being the sum of the lesser and the difference between them; hence, the attribute must possess additive structure and, so, be quantitative. Here is where the kinds of analyses performed by proponents of the logical empiricist version may play another important role. Analyses of *difference structures* from Hölder (1901) to Krantz et al. (1971) show that Bradley's reasoning is invalid. There is no logical necessity that differences between merely ordered degrees should be quantitative. Whether they are is always an empirical matter.

Consider the kind of system that Krantz et al. (1971, p. 151) call an *algebraic difference structure*. Suppose that C is an attribute, the degrees of which constitute a strict simple order (i.e., the order on the degrees is transitive, asymmetric and connected), and that the set of differences between degrees of C is weakly ordered, such that for any a, b, c, and d, degrees of C, $(a - b) \geqslant (c - d)$ means that the difference between a and b is no less than that between c and d. Krantz et al. (1971) give these axioms for this weak order on $C \times C$. For all a, b, c, d, a', b', and c' in C,

1. If $(a - b) \geqslant (c - d)$, then $(d - c) \geqslant (b - a)$.
2. If $(a - b) \geqslant (a' - b')$ and $(b - c) \geqslant (b' - c')$, then $(a - c) \geqslant (a' - c')$.
3. If $(a - b) \geqslant (c - d) \geqslant (a - a)$, then there exist d' and d'' in C, such that $(a - d') = (c - d) = (d'' - b)$.
4. Every strictly bounded standard series of elements of C is finite.

Krantz et al. (1971) prove that if the differences between degrees satisfy these conditions, then they are quantitative and Hölder (1901) long ago gave a similar proof. However, there is no necessity that axioms, such as 2 (which is analogous to the double cancellation condition for conjoint systems in being an additivity condition) must be true. If the differences between degrees do not behave as quantitative differences, then 2 will be false. These axioms display the psychometricians' fallacy by showing that qualitative increase is not necessarily the same as quantitative increase.

This is important whenever the attributes that scientists aspire to measure are experienced in the first instance only as ordered and, so, it calls into question applications of Michael Heidelberger's (1993 and 1994) 'correlative' theory of measurement (for a discussion of which see Boumans, 2007). According to this theory, one attribute, Y, may be measured via measurements of a second attribute, X, if measures of X reflect the order of degrees of attribute Y, by introducing a quantitative 'measurement formula' preserving this ordinal correlation. Heidelberger (1993) had in mind Fechner's (1960) proposal to measure the intensity of sensations via the logarithm of the magnitude of the physical stimulus eliciting the sensation involved, but it describes a pattern of practice employed in the social sciences generally, viz., that of employing numerical indices to measure ordinally associated attributes. The problem with this approach is that if attribute Y is only ever experienced as ordinal (as Fechner conceded is the case for sensation intensities), then any claim to measure Y in this way begs the question of whether Y is actually a quantitative attribute. If uncertainty over the issue of whether social and psychological attributes are really quantitative is to be resolved, then those marks capable of distinguishing quantitative from merely ordinal attributes in possible data sets need to be identified. To a significant extent, this is what proponents of the representational theory of measurement have achieved and were social scientists serious about measurement, they would attempt to employ this body of knowledge to test for quantitative structure.

2.7. Résumé

The logical empiricist doctrine that mathematics is merely a useful language, a system of symbols devoid of empirical content, is a tenacious view. Its ubiquity seems to explain the popularity of the representational theory of measurement. Yet this theory provides ammunition against that doctrine, for if the numerical representation of empirical phenomena is premised upon structural identities between empirical and numerical systems, then a structuralist interpretation of mathematics (viz., that mathematics is the science of structure, per se) is presumed. Furthermore, once it is accepted that the fundamental concept in quantitative science is the concept of a quantitative attribute, it follows that before measurement procedures are developed, quantitative attributes entail structures identical to the real number system. That is, quantity and number are part of the same package.

The representational theory of measurement could flourish only in an historical interlude between acceptance of non-empiricist views of mathematics and recognition of the central place of the concept of quantity in quantitative science. This is because it is based upon an inconsistent triad: first, there is the idea that mathematical structures, including numerical ones, are about abstract entities and not about the natural world; second, there is the idea that representation requires at least a partial identity of structure between the system represented and the system representing it; and third, there is the idea that measurement is the numerical representation of natural systems. The second and third ideas imply that natural systems instantiate mathematical structures and when the natural system involves an unbounded, continuous quantity, it provides an instance of the system of positive real numbers. Thus the second two refute the first idea, the principal *raison d'être* for the representational theory.

However, one feature of representational theory is of enduring importance. While the concept of quantity concerns the deep, theoretical structure underlying measurement, the range of empirical systems identified by proponents of the representational theory deal with the kinds of observable, surface structures enabling tests of features of quantitative structure. Cataloguing possible, surface structures provides an invaluable resource for aspiring quantitative sciences such as the human sciences to draw upon as they strive to expose the logical gaps in the quantitative program initiated under the auspices of the ideology of scientism and strive to test whether the attributes they deal with are not merely qualitative but quantitative.

References

Adams, E.W. (1966). On the nature and purpose of measurement. *Synthese* **16**, 125–169.

Armstrong, D.M. (1987). *Universals: An Opinionated Introduction*. Westview Press, Boulder.
Armstrong, D.M. (1997). *A World of States of Affairs*. Cambridge Univ. Press, Cambridge.
Boumans, M. (2007). Invariance and calibration. In: Boumans, M. (Ed.), *Measurement in Economics: A Handbook*. Elsevier, London.
Bradley, F.H. (1895). What do we mean by the intensity of psychical states? *Mind* **13**, 1–27.
Bridgman, P.W. (1927). *The Logic of Modern Physics*. Macmillan, New York.
Campbell, N.R. (1920). *Physics the Elements*. Cambridge Univ. Press, Cambridge.
Campbell, N.R. (1928). *An Account of the Principles of Measurement and Calculation*. Longmans, Green and Co., London.
Carnap, R. (1937). *The Logical Syntax of Language*. Kegan Paul, London.
Catton, P. (2004). Constructive criticism. In: P. Catton, G. Macdonald (Eds.), *Karl Popper: Critical Appraisals*. Routledge, New York, pp. 50–77.
Chao, H.-K. (2007). Structure. In: M. Boumans (Ed.), *Measurement in Economics: A Handbook*. Elsevier, London.
Cohen, M.R. (1931). *Reason and Nature: An Essay on the Meaning of Scientific Method*. Harcourt, Brace & Co., New York.
Cohen, M.R., Nagel, E. (1934). *An Introduction to Logic and Scientific Method*. Routledge & Kegan Paul, London.
Cohen, R.S., Elkana, Y. (1977). *Hermann von Helmholtz: Epistemological Writings*. Reidel, Dordrecht.
Davison, M.L., Sharma, A.R. (1988). Parametric statistics and levels of measurement. *Psychological Bulletin* **104**, 137–144.
Davison, M.L., Sharma, A.R. (1990). Parametric statistics and levels of measurement: Factorial designs and multiple regression. *Psychological Bulletin* **107**, 394–400.
De Morgan, A. (1836). *The Connexion of Number and Magnitude: An Attempt to Explain the Fifth Book of Euclid*. Taylor & Walton, London.
Dingle, H. (1950). A theory of measurement. *British Journal for Philosophy of Science* **1**, 5–26.
Fechner, G.T. (1960). *Elemente der Psychophysik*. Breitkopf and Hartel, Leipzig.
Ferguson, A., Myers, C.S., Bartlett, R.J., Banister, H., Bartlett, F.C., Brown, W., Campbell, N.R., Craik, K.J.W., Drever, J., Guild, J., Houstoun, R.A., Irwin, J.C., Kaye, G.W.C., Philpott, S.J.F., Richardson, L.F., Shaxby, J.H., Smith, T., Thouless, R.H., Tucker, W.S. (1940). Quantitative estimates of sensory events: Final report. *Advancement of Science* **1**, 331–349.
Frege, G. (1903). *Grundgesetze der Arithmetik, vol. 2*. George Olms, Hildesheim.
Heath, T.L. (1908). *The Thirteen Books of Euclid's Elements, vol. 2*. Cambridge Univ. Press, Cambridge.
Heidelberger, M. (1993). Fechner's impact for measurement theory. *Behavioral and Brain Science* **16**, 146–148.
Heidelberger, M. (1994). Three strands in the history of the representational theory of measurement. Paper delivered at a conference on Foundations of Measurement and the Nature of Number, Keil, Germany.
Hölder, O. (1901). Die Axiome der Quantität und die Lehre vom Mass. Berichte über die Verhandlungen der Königlich Sächsischen Gesellschaft der Wissenschaften zu Leipzig, *Mathematisch-Physische Klasse* **53**, 1–46. (Translated as 'The Axioms of Quantity and the Theory of Measurement', Michell and Ernst, 1996 and 1997.)
Johnson, H.M. (1936). Pseudo-mathematics in the mental and social sciences. *American Journal of Psychology* **48**, 342–351.
Kline, P. (2000). *A Psychometrics Primer*. Free Association Books, London.
Krantz, D.H., Luce, R.D., Suppes, P., Tversky, A. (1971). *Foundations of Measurement, vol. 1*. Academic Press, New York.
Locke, J. (1959). *An Essay Concerning Human Understanding, vol. 1*. Dover, New York.
Luce, R.D. (1987). Measurement structures with Archimedean ordered translation groups. *Order* **4**, 165–189.
Luce, R.D. (2005). Measurement analogies: comparisons of behavioural and physical measures. *Psychometrika* **70**, 227–251.

Luce, R.D., Krantz, D.H., Suppes, P., Tversky, A. (1990). *Foundations of Measurement, vol. 3.* Academic Press, New York.

Mari, L. (2007). Measurability. In: M. Boumans (Ed.), *Measurement in Economics: A Handbook.* Elsevier, London.

Michell, J. (1986). Measurement scales and statistics: A clash of paradigms. *Psychological Bulletin* **100**, 398–407.

Michell, J. (1993). The origins of the representational theory of measurement: Helmholtz, Hölder, and Russell. *Studies in History and Philosophy of Science* **24**, 185–206.

Michell, J. (1994). Numbers as quantitative relations and the traditional theory of measurement. *British Journal for Philosophy of Science* **45**, 389–406.

Michell, J. (1997). Bertrand Russell's 1897 critique of the traditional theory of measurement. *Synthese* **110**, 257–276.

Michell, J. (1999). *Measurement in Psychology: A Critical History of a Methodological Concept.* Cambridge Univ. Press, Cambridge.

Michell, J. (2002). Stevens's theory of scales of measurement and its place in modern psychology. *Australian Journal of Psychology* **54**, 99–104.

Michell, J. (2006). Psychophysics, intensive magnitudes, and the psychometricians' fallacy. *Studies in History and Philosophy of Science* **17**, 414–432.

Michell, J., Ernst, C. (1996). The axioms of quantity and the theory of measurement, Part I. An English translation of Hölder (1901), Part I. *Journal of Mathematical Psychology* **40**, 235–252.

Michell, J., Ernst, C. (1997). The axioms of quantity and the theory of measurement, Part II. An English translation of Hölder (1901), Part II. *Journal of Mathematical Psychology* **41**, 345–356.

Mundy, B. (1987). The metaphysics of quantity. *Philosophy Studies* **51**, 29–54.

Mundy, B. (1994). Quantity, representation and geometry. In: Humphreys, P. (Ed.), *Patrick Suppes: Scientific Philosopher, vol. 2.* Kluwer, Dordrecht, pp. 59–102.

Nagel, E. (1932). Measurement. *Erkenntnis* **2**, 313–333.

Narens, L. (1981). On the scales of measurement. *Journal of Mathematical Psychology* **24**, 249–275.

Narens, L. (2002). *Theories of Meaningfulness*. Lawrence Erlbaum, Mahwah, NJ.

Narens, L., Luce, R.D. (1990). Three aspects of the effectiveness of mathematics in science. In: Mirkin, R.E. (Ed.), *Mathematics and Science*. World Scientific Press, Singapore, pp. 122–135.

Newton, I. (1967). Universal arithmetic: Or, a treatise of arithmetical composition and resolution. In: Whiteside, D.T. (Ed.), *The Mathematical Works of Isaac Newton, vol. 2.* Unwin Hyman, London, pp. 68–82.

Ramsay, J.O. (1991). Review: Suppes, Luce, et al., Foundations of Measurement, vols. 2 and 3. *Psychometrika* **56**, 355–358.

Reinsdorf, M.B. (2007). Axiomatic price index theory. In: Boumans, M. (Ed.), *Measurement in Economics: A Handbook*. Elsevier, London.

Russell, B. (1903). *Principles of Mathematics*. Cambridge Univ. Press, Cambridge.

Russell, B. (1919). *Introduction to Mathematical Philosophy*. Routledge, London.

Stevens, S.S. (1936). A scale for the measurement of a psychological magnitude: Loudness. *Psychological Review* **43**, 405–416.

Stevens, S.S. (1939). Psychology and the science of science. *Psychological Bulletin* **36**, 221–263.

Stevens, S.S. (1946). On the theory of scales of measurement. *Science* **103**, 677–680.

Stevens, S.S. (1951). Mathematics, measurement and psychophysics. In: Stevens, S.S. (Ed.), *Handbook of Experimental Psychology*. Wiley, New York, pp. 1–49.

Stevens, S.S., Davis, H. (1938). *Hearing: Its Psychology and Physiology*. Wiley, New York.

Suppes, P. (1954). Some remarks on problems and methods in the philosophy of science. *Phil. Science* **21**, 242–248.

Suppes, P., Krantz, D.H., Luce, R.D., Tversky, A. (1989). *Foundations of Measurement, vol. 2.* Academic Press, New York.

Suppes, P., Zinnes, J.L. (1963). Basic measurement theory. In: Luce, R.D., Bush, R.R., Galanter, E. (Eds.), *Handbook of Mathematical Psychology, vol. 1.* Wiley, New York, pp. 1–76.

Swoyer, C. (1987). The metaphysics of measurement. In: Forge, J. (Ed.), *Measurement, Realism and Objectivity: Essays on Measurement in the Social and Physical Sciences*. Reidel, Dordrecht, pp. 235–290.

von Helmholtz, H. (1887). *Zählen und Messen erkenntnistheortisch betrachtet. Philosophische Aufsätze Eduard Zeller zu seinem fünfzigjährigen Doktorjubiläum gewidmet*. Fues' Verlag, Leipzig. (Translated as: Lowe, M.F. (Ed.), 'Numbering and Measuring from an Epistemological Viewpoint'. Cohen and Elkana, 1977.)

Whitehead, A.N., Russell, B. (1913). *Principia Mathematica, vol. 3*. Cambridge Univ. Press, Cambridge.

CHAPTER 3

Measurability

Luca Mari

Università Cattaneo – Liuc – Italy
E-mail address: lmari@liuc.it

Abstract

Words have nothing magic in them: there are no "true words" for things, nor "true meanings" for words, and discussing about definitions is usually not so important. Measurement assumed a crucial role in physical sciences and technologies not when the Greeks stated that "man is the measure of all things", but when the experimental method adopted it as a basic method to acquire reliable information on empirical phenomena/objects. What is the source of this reliability? Can this reliability be assured for information related to non-physical properties? Can non-physical properties be measured, and how? This paper is devoted to explore these issues.

3.1. Introduction

Measurement is an experimental and formal process aimed at obtaining and expressing descriptive information about the property of an object (phenomenon, body, substance, etc.). Because of its long history and its so diverse fields of application (see at this regards Morgan, 2007), the concept of measurement is multiform and sometimes even controversial. Indeed, while the black box model would interpret it as a "basic", and actually trivial, operation (see Fig. 3.1), measurement can become a complex and theory-laden process, as sketched in Fig. 3.2 (Carbone et al., 2006).

For this reason I will discuss here about measurability according to a bottom-up strategy: starting from what I suggest to be the simplest form of measurement (so simple that in fact someone could even consider it not measurement at all)

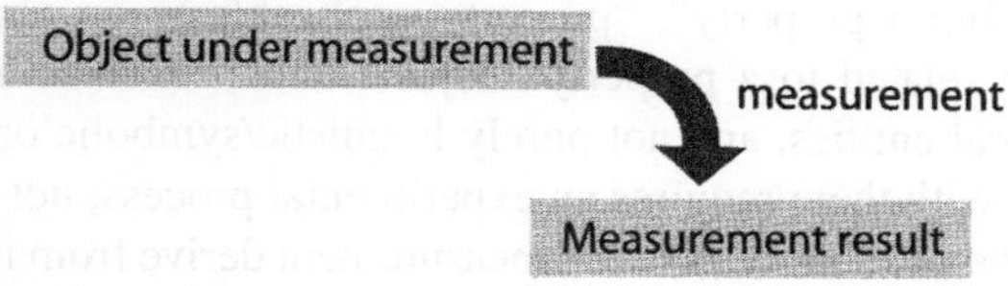

Fig. 3.1.

Measurement in Economics: A Handbook
Marcel Boumans (Editor)

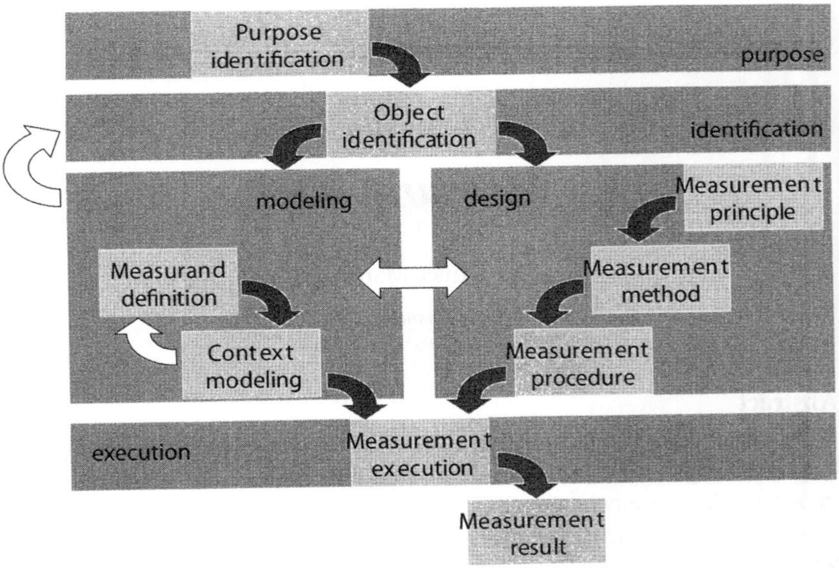

Fig. 3.2.

I will add, step by step, some of the elements leading to a more complete framework for understanding the concept. The basic theses of the paper are:

- measurability is a specific case of evaluability;
- the measurability of a property *conceptually* depends on the current state of the knowledge of the property, and therefore it is not an "intrinsic characteristic" of the property;
- the measurability of a property *operatively* depends on the availability of experimental conditions, and therefore it cannot be derived solely from formal requirements;
- the measurement of a property is an evaluation process aimed at producing intersubjective and objective information; accordingly, measurement is a fuzzy subcategory of evaluation: the more an evaluation is/becomes intersubjective and objective, the more is/becomes a measurement.

Although somehow discussed in the following pages, I will assume here as primitive the concepts of (1) property, (2) relation among objects and properties (variously expressed as "property of an object", "object having a property", "object exhibiting a property", "property applicable to an object", etc.), and (3) description related to a property. Objects under measurement are considered as empirical entities, and not purely linguistic/symbolic ones, and as such the interaction with them requires an experimental process, not a purely formal one: many of the peculiar features of measurement derive from its role of *bridge between the empirical realm*, to which the object under measurement belongs, *and the linguistic/symbolic realm*, to which the measurement result belongs.

I do not think that words have something magic in them: there are no "true" words for things, and discussing about definitions is usually not so important. Accordingly, I surely admit that the same term *measurement* can be adopted in different fields with (more or less) different meanings, and I do not think that the identification of a unified concept of measurement is necessarily a well-grounded aim for the advancement of science. On the other hand, a basic, historical, asymmetry can be hardly negated:

- measurement assumed a crucial role in Physics not when the Greeks stated that "man is the measure of all things", nor when they decided to call "measure" the ratio of a geometrical entity to a unit, but when the experimental method adopted it as a basic method to acquire reliable information on empirical phenomena/objects;
- for many centuries measurement has been exclusively adopted in the evaluation of physical properties, and it is only after its impressively effective results in this evaluation that it has become a coveted target also in social sciences.

As a consequence, I will further assume that:

- a *structural* analysis of the measuring process for physical properties should be able to highlight the characteristics which guarantee the intersubjectivity and the objectivity of the information it produces;
- as far as the analysis is maintained at a purely structural level, *its results should be re-interpretable for non-physical properties.*

3.1.1. Measurement as tool for inference

As any production process, measurement can be characterized by its aims. I suggest that measurement is primarily *a tool for inference*, whose structure can be sketched as in Fig. 3.3.

There:

- op_1 is a *sensing* operation, by which some information on the current state of a system, in the form of values of one or more of its properties, is acquired;
- op_2 is a *processing* operation, by which some conclusions is inferentially drawn from such values.

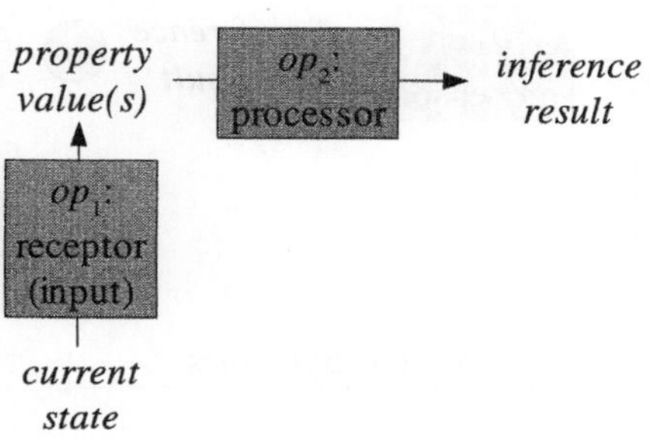

Fig. 3.3.

The following examples of this process introduce in an evolutionary way some of the topics which will be further addressed in this paper.

CASE 1. Two subsystems, x_1 and x_2, are identified, and the same property p is evaluated on them (op_1), thus obtaining the values $p(x_1)$ and $p(x_2)$. From the comparison of these values the inference can be drawn (op_2) whether x_1 and x_2 are mutually substitutable as far as the given property is concerned. As the resolution of the evaluation process increases (e.g., typically by increasing the number of the significant digits by which the values $p(x_i)$ are expressed), the inference result is enhanced in its quality.

CASE 2. The property p leads to a meaningful comparison in terms not only of substitutability or non-substitutability, as in the *Case* 1, but also of ordering. Hence, from $p(x_1) < p(x_2)$ the inference can be drawn that x_1 is "empirically less" than x_2 with respect to p. As the structure of the meaningful comparisons increases (e.g., typically by identifying a p-related metric among subsystems), the inference result is enhanced in its quality.

CASE 3. The values of $n \geqslant 2$ properties p_i of the system x are constrained by a mathematical expression, let us assume of the form $p_n = f(p_1, \ldots, p_{n-1})$. If the properties $p_1, \ldots, p_{n-1}$ are evaluated on x, then the inference can be drawn that the value of the property p_n of x is $f(p_1(x), \ldots, p_{n-1}(x))$. Moreover, if time variability of the properties p_i is taken into account, $p_i(x) = p_i(x(t))$, and the mathematical expression has the differential form:

$$\frac{dp_i}{dt} = f(p_1, \ldots, p_n)$$

sometimes called *canonical representation* for a dynamic system (it can be noted that several physical laws have this form, possibly as systems of such first-order differential equations), then the inference becomes a prediction. The diagram in Fig. 3.4 shows the basic validation criterion in this case: the values $p_i(x(t_{\text{future}}))$ obtained in t_{current} as inference result ($op_{1a} + op_2$) and by directly evaluating p_i in t_{future} (system dynamics $+ op_{1b}$) must be compatible with each other.

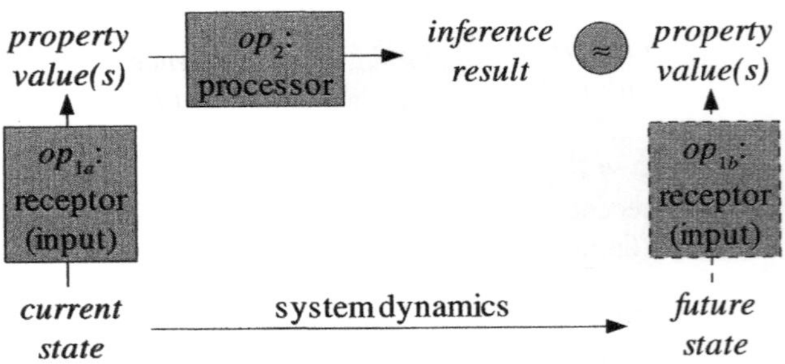

Fig. 3.4.

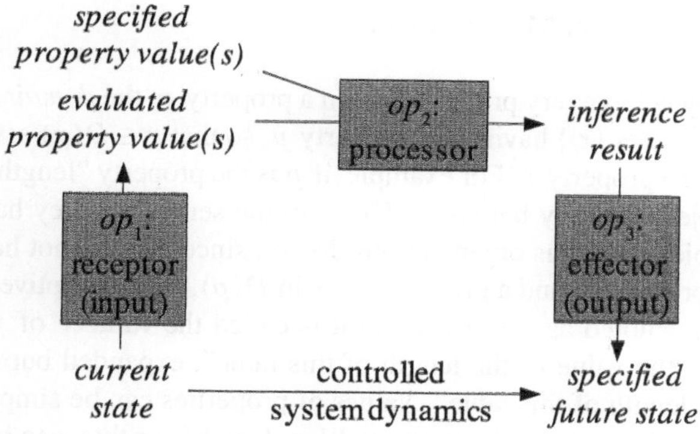

Fig. 3.5.

Furthermore, one or more property values could be specified as nominal (or target) values instead of being evaluated: in the *Case 1*, for example, this would lead to compare the values $p(x)$ and $p(nominal)$ to establish whether x is in conformance with the given specifications with respect to p. The inference result can be then interpreted as a decision on how to operate on $x(t_{\text{current}})$ so to obtain the specified state $x(t_{\text{future}})$ where therefore op_3 is an *actuation* operation (see Fig. 3.5).

In decision-making terms, the empirical outcome of having the current state $x(t_{\text{current}})$ transformed to a different state $x(t_{\text{future}})$ is achieved by acquiring some information on the current state, then processing this information together with the specifications which express the target values, and finally operatively carrying out the decision. This structure shows a general, pragmatic, constraint put on op_1 and op_2, as expressed in terms of the commutativity of the previous diagram: the empirical transformation $x(t_{\text{current}}) \rightarrow x(t_{\text{future}})$ and the composition $op_1 + op_2 + op_3$ must be able to produce the same results. Indeed, since the operation op_3 requires some empirical transformations to be performed, the good quality of the result of $op_1 + op_2$ is not sufficient to guarantee the good quality of the final outcome. On the other hand, a low quality empirical outcome must be expected from a low quality result of $op_1 + op_2$, a principle sometimes dubbed GIGO, "garbage in, garbage out" (this does not imply, of course, a related necessary condition, given the evidence that sometimes the wanted empirical outcome is obtained even from wrong decisions: since I am interested in arguing here about measurement, and not good luck, intuition, role of individual experience, etc., in decision, I will not deal with this kind of situations here).

In the jargon of the physical sciences and technologies, op_1 can be performed as a *direct measurement*, whereas a direct measurement followed by a op_2 inference is called a *derived* (or also *indirect*) *measurement*. In this sense, a data processing operation is recognized to be a possible component of measurement, provided that at least some of its inputs come from a direct measurement (and not only from specifications, guesses, etc.).

3.2. A Basic Model of Measurement

Not every object has every property. Given a property p, the *domain* of p, $D(p)$, is the set of objects $\{x_i\}$ having the property p, so that $x \in D(p)$ asserts that the object x has the property p. For example, if p is the property "length" then physical rigid objects usually belong to $D(p)$, in the sense that they have a length, but social objects such as organizations do not, since they do not have a length. For a given property p and a given object x in $D(p)$, the descriptive information on p of x is denoted as $v = p(x)$ and it is called the *value* v of p of x, as in the syntagm "the value of the length of this table", expanded but synonymous form of "the length of this table". Values of properties can be simple entities as booleans, as in the case of the property "1 m length", or they can be, for example, vectors of numbers, as for the property "RGB color" by which each color is associated with a triple of positive numbers. The set $V = \{v_i\}$ of the possible values for p *must contain at least two elements*, so that the assertion $p(x) = v_i$ conveys a non-null quantity of information, provided that the a priori probability of the assertions $p(x) = v_j$, $i \neq j$, is positive, so that $p(x) = v_i$ reduces the (objective or subjective) current state of uncertainty on the property value.[1]

Properties can be thus interpreted *as* (conceptual and operative) *methods to associate values to objects*. Accordingly, the diagram:

$$\boxed{x} \xrightarrow{p} v$$

graphically expresses the fact that $p(x) = v$.

In this paper the following terminology will be adopted (see also ISO, 1993):

- measurement is a *process* aimed at assigning a value to a property of an object;
- the measured property is called a *measurand*; measurands can be both physical and non-physical properties; they can be as simple as the length (e.g., of a rigid rod) or as complex as the reliability (e.g., of an industrial plant);
- the value $p(x)$ obtained by measuring a measurand p of an object x expresses the result of this measurement: therefore a *measurement result* is a descriptive information entity on a property p of an object x.

The basic concept for operatively characterizing properties is *mutual substitutability*: distinct objects can be recognized as mutually substitutable in attaining a purpose. For example, objects which are different in shape, color, etc.,

---

[1] This standpoint has been formalized in terms of a concept of *quantity of information* (Shannon, 1948). The quantity of information $I(v)$ conveyed by an entity v depends inversely on the probability $PR(v)$ assigned to v: as $PR(v)$ decreases, $I(v)$ increases. From a subjective standpoint, $I(v)$ expresses the "degree of surprise" generated by the entity v. The boundary conditions, $PR(v) = 1$ (logical certainty) and $P(v) = 0$ (logical impossibility), correspond respectively to null and infinite quantity of information conveyed by v. Hence, an entity v brings a non-null quantity of information only if V contains at least a second element v', such that $I(v') > 0$. The formal definition, $I(v) = -\log_2(PR(v))$ bit, only adds a few details to this conceptualization.

can be recognized as substitutable with each other as far as the purpose of filling a given round hole is considered. This recognition requires an experimental comparison to be performed among candidate objects, aimed at assessing their mutual substitutability. Since it does not involve any information handling, such a process is integrally empirical, and as such it can be considered as a primitive operation. *Properties can be operationally interpreted in terms of this concept of mutual substitutability*: if two objects, x_1 and x_2, are recognized as mutually substitutable, then there exists a property p such that both x_1 and x_2 belong to $D(p)$, and their mutual substitutability is the empirical counterpart of $p(x_1) = p(x_2)$ (this position endorses a generalized version of operationalism, whose original characterization, "the concept is synonymous with a corresponding set of operations" (Bridgman, 1927), has been acknowledged as too narrow; indeed, nothing prevents here that the same property is evaluated by different operations). As a consequence, for a given property p, an experimental *comparison process* $c_p(x_1, x_2)$ can be available:

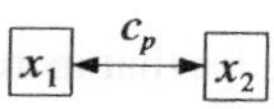

such that two objects x_1 and x_2 in $D(p)$ can be compared relatively to p. The process c_p is formalized as a relation, so that $c_p(x_1, x_2) = 1$ means that x_1 and x_2 are recognized in the comparison substitutable with each other as far as p is concerned, the opposite case being $c_p(x_1, x_2) = 0$, where 1 and 0 correspond thus to the boolean values 'true' and 'false' respectively:

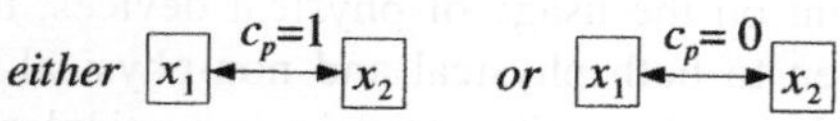

In the simplest case the result of this comparison is formalized as an equivalence relation: together with the immaterial condition of reflexivity, $c_p(x, x) = 1$, and the usually non critical condition of symmetry, $c_p(x_1, x_2) = 1$ if and only if $c_p(x_2, x_1) = 1$, the relation c_p is assumed to be transitive, if $c_p(x_1, x_2) = 1$ and $c_p(x_2, x_3) = 1$ then $c_p(x_1, x_3) = 1$. In more complex situations, both the requirements of symmetry and transitivity can be removed, and c_p can even be formalized as a non-classical, multi-valued/fuzzy, relation. In particular, in the case c_p is assumed as a non symmetric relation the following representation will be adopted:

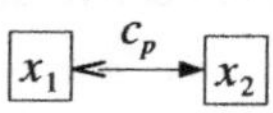

3.2.1. Conditions for measurement

Measurement is recognized to be a peculiarly effective operation for obtaining descriptive information on objects. In the course of history the *reasons of this effectiveness* have been looked for in both *ontological* characteristics of the object and *formal* characteristics of the process:

- measurement has been traditionally founded on the hypothesis that properties have a "true value", i.e., a value inherently existing in the object, which measurement has the ability to determine or at least to approximate when errors are experimentally superposed to it;
- more recently, measurement has been characterized as a process by which one or more experimentally observed relations among objects are represented by formal relations defined among property values.

With respect to other processes having comparable goals, measurement claims the ability of producing information that is reliably *intersubjective and objective* (Mari, 2003):

- *intersubjectivity* of measurement implies that its results can be interpreted in the same way by different subjects, who from the same measurement result are able to infer the same information on the measurand; this concept of intersubjectivity corresponds formally to non-ambiguity and organizationally to harmonization;
- *objectivity* of measurement implies that its results convey information only on the object under measurement and the measurand, and not on the surrounding environment, which also includes the subject who is measuring, nor on any other property of the object.

This claim of intersubjectivity and objectivity is founded on the *structural characteristics* of the measurement process: it is precisely the fact that measurement can be characterized in a purely structural way, therefore not considering any requirement on the usage of physical devices, that leaves the issue of measurability open to both physical and non-physical properties. Accordingly, measurement is *ontologically-agnostic*: in particular, it does not require measurands to have a "true value", however this concept is defined, although it does not prevent and is usually compatible with this hypothesis. The empirical content of intersubjectivity and objectivity cannot be guaranteed to measurement by formal constraints, with the consequence that *any purely formal characterization of measurement cannot be complete* if it is not able to model measurement as a process. This applies to both the classical definition of measurement as ratio to a unit and the current representational definition of measurement as scale homomorphism (Michell, 2007). Any model of measurement should be able to describe the *structure of the measurement process* as a means to obtain and express intersubjective and objective information on measurands.

3.2.2. Structure of the measurement process

In its simplest structure, the measurement process of a measurand p of an object x in $D(p)$ can be described as follows:

1. *preliminary stage* ("reference construction"): an object s ("reference object") is chosen in $D(p)$ such that:

- the value $v_1 = p(s)$ ("reference value") is assumed to be known, possibly because conventionally chosen; together with v_1, the value set V for p contains a second value, v_0;

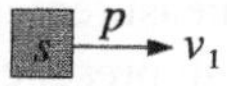

- an experimental comparison process is available, by which s can be compared to other objects x in $D(p)$, so that the value $c_p(s, x)$ can be determined;

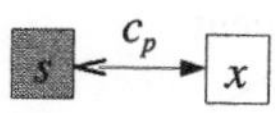

2. *determination (experimental) stage*: the object under measurement x is compared to the reference object s, and the value $c_p(s, x)$, either 1 or 0, is experimentally determined;
3. *assignment (symbolic) stage*: the value $p(x)$ is assigned according to the rule: if $c_p(s, x) = 1$ then $p(x) = v_1$, else $p(x) = v_0$ (Mari, 1997),

where thus a complete measurement process requires a calibration (first stage) and a measurement (second and third stage). Therefore:

either

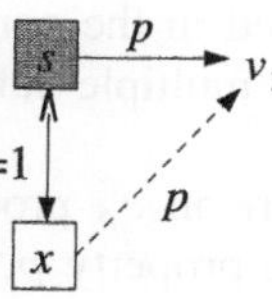

or

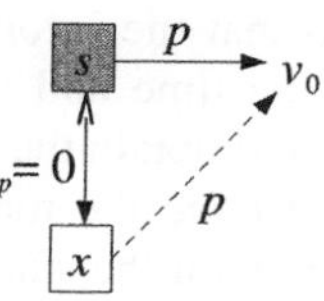

The result for this measurement process can be thus expressed as "$p(x) = v$ in reference to s by means of c_p". Whenever distinct comparisons regularly produce the same value, i.e., $c'_p(s, x) = c''_p(s, x)$ even if $c'_p \neq c''_p$, then the last specification can be removed and measurement results are expressed more customarily as "$p(x) = v$ in reference to s".

The previous diagrams assume the simplified situation in which calibration and measurement are performed synchronously, $t_{cal} = t_{meas}$: this is seldom the case. More generally, the reference object s should be then identified in its state, $s = s(t)$, that can change during time, i.e., $s(t_{cal}) \neq s(t_{meas})$ and therefore $c_p(s(t_{cal}), s(t_{meas})) = 0$. This highlights the *inferential structure of measurement*:

$$\text{if}\ \underbrace{v=p(s(t_{cal}))}_{\text{calibration}}\ \text{and}\ \underbrace{c_p(s(t_{meas}),x)=1}_{\text{comparison determination}}\ \text{and}\ \underbrace{c_p(s(t_{cal}),s(t_{meas}))=1}_{\text{reference stability}}\ \text{then}\ \underbrace{p(x)=v}_{\text{assignment}}$$

and explains why the basic requirement on reference objects is their stability.

The experimental and logical components required to perform a measurement process of a measurand p of an object x (at least: a reference object s associated to a reference value and a physical or logical device to perform the comparison process leading to determine the value $c_p(s, x)$) together constitute a *measuring system*. Both the object under measurement and the measuring system are embedded in an environment, whose presence generally influences the interaction of the former two elements. Hence, a measurement process involves three mutually interacting entities: an object under measurement, a measuring system, and a surrounding environment.

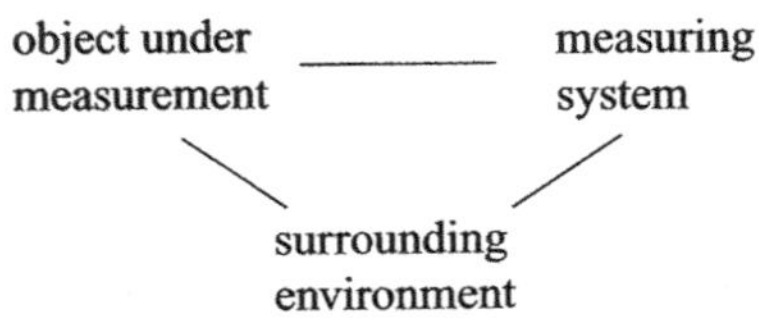

Accordingly, measurement can be thought of as *a process aimed at formally expressing the result of the experimental comparison of an object to a reference relatively to a property, performed by the suitable usage of a measuring system which interacts with the object in its environment.*

The information obtained by a measurement process is:

- the more *intersubjective* the more the reference object s is stable and widely available, so that the information obtained in the comparison can be transferred over the time and the space, and multiple subjects can perform the comparison and obtain the same results;
- the more *objective* the more the comparison c_p produces a value $c_p(s, x)$ depending only on the stated entities (the property p, the reference object s, and the measured object x), and not on any other entity of the surrounding environment.

Intersubjectivity and objectivity are thus interpreted as varying in a gradual, instead of sharp, way. By assuming the compliance to this structure as a requirement for a process to be considered a measurement, a concept of *quality of measurement* derives, such that different measurement processes can lead to results of different quality, in terms of their intersubjectivity and objectivity. It is indeed the quest for this quality that justifies an important part of the research and development done in Measurement Science and Technology.

3.2.3. Pragmatics of measurement

Among the various *pragmatic reasons* for which measurement is performed, two of them deserve specific attention for their structural implications: measurement as a first stage of an inferential process, and measurement as a means for determining the mutual substitutability of objects. Measurement can be performed as a *first stage of an inferential process*: a value $p(x)$ obtained by means of a process structured as presented above can be adopted as a premise in an inference of the form "if $p(x) = v_1$ then $q(x) = w_1$, else $q(x) = w_0$", where q is a property such that $x \in D(q)$ and $W = \{w_0, w_1\}$ is the set of its possible values. In a more general form, the premise of the inference includes the conjunction of two or more expressions "$p_i(x) = v_j$", each of them related to a distinct property: "if $p_1(x) = \cdots$ and $p_2(x) = \cdots$ and ... then ...". Physical laws are examples of this inferential structure, stating a mutual connection, and therefore a regularity, among the involved properties. The whole process of measurement of the measurands p_i together with the application of the inference rule is called *derived* (or *indirect*) *measurement*. In the case the property evaluated by the inference can be in its turn independently measured relatively to a given reference object, the comparison between the results obtained in the two situations for the same object x can be abductively adopted to validate both the processes.

Measurement can also be performed as a *means for determining the mutual substitutability of distinct objects*: in the case $c_p(s, x_1) = c_p(s, x_2)$, and therefore $p(x_1) = p(x_2)$, where x_1 and x_2 are distinct objects in $D(p)$, such objects can be inferentially assumed to be substitutable with each other with respect to p, i.e., $c_p(x_1, x_2)$. Such an inference requires a peculiar form of transitivity of the relation c_p, i.e., $c_p(s, x_1)$ and $c_p(s, x_2)$ implies $c_p(x_1, x_2)$, which becomes a transitivity in the case c_p is symmetric. The fundamental role of this property is witnessed by the first axiom in Book I of the Euclid's Elements: "Things which equal the same thing are equal to one another".

3.3. Extensions to the Basic Model

We are now ready to introduce some extensions to the simple structure presented above, with the aim of characterizing the measurement process with more details and realism.

3.3.1. Reference as a set

The information, that relatively to the measurand the measured object is either equivalent or not equivalent to the chosen reference object, can be sometimes refined, i.e., *quantitatively* increased. A whole set of reference objects, $S = \{s_i\}$, $i = 1, \ldots, n$, called a *reference set*, can be chosen such that:

- the reference objects can be compared to each other with respect to the measurand, and any two distinct objects in S are not equivalent to each other, $c_p(s_i, s_j) = 0$ if $i \neq j$, i.e., the objects in S are mutually exclusive with respect to c_p:

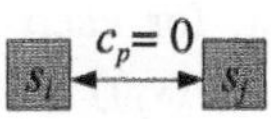

- each reference object in S can be compared to the object under measurement x, and $\exists ! s_i$ such that $c_p(s_i, x) = 1$, being $c_p(s_j, x) = 0$ for all other $s_j \neq s_i$, i.e., the objects in S are exhaustive with respect to c_p:

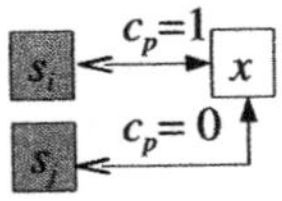

- to each reference object $s_i \in S$ a value $v_i = p(s_i)$ is associated; the value set V for p is then assumed to be $\{v_i\}$, $i = 1, \ldots, n$:

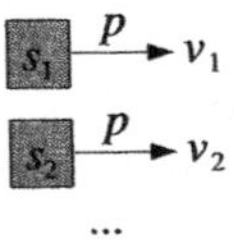

Hence, the measurand value for x is assigned so that if $c_p(s_i, x) = 1$ then $p(x) = v_i$, and the measurement result is therefore expressed as "$p(x) = v_i$ in reference to S":

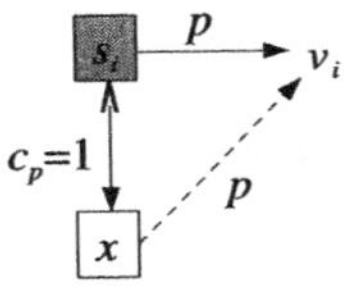

3.3.2. Reference as a scale

The information, that relatively to the measurand the measured object is equivalent to an element of the chosen reference set, can be sometimes *qualitatively* enhanced. The elements of the reference set S can be compared to each other with respect to an experimental, measurand-related, relation R_p. Assuming R_p to be binary for the sake of notation simplicity, such a relation is such that:

- for each couple (s_i, s_j) of elements in S the fact that either $R_p(s_i, s_j) = 1$ or $R_p(s_i, s_j) = 0$ can be determined, i.e., R_p is complete on $S \times S$;
- a relation R among the elements of the value set V is present in correspondence to R_p, such that, for each couple (s_i, s_j) of elements in S, $R_p(s_i, s_j) = 1$ implies $R(p(s_i), p(s_j)) = 1$, i.e., the experimental information

obtained in the comparison process R_p is preserved by R when expressed in terms of property values;

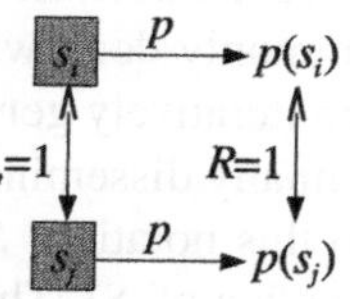

– the relation R_p is transferred by c_p to the objects under measurement $x \in D(p)$, so that if $R_p(s_i, s_j) = 1$ and $c_p(s_i, x_i) = 1$ and $c_p(s_j, x_j) = 1$ then $R_p(x_i, x_j) = 1$ and therefore $R(p(x_i), p(x_j)) = 1$.

A common relation for which such conditions hold is the experimental *ordering* $<_p$, such that if $s_i <_p s_j$ (the usual infix notation for $<_p (s_i, s_j) = 1$) then $p(s_i) < p(s_j)$: that is why a reference set S equipped with a relation R_p is called a *reference scale*. In this case measurement results are expressed as "$p(x) = v$ in reference to $\langle S, R_p \rangle$", where the couple $\langle S, R_p \rangle$ is called a relational system (in more general terms, a set $\{R_p\}$ of relations could be defined on S, so that the relational system is the couple $\langle S, \{R_p\} \rangle$; this extension, immaterial for the present discussion, is the main topic of the already mentioned representational definition of measurement, in Michell, 2007).

Considered as a first stage of an inferential process, measurement based on a reference scale leads to values that can be adopted as premises in inferences such as "if $p(x_i) = \cdots$ and $p(x_j) = \cdots$ and $R(p(x_i), p(x_j)) = 1$ then $R_p(x_i, x_j) = 1$", which thus *exploit the structure* induced by R_p on $D(p)$.

Since an n-ary operation is a specific $(n+1)$-ary relation, R_p can be sometimes expressed as an *operation* Op_p. Assuming Op_p to be binary for the sake of notation simplicity, R_p is ternary and $R_p(s_i, s_j, s_k) = 1$ if and only if $Op_p(s_i, s_j) = s_k$. Therefore a binary operation Op on the value set V corresponds to Op_p, such that if $Op_p(s_i, s_j) = s_k$ then $Op(p(s_i), p(s_j)) = p(s_k)$. Operatively important is the situation in which the binary operation Op has the properties of a sum among values in V, and a procedure for the experimental replication of the reference objects in S is available, i.e., the reflexive property $c_p(s_i, s_i) = 1$ assumes the operative meaning that the reference object s_i has a clone. In this case if $Op_p(s_i, s_i) = s_j$ then $p(s_i) + p(s_i) = p(s_j)$, and therefore $p(s_j) = 2p(s_i)$. A reference object s_1 can be then chosen so that $p(s_1) = 1$, with the role of *scale unit* by which the reference objects can be operatively generated: $s_2 = Op_p(s_1, s_1)$, $s_3 = Op_p(s_2, s_1) = Op_p(Op_p(s_1, s_1), s_1)$, etc., and $p(s_n) = np(s_1)$. Hence, in this case measurement results can be expressed as "$p(x) = n$ (in reference to) s_1", being s_1 the chosen scale unit.

3.3.3. Traceability

The goal of enhancing the intersubjectivity of measurement can be obtained by increasing the number of experimental situations, distinct in space and/or in time, in which the *same* reference S (either a set or a relational system, possibly equipped with a unit) is adopted. This requires S to be available to perform the comparisons $c_p(s_i, x)$ which constitute the experimental component of measurement. This problem is commonly dealt with by experimentally generating some replicas S_x of S, and then iteratively generating some replicas $S_{x,y}$ of the replicas S_x until required, and finally disseminating these replicas to make them widely available (according to this notation, $S_{x,y,z}$ is therefore the zth replica of the yth replica of the xth replica of S). The whole system of a reference S and its replicas is therefore based on the assumption that $c_p(S, S_x) = 1$ and that, iteratively, $c_p(S_x, S_{x,y}) = 1$, having suitably extended the relation c_p to sets and relational systems. Hence, an *unbroken chain* $c_p(S, S_x) = 1$, $c_p(S_x, S_{x,y}) = 1$, $c_p(S_{x,y}, S_{x,y,z}) = 1$, etc., makes the last term traceable to S, which thus has the role of primary reference for all the elements of the chain:

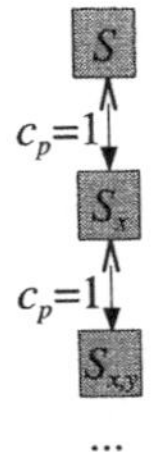

such that for example:

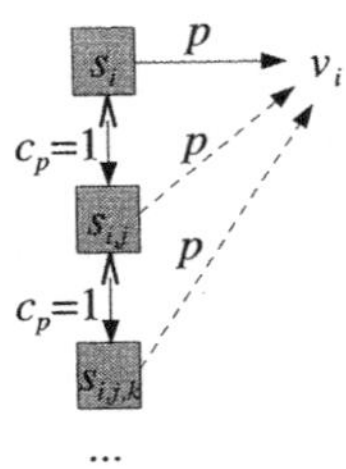

Under this assumption of *traceability*, measurement results are still expressed relatively to the primary reference S, even if this relation is only indirect, being based on the transitivity of the relation c_p. The basic characteristic of any given replica $S_{x,y}$ of a reference S_x is the guarantee that $c_p(S_x, S_{x,y}) = 1$. This is an experimental, not a formal, fact, which must be ascertained by operatively comparing the two references, and modifying the state of the replica $S_{x,y}$ in the case $c_p(S_x, S_{x,y}) = 0$, an operation called *reference calibration* (on the concept of calibration see also Boumans, 2007).

As a traceability system grows in number of the disseminated replicas, its primary reference becomes more and more intersubjectively important in the measurement of the property under consideration: therefore, the quality of measurement is not only a characteristic of the specific process under consideration but also implies some systemic components. A reference in a socially widespread traceability system is called a *measurement standard* (or simply "standard"). The primary reference in a traceability system of measurement standards is called "primary standard", and the references used to operatively perform measurements (instead of disseminating the primary standard) are called "working standards". Hence, in a traceability chain the first and the last element are the primary standard and a working standard respectively. The adoption of a traceability system modifies the structure of a measurement process as follows:

1. *preliminary stage*, in which the adopted standard S is calibrated, i.e., its traceability to a given standard is established, to assign a value $p(s_i)$ to each reference object s_i in S;
2. *determination stage*, in which the reference object s in S is identified such that $c_p(s, x) = 1$, being x the object under measurement;
3. *assignment stage*, in which the value $p(x) = p(s)$ is assigned.

3.3.4. Asynchronous comparison by means of a calibrated sensor

Despite of the dissemination of standards by a traceability system, in some routine measurements the object under measurement could not be directly compared to a standard S to determine $c_p(s_i, x)$, because of the local unavailability of a standard and/or even the unavailability of an experimental comparison process c_p which is synchronously applicable to s_i and the object under measurement x. In these situations, measurement results can be sometimes obtained by means of an *asynchronous comparison* between the object under measurement and an available standard, through the mediation of a *measuring transducer*, usually called a sensor, i.e., a device d such that:

- d has an "output property" q which can be measured;
- d is able to interact with the objects in $D(p)$, by modifying the value of its output property in function of the value of p, which thus operates in this case as an "input property".

Because of this behavior, d is interpreted as a device transducing the measurand p to the output property q, so that the structure of the measurement process is modified as follows:

1. *preliminary stage* ("sensor calibration"): the sensor d is systematically put in interaction with an available standard S whose objects $s \in D(p)$, and for each $s \in S$ the resulting value $q(s)$ is measured; since the values $p(s)$ are assumed to be known, the set of the couples $\langle p(s), q(s)\rangle$, i.e., <measurand value, corresponding output property value>, is recorded ("calibration data"), possibly in the form of a "calibration function" c, $c(p(s)) = q(s)$; such a function associates a value for the sensor output property to each measurand value obtained for a working standard (note that this characterization is in

accordance with the definition of calibration given by the International Vocabulary of Basic and General Terms in Metrology (VIM) (ISO, 1993): "set of operations that establish, under specified conditions, the relationship between values of quantities indicated by a measuring instrument or measuring system, or values represented by a material measure or a reference material, and the corresponding values realized by standards");
2. *transduction stage*: d is put in interaction with the object under measurement x, and the corresponding value $q(x)$ is obtained, called "indication", or "instrumental reading", i.e., the value of the sensor output property for the object under measurement;
3. *assignment stage*: the value $p(x)$ is assigned according to the rule: the couple $\langle p(s), q(s) \rangle$ is found in the calibration data such that $q(x) = q(s)$, and then $p(x) = p(s)$; this assignment assumes the calibration function c to be invertible, so that from the indication $q(x)$ the measurand value $p(x)$ is assigned such that $p(x) = c^{-1}(q(x))$.

This justifies the interpretation according to which *measurement and calibration are inverse operations*. Furthermore, a calibrated sensor embeds the information on the standard against which it has been calibrated. This implies that calibrated sensors can functionally operate as standards of a traceability system.

3.4. Relations With the Representational Point of View

I have already mentioned the current representational definition of measurement as scale homomorphism. Given the status of "orthodox" measurement theory of this point of view, it is worth highlighting the elements for which the concept of measurement presented here differs from the representational one. To this goal, I suggest that measurement, as any complex operation, *can be described according to multiple levels of abstraction*. Beginning from a general description, more and more specific characterizations can be obtained such that:

- each level specializes the previous one, being included in it as a special case;
- each level highlights some features of the operation that were ignored at the previous level.

I conceive of four "levels of description" for measurement, as follows:

- Level A: measurement as generic evaluation;
- Level B: measurement as homomorphic evaluation;
- Level C: measurement as homomorphic evaluation resulting from an experimental comparison to a reference;
- Level D: measurement as empirical operation.

In its most abstract interpretation, let us call it *Level A description*, measurement is simply meant to be a generic evaluation, aimed at assigning a symbol v chosen from a given set V to any candidate object x of a set X and therefore formalized as a function $p : X \rightarrow V$. Such a function admits two complementary interpretations, as it can be thought of as representing:

- the property of the objects in X whose evaluation is expressed by means of the symbols of V;
- the operation by which the objects in X are mapped to the symbols in V.

Any function p induces an equivalence relation $\approx_p$ on its domain, such that $x_i \approx_p x_j$ if and only if $p(x_i) = p(x_j)$, i.e., two objects are equivalent if and only if they are associated to the same value by p: the subset of the objects x_i which are in this sense equivalent is an equivalence class, and therefore an element of a partition of X, usually denoted by $X/{\approx_p}$. As a consequence, any function p can be decomposed into:

- a "partition function" $\pi_p : X \to X/{\approx_p}$, which maps any object to its equivalence class;
- a "labeling function" $\lambda_p : X/{\approx_p} \to V$, which maps any equivalence class to a value, and such that $p(x) = \lambda_p(\pi_p(x))$.

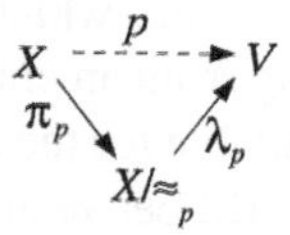

This decomposition formally justifies the initial assertion on the role of measurement of bridge between the empirical realm and the linguistic/symbolic realm: the measurement of a property p of an object x corresponds to the empirical determination of the $\approx_p$-equivalence class which x belongs to followed by the symbolic assignment of a value to this class. I see this as the main merit of the Level A description, which on the other hand is unable to specify any constraint on the evaluation (note that λ_p is 1–1 by definition), thus leading to a far too generic description of measurement.

The available knowledge on the property p could guarantee that among the objects in X one or more relations related to p can be observed together with the $\approx_p$-equivalence. For example, objects x_i and x_j which are not $\approx_p$-equivalent to each other could satisfy an order relation $<_p$ such that as far as p is concerned x_i is not only distinguishable from x_j, but also "empirically less" than it. In these cases the labeling function λ_p must be constrained, so to preserve the available structural information and to allow inferring that $x_i <_p x_j$ from $p(x_i) < p(x_j)$, as from $p(x_i) = p(x_j)$ the conclusion that $x_i \approx_p x_j$ can be drawn. To satisfy this further condition, p is formalized as a homomorphism: this *Level B description*, which clearly specializes the Level A description, emphasizes indeed the constraints that a consistent mapping p satisfies, as formalized by the concept of the scale type in which the property is evaluated. For example, an evaluation performed in an ordinal scale is defined but a monotonic transformation, so that if $p : X \to \{1, 2, 3, 4, 5\}$ is ordinal then the transformed mapping $p' : X \to \{10, 20, 30, 40, 50\}$ such that $p'(x) = \tau(p(x))$, where $\tau(y) = 10y$, conveys exactly the same information as p. Hence, each scale type corresponds to the class of the allowable transformation functions $\tau : V \to V'$ which preserve the relations defined on X.[2]

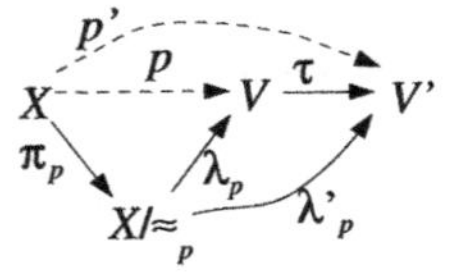

I see this link with the concept of scale type as the main merit of the Level B description, which on the other hand is unable to specify any constraint on the evaluation that guarantees its intersubjectivity and objectivity, thus leading to a description of measurement that is still too generic. The Level B description expresses the representational point of view to a theory of measurement.

The model of measurement that has been presented in the previous pages corresponds to the *Level C description*, which characterizes measurement as a homomorphic evaluation resulting from an empirical comparison to a reference. Indeed, if a reference scale is available for the property p such that, for example, an experimental order $<_p$ is defined between reference objects, then the above specified conditions on the scale require that:

– the experimental information related to the order $<_p$ must be preserved in terms of the symbolic order $<$ defined among property values:

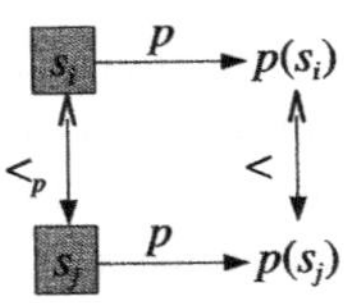

– the order $<_p$ is transferred by the comparison process c_p to the objects under measurement x, so that if $s_i <_p s_j$ and $c_p(s_i, x_i) = 1$ and $c_p(s_j, x_j) = 1$ then also $x_i <_p x_j$ and therefore $p(x_i) < p(x_j)$:

[2] As a corollary of this definition, it can be easily shown that the transformation functions τ are injective, i.e., map distinct arguments to distinct values. The algebraically weakest, and therefore more general, scale type is the nominal one, for which the only preserved relation is the $\approx_p$-equivalence, so that the only constraint on its transformation functions is injectivity. Each other scale type specializes the nominal one by adding further constraints to injectivity, for example monotonicity for the ordinal type and linearity for the interval type. It is precisely this common requirement of injectivity that justifies the fact that the transformation functions preserve the information acquired in the experimental interaction with the object under measurement, as expressed in the recognition of its membership to a given $\approx_p$-equivalence class.

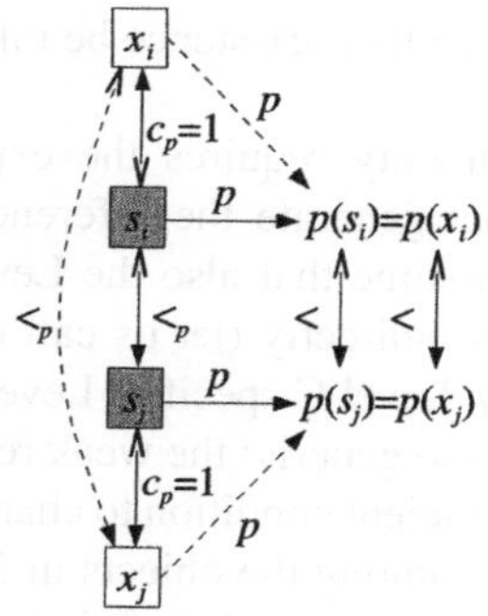

Therefore, the following chain of implications holds:

– if a reference scale is defined for p;
– and if for a given couple of reference objects s_i, s_j such that $s_i <_p s_j$ the conditions hold that $c_p(s_i, x_i) = 1$ and $c_p(s_j, x_j) = 1$;
– then also $x_i <_p x_j$ and therefore $p(x_i) < p(x_j)$.

This result is easily generalized to any relation R_p, and shows that the condition of homomorphism for the objects under measurement trivially follows from the condition of homomorphism for the reference objects, and therefore that the Level C description specializes the Level B one. I see the introduction of the concept of (traceable) reference and the formalization of the experimental comparison between the object under measurement and the reference as the main merit of the Level C description, which maintains an abstract connotation on the specific methods adopted to experimentally perform such a comparison.

Finally, a *Level D description* can be envisioned, which further specializes the Level C description by identifying the empirical operations performed to compare the object under measurement to the assumed reference. In the previous pages two of such methods have been introduced, namely, the synchronous direct comparison and the asynchronous comparison mediated by a measuring transducer. Descriptions of measurement methods can be found in most technical books on measurement. Also standard documents such as the International Vocabulary of Basic and General Terms in Metrology (VIM) (ISO, 1993) list them in various ways (indeed, according to the VIM, "measurement methods may be qualified in various ways such as: substitution measurement method; differential measurement method; null measurement method; direct measurement method; indirect measurement method").

If, as I am suggesting, it is the Level C description the one which specifically highlights the characteristics of measurement, the question arises whether the representational point of view (Level B) can be properly considered a theory of measurement. At this regards a serious ambiguity must be preliminarily solved, related to the status of the relations defined among the objects in X: is their observability an *experimental* requirement or just a *logical* one? That is: should the relations R_p be directly observed as the result of an experimental comparison process $R_p(x_i, x_j)$, or can their existence be inferred from the comparisons $R(p(x_i), p(x_j))$?

The Level C description only requires the experimental observability of the relations $R_p(s_i, s_j)$, that generate the reference scale, not necessarily of $R_p(x_i, x_j)$. Let us at first assume that also the Level B description allows the relations R_p to be obtained indirectly (let us call this a *weak* representational point of view). Accordingly, Level C specifies Level B, which is not a theory of measurement only because too generic: the weak representational point of view gives a *necessary* but not sufficient condition to characterize measurement. If, on the other hand, the relations among the objects in X are required to be directly observable (a *strong* representational point of view), the situation becomes more complex: a property evaluation could satisfy all the Level C requirements and at the same time the relations $R_p(x_i, x_j)$ could remain unobserved. The strong representational point of view gives neither a sufficient nor a necessary condition to characterize measurement (a further discussion on this subject can be found in Mari, 2000).[3]

3.5. Quality of Measurement

I have already considered that, as for any production process, measurement should be evaluated relatively to the quality of its products, i.e., measurement results. The quality of measurement results has been traditionally accounted for in terms of error, i.e., difference of the reported measurand value and the true value of the measurand itself, thus seeking an ontological solution to a pragmatic problem. I suggest that the inconclusiveness of many analyses on this topic depends on the lack of a clear distinction between the empirical realm and the linguistic/symbolic one. Indeed, the cultural tradition from which the very concept of measurement grew up, from the Pythagorean school, to Euclid, to Galileo, to Gauss, to Kelvin, *grounded measurability on the assumption that "numbers are in the world"* (as Kepler wrote in his Letter to Michael Maestlin, 1595).

Measurement was interpreted as a process of *discovery* of entities that are already in the object under measurement, so that measurement results would be empirically determined, i.e., "extracted" from the underlying objects. Quantities would be themselves inherent characteristics of objects, the concept of true value for a quantity simply being the coherent outcome of this standpoint. On the other hand, in about the last 100 years a pivotal concept appeared, and more

---

[3] In its usual interpretation, is the representational point of view *strong* or *weak*? Let us take into account a classical definition at this regards: "Measurement is the assignment of numbers to properties of objects or events in the real world by means of an objective empirical operation, in such a way as to describe them. The modern form of measurement theory is representational: numbers assigned to objects/events must represent the perceived relations between the properties of those objects/events" (Finkelstein and Leaning, 1984). This emphasis on perception seems to give a clear answer to the question.

and more became crucial for any scientific analysis and development: *the concept of model*. The current view on symbolization can be traced back to the concept of formal system as defined by David Hilbert: theories are purely symbolic constructions, and as such they can (and should) be consistent, but they are neither true nor false since, strictly speaking, they do not talk about anything. Truth is not a property of symbols, and surely not even of empirical objects, but of models, i.e., interpretations of theories that are deemed to be true whenever they manifest themselves as empirically coherent with the given domain of observation. According to our current model-based view, numbers are *not* in the (empirical) world simply because they *cannot* be part of it. Indeed, let us compare the following two statements:

- "at the instant of the measurement the object under measurement is in a definite state";
- "at the instant of the measurement the measurand has a definite value".

While traditionally such statements would be plausibly considered as synonymous, their conceptual distinction is a fundamental fact of Measurement Science: the former expresses a usual assumption of measurement (but when some kind of ontological indeterminism is taken into account, as in some interpretations of quantum mechanics); the latter is unsustainable from an epistemological point of view and however operationally immaterial (a further discussion on this subject can be found in Mari and Zingales, 2000).

The conceptual importance of the change implied in the adoption of the concept of model should not be underestimated. It is *a shift from ontology to epistemology*: measurement results report not directly about the state of the object under measurement, but on our knowledge about this state. Our knowledge usually aims at being coherent with the known objects ("knowledge tends to truth", as customarily said), but even a traditional standpoint, such as the one supported by the above mentioned VIM, is forced to recognize that "true values are by nature indeterminate". The experimental situation which at best approximates the concept of true value for a property is the check of the calibration of a sensor by means of a reference object. In this case, the value for the input property is assumed to be known before the process is performed, and therefore actually operates as a reference value. On the other hand, this operation is aimed at verifying the calibration of a device, not obtaining information on a measurand. Indeed, if the reference value is 2.345 m and the value 2.346 m is instead experimentally obtained, then the usual conclusion is not that the reference object has changed its state (however surely a possible case), but that the sensor must be recalibrated. Plausibly for describing this kind of peculiar situations the odd term "conventional true value" has been proposed (the concept of "conventional truth" is not easy to understand ...), but it should be clear that even in these situations truth is out of scope: *reference values are not expected to be true, but only traceable.* A still conservative outcome, which is adopted more and more, is of purely lexical nature: if the reference to truth is not operational, then it can simply be removed. This has been for example the choice of the Guide to the Expression of Uncertainty in Measurement (GUM) (ISO, 1995), which considers the adjective "true" to be redundant and accordingly writes "the value", by dropping "true". On the other hand, the pragmatic problem of properly evaluating the quality of measurement is not solved by a linguistic choice, and therefore remains an open issue.

3.5.1. The truth-based view

Measurement should produce information on both the measurand value and its quality, which can be interpreted in terms of reliability, certainty, accuracy, precision, etc. Each of these concepts has a complex, and sometimes controversial, meaning, also because its technical acceptation is usually intertwined with its common, non-technical, usage (as a cogent example the case of the term "precision" can be considered. The VIM (ISO, 1993) does not define it, and only recommends that it "should not be used for 'accuracy' ", whereas it defines the repeatability as the "closeness of the agreement between the results of successive measurements of the same measurand carried out under the same conditions of measurement", called "repeatability conditions". A second fundamental standard document, also released by ISO (ISO, 1998a), defines the precision as "the closeness of agreement between independent test results obtained under stipulated conditions", and then notes that the repeatability is the "precision under repeatability conditions").

I do not think discussing terminology is important: words can be precious tools for knowledge, but too often discussions are only about words. *The agreement should be reached on procedures and possibly on concepts*, not necessarily on lexicon. I subscribe at this regards the position of Willard Van Orman Quine: "science, though it seeks traits of reality independent of language, can neither get on without language nor aspire to linguistic neutrality. To some degree, nevertheless, the scientist can enhance objectivity and diminish the interference of language, by the very choice of language" (Quine, 1966). Indeed, what is important for our subject is an appropriate operative modeling on the quality of measurement, not the choice of the terms adopted to describe this modeling activity and its results.

The structure of the measurement process, that in the previous pages I have introduced and then variously extended, does not include any explicit component allowing to formally derive some information about the quality of the process itself. Such a structure can be thus thought of as an "ideal" one. Two prototypical situations are then traditionally mentioned to exhibit the possible presence of "non-idealities":

- the measurement of a property whose value is assumed to be already known (thus analogously to the check of the calibration of a sensor by means of a reference object): a difference of the obtained value from the known one can be interpreted as the effect of an error in the process, for example due to the usage of an uncalibrated sensor; this effect, which is not plausibly corrected in repeated applications of the measuring system, is traditionally called a *systematic error*;

- the measurement of a property by the repeated applications of the measuring system under the hypothesis that the state of the object under measurement does not change during the repetitions: the fact of obtaining different values in the repetitions can be interpreted as the effect of an error in the process. The superposition of several, unidentified but singularly small, causes generated by the interaction of the environment with the object under measurement and/or the measuring system is typically assumed; this effect, under the hypothesis of its statistical origin, is traditionally called a *random error*.

The concepts of systematic and random error and their relations are expressively exemplified by the operation of shooting at a target, as is shown in Fig. 3.6.

These pictures justify the (ideal) definition of "true value" as "the value obtained after an infinite series of measurements performed under the same conditions with an instrument not affected by systematic errors" (D'Agostini, 2003). On the other hand:

- systematic errors can be recognized as such only if a reference value for the measurand, i.e., the target point, is assumed to be known in advance; in this case, a "degree of systematic error" is evaluated by the distance (provided that a distance is algebraically defined) between the measurement result and the reference value;
- random errors can be recognized as such only if the state of the object under measurement does not change during the repetitions (in short: if the measurement is assumed to be repeatable), i.e., the target point is not a moving target; in this case, a "degree of random error" is evaluated by a dispersion index (provided that it is algebraically defined) of the set of the measurement results.

While both the hypotheses are demanding from an epistemological point of view, they are radically different in operative terms:

- a reference value for the measurand is typically not known in advance: indeed, measurement is usually aimed at obtaining information on a measurand, and

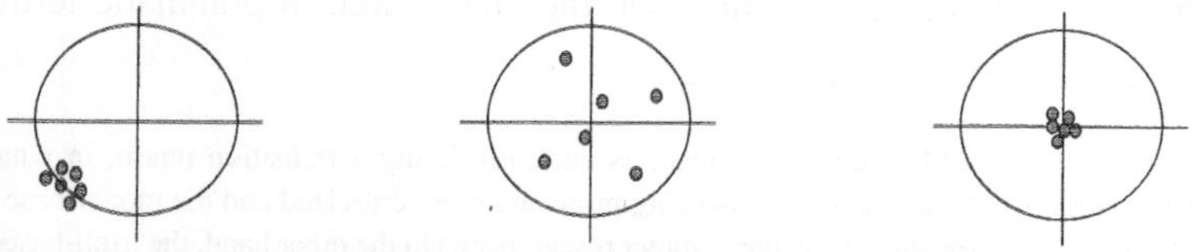

A case of systematic error with a (relatively) low random error | A case of random error with a (relatively) low systematic error | A case of (relatively) low random error and systematic error, i.e., close to "true measurement"

Fig. 3.6.

not at confirming the quality of the measuring system (which is instead the task of calibration); as a consequence, *systematic errors cannot usually be evaluated*;

- the repeatability is surely not a necessary condition for measurement, but it can be sometimes assumed as the result of the analysis of the empirical characteristics of both the measuring system and the object under measurement; as a consequence, *random errors can sometimes be evaluated.*

Apart from these epistemological issues, the traditional interpretation of quality of measurement in terms of errors is hindered by the operative *problem of formalizing these two types of error in a compatible way*, so to allow to properly combine them into a single value. None of the several solutions which have been proposed obtained a general agreement, plausibly because of their nature of ad hoc prescriptions (either "combine them by adding them linearly", or "... quadratically", or "... linearly in the case ..., and quadratically otherwise"). On the other hand, this problem has been recently dealt with in a successful way by the already mentioned GUM (ISO, 1995), according to a pragmatic standpoint which is aimed at unifying the procedure and the vocabulary while admitting different interpretations of the adopted terms. In the following this standpoint will be explicitly presented, and maintained as a background reference.

3.5.2. The model-based view

Because of the mentioned shift from ontology to epistemology, Measurement Science emphasizes now *certainty* instead of truth. Accordingly, the quality of measurement is more and more conceptualized in terms of *uncertainty*, i.e., lack of complete certainty on the value that should be assigned to describe the object under measurement relatively to the measurand, thus acknowledging that measurement is a knowledge-based process. From a conceptual standpoint this change has some traits of a scientific revolution, in the sense of the term proposed by Kuhn (1970): the truth-based view and the model-based one can be thought of as competing paradigms, and some of the current problems troubling the metrological community derive from what Thomas Kuhn calls the incommensurability of such paradigms.[4] On the other hand, in pragmatic terms the

---

[4] My opinion is that Measurement Science is currently living a transition phase, in which the historically dominant truth-based view is being more and more criticized and the model-based view is getting more and more support by the younger researchers. On the other hand, the truth-based view is a paradigm that benefits from a long tradition: the scientists and the technicians who spent their whole live thinking and talking in terms of true values and errors are fiercely opposing the change. An indicator of this situation is linguistic: in response to the critical analyses highlighting the lack of any empirical basis for the concept of true value, the term "conventional true value" has been introduced (the VIM: ISO, 1993, defines it as "value attributed to a particular quantity and accepted, sometimes by convention, as having an uncertainty appropriate for a given purpose"). Despite its

change from the truth-based view to the model-based one *is a domain extension*. Indeed, the uncertainty modeling does not prevent dealing with errors as a possible cause of quality degradation, but it does not force to assume that *any* quality degradation derives from errors. If measurement is not able to acquire "pure data", then it must be based on a model including the available relevant knowledge on the object under measurement, the measuring system and the measurand: this knowledge is generally required to evaluate the quality of a measurement. Indeed, several, not necessarily independent, situations of non-ideality can be recognized in the measurement process; in particular (denoting with x the object under measurement and with s the reference to which x is compared), it could happen that[5]:

- s is *not stable*, i.e., it changes its state during its usage, so that the value that was associated to it at the calibration time does not represent its state at the measurement time (formally: $p(s(t)) = p(s(t_0))$ even if $c_p(s(t_0), s(t)) = 0$, a comparison that can be performed only in indirect way);
- the system used to compare x to s is *not repeatable*, i.e., x and s are mutually substitutable in a given time and subsequently they result as no more substitutable even if they have not changed their state (formally: if $c_p(s(t_1), x(t_1)) = 1$, then $c_p(s(t_2), x(t_2)) = 0$ even if $c'_p(s(t_1), s(t_2)) = 1$ and $c'_p(x(t_1), x(t_2)) = 1$, where c'_p is a comparison process assumed to be more repeatable than c_p);
- the system used to compare x to the adopted reference has a *low resolution*, i.e., x is substitutable with distinct reference objects (formally: both $c_p(s_i, x) = 1$ and $c_p(s_j, x) = 1$ even if $s_i \neq s_j$) (this applies also to the relation between a reference and its replicas in the traceability system).

This list of situations of non-ideality does not include the item that the GUM (ISO, 1995) states as the first source of uncertainty in a measurement: the incomplete definition of the measurand.

Because of its relevance to the very concept of measurement uncertainty, a short analysis of *the problem of the definition of the measurand* is appropriate.

---

aim of extreme defense of the traditional paradigm, the very concept of "conventional truth" is so manifestly oxymoric that its adoption seems to be a cure worse than the illness. A further analysis on the current status of Measurement Science in terms of paradigms can be found in Rossi (2006).

[5] In more detailed way, the GUM mentions as "possible sources of uncertainty in a measurement": "a) incomplete definition of the measurand; b) imperfect realization of the definition of the measurand; c) non-representative sampling – the sample measured may not represent the defined measurand; d) inadequate knowledge of the effects of environmental conditions on the measurement, or imperfect measurement of environmental conditions; e) personal bias in reading analogue instruments; f) finite instrument resolution or discrimination threshold; g) inexact values of measurement standards and reference materials; h) inexact values of constants and other parameters obtained from external sources and used in the data-reduction algorithm; i) approximations and assumptions incorporated in the measurement method and procedure; j) variations in repeated observations of the measurand under apparently identical conditions".

3.5.3. Some considerations on the definition of the measurand

As a simple example of measurand definition, let us consider the diameter of a bore, as it is presented by Phillips et al. (2001): "The simple definition as a diameter may be sufficient for a low accuracy application, but in a high accuracy situation imperfections from a perfectly circular workpiece may be significant". According to a radically operational definition, this sentence is fallacious: if the measurand is defined by the operation by which it is measured, the experimental evidence of different "diameter values" obtained for different positions on the same bore would lead to the conclusion that the bore *has several diameters*, not that the diameter is incompletely defined. The concept of "having several diameters" is admittedly inconsistent with the geometrical meaning of the term, to which the mentioned "simple definition" implicitly refers: on the other hand, diameters, as geometrically defined, cannot be physical properties, for the obvious reason that in the physical world no "perfect circles" exist at all.

Radical operationalism is however seldom maintained: properties are a constitutive component of our knowledge, and we tend to assign them stable, and therefore transferable, meanings, to which any single operation only partially contributes. This dependence to a model can make a measurand definition incomplete: in the example, if the common, geometrical, concept of diameter is maintained, then "in a high accuracy situation imperfections from a perfectly circular workpiece may be significant", and such imperfections typically lead to uncertainties in the diameter measurement. As the observation accuracy grows, the fact that diameter is not a single-valued quantity must be recognized as depending on the discrete structure of the matter, not on manufacturing imperfections anymore: in this situation, the remaining uncertainty is therefore *intrinsic to the measurand definition*. On the other hand, it is precisely the dependence on a model (instead of ontological roots) which allows the alternative option of defining measurands on ad hoc bases. For example, again Phillips et al. (2001) note that "some standards (...) have further defined the diameter of a bore to be the maximum inscribed diameter" (or, more plausibly, the maximum distance between points on the edge of the bore, to avoid defining the concept of diameter in terms of itself ...). But this conventionality can result in arbitrariness: why not to define the diameter as the average distance between opposite points? or as the difference between the maximum and the minimum of such distances? If properties are methods to associate information entities to objects, as I have sustained above, it is possible to arbitrarily define always new properties. *Conventionality in the definition of properties avoids arbitrariness if grounded on pragmatic bases*. For example, in a system constituted of a piston and a cylinder, the internal "diameter" of the cylinder could be defined as the minimum inscribed distance and the external "diameter" of the piston as the maximum inscribed distance. Were the internal "diameter" of a cylinder c ascertained to be greater than the external "diameter" of a piston p, the passage of p through c could be inferred:

given $v_1 = \text{internal\_diameter}(c)$ and $v_2 = \text{external\_diameter}(p)$, then:

if $v_1 > v_2$ then $\text{passage}(p, c)$

an implication with formal analogies to, for example:

given $v_1 = \text{applied\_force}(x)$ and $v_2 = \text{mass}(x)$, then:

if $v_3 = v_1/v_2$ then $\text{acceleration}(x) = v_3$

(a rather lengthy expression of the known physical principle commonly written $F = ma$). Both cases express a law stating a relation among properties that in principle are defined independently of each other, in Mari (1999) I have analyzed the information conveyed by this relation, by calling it "information-from-connection" and discussing its *pragmatic* nature). These relations contribute to a complex concept of definition of properties, according to which each property is partially defined by means of other properties, in a network of mutual connections expressing the available knowledge of such properties and limiting the conventionality of their definition (Mari, 2005).

The network that connects the measurand to other properties guarantees the pragmatic usefulness of the measurand evaluation but, at the same time, is a further source of complexity for the definition of the measurand itself. Indeed, part of this network are the so called *influence quantities*, i.e., according to the definition of the VIM (ISO, 1993), those properties of the object under measurement or the environment (thus including the measuring system) that are distinct from the measurand and nevertheless affect the measurement result. As a simple example, consider the expansion of a metallic body caused by a temperature increase: if length is the measurand, then temperature is an influence quantity. The evidence that repeated measurements on the same object produce different results because of temperature variations can be modeled according to two strategies:

– temperature is maintained as a hidden variable in the definition of the measurand, whose intrinsic uncertainty should be increased correspondingly to keep into account this under-determination;
– temperature is explicitly included in the definition of the measurand, which is then denoted for example as "length at 20 °C".

The greater specificity of this second strategy offers the potential condition of obtaining measurand values of lower uncertainty, and therefore of higher quality, but requires the measurement of two properties, length and temperature, together with a control/correction system (that can be empirical or symbolic) for dealing with the situations in which the measured temperature is different from the specified one. Moreover, in this case temperature becomes a measurand in turn, with the consequence that its value could depend on further influence quantities, for which the problem of choosing a strategy for dealing with the influence quantities is iterated. Once more, this shows the model dependence of the measurand definition.

3.5.4. From analysis to expression

From the previous considerations the conclusion can be drawn that measurement is not a purely empirical operation. Indeed, any measurement can be thought of as a three-stage process (see also Mari, 2005b):

1. *acquisition*, i.e., experimental comparison of the object under measurement to a given reference;
2. *analysis*, i.e., conceptual modeling of the available information (the comparison result, together with everything is known on the measurement system: the measurand definition and realization, the instrument calibration diagram, the values of relevant influence quantities, etc.);
3. *expression*, i.e., statement of the gathered information according to an agreed formalization.

The crucial role of the analysis stage is emphasized by considering it in the light of the truth-based view. Once more, were "numbers in the world", questions such as "how many digits has the (true) length of this table?" would be meaningful, while as the power of the magnifying glass increases the straight lines limiting the table become more and more blurred, and the very concept of length looses any meaning at the atomic scale. If these questions traditionally remained outside Measurement Science it is plausibly because of the impressive effectiveness that the analytical methods based on differential calculus have shown in the prediction of the system dynamics: *this led to the assumption that the "numbers in the world" are real numbers.*[6] As a consequence, the property values are usually hypothesized to be real numbers, or however, when the previous consideration is taken into account, rationals, and therefore always scalars. On the other hand, if it is recognized that (real) numbers are linguistic means to express our knowledge, then the conclusion should be drawn that scalars are only one possible choice to formalize property values, so that other options, such as intervals, probability distributions, fuzzy subsets, could be adopted. Apart from tradition, I suggest that a single, but fundamental, reason remains today explaining why property values are so commonly expressed as scalars: such values act

[6] Direct consequence of this standpoint is the hypothesis that "true measurement" requires continuity, so that discreteness in measurement would always be the result of an approximation. I must confess that I am simply unable to understand the idea of numbers as empirical entities which grounds the position that in Mari (2005) is called the "realist view": "whether a physical phenomenon is continuous or not seems to be primarily a matter of Physics, not Measurement Science. Classical examples are electrical current and energy: while before Lorenz/Millikan and Plank they were thought of as continuously varying quantities, after them their discrete nature has been discovered, with electron charge and quantum of action playing the role of ultimate discrete entities. What is the realist interpretation of these changes in terms of the measurability of such quantities? (they were measurable before the change, no more after; they have never been actually measurable; etc.). In more general terms, from the fact that any physical measuring system has a finite resolution the conclusion follows that all measurement results must always be expressed as discrete (and actually with a small number of significant digits) entities: does it imply according to the realist view that 'real' measurements are only approximations of 'ideal' measurements, or what else?" (Mari, 2005).

as input data in inferential structures, as it is the case of physical laws, which are deemed to deal with scalars. Indeed, no logical reasons prevent to express inferences, such as the above mentioned "the acceleration generated on a body with mass m by a force F is equal to F/m", in terms of non-scalar values, e.g., intervals or fuzzy subsets, provided that the functions appearing in such inferences, the ratio in this case, are properly defined for these non-scalar values.

3.5.5. Balancing specificity and trust: a pragmatic choice

The analysis stage does not univocally determine the form of measurement results also because *quality of measurement is a multi-dimensional characteristic*. According to Bertrand Russell: "all knowledge is more or less uncertain and more or less vague. These are, in a sense, opposing characters: vague knowledge has more likelihood of truth than precise knowledge, but is less useful. One of the aims of science is to increase precision without diminishing certainty" (Russell, 1926).

The same empirical knowledge available on a measurand value can be formally expressed by balancing two components:

- one defining the specificity of the value: sometimes this component is called *precision* or, at the opposite, *vagueness*;
- one stating the trust attributed to it: neither *accuracy* nor *trueness* (the latter term is used in ISO, 1998a, but not in the VIM: ISO, 1993) have been mentioned here. If a reference value is not known, such quantities are simply undefined; in the opposite case, accuracy can be thought of as the subject-independent version of trust.

Until the available knowledge on the measurand is not experimentally enhanced, if one component is increased the other one should be decreased. An instance of such a trade-off is the probabilistic relation between confidence intervals and confidence levels. In the general case, the measurement result could be expressed as, e.g., a fuzzy subset with an associated possibility measure/distribution (see at this regard for example Benoit et al., 2005), so that the assignment of the two components stating the quality of measurement remains largely a task based on the experience of the subject.

From this point of view *the approach followed by the GUM* (ISO, 1995) *is hybrid*, being based on two complementary models, both of them probabilistic in their bases but opposite in the component of quality they emphasize (I should point out that the following analysis presents my viewpoint on the GUM, and is not literally faithful to the GUM itself, which is however repeatedly quoted henceforth; a good and synthetic (and faithful) synthesis of the GUM is Taylor and Kuyatt, 1994). Let us call them "primary" model and "secondary" model respectively.

The *primary model* assumes that the measurement result is expressed as a couple:

⟨estimated measurand value, standard uncertainty⟩

where the first term is a scalar and the second one is interpreted as a standard deviation of the estimated measurand value, either derived from an experimental frequency distribution or obtained from an assumed underlying probability density function.[7] In the first case the estimated measurand value is defined as the mean value of the experimental set $\{\nu_i\}$, $i = 1, \ldots, n$:

$$\bar{\nu} = \frac{1}{n} \sum_{1}^{n} \nu_i$$

and the *standard uncertainty* is defined as the experimental standard deviation of the mean value:

$$u(\bar{\nu}) = s(\bar{\nu}) = \sqrt{\frac{1}{n(n-1)} \sum_{1}^{n} (\nu_i - \bar{\nu})^2}.$$

If an experimental frequency distribution is not available, the standard uncertainty "is evaluated by scientific judgment based on all the available information on the possible variability" of the property (as examples of such information sources, the GUM mentions the following: "previous measurement data; experience with or general knowledge of the behavior and properties of relevant materials and instruments; manufacturer's specifications; data provided in calibration and other certificates; uncertainties assigned to reference data taken from handbooks." The focus on physical quantities is here manifest). The choice of assuming a maximally specific value for the measurand implies that its quality is entirely expressed as trust, by means of the standard uncertainty.

The *secondary model* assumes the measurement result to be expressed as an interval, whose half width is called *expanded uncertainty*, U, and is derived from

---

7 This double option highlights, once more, the pragmatic orientation of the GUM: while traditional distinctions are aimed at identifying "types" of uncertainty (or of error, of course, as in the case of random vs. systematic error), thus assuming an ontological basis for the distinction itself, the GUM distinguishes between methods to evaluate uncertainty. Furthermore, the GUM removes any terminological interference by adopting a Recommendation issued by the International Committee for Weights and Measures (CIPM) in 1980 and designating as "Type A" the evaluations performed "by the statistical analysis of series of observations", and as "Type B" the evaluations performed "by other means". The GUM itself stress then that "the purpose of the Type A and Type B classification is to indicate the two different ways of evaluating uncertainty components and is for convenience of discussion only; the classification is not meant to indicate that there is any difference in the nature of the components resulting from the two types of evaluation".

the primary model by multiplying the standard uncertainty $u(\bar{\nu})$ by a positive coefficient k, called "coverage factor", typically in the range 2 to 3, $U = ku(\bar{\nu})$. Such an interval, $\underline{\nu} = [\bar{\nu} - U, \bar{\nu} + U]$, has the goal "to encompass a large fraction of the distribution of values that could reasonably be attributed to the measurand". The quality of the value is now in principle formalized in terms of both specificity and trust, as related respectively to the expanded uncertainty and the encompassed "fraction of the distribution", interpreted as a probability measure and called "level of confidence" of the interval. On the other hand, since "it should be recognized that in most cases the level of confidence (especially for values near 1) is rather uncertain" and therefore difficult to assign, the standardized decision is made of choosing a level of confidence above 0.95, by suitably increasing the expanded uncertainty as believed to be required: the expanded uncertainty, and therefore the specificity, is thus in practice the only component which expresses the quality of measurement.

The reasons of this double modeling are explicitly pragmatic:

– the primary model is aimed at propagating uncertainties through functional relationships;
– the secondary model is aimed at comparing property values to ascertain whether they are compatible to each other.

Let us introduce the main features of these application categories.

3.5.6. Propagation of uncertainty

Let q be a property computed by a function $f, q = f(p_1, p_2, \ldots, p_k)$, where each p_j is a property whose value is assumed to be available (because either measured or in its turn computed) but uncertain, and the analytical form of the function f is assumed to be known. If the information on each input property p_j is expressed as a couple $\langle \bar{\nu}_j, u(\bar{\nu}_j) \rangle$, i.e., according to the primary model, and the information on the output property q must also be expressed as a couple $\langle \bar{\nu}_q, u(\bar{\nu}_q) \rangle$, then the problem is to derive $\langle \bar{\nu}_q, u(\bar{\nu}_q) \rangle$ from the set $\{\langle \bar{\nu}_j, u(\bar{\nu}_j) \rangle\}_j$. Since the input information is uncertain and the sought output information is also expected to be uncertain, this derivation problem is called *propagation of uncertainty*. Such a problem has been traditionally applied in derived measurement, in which the input properties are experimentally measured and the function f formalizes a (physical) law. On the other hand, the uncertainty should also be propagated when the dependence of a measurand from one or more influence quantities is analytically known and both the measurand and its influence quantities are expressed as uncertain, the output quantity being in this case the measurand specified in reference to the identified influence quantities. This shows the generality of the problem. The choice of expressing the measurement result for each property p_j as a couple $\langle \bar{\nu}_j, u(\bar{\nu}_j) \rangle$ allows to compute the output property value $\bar{\nu}_j$ and its standard uncertainty $u(\bar{\nu}_q)$ by means of separate procedures:

- $\bar{\nu}_q$ is obtained by applying the function f to the estimated values of the input properties: $\bar{\nu}_q = f(\bar{\nu}_1, \bar{\nu}_2, \ldots, \bar{\nu}_k)$;
- $u(\bar{\nu}_q)$ is obtained by assuming that the uncertainty on each property p_j produces a deviation $\Delta\nu_j$ from the mean value $\bar{\nu}_j$, so that the problem is to derive the standard deviation of $\bar{\nu}_q$ from $f(\bar{\nu}_1 + \Delta\nu_1, \bar{\nu}_2 + \Delta\nu_2, \ldots, \bar{\nu}_k + \Delta\nu_k)$.

The technique recommended by the GUM is based on the hypothesis that the function f can be approximated by its Taylor series expansion in the k-dimensional point $\langle \bar{\nu}_1, \bar{\nu}_2, \ldots, \bar{\nu}_k \rangle$. In the simplest case, in which all input properties are independent and f is "linear enough" around this point, the series expansion can be computed up to the first-order term:

$$u^2(\bar{\nu}_q) = \sum_{j=1}^{k} c_j^2 u^2(\bar{\nu}_j)$$

an expression called *law of propagation of uncertainty*, which shows that the standard uncertainty for the output property, called "combined standard uncertainty" by the GUM, depends on the weighted quadratic sum of the standard uncertainties of the input properties. Each weight c_j:

$$c_j = \left. \frac{\partial f}{\partial p_j} \right|_{\nu_1, \nu_2, \ldots, \nu_k}$$

i.e., the partial derivative of the function f with respect to the jth property as computed in the point $\langle \bar{\nu}_1, \bar{\nu}_2, \ldots, \bar{\nu}_k \rangle$, operates as a "sensitivity coefficient". This dependence becomes more and more complex as higher-order terms in the Taylor series expansion and/or the correlations among the input properties are taken into account: at this regards some further technical considerations can be found in the GUM, and several cogent examples are presented in Lira (2002).

This logic of solution to the problem of the propagation of uncertainty is based on the traditional choice of expressing the property value as a scalar entity, distinct from the parameter specifying its quality: property values are dealt with in a deterministic way and analytical techniques are applied for formally handling the uncertainty.[8]

---

[8] The working group who created the GUM is currently preparing some addenda to it, and in particular the "Supplement 1: Numerical methods for the propagation of distributions", which presents an alternative solution to the problem of uncertainty propagation. Whenever input property values can be expressed as probability density functions, the whole functions can be propagated, to obtain a "combined propagated function". This logic is in principle more general than the one endorsed by the GUM, since the mean value and its standard deviation are trivially derived from a probability density function. On the other hand, since the combined propagated function cannot generally be obtained by analytical techniques, the propagation can be performed in a numerical way, typically by the Monte Carlo method.

3.5.7. Comparison of uncertain property values

I have proposed above an operational definition of properties based on the empirical substitutability of objects: if two objects x_1 and x_2 are recognized as mutually substitutable for some purpose, then there must exist a property p such that $p(x_1) = p(x_2)$. On the other hand, whenever the property values are recognized to be uncertain (and, for example, are expressed as $\langle\bar{\nu}, u(\bar{\nu})\rangle$) such an equality at the same time:

- is ambiguous, since it is not clear whether it requires that $\bar{\nu}_1 = \bar{\nu}_2$ independently of their uncertainties, or also that $u(\bar{\nu}_1) = u(\bar{\nu}_2)$;
- constitutes a too narrow constraint, since mutual substitutability is guaranteed also in the case $\bar{\nu}_1$ and $\bar{\nu}_2$ are "close enough" relatively to their uncertainties, even if not identical.

When uncertainty is taken into account, mutual substitutability *does not require the equality of property values, but more generally their "compatibility"*. More than by means of sophisticated analytical techniques, the check of compatibility between property values is customarily performed by their direct comparison. To this goal, the simplest solution is to express property values as intervals, as in the secondary model, and to formalize their compatibility in terms of their set-theoretical intersection, which must be non-null. The GUM itself acknowledges the practical scope of the secondary model, introduced "to meet the needs of some industrial and commercial applications, as well as requirements in the area of health and safety". Indeed, this check of compatibility has at least two general applications:

- *it is a means to obtain information on the repeatability of a measurement*: while consecutive measurements produce compatible results, the inference can be drawn that the object under measurement is not changed with respect to the measurand;
- *it is a means to decide about the conformance with given specifications in presence of uncertainty*: this pragmatic issue is so important that deserves some further consideration.

A technical specification on a property is usually expressed as an interval of conformance $\underline{c}$, also called "tolerance", i.e., the subset of the property values which are considered acceptable for the given application. If also measurement results for that property are expressed as intervals $\underline{\nu}$, the decision on the conformance of $\underline{\nu}$ with the specification formalized by $\underline{c}$ requires the comparison of the two intervals. The outcome can be (see ISO, 1998b):

- (case 1) if the property value is completely within the tolerance, $\underline{\nu} \subset \underline{c}$, then the value is assumed to be in conformance with the specification;
- (case 2) else if the property value is completely outside the tolerance, $\underline{\nu} \cap \underline{c} = \emptyset$, then the value is assumed not to be in conformance with the specification;
- (case 3) otherwise, i.e., if the property value is only partially within the tolerance, $\underline{\nu} \cap \underline{c} \neq \emptyset$ but not $\underline{\nu} \subset \underline{c}$, then the situation is ambiguous.

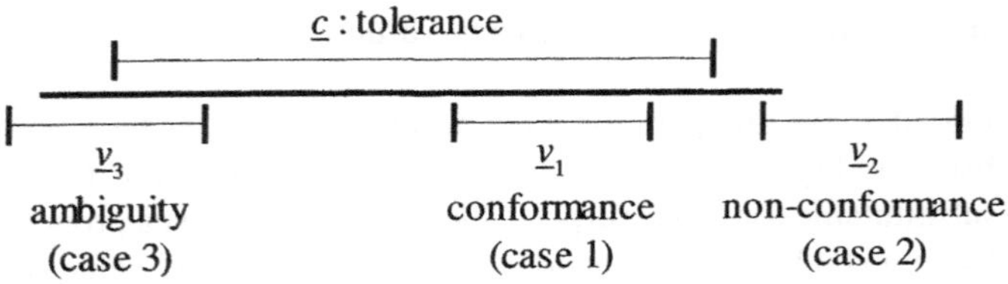

Fig. 3.7.

(See Fig. 3.7.) Whenever the property values are expressed with a non-null uncertainty, case 3 of ambiguity can always appear in the borderline situations. On the other hand, the frequency of this case statistically decreases as the width of the interval $\underline{\nu}$ decreases (whereas in the extreme situation in which the width of $\underline{\nu}$ is greater than the width of $\underline{c}$ the first case cannot occur): *the quality of measurement influences the ambiguity of the conformance decision.*

3.5.8. Uncertainty evaluation as a pragmatic decision

In presence of ambiguity, a decision can be made only on the basis of a contextual criterion. If, for example, the conformance to a specification is the condition required by a subject A (the buyer, the evaluator, etc.) to accept an entity (a product, a service, etc.) produced by a subject B (the seller, the maker, etc.), then two positions can be assumed:

- "in defense of buyer", ambiguity is dealt with as non-conformance, i.e., *in doubt refuse*;
- "in defense of seller", ambiguity is dealt with as conformance, i.e., *in doubt accept*.

This alternative maps the traditional distinction between the so called "type 1" errors (wrong acceptation) and "type 2" errors (wrong refusal). Under the hypotheses that (1) the object state can be expressed in dichotomic way, in terms of either conformance or non-conformance, and that (2) the decision can only be either "accept" or "refuse", four situations can occur:

		Object state	
		non-conformance	conformance
Decision	refuse	ok: correct refusal	type 2 error
	accept	type 1 error	ok: correct acceptation

A further position is in principle possible: if measurement results can be obtained with a reduced uncertainty, the ambiguity could be removed by reclassifying case 3 as either case 1 or case 2. This option highlights the pragmatic nature of the evaluation of measurement quality: since enhancing the measurement quality generally implies increasing the costs of the resources required to perform the measurement process, the issue arises of *balancing the costs of such resources with the quality of the measurement results*. The stated goal of the process should allow to identify a lower bound for acceptable quality and an upper bound for acceptable costs, so that the decision space can be split in three subspaces, for decisions leading respectively to (see Fig. 3.8):

- *useless* measurements, which, independently of their costs, have a quality insufficient with respect to the given goal (in conformity decision this corresponds to case 3);
- *unfeasible* measurements, which, independently of their quality, have costs unacceptable with respect to the given goal;
- *appropriate* measurements, for which the trade-off quality vs. costs is compatible with the given goal.

Accordingly, the decision should be made before measurement about its minimum acceptable quality threshold, expressed by the so called *target uncertainty*, so that the measurement process should be performed according to the following procedure:

1. decide the minimum acceptable quality, i.e., the target uncertainty, u_T, and the maximum acceptable costs, i.e., the resource budget (i.e., define the four subspaces in Fig. 3.8);
2. estimate the minimum costs required to obtain u_T: if such costs are beyond the resource budget, then stop as unfeasible measurement (the procedure stops in subspaces 2 or 3);
3. identify the components which are deemed to be the main contributions to the uncertainty budget;
4. choose an approximate method to combine such contributions, credibly leading to overestimate the combined uncertainty;
5. perform the measurement by keeping into account the identified contributions and evaluate the result by combining them, thus obtaining a measurement uncertainty u_M;
6. compare u_M to u_T: if $u_M < u_T$, then exit the procedure by stating the obtained data as the result of an appropriate measurement (area 4);
7. estimate the current costs: if such costs are beyond the resource budget, then stop as unfeasible measurement (area 2);
8. identify further contributions and/or enhance the method to combine them;
9. repeat from 5.

The pragmatic ground of this algorithm is manifest: as soon as the available information allows to unambiguously satisfy the goal for which the measurement is performed, the process should be stopped. Any further activity is not justified, because useless and uselessly costly: *the concept of "true uncertainty" is simply meaningless*.

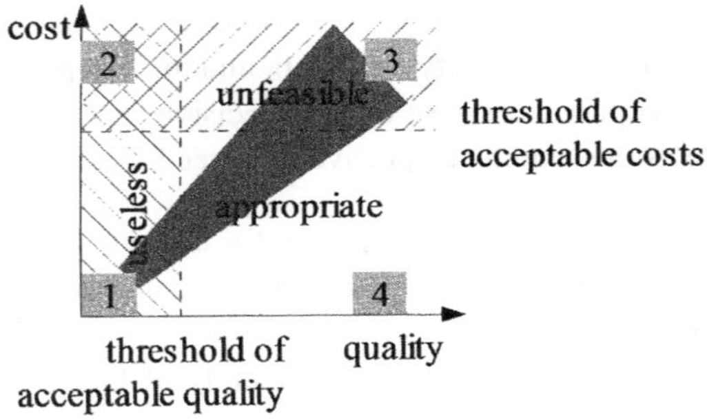

Fig. 3.8.

3.6. Conclusions

The traditional concept of measurability is grounded in ontology: each specific property, such as "the length of this table", is measurable because it inherently has a "true value", whose determination is the aim of measurement, so that the empirical inability of obtaining such true values is accounted for as caused by errors in the measurement process. The concept of measurability presented in this chapter is instead a pragmatic one: measurement results must be assigned (and not determined) according to the goals for which the measurement is performed, with the consequence that they are adequate if they meet such goals. Measurement results are evaluated and formally expressed by suitably eliciting the information on the measurand value and its quality experimentally acquired in the measurement process. In this evaluation a critical role is played by the subject; indeed, as the GUM considers, no method for evaluating the quality of measurement can be a "substitute for critical thinking, intellectual honesty, and professional skill; (...) the quality and utility of the uncertainty quoted for the result of a measurement ultimately depends on the understanding, critical analysis, and integrity of those who contribute to the assignment of its value". In this perspective, intersubjectivity and objectivity become the pragmatic target of measurement, instead of its preliminary ontological conditions. Measurement is recognized to be a model-based process, and thus it is emphasized its dependence to an interpretive activity that is pre-empirical: scientifically organized bodies of knowledge, modeling methodologies, formally-defined constraints, physical instrumentations, ethical responsibility, all contribute to the social value of measurement even in the current epistemologically relativistic world.

References

Benoit, E. Foulloy, L. Mauris, G. (2005). Fuzzy approaches for measurement. In: Sydenham, P., Thorn, R. (Eds.), *Handbook of Measuring System Design*, pp. 60–67, Wiley, ISBN 0-470-02143-8.

Boumans, M. (2007). *Invariance and calibration*. In: this book.

Bridgman, P.W. (1927). *The Logic of Modern Physics*. MacMillan, New York.

Carbone, P., Buglione, L., Mari, L., Petri, D. (2006). Metrology and software measurement: A comparison of some basic characteristics. *Proc. IEEE IMTC*, pp. 1082–1086, Sorrento, 24–27 Apr.

D'Agostini, G. (2003). *Bayesian Reasoning in Data Analysis – A Critical Introduction*. World Scientific Publishing, Singapore.

Finkelstein, L., Leaning, M. (1984). A review of the fundamental concepts of measurement. *Measurement* **2**, 1.

International Organization for Standardization (ISO) (1993). *International Vocabulary of Basic and General Terms in Metrology*. Second ed. Geneva, 1993 (published by ISO in the name of BIPM, IEC, IFCC, IUPAC, IUPAP and OIML).

International Organization for Standardization (ISO) (1995). *Guide to the Expression of Uncertainty in Measurement*. Geneva, 1993, amended 1995 (published by ISO in the name of BIPM, IEC, IFCC, IUPAC, IUPAP and OIML) (also ISO ENV 13005: 1999).

International Organization for Standardization (ISO) (1998a). *Accuracy (Trueness and Precision) of Measurement Methods and Results – Part 1: General Principles and Definitions*. Geneva.

International Organization for Standardization (ISO) (1998b). 14253-1: *Geometrical Product Specification – Inspection by Measurement of Workpieces and Measuring Instruments. Part 1: Decision Rules for Proving Conformance or Non-Conformance with Specification*. Geneva.

Kuhn, T.S. (1970). *The Structure of Scientific Revolutions*. Univ. of Chicago Press, Chicago.

Lira, I. (2002). Evaluating the measurement uncertainty – Fundamentals and practical guidance. Institute of Physics, ISBN 0-750-30840-0.

Mari, L. (1997). The role of determination and assignment in measurement. *Measurement* **21** (3), 79–90.

Mari, L. (1999). Notes towards a qualitative analysis of information in measurement results. *Measurement* **25** (3), 183–192.

Mari, L. (2000). Beyond the representational viewpoint: A new formalization of measurement. *Measurement* **27** (1), 71–84.

Mari, L. (2003). Epistemology of measurement. *Measurement* 34 (1), 17–30.

Mari, L. (2005). The problem of foundations of measurement. *Measurement* **38** (4) 259–266.

Mari, L. (2005b). Explanation of key error and uncertainty concepts and terms. In: Sydenham, P., Thorn, R. (Eds.), *Handbook of Measuring System Design*. Wiley, pp. 331–335, ISBN 0-470-02143-8.

Mari, L. Zingales, G. (2000). Uncertainty in measurement science. In: Karija, K., Finkelstein, L. (Eds.), *Measurement Science – A Discussion*. Ohmsha, IOS Press, ISBN 4-274-90398-2 (Ohmsha Ltd.)/1-58603-088-4.

Michell, J. (2007). Representational theory of measurement. In: this book.

Morgan, M.S. (2007). A brief and illustrated analytical history of measuring in economics. In: this book.

Phillips, S.D., Estler, W.T., Doiron, T., Eberhardt, K.R., Levenson, M.S. (2001). A careful consideration of the calibration concept. *Journal of Research of the National Institute of Standards and Technology* **106** (2), 371–379 (available on-line: http://www.nist.gov/jresp).

Quine, W.V.O. (1966). The scope and language of science. In: *The Ways of Paradox*. Random House.

Rossi, G.B. (2006). An attempt to interpret some problems in measurement science on the basis of Kuhn's theory of paradigms. *Measurement* **39** (6), 512–521.

Russell, B. (1926). *Theory of Knowledge*. The Encyclopedia Britannica.

Shannon, C.E. (1948). A mathematical theory of communication. *Bell System Technical Journal* **27**, 379–423, 623–656.

Taylor, B.N. Kuyatt, C.E. (1994). Guidelines for evaluating and expressing the uncertainty of NIST measurement results. Technical note 1297. National Institute of Standards and Technology (available on-line: http://physics.nist.gov/Pubs/guidelines/TN1297/tn1297s.pdf).

CHAPTER 4

Measurement With Experimental Controls

Glenn W. Harrison[a], Eric Johnson[b], Melayne M. McInnes[c] and E. Elisabet Rutström[a]

[a]*Department of Economics, College of Business Administration, University of Central Florida, USA*
E-mail addresses: gharrison@research.bus.ucf.edu; erutstrom@bus.ucf.edu
[b]*Department of Economics, Kent State University, USA*
E-mail address: ejohnson@bsa3.kent.edu
[c]*Department of Economics, Moore School of Business, University of South Carolina, USA*
E-mail address: mcinnes@moore.sc.edu

Abstract

Many predictions of economic theory depend on the assumed aversion of individuals towards risk. We examine statistical aspects of controlling for risk aversion in the lab, and the implications that these have on the ability to test expected utility theory. The concerns expressed here regarding the importance and difficulty of generating precise estimates of individual risk attitudes generalize to a wide range of other individual characteristics, such as inequality aversion and trust. We show that imprecision in estimated individual characteristics may result in misleading conclusions in tests of the underlying theory of choice. We also show that the popular instruments and statistical models used to estimate risk attitudes do not allow sufficiently precise estimates. Given existing laboratory technology and statistical models, we conclude that controls for risk aversion should be implemented using within-subjects, "revealed preference" designs that utilize the direct, raw responses of the subject. These statistical issues are generally applicable to a wide variety of experimental situations.

Experimental methods provide the promise that economists will be able to measure latent concepts with greater reliability. The reason is that experimental methods offer the possibility of controlling potential confounds.

However, the use of experimental controls might not lead to more reliable measurements. One reason is that the imposition of an artefactual control might itself lead to changes in behavior compared to the naturally occurring counterpart of interest. Concern with this problem has spurred interest in field experiments, where the controls are less artificial than in many laboratory exper-

Measurement in Economics: A Handbook
Marcel Boumans (Editor)

iments.[1] It has also spurred renewed interest in sample selection and sorting processes.[2]

Another reason that experimental controls might not generate more reliable measurements is that the latent data-generating process might simply be misspecified. If the experimental design is motivated by a model of the data-generating process that is invalid, then there can be no expectation that the controls will improve measurement and inference. For example, if there are actually two or more distinct data-generating processes at work, and we assume one, then systematically invalid inferences can result.[3]

We consider a third way in which experimental controls might influence measurement inference, by allowing "unobservables" to become "observable." Concepts that previously needed to be assumed to take on certain values or distributions a priori, can now be measured and controlled. In turn, this allows conditional measurements to be made unconditionally, akin to the integration of "nuisance parameters" in Bayesian analysis. We consider a substantively fundamental application of these ideas, to the evaluation of choice behavior under uncertainty when one has experimental control of risk attitudes.[4]

Many predictions of economic theory depend on the assumed aversion of individuals towards risk. Empirical research requires that one make a maintained assumption about risk attitudes or devise controls for risk aversion. The first strategy has the obvious disadvantage that the maintained assumption may be false. The second strategy is becoming feasible, particularly with the development of simple pre-tests for risk aversion in laboratory settings. We examine statistical aspects of controlling for risk aversion in the lab, and the implications that these have on the ability to test expected utility theory (EUT). The concerns expressed here regarding the importance and difficulty of generating precise estimates of individual risk attitudes generalize to a wide range of other individual characteristics, such as inequality aversion and trust.[5] Imprecision in estimated individual characteristics may result in misleading conclusions in tests of any underlying theory of choice.

---

[1] Harrison and List (2004) review this literature, and this concern with laboratory experiments.

[2] For example, see Botelho et al. (2005), Harrison, Lau and Rutström (2005), Kocher, Strauß and Sutter (2006) and Lazear, Malmendier and Weber (2006).

[3] Harrison and Rutström (2005) illustrate this point by comparing estimates of choice behavior when either expected utility theory or prospect theory are assumed to generate the observed data, and contrast the results with those obtained from a finite mixture model that allows both to be valid for distinct sub-samples. Similarly, Coller, Harrison and Rutström (2006) compare inferences about temporal discounting models when one assumes that subjects discount exponentially or quasi-hyperbolically, when the data is better characterized by again assuming that distinct sub-sample follow each model.

[4] Other applications include Harrison (1990), Engle-Warnick (2004) and Karlan and Zinman (2005).

[5] Methodologically related experimental procedures are being used to identify the extent of "inequality aversion" in tests of the propensity of individuals to "trust" each other. Cox (2004) discusses the need for controls in experiments in this context.

The way in which controls for risk aversion can be implemented varies with the experimental design. If a "within-subjects" design is used, in which the same subject takes part in a risk aversion test and some other task, one can directly use the results for that subject to control for theoretical predictions in the other task. In general such responses are likely to respect the individual heterogeneity that one would expect from risk aversion, which is after all a subjective preference. If a "between-subjects" design is used, in which different subjects[6] are sampled for the risk aversion test and the other task, one must construct a statistical instrument for the risk attitudes of subjects in the latter task.

Instruments for risk attitudes can be generated by constructing a statistical model of risk attitudes from the responses to the risk aversion task, and then using that model to predict the attitudes of the subjects in the other tasks. Given the time and monetary cost of eliciting risk attitudes in addition to some other experimental task, such methodological short-cuts would be attractive to experimenters if reliable. Of course, relying on a statistical model means that one must recognize that there is some sampling error surrounding the estimated risk attitude, even if one assumes that the correct specification has been used for the statistical model.

The issue of imprecision in measuring risk is readily apparent when one uses a statistical model to predict risk parameters. While less obvious, this issue still arises when one uses a "direct test" in a within subjects design. Imprecision in directly eliciting risk aversion may arise for several reasons.[7] First, our risk elicitation task may not yield precise estimates due to "trembling hand" error on behalf of the subject. For example, even when given a simple choice between two lotteries, a subject may, with some positive probability, indicate one lottery when they intended to choose the other. A second source of error occurs if our risk attitude task does not elicit enough information to make sufficiently precise inferences about the parameters of the choice model. We can reduce the imprecision by improving the design of the risk elicitation task, but we still need a way to characterize the degree of imprecision in the estimated parameters and to gage its impact on any conclusions that can be drawn based on responses in the subsequent choice task.[8]

We illustrate these procedures using a test of EUT as the "choice task" for which one needs a control for risk aversion.[9] We use data from a previous experiment in which subject choices have been shown to be inconsistent with expected

---

[6] We will assume that these are two samples drawn from the same population, and that there are no sample selection biases to worry about. These potential complications are not minor.

[7] "Imprecision" here is used in the usual econometric sense of minimizing the confidence intervals for the underlying parameter.

[8] Moffatt (2007) uses the concept of D-Optimal design to maximize the overall information content of an experiment.

[9] Rabin (2000) examines the theoretical role of risk aversion and EUT, and argues that EUT must be rejected for individuals who are risk averse at low monetary stakes. If true, then further tests of EUT are not needed for those individuals who are found to be risk averse in these low stake lottery choices. He proves a calibration theorem showing that if individuals are risk averse over

utility given the estimate of the individual's risk attitude. We begin our analysis by allowing for the possibility that subjects are noisy decision-makers. One way to incorporate subject errors is to calculate their cost and ignore those inconsistent choices that have a trivial error cost. We show that the percentage of choices violating EUT remains high even when we consider only those errors that are costly to the subject. We then ask whether these results are sensitive to the precision with which we estimated an individual subject's risk attitude. The data we use were implemented using a full within-subjects design, allowing us to compare the use of direct, raw risk aversion measures for each subject in the EUT task with the use of instruments generated by a statistical model. The method we adopt is to examine the sensitivity of our conclusions about EUT to small perturbations in the estimated risk preference parameters. We can think of this test of *empirical sensitivity* as a counterpart to the formal sensitivity tests proposed by Magnus (2007). Leamer (1978, p. 207) and Mayer (2007) remind us to consider both economic significance as well as statistical significance when evaluating estimates of a parameter of interest. Our objective is to evaluate whether our economic conclusions are sensitive to small changes in the estimated parameters. In the case of our statistical model, the estimated confidence interval provides the standard region in which to conduct the perturbation study. When we use direct measures of risk, the nature of the experiment suggests natural regions in which to check for parameter sensitivity. These methods can also be used to address the issue of precision in tests of choice models other than EUT. Tests of cumulative prospect theory, for example, are conditional on the estimated parameters of the choice function and the robustness of the conclusions will depend on the precision with which the initial parameters were estimated.[10]

In Section 4.1 we review the need for estimates of risk attitudes in tests of EUT and show how inference is affected by risk aversion. In Section 4.2 we discuss experimental procedures for characterizing risk attitudes due to Holt and Laury (2002). We present the distribution of estimated risk attitudes of our

---

low stakes lotteries then there are absurd implications about the bets those individuals will accept at higher stakes. Following the interpretation of these arguments by Cox and Sadiraj (2006) and Rubinstein (2002), a problem for EUT does indeed arise if (a) subjects exhibit risk aversion at low stake levels, and (b) one assumes that utility is defined in terms of terminal wealth. If, on the other hand, one assumes utility is defined over income, this critique does not apply. A close reading of Rabin (2000, p. 1288) is consistent with this perspective, as is the model proposed by Charness and Rabin (2002) to account for experimental data they collect. Whether or not one models utility as a function of terminal wealth (EUTw) or income (EUTi) depends on the setting. Both specifications have been popular. The EUTw specification was widely employed in the seminal papers defining risk aversion and its application to portfolio choice. The EUTi specification has been widely employed by auction theorists and experimental economists testing EUT, and it is the specification we employ here. Fudenberg and Levine (2006) provide another framework for reconciling the EUTi and EUTw approaches, by positing a "dual self" model of decision-making in which a latent EUTw-consistent self constrains choices actually observed by the EUTi-motivated self.

[10] For example Harbaugh, Krause and Vesterlund (2002) test the fourfold patten of risk attitude predicted by cumulative prospect theory. Their tests are designed based on parameter estimates from Prelec (1998) and others.

subject pool and examine its implications for subjects' preferences over lottery choices taken from the EUT choice experiments. In Section 4.3 we show that, for each subject and each choice, the cost of choosing inconsistently with EUT can be calculated. Conditional on our risk aversion estimates, we find that subjects frequently violate EUT even when the cost of doing so is high. In Section 4.4 we examine whether our risk aversion estimates provide sufficient precision for reaching meaningful conclusions about EUT. We show that the use of instruments, based on a statistical model, does not allow sufficiently precise estimates of risk aversion for our purposes. We discuss various reasons for this outcome. The implication is, however, that with existing laboratory technology and statistical models, controls for risk aversion should be implemented using within-subjects designs that utilize the direct, raw responses of the subject.[11]

4.1. Risk Aversion and Tests of EUT

Experiments that test EUT at the level of the individual typically require that the subject make two choices, so that we can compare their consistency. The first lottery choice can be used to infer the subject's risk attitude, and then the second choice can be used to test EUT, conditional on the risk attitude of the subject. Thus, preferences have to be elicited over *two* pairs of lotteries for there to be a test of EUT at all.

For a specific example of the frequently used "Common Ratio" (CR) test, suppose Lottery A consists of prizes \$0 and \$30 with probabilities 0.2 and 0.8. Lottery B, consisting of prizes \$0 and \$20 with probabilities 0 and 1. Then one may construct two additional compound lotteries, A^* and B^*, by adding a front end probability $q = 0.25$ of winning zero to lotteries A and B. That is, A^* offers a $(1 - q)$ chance to play lottery A and a q chance of winning zero. Subjects choosing A over B and B^* over A^*, or choosing B over A and A^* over B^*, are said to violate EUT.

To show precisely how risk aversion does matter, assume that risk attitudes can be characterized by the popular Constant Relative Risk Aversion (CRRA) function, $U(m) = (m^{1-r})/(1 - r)$, where r is the CRRA coefficient. The certainty equivalents (CE) of the lottery pairs AB and A^*B^* as a function of r are shown in the left and right upper panels respectively of Fig. 4.1. The CRRA coefficient ranges from -0.5 (moderately risk loving) up to 1.25 (very risk averse),

---

[11] To what extent do our conclusions transfer beyond the lab to field experiments? In that setting one often encounters apologies that it was not possible to control everything of theoretical interest, but that the tradeoff was worth it because one is able to make more "externally valid" inferences about behavior. Such claims should be viewed with suspicion, and are often made just to hide incomplete experimental designs (Harrison, 2005). One can always condition on a priori distributions that might have been generated by other samples in more controlled settings (e.g., Harrison, 1990), such that inferences based on posteriors do not ignore that conditioning information. Or one can complement "uncontrolled" field experiments with controlled lab experiments, acknowledging that controls for risk attitudes in the latter might interact with other differences between the lab and the field.

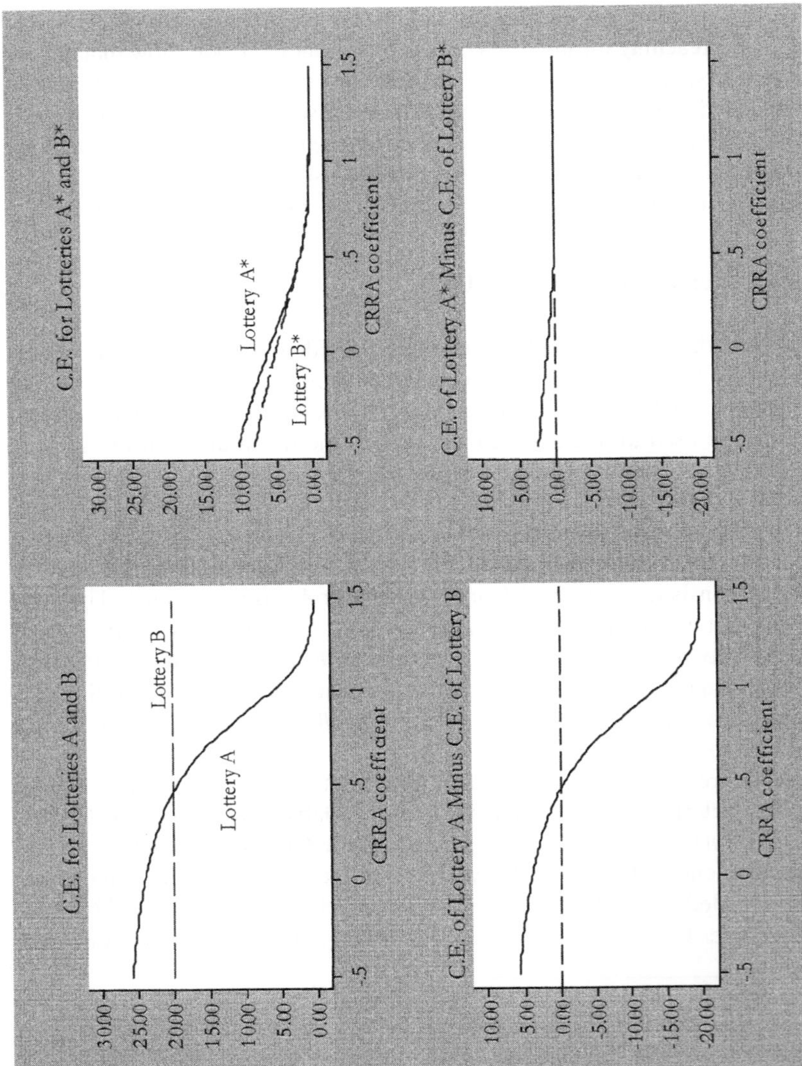

Fig. 4.1: Risk attitudes and common ratio tests of EUT.

with a risk-neutral subject at $r = 0$. The CE of lottery B, which offers \$20 for sure, is the horizontal line in the left panel. The CE of A, A^* and B^* all decline as risk aversion increases. The lower panels of Fig. 4.1 show the CE differences between the A and B (A^* and B^*) lotteries. Note that for the AB (A^*B^*) lotteries, the preferred outcome switches to lottery B (B^*) for a CRRA coefficient about 0.45.

Most evaluations of EUT acknowledge that one cannot expect any theory to predict perfectly, since any violation would lead one to reject the theory no matter how many correct predictions it makes. One way to evaluate mistakes is to calculate their costs under the theory being tested and to "forgive" those mistakes that are not very costly while holding to account those that are. For each subject in our data and each lottery choice pair, we can calculate the CE *difference* given the individual's estimated CRRA coefficient allowing us to identify those choice pairs that are most salient. A natural metric for defining "trivial EUT violations" can then be defined in terms of choices that involve a difference in CE below some given threshold.

Suppose for the moment that an expected utility maximizing individual will flip a coin to make a choice whenever the difference in CE falls below some cognitive threshold. If $r = 0.8$, the CE difference in favor of B is large in the first lottery pair and B will be chosen. In the second lottery pair, the difference between the payoffs for choosing A^* and B^* is trivial[12] and a coin is flipped to make a choice. Thus, with probability 0.5 the experimenter will observe the individual choosing B and A^*, a choice pattern inconsistent with EUT. In a sample with these risk attitudes, half the choices observed would be expected to be inconsistent with EUT.[13] With such a large difference between the choice frequencies, standard statistical tests would easily reject the hypothesis that they are the same. Thus, we would reject EUT in this case *even though EUT is true.*

Harrison et al. (2003) test EUT conditional on subjects' estimated risk aversion. Because the effects of risk aversion on our ability to test EUT depend on the particular lottery pairs used, Harrison et al. (2003) consider 6 lottery pair choices and 12 stated "selling prices" for each of those 12 lotteries taken from Grether and Plott (1979), in addition to the two CR lotteries discussed above. In this literature on Preference Reversals (PR), the term "P-bets" refers to lotteries that have a relatively high *probability* of winning a relatively low monetary prize. The alternative bets are called "\$-bets" because they have a lower probability of winning than the paired P-bet, but a higher *dollar* prize if the subject wins. PR Choice pair #1, for example, consists of the P-bet offering \$4 with probability 35/36 and a loss of \$1 with probability 1/36, and the \$-bet offering \$16 with probability 11/36 and a loss of \$1 with probability 25/36. In this case

---

12 In fact, it is less than 1 cent.

13 This example illustrates only one possible characterization of subject error. For a discussion of alternatives, see Loomes, Moffatt and Sugden (2002), Harless and Camerer (1994), Hey and Orme (1994), Hey (1995), Loomes and Sugden (1995, 1998), Ballinger and Wilcox (1997), and Carbone (1997).

the expected values are \$3.86 and \$3.85, respectively. The other five PR lottery pairs are similar. Because the lottery pairs in these experiments have virtually identical expected values, the difference in CE is zero if the CRRA coefficient $r = 0$.[14] Figure 4.2 shows that the difference in CE varies over the 6 lotteries.[15]

Based on the observed distribution of risk attitudes in our sample, we can calculate the EUT consistent choice in each of the 8 lottery pairs, assuming a CRRA utility function.[16] Abstracting from any consideration of the size of the CE difference, only 52% of observed choices were consistent with EUT when pooling over all 8 lottery pairs. Only in one PR lottery pair does one see a proportion of choices that are markedly higher than 50% and therefore consistent with EUT. However, even those observations would require us to have a high tolerance for errors in the data in order to accept EUT. One would therefore reject the predictions of EUT for this set of choices, *conditional on the point estimates of risk aversion being accepted.*

While we observe a high rate of lottery choices inconsistent with EUT, this analysis does not consider whether the apparent errors are costly from the perspective of the subject. We ask here whether consistency with EUT increases as the cost of an error increases. Moreover, we investigate whether our rejection of EUT, conditional on the point estimates of risk aversion being accepted is sensitive to the precision of our estimates of the underlying CRRA coefficients. Since the calculation of the CE differences depends critically on the CRRA estimates, we need to measure the robustness of our EUT findings to the imprecision of those estimates. While we focus on tests of EUT, this question of precision in estimating the parameters of the choice function is also relevant for tests of cumulative prospect theory, models of choice with altruism, other regarding preferences, etc.

One might ask how one can *test* EUT when one must *assume* that EUT holds in order to measure risk attitudes. Our point is that tests of EUT are incomplete if they do not also include a *joint hypothesis* about risk attitudes and consistent behavior over lottery choices. That is, one has to undertake such tests jointly or else one cannot test EUT at all, since the subject might be indifferent to the choices posed. Or, more accurately, without such tests of risk attitudes, the experimenter is unable to claim that he knows that the subject is not indifferent. So, just as EUT typically entails consistent behavior across two or more pairs of

---

[14] The payoffs in choice pair #6 have been altered slightly from the values in Grether and Plott (1979) so that a risk neutral individual is not indifferent between the two.

[15] Moffatt (2007) develops a technique to select the parameters of the experiment to maximize the information content. Rather than use his technique, we adopted familiar tests from the literature, which has the advantage of allowing comparisons to previous findings.

[16] There are 8 lotteries in total, 6 PR lotteries and 2 CR lotteries. Each individual was presented with all 6 PR choices but only one of the CR choices. Hence, we have 7 observed choices for each individual. The analysis in Harrison et al. (2003) was undertaken in the usual manner from the "preference reversal" literature: the direct binary choices of each subject were compared to the implied choices from the selling prices elicited over the underlying lotteries.

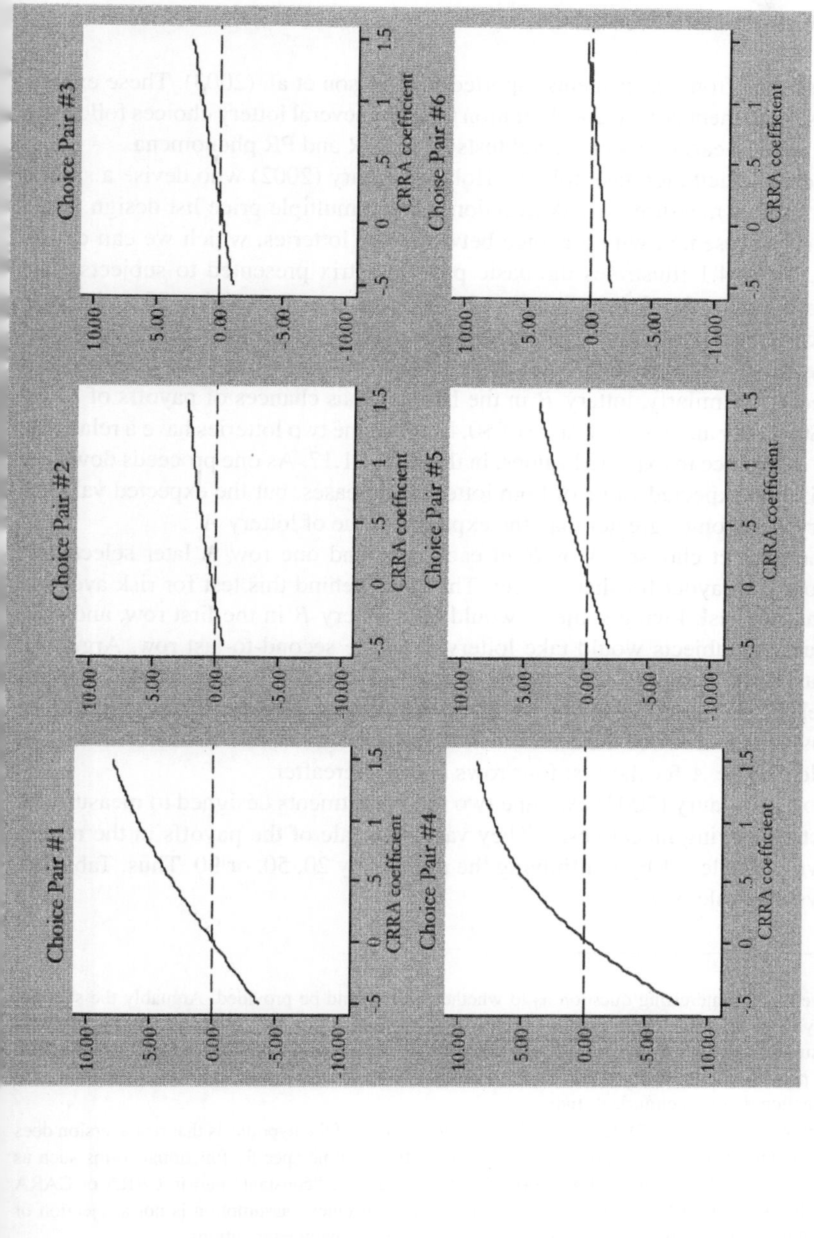

Fig. 4.2: Risk attitudes and preference reversal choice pairs
(difference in certainty equivalents favoring P-bet in each pair).

lottery comparisons, we are arguing that it necessarily entails consistent behavior across those lottery comparisons *and* a task to measure risk attitudes. Our focus, then, is on the statistical precision of the inferences from the latter task.

4.2. Experimental Procedures

We use data from experiments reported in Harrison et al. (2003). These experiments implement both a risk elicitation task and several lottery choices following those used in earlier experimental tests of the CR and PR phenomena.

The risk elicitation task follows Holt and Laury (2002) who devise a simple experimental measure for risk aversion using a multiple price list design. Each subject is presented with a choice between two lotteries, which we can call A or B. Table 4.1 illustrates the basic payoff matrix presented to subjects. The first row shows that lottery A offered a 10% chance of receiving \$2 and a 90% chance of receiving \$1.60. The expected value of this lottery, EV^{A}, is shown in the third panel as \$1.64, although the EV columns were not presented to subjects.[17] Similarly, lottery B in the first row has chances of payoffs of \$3.85 and \$0.10, for an expected value of \$0.48. Thus the two lotteries have a relatively large difference in expected values, in this case \$1.17. As one proceeds down the matrix, the expected value of both lotteries increases, but the expected value of lottery B becomes greater than the expected value of lottery A.

The subject chooses A or B in each row, and one row is later selected at random for payout for that subject. The logic behind this test for risk aversion is that only risk-loving subjects would take lottery B in the first row, and only risk-averse subjects would take lottery A in the second-to-last row. Arguably, the last row is simply a test that the subject understood the instructions, and has no relevance for risk aversion at all. A risk neutral subject should switch from choosing A to B when the EV of each is about the same, so a risk-neutral subject would choose A for the first four rows and B thereafter.

Holt and Laury (2002) examine two main treatments designed to measure the effect of varying incentives.[18] They vary the scale of the payoffs in the matrix shown in Table 4.1 by multiplying the payoffs by 20, 50, or 90. Thus, Table 4.1 shows the scale of 1.

---

[17] There is an interesting question as to whether they should be provided. Arguably the subjects are trying to calculate them anyway, so providing them avoids a test of the joint hypothesis that "the subjects can calculate EV in their heads and will not accept a fair actuarial bet." On the other hand, providing them may cue the subjects to adopt risk-neutral choices. The effect of providing EV information deserves empirical study.

[18] Holt and Laury's (2002) design provides in-sample tests of the hypothesis that risk aversion does not vary with income, an important issue for those that assume specific functional forms such as CRRA or constant absolute risk aversion (CARA), where the "constant" part in CRRA or CARA refers to the scale of the choices. A rejection of the "constancy" assumption is not a rejection of EUT in general, of course, but just these particular (popular) parameterizations.

Table 4.1: Design of the Holt and Laury risk aversion experiments
(Standard payoff matrix).

Lottery A Probability of winning $2	Probability of winning $1.60	Lottery B Probability of winning $3.85	Probability of winning $0.10	EVA (in $)	EVB (in $)	Difference in Expected value (in $)	Range of CRRA coefficient r if last lottery A choice
0.1	0.9	0.1	0.9	1.64	0.48	1.17	< -0.95
0.2	0.8	0.2	0.8	1.68	0.85	0.83	$-0.95 < r < -0.49$
0.3	0.7	0.3	0.7	1.72	1.23	0.49	$-0.49 < r < -0.15$
0.4	0.6	0.4	0.6	1.76	1.60	0.16	$-0.15 < r < 0.15$
0.5	0.5	0.5	0.5	1.80	1.98	−0.17	$0.15 < r < 0.41$
0.6	0.4	0.6	0.4	1.84	2.35	−0.51	$0.41 < r < 0.68$
0.7	0.3	0.7	0.3	1.88	2.73	−0.84	$0.68 < r < 0.97$
0.8	0.2	0.8	0.2	1.92	3.10	−1.18	$0.97 < r < 1.37$
0.9	0.1	0.9	0.1	1.96	3.48	−1.52	$1.37 < r$
1	0	1	0	2.00	3.85	−1.85	

Harrison et al. (2003) adapt the Holt and Laury (2002) procedure by scaling it appropriately for the present purposes. Multiplying by 10 the original payoff scale of 1, which has prizes ranging between \$0.10 and \$3.85, provides responses that span prizes between \$1.00 and \$38.50. These two payoffs scales are referred to as $1x$ and $10x$ hereafter. The $10x$ payoffs comfortably covers the range of prizes needed to apply the measures of risk aversion to our experiments. All subjects were given the $10x$ test, but some were also given a $1x$ test prior to the $10x$, which we refer to as the $1x10x$ treatment since these payoffs are comparable to the EUT decision tasks.[19]

Apart from conducting experiments to elicit subjects attitudes toward risk (the risk aversion experiments) Harrison et al. (2003) also conducted experiments with the same subjects in order to test for violations of EUT, controlling for risk aversion. To avoid possible intra-session effects, only one experiment was run in each session. The same subjects were contacted again by e-mail and invited to participate in subsequent experiments that were separated by at least one week.[20] Students were recruited from the University of South Carolina. In total, 152 subjects participated in a risk aversion experiment and, of those, 88 also participated in the lottery choice experiments. Overall, there were 88 subjects for whom we can match results from the risk aversion test to the lottery choice task. No attempt was made to screen subjects for recruitment into subsequent experiments based on their choices in earlier experiments.

All subjects received a fixed show-up fee of \$5 in each of the three experiments, consistent with our standard procedures.[21] This is a constant across all subjects, and does not vary with the decisions the subjects faced. No subject faced losses.

The lower left panel of Fig. 4.3 displays the elicited CRRA coefficients for our sample, based on a sample of 152 subjects. We employ the CRRA utility function introduced earlier to define the CRRA intervals represented by each row in the payoff matrix faced by the subject shown in Table 4.1, although other functional forms could also be used and would lead to similar conclusions. Each subject is assigned the midpoint of the CRRA interval at which they switch from choosing lottery A to lottery B.[22] The right column in Table 4.1 shows CRRA intervals associated with each switch point. The resulting distribution of risk attitudes is depicted in the bottom left panel in Fig. 4.3. While a small portion of

---

[19] The reason for this design was to test for "order effects" in elicited risk attitudes, as reported in Harrison et al. (2005b).

[20] The time between sessions for a given subject was usually one or two weeks. Harrison et al. (2005a) show that elicited risk attitudes for this sample are stable over time horizons of several months.

[21] The subjects were recruited in lectures for experiments run during the usual lecture time and they received no show-up fee. In our case, subjects were recruited via Ex-Lab (http://exlab.bus.ucf.edu), consisting of a combination of e-mail alerts and on-line registration schedules from a subject pool database.

[22] Several subjects switched two or more times. In this case we use the first and last switch points to define a relatively "fat" interval for that subject.

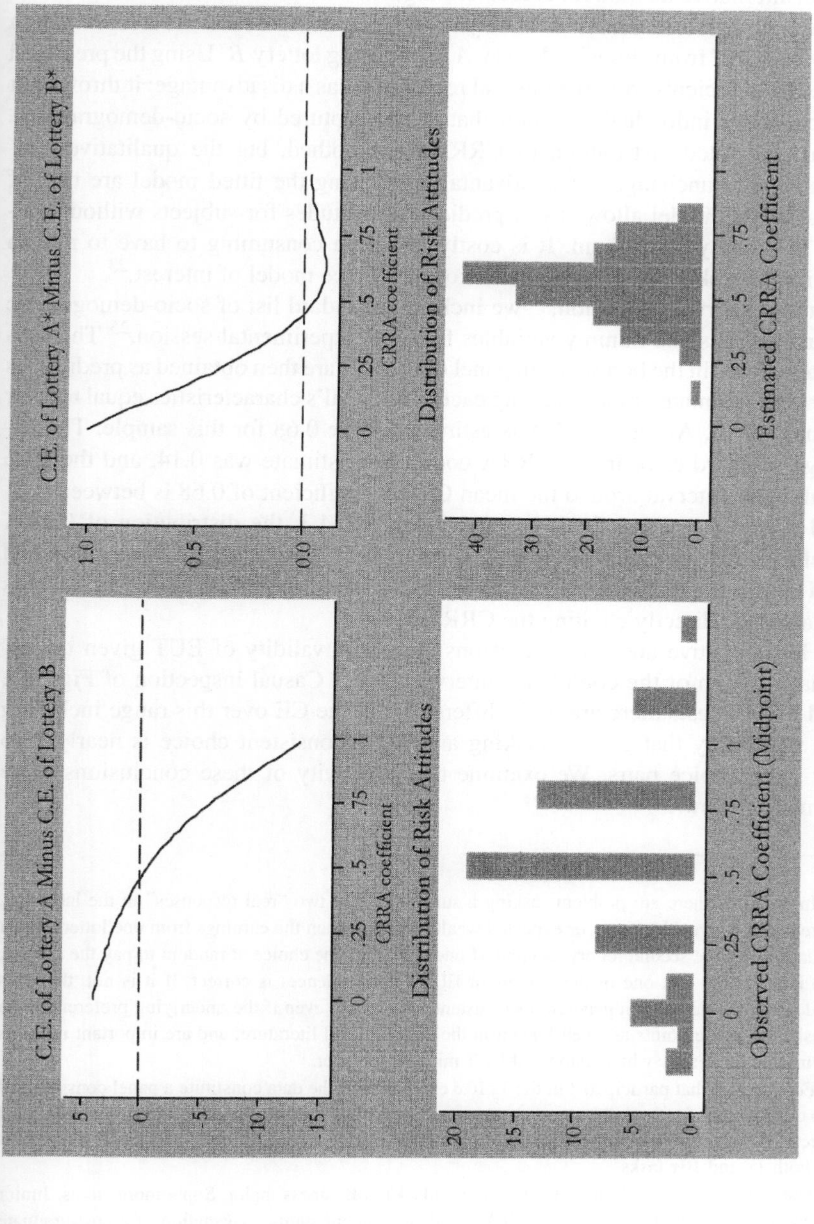

Fig. 4.3: Observed risk attitudes and common-ratio tests of EUT.

subjects appear to be risk-loving or risk-neutral, the bulk of the subjects appear to be averse to risk, with the modal response being in the neighborhood of a CRRA value of 0.5.

An alternative method for characterizing risk attitudes is an interval regression statistical model in which each subject's choice is the CRRA interval at which they "switch" from choosing lottery A to choosing lottery B. Using the predicted CRRA coefficients from the interval regression has a disadvantage: it throws out much of the individual variation that is not captured by socio-demographics. Thus, the fitted distribution of CRRA is smoothed, but the qualitative conclusions are unchanged. The advantages of using the fitted model are that, if reliable, the model allows us to predict risk attitudes for subjects without having to directly elicit them. It is costly and time consuming to have to run an elicitation task in addition to the test of the choice model of interest.[23]

In the interval regression,[24] we include a standard list of socio-demographic characteristics and dummy variables for each experimental session.[25] The estimates shown in the bottom right panel of Fig. 4.3 are then obtained as predictions from this estimated model, setting each individual's characteristics equal to their actual values. Average CRRA is estimated to be 0.68 for this sample. The average standard error in the CRRA coefficient estimate was 0.14, and the 95% confidence interval around the mean CRRA coefficient of 0.68 is between 0.41 and 0.96. Comparing the lower panels of Fig. 4.3, the distribution of CRRA coefficients from the interval regression model (right panel) is more smoothed and concentrated around the mean relative to the distribution (left panel) that is obtained by directly eliciting the CRRA values.

How sensitive are our conclusions about the validity of EUT given the estimated width of the confidence interval above? Casual inspection of Figs. 4.1 and 4.2 suggests there are wide differences in the CE over this range including the possibility that cost of making an EUT-inconsistent choice is nearly zero for some choice pairs. We examine the sensitivity of these conclusions more formally below.

---

[23] In addition, there are problems asking a subject to give two "real responses" in the lab. First, there might be wealth effects, or expected wealth effects, when the earnings from one lottery affect valuations for the second lottery. Second, if one picks out one choice at random to pay the subject, one is assuming that one of the axioms of EUT (independence) is correct. If it is not, then this random payoff device can generate inconsistent preferences even if the underlying preferences are consistent. These points are well known in the experimental literature, and are important if one is attempting to identify which axioms of EUT might be in error.

[24] For subjects that participated in the $1x10x$ experiments, the data constitute a panel consisting of two observations for that subject, so we use panel interval regression models with random individual effects. We included a binary indicator in the regression to control for order effects when subjects did both $1x$ and $10x$ tasks.

[25] These were binary indicators for sex, race (black), a Business major, Sophomore status, Junior status, Senior status, high GPA, low GPA, Graduate student status, expectation of a post-graduate education, college education for the father of the subject, college education for the mother of the subject, and US citizen status. We also included age in years.

4.3. Effects of CE Differences on Tests of EUT

We first consider the possibility that subjects may be more likely to choose inconsistently with EUT when the cost of doing so is trivial. Figure 4.4 shows the fraction of EUT consistent choices as a function of CE differences, using all the data from the two CR choices and the 6 PR choices. For each threshold listed on the bottom axis, the calculations underlying these figures drop any choice that entails a CE *difference* that is *less* than the indicated threshold. Thus, as the threshold gets above several pennies, many of the A^*B^* choices faced by risk averse subjects are naturally dropped from consideration. Figure 4.4 shows thresholds for the difference in CE varying from 0 cents up to 100 cents. The thin, dashed line shows the fraction of choices above the threshold on the bottom axis. Thus, for a threshold of 0 cents 100% of the choices are considered (i.e., the choices from the 6 PR choices plus the 2 CR choices, for all individuals). As the threshold increases, additional choices are dropped. Whether a choice is dropped depends on the estimated risk aversion of the subject and the parameters of the lotteries in each choice, since these are the factors determining the CE. The heavy, solid line shows the fraction of the remaining choices that are consistent with the EUT prediction.

Surprisingly, the ability of EUT to predict choices does not appear to increase as the threshold for CE differences is increased. Our earlier conclusion, that there is little support for EUT, is therefore not affected by excluding observations that were based on small differences in the CE of the lotteries (and where "small" is defined parametrically, so that the reader may individually decide what is

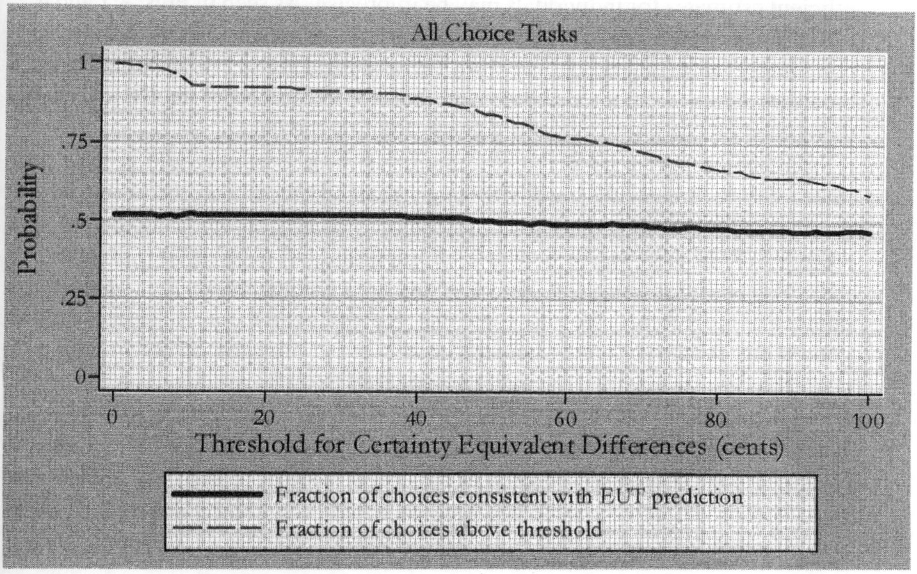

Fig. 4.4: Fraction of EUT consistent choices as a function of certainty equivalent differences.

small). Moreover, although not shown in Fig. 4.4, we find that EUT does not do better than about 50% correctly predicted even if CE differences are required to exceed $3.00. Simple random chance would explain these data better than EUT.

Figure 4.5 undertakes the same analysis at the level of each individual task.[26] These results show that the fraction of choices above the threshold, shown by the thin dashed line, stays quite high for most of the preference reversal choice tasks. This is by design, given that we have a generally risk averse subject pool. By contrast, the fraction of choices above the threshold drops rapidly in the CR task involving lotteries A^* and B^*, as implied from Fig. 4.1. In fact, given the CRRA values observed in our sample, no decisions have CE differences greater than about 30 cents for the A^*B^* pair. For this task and two of the preference reversal tasks, Pair 3 and 6, the fraction of choices consistent with EUT, shown by the heavy, solid line, does increase as the threshold increases. However, this only occurs for a small fraction of choices since the number of choices above the threshold falls rapidly for these three tasks. For the remaining tasks, there appears to be no relationship between the minimum threshold and the extent to which choices are consistent with EUT. This is particularly telling since these are the tasks for which a substantial fraction of choices exceed the threshold.

4.4. Allowing for Imprecision in Risk Elicitation

We have seen that error rates do not decline even when CE differences are large. While we do not see any persuasive evidence that the size of CE differences affects our conclusions about EUT , we must recognize that our risk aversion coefficient estimates for individuals may be imprecise. As seen in Figs. 4.1 and 4.2, CE differences are very sensitive to the CRRA coefficient. Small changes in r can change an observed choice from being considered a trivial violation to a costly violation, or to no violation. Imprecision in estimating the CRRA coefficient must be taken into account when evaluating the data.

Imprecision may arise if our risk elicitation task does not yield precise estimates due to "trembling hand" error on behalf of the subject, or to our failure to elicit sufficient information to make more precise inferences about the risk attitudes of the subject. To illustrate an important but subtle point, imagine we had collected information on hair color and used that to explain the risk aversion choices of our subject. We anticipate that this would be a poor statistical model, generating extremely wide standard errors on our forecast of the individual's risk attitudes. As a result, it would be very easy to find a predicted risk aversion coefficient within a 95% confidence interval of the mean predicted value that includes the point of indifference. Thus one could almost always find a risk attitude that makes the observed choices consistent with EUT, but only because the statistical model was so poor. We have selected individual characteristics that

[26] The lines in Fig. 4.5 are defined identically to those in Fig. 4.4.

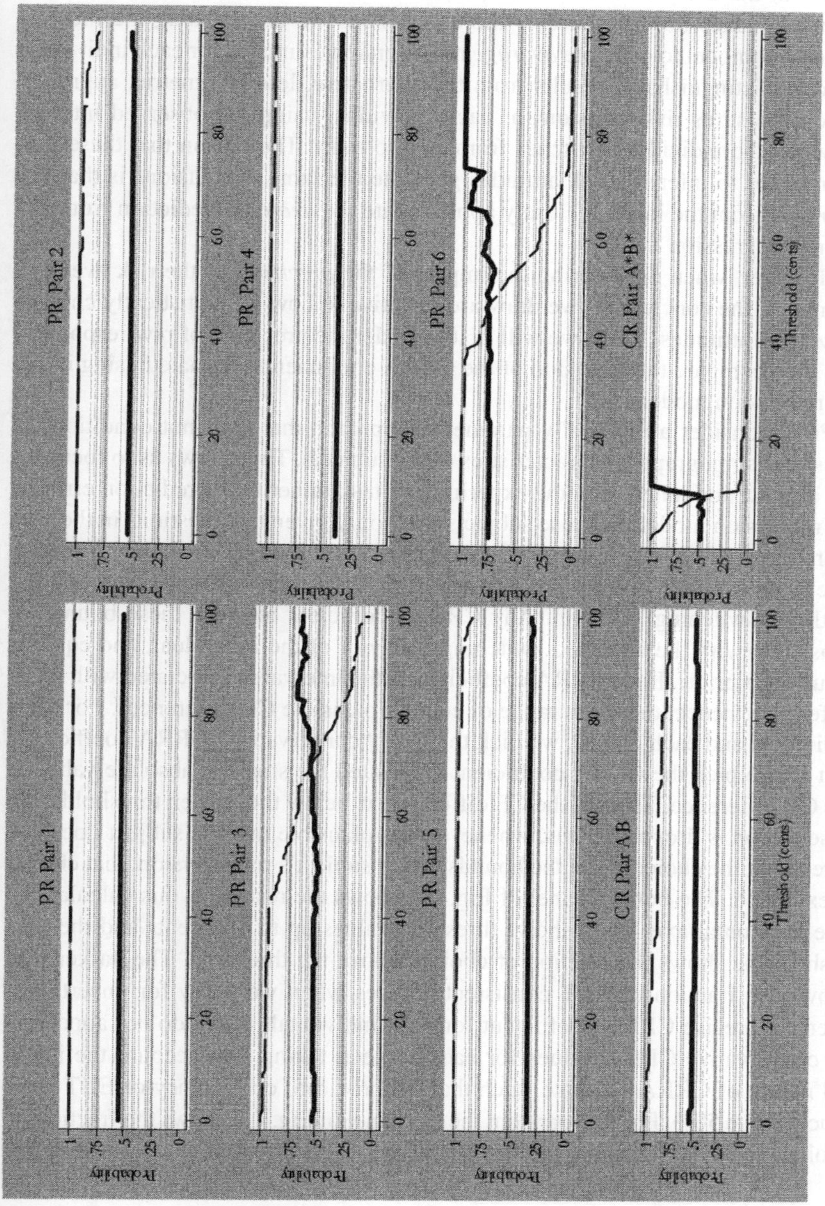

Fig. 4.5: Fraction of EUT consistent choices as a function of certainty equivalent differences.

are standard in empirical work of this kind, but there is always the risk that none of these characteristics help us predict risk attitudes carefully.

For all the analyses and tests employed so far, the way we characterize risk attitudes makes no difference to the conclusions we draw. Using the interval regression model to generate *average* risk aversion estimates for each individual yields indistinguishable results from the alternative, less parametric, approach which measures risk aversion for each individual using the observed interval at which the individual switches from safe to risky. The reason that these two approaches to inferring risk attitudes generate the same conclusions is that the *averages* from the interval closely approximate the *average* prediction from the interval regression model.

However, when considering the impact of the *precision* of the risk aversion estimates, the conclusions we draw are sensitive to how we statistically characterize risk attitudes. Thus, we will first consider the precision of raw responses, and then compare the precision of the CRRA coefficients estimated using interval regression models.

First, consider a minimally parametric approach that does not condition on the socio-demographic characteristics of the subjects. This allows us to focus on the imprecision inherent in the experimental task rather than prediction error in the regression model. Because subjects were only given ten questions in the risk aversion task, we only know the interval at which the subject switched from the safe to risky choice.[27] For each individual we know the upper and lower bounds of their "switching" interval. Any CRRA coefficient between these bounds is consistent with the observed switching behavior of the individual, and equally plausible a priori. Each CRRA coefficient in the interval is associated with a CE difference; hence, there is a range of equally plausible CE differences. For each individual and each choice, we pick the most "conservative" CRRA coefficient, that is, we pick the CRRA coefficient associated the smallest absolute value of the CE difference. Then, if the CE difference is below the chosen threshold, this observation is dropped. Thus, whenever it is plausible that the subject does not care about the choice given the bounds on the subject's risk aversion, that choice is excluded. The bottom panel of Fig. 4.6 shows the results of this calculation. The horizontal axis again shows threshold values up to 100 cents and the thin dashed line shows the fraction of choices above the threshold. The darker line shows the fraction of EUT consistent choices when we allow for uncertainty over the precise CRRA coefficient for each individual. There do not appear to be conservative CRRA values for each subject, taking into account the interval nature of CRRA estimate, such that the predicted consistency of EUT rises much above 50%. For comparison, the top panel of Fig. 4.6 shows the fraction of choices correctly predicted by EUT assuming *no* uncertainty in the risk aversion

---

27 Of course, we could have asked more questions to "pin" the individual to a smaller interval. This alternative is implemented in a risk aversion elicitation task by Harrison, Lau, Rrutström and Sullivan (2005).

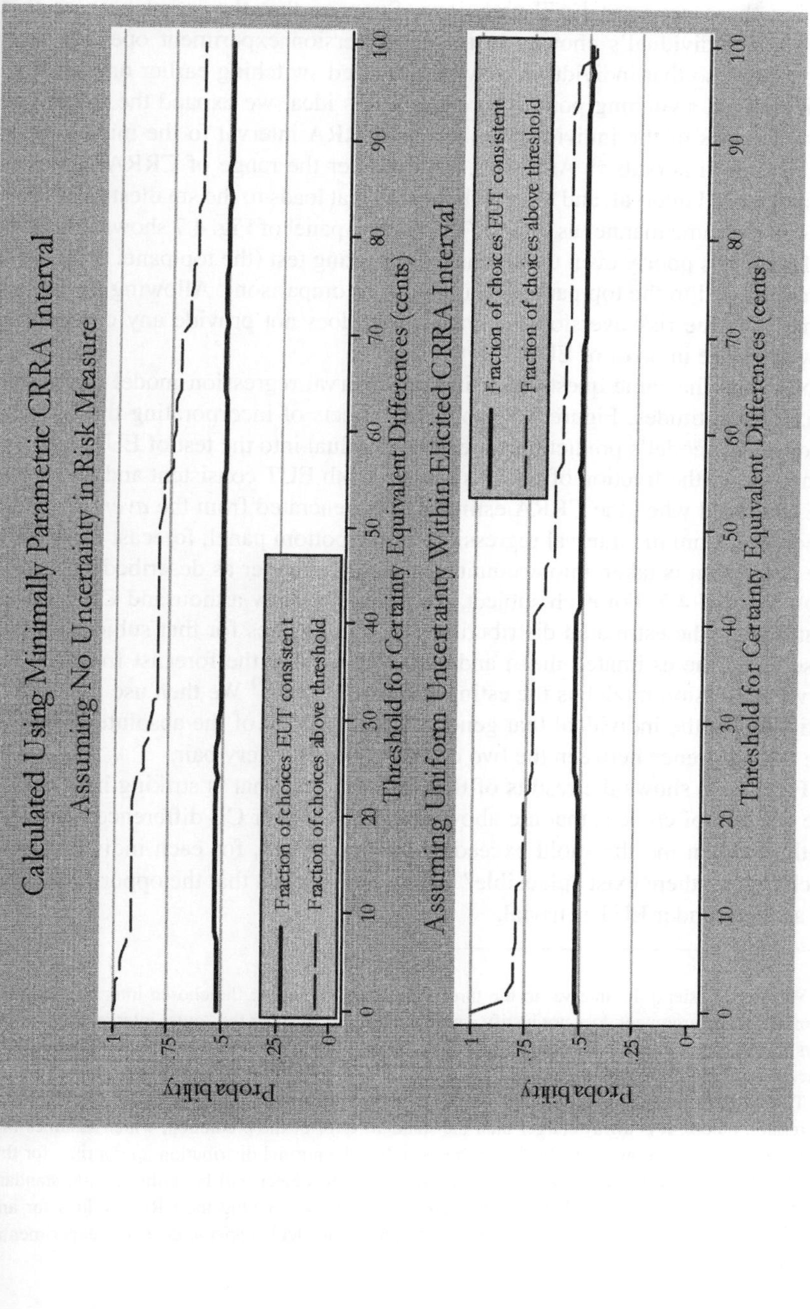

Fig. 4.6: Sample uncertainty and EUT consistent choices.

measure and using the midpoint of each individual's raw CRRA response interval. There is little difference in the fraction of EUT consistent choices between the top and bottom panels of Fig. 4.6.

We also consider whether "trembling hand" errors in risk aversion could be driving these apparent EUT violations. Suppose that the latent process that drives an individual's choices in the risk aversion experiment operates with some error, so that individuals may be observed switching earlier or later than their optimal switching points. To capture this idea, we expand the upper and lower bounds of the individual's observed CRRA interval to the midpoints of the adjacent intervals.[28] As above, we consider the range of CRRA values in this expanded interval, and then pick the one that leads to the smallest CE difference in the same manner as before. The bottom panel of Fig. 4.7 shows that EUT still preforms poorly even under this less exacting test (the top panel of Fig. 4.6 is reproduced in the top panel of Fig. 4.7 for comparison). Allowing for uncertainty over the risk aversion interval chosen does not provide any compelling new evidence in favor of EUT.

Now ask the same questions using the interval regression model to characterize risk attitudes. Figure 4.8 shows the effects of incorporating the forecast error of the model's prediction for each individual into the test of EUT. The top panel shows the fraction of choices that are both EUT consistent and above the CE threshold when the CRRA estimates are generated from the *average* of the prediction from the interval regression. In the bottom panel, forecast error from the regression is taken into account in a similar manner as described above for Figs. 4.6 and 4.7. For each subject, we randomly draw a thousand CRRA estimates from the estimated distribution of CRRA values for that subject, in this case using the estimated mean and standard error of the forecast from the interval regression model as the estimated distribution.[29] We then use the CRRA estimate for the individual that generates the smallest of the absolute values of the CE difference between the two choices in each lottery pair.

Figure 4.8 shows the results of this calculation. What is striking here is that the fraction of choices that are above the threshold for CE differences drops to nothing when the threshold exceeds 10 cents. Hence, for each individual and each lottery, there exist "plausible" CRRA values such that the opportunity cost of an error under EUT is trivial.

---

[28] We do not extend the interval to the three intervals surrounding the chosen interval, since the trembling hand argument does not justify a uniform distribution over the "outer intervals." It simply says that somebody may have had a CRRA of 0.16 but chosen the interval with upper bound 0.15 since it was "close enough."

[29] The standard error of a forecast takes into account the uncertainty of the coefficients in the interval regression model. It is always larger than the standard error of the prediction, which assumes that those estimates are known exactly. These draws reflect the normal distribution appropriate for this estimated coefficient value, so 95% of the draws for each subject will be within ± 1.96 standard errors of the point estimate. Thus, to emphasize, we are not allowing the CRRA values for any individual to take on values that are outside the realm of statistical precision given our experimental procedures.

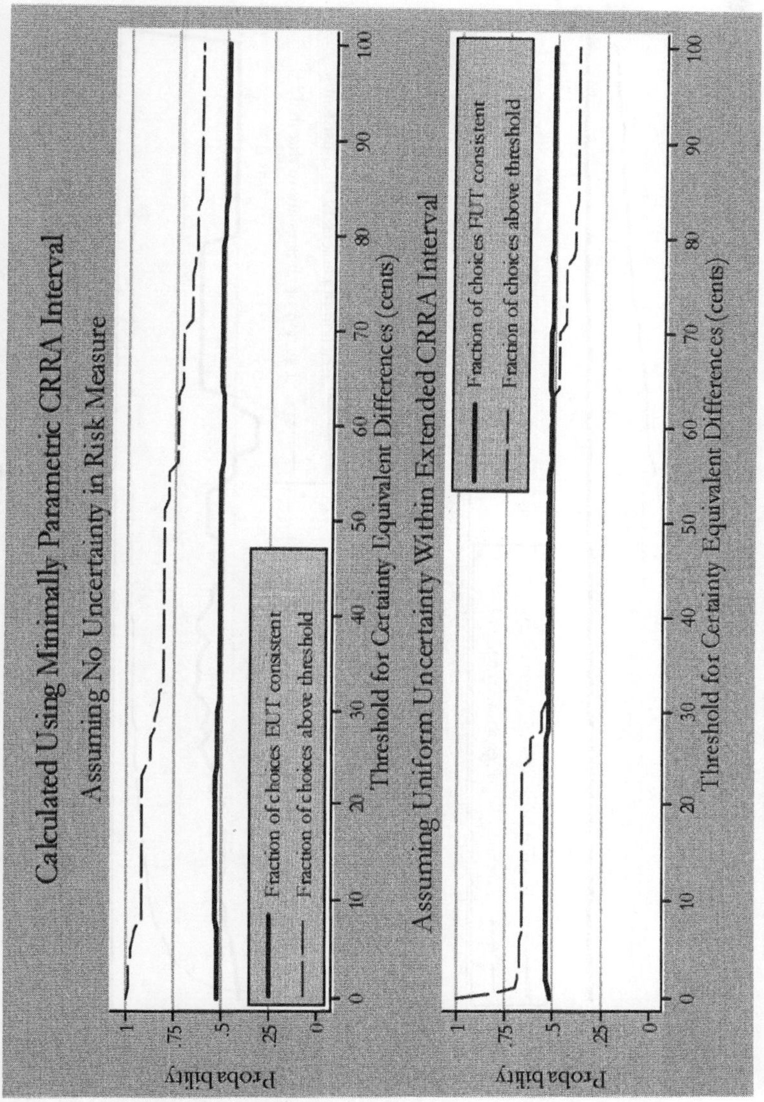

Fig. 4.7: Additional sample uncertainty and EUT consistent choices.

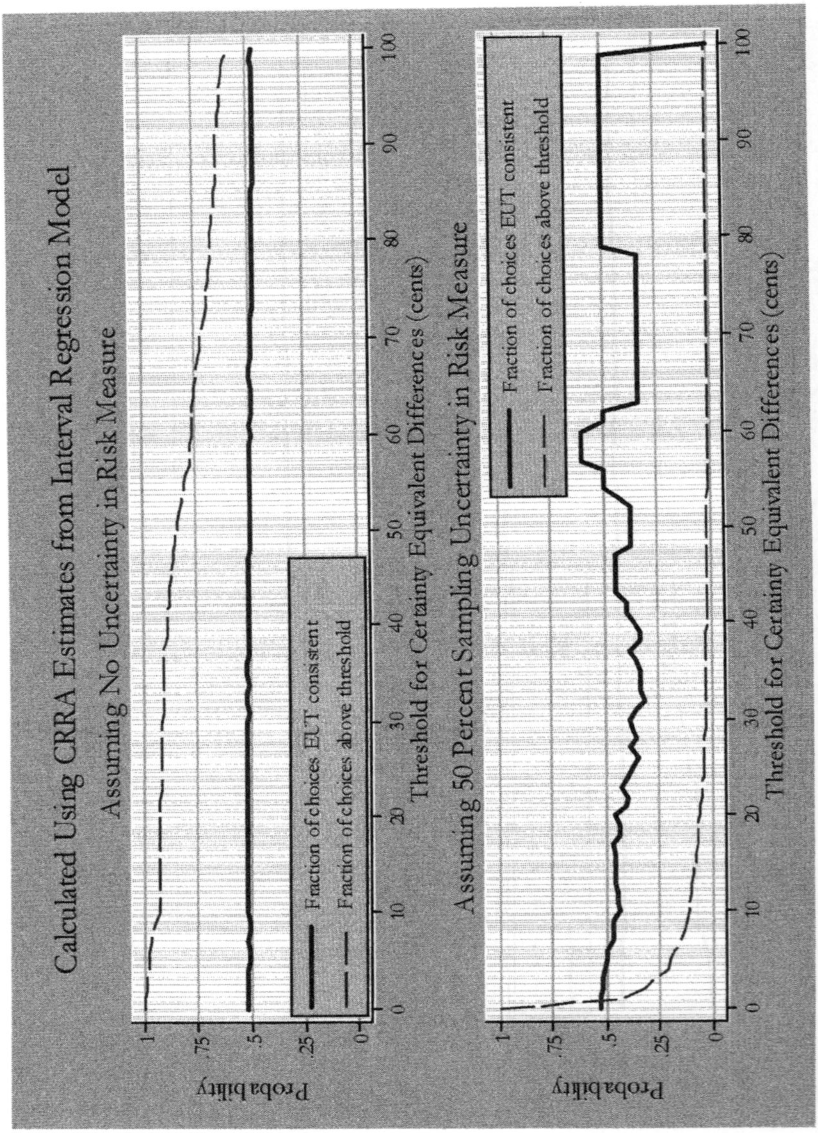

Fig. 4.8: Sample uncertainty and EUT consistent choices.

Figures 4.6 and 4.8 pose a dilemma for the interpretation of the lottery choices from the perspective of EUT. One must decide which statistical characterization of risk attitudes is the best, in terms of reflecting the precision of inferences possible from our experimental procedure. Although there is nothing wrong with the interval regression characterization, we are firmly inclined towards the minimally parametric characterization since we have that for each individual in our sample. It makes fewer assumptions about the process generating the observed risk aversion choices, can be easily relaxed to undertake robustness checks as shown in Fig. 4.7, and can be refined with simple extensions of the experimental procedures we used.[30] Thus, we conclude that *if one cannot directly elicit risk attitudes from the sample then EUT may be operationally meaningless since the estimated risk attitude coefficients suffer from too much imprecision.*

There are situations in which one might prefer the interval regression model, despite the relative imprecision of the estimates that result. Assume that the risk aversion test has been applied to a sample drawn from one population, and one wants to define a risk aversion distribution for use in interpreting data drawn from choices in a risk-sensitive task by a distinct sample drawn from the same population or a distinct population. All that one might know about the new sample are individual characteristics, such as sex and age. One could then generate conditional predictions for the new sample using the coefficient estimates from the interval regression model estimated on the first sample and the information on characteristics of the new, target sample. The minimally parametric characterization is not so attractive here, since it cannot be so easily conditioned on individual characteristics. In many experimental situations considerations of cost may necessitate using predicted rather than elicited risk attitude coefficients. However, more work on specifying good predictive models is needed before such an approach can be meaningfully applied. Furthermore, there are many situations in which one only needs to know broad qualitative properties of the risk attitudes of subjects (e.g., are they risk-neutral or not), rather than precise estimates of degrees of risk aversion. For such purposes the within-sample procedures may be overkill.

4.5. Conclusions

We address the imprecision of the empirical parameterization of risk attitude in expected utility choice models and its impact on the probability of rejecting the underlying choice model. We provide an extended case study of the inferential problems that arise, assuming a CRRA form for the utility function. However,

---

30 Harrison, Lau, Rutström and Sullivan (2005) consider two ways. One, noted earlier, is to "iterate" the MPL procedure several times so that subjects get 10 intervals *within* the interval they chose on the prior iteration. The other way in which one can tighten the CRRA interval is to administer the procedure several times over distinct lottery prizes, so as to span a more refined set of CRRA intervals.

the issue is broadly generalizable to any situation in which parameters need to be estimated prior to testing the hypothesized choice function.[31] We adopt a procedure in which the risk attitude estimates are perturbed over successively wider intervals to provide a sense of the robustness of our conclusions regarding the hypothesized EUT choice function. We constrain the perturbations to intervals that are within estimated confidence intervals of the point estimates.

We begin by considering a context in which EUT appears to be a poor predictor of choice behavior. Under the null hypothesis of EUT and CRRA, we calculate the cost of choosing inconsistently with EUT conditional on estimated individual risk parameters. We find no evidence that the predictive power of EUT improves when we restrict the sample to choices that impose nontrivial costs on subjects. We proceed to examine two methods for estimating the first stage parameters, in this case individual risk parameters. Risk measures may be directly elicited by giving each subject a test, or may be predicted based on a statistical model that utilizes the information on subject risk response and demographics. In either case we find pervasive violations of the theory even when the opportunity costs of errors are substantial for a risk averse, expected utility maximizer. Furthermore, allowing for imprecision in our estimates due to "trembling hand" error demonstrates that we can estimate coefficients of relative risk aversion with sufficient precision to test EUT. Unfortunately, this is only true for the directly elicited "within" sample method. While the point estimates from the statistical model would lead to the same conclusion as when we directly elicit risk aversion measures, the imprecision of those estimates is such that they include CRRA values for which the cost of almost any error is negligible. While our qualitative conclusions about expected utility theory are unaffected by imprecision in measuring risk aversion, this concern is generally applicable to a wide variety of experimental situations.

Acknowledgements

We thank the US National Science Foundation for research support under grants NSF/IIS 9817518 and NSF/POWRE 9973669 to Rutström, grant NSF/SES 0213974 to McInnes, and grants NSF/DRU 0527675 and NSF/SES 0616746 to

---

31 This need to account for the effect of errors that may arise in the elicitation task has been explicitly considered in the literature on using the "trade-off method" of Wakker and Deneffe (1996) to elicit the probability weighting function of rank-dependent utility theory. Using methods similar to the ones proposed here, Bleichrodt and Pinto (2000) use simulations to assess the robustness of their conclusions about the shape of the probability weighting function to subject errors. Even if errors cannot "propagate" in the elicitation task, any test of a choice theory that is formed conditional on a fitted parameter must take into account the precision with which that first stage parameter is estimated. More generally, the literature provides many examples in which predicted behavior is conditioned on risk attitudes, which then serve as a confound unless controlled for in some manner. For example, Cox, Smith and Walker (1985) and Harrison (1990) consider the effect of calibrating controls for risk attitudes on predicted bidding behavior in first-price sealed-bid auctions.

Harrison and Rutström. We are grateful to Maribeth Coller, Morten Lau, Graham Loomes, Chris Starmer, Robert Sugden, Melonie Sullivan and Peter Wakker for comments, as well as participants at the 11th Conference on the Foundations & Applications of Utility, Risk & Decision Theory in Paris. Supporting data and instructions are stored at the ExLab Digital Archive at http://exlab.bus.ucf.edu.

References

Ballinger, T.P., Wilcox, N.T. (1997). Decisions, error and heterogeneity. *Economic Journal* **107**, 1090–1105.

Bleichrodt, H., Pinto, J.L. (2000). A parameter-free elicitation of the probability weighting function in medical decision analysis. *Management Science* **46** (11), 1485–1496.

Botelho, A., Harrison, G.W., Pinto, L.M.C., Rutström, E.E. (2005). Social norms and social choice. Working paper 05-23. Department of Economics, College of Business Administration, University of Central Florida.

Carbone, E. (1997). Investigation of stochastic preference theory using experimental data. *Economics Letters* **57**, 305–311.

Charness, G., Rabin, M. (2002). Understanding social preferences with simple tests. *Quarterly Journal of Economics* **117** (3), 817–869.

Coller, M., Harrison, G.W., Rutström, E.E. (2006). Does everyone have quasi-hyperbolic preferences? Working paper 06–01. Department of Economics, College of Business Administration, University of Central Florida.

Cox, J.C. (2004). How to identify trust and reciprocity. *Games and Economic Behavior* **46** (2), 260–281.

Cox, J.C., Sadiraj, V. (2006). Small- and large-stakes risk aversion: Implications of concavity calibration for decision theory. *Games and Economic Behavior* **56** (1), 45–60.

Cox, J.C., Smith, V.L., Walker, J.M. (1985). Experimental development of sealed-bid auction theory: Calibrating controls for risk aversion. *American Economic Review (Papers and Proceedings)*, **75**, 160–165.

Engle-Warnick, J. (2004). Inferring decision rules from experimental choice data. Working paper. Department of Economics, McGill University.

Fudenberg, D., Levine, D.K. (2006). A dual self-model of impulse control. *American Economic Review* **96** (5), 1449–1476.

Grether, D.M., Plott, C.R. (1979). Economic theory of choice and the preference reversal phenomenon. *American Economic Review* **69**, 623–648.

Harbaugh, W.T., Krause, K., Vesterlund, L. (2002). Risk attitudes of children and adults: Choices over small and large probability gains and losses. *Experimental Economics* **5**, 53–84.

Harless, D.W., Camerer, C.F. (1994). The predictive utility of generalized expected utility theories. *Econometrica* **62** (6), 1251–1289.

Harrison, G.W. (1990). Risk attitudes in first-price auction experiments: A Bayesian analysis. *Review of Economics and Statistics* **82**, 541–546.

Harrison, G.W. (2005). Field experiments and control. In: Carpenter, J., Harrison, G.W., List, J.A. (Eds.), *Field Experiments in Economics, vol. 10*. Research in Experimental Economics. JAI Press, Greenwich, CT.

Harrison, G.W., List, J.A. (2004). Field experiments. *Journal of Economic Literature* **42** (4), 1013–1059.

Harrison, G.W., Rutström, E.E. (2005). Expected utility theory and prospect theory: One wedding and a decent funeral. Working paper 05-18. Department of Economics, College of Business Administration, University of Central Florida.

Harrison, G.W., Johnson, E., McInnes, M.M., Rutström, E.E. (2003). Individual choice and risk aversion in the laboratory: A reconsideration. Working paper 03-18. Department of Economics, College of Business Administration, University of Central Florida.

Harrison, G.W., Johnson, E., McInnes, M.M., Rutström, E.E. (2005a). Temporal stability of estimates of risk aversion. *Applied Financial Economics Letters* **1**, 31–35.

Harrison, G.W., Johnson, E., McInnes, M.M., Rutström, E.E. (2005b). Risk aversion and incentive effects: Comment. *American Economic Review* **95** (3), 897–901.

Harrison, G.W., Lau, M.I., Rutström, E.E. (2005). Risk attitudes, randomization to treatment, and self-selection into experiments. Working paper 05-01. Department of Economics, College of Business Administration, University of Central Florida.

Harrison, G.W., Lau, M.I., Rutström, E.E., Sullivan, M.B. (2005). Eliciting risk and time preferences using field experiments: Some methodological issues. In: Carpenter, J., Harrison, G.W., List, J.A. (Eds.), *Field Experiments in Economics, vol. 10*. Research in Experimental Economics. JAI Press, Greenwich, CT.

Hey, J.D. (1995). Experimental investigations of errors in decision making under risk. *European Economic Review* **39**, 633–640.

Hey, J.D., Orme, C. (1994). Investigating generalizations of expected utility theory using experimental data. *Econometrica* **62** (6), 1291–1326.

Holt, C.A., Laury, S.K. (2002). Risk aversion and incentive effects. *American Economic Review* **92** (5), 1644–1655.

Karlan, D., Zinman, J. (2005). Observing unobservables: Identifying information asymmetries with a consumer credit field experiment. Working paper. Department of Economics, Yale University.

Kocher, M., Strauß, S., Sutter, M. (2006). Individual or team decision-making: Causes and consequences of self-selection. *Games & Economic Behavior* **56** (2), 259–270.

Lazear, E.P., Malmendier, U., Weber, R.A. (2006). Sorting in experiments, with application to social experiments. Working paper. Department of Economics, Stanford University.

Leamer, E.E. (1978). *Specification Searches: Ad Hoc Inference with Nonexperimental Data*. Wiley, New York.

Loomes, G., Sugden, R. (1995). Incorporating a stochastic element into decision theories. *European Economic Review* **39**, 641–648.

Loomes, G., Sugden, R. (1998). Testing different stochastic specifications of risky choice. *Economica* **65**, 581–598.

Loomes, G., Moffatt, P.G., Sugden, R. (2002). A microeconometric test of alternative stochastic theories of risky choice. *Journal of Risk and Uncertainty* **24** (2), 103–130.

Magnus, J.R. (2007). Local sensitivity in econometrics. In: Boumans, M. (Ed.), *Measurement in Economics: A Handbook*. Elsevier, San Diego, CA (this book).

Mayer, T. (2007). The empirical significance of models. In: Boumans, M. (Ed.), *Measurement in Economics: A Handbook*. Elsevier, San Diego, CA (this book).

Moffatt, P.G. (2007). Models of decision and choice. In: Boumans, M. (Ed.), *Measurement in Economics: A Handbook*. Elsevier, San Diego, CA (this book).

Prelec, D. (1998). The probability weighting function. *Econometrica* **66**, 497–527.

Rabin, M. (2000). Risk aversion and expected utility theory: A calibration theorem. *Econometrica* **68**, 1281–1292.

Rubinstein, A. (2002). Comments on the risk and time preferences in economics. Unpublished manuscript. Department of Economics, Princeton University.

Wakker, P.P., Deneffe, E. (1996). Eliciting von Neumann–Morgenstern utilities when probabilities are distorted or unknown. *Management Science* **42**, 1131–1150.

CHAPTER 5

An Analytical History of Measuring Practices: The Case of Velocities of Money

Mary S. Morgan[a,b]

[a]*London School of Economics, London, UK*
[b]*University of Amsterdam, The Netherlands*
E-mail address: m.morgan@lse.ac.uk

5.1. Introduction

This paper is concerned with the kind of measurements that are often taken for granted in modern economics, namely the measurement of the entities that economists theorise about such as: prices, money, utility, *GNP*, cycles, and so forth. Two important issues are addressed here. One concerns the general constitution of such measurements in economics, or for that matter, in the social sciences more generally: What makes good economic measurements? The second is an enquiry into the historical trajectory of economists' successive attempts to provide reliable measurements for the concepts in their field. Is there a recognisable transit, and if so, what are its characteristics? I shall seek and frame answers to both these questions with the help of that useful, but perhaps unusual, concept to find in the practice of economics: namely, "measuring instruments".[1] The discussion makes extensive use of a case example: the history of attempts to measure the velocity of money – as a way of analysing the nature of economists' measuring instruments. In this case, as we will see, economists began by measuring velocity as a free standing entity using statistical data from various sources. They went on to use identities or equations from monetary theory to derive measurements of velocity that were still understood as an observable feature of the economy. More recently, economists defined and measured velocity using econometric models that embedded the mathematical idealised notions of theory in terms of statistical data relations. The case provides material for an analytical history that illuminates both general issues noted above: the criteria for measuring instruments; and the historical development of such instruments in economics.

---

[1] Marcel Boumans first introduced this terminology in an insightful series of papers on measurement in economics – see his 1999, 2001 and 2005, as well as this, volumes.

Measurement in Economics: A Handbook
Marcel Boumans (Editor)

5.2. Measuring Things

5.2.1. Ideas about measuring from philosophy, metrology and history of science

There are three kinds of literature that help us to think seriously and analytically about the history of economic measurements, particularly the problems of measuring things that are not easy to measure. These literatures come from the philosophy of science, from metrology, and from the history and social studies of science. As we shall see, they are complementary.

The mainstream philosophy of science position, known as the representational theory of measurement, is associated particularly with the work of Patrick Suppes.[2] This theory was developed by Suppes in conjunction with Krantz, Tversky and Luce, and grew out of their shared practical experience of experiments in psychology into a highly formalised approach between the 1970s and 1990s (see Michell, this volume). The original three volumes of their studies ranged widely across the natural and social sciences and has formed the basis for much further work on the philosophy of measurement.

Formally, this theory requires one to think about measurement in terms of a correspondence, or mapping: a well defined operational procedure between an empirical relational structure and a numerical relational structure. Measurement is defined as showing that "the structure of a set of phenomena under certain empirical operations and relations is the same as the structure of some set of numbers under corresponding arithmetical operations and relations" (Suppes, 1998). This theory is, as already remarked, highly formalised, but informally, Suppes himself has used the following example.[3] Imagine we have a mechanical balance – this provides an empirical relational structure whose operations can be mapped onto a numerical relational structure for it embodies the relations of equality, and more/less than, in the positions of the pans as weights are place in them. The balance provides a representational model for certain numerical relations, and there is an evident homomorphism between them. Though this informal example nicely helps us remember the role of the representation, and suggests how the numerical relations can lead to measurement, it is unclear how you find the valid representation.[4]

Finkelstein and Sydenham, both in the *Handbook of Measurement Science* (see Sydenham, 1982) offer more pragmatic accounts to go alongside and interpret the representational theory's formal requirements to ensure valid measurement. Finkelstein's informal definition talks of the assignment of numbers to properties of objects, stressing the role of objectivity and that "measurement

---

[2] For the original work, see Krantz et al. (1971). For recent versions see Suppes (1998 and 2002). A more user-friendly version is found in Finkelstein (1974 and 1982).

[3] At his Lakatos award lecture at LSE (2004).

[4] See Rodenburg (2006) on how these representations are found in one area of economics, namely unemployment measurement.

is an empirical process, ... the result of observation and not, for example, of a thought experiment" (pp. 6–7).[5]

This practical version of the representational theory closes in on the second approach – the metrology approach – developed for economics by Marcel Boumans (1999, 2001, 2005 and his chapter in this volume) at the University of Amsterdam. Boumans' innovation here entails taking seriously the notion that we have "measuring instruments" in economics. We may not recognise them as such, but Boumans shows us that the history of economics is full of mathematical formulae, models, or even parts of models, that we use as devices or instruments to enable us to put measurements (i.e. numbers) to apparently unmeasurable entities in economics.[6] For Boumans, the basis of successful measurement depends on creating or developing measuring instruments (formulae) that are, like thermometers, as far as possible invariant to extraneous changes in the broader environment while at the same time accurately capturing the variations of the entity to be measured. His work shows how these mathematical measuring devices are constructed by economists to fulfil these requirements and how they function to overcome standard problems such as extracting signal from noise, filtering, and calibrating the signal to numbers.

In parallel to these philosophical and metrological approaches, Ted Porter (1994 and 1995) in the history of the social sciences, has focussed on the ways in which social science numbers become accepted as legitimate and conventional measurements in their fields. In particular, his notion of the development of "standardised quantitative rules" focuses on the qualities necessary for social science numbers to count as "objective". All three named elements contribute to our willingness to have "trust in numbers", that is to think of them as being "objective" measurements. "Quantitative" refers to a level of precision or exactitude (see Porter, this volume) we associate with the notion of measurement; "rules" refer to the set of principles, methods and techniques by which the measurement is made; and "standardised" refers to the stability of our measuring process. Numbers produced according to methods that changed each time a measurement was taken would not constitute measurements that were usable or even meaningful.[7] That is, numbers are not trustworthy in themselves, however precise they seem, our trust depends on their means of production according to rules that don't change unduly. An important part of Porter's thesis is attention to the role of bureaucracy – preferably an independent trustworthy office such as a central statistical office – in the production of numbers, so that "rules" include not only statistical counting rules, but rules about gathering and handling

---

[5] See Mari (this volume) for an account in this pragmatic tradition that stresses the importance of processes of measurability over the purely logic approach.

[6] In this context, I should stress that this is not solely a discussion of econometrics, which uses models as measuring instruments to measure the relations between entities: on which see Chao, 2002 and this volume (and his forthcoming book).

[7] An infamous UK example of this is the way in which Thatcher's government insisted on successive changes in the definitional rules of counting unemployment so that the measurements of this entity would fall.

of information and so forth. Since these kinds of rules are obviously endemic in the production of most economic data, Porter's thesis is particularly salient to economic measurement; the onus however is on how our numbers gain trust, not on how we overcome the problem of turning our concepts and ideas about phenomena into numbers in the first place.[8]

An analysis of effective measurement in economics engages us in considering the aspects of measuring entailed in these three approaches – the philosophical, the metrological and social/historical. All of these approaches are concerned with making economic entities, or their properties, measurable, though that means slightly different things according to these different ideas. For the representational theorists, it means finding an adequate empirical relational structure for an entity or property and constructing a mapping to a numerical relational structure. This enables measurements – numbers – to be constructed to represent that entity/property. For Boumans, it means developing a model or formula which has the ability to capture the variability in numerical form of the property or entity, but itself to remain stable in that environment. For Porter, it means developing standardised quantitative rules (by the scientific or bureaucratic community or some combination thereof) that allow us to construct, in an objective and so trustworthy manner, measurements for the concepts we have. We can interpret these three notions as having in common the idea that we need a measuring instrument, though the nature of such instruments (an empirical relational structure, a model formula, or a standardised quantitative rule), and the criteria for their adequacy, have been differently posed in the three literatures.

5.2.2. Making economic things measurable with instruments

If we look back over the past century of so of how economists have developed ways of measuring things in economics, we can certainly find the kinds of formulae and models – measuring instruments – that Boumans describes. We can also interpret them using the notions of Porter's standardised quantitative rules, and the kind of representational approach outlined by Suppes. For example, Boumans (2001) analysed the construction of the measuring instrument for the case of Irving Fisher's "ideal index" number. Fisher attempted to find a formula that would simultaneously fulfil a set of axioms or requirements that he believed a good set of aggregate price measurements should have. Boumans showed how Fisher came to understand that, although these were all desirable qualities, they were, in practise, mutually incompatible in certain respects. Different qualities had to be traded-off against each other in his ideal index formula – the formula that became his ideal measuring instrument.

---

[8] The development of the measurement rules is not neglected by Porter (for example, see his 1995 discussion of the development of the rules of cost-benefit analysis), but such processes of gaining trust are less susceptible to the kinds of generalisation I seek to use here.

Fisher's initial axioms – his design criteria – can be interpreted within the representational theory of measurement as laying out the empirical relational structure that the measurements would have to fulfil. But Fisher's empirical relational structure (his axioms) could not be fully and consistently mapped onto numbers from the economic world. Only when one or two of the axioms or criteria were relaxed, could the empirical structure map onto the numerical structure.[9] While this might seem as a partial failure according to the criteria of the representational theory, the actual index number formula that Fisher developed on the modified set of axioms was interpreted by Boumans as a successful attempt to arrive at a more accurate measuring instrument given the variation in the material to be measured.[10] In addition, the kinds of rules and procedures that were developed to take measurements using Fisher's index or similar kinds of instruments[11] can be understood within Porter's discussion of standardised quantitative rules. The fact that numbers produced with such measuring instruments, are, by and large, taken for granted is evidence of our trust in these numbers, and that trust is lost when we notice something amiss with the rules or formulae used to calculate them. For example, Banzhaf (2001) gives an account of how price indices lost their status as trustworthy numbers when quality changes during the Second World War undermined the credibility of the index number formula which assumed constant qualities.[12]

Historians of economics writing about measurement issues typically focus on one particular measuring instrument such as input–output matrices or macro-accounting. But each of these particular instruments can be classified based on family likeness, for we have different kinds of measuring instruments in economics in the same way that we have different categories of musical instruments. An orchestra can be divided into classes of instrument labelled as strings, woodwind, brass, keyboard, percussion etc, according to the way that sounds are produced within each group and so to the kinds of musical noises we associate with each group. Similarly, we can define several different kinds of generic measuring instruments and associated kinds of measurements in economics (see Morgan, 2001 and 2003), and within each kind we can find a number of specific instruments. These generic measuring instrument groups are constructed

---

[9] See Reinsdorf, this volume, for a broader and deeper discussion of the issues raised here on index numbers.

[10] While Fisher decided to compromise on the axioms, an alternative is to reject the data cases that do not fit the axioms. A recent seminar paper by Steven Dowrick (see Ackland et al., 2006) at ANU on poverty measurement suggests that it is common in this field to use as a measuring instrument an ideal index in which the Afriat conditions have to be met. If a particular set of countries do not meet these tests (and thus the axioms on which the index was based), then those data points are omitted from the data set.

[11] The data requirements of Fisher's ideal index means that many index numbers are based on the simpler, less demanding, Laspeyres formula.

[12] The recent Boskin report on the US cost of living index offers another case for the investigation of trusty numbers; see the special symposium on the report in *Journal of Economic Perspectives*, 12 (1), Winter 1988.

according to strategies such as weighted averages, sampling systems, accounting systems, regressions methods, and so forth. In Morgan (2001), I suggested further that these general strategies incorporate specific principles of design; that the measuring instruments constructed according to these design principles involve techniques; and that their application involves judgement. Although such economic measuring instruments have been constructed by economists without particular regard for the requirements discussed in the previous section, it may well be that in combining principles, techniques and judgement they in fact fulfil the kinds of criteria laid out in those commentators' analyses.

Let me make this idea more concrete with an example. One of these general measuring strategies is constituted by index numbers. Of course, economists know that there are many different index number formulae, often named after their "inventors" – Laspeyres, Paasche, Fisher, Divisia, etc. (see for example, the list in Reinsdorf, this volume). We can understand all of these as providing slightly different designs of the same generic measuring instrument – namely formulae to calculate one number out of the weighted averages of many unlike elements. Although they all follow this same basic principle in construction, each of these named index numbers (and many others) has a slightly different formula, according to the kind of thing it is designed to measure. Each one also has somewhat different requirements in terms of raw data, and will also use different data according to whether it is designed to be used to take measurements of the price level, or standard of living, or money supply etc. Constructing measuring instruments of the index number kind requires a high level of technique in the art, and using the instrument to provide measurements of the price level or the money supply requires a high level of judgement as well as calculation techniques.

Each of the generic strategies for developing specific measuring instruments has a strong set of principles which provide structure to the measuring instrument, just as for example, woodwind instruments share structural features about how their sound is produced. We can think of these principles as a kind of recipe that both tells how to make something to fit such a purpose and in so doing lays down constraints: for example, woodwind instruments must have a hollow space as an air pathway, input and exit holes for breath, and so forth. Similarly, when we think of principles structuring a measuring instrument, they both shape the measuring instrument and constrain it. For example, the principles of weighted averages which underlie index number measuring instruments, or the principles of accounting which underpin national income accounting and input–output analysis, not only provide the structure of the measuring instrument but also set constraints on it. The accounting principle provides a good example of how a strategy and set of principles may spawn measuring instruments that diverge considerably in shape and in the things they measure, yet use the same kind of accounting principles and constraints in their construction (see den Butter, this volume). The accounting principles tell you that everything in the set has to be counted and must not be double counted; and its constraints mean that certain elements must balance (be equal, e.g. national income and expenditure) or that aggregates must sum to the same amount (e.g. rows and columns in input–output analysis). Such principles are really important – they are the glue that holds the necessary elements of the measuring instrument together; they give form to the standardised quantitative rules and provide constraints to the structure; they give shape to the representation of the empirical and numerical relational structures and help define the locations of variance and invariance.

In looking at the history of economic measurements then, we need to look out for the measuring instruments, to their principles of construction, and to the techniques and judgements required in their practical usefulness. The literatures on measurement from the philosophy, metrology and science studies are complementary here for they offer more general criteria relevant for all classes of instrument. Measuring instruments, regardless of their general kind or particular construction, should ideally fulfil Suppes', Boumans' and Porter's requirements for the characteristics of measuring systems. How the instruments are used, and what happens when the requirements are not fulfilled, are explored in the case below.

5.3. Case: Historical Episodes in Measuring the Velocity of Money

How should economists measure the velocity of money? This is a question which has intrigued, if not baffled, economists for several centuries. Even William Stanley Jevons, who proved to be one of the nineteenth century's most willing and innovative measurers in economics, stated:

> I have never met with any attempt to determine in any country the average rapidity of circulation, nor have I been able to think of any means whatever of approaching the investigation of the question, except in the inverse way. If we knew the amount of exchanges effected and the quantity of currency used, we might get by division the average numbers of times the currency is turned over; but the data, as already stated, are quite wanting (Jevons, 1909 [1875], p. 336).

Nowadays, this is indeed the kind of formula used in measuring velocity: some version of the values of total expenditure (usually nominal *GDP*) and of money stock are taken ready made from "official statistical sources", and velocity is measured by dividing the former by the latter. For example, the *Federal Reserve Chart Book* routinely charted something it called the "Income Velocity of Money" in the 1980s, namely *GNP*/*M1* and *GNP*/*M2* (in seasonally adjusted terms, with quarterly observations on a ratio scale): see Fig. 5.1 as an example.[13]

But such treatment accorded to velocity – as taken for granted, easily measured and charted – does not mean that the problems of adequately measuring the velocity of money have been solved, or that the Fed's modern measurements are any more useful than those of three centuries earlier. Let me begin by contrasting that standard late twentieth century method of measuring the velocity of money with one from the seventeenth century.

---

[13] For example, see *that* publication, 1984, p. 5; 1986, p. 8.

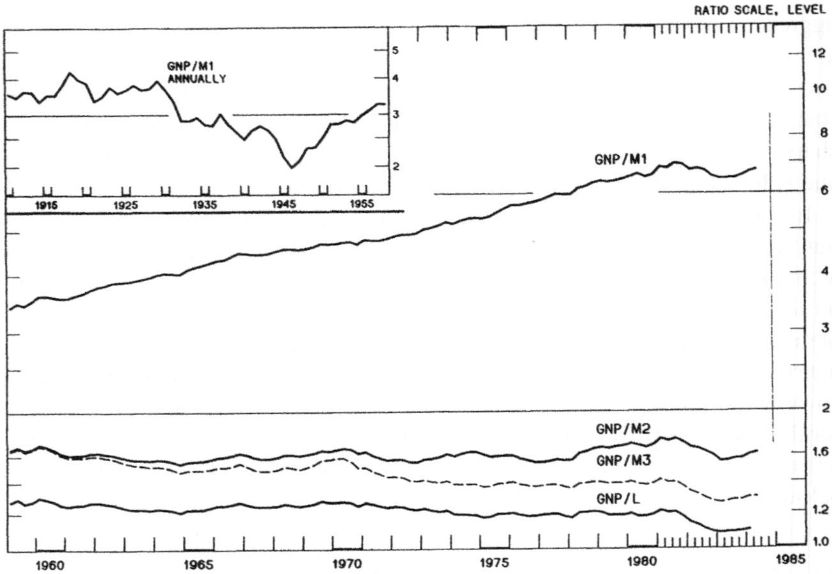

Fig. 5.1: Income Velocities of Money (seasonally adjusted, quarterly). *Source*: *Federal Reserve Chart Book*, 1984, p. 5.

William Petty undertook a series of calculations of the economic resources of England and Wales in his *Verbum Sapienti* of around 1665 and asked himself how much money "is necessary to drive the Trade of the Nation" having already estimated the total "expence" of the nation to be £40 millions. This set him to consider the "revolutions" undergone by money:

> if the revolutions were in such short Circles, viz. weekly, as happens among the poorer artisans and labourers, who receive and pay every *Saturday*, then 40/52 parts of 1 Million of Money would answer those ends: But if the Circles be quarterly, according to our Custom of paying rent, and gathering Taxes, then 10 Millions were requisite. Wherefore supposing payments in general to be of a mixed Circle between One week and 13, then add 10 Millions to 40/52, the half of the which will be 5½, so as if we have 5½ Millions we have enough (Petty, 1997 [1899], pp. 112–113).

Now Petty set out to measure the amount of necessary money stock given the total "expenses" of the nation, not to measure velocity, but it is easy to see that he had to make some assumptions or estimates of the circulation of money according to the two main kinds of payments. He supposed, on grounds of his knowledge of the common payment modes, that the circulation of payments was 52 times per year for one class of people and their transactions and 4 for the other, and guesstimated the shares of such payments in the whole (namely that payments were divided half into each class), in order to get to his result of the total money needed by the economy.

If we simple average Petty's circulation numbers, we would get a velocity number of 28 times per year (money circulating once every 13 days); but Petty was careful enough to realise that for his purpose to find the necessary money stock, these must be weighted by the relative amounts of their transactions. Such an adjustment must also be made to find a velocity measurement according to our modern ideas. If we employ the formula: velocity = total expenditure/money stock, to Petty's circulation numbers, we get a velocity equal 7.3 (or that money circulates once every 50 days).

One immediate contrast that we can notice between these two episodes is that in Petty's discussion, the original circulation figures for the two kinds of transaction – the figures relating to velocity – were needed to derive the money stock necessary for the functioning of the economy and having found this unknown, it was then possible (though Petty did not do this) to feed this back into a formula to calculate an overall velocity figure from the velocity of circulation numbers for the two classes of payments. We used the formula here to act as a calculation device for overall velocity, though that measurement was dependent on independent "guesstimates" of the two classes of such circulation by Petty. This is in contrast to the modern way used by the Fed, where the velocity number is derived only from $V = GNP/M$, this simple formula acts as a measuring device, yet there were no separate numbers constituting independent measurements (or even guesses) of monetary circulation or velocity in this calculation.

These two methods of measuring velocity – Petty's independent way and the modern derived way – are very different. It is tempting to think that the Fed's was a better measure because it was based on real statistics not Petty's guess work, and because its formula links up with other concepts of our modern theories. But we should be wary of this claim. We should rather ask ourselves: What concept in economics does the Fed's formula actually measure? And, Does it measure velocity in an effective way?

5.3.1. Independent measurements of transactions velocity

Beginning again with Petty's calculations, recall that he had guesstimated the amounts of money circulating on two different circuits in the economy of his day. He characterised the two circuits both by the kind of monetary transactions and the economic class of those making expenditures in the economy. I label these "guesstimates" because these two main circuits of transactions and their timing were probably well understood within the economy of his day but the exact division between the two must have been more like guess work. We find further heroic attempts, using a similar approach, to estimate the velocity or "rapidity" of circulation in the late 19th century. For example, Willard Fisher (1895) drew on a number of survey investigations into check and money deposits at US banks in 1871, 1881, 1890 and 1892 to estimate the velocity of money in the American economy. Although these survey data provided for two different ways of estimating the amount of money going through bank accounts, the circulation of cash was less easy to pin down, and he was unhappy with the ratio implied from the bank data that only 10% of money circulated in the form of cash transactions. On the basis of an estimate of the total currency in circulation, Willard Fisher was able to frame, with some plausibility, the limits of cash money circulation against check money circulation: that is, he argued that it would be implausible to assume a cash circulation (as for credit) of only once every 3 weeks, and that cash circulating at the more plausible 3 times a week would make credit and cash transactions roughly equal in making up the circulation of money. The method was similar to that used by Petty, except that now Willard Fisher had some statistical evidence on one part of the circulation, and his categories involved different kinds of payments rather than classes of people and types of expenditures.

This late nineteenth century was the "age of economic measurement" (see Klein and Morgan, 2001), a period when serious data collection as a means of observation and measurement was beginning to become an obsession. The question of how much work money did, and how far that had changed over the previous years, was the subject of much debate in the American economics community in the middle 1890s. Wesley Clair Mitchell (1896), for example, claimed both a substantial increase in the money in the economy and an increase in the velocity of circulation even while he estimated there had been a fall in the share of cash transactions, from 63% to 33% over the period 1860 to 1891. David Kinley's (1897) paper used evidence from an 1896 bank survey investigation, and, with a little more information at his disposal but still on the basis of guesswork on the plausible circulation of cash, he placed the figure at 75% check money and 25% cash transactions. Yet, empirical numerical information on the velocity of circulation, and cash transactions in particular, remained elusive.

A further flurry of measurement activity took place around the end of the first decade of the 20th century. Edwin Kemmerer (1909), made full use of the various banking and monetary statistics of his day, and built on these earlier 1890s investigations and estimations to arrive at an estimated velocity of money ("rate of monetary turnover") of 31 (or 47, if money was taken ex. bank reserves) for 1896. He then applied these circulation rates, and other estimates for 1896 to the whole period 1879–1908 to construct a series that summed two different kinds of money (cash and checks) times their respective velocities (i.e. MV in a Fisherian equation of exchange: *Money* × *Velocity* = *Price* × *Transactions*). In the final summary chapter of Kemmerer's book, these estimates were combined to form an index number of the "relative circulation" (i.e. MV/T) and compared with his separately constructed prices series (P) and trade series (T) to check the overall coherence of the separate measurements. These other measurements are not in themselves of interest here – rather the point is that velocity measurements were estimated independently of the other terms in the formula and directly from various banking statistics.

In terms of Suppes' representational theory of measurement, we can interpret Kemmerer's actions as taking the equation of exchange ($MV = PT$) to operate as an empirical relational structure indicating the numerical relational structure that his series of numbers needed to possess. He did not use that empirical relational formula to derive measurements for any of the unmeasured items, but did assume that the numerical relations between the separately measured series should hold in the same format as his empirically defined relations. Thus, he constructed measurements of all the elements independently and numerical differences between the two sides of the relation $MV = PT$ were taken to indicate how far his series of measurements of each side of the equation might be in error. The formula here operated neither as a calculation device nor as a measuring instrument, but it was part of a post-measurement check system which had the potential to create trust or confidence in his measurements.

This indeed was the same use that Irving Fisher made of his equation of exchange $MV = PT$, but in a much more explicit way that takes us back immediately to Suppes' informal example of the mechanical balance. In my previous examination of Irving Fisher's use of the analogy of the mechanical balance for his equation of exchange (see Morgan, 1999), I wrote briefly about the measurement functions of his mapping of the various numbers he obtained for the individual elements of the equation of exchange onto a visual representation of a double-armed balance.[14] I suggested that the mechanical balance was not the measuring instrument in this case, for, like Kemmerer, he measured all the elements depicted on the balance in separate procedures and both tabled and graphed the series to show how far the two sides of the equation were equal – see Fig. 5.2 (where money and trade are the weights on the arms; velocity and

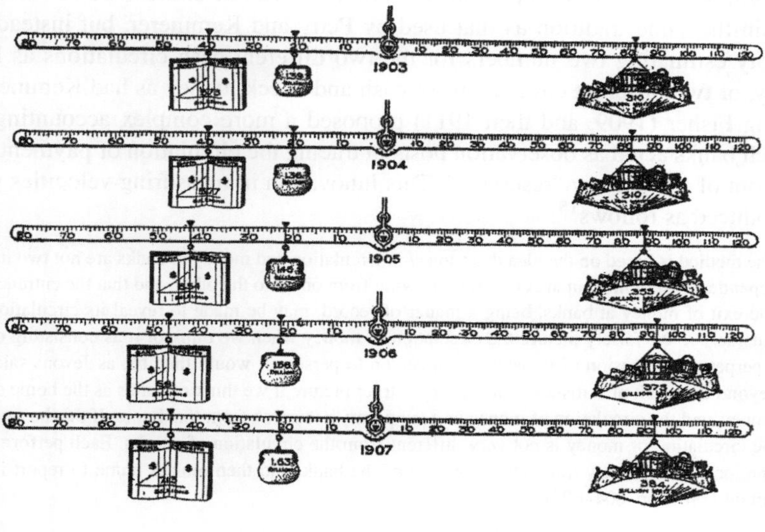

Fig. 5.2: Fisher's Mechanical Balance.

Source: Part of Fig. 17, from the 1912 edition of *The Purchasing Power of Money*, opposite p. 306.

[14] The original diagram is in his 1911 book, Fig. 17, opposite p. 306. See also Harro Maas (2001) on the way Jevons used the mechanical balance analogy to bootstrap a measurement of the value of gold, and to understand certain properties of unobservable utility; and Sandra Peart (2001) on his measurements of the wear of coins.

pries are shown on the left and right arms respectively). Nevertheless, he did use the mechanical balance visual representation to discuss various measurement issues: the mapping enabled him to show the main trends in the various series at a glance and in a way which immediately made clear that the quantity theory of money (a causal relation running from changes in money stock to changes in prices) could not be "proved" simply by studying the equation of exchange measurements. He was also prompted by this analogy to solve the problem of weighted averages by developing index number theory (which is where Boumans's case analysis of Section 5.2.2 fits in). All of this takes us somewhat away from the point at issue – the measurement of velocity – but the use of equations of exchange returns again later.

In thinking about all these measurement problems, Irving Fisher took the opportunity to develop not only the fundamentals of measuring prices by index numbers (see Boumans, 2001), but also new ways of measuring the velocity of money. He regarded his equation of exchange as an identity which defined the relationship of exchange based on his understanding that money's first and foremost function was as a means of transaction. Thus, he thought it important to measure velocity at the level of individuals: it was individuals that spent money and made exchanges with others for goods and services. From this starting point, he developed two neat new methods of measuring velocity.

I will deal with the second innovation first as it can be understood as working within the same tradition as that used by Petty and Kemmerer, but instead of simply estimating two numbers for the two different cash circulations as had Petty, or two different circulations of cash and check money as had Kemmerer, Irving Fisher (1909, and then 1911) proposed a more complex accounting in which banks acted as observation posts in tracing the circulation of payments in and out of a monetary "reservoir". This innovation in measuring velocities was introduced as follows[15]:

> The method is based on the idea that money in circulation and money in banks are not two independent reservoirs, but are constantly flowing from one into the other, and that the entrance and exit of money at banks, being a matter of record, may be made to reveal its circulation outside. ... We falsely picture the circulation of money when we think of it as consisting of a perpetual succession of transfers from person to person. It would then be, as Jevons said, beyond the reach of statistics. But we form a truer picture if we think of banks as the home of money, and the circulation of money as a temporary excursion from that home. If this be true, the circulation of money is not very different from the circulation of checks. Each performs one, or at most, a few transactions outside of the bank, and then returns home to report its circuit (1909, pp. 604–605).

He began by dividing all people into three classes: commercial depositors, other depositors, and non-depositors and thence developed two models to help

---

[15] This work was reported in his 1909 paper "A Practical Method of Estimating the Velocity of Circulation of Money" and repeated in his 1911 book under the title "General Practical Formula for Calculating *V*", Appendix to his Chapter XII, para 4, pp. 448–460.

him map the circulation of money in exchange for goods – first a visual representation, and, from using that, a second model, an algebraic formula which allowed him to calculate velocity.

The first visual model (his Fig. 18 – shown here in Fig. 5.3 – and his Fig. 19, pp. 453 and 456 of Fisher, 1911) portrayed the circulation from banks into payment against goods or services, possibly on to further exchanges, and thence back to banks. This "cash loop" representation enabled him to define all the relevant payments that needed to go into his formula and to determine which ones should be omitted. The relevant payments that he wanted to count for his calculation of velocity were ones of circulation for exchanges of money against goods and services, not those into and out of banks, that is, the ones indicated on the triangle of his diagram, not on the horizontal bars. But banks were his observation posts – they were the place where payment flows were registered and so the horizontal bars were only places where easy counting and so measurement could take place. Thus his argument and modelling were concerned with classifying all the relevant payments that he wanted to make measurable and then relating them, mapping them, in whatever ways possible, to the payments that he

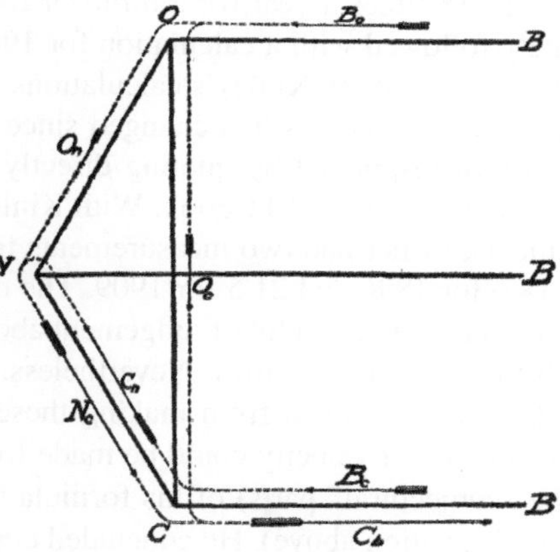

Fig. 5.3: Fisher's Cash Loop Diagram.
Source: Fig. 18 from I. Fisher, *The Purchasing Power of Money* (1911) p. 453.

On Fisher's diagram, ***B*** denote banks, ***C*** commercial depositors, ***O*** ordinary depositors (salaried men), ***N*** non-depositors (wage-earners). The main flows are bank deposits ($Oc + Nc$) and wages ($On + Cn$)

Fisher's "barometer" for measuring velocity (see text below) derives from:

$$MV = Oc + On + Cn + Nc$$

could measure using the banking accounts.[16] He used the visual model to create the mathematical equation for the calculation using the banking statistics, and this in turn used the flows that were observed (and could be measured) in order to bootstrap a measurement of the unobservable payments and thus calculate a velocity of circulation.

Irving Fisher applied his calculation formula – his measuring instrument for velocity – to the 1896 statistics on banks that Kinley had discussed earlier. This part of his work is also very careful, detailing all the assumptions and adjustments he needed to make as he went along (for example for the specific characteristics of the reporting dates). Some of these steps enabled him to improve on his model-based formula. For example, his diagram assumed that payments to non-depositors circulated straight back to depositors, so such money changes hands only twice before it returns to banks, not more. Yet in the process of making a consistent set of calculations with the statistical series, he found that he could specify how much of such circulated money did change hands more than twice. In other words, his measuring instrument formula acted not just as a rule to follow in taking the measurement, but as a tool to interrogate the statistics given in the banking accounts and to improve his measurements.

The velocity measure that Irving Fisher arrived at in 1909 by taking the ratio of the total payments (calculated using his formula) to the amount of money in circulation for 1896 was 18 times a year (or a turnover time of 20 days). Kinley (1910) immediately followed with a calculation for 1909 based on Fisher's formula and showing velocity at 19. Kinley's calculations paid considerable attention to how wages and occupations had changed since the 1890 population census, and Fisher in turn responded by quoting directly this section of Kinley's paper, and his data, in his own 1911 book. With Kinley's inputs, and after some further adjustments, Fisher had two measurements for velocity using this cash loop analysis: 18.6 for 1896 and 21.5 for 1909. The calculation procedure had been quite arduous and required a lot of judgement about missing elements, plausible limits, substitutions and so forth. Nevertheless, on the basis of this experience and the knowledge gained from making these calculations, Fisher claimed that a good estimate of velocity could be made from the "measurable" parts (rather than the "conjectural" parts) of his formula (p. 475, 1911, shown as Fisher's "barometer" equation above). He concluded confidently that "*money deposits plus wages, divided by money in circulation*, will always afford a good barometer of the velocity of circulation" (1911, p. 476). It is perhaps surprising that he did not use this modified equation, his "barometer", to calculate the figures for velocity between 1897 and 1908! Rather, the two end points acted as a calibration for interpolation. Nevertheless, the way that he expressed this shows that his cash loop model and subsequent measurement formula can be classified as a sophisticated measurement instrument in Petty's tradition of using the class of payers and payments to determine the velocity measurement.

---

[16] In doing this, he argued through an extraordinarily detailed array of minor payments to make sure that he had taken account of everything, made allowances for all omissions, and so forth.

The other new way of measuring velocity introduced by Irving Fisher was an experimental sample survey that he undertook himself and reported briefly in 1897. A fuller report of this survey was included in his *The Purchasing Power of Money* (1911). In his 1897 paper, he wrote of the possibility of taking a direct measurement of velocity:

> . . . just as an index number of prices can be approximately computed by a judicious selection of articles to be averaged, so the velocity of circulation of money may be approximately computed by a judicious selection of persons. Inquiry among workmen, mechanics, professional men, &c., according to the methods of Le Play might elicit data on which useful calculations could be based, after taking into account the distribution of population according to occupations (Fisher 1897, p. 520).

Again, this has shades of Petty's approach: investigate a groups of spenders whose varied transactions behaviour are the key to understanding the overall transactions velocity.

Fisher began this task by enlisting the help of Yale students. After an initial disappointing survey, in which he asked respondents for annual amounts of expenditure and cash balances (and which he supposed that they merely guessed), he then asked for volunteers to undertake a more systematic survey. He asked them to keep records of their cash expenditure and cash balances each day for a month as a way to get some reasonably accurate statistics on velocity or turnover of money in exchange for goods and services. He gained 116 good quality responses, of which 113 were from students: each acted as an observation post for reporting their own behaviour. These data provided him with an average velocity (money spent during the month divided by average cash balance in their pocket) of 66. The returns enabled him to divide the total sample into sub-samples according to total expenditure, and so to calculate associated velocities, showing a rising scale of velocities from 17 (for the lowest category of total expenditure) to 137 (for the highest). The average stock of money in the pocket overnight rose with the day's average expenditure, but fell as a proportion of that expenditure. These investigations fed into his discussions about the determinants of velocity and what made it change, and about what effects changes in velocity had on other entities in the equation of exchange.[17]

In this late nineteenth/early twentieth century period of work, it was taken for granted that the task of measuring velocity must be undertaken separately from measuring other elements in the equation of exchange, either by figuring out circulations of money from other payment measurements, or even by plausible guess work with them. The equations of exchange were regarded as calculation checking devices rather than measuring instruments for velocity in their own right. With Irving Fisher, as we saw, two new kinds of measuring instruments were developed to apply to the problem of measuring velocity: one based on a sampling strategy, the other on a representational model. Neither of these instruments seems to have turned into the kind of standardised quantitative rules – to

---

17 See Chapter VIII of Fisher (1911), to which the report of the Yale experiment forms an Appendix, pp. 379–382.

use Porter's terminology – that betoken well accepted measuring instruments, although as we shall see, there have been later uses of the cash-loop model, and there have been later sample survey investigations.

5.3.2. Interlude on concepts

Concepts form one of the important elements in measuring instruments. It is often held that we need a theory of what governs the behaviour of an entity before we can measure it. This seems to require too much. First, there are good examples in measurement history where reliable measuring instruments have been constructed on theories which turn out later to be wrong – e.g. thermometers.[18] Second, the history of economic measurement suggests that conceptual material is required, but not necessarily a causal account or theory of the behavioural variations in the element being measured. For example, we need a clear concept of the difference between the cost of living and the standard of living to determine relevant index number measuring formulae for them, but we don't have to commit to the causes of changes in the cost of living to determine the relevant measuring formula for that concept.

In this context, Holtrop's (1929) discussion of early theories of the velocity of circulation makes an interesting distinction between two concepts of velocity. One, held by Petty (and by Cantillon), understands the idea of velocity as a circular course in which we measure the time taken by money to travel around the circle of payments: i.e. the relation between circulation distance and time – a "motion-theory" concept. Holtrop's expression of his insight is striking: "The partisans of the motion theory are more or less inclined to regard the velocity of circulation as a property of money, as a kind of energy which is inherent to it. ... If, however, the velocity is a property of money, then the supply of money is not a singular but a compound magnitude, being constituted of the product of quantity and velocity" (1929, p. 522). In contrast, according to Holtrop, we also find in early work, the concept of a "cash-balance theory" or the total need of money as at a position of rest in the economy – to which the velocity of circulation is inversely proportional (a position he attributes to Locke). Holtrop suggests we understand this concept as a focus on the demand side of money in which "the size of cash balances is [dependent] ... on the will of the owner, which is governed by economic motives" (1929, p. 523).

In looking at these earlier methods of taking measurements of velocity (rather than theorising about it), we can see that they did indeed rely on concepts of velocity, but the positions do not seem to map onto Holtrop's account. We saw a "need of money" argument made by Petty, not for cash balances or money at rest, but as an amount of money needed for circulation – i.e. Holtrop's motion-theory concept. Irving Fisher's ideas are also difficult to characterise. Holtrop (p. 522) argues that Fisher had a cash-balance concept of velocity, but I find this doubtful

---

[18] See Chang's (2004) book on the history of measuring heat.

for his methods of measuring velocity were essentially designed to measure the money flow. Although his sample survey method appears to be measuring the cash balance (in the students' pockets overnight), Fisher's aim was to measure the cash as it went through his student subjects' pockets each day. The students were acting as his observation posts here for a flow measure, just as in his cash loop method, he used the banks as observation posts for payments into and out of a position of rest as a way to get at the flows of money. Fisher's idea of money velocity can be well characterised by Holtrop's idea of an "energy" or compound property of money, somehow inseparable from its quantity.

Open disagreement about such conceptual issues in discussions of velocity in the late nineteenth century continued into the inter-war period. The masterly treatment of these arguments by Arthur Marget (1938) in the context of the theory of prices provides an exhaustive analysis of theorising about velocity. But Marget's analysis and critique could not stem the tide; in place of the earlier "transactions velocity", the number of times *money changes hands for transactions* during a certain period (the concept that we have found in the examples of measurement from Petty to Irving Fisher), velocity was re-conceived as "income velocity": the number of times the *circular flow of income* went around during the period. Although the velocity measures of the later twentieth century are conceptualised by thinking about individuals' demand for money in relation to their income, and might even be considered a cash-balance approach in Holtrop's terms, this concept of velocity came to be "expressed" in a measuring formula of the ratio of national income to money in circulation, i.e. a macro-level instrument. And, as we shall see, the issue of compound properties comes back to strike those grappling with the problem of uncertainty and variability in these measurements of monetary aggregates at the US Federal Reserve Board.

5.3.3. Derived measurements of income velocity

Economists considering questions about velocity in the latter half of the 20th century have tended to stick with an income notion of velocity, not only in discussion, but also in measurement. Yet their measuring instruments are far from providing numbers that fit the concept of the individuals' demand for money implied by Holtrop. Rather, since 1933, measurements have been constructed on the basis of macro-aggregates, rather than at the individual level in accordance with the conceptual requirements.

Michael Bordo's elegant *New Palgrave* piece on Equations of Exchange (1987), discussed how equations of aggregate exchange, considered as identities, have been important in providing building blocks for quantity theories and causal macro-relations. Not only for theory building, for, as we have seen, equations of exchange provided resources for measuring the properties of money. In the work of Kemmerer and Fisher, their equation of exchange, the identity $MV = PT$, provided a checking system for their independent measurements of transactions circulation and so velocity. In the more recent history of velocity, the income equation of exchange, namely $M = PY/V$, has formed the basis for measuring instruments that enable the economist to calculate velocity without going through the complicated and serious work of separately measuring velocity as done by Fisher and Kemmerer.

This income equation of exchange, rearranged to provide: $V = PY/M$ (velocity = nominal income divided by the money stock), became a widely used measuring instrument for velocity in the mid-twentieth century, in which different money stock definitions provide different associated velocities, and different income definitions and categories alter the measurements of velocity made. For example, Richard Selden's (1956) paper on measuring velocity in the US reports 38 different series of "estimates" for velocity made by economists between 1933 and 1951 and adds 5 more himself. They use various versions of income as the numerator (personal, national income, even *GDP*) and various versions of M as the denominator. These are called "estimates" both because the measurers could not yet simply take their series for national income (or equivalent) and money stock ready made from some official source (national income figures were only just being developed during this time), and because many of the measurers, as Selden, wished to account for the behaviour of velocity. They wished to see if income velocity exhibited long-term secular changes, so understood themselves to be estimating some kind of function to capture the changing level of velocity as the economy developed. Like the late nineteenth century measurers of transactions velocity whose work we considered earlier, there was considerable variation in the outcome measurements.

Boumans (2005) has placed considerable emphasis on variation and invariance in measurement. It is useful to think about that question here. Clearly, we want our measuring instrument to be such that it could be used reliably over periods of time, and could be applied to any country for which there are relevant data, to provide comparable (i.e. standardised) measurements of velocity. At the same time, we want our measuring instrument to capture variations accurately, either between places or over time. In the context of this measuring instrument, clearly if the ratio of PY/M were absolutely constant over time for example, velocity measured in this way would also be unvarying, suggesting something like a natural constant perhaps. But the evidence from our history suggests that velocity is not a natural constant, so the question is: does the formula work well as a measuring instrument – like for example a thermometer – to capture that variation? From that formula, $V = PY/M$, we can see that the variations in the measurements for velocity (for example, shown in Fig. 5.1 earlier) are due to variations in either, or both, the numerator and denominator of the right hand side term. The measuring formula appears to operate as a measuring instrument to capture variations in velocity, but in fact it merely displays variations that are reflections of changes in one or both of the money supply and nominal income.[19]

---

[19] This parallels a similar confusion over testing the hypothesis that k is a constant in the equation $V = kY/M$; such a test is only valid if there are separate (independent) measurements available for V, Y and M, otherwise it is just a test of the constancy of the ratio of Y/M.

(Had Fisher used his equation of exchange: $MV = PT$ to derive measurements of velocity, the same problem of interpreting the numbers for velocity would have risen; in fact, as we saw, he used that equation as a checking device, not a measuring instrument.)

How are we to interpret the velocity that we measure in this way? And what are the sources of velocity's independent freedom for variation when the equation $V = PY/M$ is used as a measuring instrument? One economist who, without using this language of measuring instruments, has taken an interpretation close to denying the velocity measured by this instrument any independence or autonomous variation is Benjamin Friedman (1986).[20] He, for the most part, keeps "velocity" in quotes, partly to remind us that the velocity measured with nominal income is not a true velocity in the sense of the transactions velocity of the older concept, but partly as well to point to its lack of independent conceptual and so numerical content:

> ... it is useful to point out the absence of any economic meaning of "velocity" as so defined – other than, by definition, the income-to-money ratio. Because the "velocity" label may seem to connote deposit or currency turnover rates, there is often a tendency to infer that "velocity" defined in this way does in fact correspond to some physical aspect of economic behaviour. When the numerator of the ratio is income rather than transactions or bank debits, however, "velocity" is simply a numerical ratio.... The issue of money or credit movements versus their respective "velocities", in a business cycle context, is just the distinction between movements of nominal income that match movements of money or credit and movements of income that do not, and hence that imply movements in the income-to-money or in come-to-credit ratio (Friedman, 1986, pp. 411–412).

If we observe variations in the numbers produced for such "velocity", it alerts us to changes in the nominal income that are not due to increases in the money (or credit) supply. It offers a way to decompose changes in nominal income across different business cycles, but it is not something that can represent independent variation in velocity: "Saying that money growth outpaced income growth because velocity declined is like saying that the sun rose because it was morning" (Friedman, 1988, p. 58). Friedman is effectively denying an autonomous or independent status to the velocity measured using this ratio: the equation operates to produce numbers, and these are taken as an indicator for something else, but in terms of the representational theory, there is no entity – no independent well-conceptualised thing called velocity – there that can be measured with such a measuring instrument.

In the 1980s, the Governors of the Federal Reserve Board also grappled with the problem of what velocity is when measured by such an equation. For example, the transcript of the Federal Open Market Committee (FOMC) for July 6–7th of 1981 finds its members arguing over which version of *M1* to target (*M1*, *M-1A* or *M-1B*). The level of uncertainty in setting the target ranges for

---

[20] I am indebted to Tom Mayer who points out that Alvin Hansen has a strong statement of the same kind in his *The American Economy* of 1957, p. 50.

money supply growth was high, and it was an uncertainty that came from several sources. First there was the normal problem of predicting the economic future of the real economy and the monetary side of the economy in relation to that. Secondly, and equally problematic, seemed to be the uncertainty associated with the difficulty of locating a reliable measure of money supply in relation to transactions demand, the inverse of velocity. The Fed's charts show the problem of the day – after a period of trend growth, stability had broken down, as we see in the 1980s part of the graph for the *M1* velocity shown in Fig. 5.1 (above). This may have been to do with institutional changes to which people reacted by "blurring" the distinctions (and so their monetary holdings) between transactions and savings balances. As Chairman Volcker expressed it is "not that we know any of these things empirically or logically" (p. 81).

The difficulties of locating a money supply definition that provided stability for measuring the relevant concept of money was matched in – and indeed, intimately associated with – the problem of velocity measurement.[21] The target ranges discussed in the committee were understood to be dependent on both what happened to a money stock that was unstable and a velocity that was subject to change. The instability of the money stock measurements were understood to be not only normal variation as interest rates changed, but also more unpredictable changes in behaviour because of innovations in the services offered to savers.[22] Those factors in turn were likely to affect the velocity of money conceived of as an independent entity. Here though, the situation is further confused by the fact that, as the Governors were all aware, the velocity numbers that they were discussing were not defined nor measured as independent concepts, but only by their measurement equation – namely as the result of nominal income divided by a relevant money supply. Thus, variations in velocity were infected by the same two kinds of reasons for variations as the money supply.

Velocity was as problematic as the money stock. The difficulties are nicely expressed in this contribution from Governor Wallich:

> We seem to assume that growth in velocity is a special event due to definable changes in technology. But if people are circumventing the need for transactions balances right and left by using money market funds and overnight arrangements and so forth, then really all that is happening is that M-1B is becoming a smaller part of the transactions balances. And its velocity isn't really a meaningful figure; its just a statistical number relating M-1B to GNP. But it doesn't exert any constraints. That is what I fear may be happening, although one can't be very sure. But that makes a rise in velocity more probable than thinking of it in terms of a special innovation (FOMC transcript, July 1981, p. 88).

Because of these causes of variations in the money supply, velocity variations also appeared unpredictable. So, either velocity measurements were attached to

---

[21] For background to the troubles the Fed had in setting policy in this period, see Friedman (1988).

[22] This may be interpreted as Goodhart's Law, that any money stock taken as the object of central bank targeting will inevitably lose its reliability as a target. However, the reasons for the difficulty here were not necessarily financial institutions finding their way around constraints but the combination of expected savings behaviour in response to interest rate changes and unexpected behaviour by savers in response to new financial instruments.

a meaningful concept, but their variations were unpredictable, and so provided no anchor or constraints; or velocity as measured was merely the ratio of GDP to *M-1B*, and so provided no independent anchor or constraint. Either way, it was no help in the problem of predicting the future range of money supply and so targeting.

These knotty problems experienced in the early 1980s are neatly dissected in a presentation on velocity to the October 1983 meeting of the FOMC by Stephen H. Axilrod from the Fed staff:

> Velocity is of course the link between money and GNP in the equation of exchange ($MV = PY$), but whether its behavioural properties are sufficiently stable or predictable to provide a strong basis for monetary targeting as a means of attaining ultimate economic objectives over time has, as we all know, been a continuing subject of intensive economic debate. At one extreme, velocity might be considered as no more than the arithmetic by-produce of forces acting independently on the supply of money and other forces acting independently on GNP – hence, an economically meaningless number and making the whole equation of exchange useless as a policy framework. At the other extreme velocity might be found to have a trend all of its own – hence providing a reasonably predictable link between money and GNP, and giving policy content to the equation of exchange.
>
> From another viewpoint, velocity can be considered as the inverse of the demand for money relative to GNP. If we can know what influences the demand for money – and among the factors explaining money demand are income, transactions needs, interest rates, wealth and institutional change – then we can predict the money needed, for, say, a given GNP. But the more one has to go beyond income or transactions needs in explaining money demand, the weaker is the argument for pure or rigid monetary targeting (Axilrod, 1983, p. 1).

So, velocity in the equation $V = PY/M$ now has three faces or interpretations. On one side, it is simply the measured ratio between two things, each of which are determined elsewhere than the equation of exchange: because velocity has no autonomous causal connections, it provides for no measure of V that can be used for policy setting. On the second, it is thought of as an independent concept and its measurements might exhibit its own (autonomous) trend growth rate (though sometimes unreliably so) which might be useful for prediction and so monetary policy setting. On the third, it has a relationship to the behaviour of money demand, a relationship which is both potentially reliable and potentially analysable, so that it could be useful for understanding the economy and for policy work, but here the focus has been reversed: understanding the determinants of velocity now seems to be the device to understand the behaviour of the money stock, even while the measuring instrument works in the opposite direction.

Standing back from this episode and using our ideas on measuring instruments, it seems clear that the problem in the early 1980s was not so much that the instrument was just unreliable in these particular circumstances, but that the instrument itself has design flaws. In taking the formula $V =$ nominal *GDP*/money stock as a measuring instrument that is reliable for measuring velocity, there is a certain assumption of stability between the elements that make up the measuring instrument and within their relationships. If the dividing line between velocity and money supply (that is, between one property or stuff that is defined as velocity and another property or stuff that constitutes money) is not strict, the latter cannot be used as a reliable component in a measuring device intended for the former. It would be rather like using a thermometer where the glass tube and the mercury column keep dissolving into each other.

This problem of maintaining a definitional division between M and V, between money stock and velocity of circulation is not simply a question of logical or conceptual clarity, but a problem of the fit between concepts and the economic world.[23] There are two senses in which this problem might be understood in the velocity case. First the changes in behaviour of people and in their categorisation of elements mean that there is a switching between what counts as the money quantity and what counts as the velocity category. This seems to be a generic problem in this field of economics, for as Tom Humphrey has so astutely remarked in his history of the origins of velocity functions, "one era's velocity determinants become another's money-stock components" (Humphrey, 1993, p. 2).[24] The second is, as Holtrop characterised it – we may really have a compound property, and so, despite the measurement formula, velocity cannot be separated out from the money stock. In terms of Porter's trust in numbers, we have a standardised quantitative rule to measure velocity, one supported by a well-respected bureaucracy and vast amounts of data collection and manipulation, but the measuring device lacks certain characteristics which make us believe that its numbers are trustworthy. It lacks the requirements of invariance specified by Boumans for measuring instruments because the device does not capture the independent variations in the thing being measured. It fails also in Suppes' representational theory of measurement in that the mapping between empirical and numerical structures seems not to be operational.

5.3.4. Measures of idealised velocity

These second and third faces mentioned by Axilrod are ones that many economists have taken up when they assume that velocity does indeed have its own behaviour. Arguments over what determines the behaviour of velocity and whether it declines or rises with commercialisation were a feature of those late 19th and early 20th century measurers. They can be seen as following suggestions made by many earlier economists (mostly non-measurers) who discussed both economic reasons (such as changes in income and wealth) as well as institutional reasons (changes in level of monetisation or in financial habits) for velocity to change over time.[25]

In the twentieth century, economists have assumed that velocity's behaviour can be investigated just like that of any other entity through an examination of

---

[23] See also Fixler, and den Butter, both in this volume.

[24] Similar definitional problems have occurred in the history of measuring consumption and investment.

[25] Excellent accounts of economists' attempts to explain velocity behaviour can be found in Humphrey, 1993 and of these institutional changes can be found in Friedman, 1986.

the patterns made by its measurements. Some, like Selden (1956) have used correlations and regressions to try to fix the determinants of variations in velocity. Particular attention was paid to the role of interest rates in altering people's demand for money and so its velocity. Selden himself reported regressions using bond yields, wholesale prices and yields on common stocks to explain the behaviour of velocity (though without huge success). More recently and notably, Michael Bordo with Lars Jonung (1981 and 1990), have completed a considerable empirical investigation into the long run behaviour of velocity measurements using regression equations to fix the causes of these behaviours statistically and thence to offer economic explanations for the changes implied in the velocity measurements. Others have argued that there is no economically interesting behavioural determinant, that velocity follows a random walk and can be characterised so statistically (for example Gould and Nelson, 1974).[26]

The use of regression equations in the context of explaining the behaviour of velocity is but one step removed from using regression equations as a measuring instrument to measure velocity itself. Regression forms a different kind of generic measuring instrument (see Section 5.2.2) from the calculations based on bank and individual sample surveys used from Petty to Irving Fisher and from the calculating formulae provided by equations of exchanges (such as those surveyed by Seldon or in the Fed's formulae). The principles of regression depend on the statistical framework and theories which underlay all regression work. An additional principle here is that by tracing the causes which make an entity change, we can track the changes in the entity itself. Alfred Marshall suggested this as one of the few means to get at monetary behaviour: "The only practicable method of ascertaining approximately what these changes [in prices or velocity of money] are is to investigate to what causes they are due and then to watch the causes" (Marshall, 1975, p. 170). Marshall did not of course use regression for this, but his point is relevant here: regression forms a measuring instrument not only for tracing these changes but for measuring them – and so velocity – too.[27]

One option has been to use regression to measure or "estimate" velocity by using the opportunity cost of holding money as the estimator (see for example, Orphanides and Porter, 1998). The velocity concept measured here is a different one from the kind supposed and measured by Fisher. It is, by constitution an idealised entity named the "equilibrium velocity"; it may be well defined con-

---

[26] William Barnett has used Divisia index numbers to try to isolate a stable velocity; see Chapter 6 of Barnett and Serlitis (2000).

[27] See Backhouse, this volume, for a more general account of representational issues of models and measurement and Chao, this volume, for a considered account of issues or representation particularly related to econometrics.

ceptually, but it is a different concept altogether from those concrete, empirically defined concepts sought and measured in earlier times.[28]

Another interesting example combines the regression measuring instrument with that of Fisher's transactions loop model. J.S. Cramer (1986) set out to measure the transactions velocity for the US in the post-war period. He began with Fisher's cash loop idea to get at measures of currency velocity, and then developed the equation of exchange into a form which included a parameter for "hypothetical pure transactions velocity". This parameter was measured using regression and then plugged back into his equation of exchange to provide the series of measurements of velocity over the period showing a rise in the transaction velocity of demand deposits. Clearly, Cramer rivals Irving Fisher's inspired ingenuity as a measurer. And he appears to bring us back almost to where we started, but not quite – for he too is now purporting to measure a different concept: the "hypothetical" version of the transactions velocity from an idealised economic model.

5.4. Conclusions: The Historical Trajectory of Measurement in Economics

It is easy to put a number to the *income velocity of money* by calculating it from an equation of exchange $V = PY/M$, but velocity is a difficult thing to measure with any confidence using that well-worn method. The standardised quantitative rules that measuring instrument entails do not seem to provide numbers that adequately represent the property we are trying to measure even though the raw numbers fed in come from trustworthy series. The equation there acts as a measuring instrument, yet by its design does not have the reliability we require in such instruments. We can understand this equation of exchange as a numerical relational structure, but it is not clear that it relates to an empirical relational structure for velocity. In other words, this is a case of feeding trustworthy data into an untrustworthy measuring instrument. The velocity numbers it produces are not trustworthy.

We have also seen that earlier economists tried to secure trustworthy measurements of a *transactions velocity* of money using a variety of other kinds of measuring instruments: sample surveys, bank surveys, and so forth that aimed at measuring velocity independently of the money stock. These often relied on feeding in guesstimated data, of rather poor quality compared to modern data. Yet these measuring instruments were rather better designed to create good measurements. Even though these instruments have their individual problems, their design treats velocity as a separate, conceptually well defined, entity, and so the measurements they produce may well be more sustainable and so trustworthy.

---

[28] Even if such models locate the actual velocity in an error term, this too would be a velocity measured with respect to some hypothetical equilibrium level.

In a further contrast, the regression methods of the most recent work rely on well-established measuring instruments (the statistical family of regression methods), and use a variety of good quality input data on other variables that are causally related to the velocity that modern economists seek to measure. Notably, these instruments are aimed at a different concept of velocity, one defined by *idealised economic models* rather than one that might be immediately valid in the real economy. In this respect, there is a step change in the kind of entity being made measurable from the earlier transactions and income velocities, both of which had seemed to have the status of empirically valid entities (however difficult it was to get at them and make them measurable), to ones that in principle seem non-observable.

Time	Concept	Measuring Instrument
Late 19th century	Transactions Velocity	Bank surveys and statistics; individual surveys
Mid 20th century	Income Velocity	$V = PY/M$ identity
Late 20th century	Idealised (equilibrium) Velocity	Regression models

The historical trajectory of this case suggests that economists in the later nineteenth century began by treating the things they wanted to measure as independent free standing entities which could be measured using clever designs for collecting and then manipulating statistical data: an approach that understood observation as close to measurement and fashioned measuring instruments accordingly. This was not a naive empiricist approach to measuring, for well defined conceptual properties and relations were used to help define measuring instruments (e.g. surveys), but the relationships (causal relations, accounting identities) in which velocity was thought to be embedded were cast as background constraints or as checking systems not as measuring instruments in themselves. In the middle of the twentieth century, economists' approach had changed to using those same kinds of descriptive identities or relationships as the measuring instruments themselves: enabling economists to derive measurements of velocity by easy application of equations in which other elements had already been observed and measured. In the late twentieth century, economists moved further away from an empirical starting point to focus on measuring concepts that were defined in, and by, the idealised, theory-based, economic models which had come to dominate economics. Such concepts of velocity could be considered unobservables in the sense that they were hypothesised, though the point of the measurement process was to bring them into measurable status by using their causal and functional relationships to other entities – both idealised and pragmatic – so as to put numbers to them.

This trajectory of beginning by measuring some economic quantity by independent means, to processes of making measurable some empirical entity by deriving it from some other measurements, to the measurement of an idealised, or non-observable, entity defined in relation with other theoretically defined concepts may be a general feature of the history of economic measurement. We can think for example of how early political arithmetik's indicative listing of the incomes of the nation were replaced by more sophisticated and comprehensive adding-up attempts in the nineteenth century measures of gross output, to be replaced in the twentieth century by the more closely-theorised, national income measurements conceptualised in accounting models formulated in scientific rather than everyday terms. Peter Rodenburg (2006), in a recent thesis, has found the same pattern of development in the measurement of unemployment: first unstandardised counts collected by trades unions and local councils, giving way to more inclusive and standardised measurement at national level, giving way to economists seeking numbers for theorised, but unobservable, kinds of unemployment (such as voluntary or involuntary, frictional, natural and so forth) using measuring instruments in the form of the diagrams, models and formulae that are habitually found in modern economics.

Over time, the quality of input data has improved, the measuring instruments have become more sophisticated, and the entities themselves have become less observable. Though the measuring work for the latter non-observables attains a high level of sophistication, and involves real economic data, such processes of measuring seem to be more like the complicated, mathematical model, glorified thought experiments of theoretical economics (see Morgan, 2002) than the workings of measuring instruments. This historical experience invites us to recall the injunction by Finkelstein quoted earlier: "measurement is an empirical process, . . . the result of observation and not, for example, of a thought experiment" (1982, p. 6–7).

Acknowledgements

This paper was originally written for the "History and Philosophy of Money" Workshop, Peter Wall Institute for Advanced Study, University of British Columbia, 12–14th November 2004 and then given at the Cachan/Amsterdam Research Day, 10th December 2004. Later versions were given at the ESHET conference in Stirling (June 2005), at the HES sessions at the ASSA, January 2006, at departmental seminars at LSE and Australian National University in 2005 and at the Tinbergen Institute, University of Amsterdam, April 21–22nd 2006 for the workshop for the Elsevier *Measurement in Economics: A Handbook* (editor: Marcel Boumans). I thank participants for comments on all these occasions, but particularly Malcolm Rutherford, David Laidler, Marshall Reinsdorf, Tom Mayer, Frank den Butter and Janet Hunter. I thank Arshi Khan, Xavier Duran and Sheldon Steed for research assistance; Peter Rodenburg, Hsiang-Ke Chao and Marcel Boumans (editor of this volume) for teaching me about measurement in economics; and The Leverhulme Trust and ESRC funded project "How Well Do 'Facts' Travel?" (Grant F/07 004/Z, held at the Department of Economic History, LSE) who sponsored the research.

References

Ackland, R., Dowrick, S., Freyens, B. (2006).Measuring global poverty: Why PPP methods matter. Working paper. ANU.

Axilrod, S.H. (1983). Velocity presentation for October FOMC Meeting. At http://www.federalreserve.gov/FMC/transcripts/1983/831004StaffState.pdf.

Banzhaf, S. (2001). Quantifying the qualitative: Quality-adjusted price indexes in the United States, 1915–1961. In: Klein, J.L., Morgan, M.S. (Eds.) (2001). *The Age of Economic Measurement*. Annual Supplement to vol. 33: *History of Political Economy*. Duke Univ. Press, Durham, pp. 345–370.

Barnett, W., Serlitis, A. (Eds.) (2000). *The Theory of Monetary Aggregation*. Elsevier, Amsterdam.

Board of Governors of the Federal Reserve System (1984, 1986). *Federal Reserve Chart Book*.

Bordo, M.D. (1987). Equations of exchange. In: Eatwell, J., Milgate, M., Newman, P. (Eds.), *The New Palgrave: A Dictionary of Economics, vol. 2*. Macmillan, London, pp. 175–177.

Bordo, M.D., Jonung, L. (1981). The long-run behaviour of the income velocity of money in five advanced countries, 1870–1975: An institutional approach. *Economic Inquiry* **19** (1), 96–116.

Bordo, M.D., Jonung, L. (1990). The long-run behaviour of velocity: The institutional approach revisited. *Journal of Policy Modeling* **12** (2), 165–197.

Boumans, M. (1999). Representation and stability in testing and measuring rational expectations. *Journal of Economic Methodology* **6** (3), 381–401.

Boumans, M. (2001). Fisher's instrumental approach to index numbers. In: Klein, J.L., Morgan, M.S. (Eds.) (2001). *The Age of Economic Measurement*. Annual Supplement to vol. 33: *History of Political Economy*. Duke Univ. Press, Durham, pp. 313–344.

Boumans, M. (2005). *How Economists Model the World into Numbers*. Routledge, London.

Chang, H. (2004). *Inventing Temperature: Measurement and Scientific Progress*. Oxford Univ. Press, Oxford.

Chao, H.-K. (2002). *Representation and Structure: The Methodology of Economic Models of Consumption*. University of Amsterdam thesis, and Routledge, London (in press).

Cramer, J.S. (1986). The volume of transactions and the circulation of money in the United States, 1950–1979. *Journal of Business & Economic Statistics* **4** (2), 225–232.

Federal Open Market Committee (1981). Transcripts of July 6–7 Meeting at http://www.federalreserve.gov/FOMC/transcripts/1981/810707Meeting.pdf.

Finkelstein, L. (1974). Fundamental Concepts of Measurement: Definition and Scales. *Measurement and Control* **8**, 105–111 (Transaction paper 3.75).

Finkelstein, L. (1982). Theory and philosophy of measurement. Chapter 1. In: Sydenham, P.H. (Ed.), *Handbook of Measurement Science, vol. 1: Theoretical Fundamentals*. Wiley, New York.

Fisher, I. (1897). The role of capital in economic theory. *Economic Journal* **7**, 511–537.

Fisher, I. (1909). A practical method of estimating the velocity of circulation of money. *Journal of the Royal Statistical Society* **72** (3), 604–618.

Fisher, I. (1911). *The Purchasing Power of Money*. Macmillan, New York.

Fisher, W. (1895). Money and credit paper in the modern market. *Journal of Political Economy* **3** (4), 391–413.

Friedman, B.M. (1986). Money, credit, and interest rates in the business cycle. In: Gordon, R.J. (Ed.), *The American Business Cycle, vol. 25*. NBER Studies in Business Cycles. Univ. of Chicago Press, Chicago, pp. 395–458.

Friedman, B.M. (1988). Lessons on monetary policy from the 1980s. *Journal of Economic Perspectives* **2** (3), 51–72.

Gould, J.P., Nelson, C.R. (1974). The stochastic structure of the velocity of money. *American Economic Review* **64** (3), 405–418.

Hansen, A. (1957). *The American Economy*. McGraw–Hill, New York.

Holtrop, M.W. (1929). Theories of the velocity of circulation of money in earlier economic literature. *Economic Journal Supplement: Economic History* **4**, 503–524.

Humphrey, T.M. (1993). The origins of velocity functions. *Economic Quarterly* **79** (4), 1–17.

Jevons, W.S. (1909) [1875]. *Money and the Mechanism of Exchange*. Kegan Paul, Trench, Trübner & Co., London.

Kemmerer, E.W. (1909). *Money and Credit Instruments in their Relation to General Prices 2nd ed.* Henry Hold & Co., New York.

Kinley, D. (1897). Credit instruments in business transactions. *Journal of Political Economy* **5** (2), 157–174.

Kinley, D. (1910). Professor Fisher's formula for estimating the velocity of the circulation of money. *Publications of the American Statistical Association* **12**, 28–35.

Klein, J.L., Morgan, M.S. (Eds.) (2001). *The Age of Economic Measurement*. Annual Supplement to vol. 33: *History of Political Economy*. Duke Univ. Press, Durham.

Krantz, D.H., Luce, R.D., Suppes, P., Tversky, A. (1971). *Foundations of Measurement, vol. 1*. Academic Press, New York.

Maas, H. (2001). An instrument can make a science: Jevons's balancing acts in economics. In: *Klein and Morgan,* 2001, pp. 277–302.

Marget, A.W. (1938). *The Theory of Prices*, Vol I. New York, Prentice Hall.

Marshall, A. (1975). *The Early Economic Writings of Alfred Marshall, vol. 1*. Whitaker, J.K. (Ed.), Macmillan for the Royal Economic Society.

Mitchell, W.C. (1896). The quantity theory of the value of money. *Journal of Political Economy* **4** (2), 139–165.

Morgan, M.S. (1999). Learning from models. In: Morgan, M.S., Morrison, M. (Eds.), *Models as Mediators: Perspectives on Natural and Social Science*. Cambridge Univ. Press, Cambridge, pp. 347–388.

Morgan, M.S. (2001). Making measuring instruments. In: Klein, J.L., Morgan, M.S. (Eds.) (2001). *The Age of Economic Measurement*. Annual Supplement to vol. 33: *History of Political Economy*. Duke Univ. Press, Durham, pp. 235–251.

Morgan, M.S. (2002). Model experiments and models in experiments. In: *Model-Based Reasoning: Science, Technology, Values*. Magnani, L., Nersessian, N.J. (Eds.), Kluwer Academic/Plenum, pp. 41–58.

Morgan, M.S. (2003). Business cycles: Representation and measurement. In: *Monographs of Official Statistics: Papers and Proceedings of the Colloquium on the History of Business-Cycle Analysis*. Ladiray, D. (Ed.), Office for Official Publications of the European Communities, Luxemborg, pp. 175–183.

Orphanides, A., Porter, R. (1998). P* revisited: Money-based inflation forecasts with a changing equilibrium velocity*. Working paper. Board of Governors of the Federal Reserve System, Washington, DC.

Peart, S.J. (2001). "Facts carefully mershalled" in the empirical studies of William Stanley Jevons. In: Klein, J.L., Morgan, M.S. (Eds.) (2001). *The Age of Economic Measurement*. Annual Supplement to vol. 33: *History of Political Economy*. Duke Univ. Press, Durham, pp. 252–276.

Petty, W. (1997) [1899]. *The Economic Writings of Sir William Petty, vol. I*. Cambridge Univ. Press, Cambridge. Reprinted Routledge: Thoemmes Press.

Porter, T.M. (1994). Making Things Quantitative. In: *Accounting and Science: Natural Enquiry and Commercial Reason*. Power, M. (Ed.), Cambridge Univ. Press, Cambridge, pp. 36–56.

Porter, T.M. (1995). *Trust in Numbers: The Pursuit of Objectivity in Science and Public Life*. Princeton Univ. Press, Princeton.

Rodenburg, P. (2006). *The construction of measuring instruments of unemployment*. University of Amsterdam thesis.

Selden, R.T. (1956). Monetary velocity in the United States. In: *Studies in the Quantity Theory of Money*. Friedman, M. (Ed.), Univ. of Chicago Press, Chicago, pp. 179–257.

Suppes, P. (1998). Measurement, theory of. In: Craig, E. (Ed.), *Routledge Encyclopedia of Philosophy*. London, Routledge. Retrieved October 27, 2004, from http://www.rep.routledge.com/article/QO66.

Suppes, P. (2002). *Representation and Invariance of Scientific Structures*. CSLI, Stanford.

Sydenham, P.H. (1982). Measurements, models, and systems. Chapter 2. In: *Handbook of Measurement Science, vol. 1: Theoretical Fundamentals*. Sydenham, P.H. (Ed.), Wiley, New York.

PART II

Representation in Economics

CHAPTER 6

Representation in Economics

Roger E. Backhouse

University of Birmingham and London School of Economics, UK
E-mail address: R.E.Backhouse@bham.ac.uk

6.1. Representation through Modelling

Economists see themselves as modellers. There is a sense in which all thought involves abstraction, and hence the use of models. However, when economists use the word they refer to systems that can be presented using mathematical notation – using algebra or geometry. This approach to the subject is the method that is best articulated, and as a result it is the most visible. It has much in common with the assumptions underlying the representational theory of measurement (see Michell, Chapter 2), where models are seen as logical-mathematical structures and measurement is analysed in terms of mappings – formal relationships – between different entities. If students are exposed to formal discussions of methodology, it is modelling (understood in this way) to which they are exposed. They will typically be taught some variant of the hypothetico-deductive method, or even falsificationism.[1] A classic example is Lipsey's *Introduction to Positive Economics* (1975, p. 15) which argues that definitions and assumptions about behaviour are used to generate predictions that are tested against data: if the theory provides a better explanation of the data than competing ones, it is used, but is subjected to continuing scrutiny. Otherwise, it is amended or rejected, and a new theory developed, this in turn being tested against the data.[2]

In practice, however, the process of representation through modelling is much more complex. An attempt to summarise it is made in Fig. 6.1. This distinguishes the stock of knowledge (of representations of the economy), which constitute the background knowledge for any specific piece of work, from economic theory and empirical work. It shows the channels through which modelling interacts with the stock of knowledge.

The first and fundamental point is that representations of the economy are of many types. Though they overlap and cannot be disentangled completely from

---

[1] The word "even" is used, because it is widely accepted, by supporters as well as critics, that falsificationism is not what goes on in economics. See Hausman (1992), Blaug (1992).

[2] Lipsey's flow chart and Figures 1 and 2 can be compared with the ones offered in Backhouse (1997, pp. 140–142).

Measurement in Economics: A Handbook
Marcel Boumans (Editor)

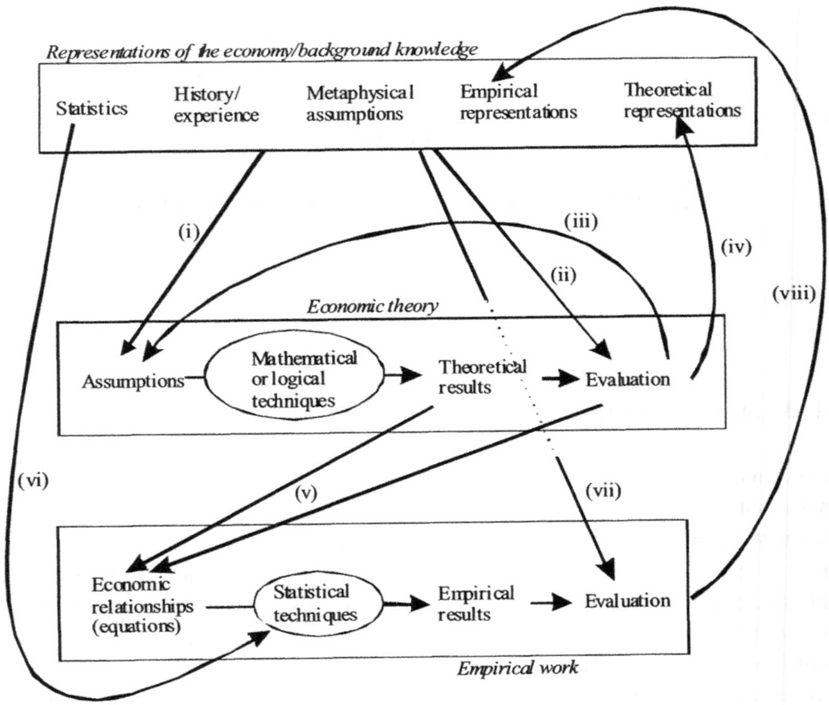

Fig. 6.1: Theory, empirical work and representations of the economy.

one another, it is helpful to think of them in five categories. Together, they constitute the background knowledge relevant to economists' modelling activities.

(a) Statistics are numerical measurements of the economy. There is, of course, much to be said about the creation of statistics, which are themselves representations, and what they measure – for example about how the national accounts are constructed (see den Butter, Chapter 9) or whether index numbers can have the properties that economists want them to have (see Reinsdorf, Chapter 8). Taking into account the process whereby statistics are created reinforces the argument given here: it adds to the complexity of the picture, making the contrast with the conventional view even more pronounced; and it provides further places through which informal arguments enter, raising further questions about whether representation can be understood in terms of formal mappings between entities.
(b) History/experience is a very loose label for knowledge about the economy that is not the result of any formal modelling process. It is discussed further in Section 6.2.
(c) Metaphysical assumptions are included as a separate category as a reminder that economists appear, much of the time, to be committed to some of many of the assumptions made in their models for reasons that appear to have

little to do with evidence. Utility maximisation is strictly unfalsifiable, for if evidence were found to contradict it, the notion could be redefined so as to make it fit the evidence.[3] For example, if it is shown that agents do not maximise utility, then utility can be redefined as an expectation, or the maximisation process can be made conditional on other factors such as limited information. This is not to claim that the assumption of utility maximisation is in itself metaphysical, for it may reflect accumulated experience, or introspection: what is suggested is that there may be metaphysical assumptions that underlie it, or other assumptions being made.

(d) Empirical representations are added to describe the output of economists empirical modelling activities. Clearly this category overlaps with the first two. It covers representations ranging from the equations found in econometric forecasting models to estimates of elasticities of demand and supply, or elasticities of substitution.

(e) Theoretical representations are a further category to represent relationships between economic variables that economists have established using theory, without any formal empirical testing. Examples might include the proposition that, where there is asymmetric information about product quality, adverse selection will ensure that price is forced down to zero. Clearly, assumptions about the world underlie such results, but they involve no formal testing as described below.

Knowledge about the economy could, of course, be classified differently. For example, Boumans (1999, p. 93) distinguishes metaphors, analogies, policy views and stylised facts from empirical data. The reason for the classification adopted here is to focus on a number of distinctions: between knowledge that results directly from economists' modelling activities and that which does not; between knowledge that results from theoretical and empirical modelling; and between statistical representations that enter economists' formal testing procedures and informal knowledge that affects theory through other mechanisms.

Economic theory starts with assumptions from which results are derived using formal mathematical or logical techniques. These typically involve algebra (typically differential and integral calculus or more abstract algebra) or geometry, though they need not do so. The assumptions reflect the background knowledge (i),[4] the importance of the different types of representation varying greatly from problem to problem. Theoretical results may then be evaluated against the background knowledge (ii): they might, for example, be rejected because they seem so silly that the economist concludes something must be wrong with the theory, or because they are inconsistent with some other result that is considered well-established. The result may be to change the assumptions, without any empirical work taking place (iii). Or, as with the adverse selection example just

[3] Hausman (1992) makes a similar, though not identical, point.

[4] Lower case roman numbers refer to links in Fig. 6.1.

mentioned, economists may decide that the result is so clearly right that it does not need empirical testing: the stock of knowledge has been enlarged (iv). A third possibility is that the result may feed into empirical work (v). Two arrows are shown here, to denote the fact that economists may decide to test theoretical results with or without evaluating them first.

Empirical work starts with a set of economic relationships, formulated in such a way that they can be confronted with data using formal, statistical techniques. These relationships may be the theoretical results discussed above, but typically they will be different. The reason for this is the requirement that they can be confronted with data: they must refer to variables on which statistical data exist, or for which proxies can be found; functional forms must be precisely specified and amenable to statistical implementation. These equations are then confronted with statistics (vi), and empirical results are derived. These results are then evaluated against the background knowledge (vii). They augment that background knowledge (viii) either positively (the results are considered to stand up) or negatively (the results indicate that the model is inferior to some other representation of the phenomenon). The process then starts again given the new set of representations of the economy.

The significance of this view can best be seen by comparing it with the conventional, hypothetico-deductive model. This is depicted in Fig. 6.2, which is kept as close as possible to Fig. 6.1, to aid comparison. The economist starts with assumptions that reflect what has been leaned from previous modelling exercises and logical or mathematical methods are used to derive results. These results are then tested (note that the step of evaluating the theoretical results is dropped) against statistical data (it is assumed that it is the theoretical results themselves that are tested, cutting out another element in Fig. 6.1). Empirical results are then evaluated against previous results, and the stock of knowledge is augmented, either positively or negatively, as before.

This is might be thought an oversimplification of the hypothetico-deductive model, which allows for the possibility that assumptions may come from anywhere, so long as their implications are tested empirically. There should perhaps also be direct feedback from evaluation of the empirical results to theoretical assumptions, the process iterating until some results receive a positive evaluation. However, the heart of the hypothetico-deductive model is represented here, for there is a clear link from assumptions to evaluation of empirical results (as in Lipsey, 1975, p. 15). In addition, Fig. 6.2 captures the fact that in the hypothetico-deductive model, testing leads to progressive improvement in the empirical representation of the phenomenon.

The process of representation outlined in Fig. 6.1 thus encompasses the hypothetico-deductive model, but is more complex. This additional complexity points to additional questions concerning representation in economics:

(a) What is the origin of representations that are not the outcome of the formal modelling analysed here (notably History/experience)?
(b) How are theories and the evaluation of theories related to existing representations (i) and (ii)?

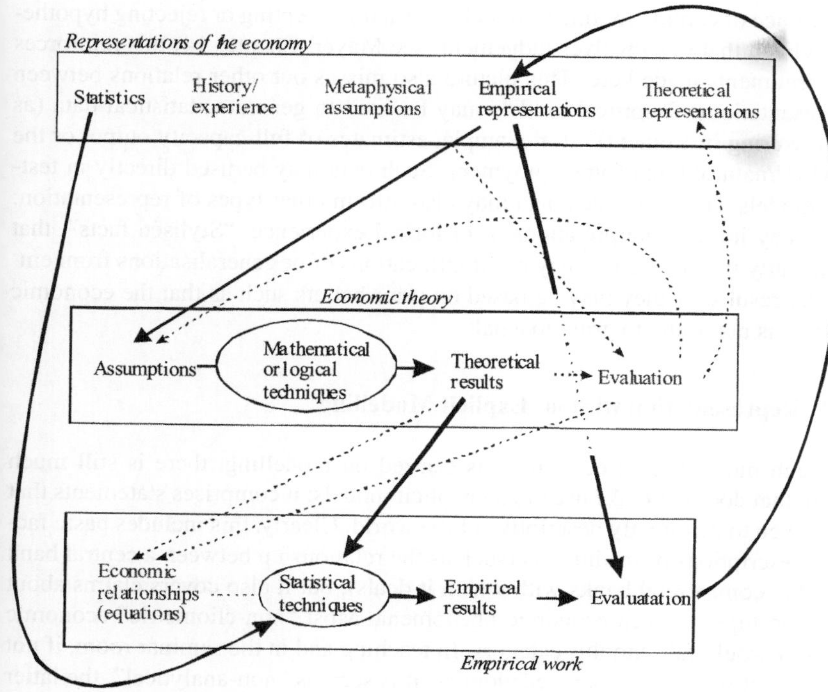

Fig. 6.2: The hypothetico-deductive model.

(c) What is the relationship theoretical models, data and empirical models (v)?
(d) How do economists learn from the results of their modelling activities (iv) and (viii)?

The conventional view has simple answers to all of these. In other words, the conventional view, represented by the hypothetico-deductive model, presumes the following:

(a) Models are based on assumptions that reflect what is known about the economy as a result of preceding empirical work.
(b) Theoretical models are used to generate predictions that are then tested.
(c) These predictions typically take the form of equations, and testing them implies estimating the parameters of these equations, thereby generating an empirical model.
(d) These numerical parameters provide quantitative knowledge of the phenomena under analysis, thereby increasing the stock of knowledge.

In practice, however, the picture is much more complicated: none of these four links is as simple as the conventional view suggests. Each will be considered in turn. It is worth noting that even this picture is not comprehensive in that little attention is paid to the statistical estimation process itself and to issues such as the choice of confidence intervals and criteria for accepting or rejecting hypotheses. Given that this involves judgement (see Mayer, Chapter 14) this reinforces the arguments made here. This picture also misses out other relations between representations. Empirical models may be used to generate statistical data (as a measuring instrument) – for example, estimates of full-capacity output or the NAIRU/natural rate of unemployment. Such data may be used directly in testing models. However, such data may also inform other types of representation: they may inform interpretations of historical experience. "Stylised facts", that frequently inform theory, may be simplifications of or generalisations from empirical results, or they may be based on prior beliefs such as that the economic system is not going to grind to a halt.

6.2. Representation without Explicit Modelling

Though most modern economics is centred on modelling, there is still much work that does not make use of any explicit models: it comprises statements that are taken to be directly descriptive of the world. Clearly, this includes basic factual descriptions of institutions (such as the relationship between a central bank and the commercial banks with which it deals), but it also covers claims about relationships between economic phenomena. Most "non-cliometric" economic history would fall into this category. In teaching and in the seminar room, if not in print, it is seen my many economics, it is seen as "non-analytical", the latter being associated with the use of mathematics, of one form or other.[5]

The main characteristic of such work for the present discussion is that the statements about economic phenomena that comprise such work are conceived as statements about the world, not as abstractions from it. Much non-academic writing, such as economic or financial journalism, is of this type, but it merges into academic economics. It was also a much more common approach amongst academic economics before the Second World War, when many economists simply did not think in terms of models that abstracted from reality, instead making deductions on the basis of assumptions that were assumed to describe the real world.[6] On what could they rest?

(1) Institutional/legal descriptions.
(2) The lore of the market place: beliefs that are the result of experience of how markets work.[7]
(3) Beliefs about what rational people do, or about what the analyst would do in such a situation.
(4) Ideas learned from economists who have used more formal methods to develop them.

[5] It should go without saying that it is ridiculous to describe work as non-analytical simply because it does not use mathematics.
[6] See Backhouse (1998).
[7] The wording reflects McCloskey (1986).

If the last of these is very important, it is arguable that "descriptive" work is does not avoid explicit modelling, but is based on it. However, that judgement would be inappropriate, for the links with any formal modelling may be very loose, with the caveats that surround models having been dropped completely.

Also descriptive, though worth considering as a separate category are statistical descriptions, where the descriptions are not derived using any formal economic modelling. One type of such analysis is found in the national accounts which provide a representation of the economy as a whole. As den Butter (Chapter 9) points out, the national accounts are based on accounting rules, many of which involve judgement – such as how to classify multi-product firms, and where to draw the boundaries between industries. There is frequently no single answer to the question, 'What is the correct measure to use?'

Two other types of 'model-free' representation are illustrated by Stephen Nickell's "A picture of male unemployment in Britain" (1980) is a good example. This examines data from the General Household Survey in 1972, in two ways. One is breaking down the sample into various categories (age, reasons for becoming unemployed, benefits received, socio-economic group, family make-up and so on) and finding patterns in the incidence of unemployment across the some of the categories so defined. This is description that is independent of any model.

The other approach used by Nickell is to use a Logit model to relate unemployment incidence to a list of personal characteristics (including many of those listed in the previous sentence). Clearly, the selection of variables was informed by Nickell's knowledge of economic theory, but the choice of model was determined by the statistical properties of the data, not by any economic theory. More important, many of the relationships have little theory, in the sense of theory that hardly goes beyond common sense, behind them. Examples are whether unemployment incidence should be higher for men living in private or public rented accommodation, or owner-occupiers; or how unemployment incidence should vary with the number of dependent children. Even where relationships are the subject of formal theorising, such as the link between unemployment incidence and the level of benefits received, which certainly influenced Nickell's decision to explore this relationship, his analysis does not depend on that theory. There is a statistical model, but it is arguable that there is not really any economic theoretical model behind the analysis. It is data description rather than testing an economic model.

Macroeconomic time-series models fall into a similar category, though with differences. Data are usually index-numbers, or aggregates such as appear in the national accounts which bear only a tenuous relationship to formal economic theory.[8] Monetary aggregates rest on little formal theory, for economic models say little about which types of bank deposit (or deposits with other financial institutions) should be counted as money. The categories into which national

[8] On the meaning of economic aggregates, see Hoover (2002b).

income is broken up do have links to formal economic theory (consumption, investment, exports, imports), but are in practice largely independent of it. Unemployment statistics are based on counts of those meeting certain criteria, whether in receipt of benefits, or how certain questions in a survey are answered. When such data are plotted or tabulated, the result is something that, as regards any direct relation with formal theory, can be seen as purely descriptive.

The term "descriptive" can also be applied to the results of more formal time-series modelling, where more elaborate statistical techniques are employed to provide a robust description of the data. The selection of variables and the formulation of the model will clearly reflect background knowledge, including economic theory, but it is analysis that stands as a description of the data, independently of any economic theory and belong here as much as Nickel's statistical techniques discussed above, even though the result may be an equation, or even set of equations that describe the economy.

Some experimental work comes into this category. An interesting example is the early studies of preference reversals by Kahneman and Tversky (see Hausman, 1992 for a discussion). Faced with a choice between two carefully-chosen lotteries, a significant proportion of subjects (around 30%) choose the lottery to which, as revealed by other questions, they attached lowest value. Though Kahneman and Tversky had what, as psychologists, they considered a theoretical explanation of this phenomenon, as far as many economists were concerned, this was a result not founded on any theory worthy of the name. It was tantamount to pure description of how subject behaved (assuming, of course, that the results were believed).

The point that representations may be based on theories that economists do not recognise as theories, perhaps because they are not instantiated in formal models, also applies to historical work. In the past half century, the advent of 'Cliometrics' has meant that much work in economic history is indistinguishable from applied economics or even from applied econometrics. However, before that, historians spurned the use of formal techniques: they might classify factors in terms of supply and demand, or distinguish between the quantity of money and its velocity (using the equation of exchange) but in an informal way. Theories about the role of Protestantism in the rise of European capitalism, or even the preconditions for a take-off into self-sustained growth created what might be thought representations, but were not based on formal modelling.

Economists' representations of the economy rest in large part on such "descriptive" work, which bears only tenuous, or indirect, relation to formal theory and model building. Its precise relation to model-building depends very much on definitions. Statistical models are of course models, but from an economic point of view, it arguably makes more sense to bracket models that have only a loose relationship, if any, to economic theory, with simpler procedures such as the calculation of means and index numbers, rather than associating them with economic models. Furthermore, though it can be argued that such work, and work that deduces relationships between economic phenomena from such evidence, rests on implicit models, the point is that the models are not explicit and their relationship to the results is, at best, tenuous.

6.3. Economic Theory and Existing Representations

Theoretical models can be thought of as logical structures that rest on abstractions from reality.[9] Abstraction is necessary to create structures that are sufficiently precise that deductive logic can be applied, so that the implications of assumptions can be worked out and confronted with evidence. If models are tested, and inadequate ones are abandoned or at least modified, it should not matter where they come from: all that matters is that economists do not go round in circles. However, given the infinite number of models that could be used, and the impossibility of testing them all, this may not be enough. The price of using abstract models is that theorising is constrained by theoretical choices as much as by evidence. The principles underlying economic models matter.

Knowledge relevant to the construction of models falls into several categories.

(1) Knowledge of institutions in the broadest sense. This ranges from knowledge about what products are bought and sold, by whom they are produced, the number of firms in an industry, whether products are close substitutes for each other or complements, legal constraints, the nature of contractual arrangements, and so on. Though its interpretation may be open to question, much of this knowledge is comparatively unproblematic and does not need further discussion here.[10]
(2) Statistical and historical evidence on relevant phenomena.
(3) Beliefs about agents' motivations and behaviour.
(4) Propositions derived from theoretical models.
(5) Propositions derived from empirical models.

These are not necessarily independent of each other. Statistical and historical evidence, and the results of empirical models should not only feed into economists' knowledge of institutions, but should also affect their beliefs about agents' motivations and behaviour. If the hypothetico-deductive method is to work as described by Lipsey, this needs to happen. However, in practice, the links are looser than one might expect.

One problem is that economists' knowledge of economic agents is not derived simply from observations of behaviour: it is different from, for example, the

---

[9] I make no claim that this is the only, or even the best, way to view models, merely that it is the appropriate one for the arguments being made here.

[10] I use the word "comparatively" because even apparently simple data may be open to question. Take the assertion that the market for groceries in the UK is dominated by four large firms. This depends on how that market is defined: on whether "convenience stores" are considered to be a distinct market from "supermarkets".

chemist's knowledge of how sodium and water behave when they come together. Economists are themselves economic agents, so can draw upon introspection: they can consider how they would themselves behave in the situation they are considering. Thus one prominent economist could go so far as to claim that "The method of economics remains ... that of the mental experiment aided by introspection" (Georgescu-Roegen, 1936, p. 546). Not exactly the same, but in the same broad category are arguments from rationality. Maximisation of expected utility is a normative theory in that it describes how agents ought to behave, which provides economists with a strong reason for assuming that economists do behave in this way. In addition, for many economists, explanation *means* explaining observed behaviour as the outcome of rational behaviour. Some explore other assumptions about behaviour, such as bounded rationality, or other characterisations of behaviour derived from experimental work ("behavioural economics") but that is a minority.

Thus most theoretical models are based not on empirically observed behaviour but on the assumption of rationality. Agents are assumed to be rational, and to maximise an objective function subject to the relevant constraints. These constraints are drawn from economists knowledge of institutions, which determine, for example, how market structures are modelled (as perfect competition, monopoly, or interaction between a small number of agents, each of whom has to take account of how others will respond to his or her own actions). However, increasingly, economists have ceased to take institutions as constraints, but as part of what is to be explained. Contracts, for example, should not be seen as constraints, but as the result of a process involving decisions by rational agents. Government decisions are the result, not of policy-makers standing "outside" the system, taking decisions based on what improves social welfare, but of decisions taken by politicians and bureaucrats who are seeking to achieve their own ends. Though they are more reticent in print, in less formal situations, economists will talk about analysing the implications of rational choice as "the" method of economics.

This approach, defining economics not in terms of its subject matter but in terms of its method, has a history going back at least to Lionel Robbins (1932) who provided the most commonly cited definition of economics: the science which studies the allocation of scarce resources, which have alternative uses, between competing ends. The whole of economic theory, he suggested, could be derived from the assumption of scarcity, taken to be a fundamental feature of the human condition. It resulted in an approach to economics that paid little attention to empirical work, and which provoked the move to "positive economics", represented by Friedman (1953) and Lipsey (1975). Under the banner of positive economics, and facilitated by increased quantities of economic data and improved computing facilities, statistical work aimed at testing theories became more and more common.

Despite the mass of empirical work, the assumption of rationality has continued to drive economic theory. One reason for its persistence has been that, the assumption of rationality is hard to falsify. However, the attractions of the model would appear to go deeper than this. Hausman (1992) has argued that, not only have economists frequently attached more weight to such theoretical arguments than to empirical results, but that there are reasons why they should do this. Not only are the arguments in favour of rationality compelling, to the extent that economists find ways to preserve it rather than accept apparently conflicting experimental evidence, but also the data available to economists are often of low quality, containing many errors, and not measuring precisely what economists want them to measure. The result is that, faced with a conflict between theory and data, it is the data that they call into question. The result is that propositions from economic theory, even if not tested against data, or even if they have been tested and found inadequate, may influence subsequent work. The assumption of rationality may exert a more powerful influence on models than does the result of statistical testing.

6.4. From Theoretical Models to Empirical Models

In an ideal world, the models that economists confront with data (assumed in this section to be statistical) would be the same as their theoretical models. In practice this is not always possible: theories may involve unobservable variables; other variables may be not be measurable or measured properly; theories may specify functional forms that cannot be estimated given the available techniques; and theories may simply be too complicated or too imprecise to be testable (see Mayer, Chapter 14). The result is that, probably in most cases, the model that is tested is not the same as the one that is produced by the theory. It may not even be a special case of the theoretical model, but one that has been modified in ways that make it possible to confront it with data.

Cartwright (2002) suggests that when there is such a gap between theoretical and empirical models, the link between them is too weak to consider the empirical work a meaningful test of the theoretical model; empirical models do not have any nomological machine underlying them, but are effectively plucked from the air. Against this, it can be argued that the theoretical model should be seen as interpretive, the lack of a precise correspondence between the two models being the result of the model being an incomplete representation of reality (Hoover, 2002a). The model leads us to discover robust regularities in the data. An alternative way to put this is that the theoretical model establishes possible causal links between variables, and that those causal links then form building blocks for the empirical model that is confronted with the data (Backhouse, 2002a). Whichever interpretation of the link we accept, the result is the same: the nature of economic data mean that the links between theory and empirical models involve a degree of informality.

The most highly visible, though not necessarily the most commonly-used, way of confronting models with data involves the imprecisely-defined package of techniques going under the name of econometrics. These methods are covered by Qin and Gilbert in Chapter 11, but some features of this process need to be discussed here. The most important point is that, though econometricians emphasise the statistical foundations of their work, economic considerations and consequently less formal forms of reasoning become important when statistical methods are employed in practice. These come in both in formulating and estimating the model, and in drawing conclusions.

Econometric models rarely work properly the first time they are applied to data – say, the first time a regression equation is calculated. Theory typically does not tell the economist what functional form to use. Often it merely say that a function should be increasing, decreasing, or perhaps that it should be convex or concave, leaving room for an infinite number of functional forms. Decisions need to be made about which variable to include, and how they are measured. Even something apparently simple such as a price index can be measured in many ways, none of which is clearly better than the others. Lag structures and control variables (particularly important in cross-section data sets on individuals) are something else over which it is hard to make a decision before coming to the data. Where theory does indicated clearly that variables should be included, their statistical properties in the particular data set may make it impossible to include them in the way that theory suggests they should be. The result is that decisions on these matters have to be made in the light of initial empirical results. Variables are added or dropped; alternative functional forms and lags are tried out; and the economist experiments with different measures of included variables.

Such practices are often referred to, derogatorily, as data mining. Mayer (Chapter 14) offers a parallel discussion of this problem, and suggests remedies. Given conventional statistical theory, it undermines the theoretical foundations of the hypothesis tests on which econometricians rely: at its simplest, if the econometrician will carry on calculating regressions until he or she finds one where a particular coefficient is positive, a statistical test that shows it to be positive is meaningless. In practice, however, not only does data mining occur – it has to occur. It can be compared with the way experimental scientists have to tune their experiments before they work, whether working means that anticipated results are found or are not found (Backhouse and Morgan, 2000). There are no rules for such tuning, and economic criteria enter. Attempts have been made to formalise the process, even incorporating such strategies into automated computer software routines but choices have to be made before even the most sophisticated software can be applied. For example, to use PcGets,[11] which automates the process of model selection, requires the user to input a list of variables and to specify basic parameters such as lag lengths to be analysed.

Even once a satisfactory empirical model is found, judgements have to be made about its economic significance. Of particular importance is the generality of the conclusions reached – about the domain of the theory – a process that is

[11] See http://www.pcgive.com/pcgets/index.html.

not independent of the estimation process (Backhouse, 1997). Suppose a consumption function is estimated for the UK during the 1980s. Does this tell us anything about consumption in the UK in general, or about consumption in European economies in general? This is relevant for decisions about the results: if the domain is UK consumption in general, then data for the 1990s is relevant, otherwise it is not. If it is believed to say something about consumption in European economies, then data for France and Germany is relevant too. The point is that these decisions involve economic criteria (for example, the introduction of the Euro may have changed the way foreign exchange markets operate, or the 1997 change in the UK monetary regime might be thought to have changed the structure of the UK market for money). One of the difficulties is that decisions about these matters will depend on the empirical results, but the empirical results depend on the decisions made.[12]

6.5. Learning from Models

Empirical models clearly add to the stock of knowledge. What is less clear is how they add to the stock of economic knowledge, rather than simply knowledge of the form "If you correlate x, y and z, the result is p". Econometric results *can* establish generalisations (see Hoover, 2002a; Sutton, 2000) but the stock of economic knowledge resulting from such work is arguably much less than the stock of results. Summers (1991) has argued that econometric results have had much less influence on macroeconomics than much more informal work, such as the calculation of averages, trends, and other "low level" techniques. The reason, he contends, is that the latter are more robust. This is related to the problem of the domain of the results discussed above. Typically, economists are not concerned, say, with the properties of UK demand for money between 1979 and 1987, but with the properties of money demand functions in general. For example, if someone is constructing a model of the business cycle, is it more realistic to assume that the elasticity of substitution between labour and leisure is zero, a half or one? Meta-analysis works in some disciplines, but in economics it has not been particularly effective in narrowing the range of disagreement.[13] However, if it became more widespread, the effects might be greater: knowing that their results would be subject to meta-analysis, and compared systematically with other results, researchers might alter their behaviour.

The issue of how economists learn from empirical and theoretical results is not merely a practical problem, but a profound conceptual one. The stock of knowledge is multi-dimensional, the various elements being, at least in part, incommensurable. Furthermore, there is no formal procedure that can specify

---

[12] Backhouse (1997), following Harry Collins's "experimenter's regress" calls this the "econometrician's regress".

[13] See Backhouse (1997) and Goldfarb (1995).

the knowledge contained in a particular empirical result; in one sense, an equation (for example) is itself a representation, but more important is its effect on economists beliefs about the economy. It is the representations that are implicit or explicit in economists beliefs that matter. This means that to make sense of the last link in the chain, from empirical results to knowledge about the economy, it is necessary to see how empirical results are used by economists.

Models are clearly used in policy-making: not only do policy makers use economic models, but "the requirements and questions of policy makers play an important role in the development and revision of economic models" (den Butter and Morgan, 2000, p. xiv). Den Butter and Morgan describe two-way interaction between policy makers and modellers as "widespread". Policy failures may be even more important than formal tests in causing economists to revise their views of how the economy operates.[14]

The Bank of England, for example, uses both large-scale models and smaller models (such as Phillips curves) in the design of policy.[15] Models provide forecasts, though with error bands that increase the further into the future the forecast is made. But the knowledge provided by the model is heavily circumscribed. Decisions are made on the basis of judgement: this is informed by models, but not in a mechanical way. The forecasts produced by models have errors attached, but there are also uncertainties that go beyond these. There will often be evidence about, for example, future developments in energy markets, future trends in house prices, or consumer confidence that are not incorporated in the models. In considering model forecasts, therefore, members of the Monetary Policy Committee (MPC) balance the risks that the models may be wrong in different directions. The implication of this is that the MPC members' knowledge of the economy is informed by empirical models, but in a complex way.[16]

The same is true of the Netherlands Central Planning Bureau (CPB). Den Butter (Chapter 9) points out that the CPB tries to establish 'a consensus view' on what is going on in the economy and on the effects that policy changes are likely to have. This implies that, even on questions of positive economics, there is scope for legitimate disagreements on how to interpret the results of formal modelling: if it were a matter of simply eliminating technical mistakes, searching for consensus would not make sense.

In economics more generally, models are used in different ways. Economists doing research into a field will typically, one assumes, start with the existing literature. In this sense, the models are directly part of the relevant stock of

---

[14] They approach the complexity of the relationships between models and the policy process by analysing their case studies as examples of different market structure, characterised by the variables of number and the degree of product differentiation (den Butter and Morgan, 2000, p. 283).

[15] See Bank of England (2000).

[16] Downward and Mearman (2005) use the metaphor of 'triangulation', which has recently entered British political discourse, to describe this use of a variety of methods and sources. It is typical of the way economists use empirical evidence (see Backhouse, 1997, 2002b, two examples from which are discussed below).

knowledge. However, it is the models themselves, rather than what they say about the economy that is relevant, for the aim is to produce other models that can be judged superior. It is not even *necessary* that the models are taken seriously as representations of the economy for them to play a role in subsequent research.

Perhaps more interesting is the way that econometric results are used by economists in constructing economic theories. Generally, economists have been reluctant to rely on generalisations established by economists, these doubts going beyond the widely-known Lucas critique (Lucas, 1976). There is usually scepticism about whether quantitative generalisations will be robust in the presence of exogenous shocks and changes within the systems being considered. Thus, whereas economists were at one time willing to assume that the propensity to save was approximately constant, and might have considered using evidence on its value, they would nowadays not be willing to do this. Yet empirical results are not irrelevant. Rather, they inform theory in ways that have something in common with the way the MPC uses the results of models (Backhouse, 1997, Chapter 13). Two examples make this point.[17] These may be particularly good examples, but the conclusions drawn are probably representative of much theoretical work.

Peter Diamond (1994) is concerned with theory, seeking to go beyond the statics of Marshallian period analysis and the textbook IS-LM model, to construct a more dynamic theory. Though his purpose is theoretical, and he does not even try to derive empirical models, he makes extensive use of evidence, some of which came from models, some of which did not. This ranged from survey evidence on the frequency of price changes and price dispersion to evidence on the link between US monetary policy decisions and subsequent change in national output. He does not use numbers directly in his theory, but quantitative results are important in establishing that things are important. Thus he establishes that flows into and out of unemployment are very large in relation to the stock of unemployment, that entry is more concentrated than exit, that seasonal changes are large relative to the growth of national product. Because he is interested in propositions that are more general – more abstract – than those offered by the studies he cites, he brings together evidence from a range of sources, looking informally for common patterns. Thus price stickiness is established by bringing together evidence on input prices, mail order catalogue prices and news-stand prices of magazines.[18]

Another example is Seater's (1993) survey or Ricardian equivalence. This brings together evidence from econometric studies of the life-cycle theory of consumption, in which Ricardian equivalence depends, tests relating to assumptions made in theory, direct evidence (effectively from reduced-form models)

---

[17] Both are taken from Backhouse (1997, pp. 190—203), where they are discussed in much more detail.

[18] Backhouse (1997, pp. 203–205) argues that this can be thought of as replication, comparable to the replication of experimental results.

on the effects of tax changes on consumption, and a range of other evidence, such as the proportion of couples that are childless (and hence cannot care about their descendants' welfare as the theory requires). They reach a heavily qualified conclusion about the limited relevance of Ricardian equivalence.

In both examples, evidence is used to reach conclusions about what the world is like. It is hard to point to a single study that causes either Diamond or Seater to reach the conclusions that they reach, but evidence from models and more formal evidence do play a role in guiding their theorising. A further role of empirical models is the negative one, of showing that simple theories are inadequate, opening up a space for more complex models.[19]

6.6. Conclusions: Representations and Reality

Representation does not imply resemblance, even in visual arts. This is doubly true in economics. Economic models, even though they may be thought adequate representations of the economic world, rest on assumptions that are often wildly unrealistic as descriptions of the world. Indeed, in his classic analysis of the issue, Friedman (1953) made a virtue of models being unrealistic. Models are based on caricatures of agents.[20] Furthermore, in some cases it is hard even to think about resemblance, for models deal with concepts for which it is hard to identify real-world counterparts with which a comparison can be made. Take markets as an example. The market for equities may correspond to an identifiable institution, defined in space and time, but many of the markets that appear in economic models have no such counterparts. Many markets are, at most, loose networks of buyers and sellers with no tangible existence.

This has led many economists to be sceptical about the link between models and understanding reality, this scepticism extending both to economic theory and to econometric work. On economic theory, many would echo the following critique:

> More often than not, the method of economics consists either of the application of an existing theory with little attention to whether it is closely related to the system being considered or, worse still, of recommending that the system be changed to bring it into conformity with the assumptions of theory (Phillips, 1962, p. 361).

On econometrics, Summers's scepticism has been mentioned. In similar vein, Keuzenkamp and Magnus (1995, p. 21) challenged readers of the *Journal of Econometrics* "to name a paper that contains significance tests which significantly changed the way economists think about some economic proposition".

But if account is taken of informal ways in which evidence is used, wherever that evidence comes from, a different picture emerges. It is not correct to say

---

[19] Backhouse (1997, pp. 194–199) uses the example of the textbook by Blanchard and Fischer to make this point.

[20] See Gibbard and Varian (1978).

that the informality of this process means that models are dispensable. As the Bank of England (2000, p. 3) put it,

> Why bother with models at all? Could policy judgements not simply be based on observation of current economic developments, in the light of lessons from past experience of how the economy works? That is indeed the basis for policy judgements, but *making them without the aid of models would be extraordinarily difficult*, not simple.

The same could be applied, *mutatis mutandis*, to the use of models elsewhere in economics, for purposes other than monetary policy.

Where does this leave representation in economics? The main lesson is that representation is multi-dimensional or multi-layered.[21] It is trivial to say that economics is full of representations of economic phenomena. What is interesting is how these relate to each other, how they evolve, and how they contribute to the economist's stock of knowledge. Individual representations, whether based on experiments, econometric work or "lower-level" methods, should not be seen in isolation. This has been widely recognised. Friedman (1953) stressed the importance of looking at the data before theorising, reflecting the view associated with the National Bureau of Economic Research that empirical work was an engine of discovery as much as a way of testing theories. Boumans (1999) has drawn attention to the variety of roles played my models and the way evidence affects theorising at different levels. "Data mining" is acknowledged to be a widespread practice in econometrics, implying a more complex relationship between theory and data than standard views about hypothesis testing would imply. When this broader view is taken, the common theme is that formal rules, such as the rules of experimental or econometric practice, fail to encompass the process. Insofar as it implies formal mappings between entities, and sees models purely as logical-mathematical structures, this involves moving away from the representational theory of measurement. The wider picture may be less precise and highly informal, but this is not to say it is not systematic.[22]

Acknowledgements

This chapter was finished while Ludwig Lachmann Research Fellow in the Department of Philosophy, Logic and Scientific Method at the London School of Economics. I am grateful to the Charlottenberg Trust for its support. I am grateful to Marcel Boumans and Thomas Mayer for helpful remarks on this paper.

References

Backhouse, R.E. (1997). *Truth and Progress in Economic Knowledge.* Edward Elgar, Cheltenham.

Backhouse, R.E. (1998). If mathematics is informal, perhaps we should accept that economics must be informal too. *Economic Journal* **108**, 1848–1858.

---

21 The latter implies a hierarchy of representations, the former does not.

22 This point is argued in Backhouse (1998, 2002a).

Backhouse, R.E. (2002a). Economic models and reality: The role of informal scientific methods. In: Maki, U. (Ed.), *Fact and Fiction in Economics: Models, Realism and Social Construction*. Cambridge Univ. Press, Cambridge, pp. 202–213.

Backhouse, R.E. (2002b). How do economic theorists use empirical evidence? Two case studies. In: Dow, S.C., Hillard, J. (Eds.), *Beyond Keynes, vol. 1: Post-Keynesian Econometrics, Microeconomics and the Theory of the Firm*. Edward Elgar, Cheltenham and Lyme, VT, pp. 176–190.

Backhouse, R.E., Morgan, M.S. (2000). Is data mining a methodological problem? *Journal of Economic Methodology* **7** (2), 171–181.

Bank of England (2000). *Economic Models at the Bank of England*. Bank of England, London. Available at http://www.bankofengland.co.uk/publications/other/beqm/modcobook.htm.

Blaug, M. (1992). *The Methodology of Economics*, second ed. Cambridge Univ. Press, Cambridge.

Boumans, M.J. (1999). Built-in justification. In: Morgan, M.S., Morrison, M. (Eds.), *Models as Mediators: Perspectives on Natural and Social Science*. Cambridge Univ. Press, Cambridge, pp. 66–96.

Cartwright, N. (2002). The limits of causal order, from economics to physics. In: Maki, U. (Ed.), *Fact and Fiction in Economics: Models, Realism and Social Construction*. Cambridge Univ. Press, Cambridge, pp. 137–151.

den Butter, F.A.G., Morgan, M.S. (2000). *Empirical Models and Policy-Making: Interaction and Institutions*. Routledge, London.

Diamond, P. (1994). *On Time: Lectures on Models of Equilibrium*. Cambridge Univ. Press, Cambridge.

Downward, P., Mearman, A. (2005). Methodological triangulation at the Bank of England: An investigation. Discussion paper 05/05. School of Economics, University of the West of England.

Friedman, M. (1953). The methodology of positive economics. In: Friedman, M. (Ed.), *Essays in Positive Economics*. Chicago Univ. Press, Chicago, IL.

Georgeseu-Roegen, N. 1936. The pure theory of consumer's behaviour. *Quarterly Journal of Economics* **50** (4), 545–593.

Gibbard, A., Varian, H.R. (1978). Economic models. *Journal of Philosophy* **75**, 664–677.

Goldfarb, R. (1995). The economist-as-audience needs a methodology of plausible inference. *Journal of Economic Methodology* **2** (2), 201–222.

Hausman, D.M. (1992). *The Inexact and Separate Science of Economics*. Cambridge Univ. Press, Cambridge.

Hoover, K.D. (2002a). Econometrics and reality. In: Maki, U. (Ed.), *Fact and Fiction in Economics: Models, Realism and Social Construction*. Cambridge Univ. Press, Cambridge, pp. 152–177.

Hoover, K.D. (2002b). *The Methodology of Empirical Macroeconomics*. Cambridge Univ. Press, Cambridge.

Keuzenkamp, H.A., Magnus, J.R. (1995). On tests and significance in econometrics. *Journal of Econometrics* **67** (1), 5–24.

Lipsey, R.G. (1975). *An Introduction to Positive Economics, fourth ed*. Weidenfeld and Nicolson, London.

Lucas, R.E. (1976). Econometric policy evaluation: A critique. In: Brunner, K., Meltzer, A. (Eds.), *The Phillips Curve and Labor Markets*. North-Holland, Amsterdam.

McCloskey, D.N. (1986). *The Rhetoric of Economics*. Wheatsheaf Books, Brighton.

Nickell, S.J. (1980). A picture of male unemployment in Britain. *Economic Journal* **90**, 776–794.

Phillips, A. (1962). Operations research and the theory of the firm. *Southern Economic Journal* **28** (4), 357–364.

Robbins, L.C. 1932. *An Essay on the Nature and Significance of Economic Science*. MacMillan, London.

Seater, J. (1993). Ricardian equivalence. *Journal of Economic Literature* **31**, 142–190.

Summers, L. (1991). The scientific illusion in empirical macroeconomics. *Scandinavian Journal of Economics* **93** (2), 129–148.

Sutton, J. (2000). *Marshall's Tendencies: What Can Economists Know?* MIT Press, Cambridge, MA.

CHAPTER 7

Axiomatic Price Index Theory

Marshall B. Reinsdorf

US Bureau of Economic Analysis, USA
E-mail address: Marshall.Reinsdorf@bea.gov

7.1. Objective of Axiomatic Index Theory

Price indexes summarize changes in price for a heterogeneous set of commodities over time or between geographic areas. They are sometimes paired with quantity or volume indexes, which are analogous summarizations of the changes in economic volumes of a set of commodities consumed or produced in some definite interval of time. In axiomatic price index theory, "tests" or "axioms" specify mathematical properties that are essential or desirable for a price index formula, and formulas are sought that exhibit those properties. The term "test" was used by Irving Fisher in two books that effectively launched this field of research in the early twentieth century, while "*axiom*" is used by more recent authors to refer to core properties that are essential for any price index.

Two alternatives to the axiomatic approach are also used to design or to evaluate price indexes. The *stochastic approach* (also known as the statistical approach) models individual price changes as draws from a statistical distribution whose central tendency is to be estimated. The *economic approach* models the quantities as functions of the prices and income that describe the solution to an optimization problem. The problem may be one of revenue maximization via substitution among outputs by a producer subject to constraints on inputs, cost minimization via substitution among inputs by a producer subject to a constraint on output, or utility maximization by a consumer subject to a budget constraint. The two kinds of producer indexes are often used to measure productivity change. The consumer problem, which defines the *cost of living index*, is often treated as representative of the entire approach in theoretical discussions.

The axiomatic approach is sufficiently adaptable to be universally applicable, but the applicability of the alternative approaches generally depends on the level of aggregation. At the lowest level of aggregation, the assumptions of the stochastic approach are well-suited for the problem of combining price quotes from individual sellers into an index for a single commodity. Most index number problems involve higher levels of aggregation, however. A critical feature of these problems – the weighting of different commodities to reflect their economic importance – is handled most naturally by the economic approach. At this level of aggregation the stochastic approach is also subject to two criticisms

Measurement in Economics: A Handbook
Marcel Boumans (Editor)

made by John Maynard Keynes (1930), who argued that commodity price trends diverge in ways that are too persistent to be explainable as differences in random draws from some distribution, and that the prices in an economy are functionally interdependent and simultaneously determined. Nevertheless, after a long period of neglect, the stochastic approach has recently enjoyed something of a revival, particularly for applications to inter-area comparisons.

7.2. History of the Field

7.2.1. Early efforts

Although the first systematic uses of price index tests occurred in late in the nineteenth century, people have been selecting index formulas to achieve certain properties for as long as they have sought to go beyond the use of a single, purportedly representative, commodity for measurement of aggregate price change. Perhaps the earliest discussion of a price index property (quoted in Wirth Ferger, 1946, p. 56) concerned the ability to track the cost of a constant basket of commodities. This discussion was in a treatise written in 1707 by William Fleetwood, Bishop of Eli, on the change in the cost of living for Fellows at Oxford since the establishment of a cap on their outside income of £5 per year in the time of Henry VI. Letting $\mathbf{p}_0$ and $\mathbf{p}_t$ represent the vectors of prices in periods 0 and t and letting $\mathbf{q}^*$ be a vector of quantities that is taken as representative of both periods, the fixed basket price index $P^{FB}(\mathbf{p}_0, \mathbf{p}_t, \mathbf{q}^*)$ compares the cost of purchasing the same quantities at the different vectors of prices from the reference time period 0 and the comparison time period t:

$$P^{FB}(\mathbf{p}_0, \mathbf{p}_t, \mathbf{q}^*) = \frac{\mathbf{p}_t \cdot \mathbf{q}^*}{\mathbf{p}_0 \cdot \mathbf{q}^*}. \qquad (7.1)$$

Unfortunately, William Fleetwood does not get the credit for the first use of the fixed basket index formula: surprisingly enough, he departed from Eq. (7.1) in calculating his results. The groundwork for the first documented use of the fixed basket index came a few years later in 1747, when the Massachusetts Bay Colony passed legislation calling for the use of "the prices of provisions and other necessaries of life" for the escalation of inflation-adjusted public debt to avoid the spurious volatility and manipulation that had occurred when a single commodity (silver) was used (Willard Fisher, 1913, p. 426). Since keeping track of the prices of the "necessaries of life" was impractical given the resources available at the time, the idea had to be simplified before it could be implemented. This was done in 1780, when Massachusetts specified a basket of consisting of 5 bushels of corn, 68 4/7 pounds of beef, 10 pounds of wool, and 16 pounds of sole leather for indexation of interest-bearing notes used to pay its soldiers in the Revolutionary War.

The rudimentary Massachusetts basket was not an approximation to the average basket that was actually consumed by the erstwhile colonists, so it also falls short of complete implement of the fixed basket index idea. The first index basket design that included a plan for making the weights truly reflect expenditure patterns came nearly a half century later in 1823, when Joseph Lowe proposed such a consumer price index for Britain (W. Erwin Diewert, 1993, p. 34).

Another index number property that early measures of price change were designed to achieve is independence from the definitions of the units of measurement of the items in the index. Letting $\boldsymbol{A}$ represent a matrix with arbitrary positive values on its main diagonal and zeros elsewhere, the *commensurability axiom*, also known as the "change of units test," requires that the index formula $P(\mathbf{p}_0, \mathbf{p}_t, \mathbf{q}_0, \mathbf{q}_t)$ have the property:

$$P(\mathbf{p}_0, \mathbf{p}_t, \mathbf{q}_0, \mathbf{q}_t) = P(\boldsymbol{A}\mathbf{p}_0, \boldsymbol{A}\mathbf{p}_t, \boldsymbol{A}^{-1}\mathbf{q}_0, \boldsymbol{A}^{-1}\mathbf{q}_t). \tag{7.2}$$

A formula that fails to satisfy this axiom is useful only for items that are homogeneous and measured in identical units. An example such a formula was used by Dutot in 1738:

$$P^{Dutot}(\mathbf{p}_0, \mathbf{p}_t) = \frac{\sum_i p_{it}}{\sum_i p_{i0}}. \tag{7.3}$$

The commensurability axiom is critical for the main purpose of price indexes, which Ragnar Frisch (1936, p. 1) identified as the uniting of individual measurements for which no common physical unit exists. If the units of measurement for diverse commodities could all be converted into some common unit by means of physical equivalency ratios, index numbers would be unnecessary. Instead, the aggregate price level could be measured by the unit value (the ratio of total expenditures to total equivalency units consumed) of the single composite commodity. Price change would then be measured by the change in the aggregate unit value:

$$\text{unit value ratio} = \frac{[\sum_i p_{it}q_{it}]/[\sum_i q_{it}]}{[\sum_i p_{i0}q_{i0}]/[\sum_i q_{i0}]}. \tag{7.4}$$

In the absence of a system of physically equivalent units for diverse commodities, the only recourse is to use prices for conversions into units that are equivalent in monetary terms.

The commensurability axiom is satisfied by any index formula that can be written as a function of the price relatives and weighting parameters that do not depend on the prices (which means that the weights must either be predetermined or else depend on observed item expenditures). The simplest function of this type is an unweighted average of price relatives. Carli used this formula (which is also known as the Sauerbeck index) in his 1764 investigation of the effect of the discovery of America on the purchasing power of money:

$$P^{Carli}(\mathbf{p}_0, \mathbf{p}_t) = \frac{1}{N} \sum_{i=1,\dots,N} p_{it}/p_{i0}. \tag{7.5}$$

A fixed basket index satisfies the commensurability axiom if and only if the elements of $\mathbf{q}^*$ in Eq. (7.1) are determined in a way that takes units of measurement into account. The basket used by Massachusetts in 1780, for example, assumed equal expenditures in the base period. This procedure insures that a change in units will have no effect on the index; indeed, it makes the fixed basket index equivalent to the Carli index. Two more substantive examples of fixed basket indexes that satisfy the commensurability axiom are the Laspeyres index, defined as $P^{FB}(\mathbf{p}_0, \mathbf{p}_t, \mathbf{q}_0)$, and the Paasche index, defined as $P^{FB}(\mathbf{p}_0, \mathbf{p}_t, \mathbf{q}_t)$. Defining s_{i0} as $(p_{i0}q_{i0})/(\mathbf{p}_0 \cdot \mathbf{q}_0)$, the reference period expenditure share of commodity i, the Laspeyres index is shown to satisfy the commensurability axiom by writing it as a weighted average of the price relatives:

$$P^{Laspeyres} = \sum_i s_{i0}(p_{it}/p_{i0}). \tag{7.6}$$

Similarly, the Paasche index is shown to satisfy the commensurability axiom by writing it as a weighted harmonic mean of the price relatives:

$$P^{Paasche}(\mathbf{p}_0, \mathbf{p}_t, \mathbf{q}_t) = \frac{1}{\sum_i s_{it}(p_{i0}/p_{it})}. \tag{7.7}$$

7.2.2. Emergence as a field of study

In the latter half of the nineteenth century, explicit discussions of properties that could be used to evaluate price index formulas began to appear. Etienne Laspeyres discussed the *strong identity test*, which requires that $P(\mathbf{p}, \mathbf{p}, \mathbf{q}_0, \mathbf{q}_t) = 1$. The test of *independence from the choice of the base* for comparisons of periods other than the base period was discussed by W. Stanley Jevons and F.Y. Edgeworth. This test requires that the change in the index between periods s and t be unaffected by the choice of the base period, or $P(\mathbf{p}_0, \mathbf{p}_t, \mathbf{q}_0, \mathbf{q}_t)/P(\mathbf{p}_0, \mathbf{p}_s, \mathbf{q}_0, \mathbf{q}_s) = P(\mathbf{p}_1, \mathbf{p}_t, \mathbf{q}_1, \mathbf{q}_t)/P(\mathbf{p}_1, \mathbf{p}_s, \mathbf{q}_1, \mathbf{q}_s)$. Jevons proposed an unweighted geometric mean index that satisfies this test, as well as the commensurability test:

$$P^{Jevons}(\mathbf{p}_0, \mathbf{p}_t) = \prod_{i=1,\ldots,N} (p_{it}/p_{i0})^{1/N}. \tag{7.8}$$

A closely related test that is satisfied by any index that satisfies the base-independence test was discussed by Harald Westergaard. This test is known as the *circularity test*, and is much-discussed in the subsequent price index literature. It requires that a chained index calculated as the product of the index from period 0 to period s and the index from period s to period t equal the direct index from period 0 to period t:

$$P(\mathbf{p}_0, \mathbf{p}_s, \mathbf{q}_0, \mathbf{q}_s)P(\mathbf{p}_s, \mathbf{p}_t, \mathbf{q}_s, \mathbf{q}_t) = P(\mathbf{p}_0, \mathbf{p}_t, \mathbf{q}_0, \mathbf{q}_t). \tag{7.9}$$

Another much-discussed test is, in turn, satisfied by any index that satisfies the circularity test and the identity test. The *time reversal test* requires agreement between the value that a price index formula assigns to a set of price changes, and the value that the formula assigns to a reversal of those price changes, given that quantities also return to their original values:

$$P(\mathbf{p}_0, \mathbf{p}_t, \mathbf{q}_0, \mathbf{q}_t)P(\mathbf{p}_t, \mathbf{p}_0, \mathbf{q}_t, \mathbf{q}_0) = 1. \tag{7.10}$$

N.G. Pierson (1896) (who also pointed out the failure of the commensurability axiom by the Dutot index) thought this test of such importance that its failure by the indexes known to him caused him to recommend that the entire enterprise of trying to construct price indexes be abandoned.

A failure of the time reversal test that reveals a bias occurs in the case of the Carli index. Let $\mathbf{r}$ be the column vector of the price relatives and $\mathbf{r}^{-1}$ be the vector of their inverses p_{i0}/p_{it}. Letting $\boldsymbol{\iota}$ be a vector of ones, the product of the Carli index $(1/N)\boldsymbol{\iota}'\mathbf{r}$ and its time-reversed counterpart $(1/N)\boldsymbol{\iota}'\mathbf{r}^{-1}$ is the quadratic form $(1/N^2)\boldsymbol{\iota}'[\mathbf{r}(\mathbf{r}^{-1})']\boldsymbol{\iota}$. The main diagonal of the matrix $\mathbf{r}(\mathbf{r}^{-1})'$ consists of 1s, and the average of all the elements of $\mathbf{r}(\mathbf{r}^{-1})'$ equals the chained Carli index.

We can calculate this average in two stages. The first stage combines each element above the main diagonal of $\mathbf{r}(\mathbf{r}^{-1})'$ with a counterpart from below the main diagonal. Letting $\delta_{ij} = (p_{it}/p_{i0})(p_{j0}/p_{jt}) - 1$, the average of element ij and element ji of the matrix $\mathbf{r}(\mathbf{r}^{-1})'$ is:

$$\frac{(1+\delta_{ij}) + 1/(1+\delta_{ij})}{2} = \frac{2(1+\delta_{ij}) + \delta_{ij}^2}{2(1+\delta_{ij})}.$$

This average is greater than 1 if $\delta_{ij} \neq 0$, so unless $\mathbf{p}_t = \mathbf{p}_0$, the average of all the pairwise averages exceeds 1. Paradoxically, after every price and every quantity has returned to its original value, the chained Carli index registers positive inflation!

The beginning of the twentieth century saw the first systematic use of the test approach to evaluate and design price index formulas. A book by Correa M. Walsh (1901) discussed a version of the circularity test that adds a third link to the chain and makes the ultimate prices and quantities identical to the original ones, as they are in the time reversal test. Walsh also discussed a *proportionality axiom* (also known as the *strong proportionality test*), which requires that an index containing identical price relatives equal that price relative:

$$P(\mathbf{p}_0, \lambda\mathbf{p}_0, \mathbf{q}_0, \mathbf{q}_t) = \lambda. \tag{7.11}$$

Finally, Walsh applied the *constant basket test* to price index formulas that attempt to account for the effects of changes in the basket that is consumed.

These formulas should agree with the fixed basket formula in the special case of an unchanging consumption basket:

$$P(\mathbf{p}_0, \mathbf{p}_t, \mathbf{q}, \mathbf{q}) = \frac{\mathbf{p}_t \cdot \mathbf{q}}{\mathbf{p}_0 \cdot \mathbf{q}}. \tag{7.12}$$

The constant basket test is trivially satisfied either by a fixed basket index formula that uses only the base period market basket, disregarding the basket from the other period, or by a fixed basket index formula that uses only the comparison period market. Use of the base period basket had been suggested by Laspeyres in 1871, and use of the comparison period basket had been suggested by Hermann Paasche in 1874. Yet Walsh inferred from numerical trials that the Laspeyres price index $P^{FB}(\mathbf{p}_0, \mathbf{p}_t, \mathbf{q}_0)$ and the Paasche price index $P^{FB}(\mathbf{p}_0, \mathbf{p}_t, \mathbf{q}_t)$ were both biased.

To satisfy the constant basket test while allowing the opposite biases of the Laspeyres and Paasche indexes to offset one another, Walsh favored an average of the baskets from the base and comparison periods. The simple average of the quantities in the two baskets proposed earlier by Edgeworth and Alfred Marshall was acceptable. Walsh found, however, that a geometric mean performed better, so his preferred index was:

$$P^{Walsh}(\mathbf{p}_0, \mathbf{p}_t, \mathbf{q}_0, \mathbf{q}_t) = \frac{\sum_i p_{it}(q_{i0}q_{it})^{0.5}}{\sum_i p_{i0}(q_{i0}q_{it})^{0.5}}. \tag{7.13}$$

7.2.3. Irving Fisher's systematic approach

A decade after Walsh's book appeared, Irving Fisher wrote *The Purchasing Power of Money*. This book contained some important new tests, but it is even more notable because Fisher took a systematic and thorough approach that elevated the question of index number properties to the level of a formal field of study.

Inspired by the right hand side of the equation of exchange $MV = PT$, where M is the stock of money in circulation, V is its velocity of circulation, P is the price level and T is the volume of trade, Fisher proposed the *product test*.[1] This test states that when a price index and a quantity index are specified simultaneously, their product must equal the expenditure relative $\mathbf{p}_t \cdot \mathbf{q}_t / \mathbf{p}_0 \cdot \mathbf{q}_0$. Using the product test, Fisher developed the concept of the "correlative form" of the quantity index corresponding to a price index, a concept that is now known as the *implicit quantity index*.

---

[1] As den Butter [this volume] explains, today National Accounts use index numbers to decompose changes in nominal expenditure into price and volume effects. This procedure has its origins in Fisher's (1911) discussion of the product test. The Laspeyres quantity index derived there is used to measure real GDP in most countries.

The product test can also be used to derive the *implicit price index* corresponding to a directly specified quantity index. To avoid a violation of the commensurability axiom, Fisher defined the units for each item in T as a "dollar worth" in the base year, which makes T equal to the numerator of the Laspeyres quantity index $\mathbf{p}_0 \cdot \mathbf{q}_t$. By substituting $\mathbf{p}_t \cdot \mathbf{q}_t$ for MV in the equation $MV = PT$ and solving for P, Fisher obtained the implicit price index implied by the use of base period prices to measure volume change. The result showed that for the Laspeyres quantity index, the implicit price index is a Paasche price index. Divide both sides of the equation $\mathbf{p}_t \cdot \mathbf{q}_t = P(\mathbf{p}_0 \cdot \mathbf{q}_t)$ by base period nominal expenditures $\mathbf{p}_0 \cdot \mathbf{q}_0$ to obtain $\mathbf{p}_t \cdot \mathbf{q}_t / \mathbf{p}_0 \cdot \mathbf{q}_0 = P(\mathbf{p}_0 \cdot \mathbf{q}_t / \mathbf{p}_0 \cdot \mathbf{q}_0)$, where $\mathbf{p}_0 \cdot \mathbf{q}_t / \mathbf{p}_0 \cdot \mathbf{q}_0 = Q^{Laspeyres}$. Then the price index P must equal:

$$P = \frac{\mathbf{p}_t \cdot \mathbf{q}_t / \mathbf{p}_0 \cdot \mathbf{q}_0}{Q^{Laspeyres}} = \frac{\mathbf{p}_t \cdot \mathbf{q}_t}{\mathbf{p}_0 \cdot \mathbf{q}_t}. \tag{7.14}$$

Another advance in *The Purchasing Power of Money* was the assembly of a battery of all tests known to Fisher for purposes of screening for the best price index formulas. As a reflection of Fisher's interest in the equation of exchange, his list of tests included ones that concerned the behavior of the implicit quantity index that the price index implied. A further novelty was the inclusion of tests of comparative index behavior, which apply to not to index itself but rather to the change in an index between periods other than the base period, i.e. $P(\mathbf{p}_0, \mathbf{p}_t, \mathbf{q}_0, \mathbf{q}_t)/P(\mathbf{p}_0, \mathbf{p}_s, \mathbf{q}_0, \mathbf{q}_s)$.

Eight tests were on Fisher's original list. Using names from today's literature, they are:

1. *The proportionality axiom.*
2. *The proportional baskets test.* The price index must satisfy $P(\mathbf{p}_0, \mathbf{p}_t, \mathbf{q}_0, \lambda\mathbf{q}_0) = \mathbf{p}_t \cdot \mathbf{q}_0 / \mathbf{p}_0 \cdot \mathbf{q}_0$. The proportional baskets test is necessary because the quantity index in the equation $\mathbf{p}_t \cdot \mathbf{q}_t = P(\mathbf{p}_0, \mathbf{p}_t, \mathbf{q}_0, \mathbf{q}_t) Q(\mathbf{p}_0, \mathbf{p}_t, \mathbf{q}_0, \mathbf{q}_t)(\mathbf{p}_0 \cdot \mathbf{q}_0)$ must equal λ if $\mathbf{q}_t = \lambda\mathbf{q}_0$. This test includes the constant basket test as a special case by letting λ equal 1.
3. *Test of determinateness in prices*: The price index does not become indeterminate or converge to 0 as a price goes to 0. Although this test is sometimes defined with the outlier price equal to 0, stating it as a requirement of a finite, positive limit as any price approaches 0 avoids some unhelpful complications.
4. *Test of determinateness in quantities:* The quantity index does not become indeterminate or equal 0 if a quantity goes to 0.
5. *Test of withdrawal or entry of prices*: The price index is unaffected by the withdrawal or entry of a price relative that has the same value as the price index.
6. *Test of withdrawal or entry of quantities*: The quantity index is unaffected by the withdrawal or entry of a quantity relative that has the same value as the quantity index.

7. *Test of independence from the choice of base* and the closely related *circularity test* and *time reversal test*. Given the identity axiom (i.e., given that $P(\mathbf{p}, \mathbf{p}, \mathbf{q}, \mathbf{q}) = 1$), these latter tests are special cases of the base-independence test.
8. *The commensurability axiom.*

None of the 44 price indexes that Fisher considered passed all these tests. (Indeed, no index can.) Fisher, however, emphasized the test of proportionality in quantities because of the importance he attached to the equation of exchange. If we restrict attention to indexes that also satisfy the proportionality axiom in prices, only the Paasche price index is able to satisfy the implicit quantity index version of the *comparative proportionality test*, which considers time periods other than the base period. Substituting $\lambda\mathbf{q}_s$ for $\mathbf{q}_t$, the change in the Laspeyres quantity index implied by the Paasche price index from time s to time t is:

$$Q(\mathbf{p}_0, \mathbf{p}_t, \mathbf{q}_0, \lambda\mathbf{q}_s)/Q(\mathbf{p}_0, \mathbf{p}_s, \mathbf{q}_0, \mathbf{q}_s) = \frac{\mathbf{p}_0 \cdot \lambda\mathbf{q}_s/\mathbf{p}_0 \cdot \mathbf{q}_0}{\mathbf{p}_0 \cdot \mathbf{q}_s/\mathbf{p}_0 \cdot \mathbf{q}_0} = \frac{\mathbf{p}_0 \cdot \lambda\mathbf{q}_s}{\mathbf{p}_0 \cdot \mathbf{q}_s} = \lambda. \tag{7.15}$$

As an illustration of how other indexes fail the comparative proportionality test, consider the Laspeyres price index. The implicit quantity index that it implies has a Paasche form. Substituting $\lambda\mathbf{q}_s$ for $\mathbf{q}_t$ in the Paasche formula, a test of the Paasche quantity index for the comparative proportionality property gives:

$$\frac{\mathbf{p}_t \cdot \lambda\mathbf{q}_s/\mathbf{p}_t \cdot \mathbf{q}_0}{\mathbf{p}_s \cdot \mathbf{q}_s/\mathbf{p}_s \cdot \mathbf{q}_0} = \frac{\mathbf{p}_t \cdot \lambda\mathbf{q}_s/\mathbf{p}_s \cdot \mathbf{q}_s}{\mathbf{p}_t \cdot \mathbf{q}_0/\mathbf{p}_s \cdot \mathbf{q}_0} \neq \lambda \quad \text{except in special cases.} \tag{7.16}$$

Based on its ability to satisfy the comparative test of proportionality in quantities, Fisher selected the Paasche price index as best. In the context of national product accounts, Fisher's emphasis on this test is reasonable. The single number of greatest interest to the users of these accounts is the most recent change in real gross domestic product (GDP). National statistical agencies that use a fixed base approach calculate the percentage change in real GDP as $100[Q(\mathbf{p}_0, \mathbf{q}_t, \mathbf{q}_0, \mathbf{q}_t)/Q(\mathbf{p}_0, \mathbf{p}_s, \mathbf{q}_0, \mathbf{q}_s) - 1]$. The national accounts of most countries still follow Fisher's recommendation in their choice of formula for the "implicit deflator" for GDP.

Of course, price indexes are used for many purposes besides the measurement of the volume of domestic production. Fisher next turned his attention to selecting the best index number for all purposes. For this, he drew on his work on quantity indexes and the equation of exchange to develop a new test. Fisher's *factor reversal test* requires that the price index and its implicit quantity index have the *same* functional form:

$$P(\mathbf{p}_0, \mathbf{p}_t, \mathbf{q}_0, \mathbf{q}_t)P(\mathbf{q}_0, \mathbf{q}_t, \mathbf{p}_0, \mathbf{p}_t) = (\mathbf{p}_t \cdot \mathbf{q}_t)/(\mathbf{p}_0 \cdot \mathbf{q}_0). \tag{7.17}$$

In a paper presented to the American Statistical Association Fisher (1921) used this test, and the time reversal test to identify an "ideal" price index for any purpose.[2] The form of Fisher's index was a geometric mean of the Laspeyres index and the Paasche index:

$$P^{Fisher} = \sqrt{\frac{\mathbf{p}_t \cdot \mathbf{q}_0}{\mathbf{p}_0 \cdot \mathbf{q}_0} \frac{\mathbf{p}_t \cdot \mathbf{q}_t}{\mathbf{p}_0 \cdot \mathbf{q}_t}}. \tag{7.18}$$

Fisher's *magnum opus* on index numbers, *The Making of Index Numbers*, appeared a year later. This book tabulated the performance of nearly 150 formulas on the tests of proportionality, determinateness, and withdrawal or entry, and it identified the class of formulas that failed to satisfy the fundamentally important commensurability test. It supplemented this deductive reasoning based on tests with inductive reasoning based on trials of how formulas performed with actual data. These trials gave empirical evidence of such properties as the upward bias of arithmetic averages of price relatives and the downward bias of harmonic averages (which are simply reciprocals of time-reversed arithmetic averages).

Fisher's new treatment of tests differed from his original one in some important ways. Fisher renounced the circularity test and also the "comparative" tests, which focused on the change in the index rather than the index itself. Fisher also dismissed the base-independence test as irrelevant because of its inapplicability to the chained indexes that he now favored. (Chained price indexes use the baskets from years being compared, not the basket from some base year of questionable germaneness.) Finally, these changes in approach implied an abandonment of the recommendation of the Paasche price index as the best formula for deflation purposes.

Three tests that were unknown at the time of Fisher's earlier book are mentioned in *The Making of Index Numbers*. Fisher's discussion of index formulas that behaved "erratically" or "freakishly" implied a test of continuity in prices and quantities. Second, Fisher (1922, pp. 220–221 and 402) justified his preference for "crossing" formulas (as is done in the Fisher index) rather than crossing weights (as is done in the Edgeworth–Marshall and Walsh indexes) by arguing that only the former procedure would insure that the final index remained within the bounds of the Laspeyres index and the Paasche index. (This was not the first mention of the Laspeyres–Paasche bounds test; it had already been discussed by Arthur L. Bowley and by Pigou, 1912 and 1920.) Third, Fisher placed great emphasis on his new factor reversal test. After excluding erratic or freakish index formulas and focusing on crosses of formulas rather than of weights, Fisher identified P^{Fisher} as "ideal" because it was the only straightforward formula that satisfied the time reversal test and the factor reversal test.

---

[2] In his discussant's comments Walsh (1921) showed how to derive other formulas that satisfied Fisher's new test besides P^{Fisher}, thereby undermining Fisher's initial argument for the superiority of P^{Fisher}. The name later given to this formula reflects Fisher' role in demonstrating its axiomatic advantages; Walsh was the first to mention it.

Indeed, P^{Fisher} also satisfies all the tests on Fisher's original list if they are properly framed. The circularity test or base-independence test, which Fisher now disavowed, becomes the time reversal test when applied to two periods only. Of the remaining seven tests, Fisher reported that five were satisfied. The two tests that Fisher reported as violated by his ideal index are the price withdrawal or entry test, and the quantity withdrawal or entry test. Fisher, however, made no restriction on the quantities when he tested the effect on the price index of withdrawal or entry of an item with a price relative equal to P^{Fisher}. The appropriate assumption for testing an index that depends on prices and quantities in both periods is that the entering or withdrawing item matches *both* the original price index and the original quantity index. A simultaneous test of price and quantity withdrawal or entry is satisfied by P^{Fisher} and Q^{Fisher}.

7.2.4. Criticisms of Fisher's tests and the rise of the economic approach

Following the publication of *The Making of Index Numbers*, the focus of index number research shifted to the economic approach, with a host of contributions advancing the field far beyond the state in which Pigou and other pioneers of this approach had left it.[3] Furthermore, the test approach research that continued to be performed shifted in focus from the use of tests to select index formulas to the selection of the tests themselves. Certain tests were singled out for criticism as unjustifiable according to the economic approach or as incompatible with other tests. For example, Samuelson and Swamy (1974, p. 575) discussed the lack of an economic justification for the factor reversal test, concluding: "A man and his wife should be properly matched, but that does not mean I should marry my identical twin!"

The discovery that important tests can be incompatible with each other pointed to a weakness of the axiomatic approach: the question of which axioms are vital can neither be avoided by finding a formula that simultaneously satisfies them all, nor answered in a way that is beyond all controversy.[4] A noteworthy example of controversy involves three tests from Fisher's list that Frisch (1930) identified as impossible to satisfy simultaneously. These are the circularity (or base-independence) test, the commensurability test, and the determinateness test.[5] At different times, each member of Frisch's set of incompatible tests has been identified as the one to abandon. Frisch (1930, p. 405) suggested the sacrifice of the commensurability test. Fisher had, of course, discarded the circularity

---

[3] Important contributions to the economic approach from this era include Corrado Gini (1924, 1931), Gottfried Haberler (1927), Bowley (1928), R.G.D. Allen (1935 and 1949), Hans Staehle (1935), Abba P. Lerner (1935), A.A. Konus (1939) and Erwin Rothbarth (1941).

[4] The impossibility of satisfying every axiom is interpreted within the representational theory of measurement by Morgan [this volume]. She also discusses two approaches that have been used to respond to this problem.

[5] Frisch overlooked the need for the proportionality axiom, without which the expenditure relative $\mathbf{p}_t \cdot \mathbf{q}_t / \mathbf{p}_0 \cdot \mathbf{q}_0$ would satisfy all the tests on the list (Eichhorn, 1976, p. 251).

test, and had – like Frisch in 1936 – identified the commensurability test as fundamental. Finally, Swamy (1965, p. 625) discarded the determinateness test.

The circularity test is particularly prone to incompatibility with other axioms, including some that are indispensable. In particular, an important impossibility theorem states that it is impossible to satisfy the axioms of circularity, commensurability and proportionality simultaneously if the price index uses information on the quantities (see Appendix A). These three axioms constitute a *characterization* for a geometric average of price relatives that has exponents that are constants that sum to 1 but that need not be identical, as they are in the Jevons index. (A characterization for an index is a combination of tests and axioms that is uniquely satisfied by that index.) An additional axiom that prevents negative exponents must also be included to make the formula that is characterized admissible as a price index. One such axiom, introduced in a later vein of the literature by Wolfgang Eichhorn and Joachim Voeller, is the *monotonicity axiom*. This axiom requires that the price index be strictly increasing in comparison period prices and strictly decreasing in base period prices. Combining this axiom with the other three, we have a characterization for a version of the *Cobb–Douglas index* that has predetermined weights $\mathbf{s}^*$.[6] In log-change form, this index is:

$$\log P^{Cobb\text{–}Douglas}(\mathbf{p}_0, \mathbf{p}_t, \mathbf{s}^*) = \sum_i s_i^* \log(p_{it}/p_{i0}). \tag{7.19}$$

Another perspective on the difficulty of satisfying the circularity test was offered by Samuelson and Swamy. They showed that a price index *can* use the quantity data and still satisfy the circularity test if the quantities behave in a way that is consistent with homothetic utility maximization.[7] This price index need not sacrifice the proportionality test nor the commensurability axiom. Unfortunately, however, homotheticity is a strong assumption: it means that marginal rates of substitution do not depend on the utility level, making the composition of the consumption basket invariant to income and dependent only on prices. Samuelson and Swamy conclude:

> [I]n the nonhomothetic cases of realistic life, one must not expect to be able to make the naïve measurements that untutored common sense always longs for; we must accept the sad facts of life, and be grateful for the more complicated procedures economic theory devises (p. 592).

7.2.5. The resurgence of interest in the axiomatic approach

The rise of the economic approach to index numbers did not mean the end of progress on index number axiomatics, nor even the limiting of axiomatic

[6] The name comes from the economic approach. Constant expenditure shares are implied by a Cobb–Douglas utility function. Used as weights in a log-change price index, these shares yield the Cobb–Douglas cost of living index.

[7] They were not the first to show this: the homotheticity condition had been identified a year earlier by Charles Hulten using a method that is discussed in the appendix.

research to the identification of tests with an economic justification. Notably, G. Stuvel (1957) and K.S. Banerjee (1959) used the factor reversal test to derive a novel ideal index number formula, which we discuss below. Furthermore, Jan van IJzeren (1952) derived a useful and illuminating alternative formula for the Fisher index. Although van IJzeren's use of the test approach was rather informal, his equations reveal how the Fisher index corrects an axiomatic weakness of the Edgeworth–Marshall price index.[8] Deflating the period t quantities (prices) by the quantity index Q (price index P) before forming the simple averages used as the basket of the Edgeworth–Marshall index yields a pair of simultaneous equations in P and Q:

$$P = \frac{\sum_i p_{it}(q_{i0} + q_{it}/Q)}{\sum_i p_{i0}(q_{i0} + q_{it}/Q)}, \tag{7.20}$$

$$Q = \frac{\sum_i q_{it}(p_{i0} + p_{it}/P)}{\sum_i q_{i0}(p_{i0} + p_{it}/P)}. \tag{7.21}$$

The solution to Eqs. (7.20) and (7.21) is $P = P^{Fisher}$ and $Q = Q^{Fisher}$.

Deleting Q from the numerator and denominator equation (7.20) would turn it into the Edgeworth–Marshall price index. The value of the Edgeworth–Marshall price index depends arbitrarily on whether growth is negative or positive, since with a low Q it resembles a Paasche price index and with a high Q it resembles a Laspeyres index. Consequently, the Edgeworth–Marshall index fails to satisfy the *test of homogeneity of degree zero in base period quantities and in comparison period quantities*, which requires that for $\lambda > 0$:

$$P(\mathbf{p}_0, \mathbf{p}_t, \lambda\mathbf{q}_0, \mathbf{q}_t) = P(\mathbf{p}_0, \mathbf{p}_t, \mathbf{q}_0, \lambda\mathbf{q}_t) = P(\mathbf{p}_0, \mathbf{p}_t, \mathbf{q}_0, \mathbf{q}_t). \tag{7.22}$$

Note also that Eq. (7.20) allows an additive decomposition of the change in P^{Fisher}, and similarly for Eq. (7.21) and Q^{Fisher}. These equations are therefore used in the national economic accounts of the US and Canada to calculate the tables of contributions to change in their Fisher indexes of price and volume change (Reinsdorf et al., 2002).

Starting in the 1970s, the field of axiomatic index theory began to experience a renaissance. Yrjö Vartia (1976) introduced the test of *consistency in aggregation*, which requires that a multi-stage application of the index formula in various levels of aggregation yield the same result as a single stage application that calculates the top-level aggregate directly from the detailed data.[9] Another watershed event was the independent discovery by Kazuo Sato (1976) and Vartia (1976) of the ideal log-change (i.e. geometric) index, where "ideal" means that an index satisfies the factor reversal and time reversal tests. This index has

---

8 This weakness of the Edgeworth–Marshall index is also avoided by the Walsh index.

9 Diewert (2005, fn. 24) notes that a variant of this test had already appeared in a book by J.K. Montgomery (1937). This test is also discussed in Charles Blackorby and Diane Primont (1990).

weights proportional to logarithmic means of expenditure shares. The logarithmic mean of two positive and unequal shares is defined as:

$$\text{logmean}(s_{i0}, s_{it}) \equiv (s_{it} - s_{i0})/(\log s_{it} - \log s_{i0}), \tag{7.23}$$

with $\text{logmean}(s_{i0}, s_{i0}) \equiv s_{i0}$. Normalizing the weights so that they sum to 1, the natural logarithm of the Sato–Vartia index (also known as the Vartia II index), has the form:

$$\log P^{\textit{Sato-Vartia}} = \sum_i \frac{\text{logmean}(s_{i0}, s_{it}) \log(p_{it}/p_{i0})}{\sum_j \text{logmean}(s_{j0}, s_{jt})}. \tag{7.24}$$

At about the same time as the research leading to the Sato–Vartia index, the study of index number tests themselves experienced a rebirth as "the axiomatic theory of index numbers," which was the name of a paper by Eichhorn. Eichhorn, with his student Voeller, and also Janos Aczél, replaced Fisher's pragmatic quest for good measurement tools – termed the "instrumental approach" by Marcel Boumans (2001, p. 336) – with the functional equation approach. This literature provided further theorems on the mutual inconsistency of various sets of axioms, but it also introduced the new concerns of identifying mathematically independent sets of axioms and the discovery of *characterizations* for the important price index formulas. Theorems on mutual inconsistency and independence of sets of axioms were proven by Eichhorn (1976), for example. For examples of characterizations for the Fisher index, see Bert Balk (1995), H. Funke and Voeller (1978, 1979) and for characterizations for other indexes see Manfred Krtscha (1984, 1988), and Arthur Vogt (1981).

A set of independent axioms than can be viewed as a definition of the fundamental properties of a price index function was introduced by Eichhorn and Voeller (1983). This set consists of the monotonicity axiom, the proportionality axiom, the commensurability axiom and the price dimensionality axiom. The *price dimensionality axiom* requires that multiplying all base and comparison period prices by the same positive scalar leave the index unchanged, so Balk (1995, p. 72) calls it "homogeneity of degree zero in prices."

These four axioms are independent because price indexes exist that violate any one of them while satisfying all others. Eichhorn and Voeller show that any index that satisfies them all also satisfies some additional tests, most notably the *mean value test*. The mean value test requires that $P(\mathbf{p}_0, \mathbf{p}_t, \mathbf{q}_0, \mathbf{q}_t)$ lie within the range defined by the smallest and largest price relative:

$$\min\{p_{1t}/p_{10}, p_{2t}/p_{20}, \ldots, p_{Nt}/p_{N0}\} \leqslant P(\mathbf{p}_0, \mathbf{p}_t, \mathbf{q}_0, \mathbf{q}_t) \leqslant \max\{p_{1t}/p_{10}, p_{2t}/p_{20}, \ldots, p_{Nt}/p_{N0}\}. \tag{7.25}$$

7.2.6. Axiomatic theory for inter-area price indexes

Axiomatic price index theory continues to be a lively field of research. Diewert (2005), for example, extends this theory from the measurement of ratios to measures of level differences, and the 2004 International Labor Organization Manual on Consumer Price Indexes develops an axiomatic theory of price index formulas where item expenditures replace the quantities as arguments. Yet inter-area price indexes may be the most active topic of current research on axiomatic index theory.

When indexes are used for inter-area comparisons, such as determining the relative price levels of a set of countries, the kind of transitivity called for by the circularity test is critical. Transitivity is also more feasible to achieve in the inter-area index context than in a time series context, because the static membership of geographic groups is generally allows the use of quantities or prices that reflect a combination of all the included countries. (Use of different quantity weights for each bilateral comparison is incompatible with transitivity.) The grand geometric mean of country quantity indexes, first proposed by Gini, is known as the EKS method, because it was independently derived and justified by Ö. Eltetö and P. Köves (1964) and by Bohdan Szulc (1964). Another approach is to solve a system of equations that uses a common set of average commodity prices to value each country's commodity quantities. This method, proposed by Robert C. Geary (1958) and validated by Salem H. Khamis (1972), satisfies a test of additivity that is convenient for inter-area volume comparisons. Balk (2003) finds that it fails just one of his core inter-area index tests, along with a test of monotonicity in quantities for inter-area indexes first proposed by Diewert (1999). Diewert (who is skeptical about the test of additivity) evaluates the test performance of the Geary–Khamis method less favorably than does Balk, and recommends the EKS method for the calculation of purchasing power parities (1999, p. 52). Armstrong (2003) finds that a specialized, restricted domain version of the EKS method has superior axiomatic properties, though without these restrictions the GKS does better. All these authors also distinguish some other methods for their good test properties, however. Also methods derived from the stochastic approach, such as weighted country-product regression dummies (WCPD), are more convenient to calculate than the EKS system yet still satisfactory in their axiomatic properties.

7.3. Issues in Axiomatic Price Index Theory

7.3.1. Superiority of the Fisher index

The superiority of the Fisher index is the subject of a longstanding debate in the literature on the axiomatic theory of index numbers that has continued into recent years. Diewert (1992) implicitly claims superiority for the Fisher index, as it satisfies a battery of 20 tests (21 if the factor reversal test is included) that none of its main rivals can satisfy completely. A particularly noteworthy rival to the Fisher index is the Leo Törnqvist (1936) index:

$$\log P^{Törnqvist} = \sum_i \frac{1}{2}(s_{i0} + s_{it}) \log(p_{it}/p_{i0}). \tag{7.26}$$

Many researchers who prefer the economic approach think of the Törnqvist price index as superior because, in a much-celebrated paper, Diewert (1976) demonstrated its exact equality to a cost of living index from the versatile translog model of economic behavior.[10] This claim to superiority from the economic approach made Diewert's subsequent finding of a relatively poor performance for the Törnqvist index on axiomatic criteria all the more striking. The test violations of the Törnqvist index generally involve only small discrepancies, but they are surprisingly numerous and they include some important properties. The constant basket test, the Laspeyres–Paasche bounds test, the determinateness test (which was omitted from Diewert's list), the monotonicity axiom, and the mean value test for the implicit quantity index are not satisfied by the Törnqvist index.[11] The violation of the Laspeyres–Paasche bounds test may seem inconsistent with the equivalence of the Törnqvist index to a cost of living index in the translog case, but when the data do not fit the translog model, the Törnqvist index may not mimic a cost of living index so well.

The next round in the debate came in a survey of axiomatic price index theory. Here Balk (1995, p. 87) observed that every known characterization of the Fisher index includes a questionable test. This leaves open the possibility that some other index could fulfill just as many of the important tests as the Fisher index does. Indeed, Balk singled out the Sato–Vartia index as doing just that. Though Balk did not explore the properties of the Sato–Vartia index in detail, remarkably, it can be shown to satisfy the same slightly weakened version of Fisher's original list of tests that the Fisher index satisfies.

Tests not found on Fisher's (1911) list are a different matter, however. The question of the test parity of the Sato–Vartia index with the Fisher index turns on how much importance is attributed to two of these tests. First, Reinsdorf and Alan Dorfman (1999) demonstrated that the Sato–Vartia index fails to satisfy the monotonicity axiom. Since the monotonicity axiom has been viewed as fundamental – Balk lists it first among his core axioms – there would seem to be no hesitation in proclaiming the Fisher index superior.

---

[10] The paper also categorized the Fisher index and some other indexes as superlative, but the Törnqvist index is exact for the economic model with the widest use and the most appeal. The intuition that the superlative index corresponding to the best model must itself be best has recently been vindicated in research by Robert J. Hill (2006).

[11] Diewert subsequently discovered some axiomatic advantages of the Törnqvist index, which he details in chapter 16 of the International Labor Organization (2004) manual on consumer price indexes.

Yet the economic approach shows that things are not so simple. The relationship between price changes and quantity changes implies a value for the elasticity of substitution in the economic model that generates the Sato–Vartia index, so with quantities held constant, a different price change implies a different degree of item substitutability. For large price changes, the degree of substitutability matters greatly. A larger price increase (or smaller price decline) for a highly substitutable item can therefore have less effect on the cost of living than a smaller price increase (larger decrease) for a less substitutable item. A believer in the economic approach could, then, argue that the fault lies with the monotonicity axiom, not the Sato–Vartia index. In particular, according to the economic approach, the property of monotonicity should be required *locally* in the region where price log-changes do not exceed 1 in absolute value. The Sato–Vartia index indeed satisfies such local monotonicity.

The second important test failure of the Sato–Vartia index – which occurs only when it includes three or more items – is of the Laspeyres–Paasche bounds test. As is argued below, the economic approach *does* support the validity of the Laspeyres–Paasche bounds test. Thus, if the economic approach is used to excuse the failure of the monotonicity axiom, the failure of the Laspeyres–Paasche bounds test cannot at the same time be dismissed.

The failure of the Sato–Vartia index to equal the test performance of the Fisher index does not by itself rule out the possibility that some new rival to the Fisher index could be discovered. We can rule out this possibility, however, if we accept the importance of the Laspeyres–Paasche bounds test. Fisher's contention that this test rules out a crossing of the weights can be proven under the assumptions that more than two goods are present and that the index satisfies tests of time reversal, continuity, and proportionality. Consistent with this, Hill (2006) shows that the only superlative index that satisfies the Laspeyres–Paasche bounds test is the Fisher index.

7.3.2. The Laspeyres–Paasche bounds test

Since Pigou, the main argument for the Laspeyres–Paasche bounds test has come from the economic approach. The basic logic is straightforward: adjusting consumers' base period income $\mathbf{p}_0 \cdot \mathbf{q}_0$ for the price change to $\mathbf{p}_t$ by means of the Laspeyres index would enable them to purchase basket $\mathbf{q}_0$ again, though they would likely choose a better basket that would also cost $\mathbf{p}_t \cdot \mathbf{q}_0$. A change in income in proportion to the Laspeyres index is, therefore, at least adequate to maintain the base period standard of living, and quite possibly more than an adequate. This makes the Laspeyres index an upper bound for the cost of living index evaluated at the base period standard of living. Similarly, consumers' comparison period income $\mathbf{p}_t \cdot \mathbf{q}_t$ deflated by the Paasche index is adequate at base period prices $\mathbf{p}_0$ to purchase basket $\mathbf{q}_t$, or some other, possibly better, basket that also costs $\mathbf{p}_0 \cdot \mathbf{q}_t$. Therefore the Paasche index is a lower bound for the index that compares the cost of the comparison period standard of living at comparison period prices to the cost of that same standard of living at base period prices.

The existence of two relevant standards of living creates complications that easily lead to mistakes. Only in the simple case of homotheticity are the Laspeyres and Paasche indexes upper and lower bounds for the *same* cost of living index. One possible mistake is, therefore, to ignore the need to assume homotheticity to make the cost of living index a function of prices alone.

A sound theory should allow for the possibility of changes in the composition of the consumption basket due to income effects. For small changes in the standard of living, income effects are generally so dominated by price effects that they may be ignored. At the other extreme, if $\mathbf{q}_0$ and $\mathbf{q}_t$ represent very disparate standards of living, the Laspeyres–Paasche bounds may plausibly contain neither the cost of living index for the standard of living of period 0, nor the one for the standard of living of period t. A relaxation of the Laspeyres–Paasche bounds test is justifiable when the value of the quantity index is far below 1 or far above 1, because large effects on consumption patterns attributable to a changing standard of living widen the range of possible values for the relevant cost of living indexes beyond the Laspeyres and Paasche bounds.

Nevertheless, to discard the Laspeyres–Paasche bounds test entirely is a second possible mistake. Under a wide variety of assumptions, any cost of living index that is outside the desired bounds will be *approximately* equal to a Laspeyres or Paasche index and hence be at least approximately inside their bounds. Furthermore, the regions of the index domain where the relevant cost of living indexes are outside the Laspeyres–Paasche bounds are limited to subspaces of the domain where the standard of living varies widely. As a result, an index number formula that violates the Laspeyres–Paasche bounds test is likely to do so in the region where the relevant cost of living indexes *are* necessarily between those bounds.

To identify the region where the index must lie within the range defined by the Laspeyres and Paasche indexes, we can use the *weak axiom of revealed preference* (WARP). According to revealed preference theory, if bundle $\mathbf{q}_0$ ($\mathbf{q}_t$) is chosen when $\mathbf{q}_t$ ($\mathbf{q}_0$) would be less expensive, the costlier bundle is superior ("revealed preferred") to less expensive one. In terms of index numbers, this means that $Q^{Laspeyres}(\mathbf{p}_0, \mathbf{p}_t, \mathbf{q}_0, \mathbf{q}_t) \leqslant 1$ implies that $\mathbf{q}_0$ is at least equivalent to $\mathbf{q}_t$, and that $Q^{Paasche}(\mathbf{p}_0, \mathbf{p}_t, \mathbf{q}_0, \mathbf{q}_t) \geqslant 1$ implies that $\mathbf{q}_t$ is at least equivalent to $\mathbf{q}_0$. Letting Q^* represent the implicit quantity index implied by the price index being tested, WARP requires that $Q^* \leqslant 1$ if $Q^{Laspeyres}(\mathbf{p}_0, \mathbf{p}_t, \mathbf{q}_0, \mathbf{q}_t) \leqslant 1$, and that $Q^* \geqslant 1$ if $Q^{Paasche}(\mathbf{p}_0, \mathbf{p}_t, \mathbf{q}_0, \mathbf{q}_t) \geqslant 1$. If $Q^{Laspeyres} = Q^{Paasche} = 1$, then Q^* must equal 1.

Moreover, the version of revealed preference theory for strictly quasi-concave preferences (Vartia and Weymark, 1981, p. 411) implies that $Q^{Paasche} < Q^{Laspeyres}$ when prices change in a way that keeps the standard of living unchanged. In this case, in a region of positive measure consisting of a neighborhood around the locus of points where the standard of living is constant, the cost of living index evaluated at the comparison period or reference period utility is in $[P^{Paasche}, P^{Laspeyres}]$. A price index that strays outside of the Laspeyres–Paasche bounds in this region is likely to get the direction of the welfare change wrong.

Unfortunately, this is not the end of the story regarding the Laspeyres–Paasche bounds test. Besides non-homotheticity, a second source of conceptual difficulties in the economic theory of the Laspeyres–Paasche bounds is the problem of aggregation over consumers. Applications of revealed preference theory to aggregate demand data are subject to the criticism that they presume the existence of a representative consumer, ignoring the fact that aggregate demands of a heterogeneous, nonhomothetic population fail to exhibit key properties that utility maximization confers on individual demands. A theory of the Laspeyres index as an upper bound of a social cost of living index for a population was developed by Robert Pollak (1981). This social cost of living index is based on a Scitovsky contour, which means that it tracks the amount of aggregate income needed for every household to keep its own reference standard of living. Pollak's upper bound result follows because the Laspeyres index and Scitovsky–Laspeyres social cost of living index can both be written as weighted averages of corresponding household level indexes using the same set of weights – households' base period shares of aggregate expenditures. A symmetric result establishing the Paasche index as a lower bound on a social cost of living index was derived by Diewert (1984). In the Paasche case, the weights reflect comparison period household expenditures, and a harmonic mean formula is used both to average the household level Paasche indexes and the corresponding household level cost of living indexes.

The Scitovsky–Pollak social cost of living index bounded by the Laspeyres index is again not the same as the social cost of living index concept bounded by the Paasche index, except in very special cases. Nevertheless, an index that satisfies the Laspeyres–Paasche bounds test has some clear advantages. In the absence of detailed information on the individual cost of living indexes of the members of the population, the presumption that our summary statistic for those indexes should lie in between the two bounds identified as important by theory is a reasonable one. Furthermore, for consistency with the Pareto principle, at least one member of the population must have a welfare change in the direction indicated by the implicit quantity index. An index that is less than or equal to the Laspeyres index and greater than or equal to the Paasche index is consistent with the Pareto principle, something we can generally not be sure of for an index outside these bounds.

7.3.3. Existence of an economic interpretation for indexes that satisfy ordinal circularity

Samuelson and Swamy counsel us to accept the sad facts of life regarding the circularity test because our hopes for satisfying this test must depend on an unrealistic assumption of homotheticity. Yet price indexes that take expenditure patterns into account via their weighting structure must exhibit at least a minimal amount of internal consistency to be meaningful. This requisite internal consistency can be defined as the absence of contradictions in the ordinal ranking of consumption (or output) bundles: a price measure that simultaneously implies that real consumption is up and that it is down does not seem to measure anything useful. Fortunately, economic optimization based on some stable utility or production function – a much weaker assumption than homotheticity! – is sufficient to rule out such contradictions.

The *ordinal circularity axiom* uses the absence of ranking contradictions as a criterion for determining whether the quantities and prices behave too inconsistently for construction of indexes that conform to the Laspeyres–Paasche bounds test. Recalling the logic of the weak axiom of revealed preference for consumption, purchase of $\mathbf{q}_t$ at price $\mathbf{p}_t$ when $\mathbf{q}_0$ would have cost less implies that $\mathbf{q}_t$ yields more utility than $\mathbf{q}_0$. That is, $Q^{Paasche}(\mathbf{p}_0, \mathbf{p}_t, \mathbf{q}_0, \mathbf{q}_t) > 1$ implies that $\mathbf{q}_t$ can be ranked as a higher level of real consumption (consumer welfare or producer use of inputs) than $\mathbf{q}_0$. Similarly, $Q^{Laspeyres}(\mathbf{p}_0, \mathbf{p}_t, \mathbf{q}_0, \mathbf{q}_t) < 1$ implies that $\mathbf{q}_0$ can be ranked as superior. An analogous theory for a producer of multiple outputs states that $Q^{Laspeyres}(\mathbf{p}_0, \mathbf{p}_t, \mathbf{q}_0, \mathbf{q}_t) > 1$ implies that $\mathbf{q}_t$ represents a higher level of real output than $\mathbf{q}_0$, while $Q^{Paasche}(\mathbf{p}_0, \mathbf{p}_s, \mathbf{q}_0, \mathbf{q}_s) < 1$ implies that $\mathbf{q}_0$ is superior. In the producer case, the logic is that selling $\mathbf{q}_0$ when $\mathbf{q}_t$ would have yielded more revenue shows that $\mathbf{q}_t$ is on a higher production possibility frontier. Of course, these restrictions on the quantity indexes imply restrictions on the Laspeyres and Paasche price indexes via the product test.

The ordinal circularity axiom forbids a transitive contradiction in rankings when we form a closed loop of Laspeyres and Paasche indexes. The simplest version of this axiom uses just three time periods to form the loop, though a complete characterization of this axiom would allow for loops of any length. Letting the first link in the loop run from period 0 to period s, if $\min[Q^{Laspeyres}(\mathbf{p}_0, \mathbf{p}_s, \mathbf{q}_0, \mathbf{q}_s), Q^{Paasche}(\mathbf{p}_0, \mathbf{p}_s, \mathbf{q}_0, \mathbf{q}_s)] > 1$, then $\mathbf{q}_s$ represents a larger volume of production or consumption than $\mathbf{q}_0$. Similarly, if $\min[Q^{Laspeyres}(\mathbf{p}_s, \mathbf{p}_t, \mathbf{q}_s, \mathbf{q}_t), Q^{Paasche}(\mathbf{p}_s, \mathbf{p}_t, \mathbf{q}_s, \mathbf{q}_t)] > 1$, then $\mathbf{q}_t$ represents a larger volume of consumption or production than $\mathbf{q}_s$. The ordinal circularity axiom states that if $\mathbf{q}_s$ is an improvement on $\mathbf{q}_0$ and $\mathbf{q}_t$ is an improvement on $\mathbf{q}_s$, then a return to $\mathbf{q}_0$ cannot be still another improvement. That is:

$$\begin{aligned}&\min\left[Q^{Laspeyres}(\mathbf{p}_0, \mathbf{p}_s, \mathbf{q}_0, \mathbf{q}_s), Q^{Paasche}(\mathbf{p}_0, \mathbf{p}_s, \mathbf{q}_0, \mathbf{q}_s)\right] \geqslant 1 \quad \text{and} \\ &\min\left[Q^{Laspeyres}(\mathbf{p}_s, \mathbf{p}_t, \mathbf{q}_s, \mathbf{q}_t), Q^{Paasche}(\mathbf{p}_s, \mathbf{p}_t, \mathbf{q}_s, \mathbf{q}_t)\right] \geqslant 1 \\ &\quad\Rightarrow\quad \max\left[Q^{Laspeyres}(\mathbf{p}_0, \mathbf{p}_t, \mathbf{q}_0, \mathbf{q}_t), Q^{Paasche}(\mathbf{p}_0, \mathbf{p}_t, \mathbf{q}_0, \mathbf{q}_t)\right] \geqslant 1. \qquad (7.27)\end{aligned}$$

Assume a violation of the ordinal circularity axiom. Then when we reverse the direction of time in the last inequality in (7.27), we obtain:

$$\min\left[Q^{Laspeyres}(\mathbf{p}_t, \mathbf{p}_0, \mathbf{q}_t, \mathbf{q}_0), Q^{Paasche}(\mathbf{p}_t, \mathbf{p}_0, \mathbf{q}_t, \mathbf{q}_0)\right] > 1. \qquad (7.28)$$

In the loop formed by combining inequality (7.28) with the first two inequalities in expression (7.27), the transitive property implies that each point is strictly superior to itself!

The Laspeyres and Paasche indexes will satisfy the ordinal circularity test if and only if the price and quantity data are consistent with economic optimization behavior (utility maximization, cost minimization, profit maximization). If we accept that the absence of ranking contradictions is necessary for indexes to be meaningful, we must conclude that the construction of Laspeyres, Paasche or similar indexes implies a belief in the existence of some economic concept that is being maximized, such as utility or profits. This belies the claims that are occasionally made that Laspeyres and Paasche indexes are devoid of economic content.

Tests of ordinal circularity have an interesting history. The economic significance of the existence of intransitive loops was first pointed out by Jean Ville (1951–1952), an engineer who was called upon to teach economics at the University of Lyon because of a post-war faculty shortage. Ville, however, based his tests on a purely theoretical construct known as a Divisia index, which is explained in Appendix B. Ordinal circularity of Laspeyres and Paasche indexes was first used to test for the existence of a utility function that rationalizes the data by Sidney Afriat (1967), who also developed non-parametric bounds for the cost of living index. The narrowing of the hypothesis to be tested to one of utility maximization allows Eq. (7.27) to be simplified by substituting $Q^{Paasche}$ for $\min[Q^{Laspeyres}, Q^{Paasche}]$ and $Q^{Laspeyres}$ for $\max[Q^{Laspeyres}, Q^{Paasche}]$.

The importance of Afriat's tests was explained in Diewert (1973), and they were extended to include a test for homothetic utility maximization in Diewert (1981). Hal Varian (1982 and 1984) developed algorithms for the implementation of these tests, and Dowrick and Quiggin (1994 and 1997) adapted these algorithms for use in inter-area comparisons. Varian's algorithms were used by Marilyn Manser and Richard McDonald (1988), with the surprising result that US aggregate consumption data were consistent with homothetic utility maximization. Finally, using enhanced algorithms, Blow and Crawford (2001) found that data from the British Family Expenditure Survey, which furnishes the weights for the British Retail Price Index (RPI), were consistent with utility maximization. They also determined ranges for the annual substitution bias of the Laspeyres index used for the official RPI. The range was centered somewhere between 0.1 and 0.25 percentage points in most years, a result that agrees with Manser and McDonald's estimates of substitution bias in a Laspeyres price index for the US.

7.3.4. Axiomatic advantages of Laspeyres and Paasche indexes

Formulas with better axiomatic properties than the Laspeyres and Paasche formulas have been recommended since the earliest days of the field in the late 1800s, and the economic approach also implies that other formulas are better.

Nevertheless, the Laspeyres and Paasche indexes remain in widespread use, to such an extent that they were relied on almost exclusively by national statistical agencies until the last days of the twentieth century. It is therefore natural to ask whether these indexes have axiomatic advantages that can justify their use.

An affirmative answer to this question was suggested by Balk (1995 and 1996) based on the test of consistency in aggregation. This test is important for price indexes that are calculated in stages or that comprise components that are themselves of interest, such as a consumer price index. To calculate an index in stages, at each stage of aggregation, the price indexes for lower level aggregates (or basic components) are treated just as if they were price relatives.

The consistency in aggregation test requires that successive use of the index formula in multiple levels of aggregation yield the same answer as a single stage application of that formula that calculates to top-level index directly from all of the detailed data. The Laspeyres index provides an illustration of this property. Partition the detailed items i into K lower-level aggregates J_k with base-period expenditure shares $S_{k0} = \sum_{i \in J_k} s_{i0}$, price vectors $\mathbf{p}_0^k$ and $\mathbf{p}_t^k$, and quantity vectors $\mathbf{q}_0^k$ and $\mathbf{q}_t^k$. Then the Laspeyres index equals:

$$
\begin{aligned}
P^{Laspeyres} &= \sum_i s_{i0}(p_{it}/p_{i0}) \\
&= \sum_{k=1,\ldots,K} \left[\sum_{i \in J_k} s_{i0}(p_{it}/p_{i0}) \right] \\
&= \sum_{k=1,\ldots,K} S_{k0} P^{Laspeyres}(\mathbf{p}_0^k, \mathbf{p}_t^k, \mathbf{q}_0^k, \mathbf{q}_t^k).
\end{aligned} \tag{7.29}
$$

Balk (1996, p. 357) provides a general characterization for the price indexes that satisfy consistency in aggregation. He shows that this set of indexes P can be defined implicitly by requiring the existence of a function $f(P, \mathbf{p}_0 \cdot \mathbf{q}_0, \mathbf{p}_t \cdot \mathbf{q}_t)$ such that:

$$
f(P, \mathbf{p}_0 \cdot \mathbf{q}_0, \mathbf{p}_t \cdot \mathbf{q}_t) = \sum_i f(p_{it}/p_{i0}, p_{i0}q_{i0}, p_{it}q_{it}). \tag{7.30}
$$

For example, a generalization of the Laspeyres index that depends on the unobservable elasticity of substitution parameter σ from the CES utility function is the Lloyd–Moulton index. This index satisfies condition (7.30) because $(\mathbf{p}_0 \cdot \mathbf{q}_0) P^{Lloyd\text{–}Moulton} = [\sum_i (p_{i0}q_{i0})(p_{it}/p_{i0})^{\sigma}]^{(1/\sigma)}$.

A formula that depends exclusively on observables is the Vartia I or Montgomery index:

$$
P^{MontGomery} = \sum_i \frac{\text{logmean}(p_{i0}q_{i0}, p_{it}q_{it}) \log(p_{it}/p_{i0})}{\text{logmean}(\mathbf{p}_t \cdot \mathbf{q}_t, \mathbf{p}_0 \cdot \mathbf{q}_0)}. \tag{7.31}
$$

The Montgomery index is the only formula that is consistent in aggregation and that satisfies the factor reversal test. Unfortunately, it gains these remarkable properties at the cost of sacrificing the vital proportionality axiom. Its usefulness is therefore limited to theoretical purposes, such as Diewert's (1978) proof that the Törnqvist and Fisher indexes satisfy approximate versions of the consistency in aggregation test.

If we restrict $f(\cdot)$ to be a linear combination of $(\mathbf{p}_0 \cdot \mathbf{q}_0)P$ and $(\mathbf{p}_t \cdot \mathbf{q}_t)P$, then the family of generalized Stuvel indexes comprises the admissible indexes that solve Eq. (7.30) exactly. To derive the Stuvel indexes, begin by recalling that a pairing of the Paasche price index with the Laspeyres quantity index passes the product test, but a pairing of two Laspeyres indexes does not. Since raising a quantity index has the effect of lowering the implicit price index that it implies, we can adjust the Laspeyres price index and the Laspeyres quantity index in the same direction to arrive at a pair of indexes P and Q that pass the product test. Moreover, by making both adjustments identical, we can derive a formula that satisfies the factor reversal test.

Two ways to do this were identified by van IJzeren (1958). The system of equations formed by the product test $PQ = (\mathbf{p}_t \cdot \mathbf{q}_t)/(\mathbf{p}_0 \cdot \mathbf{q}_0)$ and an equality of proportional adjustments can be solved for P and Q to obtain the Fisher indexes. The proportional adjustments equality is:

$$P/P^{Laspeyres} = Q/Q^{Laspeyres}. \tag{7.32}$$

Alternatively, we can make the adjustments equal in absolute terms. This leads to the equation:

$$P - P^{Laspeyres} = Q - Q^{Laspeyres}. \tag{7.33}$$

Solving for P and Q in the system of simultaneous equations formed by $PQ = (\mathbf{p}_t \cdot \mathbf{q}_t)/(\mathbf{p}_0 \cdot \mathbf{q}_0)$ and the equality of absolute adjustments gives the Stuvel (1957) indexes:

$$P^{Stuvel} = \frac{P^{Laspeyres} - Q^{Laspeyres}}{2} + \frac{[(P^{Laspeyres} - Q^{Laspeyres})^2 + 4(\mathbf{p}_t \cdot \mathbf{q}_t)/(\mathbf{p}_0 \cdot \mathbf{q}_0)]^{1/2}}{2}, \tag{7.34}$$

$$Q^{Stuvel} = \frac{Q^{Laspeyres} - P^{Laspeyres}}{2} + \frac{[(Q^{Laspeyres} - P^{Laspeyres})^2 + 4(\mathbf{p}_t \cdot \mathbf{q}_t)/(\mathbf{p}_0 \cdot \mathbf{q}_0)]^{1/2}}{2}. \tag{7.35}$$

The Stuvel indexes are "ideal" because they satisfy both the time reversal test and the factor reversal test. They can also be generalized. The family of generalized Stuvel indexes is defined by weighting the absolute price and quantity index adjustments by some $\lambda \in [0, 1]$:

$$\lambda\big(P - P^{Laspeyres}(\cdot)\big) = (1 - \lambda)\big(Q - Q^{Laspeyres}(\cdot)\big). \tag{7.36}$$

The resulting indexes satisfy Balk's condition for consistency in aggregation with $f(\cdot)$ from Eq. (7.30) specified as follows:

$$\lambda(\mathbf{p}_0 \cdot \mathbf{q}_0)P - (1-\lambda)(\mathbf{p}_t \cdot \mathbf{q}_t)P^{-1}$$
$$= \sum_i [\lambda(p_{i0}q_{i0})(p_{it}/p_{i0}) - (1-\lambda)(p_{it}q_{it})(p_{it}/p_{i0})^{-1}]. \quad (7.37)$$

If λ equals 1, the generalized Stuvel price index becomes a Laspeyres index, and if λ equals 0, it becomes a Paasche index. Balk (1996) observes that the generalized Stuvel indexes fail to satisfy the axiom of linear homogeneity in comparison period prices unless $\lambda = 0$ or $\lambda = 1$. Therefore, the Laspeyres index and the Paasche index are unique in their ability to exhibit consistency in aggregation and linear homogeneity in comparison period prices.

Balk argues that this property of linear homogeneity is important because it is called for by the economic approach and because it is required to obtain sensible results in a common use of price indexes, the measurement of price change between periods other than the base period. The latter assertion is a reference to the comparative proportionality test, ironically, the very test that led Fisher to favor the Paasche index in *The Purchasing Power of Money*.

In *The Making of Index Numbers* Fisher reversed his position and dismissed the test of comparative proportionality because of its inapplicability to chained indexes. This castes doubt of Balk's rationale for preferring the Laspeyres and Paasche indexes to other types of generalized Stuvel indexes. The Laspeyres and Paasche indexes have another axiomatic advantage over the other Stuvel indexes, however. Like the Edgeworth–Marshall index, P^{Stuvel} defined in Eq. (7.34) grows closer to the Paasche index as $\mathbf{q}_t$ rises. This violation of the axiom of homogeneity of degree 0 in comparison period quantities is avoided by the Laspeyres and Paasche price indexes.

7.4. Selection and Application of Axioms and Tests

7.4.1. A core set of axioms

Despite the controversies over which tests to set aside in light of the impossibility of simultaneously satisfying all of them, some sets of axioms have gained acceptance as ways of defining an admissible price index. Balk (1995, p. 86) identifies two such sets of fundamental axioms. One combination consists of the monotonicity axiom, the proportionality axiom, the price dimensionality axiom and the commensurability axiom, as discussed by Eichhorn and Voeller (1983). The other combination of axioms, which Balk prefers, replaces the proportionality axiom with two axioms, the strong identity test and an axiom requiring *linear homogeneity in comparison period prices*, i.e. that $P(\mathbf{p}_0, \lambda\mathbf{p}_t, \mathbf{q}_0, \mathbf{q}_t) = \lambda P(\mathbf{p}_0, \mathbf{p}_t, \mathbf{q}_0, \mathbf{q}_t)$. A formula can satisfy proportionality yet fail to exhibit linear homogeneity in comparison prices. Whether such a formula should be excluded from consideration as a price index is debatable, so either treatment of the axiom of linear homogeneity in comparison prices is defensible.

Nevertheless, both sets of axioms are too restrictive to be accepted as fundamental. The problem lies with the monotonicity axiom. Besides its inconsistency with economic theory discussed above, this axiom is incompatible with some formulas that are clearly acceptable. These are the log-change indexes that use expenditure shares as weights, including the Törnqvist index, the Sato–Vartia index, and the version of the Cobb–Douglas index with weights of $s_{i0} = p_{i0}q_{i0}/(\mathbf{p}_0 \cdot \mathbf{q}_0)$. Moreover, if monotonicity is also required for the implicit quantity indexes, as is logically consistent for a price index that is used as a deflator, more formulas are ruled out, most notably the Walsh index. The Walsh index is remarkable for the number of tests that it satisfies; indeed, it was classified by Fisher (1922, p. 247) as superlative.

As an illustration of the non-monotonicity of the log-change indexes, consider the endogenous weight version of the Cobb–Douglas index, $P^{Cobb\text{–}Douglas}(\mathbf{p}_0, \mathbf{p}_t, \mathbf{s}_0)$. Substituting $p_{i0}q_{i0}/(\mathbf{p}_0 \cdot \mathbf{q}_0)$ for s_i^* in Eq. (7.18) and differentiating, we have:

$$\partial \log P^{Cobb\text{–}Douglas} / \partial \log p_{i0} = s_{i0}(1 - s_{i0}) \log(p_{it}/p_{i0}) - s_{i0}. \tag{7.38}$$

If $\log(p_{it}/p_{i0}) \geqslant 1 - s_{i0}$, the index is increasing in p_{i0}, thus violating the monotonicity axiom.[12]

The problems of severe implications and lack of theoretical justification can be resolved by weakening the monotonicity axiom whenever a log price changes by more than one. We retain the *local monotonicity axiom* as a requirement on the price index in the region defined by $|\log(p_{it}/p_{i0})| \leqslant -1\ \forall i$ because this axiom guarantees that $P(\mathbf{p}_0, \mathbf{p}_t, \mathbf{q}_0, \mathbf{q}_t) > 1$ whenever $p_{it} \geqslant p_{i0}\ \forall i$ with at least one inequality strict, and that $P(\mathbf{p}_0, \mathbf{p}_t, \mathbf{q}_0, \mathbf{q}_t) < 1$ when $\mathbf{p}_0 < \mathbf{p}_t$. We also maintain the global necessity of a monotonicity axiom that holds item expenditures constant by treating the quantities as inversely dependent on prices. Using the diagonal matrix $\boldsymbol{\Lambda}$ from the commensurability axiom to adjust prices and quantities in one period only, the *weak monotonicity axiom* requires that:

$$\partial P(\boldsymbol{\Lambda}\mathbf{p}_0, \mathbf{p}_t, \boldsymbol{\Lambda}^{-1}\mathbf{q}_0, \mathbf{q}_t)/\partial \Lambda_{ii} < 0 \tag{7.39a}$$

and

$$\partial P(\mathbf{p}_0, \boldsymbol{\Lambda}\mathbf{p}_t, \mathbf{q}_0, \boldsymbol{\Lambda}^{-1}\mathbf{q}_t)/\partial \Lambda_{ii} > 0. \tag{7.39b}$$

Eichhorn and Voeller's set of four core axioms is valid if the monotonicity axiom is replaced with a combination of the local monotonicity axiom and the

---

[12] To obtain a general result for the log-change indexes, note that functions of the form x^{ap+b} are non-monotonic for small p if $a > 0$ and $0 \leqslant b < e^{-2}a$. Let p represent a price and let a and b be parameters such that $ap + b$ approximates the function for the weight of the Cobb–Douglas, Törnqvist or Sato–Vartia index.

weak monotonicity axiom. Alternatively, to rule out negative weights without relying on a monotonicity axiom, we can strengthen the strong identity test to the mean value test. The mean value test formalizes the appealing principle that a measure of central tendency must not stray outside the range of the values that it is supposed to summarize. Eichhorn and Voeller (1983) showed that this property is implied by their set of fundamental axioms, so adding it to their set of axioms, or, by extension, to Balk's set of five axioms, does not have the effect of excluding any index previously admissible. If linear homogeneity in comparison period prices is maintained as an axiom, the mean value axiom is particularly appealing because it reduces Balk's set of five axioms to a set of just four axioms. These axioms are linear homogeneity in comparison period prices, the mean value axiom, the price dimensionality axiom and the commensurability axiom.

7.4.2. Choosing the right set of tests

The specifics of the problem at hand, including the purpose of the index and the characteristics of the data, determine the relative merits of the possible attributes of the index formula. In selecting tests, therefore, the key principle is that the answer depends on the question. Even formulas with serious defects, such as the Dutot index and the ratio of unit values, can be useful in the right context. However Fisher's (1922, p. 361) oft-neglected warning about the Carli index – "[it] should not be used under any circumstances" – is best observed.

Six kinds of tests are of practical value for comparison of prices over time. First, failure to satisfy the time reversal test is a sign of bias if the discrepancies tend to be in one direction, and if the discrepancies are necessarily in one direction, the bias is severe. Second, the requirements of continuity in prices and quantities may be necessary for avoiding erratic behavior of the index. Third, if the data contain extreme price relatives, the determinacy test is important for avoiding excessive sensitivity to outliers. Fourth, the test of consistency in aggregation is relevant when an index is constructed in stages, especially if index users are interested in the index components along with the top level aggregate.

Fifth, for indexes that have an interpretation using the economic approach, such as a cost of living index, item weights must reflect expenditure patterns. An index that stays within the bounds defined by the Laspeyres and Paasche indexes will do this, but treating this test may be treated as approximate to avoid automatically limiting the choice of index to a Laspeyres index, a Paasche index, or some kind of average of the two.

Lastly, if the index is to be used for deflation of nominal expenditures, the product test, and tests of the properties of the implicit quantity index that is implied by the product test are critical. Satisfaction of the factor reversal test (which requires that the implicit quantity index have the same functional form as the price index) is a convenient way to insure that the implicit quantity index has axiomatic properties that are as good as those of the price index, but this test is intrinsically important only if an identical approach to price and quantity indexes is desired.

7.4.3. Hard tests or soft tests?

Mathematically, a theorem is determined to be false if a single example that violates it is discovered, regardless of whether the conditions that generate the example are aberrant. Yet for the instrumentalist's goal of finding price measurement tools that work well in practice, the circumstances and magnitude of test violations *are* relevant. Measurement errors caused by a test violation may be rare if the test is locally satisfied in the region that contains most data, or they may be inconsequential if the test is approximately satisfied.

Unnecessary errors are, of course, to be avoided, even if they are infrequent and small. An exposure to minor errors that is necessary to gain other advantages may be warranted, however. Many tests hypothesize conditions that are rarely encountered in actual practice, so a failure of a test because of a small discrepancy is not always an indication that an index will perform poorly.

The Törnqvist index is the best example of this. It has long been a staple of the productivity measurement literature, sometimes under the name "Divisia index."[13] Extensive experience with the Törnqvist index in applied research shows that it generally produces very credible results, yet it has a mediocre score of satisfied tests. The explanation for this paradox is that the Törnqvist index approximately satisfies the critical tests that it does not satisfy exactly, and its test violations occur in narrow or extreme ranges of prices and quantities. For example, when the gap between the Laspeyres and Paasche indexes is close to vanishing, the Törnqvist index will generally violate the Laspeyres–Paasche bounding test – albeit by a small amount – but the probability of the Laspeyres and Paasche indexes coinciding is small, absent some mechanism that artificially guarantees such an outcome. In most practical applications, therefore, the Törnqvist index falls inside the required bounds. Indeed, most of the time, it closely mimics the high-scoring Fisher and Sato–Vartia indexes, as is demonstrated formally for the Fisher index case by Diewert (1978). It may even be superior to them in its resistance to chain drift, which occurs when a chained index exhibits large or systematic violations of the circularity test (Ehemann, 2005).

7.5. Future of the Field

The pendulum that swung so strongly towards the economic approach starting in the 1930s began to swing back starting in the 1970s. One cause of this revitalized interest is an increased recognition of the usefulness of the axiomatic

[13] A chained Törnqvist index is a good discrete time approximation for François Divisia's continuous time concept, as explained in Pravin K. Trivedi (1981) and Balk (2005).

approach. The problem of formula bias in the US Consumer Price Index (CPI), which caused hundreds of billions of dollars in excess payments and played a key role in the decision to name a commission to investigate the CPI led by Michael Boskin, provides a dramatic example of this. In the early 1990s, research revealed that a narrow focus on the stochastic approach had prevented a full consideration in the 1970s of the axiomatic properties of a formula for the lowest-level aggregates of the CPI that had the characteristics of a Carli index (Reinsdorf, 1998). Another example of the usefulness of the axiomatic approach comes from the selection in the 1990s of the Fisher index for the US and Canadian national economic accounts. Even though the factor reversal test has been criticized for its lack of support from the economic approach, this test showed that the alternatives to the Fisher index (such as the Törnqvist index) do not permit the kind of unified approach to the construction of both price indexes and quantity indexes that is desirable for national accounts.

A second cause of revitalized interest in the axiomatic approach is disillusionment with its competitor, the economic approach. Concerns about the applicability of the economic approach to groups of heterogeneous households have received renewed emphasis from some researchers (e.g. Angus Deaton, 1998). Furthermore – although having an imperfect but explicit conceptual framework would seem preferable to having a framework that cannot be articulated or that is not relevant to important elements of the problem – a few index number users question whether the underlying assumptions of the economic approach are sufficiently descriptive of reality to constitute a useful paradigm. Because of such controversies, a recent US National Academy of Sciences Panel was unable to reach a consensus on the question of whether the underlying measurement concept for the US Consumer Price Index should be based on the economic approach or on a kind of basket test (National Research Council, 2002). A turning of the tables on the economic approach by the axiomatic approach is not on the horizon, for the reasons discussed by Jack Triplett (2001). Instead, we can hope that index number researchers in either tradition will become increasingly aware that both traditions offer critical advantages.

Acknowledgements

I am grateful to Keir Armstrong, Bert Balk, Erwin Diewert and Jack Triplett for helpful comments. The views expressed are my own and should not be attributed to the Bureau of Economic Analysis.

Appendix A7. The Circularity Test in Characterizations for the Cobb–Douglas Index

PROPOSITION 1. *If an index that satisfies the circularity test, the commensurability axiom, the proportionality test, and the monotonicity axiom, then it is the Cobb–Doublas index.*

PROOF. The commensurability axiom states that a change in the quantity units for any item i must have no effect on the index. A change in the units of measurement for the arbitrary item i will change the values of q_{i0} and q_{it} and the values of p_{i0} and p_{it}, so an index that satisfies the commensurability axiom must be expressible as a function that does not have the q_{i0}, the q_{it}, the p_{i0}, or the q_{it} as arguments. In particular, all the information about item i that matters for the index must be contained in three functions of $(q_{i0}, q_{it}, p_{i0}, q_{it})$ that are unaffected by a change in its units of measurement: (a) the price relative p_{it}/p_{i0}; (b) the expenditure $p_{i0}q_{i0}$; and (c) $p_{it}q_{it}$. Therefore, an index that satisfies the commensurability axiom is expressible in the form:

$$f(p_{1t}/p_{10}, \ldots, p_{Nt}/p_{N0}, s_{20}, \ldots, s_{N0}, s_{2t}, \ldots, s_{Nt}, \mathbf{p}_0 \cdot \mathbf{q}_0, \mathbf{p}_t \cdot \mathbf{q}_t), \tag{A7.1}$$

where s_{10} and s_{1t} are omitted from the argument list because they are determined from the other shares as $1 - (s_{20} + \cdots + s_{N0})$ and $1 - (s_{2t} + \cdots + s_{Nt})$, respectively.

The circularity test states that:

$$\begin{aligned} &f\big((p_{1s}/p_{10})(p_{1t}/p_{1s}), \ldots, (p_{Ns}/p_{N0})(p_{Nt}/p_{Ns}), \cdot\big) \\ &\quad = f(p_{1s}/p_{10}, \ldots, p_{Ns}/p_{N0}, \cdot) f(p_{1t}/p_{1s}, \ldots, p_{Nt}/p_{Ns}, \cdot). \end{aligned} \tag{A7.2}$$

Equation (A7.2) implies that multiplying p_{is}/p_{i0} by any positive scalar k must change $\log f(p_{1s}/p_{10}, \ldots, p_{Ns}/p_{N0}, \cdot)$ by minus the amount that dividing p_{it}/p_{is} by k changes $\log f(p_{1t}/p_{1s}, \ldots, p_{Nt}/p_{Ns}, \cdot)$. Let $\mathbf{r}$ represent the vector of price relatives from time 0 to time s and $\boldsymbol{\rho}$ represent the vector of price relatives from time s to time t. Then, using the first price relative as the representative case, for all $(\mathbf{r}, \boldsymbol{\rho})$ we have the equality:

$$\begin{aligned} &\log f(kr_1, \ldots, r_N, \cdot) - \log f(r_1, \ldots, r_N, \cdot) \\ &\quad = \log f(\rho_1, \ldots, \rho_N, \cdot) - \log f\big(k^{-1}\rho_1, \ldots, \rho_N, \cdot\big). \end{aligned} \tag{A7.3}$$

This equality holds if and only if, for some predetermined constant w_1,

$$\log f(kr_1, \ldots, r_N, \cdot) - \log f(r_1, \ldots, r_N, \cdot) = w_1 \log k. \tag{A7.4}$$

Similar requirements for items 2 through N imply that

$$\log f(r_1, \ldots, r_N, \cdot) = \sum_{i=1,\ldots,N} w_i \log r_i. \tag{A7.5}$$

Now suppose that $p_{it}/p_{i0} = \lambda > 0$ for all i. Then $\lambda(p_{i0}/p_{is})$ can be substituted for p_{it}/p_{is} in Eq. (A7.2). Furthermore, using the proportionality test, λ can be substituted for $f(p_{1t}/p_{10}, \ldots, p_{Nt}/p_{N0}, \cdot)$. Equation (A7.2) then becomes:

$$\begin{aligned} \log\lambda &= \log f(p_{1s}/p_{10}, \ldots, p_{Ns}/p_{N0}, \cdot) \\ &\quad + \log f\big(\lambda(p_{1s}/p_{10})^{-1}, \ldots, \lambda(p_{N0}/p_{Ns})^{-1}, \cdot\big) \\ &= \log\lambda\left[\sum_{i=1,\ldots,N} w_i\right]. \end{aligned} \tag{A7.6}$$

Consequently, $\sum_{i=1,\ldots,N} w_i = 1$. Finally, monotonocity of $f(\cdot)$ implies that $w_i \geqslant 0\ \forall i$. □

PROPOSITION 2. *If an index that satisfies the circularity test, the commensurability axiom, the proportionality test, and the mean value test, then it is the Cobb–Doublas index.*

PROOF. Identical to proof of Proposition 1, except that $w_i \geqslant 0\ \forall i$ follows from the mean value test instead of from the monotonicity test. □

Appendix B7. Divisia Indexes and the Assumptions of the Economic Approach

In the economic approach, the price index concept is a ratio of expenditure functions, cost functions or revenue functions. These functions are derived from the primal economic utility or production functions via the maximization and minimization problems studied in duality theory. They therefore exist if and only if the demand system or output system could have been generated by some form of economic optimization behavior, such as utility maximization.

To identify the implications of economic optimization behavior, we need an index concept that does not presume the existence of expenditure functions, cost functions, or revenue functions, which are used to define the economic indexes. The Divisia index can be adapted to this purpose. The Divisia index may be considered a generalization of the economic index concept (such as the cost of living index) because in cases where the functions needed to define an economic index exist, the Divisia index can be evaluated in a way that makes it equal to the economic index. A detailed explanation of this point is beyond the scope of this appendix, but briefly, to equal the economic index based on some indifference curve (or isoquant), the line integral that defines the Divisia index must be evaluated over a path consisting of a segment that runs along the indifference curve (or isoquant) in price space, and a segment (or possibly a pair of segments) that runs along a ray emanating from the origin.

A derivation of the Divisia index of consumption is as follows. Let $\{(\mathbf{p}_t, Y_t);\ t \in [0, 1]\}$ define a continuously differentiable mapping from t to the price vector $\mathbf{p}_t$ and income level Y_t. François Divisia defined an analogous path for the quantity vector, but in the version of the Divisia index used to study the properties of a demand model, the quantities must be specified as functions of prices and income. To represent the demand model, let $\mathbf{s}(\mathbf{p}, Y)$ be a continuously differentiable mapping of prices and income to a vector of expenditure shares. Letting s_{it} and p_{it} represent the share and price of the ith item at time t, a price change from $\mathbf{p}_t$ to $\mathbf{p}_{t+\Delta t}$ implies a Laspeyres index of $\sum_i s_{it}(p_{i,t+\Delta t}/p_{it})$. In the limit as Δt approaches 0, the log-change in this Laspeyres index equals $\mathbf{s}(\mathbf{p}_t, Y_t) \cdot (\partial \log(\mathbf{p}_t)/\partial t)\Delta t$, and the log-change in the Paasche index has an identical limit. We therefore define the Divisia price index as the solution to the differential equation:

$$\partial \log\left(P_t^{Divisia}\right)/\partial t = \mathbf{s}(\mathbf{p}_t, Y_t) \cdot \left(\partial \log(\mathbf{p}_t)/\partial t\right). \tag{B7.1}$$

A similar derivative of a Laspeyres or Paasche implicit quantity index defines the Divisia quantity index:

$$\partial \log\left(Q_t^{Divisia}\right)/\partial t = \partial \log(Y_t)/\partial t - \mathbf{s}(\mathbf{p}_t, Y_t) \cdot \left(\partial \log(\mathbf{p}_t)/\partial t\right). \tag{B7.2}$$

Failure of this Divisia index to satisfy ordinal circularity is indicated by the existence of a path with $\mathbf{p}(1) = \mathbf{p}(0)$ and $\partial \log(Q_t^{Divisia})/\partial t > 0$ everywhere. The existence of such a cycle implies that the demand system is inconsistent with utility maximization (Ville, 1951–1952, and Leonid Hurwicz and Marcel Richter, 1979).

In a paper that anticipated Samuelson and Swamy's result, Charles Hulten (1973) showed that the Divisia index satisfies the circularity test (in cardinal form) if and only if the utility function is homothetic. If $\mathbf{s}(\mathbf{p}, Y)$ is consistent with maximization of a homothetic utility function, then $\mathbf{s}(\mathbf{p}, Y) = \partial \log(e(\mathbf{p}, u))/\partial \log \mathbf{p}$, where $e(\mathbf{p}, u)$ is the expenditure function. Substituting this vector of derivatives for $\mathbf{s}(\mathbf{p}_t, Y_t)$ in (B7.2), we can show the "if" part of Hulten's result, by writing the line integral defining the Divisia index as:

$$\int_1^0 \left[\partial \log(Y_t)/\partial t - \left(\partial \log\left(e(\mathbf{p}, u)\right)/\partial \log \mathbf{p}\right) \cdot \left(\partial \log(\mathbf{p}_t)/\partial t\right)\right] dt. \tag{B7.3}$$

This integral equals $\log(Y(1)/Y(0)) - \log(e(\mathbf{p}(1), u)/e(\mathbf{p}(0), u))$ regardless of the path.

For more information on Divisia indexes see Balk (2005).

B7.1. Glossary

B7.1.1. Tests and axioms

Base-independence. Requires that $P(\mathbf{p}_0, \mathbf{p}_t, \mathbf{q}_0, \mathbf{q}_t)/P(\mathbf{p}_0, \mathbf{p}_s, \mathbf{q}_0, \mathbf{q}_s) = P(\mathbf{p}_1, \mathbf{p}_t, \mathbf{q}_1, \mathbf{q}_t)/P(\mathbf{p}_1, \mathbf{p}_s, \mathbf{q}_1, \mathbf{q}_s)$.

Basket, constant. Requires that $P(\mathbf{p}_0, \mathbf{p}_t, \mathbf{q}, \mathbf{q}) = \frac{\mathbf{p}_t \cdot \mathbf{q}}{\mathbf{p}_0 \cdot \mathbf{q}}$, where $\mathbf{q}$ represents a fixed consumption basket that is assumed to be representative of purchasing patterns. The proportional baskets test imposes the same requirement on $P(\mathbf{p}_0, \mathbf{p}_t, \mathbf{q}, \lambda\mathbf{q})$ for any positive scalar λ.

Change of units. See "Commensurability."

Circularity. Requires that $P(\mathbf{p}_0, \mathbf{p}_s, \mathbf{q}_0, \mathbf{q}_s)P(\mathbf{p}_s, \mathbf{p}_t, \mathbf{q}_s, \mathbf{q}_t) = P(\mathbf{p}_0, \mathbf{p}_t, \mathbf{q}_0, \mathbf{q}_t)$.

Commensurability. Requires that simultaneously multiplying the prices of the arbitrary item i by Λ_{ii} and dividing its quantities by Λ_{ii} leave the index unchanged. Letting $\boldsymbol{\Lambda}$ be a matrix with the Λ_{ii} on its main diagonal and 0s elsewhere, this requirement may be written as $P(\mathbf{p}_0, \mathbf{p}_t, \mathbf{q}_0, \mathbf{q}_t) = P(\boldsymbol{\Lambda}\mathbf{p}_0, \boldsymbol{\Lambda}\mathbf{p}_t, \boldsymbol{\Lambda}^{-1}\mathbf{q}_0, \boldsymbol{\Lambda}^{-1}\mathbf{q}_t)$. Also known as "the change of units" test.

Consistency in aggregation. Requires that an iterated application of the index formula in multiple stages of aggregation, with index values from lower stages of aggregation treated as price relatives, yield the same answer as a single-stage application of the index formula.

Continuity. Requires that the function $P(\mathbf{p}_0, \mathbf{p}_t, \mathbf{q}_0, \mathbf{q}_t)$ be continuous in all of its arguments.

Determinateness. Requires that $P(\mathbf{p}_0, \mathbf{p}_t, \mathbf{q}_0, \mathbf{q}_t)$ have limit that remains within some definite finite positive bounds as a price approaches 0 or infinity.

Factor reversal. Requires that the price index and its implicit quantity index have the *same* functional form; i.e. $P(\mathbf{p}_0, \mathbf{p}_t, \mathbf{q}_0, \mathbf{q}_t)P(\mathbf{q}_0, \mathbf{q}_t, \mathbf{p}_0, \mathbf{p}_t) = (\mathbf{p}_t \cdot \mathbf{q}_t)/(\mathbf{p}_0 \cdot \mathbf{q}_0)$.

Linear homogeneity in comparison period prices. A generalization of the proportionality test that requires that the index satisfy $P(\mathbf{p}_0, \lambda\mathbf{p}_t, \mathbf{q}_0, \mathbf{q}_t) = \lambda P(\mathbf{p}_0, \mathbf{p}_t, \mathbf{q}_0, \mathbf{q}_t)$.

Laspeyres–Paasche bounds. Prohibits the index from ranging outside the bounds defined by the Laspeyres index and the Paasche index.

Mean value. Prohibits the index from ranging outside the bounds defined by the largest and smallest price relative.

Monotonicity. The derivative of the index with respect to any comparison period price is non-negative and the derivative with respect to any base period price is non-positive. Applied holding quantities constant.

Monotonicity, weak. The derivative of the index with respect to any comparison period price with quantities adjusted simultaneously to hold expenditures constant is non-negative; i.e. for any non-negative diagonal matrix $\boldsymbol{\Lambda}$, $\partial P(\mathbf{p}_0, \boldsymbol{\Lambda}\mathbf{p}_t, \mathbf{q}_0, \boldsymbol{\Lambda}^{-1}\mathbf{q}_t)/\partial \Lambda_{ii} > 0$.

Ordinal circularity. Prohibits transitive contradictions in the ranking of consumption or output bundles. If the quantity indexes imply that $\mathbf{q}_s$ is a greater level of real consumption (or real output) than $\mathbf{q}_0$ and that $\mathbf{q}_t$ is a greater level of real consumption (or real output) than $\mathbf{q}_s$, then they cannot at the same time imply that $\mathbf{q}_0$ is a greater level of real consumption (or real output) than $\mathbf{q}_t$.

Price dimensionality. Requires that multiplying all base and comparison period prices by the same positive scalar λ leave the index unchanged. Also known as "homogeneity of degree zero in prices."

Product. Requires that the price index and the quantity index together decompose the expenditure change; i.e. $P(\mathbf{p}_0, \mathbf{p}_t, \mathbf{q}_0, \mathbf{q}_t)Q(\mathbf{p}_0, \mathbf{p}_t, \mathbf{q}_0, \mathbf{q}_t) = (\mathbf{p}_t \cdot \mathbf{q}_t)/(\mathbf{p}_0 \cdot \mathbf{q}_0)$.

Proportionality. $P(\mathbf{p}_0, \lambda\mathbf{p}_0, \mathbf{q}_0, \mathbf{q}_t) = \lambda$. Also known as "strong proportionality" to distinguish it from the weaker requirement that $P(\mathbf{p}_0, \lambda\mathbf{p}_0, \mathbf{q}_0, \lambda\mathbf{q}_0) = \lambda$.

Proportionality, comparative. $P(\mathbf{p}_0, \lambda\mathbf{p}_s, \mathbf{q}_0, \mathbf{q}_t)/P(\mathbf{p}_0, \mathbf{p}_s, \mathbf{q}_0, \mathbf{q}_s) = \lambda$, where $\mathbf{p}_t$ has been assumed to equal $\lambda\mathbf{p}_s$.

Time reversal. $P(\mathbf{p}_0, \mathbf{p}_t, \mathbf{q}_0, \mathbf{q}_t)P(\mathbf{p}_t, \mathbf{p}_0, \mathbf{q}_t, \mathbf{q}_0) = 1$.

Weak axiom of revealed preference. Implies that the standard of living index is greater than or equal to 1 whenever the Paasche quantity index is greater than 1 and that the standard of living index is less than or equal to 1 whenever the Laspeyres quantity index is less than 1. If expenditures are constant, equivalent conditions are that the cost of living index is greater than or equal to 1 whenever the Paasche price index is greater than 1, and the cost of living index is less than or equal to 1 whenever the Laspeyres index is less than 1.

B7.1.2. Price index formulas

Carli. A simple average of price relatives. Also known as the Sauerbeck index.

Cobb–Douglas. In log-change form, a weighted average of price log-changes, with fixed weights that reflect a set of constant expenditure shares.

Cost of Living. Also known the "Konüs index." Tracks the change in the expenditure needed to keep the standard of living constant at some reference level taking substitution possibilities into account.

Divisia. Define prices and quantities as continuous functions of time. The limit of log-change in the chained Laspeyres (or, equivalently, Paasche) index as the frequency of chaining becomes infinite is the log-change in the Divisia index.

Dutot. Ratio of simple averages of prices.

Edgeworth–Marshall. Uses a simple two-period average of quantities as its fixed basket.

Fisher. Geometric mean of the Laspeyres and Paasche indexes.

Implicit. An implicit price index is derived from a specified quantity index via the product test, and is equal to the expenditure relative divided by the quantity index.

Jevons. An unweighted geometric mean of price relatives.

Laspeyres. Uses initial (base) period quantities as its basket. If price relatives are averaged, the weights are always the expenditure shares from the same period as the denominator in the price relatives.

Laspeyres–Scitovsky. A social cost of living index concept that measures the change in the aggregate expenditure needed to keep all individuals at their base period utility level.

Lowe. Uses a representative basket based on expenditure patterns from a year or set of years immediately preceding the period furnishing the initial prices. This basket can be more practical to estimate than the precise basket corresponding to the initial prices called for by the Laspeyres index formula.

Paasche. Uses final (comparison) period quantities as its basket. If price relatives are averaged, the averaging formula is a weighted harmonic mean, and the weights are the expenditure shares from the same period as the numerator of the price relatives.

Sato–Vartia. In log-change form, an average of price log-changes with weights proportional to logarithmic means of base and comparison period expenditure shares.

Stuvel. Uses the quadratic formula to define implicitly an average of the Laspeyres and Paasche indexes that satisfies the factor reversal test and the time reversal test.

Törnqvist. In log-change form, an average of price log-changes with weights equal to simple averages of base and comparison period expenditure shares. Some authors refer to the chained Törnqvist index as a "Divisia index."

Walsh. Uses a two-period geometric mean of quantities as its fixed basket.

B7.1.3. Other terms

Characterization. For an index formula, a set of axioms and tests that the formula uniquely satisfies.

Homotheticity. Assumption in economic models of optimization behavior that changes in income (aggregate expenditures) with prices held constant have no effect on consumption patterns. In a homothetic utility function, marginal rates of substitution between commodities are independent of the utility level, which equals a monotonic transformation of a function that is linear homogeneous in quantities.

Impossibility theorem. A result that some set of axioms and tests cannot be satisfied simultaneously. Also known as an inconsistency theorem.

Logarithmic mean. For two positive real numbers a and b, equals a if $a = b$, or $(b - a)/(\log b - \log a)$ if $a \neq b$. It is in between the arithmetic mean and the geometric mean, with the distance from the geometric mean approximately half the distance from the arithmetic mean.

Log-change. For the ith price between period 0 and period t, equals $\log p_{it} - \log p_{i0}$.

Standard of living index. The quantity index counterpart of the cost of living index that tracks the change in the money metric utility function. Also known as the Allen index.

References

Afriat, S.N. (1967). The construction of utility functions from expenditure data. *International Economic Review* **8**, 67–77.

Allen, R.G.D. (1935). Some observations on the theory and practice of price index numbers. *Review of Economic Studies* **3**, 57–66.

Allen, R.G.D. (1949). The economic theory of index numbers. *Economica* **16**, 197–203.

Armstrong, K. (2003). A restricted-domain multilateral test approach to the theory of international comparisons. *International Economic Review* **44**, 31–86.

Balk, B.M. (1995). Axiomatic price index theory: A survey. *International Statistical Review* **63**, 69–93.

Balk, B.M. (1996). Consistency-in-aggregation and Stuvel Indices. *Review of Income and Wealth* **42**, 353–364.

Balk, B.M. (2003). Aggregation methods in international comparisons, ERIM Report Series Reference No. ERS-2001-41-MKT. http://ssrn.com/abstract=826866.

Balk, B.M. (2005). Divisia price and quantity indices: 80 years after. *Statistica Neerlandica* **59**, 119–158.

Banerjee, K.S. (1959). A generalisation of Stuvel's index number formulae. *Econometrica* **27**, 676–678.

Blackorby, C., Primont, D. (1990). Index numbers and consistency in aggregation. *Journal of Economic Theory* **22**, 87–98.

Blow, L., Crawford, I. (2001). The cost of living with the RPI: Substitution bias in the UK retail prices index. *Economic Journal* **111**, F357–F382.

Boumans, M. (2001). Fisher's instrumental approach to index numbers, In: Klein, J.L., Morgan, M.S. (Eds.), *The Age of Economic Measurement*, Duke Univ. Press, Durham, pp. 313–344.

Bowley, A.L. (1928). Notes on index numbers. *Economic Journal* **38**, 216–237.

Deaton, A. (1998). Getting prices right: What should be done? *Journal of Economic Perspectives* **12**, 37–46.

Diewert, W.E. (1973). Afriat and revealed preference theory. *Review of Economic Studies* **40**, 419–426.

Diewert, W.E. (1976). Exact and superlative index numbers. *Journal of Econometrics* **4**, 115–145. Reprinted in: Diewert, W.E., Nakamura, A.O. (Eds.), *Essays in Index Number Theory, vol. 1*. Elsevier Science Publishers, Amsterdam, 1993, pp. 223–252.

Diewert, W.E. (1978). Superlative index numbers and consistency in aggregation. *Econometrica* **46**, 883–900. Reprinted in: Diewert, W.E., Nakamura, A.O. (Eds.), *Essays in Index Number Theory, vol. 1*. Elsevier Science Publishers, Amsterdam, 1993, pp. 253–275.

Diewert, W.E. (1981). The economic theory of index numbers: A survey. In: Deaton, A. (Ed.), *Essays in the Theory and Measurement of Consumer Behavior in Honour of Sir Richard Stone*, Cambridge Univ. Press, London, 163–208. Reprinted in: Diewert, W.E., Nakamura, A.O. (Eds.), *Essays in Index Number Theory, vol. 1*. Elsevier Science Publishers, Amsterdam, 1993, pp. 177–222.

Diewert, W.E. (1984). Group cost of living index: Approximations and axiomatics. *Methods of Operations Research* **48**, 23–45.

Diewert, W.E. (1992). Fisher ideal output, input, and productivity indexes revisited. *Journal of Productivity Analysis* **3**, 211–248.

Diewert, W.E. (1993). The early history of price index research. In: Diewert, W.E., Nakamura, A.O. (Eds.), *Essays in Index Number Theory, vol. 1*, Elsevier Science Publishers, Amsterdam, pp. 33–66.

Diewert, W.E. (1999). Axiomatic and economic approaches to international comparisons. In: Heston, A., Lipseys, R.E. (Eds.), *International and Inter-Area Comparisons of Income, Output and Prices*, pp. 13–87.

Diewert, W.E. (2005). Index number theory using differences rather than ratios. *American Journal of Economics and Sociology* **64**:1, 311–360.

Dowrick, S., Quiggin, J. (1994). International comparisons of living standards and tastes: A revealed preference analysis. *American Economic Review* **84**, 332–341.

Dowrick, S., Quiggin, J. (1997). True measures of GDP and convergence. *American Economic Review* **87**, 41–64.

Ehemann, C. (2005). Chain drift in leading superlative indexes. Working paper WP2005-09 BEA. Available at http://www.bea.gov/bea/working_papers.htm.

Eichhorn, W. (1976). Fisher's tests revisited. *Econometrica* **44**, 247–256.

Eichhorn, W., Voeller, J. (1983). The axiomatic foundation of price indexes and purchasing power parities. In: Diewert, E., Montmarquette, C. (Eds.), *Price Level Measurement*. Ministry of Supply and Services, Ottawa.

Eltetö, Ö. Köves, P. (1964). On the problem of index number computation relating to international comparisons. *Statisztikai Szemle* **42**, 507–518 (in Hungarian).

Ferger, W.F. (1946). Historical note on the purchasing power concept and index numbers. *Journal of the American Statistical Association* **41**, 53–57.

Fisher, I. (1911). *The Purchasing Power of Money*. MacMillan, New York.

Fisher, I. (1921). The best form of index number. *Quarterly Publications of the American Statistical Association* **17**, 533–537.

Fisher, I. (1922; 3rd ed. 1927). *The Making of Index Numbers: A Study of Their Varieties, Tests, and Reliability*. Houghton Mifflin Co., Boston.

Fisher, W.C. (1913). The tabular standard in Massachusetts history. *Quarterly Journal of Economics* **27**, 417–452.

Frisch, R. (1930). Necessary and sufficient conditions regarding the form of an index number which shall meet certain of Fisher's Tests. *Journal of the American Statistical Association* **25**, 397–406.

Frisch, R. (1936). Annual survey of general economic theory: The problem of index numbers. *Econometrica* **4**, 1–38.

Funke, H., Voeller, J. (1978). A note on the characterization of Fisher's ideal index. In: Eichhorn, W., Henn, R., Opitz, O., Shephard, R.W. (Eds.), *Theory and Applications of Economic Indices*. Physica-Verlag, Würzburg, pp. 177–181.

Funke, H., Hacker, G., Voeller, J. (1979). Fisher's circular test reconsidered. *Schweizerische Zeitschrift für Volkswirtschaft und Statistik* **115**, 677–687.

Gini, C. (1924). Quelques considérations au sujet de la construction des nombres indices des prix et des questions analogues. *Metron* **2**.

Gini, C. (1931) On the circular test of index numbers. *Metron* **9**, 3–24.

Geary, R.C. (1958). A note on the comparison of exchange rates and purchasing power between countries. *Journal of the Royal Statistical Society* **121**, 97–99.

Haberler, G. (1927). *Der Sinn der Indexzahlen*. Mohr, Tübingen.

Hill, R.J. (2006). Superlative index numbers: Not all of them are super. *Journal of Econometrics* **130**, 25–43.

Hulten, C.R. (1973). Divisia index numbers. *Econometrica* **41**, 1017–1025.

Hurwicz, L., Richter, M. (1979). Ville axioms and consumer theory. *Econometrica* **47**, 603–620.

International Labor Organization (2004). *Consumer Price Index Manual: Theory and Practice*. ILO Publications, Geneva.

Keynes, J.M. (1930). *A Treatise on Money*. MacMillan, London.

Khamis, S.H. (1972). A new system of index numbers for national and international purposes. *Journal of the Royal Statistical Society* **135**, 96–121.

Konus, A.A. (1939). The problem of the true index of the cost of living. *Econometrica* **7**, 10–29.

Krtscha, M. (1984). *A Characterization of the Edgeworth–Marshall Index*. Athenaüm/Hain/Hanstein, Königstein.

Krtscha, M. (1988). Axiomatic characterization of statistical price indices. In: Eichhorn, W. (Ed.), *Measurement in Economics*. Physical-Verlag, Heidelberg.

Lerner, A.P. (1935). A note on the theory of price index numbers. *Review of Economic Studies* **3**, 50–56.

Manser, M., McDonald, R. (1988). An analysis of substitution bias in measuring inflation. *Econometrica* **46**, 909–930.

Montgomery, J.K. (1937). *The Mathematical Problem of the Price Index*. Orchard House, P.S. King & Son, Westminster.

National Research Council (2002). At what price? Conceptualizing and measuring cost-of-living and price indexes. In: Schultze, C.L., Mackie, C. (Eds.), *Panel on Conceptual Measurement, and Other Statistical Issues in Developing Cost-of-Living Indexes*. Committee on National Statistics, Division of Behavioral and Social Sciences and Education, National Academy Press, Washington, DC.

Pierson, N.G. (1896). Further considerations on index numbers. *Economic Journal* **6**, 127–131.

Pigou, A.C. (1912). *Wealth and Welfare*. Macmillan, London.

Pigou, A.C. (1920). *The Economics of Welfare*. 4th ed., Macmillan, London.

Pollak, R. (1981). The social cost-of-living index. *Journal of Public Economics* **15**, 311–336.

Reinsdorf, M.B. (1998). Formula bias and within-stratum substitution bias in the US CPI. *Review of Economics and Statistics* **80**, 175–187.

Reinsdorf, M., Dorfman, A. (1999). The monotonicity axiom and the Sato–Vartia Index. *Journal of Econometrics* **90**, 45–61.

Reinsdorf, M.B., Diewert, W.E., Ehemann, C. (2002). Additive decompositions for Fisher, Törnqvist and geometric mean indexes. *Journal of Economic and Social Measurement* **28**, 51–61.

Rothbarth, E. (1941). The measurement of changes in real income under conditions of rationing. *Review of Economic Studies* **8**, 100–107.

Samuelson, P.A., Swamy, S. (1974). Invariant economic index numbers and canonical duality: Survey and synthesis. *American Economic Review* **64**, 566–593.

Sato, K. (1976). The ideal log-change index number. *Review of Economics and Statistics* **58**, 223–228.

Staehle, H. (1935). A development of the economic theory of price index numbers. *Review of Economic Studies* **2**, 163–188.

Stuvel, G. (1957). A new index number formula. *Econometrica* **25**, 123–131.

Swamy, S. (1965). Consistency of Fisher's tests. *Econometrica* **33**, 619–623.

Szulc, B. (1964). Indices for multiregional comparisons. *Przeglad Statystyczny* **3**, 239–254.

Törnqvist, L. (1936). The bank of Finland's consumption price index. *Bank of Finland Monthly Bulletin* **10**, 1–8.

Triplett, Jack E. (2001). Should the cost-of-living index provide the conceptual framework for a Consumer Price Index? *Economic Journal* **111**, F311–F334.

Trivedi, P.K. (1981). Some discrete approximations to Divisia integral indices. *International Economic Review* **22**, 71–77.

van IJzeren. J. [van Yzeren] (1952). Over de plausibiliteit Van Fisher's ideale indices (On the plausibility of Fisher's ideal indices). *Statistiche en Econometrische Onderzoekingen (C.B.S.)* **7**, 104–115.

van IJzeren, J. [van Yzeren] (1958). A note on the useful properties of Stuvel's index numbers. *Econometrica* **26**, 429–439.

Varian, H.R. (1982). The non-parametric approach to demand analysis. *Econometrica* **50**, 945–974.

Varian, H.R. (1984). The non-parametric approach to production analysis. *Econometrica* **52**, 579–597.

Vartia, Y.O. (1976). Ideal log-change index numbers. *Scandinavian Journal of Statistics* **3**, 121–126.

Vartia, Y.O., Weymark, J.A. (1981). Four revealed preference tables. *Scandinavian Journal of Economics* **83**, 408–418.

Ville, J. (1951–1952). The existence-conditions of a total utility function. *Review of Economic Studies* **19**, 123–128.

Vogt, A. (1981). Characterizations of indexes, especially of the Stuvel index and the Banerjee index. *Statistische Hefte* **22**, 241–245.

Walsh, C.M. (1901). *The Measurement of General Exchange Value*. Macmillan and Co., New York.

Walsh, C.M. (1921). The best form of index number: Discussion. *Quarterly Publications of the American Statistical Association* **17**, 537–544.

CHAPTER 8

National Accounts and Indicators

Frank A.G. den Butter

Vrije Universiteit, Department of Economics, De Boelelaan 1105, NL-1081 HV Amsterdam, The Netherlands
E-mail address: fbutter@feweb.vu.nl

Abstract

National accounts generate a variety of indicators used in economics for determining the value of goods and services. This chapter highlights two problems in the measurement of such indicators, namely the construction of the data at the macro level using individual observations from different sources, and the interpretation of the data when economic relationship are empirically investigated using these data at the macro level. The chapter pays ample attention to the institutional set-up of national accounting, and to the use of indicators derived from the national accounts in policy analysis in various industrialised countries. Major difficulties in interpretation arise when the indicators are used in the assessment of (social) welfare and in separating developments in prices and volumes.

8.1. Introduction

National accounts provide a quantitative description of the state of the economy at the macro level. Indicators derived from national accounts are widely used in economic policy analysis. Examples are national income, price and wage deflators as measures of inflation, purchasing power, total employment, imports, exports, current account of the balance of payments, government receipts and expenditure, government deficit, total consumption, investments, stock building, etc.. In almost all countries data of the national accounts are compiled by the National Statistical Offices (NSOs) following uniform international guidelines.

National accounts' data are based on individual observations of persons, households, firms and government bodies. Most of these observations stem from administrative records and are supplemented by evidence from surveys and field observations. The major conceptual problem of the construction and use of these data is that observations at the micro level are to be combined and aggregated to the macro level in order to comply with concepts from economic theory used in policy analysis. It implies that there will always be a discrepancy between interpretations and semantics of concepts at the macro level, and the way they are

Measurement in Economics: A Handbook
Marcel Boumans (Editor)

given empirical content by the statistics from the national accounts. National income may have different meanings and connotations in various macro economic analyses. However, when national accounts' data are used in these analyses to represent the concept of national income empirically, it is the definition of national income according to the rules of national accounting which determines how this concept is made operational. To give another example: many inhabitants of the European Union had the impression that after the introduction of the Euro life had become much more expensive. Yet, according to the price deflators computed by the NSOs, following the standard aggregation methods, "in reality" only a slight increase of inflation could be observed. Obviously there was a discrepancy between the men and women in the streets' view on inflation, and the way this concept is made operational in statistical accounting.

This chapter focuses on the conceptual problem of the construction and use of indicators from the national accounts in policy analysis. As the author is especially familiar with the situation in the Netherlands, most examples and historical anecdotes stem from that country. The contents of the article is as follows. The next section describes the characteristics and methodology of the national accounts. Section 8.3 surveys the history of national accounting and Section 8.4 discusses the interaction between the collection and use of data at the macro level in the last two centuries in the Netherlands. Section 8.5 considers the role of statistics and economic policy analysis in the institutional set-up of the polder model in the Netherlands. Section 8.6 discusses the history of national accounting and the institutional set-up of policy preparation in some other industrialised countries. Sections 8.3–8.6 provide insight into the confrontation between scientific knowledge and practical policy needs, which has been crucial in the development of the national accounts. Section 8.7 examines the present situation, issues for discussion and prospects for national accounting. The relationship between construction and use of various main economic indicators from the national accounts is discussed in Section 8.8. This section also gives examples where the conceptual problem of measurement and use has been subject of fierce debate, such as the use of NA statistics as welfare indicators and the correction of national income for environmental degradation. Finally Section 8.9 concludes.

8.2. National Accounts as Indicators of the State of the Economy

The national accounts (NA) or the national bookkeeping of an economy provide a quantitative description of the economic process at the level of the state during a certain period. Particularly those aspects of the economic activities are described which are directly or indirectly related to the formation, distribution, spending and financing of the domestic product or national income. Moreover the national accounts provide insight in the economic relations with foreign countries.

More specifically three different approaches are used in national accounting in order to describe economic developments at the level of the state. The first one is the *expenditure approach,* which determines aggregate demand, or gross national expenditure, by summing consumption, investments, government expenditure and net exports. The second way of measurement is the *output (or production) approach*. Here total production of a nation is calculated by summing added value in production in all sectors of the economy and net income from abroad. The third method of measurement is the *income (distribution) approach*. This method illustrates how national income has been earned and has been distributed amongst the income factors (wages, rents, profits). All three methods use different sources for the compilation of data, but, in the end, must yield the same outcomes for national income and expenditure data. Total expenditures on goods and services must by definition be equal to the value of goods and services produced, which must be equal to the total income paid to the factors that produce these goods and services. In fact there will be minor differences in the results obtained from the three different methods. A source of these differences are inventories that have been produced but not sold. But also the use of various sources for compilation of the data may be a reason that the definition equations, which are balancing identities in the double (or even triple) bookkeeping of the national accounts, do not hold. A solution is to have one of the items as the residual item to be determined by the definition equation (e.g. stock building in the production approach, and profits in the income approach). However, most NSOs use much more sophisticated methods to distribute discrepancies between the various approaches so that the balancing definitions hold and the system is made consistent.

In this confrontation of income and expenditures, national accounts' data generate a number of important economic indicators, such as the domestic product and national income. The domestic product is the sum of all goods and services produced in the country. More specifically it is the difference between the output value of the production and the input value of goods and services used in production. This is the added value of production in the country. National income, in its turn, indicates how much all residents of a country earned in a specific period. These loose definitions of both indicators only give a first impression of the core indicators from the system of national accounts. For more formal definitions of the various ways income and production are measured at the macro level we refer to the official guidelines for the construction of the national accounts, and to the publications of the various NSOs which specify how these guidelines are implemented in the specific case of the country concerned

National accounting does not aim at explaining the past, nor at forecasting future developments. It is solely directed at the *recording of the economic activity in the past*. This knowledge of the macroeconomic data from the past is indispensable for the construction and testing of economic theories, and for the building of empirical models, such as the macroeconomic models, which are nowadays used all over the world in order to examine economic developments and to calculate effects of measures of economic policy. This knowledge is also essential for formulating concrete policy goals, for example with respect to the development of the purchasing power or with respect to the extent that the collective sector makes use of national resources. National accounts data also give an answer to the question to what extent the policy goals have been realised. This illustration of the scope and use of the national accounts is indicative for what must be included in the description of the economic process. On the one hand the selection of data is motivated by the needs from economic theory, and on the other side by the demands from policy analysis. With respect to the latter, demands do not only stem from the government. Trade unions and employer associations base their policy likewise on data from the national accounts. An example is the development of prices and labour productivity, which play a major role in the wage negotiations.

The system of the national accounts can be characterised as a coherent and integrated data set at the macro level. The consistency of the data in the accounting scheme is guaranteed by using definition equations and identities, which relate the underlying observations from various statistical sources to each other. This quality of the system is crucial for its use in economic analysis and policy: its structure of interdependent definitions enables a uniform analysis and comparison of various economic phenomena. However, it also makes the system rather rigid. It is impossible to change individual concepts and/or definitions in the system. For instance, inclusion of a new component to domestic production is only possibly if at the same time the concepts of income, consumption, savings and investments are adapted.

The consistency of the system of national accounts is of great importance for the way the data are used in practice. A number of possibilities has already been mentioned. The domestic product and national income are frequently used as an overall indicator for the functioning of the national economy. The success of the economic policy and the financial power of a nation are based on these indicators. In this line of reasoning the extent to which a country should provide development aid is expressed as a percentage of national income. National income is also the benchmark for payments of the various member states to the European Union. A higher national income means more payments. Therefore, it is extremely important that the calculation of national income is based as much as possible on objective criteria and is calculated according to international guidelines. It should not become subject of dispute between countries, and of political manipulation.

The same applies when the national income is taken as a basis for various economic indicators to guide and judge government policy. See for instance the debt and budget deficit of the government, which are, according to the Maastricht criteria and the limits set in the Stability and Growth Pact (SGP) of the EU, expressed as a percentage of national income. Moreover the relative importance of a specific economic sector, e.g. agriculture, industry or retail trade, can be illustrated by calculating its relative share in domestic production. However, the fact that national account data should be undisputed when used in policy practice, does not exclude that there can be much dispute between experts on proper definitions. By way of example Mellens (2006) discusses the various definitions of savings.

8.2.1. Methodology

National accounts are set-up for a number of possible uses. The consequence of such diversity is that the definition of the various concepts in the national accounts (e.g. of income) is not always completely in accordance with the intention and wishes of the users. An important choice in this respect is that between providing a description from the angle of the economic actors versus reproducing as correctly as possible economic processes. The first is called the *institutional approach* and the second the *functional approach*.

In the institutional approach the producers are the focus of the description of the production process. Their value added in production is classified on the basis of their main activities in sectors of the economy. Producers who perform mainly transport activities, therefore will be classified in the transport sector. This provides good information on total production value of producers in a specific branch of industry or services. However, it also implies that other activities of the producers in the transport sector, for instance some trading activities, are not counted as such in the national accounts. When the analysis focuses on the characteristics of the production activities themselves, such institutional approach is not very adequate and a functional approach is warranted.

The question of how to define a concept plays an important role in the national accounts and in the interpretation of the data from these accounts. Examples are construction and decorating activities of house owners and their families, and unpaid domestic work. Should these be included in the domestic product? One can think of pros and cons. The argument for inclusion is that they are productive services that would be included in the domestic product if they would be performed on payment by third parties. The counter argument is that inclusion would imply large changes in the domestic production, which would limit the use of this indicator in analysing the developments of the market economy. In fact, taxable income is used here as criterion (see Bos, 2003, pp. 145–147). The problem of definition is, of course, very much connected to the desire for international comparability. An individual country or a statistical office does not decide about the definition of, for instance, income autonomously, but has to follow the definition laid down in the international directives. Of course there are always border cases and grey areas in these definitions. A typical example in the Netherlands is the (home) production from small rented gardens at distance from the homes (so called "volkstuintjes"). It is now included in the production statistics because the official directives suggest it should, but only after a foreign expert asked questions about the production of these gardens when he had seen them when travelling to the CBS (Netherlands Central Bureau of Statistics). However, most of such cases relate to small amounts which will not influence interpretation of the data.

8.2.2. National accounts and the theory of measurement

A major question of this chapter is how national accounts' data can be used in measurement of economic phenomena and relationships. From a theoretical perspective this question relates to the way the construction and compilation of data of the national accounts are related to the theory of measurement. According to Boumans (2007, this volume) today's measurement theory is the Representational Theory of Measurement. It is described as taking "measurement as a process of assigning numbers to attributes of the empirical world in such a way that the relevant qualitative empirical relations among these attributes are reflected in the numbers themselves as well in important properties of the number system". Boumans distinguishes two different foundational approaches in economics in the theory of measurement: the axiomatic and the empirical approach.

When considering measurement and national accounts the empirical approach is most relevant. For the use of these data in policy analysis modelling economic relationships based on economic theory plays a major role. That is why this chapter pays ample attention to the interaction between the provision of data at the macro level, the empirical analysis of economic relationships using these data and the policy analysis based on these relationships, or "models" of the economy. Loosely speaking, measurement theory is, in this respect, concerned with determining the parameter values of these models using the data constructed by the methodology of the national accounts. Modern econometric methodology, time series analysis in particular, teaches us how to establish this empirical link between data and characteristics of the model (see e.g. Chao, this volume). However, a number of methodological issues remains unsolved which nowadays have considerably reduced the role of econometric methodology in macroeconomic model building (see e.g. Don and Verbruggen, 2006). Three issues can be mentioned. A first issue is that consistency of the models with theoretical requirements and with long run stylised facts is often at variance with parameter estimates which are a mere result of applying econometric methods to one specific data set. A second issue is that econometric methodology requires specific conditions of the specification of a model, e.g. linearity, which are too binding for a proper use of the model. Thirdly, the relationship between the theoretical concept warranted in the model may be much at variance with the practical construction method according to which the data in the empirical analysis are obtained. This latter issue is most relevant for this chapter.

8.3. History of National Accounts

Important historical events such as wars, economic crises and revolutions have always called the need for good quantitative data on the economy at the macro level, and have therefore contributed considerably to the development of national accounting. A look into the early history teaches us that a need for such data for policy analysis formed the reason for the first estimates of national income. They were made respectively by Sir William Petty and Gregory King in 1665 and 1696 for United Kingdom (see Kendrick, 1970; Bos, 1992, 2003). Petty tried to show that the state could raise a much larger amount of taxes to finance the war expenditure than it actually did, and that the way of collecting taxes could be much improved. Moreover, Petty wanted to show that the United Kingdom was not ruined by its revolutions and by the wars with the foreign enemies, and that it could compare itself with the Netherlands and France with respect to the amount of trade and military potential.

The estimates by King can be regarded as an improvement to those of Petty. In his calculation method, King used a broad concept of income and production, similar to what it is today according to the guidelines of the United Nations. Production comprises the added value of both the production of goods and of services. This concept is in strong contrast with that of the physiocrats, who reasoned that only agriculture produces value added and that all remaining production is 'sterile'. Yet already Adam Smith argued that not only agriculture but also occupations in the trade and the industry produce added value. However, according to Smith, services, both by the government and by private businesses, do not generate additional value. In that sense the income concept of King was even broader and more modern than that of Smith. Beside the use of a 'modern' concept of income, a second important characteristic of the estimates of King is that he calculated national income already in three different ways, as it is done today, namely from the perspective of (i) production, (ii) income distribution and (iii) expenditure. Moreover, the calculations by King showed remarkably much detail. He did not restrict himself to the outcomes for total annual national income and the total annual expenditure and savings, but made a split up of these data with respect to social groups, to the various professions, and to different income groups. He also made an estimate of the national wealth (gold, silver, jewels, houses, livestock, etc.). King compared national income and national wealth of United Kingdom with those of the Netherlands and France. It is interesting to note that this aspect of international comparability – an important aim of the international guidelines – already played a role in the first estimates of national income ever. King constructed time series for national income for the period 1688–1695. Using these time series he calculated income forecasts for the years 1696, 1697 and 1698.

At about the same time in France estimates of national income were made by Boisguillebert and Vauban. It is unclear to what extent these estimates were influenced by the way national income was originally calculated in United Kingdom. However, the estimates of the English national income by Petty and King can be regarded unique as far as the quality and the scope of these estimates were hardly matched in the following two centuries. After the pioneering work of King the number of countries for which national bookkeeping's were established, gradually increased. Around 1900, estimates were available for eight countries: United Kingdom, France, the United States, Russia, Austria, Germany, Australia and Norway. Compiling national accounts was not yet always considered as a task for the government. In this respect Australia was an early bird: here the government already started in 1886.

8.3.1. The Netherlands

International historic reports do not include the Netherlands in the above list of eight countries. Nevertheless the first estimates of national income in the Netherlands were already made much earlier (see Den Bakker, 1993). In fact the history of the national bookkeeping in the Netherlands starts at the beginning of the 19th century, with the calculations of national income by Hora Siccama and Van Rees in 1798, by Keuchenius in 1803, and by Metelerkamp in 1804. And again war was the reason for making these calculations. The major goal of these calculations was that they enabled a comparison of the wealth in the Netherlands with that of the neighbouring countries from the economic and military perspective. The calculations by Hora Siccama and Van Rees were part of a plan at the request of the national assembly of the new Batavian republic for revision of the tax system. The reason was to see how taxes could be levied efficiently, in proportion to personal wealth (see Bos, 2006). Keuchenius, a member of the city council of Schiedam, constructed a hypothetical estimate of national income which was based on the situation as if war in Europe would have ended and peace would have been established. Keuchenius estimated national income of the Netherlands to be about 221 million guilders, it is 117 guilders per head of the population. The share of agriculture and fishery in this income amounted to 45%, whereas 27% was transfer income from abroad (think of the rich import from the colonies). Metelerkamp, who knew the work of Keuchenius, introduced some improvements, and arrived at an estimate of national income for the Netherlands in 1792 of 250 million guilders, that is 125 guilders per head of the population.

The first systematic estimates of national income in the Netherlands were made by Bonger. The first year for which data were calculated, was 1908. It was published in 1910. The first official calculations of national income by the Netherlands Central Bureau of Statistics (CBS) were published in 1933 and refer to the year 1929. Finally it was Van Cleeff who constructed a coherent system of national accounts for the Netherlands in a two article publication in the Dutch periodical 'De Economist' in 1941. Subsequently, on 19 January 1943 a commission for national accounting was installed at CBS. Today the installation of this commission is considered the official beginning of the Netherlands' national accounting (see Bos, 2006, for an extensive review of the history of national accounting in the Netherlands).

8.3.2. Modern systems of NA

The 1930s and 1940s provided inspiration for the modern system of national accounts. Three aspects played an important role. In the first place the discussion on what concepts of income to use at the macro level revived. Secondly developments in economic theory underlined the importance of national accounting. Thirdly the first coherent and approved systems of national accounts were developed. The two most important protagonists in the discussions on the problems of the definition of national income (what should, and should not be included in income data) in the inter-bellum were Clark and Kuznets. Clark argued that services from house ownership were to be included in income, but services of durable consumer goods were not to be included. Clark already suggested to subtract every verifiable exhaustion of natural resources from income. Moreover he considered problems of purchasing power and international and intertemporal comparability of the national income data. This discussion of comparability continues today and has, for instance, resulted in the large PENN World Table-project of data collection and construction, where national income data are made comparable by using a constructed international price. More specifically, for each country the costs of a differentiated basket of goods are calculated and the national income data are corrected by means of the observed cost differences (see Summers and Heston, 1991).

Much more than Clark, Kuznets was also a prominent theoretician. He published on the link between changes in national income and welfare, on the valuation of production by the government and on the difference between intermediate and final production. Moreover he contributed a number of technicalities in data processing (interpolation, extrapolation). In 1936, Leontief made a next major step in the statistical description of an economy by presenting input/output tables. Although the basic idea of the input/output table is already present in Quesnay's 'tableau économique' and in the way Walras described the working of the economy, Leontief's main innovation was the formulation of the model that directly connects the outputs with the inputs in an operational manner. In this way it portrays the complete production structure of a country and it enables to calculate which changes in inputs are needed in order to bring about a warranted change of the outputs. It should be noticed that there does not need to exist a direct link between the input/output tables and the national accounts. As a matter of fact in a large number of countries input/output tables are calculated only on an incidental basis, and outside the framework of the annual calculation of the national accounts. The Netherlands is an exception. Already for a long time in this country input/output tables are published annually together with the tables of the national accounts. In this case the input/output tables do not only form a separate source of information, but are also exploited as the main statistical tool to calculate the data from the production accounts.

8.3.3. Importance of macroeconomic model building

In the 1930s, the start of macro economic model building and the consequent development of new econometric techniques were important innovations that increased the need for statistical data collection at the macro level, and hence for national accounting. In 1936, Tinbergen constructed the first macro model for the Dutch economy. In order to make the model describe the actual working of the economy empirically, the behaviour parameters of the model were estimated using time series data on all endogenous and exogenous variables of the model. For that reason other and longer time series at the macro level were needed than originally available. Moreover, the quality of the existing data had to be improved. Although Tinbergen realised the need of a good and comprehensive system of national accounts, he himself has not been involved directly in the drawing up of such a social accounting system. However, the CBS started already in 1937 at the request of Tinbergen a project that aimed at improved estimates of the national income. Its focus was a better statistical foundation of cyclical analysis. At the CBS it was Derksen who managed this project that contributed much to improve the calculation methodology of income data. Nowadays the demands of the builders and users of macro economic models still play a major role in the set-up and development of national accounting.

8.3.4. Keynes and the national accounts

Undoubtedly the most important support for further elaboration of the national bookkeeping was the publication of Keynes' "General Theory" in 1936. It marks the beginning of macro economic analysis. This Keynesian analysis directly connects economic theory with national accounting: both use the same set of identities. The consequence of the theory of Keynes was that a shift occurred in the main concept of income used in policy analysis: net national income in factor costs was more and more replaced by gross national income in market prices. The reason was to provide a better insight into the link between the different expenditure categories and income. The Keynesian revolution also prompted the governments to an active countercyclical policy. This created a need for a system of national accounts where the government sector was added to the sector accounts. All in all, thanks to the Keynesians revolution it was widely recognised how important national accounting for preparation and conduct of economic policy is. Keynes himself actively stimulated the advancement of national accounting schemes, particularly in the United Kingdom. At his initiative the most important experts of the national accounting in the United Kingdom, Stone and Meade, made estimates of national income and expenditures in 1941. These data were used to assess the receipts and expenditures of the government into a scheme of balances for the whole economy. And again it was a war which contributed to a prompt implementation of this work. According to Stone the major aim of this exercise was to map the problem of financing the war expenditures. These data were indeed used in the discussions on the government budget during war time.

8.3.5. International comparability

This marks also the beginning of the era in which national accounting was conducted on the basis of international guidelines in order to promote international comparability. For that reason, the League or Nations (the pre-war predecessor of the United Nations) had already asked for such guidelines in 1939. However, the activities were postponed because of the war. At last, in 1947, the first guidelines were published by the United Nations in a report which consisted mainly of an appendix, drafted by Stone. This appendix can be regarded as the first fully fledged and detailed description of a system of national accounts. The next step were the guidelines that Stone published in 1951 at the request of the Organisation of European Economic Co-operation (OEEC, the predecessor of the OECD). These guidelines were a simplification as compared to those of the United Nations: in fact the guidelines of the United Nations were much too ambitious for most European countries. After a number of following rounds with new guidelines the United Nations published in 1968 a fully revised and very detailed set of guidelines for the construction of national accounts (SNA). Together with the guidelines of the EC from 1970, which were mainly meant to clarify the guidelines of the United Nations, these guidelines have, for a long period, been the basis for the set-up of the systems of national accounts in the world. As a matter of fact, in order to guarantee the continuity in national accounting, modification of the guidelines should not take place too frequently. It was only in 1993 that the United Nations issued new guidelines.

8.4. History of Statistics and Economic Analysis in the Netherlands

The previous survey of the history of national accounts illustrates the long road from the early calculations of total income and wealth of a nation to today's extended and sophisticated systems of national accounts. In order to obtain a better view on how indicators from the national accounts are used in economic policy analysis, a look into the history of the interaction between data collection and policy analysis is also useful. Here the history in the Netherlands is taken as an example. A historical overview for other countries, especially the United Kingdom, Norway and the United States, is given by Kenessey (1993).

Today empirical analysis and measurement play an essential role in the debate on policy measures in the Netherlands. This interest in actual measurement only slowly and partially emerged between 1750 and 1850 (see Klep and Stamhuis, 2002; Den Butter, 2004). Yet, it were mainly private initiatives of individual scientists and practitioners, and not so much of the government, which brought about this attitude. The estimates by the forerunners Hora Siccama, Van Rees, Keuchenius and Metelerkamp were already mentioned in the previous section.

8.4.1. Kluit and Vissering

An early protagonist of actual measurement in the Netherlands was Adriaan Kluit (1735–1807). He was the first Dutch professor to teach statistics under that name. One of the reasons that Kluit started to deliver lectures in statistics was a prize contest by the "de Hollandsche Maatschappij der Wetenschappen" (Dutch Society of Sciences) at Haarlem, which is a learned society founded in 1752 and still existing, and which, in those days, tried to promote scientific research by posing practical questions. The question to which Kluit reacted was 'What is the overall situation, both in general and especially with respect to the economy in our fatherland, and what are the reasons why our country lacks so far behind, compared to our neighbours?' So it was in fact a quest for economic data which inspired Kluit to get involved in statistics. Kluit did not distinguish between political economy and statistics, and in his specification the state was the centre of attention. So in his work we are at the beginning of the connection between the working of political economy (in Dutch: "staatkunde" or "staathuishoudkunde") and statistics. In this respect it is noteworthy that in Germany political economy or economic political science was called *Statistica* or *Statistik*. This connection can also be traced back to the Italian word 'Statista' or 'Statesman', which has given the discipline of statistics its name.

Although he was a lawyer by education, Simon Vissering (1818–1888) can be regarded as one of the main advocates of statistical quantification of the state of the economy at the macro level in the Netherlands. He was one of the leaders of the "Statistical Movement", a group of lawyers who dedicated themselves to the development of statistics. Although Vissering was more quantitatively oriented than his predecessors in political economy, his ideas about which data are needed for the description of the national economy, are still rather naïve as compared to the data which are nowadays used to analyse the economy. In the course of the 19th century quantification came to play a more important role, but it was still Vissering's opinion that qualitative information was needed to make the statistical description of a state complete (see Klep and Stamhuis, 2002).

8.4.2. Descriptive versus mathematical statistics

It is interesting to note that in the development of measuring the state of the economy (and society) in the 19th century no much reference seems to be made to the work of early "quantitative" economists such as Petty and King in the UK, or Keuchenius and Metelerkamp in the Netherlands, as discussed in the previous section. Moreover, there was still a large gap between descriptive and mathematical statistics. In the latter discipline the Belgian statistician Lambert Adolphe Jaques Quetelet (1796–1874) was a forerunner. In 1834 Quetelet was one of the founders of the London Statistical Society, nowadays the Royal Statistical Society. Morgan (1990) describes how, in the history of statistics, Quetelet's statistical characterisation of human behaviour proved to be of great importance. He noted that individuals behave in an unpredictable way, but that taken together these apparently disorganised individuals obey the law of errors in deviating from the ideal "average man". Obviously this is one of the basic notions in econometric methodology, used in the evaluation of economic policy measures. So Quetelet can be seen as a first bridge-builder between the mathematically oriented statistical approach and the descriptive and qualitative-quantitative approach. However, Quetelet's ideas did not reach Vissering and his people. It was only after the 1930s that, with Tinbergen as the great inspirer and teacher, a full integration of both lines of thought in statistics took place in the Netherlands. It is remarkable that, whereas these two lines in statistics had been separated for such a long time, from then on the Netherlands obtained a strong position in econometrics and applied economics.

8.4.3. Statistics as a public good

Vissering and his people have played a major role in promoting that the government should regard statistical data collection as a public good and therefore should take its responsibility in collection these data. However, in the second half of the 19th century the government was very reluctant to take up this responsibility. Therefore, in 1866 Vissering took a private initiative to compose and publish general statistics for the Netherlands. However, this large project has never been finished (see Stamhuis, 1989, 2002). In 1884, when the Dutch government was still not willing to collect statistical data in the public domain, a Statistical Institute was established by these private people. At last, in 1892, after questions in the Second Chamber of the Parliament by, amongst others, the socialist member of parliament, F.J. Domela Nieuwenhuis, de "Centrale Commissie voor de Statistiek" (Central Committee for Statistics) was installed. Finally, in 1899 the Central Bureau of Statistics (CBS) was founded, which from then on conducts its task to collect independent and undisputed data for public use in the Netherlands. The Central Committee for Statistics still exists and has a role as supervisory board for the Central Bureau of Statistics. Its responsibilities were even expanded by decision of the Parliament in 2003. In fact, the lobby to have the government collect statistical data at the level of the state was much conducted by the "Society of Statistics", founded in 1849 (see Mooij, 1994). After 1892, now that the lobby of the society for data collection by the government had finally been successful, the main focus of the society became more and more on economics. Therefore, in 1892, its name was changed in Society for Political Economy and Statistics. Yet it was more than half a century later, namely in 1950, that the focus of the society was really reflected in its name which now became Netherlands Economic Association. Finally, in 1987 the Queen honoured the society by granting it the label "Royal". So since 1987 we have the Royal Netherlands Economic Association, which, given its start in 1849, is probably the oldest association of political economists in the world.

8.4.4. Micro versus macro data

As mentioned before, a major question in national accounting is on how to aggregate individual data to the macro level. In this respect Van den Bogaard (1999, Chapter 5) gives an interesting description of the long discussions between Tinbergen and the CBS on transforming individual data from budget surveys to national data on consumption which could be used in consumption functions of the Keynesian macro models of those days. In the 1930s consumption was still something related to individual incomes, classes of people and their social role in society. It was indeed only in the early 1950s that data collection and statistical methodology to analyse data at the macro level, were really integrated.

8.5. The Tinbergen Legacy and the Institutional Set-up of Policy Preparation in the Netherlands

This integration of data collection and statistical methodology is an important aspect of how indicators of the national accounts are used in economic policy analysis. For a more comprehensive answer to that question it is useful to look at the institutional set-up of economic policy preparation of a country. Again the Netherlands is taken as an example. The present institutional set-up of policy preparation in the Netherlands can, in a way, be seen as a spring-off of Tinbergen's theory of economic policy, where scientific insights on how instruments may affect policy goals are separated from political preferences on trade-off between these policy goals (see Tinbergen, 1952, 1956). These ideas were, of course, very much inspired by the political and societal landscape in the Netherlands in the period between the First and the Second World Wars (see also Van Zanden, 2002, for a broad historic perspective). In the years just after the Second World War, when Tinbergen designed his theory of economic policy and was active in the institutional set-up of policy preparation in the Netherlands, the Dutch society was still very much "pillarised". The four main pillars were the liberals, the Catholics, the Protestants and the socialists. Each of them were represented by one or more political parties with implicit preferences on policy goals in their own, so to say, social welfare function. As they all are minority parties, there has been always a need for the formation of a coalition government. The leaders of the political parties or pillars did realise that it is impossible to meet all of their own policy goals in such a coalition government. Although the pillarised society has changed very much since then and there has been a steady "depillarasation", still all parties are minority parties, even more so then before, so that the need for a compromise agreement for the coalition government has remained.

8.5.1. The CPB Netherlands Bureau for Economic Policy Analysis

The analysis of the Dutch Central Planning Bureau has from its start played an important role in the design of the policy preparation in the Netherlands.

Nowadays the bureau calls itself CPB Netherlands Bureau for Economic Policy Analysis, because there is no true "planning" involved in the activities of the bureau. More specifically the analysis is an important input for the negotiations and social dialogue on policy issues in what has become known as the Dutch "polder model". It has already be noted that Tinbergen, who became the CPB's first director in 1945, has built the first econometric policy model (Tinbergen, 1936). Therefore, it is understandable that model based policy analysis has, from the origin, constituted an important part of the work of the CPB. The CPB's 'model' early acquired a high status in academic circles and has come to be regarded in the Dutch society as an more or less "objective" piece of economic science (Den Butter and Morgan, 1998).

However, in the first few years of the CPB there was a fierce internal discussion in the CPB about the way the bureau should give shape to its advices (see Van den Bogaard, 1999). On the one side was Van Cleeff, who had the view that the CPB should follow a normative approach, while on the other side Tinbergen supported the idea of disentangling the positive and normative elements of the analyses. The crucial question in this controversy was about the way economic policy advice would be the most successful in the pillarised economy. Van Cleeff tried to develop an all-embracing normative theory which would integrate the ideas of the different pillars. Like in industry that would lead to a formal policy "plan" which could be implemented by the government in a coordinated effort of all citizens, On the other hand, Tinbergen wanted to develop a method that would give the most objective description of reality. The differences between the pillars would then be minimised to their different normative proportions. In other words, he wanted to make a clear distinction between the working of the economy (model) and the policy goals (welfare functions), and then "try to agree on the first and compromise on the second issue". Tinbergen won this battle. Since then, economic policy preparation in the Netherlands is organised in three autonomous parts: data, model and norms. As discussed in the previous section, the data and statistics are collected by the Central Bureau of Statistics (CBS) in an independent and (hopefully) undisputed manner, the working of the economy is described by the models of the CPB and the balancing of different points of view is done by the government in dialogue with unions, employer organisations and other associations of organised interest. This method of splitting facts and politics has, up to now, always been a prominent feature in creating consensus in the Dutch society where all belong to a cultural minority or minority party.

In this institutional set-up the CPB has a major role in describing the working of the economy. It takes the data, collected, and in the case of national accounts, constructed by the CBS, as given. The task of the CPB is to provide a quantitative analysis of the state of the Dutch economy, based on scientific knowledge. In doing so it tries to establish a *consensus view* on economic developments and the effects of policy measures. Of course others (other institutions) also have a say in this analysis of the Dutch economy based on scientific insights. An example is the Dutch central bank, that makes its own model based analysis of developments and policy measures in the Netherlands. Moreover, in some cases a major discussion emerges with academics and other scientists working outside the CPB (e.g. the Ministry of Economics Affairs, private research institutes) on matters of interpretation of economic developments. Examples are discussions on Keynesian demand policies versus neo-classical policies in the second half of the 1970s, on the need for general equilibrium modelling in the early 1990s, and on the effectiveness of a prolonged policy of wage moderation in the early 2000s. However, these disputes did not refer to the measurement of economic data at the macro level, nor to the construction methods of data.

Nowadays, the analyses of the CPB are widely used as input for social economic policy discussions, e.g. in the Social Economic Council (see below). A typical example of the role of the CPB in using their model based analysis for policy purposes is the calculation of the effects of the policy proposals in the election programmes of the political parties on economic growth, employment, income distribution and so on. Seemingly, it is almost a realisation of Tinbergen's dream to separate the knowledge on the working of the economy, which is contained in the models used by the CPB, and the normative preferences on trade-offs between policy goals, which will differ for each political party. In fact, the CPB has two major tasks. The first is that of national auditor: this implies economic forecasting and assessment of the effects of policy measures for the government and for other groups involved in the policy making process. The second task consists of the CPB conducting, in a more general sense, applied economic research (see Don, 1996). Nowadays the latter task gains importance: extensive scenario analyses and cost benefit analyses are conducted with respect to various aspects of the Dutch economy. There is also a shift towards microeconomic research and evaluation studies. Typical for the institutional set-up of Dutch policy-making are the numerous formal and informal contacts between the staff of the CPB and the economists at ministries, researchers in academia and the staff of the social partners. On the one hand, they provide relevant information to the CPB, but, on the other hand, they will, if needed, be critical on the work of the CPB.

An other major institution in the set-up of policy preparation in the Netherlands is the Social Economic Council (SER) that plays (together with the Foundation of Labour) the central role in negotiations between the various stakeholders to come to a *compromise agreement* on matters of economic and social policy (see for a more elaborate survey: Den Butter and Mosch, 2003; Den Butter, 2006). This is the arena where interaction between scientific knowledge and the policy dispute takes place. The SER is the main policy advisory board for the government regarding social economic issues. Its constellation is tripartite. Labour unions, employer associations and independent "members of the crown" each possesses one third of the seats. The "members of the crown" consist of professors in economics or law, politicians, the president of the Dutch Central Bank and the director of the CPB.

It is through these independent members that the policy discussions within the SER benefit from the insights of scientific research. The analyses of the CPB and also of the Dutch Central Bank carry a large weight in these discussions. Policy advices by the SER are prepared in committees, wherein representatives of the three categories discuss and amend texts drafted by the SER's Secretariat. Representatives of various ministries attend these committee meetings, but formally they are observers. They will not take part in discussions unless they are asked to provide relevant information. So, unlike in other countries, where the third party in tripartite council discussions is the government, in the Netherlands scientists, as independent third party in the discussion, see to it that the social partners do not come to agreements which are harmful to society as a whole. This would be the case when the costs of the policy measures agreed upon, are shifted away from the social partners to the society as a whole.

Obviously it is important for the impact of the SER recommendations that they are supported unanimously. It is quite exceptional that the government would disregard a SER unanimous policy recommendation. The independent members (which, by the way, represent the various pillars in the Dutch society, so that their political colour mimics the political landscape in the country) can be helpful in reaching a unanimous recommendation in informal discussions. The SER chairman, who is also an independent member and understandably has a crucial position in this institutionalised social dialogue, plays a major role.

8.6. National Accounts and Policy Preparation in other Industrialised Countries

The role of the CBS in the institutional set-up of economic policy preparation in the Netherlands is much linked to Tinbergen's strict separation of the task of independent data collection form the tasks of consensus and compromise formation on economic policy analysis and political decision making. In this respect the institutional set-up in other countries differs from that in the Netherlands, albeit that independence of data collection and compilation carries a large weight in all industrialised and democratic economies.

8.6.1. Statistics and policy analysis in the UK[1]

The 19th and early 20th century history of data collection at the macro level in the UK is somewhat comparable to that in the Netherlands. The major government body to collect data at a national level was the statistical department of the Board of Trade. After two journalists had been head of that department, in the early 1870s there were great concerns about the quality of the data. The idea was to establish a central statistical department to service the requirements of all Departments of State. Recommendations were continually made over the years to establish a small central statistical department but they were rejected because of difficulties arising from the laws, customs and circumstances under

[1] This section is partly based on information from http://www.bized.ac.uk.

which the different statistics were collected. In addition to the objections raised by the Board of Trade, Mr Gladstone, then the first Chancellor of the Exchequer, feared that such a central Department might extend its functions beyond the limits required by economy and expediency, and so the recommendations to form a Central Statistical Office were rejected.

Calls for improvements in statistical services continued throughout the 1920s and the 1930s. The outbreak of the Second World War saw proponents for change brought together in the team supporting the War Cabinet. Finally the Central Statistical Office (CSO) was set up on 27 January 1941 by Sir Winston Churchill with the clear aim of ensuring coherence of statistical information and to service the war effort. It quickly established itself as a permanent feature of government. It is interesting to note that again it was during wartime that a major step in the provision of statistical data at the macro level was taken. After 1945 there was an expansion in the work of official statisticians. This resulted mainly from the aim to manage the economy through controlling government income and expenditure by the use of an integrated system of national accounts. The passing of the Statistics of Trade Act in 1947 made it possible to collect more information from industry on a compulsory basis.

The late 1960s saw the performance of the statistical system again come under scrutiny. Following a report of the Estimates Committee of the House of Commons a reorganisation was effected. This reorganisation had four central elements:

- Establishment of the *Business Statistics Office* (BSO) to collect statistics from businesses irrespective of the department requiring information.
- Establishment of the *Office of Population Censuses and Surveys* to collect information from individuals and households through programmes of censuses, surveys and registers.
- An enhanced role for the CSO in managing government statistics.
- Development of the *Government Statistical Service* (GSS), including a cadre of professional statisticians across government.

A new, expanded CSO was established in July 1989. This brought together responsibility for collecting business statistics (previously with the BSO), responsibility for compilation of trade and financial statistics (previously with the Department of Trade and Industry) and responsibility for the retail prices index and family expenditure survey (previously with the Employment Department) with the old responsibilities of the CSO. In early 1990 the quality of economic statistics continued to be of concern to the Treasury and to the CSO. John Major, then the Chancellor of the Exchequer, indicated to Parliament his continuing concern about the statistical base. This was quickly followed by an announcement in May 1990 of a package of measures (known as the Chancellor's Initiative), backed up by substantial additional resources, to improve quality. Finally the CSO was renamed *Office for National Statistics* (ONS) on 1 April 1996 when it merged with the Office of Population, Censuses and Surveys (OPCS).

Economic policy preparation in the UK is very much the responsibility of the Chancellor of the Exchequer, which is the head of *Her Majesty's Treasury*. This institution combines the tasks of the Ministry of Finance, the Ministry of Economic Affairs and a bureau for economic policy analysis (such as the CPB in the Netherlands), and therefore holds a very powerful position in economic policy preparation in the UK. Civil servants of Her Majesty's Treasury make economic forecasts and policy analyses using their own model of the UK economy. The Cabinet uses these services for the calculation of the economic effects of their policy plans. So the separation between the more or less "objective" discussions on the working of the economy, and on political preferences and trade-offs, is less strict in the UK than in the Netherlands. On the other hand, much model based policy analysis in the UK is done by universities and institutes linked to universities. The Macroeconomic Modelling Bureau (MMB) of the University of Warwick compares and publishes the outcomes of the various UK models (and interprets the differences) so that there is some countervailing power to the policy analysis of the government. The *Bank of England* also conducts model based policy analysis but the citation reproduced by Backhouse (this volume) sheds some doubts on its influence.

8.6.2. Statistics and economic policy analysis in Norway[2]

In Norway, national accounts was, earlier than in most other countries, defined as the framework for the overall economic policy. It was Ragnar Frisch, with Tinbergen the first Nobel price winner in economics, who was responsible for this special type of integration of national accounting and economic policy analysis in Norway, which differed from the Anglo-American approach. Frisch had already in the late 1920s worked on a system of accounting concepts for describing the economic circulation. In 1933 Frisch had recommended the construction of 'national accounts', introducing this term for the first time in Norwegian. Frisch reworked his national accounting ideas several times in the following years, adopting the *eco-circ system* as the name for his accounting framework (and elaborate *eco-circ graphs* as a way of presenting it).

Frisch's national accounting ideas and his active role in the economic policy discussion in the 1930s led in 1936 to a project with colleagues at the University of Oslo, where he started to develop national accounts for Norway. Funds were provided by the Rockefeller Foundation and by private Norwegian sources. In 1940 Frisch had elaborated the eco-circ system from a theoretical level to a quite sophisticated system of national accounts.

The compilation of national accounts tables according to Frischian ideas was continued by some of his former students within the Central Bureau of Statistics (renamed Statistics Norway in 1991). In the first years after WWII, national accounting was at a preliminary stage and international standards were still years

[2] This section is based on Bjerkholt (1998).

away. That is why the early national accounting in Norway in the Frischian tradition had distinct national features, which made it differ from the standard national accounting framework. In the Frischian conception of national accounts above all it were the 'real phenomena' that mattered. The accounts should distinguish clearly between the real sphere and the financial sphere and show the interplay between them. The entries in the accounts should represent flows (or stocks) of real and financial objects. This 'realist' conception of national accounting, supported by Frisch's detailed structure of concepts, was later modified by adopting elements from Richard Stone's work, and further enhanced by embracing the input–output approach of Wassily Leontief as an integral part. For years the Norwegian approach was one of very few accounting systems producing annual input–output tables. The result was a detailed set of accounts comprising thousands of entries, rather than just a few tables of aggregate figures. It gave the impression that an empirical representation of the entire economic circulation had been achieved and it looked like a wholly new foundation for scientifically-based economic policy analysis.

The use of macroeconomic models for economic policy in Norway has been closely related to the reliance upon 'national budgeting' in the management of economic policy. The idea was that of a budget, not for the government's fiscal accounts, but in real terms for the entire national economy, spelt out in the spirit and concepts of the Frischian national accounts. The national budget served as a conceptual framework as well as a quantitative instrument for economic planning. The national budgeting process was organised by the Ministry of Finance as a network of ministries, other government agencies, semi-official bodies, and coordinating committees. The national budgeting in the early postwar period took place in a highly-regulated and rationed economy, and called for the kind of detail that the new national accounts could provide. The value of the national budget was seen in its role as an integrating tool, linking the sub-budgets of ministries, subordinate government agencies and semi-official bodies in the process of working out the economic prospects and economic policies for the coming year.

This programmatic national budget as something different from a forecast of national accounting aggregates raised problems of interpretation and realism. The national budget would not constitute a plan in a meaningful sense unless it was based upon a realistic assessment of the functioning of the economy. The various sub-budgets had to be combined in a such way that all relationships in the economy would be taken into account. However, with national accounts still in their infancy, large-scale models unavailable and computers in a modern sense non-existent, this was a daunting task. In fact it was resolved by the 'administrative method' which at best was an imperfect iterative administrative procedure.

As yet, together with the Netherlands, Norway is the example of a country where interaction between data collection at the macro level and model based economic analysis had an early start. Even more so than in the Netherlands, the Norwegian experiment was, in those early days, directed at detailed economic planning, where the economy was run like an enterprise. In that sense the planning exercise in Norway was much in line with the proposals of Van Cleeff for 'central planning' in the Netherlands. A remarkable difference with the Netherlands (and reflecting differences in opinion between Tinbergen and Frisch) is that in Norway model based economic policy analysis and forecasting has originally been conducted at the same institute as the data collection, namely Statistics Norway. As mentioned before, in the Netherlands Tinbergen advocated a strict separation between on the one hand data collection and on the other hand economic policy analysis and forecasting.

8.6.3. Statistics and policy analysis in the US

Unlike in other countries, the US has no single NSO which collects all statistical data. There are several institutions financed by the government which collect and compose data on the state of the economy. The *Bureau of Labour Statistics* publishes inflation and unemployment figures. The *Census Bureau* collects statistics specifically with respect to production, stock building, and population data. The *Bureau of Economic Analysis* (BEA) composes the national accounts based on data collected using by the Census Bureau. Finally the *Federal Reserve Board* (Fed), apart from monetary data, also collects and composes data on the cyclical situation of the economy. This division of labour between the various institutes brings about coordination problems. The different institutions, in many cases, use their own methodology, which makes the data difficult to compare, and makes policy analysis based on the data somewhat troublesome. It also leads to much discussion on the quality of the data between the various producers, so that data are less undisputed as, for instance, in the Netherlands.

A powerful institution in the US where economic policy analysis of statistical data at the macro level takes place is the *Council or Economic Advisers (CEA)*. The council consists of a chairperson and two members, appointed by the President of the US. The members are assisted by a relatively small staff. Most of them are university professors on leave from their university, and statistical assistants and graduate students. For this reason the CEA has been strongly related to the academic world. Each year the CEA makes forecasts of macroeconomic developments. An important publication is The Economic Report of the President, which contains the political vision of the CEA. Obviously the composition of this advisory body changes with the political colour of the President. As a consequence, both the contents of the recommendations and the advice process itself depend much on the composition of the government. Although the major obligation of the CEA is to give policy recommendations to the President, it has a broader task in policy preparation. The members of the CEA frequently take part in committee meetings at several levels and can therefore try to persuade, beside the President, other policy makers of their vision. This strong link between the political colour of the President and the composition of the CEA resulted that policy advices have been less consistent than for example at the

German Sachverständigenrat (see later). Particularly in the field of the macroeconomic stabilisation policy diverging recommendations have been given by various councils of different political colour. However, on other issues such as the support for free trade and the correction of market failures the CEA has followed a more consistent line.

Another powerful institution in policy making in the US is its independent central bank, the *Fed*. It collects data on the monetary side of the economy and has a large research staff for analysis of all kinds of economic data. Another institute for economic policy analysis is the *Congressional Budget Office*, which is part of the advisory bodies of the Congress. A major task is to make forecasts in a way similar to that of the CPB in the Netherlands.

A difference between the United States and, for instance the Netherlands and Germany, is that there are much less formal and institutionalised channels of contact between scientists and policy makers. On the other hand, the US has a number of private institutions, which conduct fundamental policy oriented research. The *National Bureau of Economic Research* (NBER) is such private non-profit research organisation of top people from the academic world. Enterprises, several 'foundations' and the federal government finance this institution with general funds or funds for specific projects. Another institution, the *Brookings Institution*, tries, by organising all kinds of activities, to make a bridge between scientific research and policy. The institute is financed by the turnovers of contract research, donations by charitable institutions, grants and sale of books. Similarly the American Enterprise Institute has much influence as opinion leader on a broad range of topics, albeit in an informal way.

8.6.4. Statistics and policy analysis in Germany

The *Statistische Bundesamt* is the central institution for collecting statistical data in Germany. Some 2780 staff members collect, process, present and analyse statistical information in this Federal Statistical Office. Seven departments and the offices of the President and the Vice-President are located in Wiesbaden's main office, two further departments are situated in the Bonn branch office. The Berlin Information Point directly provides information and advisory services based on official statistical data to Members of the Bundestag, the German federal government, embassies, federal authorities, industry associations, and all those who are interested in official statistics in the Berlin–Brandenburg region.

In accordance with the federal state and administrative structure of the Federal Republic of Germany, federation-wide official statistics (federal statistics) are produced in cooperation between the Federal Statistical Office and the statistical offices of the 16 Länder. This means that the system of federal statistics is largely decentralised. In the context of that division of labour, the Federal Statistical Office has mainly a coordinating function. Its main task is to ensure that federal statistics are produced without overlaps, based on uniform methods, and in a timely manner. The tasks of the Federal Statistical Office include (i) the methodological and technical preparation of the individual statistics, (ii) the further development of the programme of federal statistics, (iii) the coordination of individual statistics, (iv) the compilation and publication of federal results. With just few exceptions, conducting the surveys and processing the data up to the Land results fall within the competence of the statistical offices of the Länder.

So in fact a major part of the statistical data in Germany are collected by these regional statistical institutions. Many cyclical indicators are constructed and published by the *Bundesbank*. Moreover the *Institut für Arbeidsmarkt- und Berufsforschung der Bundesagentur für Arbeit* (IAB) collects, publishes and analyses data on developments at the labour market.

An important link between science and policy advice in Germany is the *Sachverständigenrat zur Begutachtung der gesamtwirtschaftlichen Entwicklung* (SVR). This council consists of five members, in most cases university professors. They are the so-called 'five wise'. The members of the council are appointed for five years on proposal of the federal government by the Bundespresident. In practice three members have no links with political parties and interest groups. For the remaining places the employees and employers organisations can present a candidate, but also the current members of the SVR have a say in these appointments. The Sachverständigenrat publishes each year before November 15th a report on economic developments. Important topics in the analysis are the stability of the price level, developments on the labour market, including the unemployment problem, steady economic growth and an assessment of the position of the balance of payment. Moreover the council must take the income distribution in consideration. The council is asked to propose several policy measures for reaching the policy goals, but no choice should be make. The advice of the council is not bound to be unanimous; members may include a minority opinion in the report. The Sachverständigenrat regularly commissions research to other scientists. In contrast to the CEA in the US, the Sachverständigenrat is politically independent. Moreover, the way new members are appointed ensures that their economic views will not differ radically from those of their predecessors.

Both the Ministry of Finance and the Ministry of Economic Affairs also have their own scientific advisory councils (wissenschaftliche Beiräte), composed of university professors. The current members of these councils propose the new members, so that here there is also some continuity in the line of advice. The task of members of these councils is to give opinions on policy suggestions and to suggest proposals themselves.

An important role in economic policy analysis in Germany is played by the *six independent research institutes*. These have each their own specialisations, although all report on the (inter)national economic development. Although none of these institutes has a specific political background, or is linked to a political party, they do represent different schools of economic thought. For instance, the *Deutsches Institut für Wirtschaftsforschung* (DIW) in Berlin has a more Keynesian orientation, whereas the *Institut für Weltwirtschaft* (IfW) of the university of Kiel frequently pleads for letting the market forces work and for less government regulation. Twice a year these institutes meet in order to draft a report on the stance of the business cycle for the current year (in April) and for the coming year (in October). It is possible to add a minority opinion to the report. Especially the DIW has often used this possibility. Moreover each of the research institutes publishes its own monthly report. So there is no equivalent to the CPB in Germany. The common (consensus) forecast of the research institutes is not the outcome based on one macroeconomic model, but the result of consultation between the institutes. An important aspect is also that policy makers and politicians in Germany are not very familiar with, and enthusiastic about model based policy analysis.

In Germany the social partners also have their own research institutes. The *Institut der Deutschen Wirtschaft* (IW) in Cologne, financed by the employers organisations, is even one of the largest scientific research institutes in Germany. The counterpart of the trade unions, the *Wirtschafts und Sozialwissenschaftliche Institut* of the DGB (WSI), is somewhat smaller. These institutes publish their own bulletins with analyses of the economic situation and prospects in advance of the autumn report of the six independent institutes, in order to influence the discussion.

8.6.5. Statistics and policy analysis in France

Like in the UK, the most powerful institution in economic policy analysis and policy preparation in France is the Ministry of Finance. The power of the Minister for Finance over its colleagues stems from delegation by the President of the Republic. Because of this, a situation can arise where the Prime Minister has no influence on economic policy, because the President imposes another opinion by means of the Minister for Finance.

National accounts' data and other data on the state of the French economy are collected by the *Institut National de la Statistique et des Études Économiques (INSEE)*. It is a "General Directorate" of the French Ministry of Finance and it is subjected to government-accounting rules: it is mainly funded from the central-government's general budget. The INSEE has a rather long history. In 1833 Adolphe Thiers (then Minister of the Interior) founded the Bureau de la Statistique. It became the Statistique Générale de la France (SGF) in 1840. In 1946 the National Institute of Statistics and Economic Studies for Metropolitan France and Overseas Possessions (Institut National de la Statistique et des Études Économiques pour la Métropole et la France d'Outre-Mer) was established. It was later renamed as the INSEE.

Around 1960, the formulation of "Le Plan" in France led to the application of statistics to economic planning and economic-regulation policies. Immediately after the war, a task force had engaged in preliminary national-accounting work. The program was originally carried out by the Finance Ministry's Economic and Financial Studies Office (Service des Études Économiques et Financières: SEEF), and then transferred to the INSEE. National accounting and medium-term forecasting gained momentum in the 1960s. The contacts with potential "customers" of statistics were implemented in the National Council for Statistics (which later became the National Council for Statistical Information: CNIS), established in 1972: statistical programs were now discussed with organisations representing the social partners (employers and trade unions). From 1974–1987 one of the most prominent French economists, Edmond Malinvaud, has been director general of the INSEE. This period saw a move toward greater independence for the Institute – a trend begun under the previous directors-general. Many large-scale computing resources were set up, the leading classifications were revised and intermediate accounts, satellite accounts (see later), and major macroeconomic models (DMS, METRIC) were introduced. So, like the situation in Norway, the French NSO does not only collect data but has the combined role of a bureau of statistics and of an institute of applied economic research. Besides data collection and its analysis the INSEE is actively involved in economic research and education. In addition to applied research, focused on policy making, the INSEE also conducts high quality fundamental research.

Another institute in France that resorts under the Ministry of Finance is the *Direction de Prévision* (DP). Although both the INSEE and the DP are involved in economic forecasting, each institute has its own specific responsibilities. The DP focuses primarily on short-term forecasting for economic policy making concerning public finance, foreign relations and the financial sector. The INSEE specialises on the one hand in extremely short term forecasting and on the other hand on long term forecasting. In order to built in some independence between data collection and policy analysis, forecasting and analysis of policy proposals, which are relevant for actual policy making, are prepared by the DP, and not by the INSEE.

An important feature of the French system is the close interrelations between the Ministry of Finance, the INSEE and the DP. Staff members are often employed by one of those institutions through short term contracts, which result in frequent mutual rotations and increased interaction possibilities.

8.7. National Accounts Today

In an early stage one of the main protagonists of national accounting, Richard Stone, realised that the data constructed by the system of national accounts, are to be used in economic analysis in various different contexts. So there always is a tension between the way national accounts data are constructed, and defined, and the theoretical concepts that they are to represent. In other words, Stone was one of the first to pay attention to the issue of what criteria should be used to assess the quality of measurement (see Comim, 2001). The main criteria that the construction of national accounting data should comply with, namely (i) consistency, (ii) flexibility, (iii) invariance and (iv) standardised forms, were already formulated by Stone at the beginning of the 1940s.

The conception of *consistency* viewed the measurement of national income not merely as a quantification of isolated single magnitudes, but as a quantification of an integrated accounting system in which magnitudes from different sources had to agree. This consistency as a balance between measures from different sources was achieved through the principle of double entry applied to a system of four balancing accounts: domestic product account, income and expenditure account, capital transactions account and the balance of payments account. The balancing identities close this system of accounts where each item appears once on the credit side of the balance and once at the debit side. The problem of consistency is the analogue of that described in Section 8.2 where there has to be a balance between the expenditure approach, the production approach and the income distribution approach.

The '*flexibility*' in the formulation of national accounts is, from the perspective of the tension between the construction and economic interpretation of national accounts' data, the most important measurement criterion. The remainder of this section discusses various recent developments in national accounting that comply with this criterion. In 1944 Meade and Stone noted that "there are many admissible ways of defining national income, and there is nothing absolutely right or wrong about any of these definitions" (cited by Comim, 2001). In a broader sense Stone suggested that measurement and economic theory should be tailored to each other's needs. On the one hand the social accounting system should preserve conceptual distinctions that are needed for economic analysis. On the other hand economic analysis should restate its needs in a terminology that could be measured. In modern terminology, one could reformulate this criterion of flexibility as a plea for an open standard for the system of national accounts, where the core of the system is fixed, but which enables changes in the semantics of the various aggregates. In this vein Stone advocated a system of multiple classifications.

In this respect there is also a tension between the criterion of flexibility and the criteria of *invariance* and *standardisation*. The latter criteria concerned the formal aspects of national accounts and consisted of homogenising definitions, classifications and procedures in order to narrow the variability of measurement. The apparent contrary criterion of flexibility concerned the human context of national accounts and would advocate extending the scope of measurement by introduction of new dimensions of measurement of national accounts.

8.7.1. Timeliness and accuracy of NA data

Today, most NSOs publish quarterly national account data and some data are even available at a monthly basis. An important aim of the quarterly estimates is providing consistent and timely information on the recent economic developments in the country. However, NA data, and also the quarterly estimates, suffer from long publication delays. In most cases it will take more than two years when final data can be published. Data published previously are all preliminary and provisional data, bound to revisions. Therefore the analysis of the recent development takes place by means of data which may change considerably. In spite of these uncertainties with respect to the quality of the data, most NSOs provide a quarterly "flash estimate" in order to cope with the need for very recent information. In the case of the CBS this is an estimate of the development of gross domestic product, released by means of a press bulletin eight weeks after the end of the respective quarter. Magnus et al. (2000) designed a methodology using available information on indicator ratio's, which can be helpful to enhance the accuracy of recent national accounts estimates. Yet, there always is a trade-off between timelines and accuracy in these estimates (see also Fixler, 2007, this volume). It can pose a problem when much weight is attached to these recent data, for instance by financial markets. Market developments and strategic decisions may, with the benefit of hindsight, be based on data which had a very poor information contents. Therefore NSOs should very well monitor the quality of their flash estimates and refrain from publishing them when quality is too poor. They should do that in spite of public pressure to come up with recent information.

8.7.2. Revisions of NA

On average each five to seven years a major revision of the national accounts data takes place (see e.g. Blades, 1989). Reasons for these revisions are (i) new basic observations becoming available; (ii) improvement in the construction method and (iii) changes in the definitions and set-up of the system (for instance in response to new international guidelines). These revisions may bring about substantial changes in the final figures of the national accounts. In the Netherlands the last revision was published in 2005 and related to 2001 as the year of revision. This revision had the following consequences for the assessment of the state of the economy and for the economic policy indicators:

1. Gross domestic product was enhanced with 18.4 billion Euros which implies an increase of 4.3%. This increase was mainly caused by introduction of new insights in the use of statistical information.
2. Gross national income increased with 24.8 billion Euros.
3. The financial deficit of the government (according to the EMU definition) now amounted to 0.2% of gross domestic product instead of 0.1% according to the original calculations.

Obviously these revisions have considerable consequences for the interpretation of historic economic developments, and also, in the above case, in the ranking of nations according to their per capita income. This ranking is often used to illustrate the relative prosperity of nations (see also Table 8.1).

8.7.3. Modules at national accounts – core module system

National accounts, in their current form, are a consistent description of economic processes on the basis of one, internationally used framework and terminology.

Table 8.1: Ranking of countries according to UN Human Development Index, 2005.

Country ranked according to HDI	Rank of country according to GDP per capita, pp US$
1. Norway	3
2. Iceland	6
3. Australia	10
4. Luxemburg	1
5. Canada	7
6. Sweden	20
7. Switzerland	8
8. Ireland	2
9. Belgium	12
10. United States	4
11. Japan	13
12. Netherlands	11
13. Finland	16
14. Denmark	5
15. United Kingdom	18
16. France	15
17. Austria	9
18. Italy	19
19. New Zealand	22
20. Germany	14

Source: Human Development Report 2005, United Nations.

Of course this is not by definition the most suitable system for an analysis of the national economy with its specific institutional characteristics. Although already in its current form the accounting framework satisfies to a large number of user wishes, information relevant for a specific policy analysis may not be contained in the system. Here the trade-off between the criteria of flexibility and invariance (and international comparability) referred to above, plays a part. Moreover the current NA in principle has been set up from the institutional approach (see Section 8.2). The international guidelines have chosen a specific definition of income, which excludes, for instance, domestic production but also the negative consequences of the use of the environment in production. More in general, NA do not provide information on other aspects which are, beside financial income and wealth, of importance for the prosperity of a country (see the next section).

In order to meet the need of multi-purpose information a more flexible system of NA has been designed. It consists of a (institutional oriented) core and various types of modules (see Bloem et al., 1991; Bos, 2006). The core focuses on transactions which are in reality expressed in money terms. These transactions are booked (exclusively) for the actors who are actually involved in the transactions. This core module system offers a number of clear advantages above the current system of presentation of NA. In this alternative set-up the users avail of a number of parallel definitions and classifications for various types of analyses. An example is a definition of national income which excludes imputed rents on owner occupied dwellings, which may be relevant representing the transactions motive in a demand for money equation. As a matter of fact this imputed rent does not represent an actual transaction for which money is needed.

Definitions and classifications used in the core can rather easily be understood by general users of NA, because they are in conformity with the international standards, adapted to the specific situation of the country. The modules make it possible to zoom in on a specific topic of research by using alternative definitions and classifications. In this way the modular approach enables to illustrate in detail various relationships between economic, social and technical phenomena, whereas on the other hand the connection with the core system remains preserved. An example is the relationship between economic developments as registered in the national accounts, and total spending of time by a population. An advantage is also that the description in a module must not inevitably be registered in monetary terms (for example, it is preferable to register unpaid labour in terms of time spent). A difference between the modular system and the traditional system is that the core of the modular system may contain much more side information.

The general idea of a building-block system with a core and satellite modules has been incorporated in the most recent official guidelines of the United Nations and of the European Union. For example, the United Nations guidelines contain a separate chapter on satellite accounts, (to be) supplemented by various handbooks, e.g. on environmental accounting (see Bos, 2006). In the Netherlands, the CBS has been an early promoter of satellite accounts, and a number of modules have been developed and made operational, namely (i) the relationship between the environment and the national economy; this extensive environmental module can also be used to illustrate trade-offs between production and environmental degradation; (ii) human capital and research and development; (iii) social protection; (iv) non-market production; (v) the illegal economy; (vi) income and expenditure by socio-economic group: the so called Social Accounting Matrix (SAM) (see Keuning and De Ruijter, 1988; Keuning, 1991).

8.7.4. Flexibility and transaction costs

Today's emphasis on the on the flexibility of the system of national accounts reflects the wishes of national accountants to make the system more user friendly and to adapt to changes in the needs for data in economic analysis. In this perspective there is an analogy to the argument by Mayer (this volume). He describes the relationship between readers and authors of scientific articles as a principal agent relationship. The author (as agent) has more information on his/her research, but the description of the research should, in a concise way, provide the essentials of the information so that the reader (as principal) can make a good judgement on the value and importance of the research. Likewise the national accountant (as agent) should in the construction of the data provide as much as possible the information which the user of the data (the principal) needs. Tinbergen's organisational set-up of economic policy preparation can, along these lines, be seen as a multilayered principal agent relationship. The CSO is the agent for the modelling and forecasting agency, and on their turn, these model builders, model users and forecasters are the agents of the policy makers who use these analyses in their debates and compromise agreements on proper policy measures. A major advantage of such strict organisation and separation of responsibilities is that it minimizes transaction costs in the policy discussions. In the context of the principal agent model these transaction costs can be associated with bonding costs, monitoring costs and residual loss. The more the national accountants are prepared and able to fulfil the wishes of the users, and communicate the information contents of the data in an adequate manner, the less effort the users of the data have to conduct their research in a proper manner. In the multilayered principal agent model discussed above, all experts involved in policy preparation – statisticians, model builders and model users, policy makers – should familiarise themselves with the concepts used in the analysis. Such common economic framework, where all "speak the same language", greatly contributes to the efficiency in the policy discussions. Of course, as Den Butter and Morgan (1998) note, there is much interaction between policy makers, model builders and model users. So there is no one way stream of information from agent to principal (or vice versa). In the context of the principal agent model this interaction could be seen as a way of goal alignment, so that the residual loss (agent has different goals than principal, or principal has no clear goals given the external conditions) as part of transaction costs is minimized.

8.8. The Use of NA Indicators in Welfare and Policy Analysis

The major aggregate economic indicators from the national accounts are national income and national product in their various definitions. These data are often used as indicators for economic welfare and prosperity. There is ample theoretical literature on the representation of economic welfare by national accounting (e.g. Weitzman, 1976; Asheim, 1994). Asheim and Buchholz (2004) developed a framework for national income accounting using a revealed welfare approach that covers both the standard utilitarian and the maximin criteria for welfare as special cases. They show that the basic welfare properties of national income accounting do not only cover the discounted utilitarian welfare functions, but extend to a more general framework of welfare functions. In particular, under a wider range of circumstances, it holds that real NNP growth indicates welfare improvement. Also from the empirical perspective developments in real national income (per capita) show a substantial correlation with indicators which are specifically used as indicators of non material welfare, such as child mortality, literacy, educational attainment and life expectancy. The

Human Development Index (HDI), published annually by the UN, ranks nations according to their citizens' quality of life rather than strictly by a nation's traditional economic figures. The ranking of countries according to HDI in Table 8.1 shows that the top of the list consists only of industrialised countries with high national per capita incomes. The table uses the 2005 index which is based on 2003 figures. Yet, the table also shows that within this group of industrialised countries, the ranking according to HDI and according to GDP per capita may differ considerably. For instance, Australia and Sweden obtain much better scores for HDI than for GDP per capita. The opposite holds for the United States, and, surprisingly, for Ireland and Denmark.

However, from a more operational perspective there is much criticism and discontent with national accounting data as indicators for welfare and specific economic developments. For instance, Van Ark (1999) mentions a number of problems when national account data are used for the analysis of long term economic growth. In that case long and internationally comparable time series are needed on (changes) in real GDP and its components. Van Ark's first concern is the *weighting procedure*. Changes in volume terms need necessarily be related to a benchmark year with a given basket of goods and services. The weights of the benchmark year are representative for the volume index or price index used for the calculation of volume data over the whole time period. Ideally one would wish to use the regular shifts in weights in benchmark years every five or ten years, and some coordination amongst various countries would be highly desirable. However, such data are not available and one has to rely at most on a few benchmark years, and sometimes even on only one benchmark year. The second concern by Van Ark is the *estimation of intermediate inputs, capital and labour*, which are important ingredients of an empirical study of economic growth. With the exception of manufacturing, which in many (trading) countries comprises only a relative small part of total production, there is very little comprehensive evidence on intermediate inputs in the production process before the era of input–output tables. Historical sources on capital stock and capital services are only available for a very limited number of countries and the consistency of historical labour statistics with national accounts is weak in many cases. The third concern of Van Ark is the *treatment of services*. The measurement of real output in services remained somewhat neglected as much of the work of historical accounts focused primarily on the commodity sectors of the economy. Historical accounts often assume no productivity changes in services and rely largely on changes in the wage bill of services. It appears that on the whole real output growth in services is likely to be understated in most accounts, because the no productivity growth assumption seems to be unrealistic. It may also imply that productivity increases in services are attributed to industry and commodity sectors.

8.8.1. Prices and volumes

More in general one of the most troublesome parts of national accounting from the perspective of the interpretation of the data is the separation of the observed (changes in) nominal values in prices and volumes (for reviews see Diewert, 2004 and Reinsdorf, 2007, this volume). Index number theory gives statistical agencies some guidance on what is the "right" theoretical index for determining prices of commodities and services and for aggregation of these prices. The problem, however, is that there have been many alternative index number theories and that statistical agencies have been unable to agree on a single theory to guide them in the preparation of their consumer price indices or their indices of real output.

One of major operational problems is to adjust prices for the quality changes in the attributes of goods and services. For instance, a price increase of a new version of a car may come together with some improvements (higher engine power, more luggage space, new safety provisions) as compared to the older version of the same car. In that case a correction has to be made for these improvements which may imply that the corrected price change is much lower, or even negative, as compared to the actual price change. These implicit changes in the quality of goods and services in the basket of consumer goods used for determining the consumer price index (CPI) has been a major concern for the Boskin commission.[3] When quality changes are not properly taken into consideration, price indices overestimate inflation and hence underestimate volume changes and productivity increases. A method of adjusting prices for quality changes is the so called hedonic method where prices of goods and services are regressed with (quality) changes in the attributes of those goods and services. As yet one should be cautious in the use of hedonic regressions because many issues have not yet been completely resolved. Moreover questions have been raised about the usefulness of hedonic regressions as several alternative hedonic regression methodologies proved to yield different empirical results. Therefore Diewert (2004) notes that there is still some work to be done before a consensus on "best practice" hedonic regression techniques emerges.

A related problem with respect to the construction of price indices is introduction of new products. Here the solution is the reservation price methodology, already suggested by Hicks, which has, however, not been adopted by any statistical agency as yet. Moreover, a final solution for the problem of separating price and volume movements will never be possible as there are, especially in services, categories of products where prices are difficult, or even impossible to be observed. Diewert (2004) gives the following list: (i) *unique products*: that is, in different periods, different products are produced; it prevents routine matching of prices and is a pervasive problem in the measurement of the prices of

---

[3] It is acknowledged that measuring inflation by the CPI using a basket of consumer commodities is, strictly speaking, not part of national accounting.

services; (ii) *complex products*: many service products are very complicated; e.g., telephone service plans; (iii) *tied products*: many service products are bundled together and offered as a single unit; e.g., newspapers, cablevision plans, banking services packages; (iv) *joint products*; for this type of product, the value depends partially on the characteristics of the purchaser; e.g., the value of a year of education depends not only on the characteristics of the school and its teachers but also on the social and genetic characteristics of the student population; (v) *marketing and advertising products:* this class of service sector outputs is dedicated to influencing or informing consumers about their tastes; a standard economic paradigm for this type of product has not yet emerged; (vi) *heavily subsidized products*: in the limit, subsidized products can be supplied to consumers free of (explicit) charges: the question than is whether zero is the "right" price for this type of product? (vii) *financial products*: what is the "correct" real price of a household's monetary deposits? (viii) *products involving risk and uncertainty*: what is the correct pricing concept for gambling and insurance expenditures? What is the correct price for a movie or a record original when it is initially released?

Diewert also mentions the problem for statistical agencies of how to deal with transfer prices when constructing import and export price indexes. A transfer price is a border price set by a multinational firm that trades products between subsidiaries in different countries. It is unlikely that currently reported transfer prices represent "economic" prices that reflect the resource costs of the exports or imports. As the proportion of international trade that is conducted between subsidiaries of multinational firms is about 50%, it becomes an increasingly difficult challenge for statistical agencies to produce price indexes for exports and imports that are meaningful.

8.8.2. A more fundamental critique on national income as welfare indicator

Beside the practical problems of measurement described above, more fundamental critique has been raised against the use of national income data from the national accounts for economic welfare analysis. A recent example is van den Bergh (2005) who advocates to completely abolish the use of GNP in economic analysis because it provides 'misleading information and does harm to welfare'. He repeats a number of arguments from the literature such as the mixing up of costs and benefits in national accounting, government expenditures connected with government failure which reduce welfare instead of increasing it, welfare reductions through market failures which national accounting does not take into account, exclusion of the informal economy and household production from the national accounts (although, as described above, provisions for this are taken in the modules at the national accounts), the neglect of questions of income distribution and loss of information in the aggregation process. A major argument for Van den Bergh are the results of recent empirical studies on subjective welfare, which connect individual welfare with happiness. These studies show that somewhere between 1950 and 1970 the increase in individual welfare (or happiness) has stopped, or even has changed into a negative trend in most industrialised (OECD) countries, whereas there has been a steady and continuous growth of real GNP. There seems to be a 'decoupling' between income and individual subjective welfare at the level of about 15 000 to 20 000 dollars income per year (see also Layard, 2006; Helliwell, 2006).

8.8.3. National accounts and the environment

In the assessment of the relationship between national accounting and welfare much attention has been paid to environmental issues (see e.g. Mäler, 1991). A major criticism on national income as welfare indicator is that it does not take environmental degradation, or the use of the environment in production, into account. In principle two solutions have been proposed for this problem (see also Den Butter and Verbruggen, 1994). The first solution is to consider environmental quality as a separate variable (or policy target) in the social welfare function. In that case the argument is on the trade-off between environmental quality and material welfare – as indicated by national income – given the other variables in the welfare function. The problem in this case is how to determine the composite indicator of environmental quality which reflects this respect of social welfare. The second solution is to correct, in one way or another, GNP for environmental change and arrive at a so called environmentally adjusted GNP: 'green' GNP, eco-GNP or (environmentally) sustainable GNP. Now the problem is how to make this correction which gives an implicit weight to the trade-off between environmental quality and income in the welfare function. Such correction was, by the way, already alluded to by, Clark (1937, p. 9) who indicated a possible 'deduction for any demonstrable exhaustion of natural resources'.

Both methods obviously represent opponent strategies, which stem from different schools of economic thought. A correction of GNP implies a monetising of environmental degradation (or upgrading) by the statistical agency that publishes these data. It affects the definition of national income and requires an amendment of the theory of national accounting. On the other hand, the calculation of physical indicators leaves the final valuation of the trade-off between economic growth and a clean environment to the users of the data. Then, it may become a political rather than an economic valuation. However, both strategies are not opponent in every respect. For the construction of composite indicators of the state of the environment some valuation cannot be avoided as various aspects of pollution are to be added up, whereas calculation of a green or sustainable GNP implicitly defines an overall indicator for the state of the environment, namely the difference between the traditional GNP and the corrected figure for GNP.

Physical indicators for the state of the environment can be constructed within the framework of national accounts, namely by adding, by way of satellite account, an environmental module to the system (see the description of the modular approach above). In the Netherlands the design for an environmental module to the NA, which yields such satellite account, was made by De Boo et al. (1991). Indicators for the state of the environment can be derived from the physical accounts of this environmental module (see e.g. Keuning, 1993; De Haan and Keuning, 1996). A related method is to combine various aspects of environmental quality by using theme indicators. In their environmental indicators for respectively the UK and the Netherlands, Hope et al. (1992) and Den Butter and Van der Eyden (1998) have aggregated such theme indicators of environmental policy (such as greenhouse emissions, acidification, eutrophication, etc.) to one overall index. For the aggregation weights of these indices evidence from public opinion polls on the concern for environmental problems is used. In this way preferences with respect to trade-offs between various aspects of the environment are taken into account in the overall indicator.

The second way to incorporate the environment in national accounting is, as mentioned before, to correct GNP for environmental damage. A strong proponent of this methodology is one of the pioneers in environmental economics, Hueting. In many publications he has proposed a practical methodology for the calculation of an environmental correction, which is based on sustainability norms (e.g. see Hueting et al., 1992). Hueting's proposals for the correction of GNP for environmental loss has been made operational for the Netherlands by a research team at the Institute for Environmental Studies (IvM) of the Vrije Universiteit chaired by Verbruggen (see Gerlagh et al., 2002). They use a computable general equilibrium model calibrated to a benchmark year. The equilibrium obtained with an unrestricted version of the model is compared with the equilibrium obtained when the sustainability standards are included as constraints in the model. GNP in this new equilibrium, which appears to be (much) lower that the original equilibrium because all standards are binding, is labelled "the sustainable national income according to Hueting" for the benchmark year. Clearly this calculation of the sustainable NI cannot be taken as a simple statistic-technical correction in the system of the national accounts. That is why, in Tinbergen's set-up of separated responsibilities in economic policy preparation, this model based calculation should not be conducted by the NSO (CBS in this case) but by outsiders (in this case the IvM).

8.8.4. The road back from macro to micro?

The main skill of national accounting is to construct, in a consistent framework, meaningful data at the macro level from individual observations. However, today there is a tendency of data users to ask for more and more detail in the economic indicators: the road back to the micro level. Below three examples are given of this tendency.

Firstly there is a growing need for detailed information on various sectors of the economy. The problem here is how to define the various sectors and how to allot individual observations at the firm level to these various sectoral accounts. Sectoral disaggregation becomes even more difficult now that more and more production processes are split up due to subcontracting and outsourcing. Even at the plant level firms fulfil various different functions in the production chain so that a functional approach would be better suited for the purposes of data analysis than the present institutional approach in sectoral accounting. Think of multinationals like Shell, Unilever and Philips, which are in the statistics part of the industry sector, but which have in their home countries mainly an orchestrating function where goods and services are produced all over the world at lowest prices and sold at highest prices. Reductions of transaction costs (e.g. by innovations in subcontracting and outsourcing, or by creating much value by smart marketing) will, according to the sectoral accounting, result in productivity gains of the industry. The economic interpretation of such productivity increase is often that it is caused by product innovations, which is not true in this case (see WRR, 2003). In fact, macroeconomic research in this field of productivity analysis and growth accounting increasingly use microeconomic data sets with individual firm data which cover the whole economy. Modern computer facilities and empirical methodology facilitates such analysis. NSOs are capable and willing to make these data sets available for professional researchers.

The second example relates to the consumer price index (CPI). The CPI is used for indexation of all kinds of economic quantities such as wages and pension income. Calculation of the CPI is based on an basket of goods and services for the average of all individuals. However, the price inflation calculated by the CPI differs for each individual and group. Frequently specific groups, such as the elderly, are dissatisfied with indexation according to the average CPI when they believe that inflation has been above average for their group. On that occasion they ask the NSO to calculate a CPI for their specific group – obviously no demand for a group CPI occurs when the inflation of that group is believed to be below average. In principle NSOs are able to calculate a CPI for each individual person – or to be more precise: for each individual basket of goods and services. So they can comply with the demand for CPIs for various (sub)groups of the population. The question is whether such proliferation of CPIs is wise from both a political and a statistical viewpoint. From a political viewpoint it is not wise because the use of these disaggregated CPIs will always be asymmetric and biased to bring more inflation. From a statistical viewpoint, researchers at the Netherlands CBS, Pannekoek and Schut (2003) have shown that it is not wise either. They looked at price increases within and between four different groups of income earners, namely (i) households with wage incomes (workers); (ii) households with income from capital and own occupation (self employed); (iii) households living on social security and assistance; (iv) household with old age pensions (elderly). There appeared to be some persistent (but hardly significant) differences in inflation rates between these groups. However, differences within these groups appeared to be much larger. Therefore the CBS decided, for the time being, not to comply with the demand to publish regularly CPIs for various groups.

The third example is somewhat related to the previous one, albeit that the result here is a presentation of data at the micro level rather than (solely) at the macro level. Traditionally the Netherlands CPB calculates short term prospects for the purchasing power of Dutch households. The outcome of these calculations carry a heavy weight in the policy discussions in the Netherlands. The effect of each policy measure on purchasing power is closely looked at by politicians and the media, and often policy measures are very much fine tuned (and therefore sometimes made too specific and complicated) in order to avoid losses of purchasing power, especially for low income groups. As a matter of fact, in the Netherlands it is the indicator which carries the largest weight in policy discussions on measures which affect the income distribution and in the yearly negotiations on the government budget. The CPB used to present (and still is presenting) the effects on purchasing power for the average of different income groups: minimum wage earner; modal wage earner; two times modal wage earner, etc. However it was perceived that these average outcomes at the macro level did not provide a sufficient picture of the underlying effects at the individual level. For instance, when the government declared that, on the basis of the average outcomes, through a combination of policy measures, the purchasing power of the whole population would increase, the media and politicians of the opposition were always able to find an unfortunate and poor individual, who suffered a substantial decrease in disposable income by the combination of the policy measures. The Social Economic Council even published a lengthy advice on how to present indicators of purchasing power. It made the CPB decide to present the development of purchasing power in scatter diagrams, where each point in the scatter represents a specific small groups of similar households. These scatters for six different categories of households are reproduced in Fig. 8.1. They show for most households of all categories an increase of purchasing power in 2006 as compared to 2005. Policy measures seem to be most favourable to households with a single wage earner. Most households with two wage earners will also see their purchasing power increase, but here there is a considerable number of households that will not profit from the policy measures (and in this case, start of the cyclical upturn). The same holds true for the other categories of the figure. So the scatter diagram brings more sophistication to the policy discussions than a simple presentation of averages at the macro level in a table. Although the scatter diagrams may seem complicated and difficult to understand at first sight, nowadays all participants in the social economic policy debate in the Netherlands know perfectly well how to interpret this representation of the indicator. A disadvantage of this indicator is, like in the case of aggregated purchasing power indicators, that it does not reveal the dynamics of moving to another group (e.g. from unemployed to employed). Policy measures often aim to give incentives for such transitions.

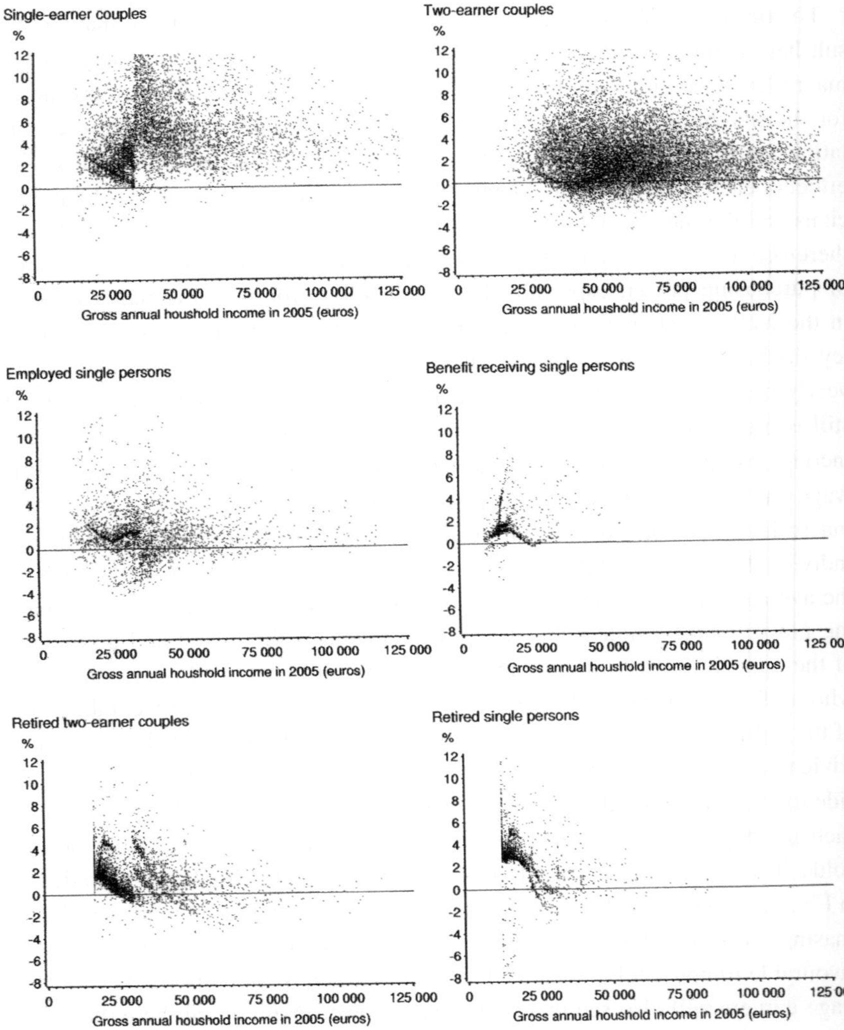

Fig. 8.1: Purchasing power by household type, source of income and household income (changes in %), 2006. Source CPB: Purchasing power in 2006 according to MEV 2007.

8.9. Conclusions

National accounts (NA) and the indicators derived from the system of national accounts play a major role in economic policy preparation and in the political debate on welfare and well being. For a structured discussion on these matters it is essential that technical aspects of data construction are as much as possible separated from the policy interpretation of these composed data which often has a normative and political character. This separation of responsibilities leads to a considerable reduction of transaction costs in discussions on the effects of policy measures as in that case the discussions are based on the same undisputed data and use the same concepts known to all participants in the discussions.

This chapter lays much emphasis on the institutional set-up of (economic) data collection at the macro level, with the Netherlands as an example. National accounts' data, and all other data which describe developments at the level of the state (or parts thereof) have the character of a public good and should be collected by an independent National Statistical Office. The first problem is an aggregation problem: how to come from individual data at the micro level to aggregate data at the macro level so that, as much as possible, normative elements are excluded from the aggregation process. National accountants have solved this problem by being very precise about the definitions of the various concepts of the NA. Consistency is obtained by an accounting framework of double (or even triple) bookkeeping where total income should be equal to total expenditure. International comparability of the data is obtained by following international guidelines.

The second problem, however, is that of interpretation of indicators derived from the NA. Here different users of the data may warrant different definitions in order to let the data conform to the specific concept used in the analysis. The chapter extensively discusses the concept of welfare, but similar arguments hold for the discussions on poverty: NSOs collect data on income distribution, but the transformation of these data into one of the many indices of poverty contains normative elements. So, besides internal consistency and international comparability, flexibility is another criterion for NA. As yet this criterion of flexibility does not imply that national accountants and NSOs themselves are to publish various concepts according to alternative definitions which have a specific normative interpretation. They should allow others, by kind of open standards, to make such calculations. Satellite accounts are useful in that respect.

On several occasions interpretation of indicators at the macro level is troublesome anyhow. The discussion on purchasing power in the Netherlands is a clear example. In such cases, presentation of micro data in other forms than as aggregate indicators can be a solution. This road back from macro to micro is an apparent trend in economic analysis. Therefore, making relevant sets with individual data available for professional users has become an important task for NSOs.

References

Asheim, G.B. (1994). Net national product as an indicator of sustainability. *Scandinavian Journal of Economics* **96**, 257–265.

Asheim, G.B., Buchholz, W. (2004). A general approach to welfare measurement through national income accounting. *Scandinavian Journal of Economics* **106**, 361–384.

Bjerkholt, O. (1998). Interaction between model builders and policy makers in the Norwegian tradition. *Economic Modelling* **15**, 317–339.

Blades, D. (1989). Revision of the system of national accounts: A note on the objectives and key issues. *OECD Economic Studies* **12**, 205–219.

Bloem, A.M., Bos, F., Gorter, C.N., Keuning, S.J. (1991). Vernieuwing van de Nationale rekeningen (Improvement of national accounts). *Economisch Statistische Berichten* **76**, 957–962.

Bos, F. (1992). The history of national accounting. National Accounts Occasional Paper Nr. NA-048. CBS, Voorburg.

Bos, F. (2003). The national accounts as a tool for analysis and policy; past, present and future. Academic thesis. University of Twente.

Bos, F. (2006). The development of the Dutch national accounts as a tool for analysis and policy. *Statistica Neerlandica* **60**, 215–258.

Boumans, M.J. (2007). Representational theory of measurement. In: Durlauf, S., Blume, L. (Eds.), *New Palgrave Dictionary of Economics, 2nd ed.* Macmillan, to appear.

Clark, C. (1937). *National Income and Outlay*. MacMillan, London.

Comim, F. (2001). Richard Stone and measurement criteria for national accounts. In: *History of Political Economy*. Annual Supplement to vol. 33, pp. 213–234.

de Boo, A.J., Bosch, P.R., Garter, C.N., Keuning, S.J. (1991). An environmental module and the complete system of national accounts. National Accounts Occasional Paper Nr. NA-046. CBS, Voorburg.

de Haan, M., Keuning, S.J. (1996). Taking the environment into account: The NAMEA approach. *Review of Income and Wealth* **42**, 131–148.

den Bakker, G.P. (1993). Origin and development of Dutch National Accounts. In: de Vries, W.F.M., et al. (Eds.), *The Value Added of National Accounting*. CBS, Voorburg/Heerlen, pp. 73–92.

den Butter, F.A.G. (2004). Statistics and the origin of the Royal Netherlands Economic Association. *De Economist* **152**, 439–446.

den Butter, F.A.G. (2006). The industrial organisation of economic policy preparation in the Netherlands. Paper presented at the conference on Quality Control and Assurance in Scientific Advice to Policy. Berlin–Brandenburg Academy of Sciences and Humanities, Berlin, January 12–14, 2006.

den Butter, F.A.G., Morgan, M.S. (1998). What makes the models-policy interaction successful? *Economic Modelling* **15**, 443–475.

den Butter, F.A.G., Mosch, R.H.J. (2003). The Dutch miracle: Institutions, networks and trust. *Journal of Institutional and Theoretical Economics* **159**, 362–391.

den Butter, F.A.G., van der Eyden, J.A.C. (1998). A pilot index for environmental policy in the Netherlands. *Energy Policy* **26**, 95–101.

den Butter, F.A.G., Verbruggen, H. (1994). Measuring the trade-off between economic growth and a clean environment. *Environmental and Resource Economics* **4**, 187–208.

Diewert, W.E. (2004). Index number theory: Past progress and future challenges. Paper presented at SSHRC Conference on Price Index Concepts and Measurement, Vancouver, Canada, June/July 2004.

Don, F.J.H. (1996). De positie van het Centraal Planbureau (The position of the Central Planning Bureau). *Economisch Statistische Berichten* **81**, 208–212.

Don, F.J.H., Verbruggen, J.P. (2006). Models and methods for economic policy: An evolution of 50 years at the CPB. *Statistica Neerlandica* **60**, 145–170.

Gerlagh R., Dellink, R., Hofkes, M.W., Verbruggen, H. (2002). A measure of sustainable national income for the Netherlands. *Ecological Economics* **41**, 157–174.

Helliwell, J.F. (2006). Well-being, social capital and public policy: What's new? *Economic Journal* **116**, C34–C45.

Hope, C., Parker, J., Peake, S. (1992). A pilot environmental index for the UK in the 1980s. *Energy Policy* **20**, 335–343.

Hueting, R., Bosch, P., de Boer, B. (1992). Methodology for the calculation of sustainable national income. *Statistical Essays* M44 (Central Bureau of Statistics, Voorburg).

Kendrick, J.W. (1970). The historical development of National-Income accounts. *History of Political Economy* **2**, 284–315.

Kenessey, Z. (1993). Postwar trend in national accounts in the perspective of earlier developments. In: de Vries, W.F.M., et al. (Eds.), *The Value Added of National Accounting*. CBS, Voorburg/Heerlen, pp. 33–70.

Klep, P.M.M., Stamhuis, I.H. (Eds.) (2002). *The Statistical Mind in a Pre-statistical Era: The Netherlands 1750–1850*. Aksant, Amsterdam, NEHA Series III.

Keuning, S.J. (1991). Proposal for a social accounting matrix which fits into the next system of national accounts. *Economic Systems Research* **3**, 233–248.

Keuning, S.J. (1993). An information system for environmental indicators in relation to the National Accounts. In: de Vries, W.F.M., et al. (Eds.), *The Value Added of National Accounting*. Netherlands Central Bureau of Statistics, Voorburg/Heerlen, pp. 287–305.

Keuning, S.J., de Ruijter, W.A. (1988). Guidelines to the construction of a social accounting matrix. *Review of Income and Wealth* **34**, 71–100.

Layard, R. (2006). Happiness and public policy: A challenge to the profesion. *Economic Journal* **116**, C24–C33.

Magnus, J.R., van Tongeren, J.W., de Vos, A.F. (2000). National accounts estimation using indicator ratios. *Review of Income and Wealth* **46**, 329–350.

Mäler, K.-G. (1991). National accounts and environmental resources. *Environmental and Resource Economics* **1**, 1–15.

Mellens, M. (2006). Besparingen belicht: Samenhang en verschillen tussen definities (A look at savings: Links and differences between definitions). *CPB Memorandum* 145. The Hague, February.

Mooij, J. (1994). *Denken over Welvaart, Koninklijke Vereniging voor de Staathuishoudkunde, 1849–1994*. Lemma, Utrecht.

Morgan, M.S. (1990). *The History of Econometric Ideas*. Cambridge Univ. Press, Cambridge.

Pannekoek, J., Schut, C.M. (2003). Geen inflatie op maat (No inflation index at request). *Economisch Statistische Berichten* **88**, 412–414.

Stamhuis, I.H. (1989). 'Cijfers en Aequaties' en 'Kennis der Staatskachten'; Statistiek in Nederland in de negentiende eeuw. Rodopi, Amsterdam/Atlanta.

Stamhuis, I.H. (2002). Vereeniging voor de Statistiek (VVS); Een gezelschap van juristen (The Statistical Society; A society of lawyers). *STAtOR* **3** (2), 13–17.

Summers, R., Heston, A. (1991). The PENN world table (mark 5); an expanded set of international comparisons, 1950–1988. *Quarterly Journal of Economics* **106**, 327–368.

Tinbergen, J. (1936). Kan hier te lande, al dan niet na overheidsingrijpen een verbetering van de binnenlandse conjunctuur intreden, ook zonder verbetering van onze exportpositie? Welke lering kan ten aanzien van dit vraagstuk worden getrokken uit de ervaringen van andere landen? In: *Praeadviezen voor de Vereeniging voor de Staathuishoudkunde en de Statistiek*. Nijhoff: Den Haag, pp. 62–108.

Tinbergen, J. (1952). *On the Theory of Economic Policy*. North-Holland, Amsterdam.

Tinbergen, J. (1956). *Economic Policy: Principles and Design*. North-Holland, Amsterdam.

Wetenschappelijke Raad voor het Regeringsbeleid (2003). Nederland handelsland: Het perspectief van de transactiekosten (The Netherlands as a nation of traders: The transaction costs' perspective). *Reports to the Government* No. 66. Sdu Publishers, The Hague.

Weitzman, M.L. (1976). On the welfare significance of national product in a dynamic economy. *Quarterly Journal of Economics* **90**, 156–162.

van Ark, B. (1999). Accumulation, productivity and technology: Measurement and analysis of long term economic growth. *CCSO Quarterly Journal* **1** (2). June.

van den Bergh, J.C.J.M. (2005). BNP, weg ermee (BNP, let's get rid of it). *Economisch Statistische Berichten* **90**, 502–505.

van den Bogaard, A. (1999). Configuring the economy, the emergence of a modelling practice in the Netherlands, 1920–1955. Thela-Thesis.

van Zanden, J.L. (2002). Driewerf hoera voor het poldermodel (Three hoorays for the polder model). *Economisch Statistische Berichten* **87**, 344–347.

CHAPTER 9

Invariance and Calibration

Marcel Boumans

Department of Economics, University of Amsterdam, Amsterdam, The Netherlands
E-mail address: m.j.boumans@uva.nl

Abstract

The Representational Theory of Measurement conceives measurement as establishing homomorphisms from empirical relational structures into numerical relation structures, called models. Models function as measuring instruments by transferring observations of an economic system into quantitative facts about that system. These facts are evaluated by their accuracy. Accuracy is achieved by calibration. For calibration standards are needed. Then two strategies can be distinguished. One aims at estimating the invariant (structural) equations of the system. The other strategy is to use known stable facts about the system to adjust the model parameters. For this latter strategy, the requirement of models as homomorphic mappings is not required anymore.

9.1. The Representational Theory of Measurement

In the formal representational theory (see Chapter 2), measurement is defined set-theoretically as:

Given empirical relations $R_1, \ldots, R_n$ on a set of extra-mathematical entities **Y** and numerical relations $P_1, \ldots, P_n$ on the set of numbers **N** (in general a subset of the set of real numbers), a function ϕ from **Y** into **N** takes each R_i into P_i, $i = 1, \ldots, n$, provided that the elements $Y_1, Y_2, \ldots$ in **Y** stand in relation R_i if and only if the corresponding numbers $\phi(Y_1), \phi(Y_2), \ldots$ stand in relation P_i.

In other words, measurement is conceived of as establishing homomorphisms from empirical relational structures $\Psi = \langle \mathbf{Y}, R_1, \ldots, R_m \rangle$ into numerical relational structures $N = \langle \mathbf{N}, P_1, \ldots, P_m \rangle$. We say then that the ordered triple $\langle \Psi, N, \phi \rangle$ is a *scale*. Figure 9.1 shows a diagrammatic representation of this set-theoretical definition of measurement.

A numerical relational structure representing an empirical relational structure is also called a model. For this reason RTM is sometimes called the Model Theory of Measurement.

The problem of this representational view on measurement is that when the requirements for assessing the representations or models are not further qualified,

Measurement in Economics: A Handbook
Marcel Boumans (Editor)

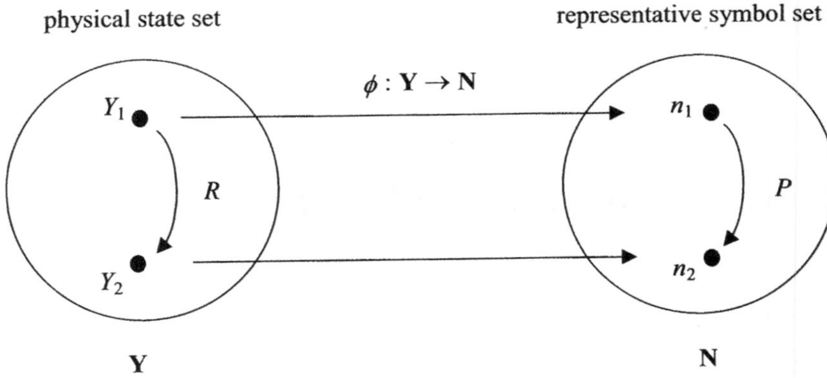

Fig. 9.1: Representational theory of measurement.

it can easily led to an operationalist interpretation. This operationalist interpretation is best illustrated by Stevens' dictum: Measurement is 'the assignment of numerals to objects or events according to rule – any rule' (Stevens, 1959, p. 19). As a result, measurement according to this interpretation does not inform us about empirical phenomena. To avoid this, a model should meet certain criteria to be considered homomorphic to an empirical relational structure. This is the so-called *representation problem*.

9.2. Data and Phenomena

The objects of economic measurements have a different ontology than the objects of classical theories of measurement. Measurement is assigning numbers to properties. In the classical view of measurement, which arose in the physical sciences and received its fullest exposition in the works of Campbell (1928), these numbers represents properties of *things*. Measurement in the social sciences does not necessarily have this thing-relatedness. It is not only properties of 'things' that are measured but also those of other kinds of phenomena: states, events, and processes.

To arrive at an account of measurement that acknowledges this different ontology, Woodward's (1989) distinction between phenomena and data is helpful. According to Woodward, phenomena are relatively stable and general features of the world and therefore suited as objects of explanation and prediction. Data, that is, the observations playing the role of evidence for claims about phenomena, on the other hand involve observational mistakes, are idiosyncratic and reflect the operation of many different causal factors and are therefore unsuited for any systematic and generalizing treatment. Theories are not about observations – particulars – but about phenomena – universals.

Woodward characterizes the contrast between data and phenomena in three ways. In the first place, the difference between data and phenomena can be indicated in terms of the notions of error applicable to each. In the case of data the notion of error involves observational mistakes, while in the case of phenomena one worries whether one is detecting a real fact rather than an artifact produced by the peculiarities of one's instruments or detection procedures. A second contrast between data and phenomena is that phenomena are more 'widespread' and less idiosyncratic, less closely tied to the details of a particular instrument or detection procedure. A third way of thinking about the contrast between data and phenomena is that scientific investigation is typically carried on in a noisy environment, an environment in which the observations reflect the operation of many different causal factors.

> The problem of detecting a phenomenon is the problem of detecting a signal in this sea of noise, of identifying a relatively stable and invariant pattern of some simplicity and generality with recurrent features – a pattern which is not just an artifact of the particular detection techniques we employ or the local environment in which we operate. Problems of experimental design, of controlling for bias or error, of selecting appropriate techniques for measurement and of data analysis are, in effect, problems of tuning, of learning how to separate signal and noise in a reliable way (Woodward, 1989, pp. 396–397).

Underlying the contrast between data and phenomena is the idea that theories do not explain data, which typically will reflect the presence of a great deal of noise. Rather, an investigator first subjects the data to analysis and processing, or alters the experimental design or detection technique, in an effort to separate out the phenomenon of interest from extraneous background factors. Although phenomena are investigated by using observed data, they themselves are in general not directly observable. To 'see' them we need instruments, and to obtain numerical facts about the phenomena in particular we need measuring instruments. In social science, we do not have physical instruments, like thermometers or galvanometer. Mathematical models function as measuring instruments by transforming sets of observations into a measurement result.

Theories are incomplete with respect to the quantitative facts about phenomena. Though theories explain phenomena, they often (particularly in economics) do not have built-in application rules for mathematizing the phenomena. Moreover, theories do not have built-in rules for measuring the phenomena. For example, theories tell us that metals melt at a certain temperature, but not at which temperature (Woodward's example); or they tell us that capitalist economies give rise to business cycles, but not the duration of recovery. In practice, by mediating between theories and the data, models may overcome this dual incompleteness of theories. As a result, models that function as measuring instruments mediate between theory and data by transferring observations into quantitative facts about the phenomenon under investigation:

Data $\rightarrow$ Model $\rightarrow$ Facts about the phenomenon.

Because facts about phenomena are not directly measured but must be inferred from the observed data, we need to consider the reliability of the data. These considerations cannot be derived from theory but are based on a closer investigation of the experimental design, the equipment used, and need a statistical underpinning. This message was well laid out for econometrics by Haavelmo

(1944, p. 7): 'The data [the economist] actually obtains are, first of all, nearly always blurred by some plain errors of measurement, that is, by certain extra "facts" which he did not intend to "explain" by his theory'.

If we look at the measuring practices in economics and econometrics, we see that their aims can be formulated as: Measurements are results of modeling efforts for their goal of obtaining quantitative information about economic phenomena. To give an account of these economic measurement practices, the subsequent sections will explore in which directions the representational theory has to be extended. This extension will be based on accounts that deal explicitly with measuring instruments and measurement errors.

9.3. Instrument Measurement

The danger of operationalism, that is, lack of empirical significance in RTM is discussed by Heidelberger (1994a, 1994b), who argues for giving the representational theory a 'correlative interpretation', based on Fechner's principle of mental measurement.

The disadvantage of a general RTM is that it is much too liberal. As Heidelberger argues, we could not make any difference between a theoretical determination of the value of a theoretical quantity and the actual measurement. A correlative interpretation does not have this disadvantage, because it refers to the handling of a measuring instrument. This interpretation of the representational theory of measurement is based on Fechner's correlational theory of measurement. Fechner had argued that

> the measurement of any attribute Y generally presupposes a second, directly observable attribute X and a measurement apparatus A that can represent variable values of Y in correlation to values of X. The correlation is such that when the states of A are arranged in the order of Y they are also arranged in the order of X. The different values of X are *defined* by an intersubjective, determinate, and repeatable calibration of A. They do not have to be measured on their part. The function that describes the correlation between Y and X relative to A (underlying the measurement of Y by X in A) is precisely what Fechner called the measurement formula. Normally, we try to construct (or find) a measurement apparatus which realizes a 1:1 correlation between the values of Y and the values of X so that we can take the values of X as a direct representation of the value of Y (Heidelberger, 1993, p. 146).[1]

To illustrate this, let us consider an example of temperature measurement. We can measure temperature, Y, by constructing a thermometer, A, that contains a mercury column which length, X, is correlated with temperature: $X = F(Y)$. The measurement formula, the function describing the correlation between the values of Y and X, $x = f(y)$, is determined by choosing the shape of the function, f, e.g. linear, and by calibration. For example, the temperature of boiling water is fixed at 100, and of ice water at 0.

---

[1] I have replaced the symbols Q and R in the original text by the symbols Y and X, respectively, to make the discussion of the measurement literature uniform.

The correlative interpretation of measurement implies that the scales of measurement are a specific form of indirect scales, namely so-called associative scales. This terminology is from Ellis (1968). To understand what these scales entail, we first have a closer look at direct measurement; thereupon we will discuss Ellis' account of indirect measurements and finally explicate instrument measurement.

A *direct* measurement scale for a class of measurands is one based entirely on relations among that class and not involving the use of measurements of any other class. This type of scale is implied by the definition of the representational theory of measurement above, see Fig. 9.1, and is also called a *fundamental* scale. Direct measurement assumes direct observability – human perception without the aid of any instrument – of the measurand.

However, there are properties, like temperature, for which it is not possible or convenient to construct satisfactory direct scales of measurement. Scales for the measurement of such properties can, however, be constructed, based on the relation of that property, Y, and quantities, X^i $(i = 1, \ldots, m)$, with which it is associated and for which measurement scales have been defined. Such scales are termed *indirect*. *Associative* measurement depends on there being some quantity X associated with property Y to be measured, such that when things are arranged in the order of Y, under specific conditions, they are also arranged in the order of X. This association is indicated by F in Fig. 9.2. An associative scale for the measurement of Y is then defined by taking $h(\phi(X))$ as the measure of Y, where $\phi(X)$ is the measure of X on some previously defined scale, and h is any strictly monotonic increasing function. Associative measurement can be pictured as an extended version of direct measurement, see Fig. 9.2.

We have *derived* measurement if there exists an empirical law $h = h(\phi_1(X^1), \ldots, \phi_m(X^m))$ and if it is the case that whenever things are ordered in the order of Y, they are also arranged in the order of h. Then we can define $h(\phi_1(X^1), \ldots, \phi_m(X^m))$ as a derived scale for the measurement of Y.

The measurement problem then is the choice of the associated property X and the choice of h, which Ellis following Mach called the 'choice of principle of correlation'.[2] The central idea of associative measurement, which stood in the center of Mach's philosophy of science, is that 'in measuring any attribute we always have to take into account its empirical lawful relation to (at least) another attribute. The distinction between fundamental [read: direct] and derived [read: indirect] measurement, at least in a relevant epistemological sense, is illusory' (Heidelberger, 1994b, p. 11).

In addition to direct (fundamental) and indirect (associative and derived), a third type, called *instrument measurement*, may be noted. This kind of measurement, involving an instrument, was also mentioned by Suppes and Zinnes

---

[2] Ellis' account of associative measurement is based on Mach's (1968) chapter 'Kritik des Temperaturbegriffes' from his book *Die Principien der Wärmelehre* (Leipizg, 1896). This chapter was translated into English and added to Ellis' (1968) book as Appendix I.

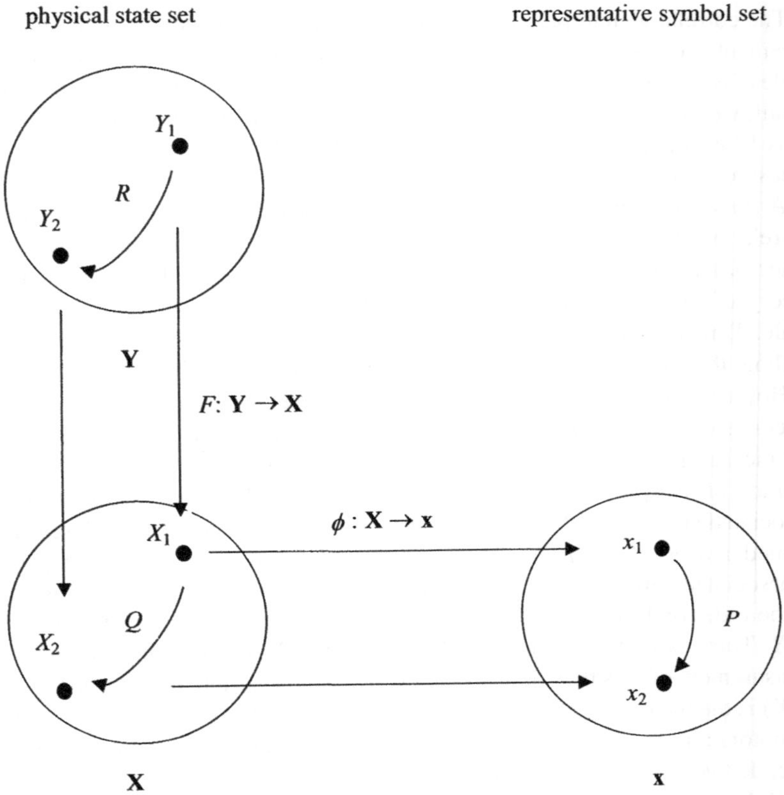

Fig. 9.2: Associative measurement.

(1963), where it was called 'pointer measurement', but its discussion disappeared in later accounts of RTM. Generally, by instrument measurement we mean a numerical assignment based on the direct readings of some validated instrument. A measuring instrument is validated if it has been shown to yield numerical values that correspond to those of some numerical assignments under certain standard conditions. This is also called calibration, which in metrology is defines as: 'set of operations that establish, under specified conditions, the relationship between values of quantities indicated by a measuring instrument or measuring system, or values represented by a material measure or a reference material, and the corresponding values realized by standards' (IVM, 1993, p. 48). To construct a measuring instrument, it is generally necessary to utilize some established empirical law or association.

One difference between Ellis' associative measurement and Heidelberger's correlative interpretation of measurement, that is instrument measurement, is that, according to Heidelberger, the mapping of X into numbers, $\phi(X)$, is not the result of (direct) measurement but is obtained by calibration (see Heidelberger's quote above). To determine the scale of the thermometer no prior measurement of the expansion of the mercury column is required; by convention it is decided in how many equal parts the interval between two fixed points (melting point and boiling point) should be divided.

Another difference between both accounts is that Heidelberger's account involves the crucial role of measuring devices to maintain the association between Y and X. To represent the correlative interpretation, Fig. 9.3 is an expansion of Fig. 9.2 by adding the measurement apparatus A to maintain the association F between the observations $X \in \mathbf{X}$ and the not-directly-observable states of the measurand $Y \in \mathbf{Y}$. A correlative scale for the measurement of Y is then defined by taking

$$x = \phi(X) = \phi\big(F(Y, OC)\big) \tag{9.1}$$

where $\phi(X)$ is the measure of X on some previously defined scale. The correlation F also involves other influences indicated by OC. OC, an acronym of

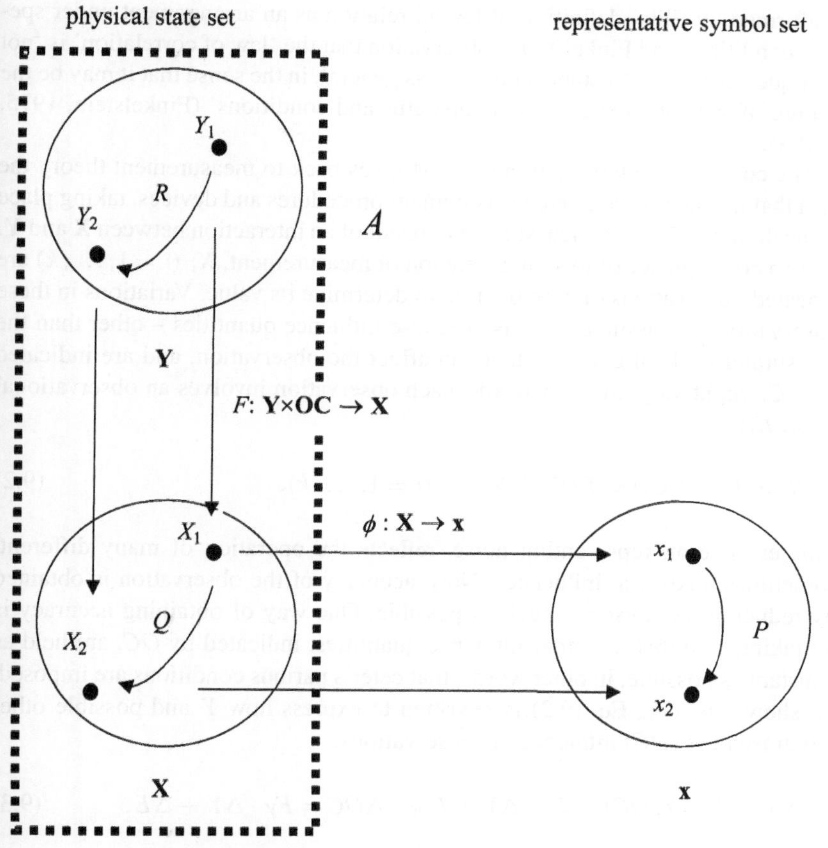

Fig. 9.3: Instrument measurement.

'other circumstances', is a collective noun of all other quantities that might have an influence on X.

The central idea of instrument measurement is that in measuring any attribute Y we always have to take into account its empirical lawful relation to (at least) another attribute X. To establish this relation we need a measurement apparatus or experimental arrangement, A. In other words, a measuring instrument had to function as a nomological machine. This idea is based on Cartwright's account that a law of nature – necessary regular association between properties – hold only relative to the successful repeated operation of a 'nomological machine', which she defines as:

> a fixed (enough) arrangement of components, or factors with stable (enough) capacities that in the right sort of stable (enough) environment will, with repeated operation, give rise to the kind of regular behavior that we represent in our scientific laws (Cartwright, 1999, p. 50).

It shows why empirical lawful relations on which measurement is based and measuring instruments are two sides of the same coin. The measuring instrument must function as a nomological machine to fulfill its task. This interconnection is affirmed by Ellis' definition of lawful relation as an arrangement under specific conditions and Finkelstein's observation that the 'law of correlation' is 'not infrequently less well established and less general, in the sense that it may be the feature of specially experimental apparatus and conditions' (Finkelstein, 1975, p. 108).

The correlative interpretation of RTM gives back to measurement theory the idea that it concerns concrete measurement procedures and devices, taking place in the domain of the physical states as a result of an interaction between **X** and **Y**.

As a consequence of this interpretation of measurement, X_i $(i = 1, \ldots, k)$ are repeated observations of Y to be used to determine its value. Variations in these observations are assumed to arise because influence quantities – other than the measurand itself of course – that can affect the observation, and are indicated by OC, might vary. In other words, each observation involves an observational error, E_i:

$$X_i = F(Y, OC_i) = F(Y, 0) + E_i \quad (i = 1, \ldots, k). \tag{9.2}$$

This error term, representing noise, reflects the operation of many different, sometimes unknown, influences. Now, accuracy of the observation is obtained by reducing the noise as much as possible. One way of obtaining accuracy is by taking care that the other influence quantities, indicated by OC, are held as constant as possible, in other words, that ceteris paribus conditions are imposed. To show this idea, Eq. (9.2) is rewritten to express how Y and possible other circumstances (OC) influence the observations:

$$\Delta X = \Delta F(Y, OC) = F_Y \cdot \Delta Y + F_{OC} \cdot \Delta OC = F_Y \cdot \Delta Y + \Delta E. \tag{9.3}$$

Thus, imposing ceteris paribus conditions, $\Delta OC \approx 0$, reduces noise $\Delta E \approx 0$.

Equation (9.3) shows that accuracy can be obtained 'in the right sort of stable (enough) environment' by imposing ceteris paribus conditions (*cp*), which also might include even stronger ceteris absentibus conditions: $OC \approx 0$. As a result the remaining factor Y can be varied in a systematic way to gain knowledge about the relation between Y and X:

$$F_Y = \frac{\Delta X_{cp}}{\Delta Y}. \tag{9.4}$$

If the ratio of the variation of X_{cp} and the variation of Y appears to be stable, the correlation is an invariant relationship and can thus be used for measurement aims.

So, an observation in a controlled experiment is an accurate measurement because of the stabilization of background noise ($\Delta E = 0 \rightarrow E$ is stable: $E = S$).

$$x_{cp} = \phi(X_{cp}) = \phi\big(F(Y, S)\big). \tag{9.5}$$

Knowledge about stable conditions S is used for calibrating the instrument.

However, both kinds of conditions imply (almost) full control of the circumstances and (almost) complete knowledge about all potential influence quantities. Besides uncertainty about the observations, in both natural and social science, due to inadequate knowledge about the environmental conditions OC, there is an additional problem of control in economics. Fortunately, a measuring instrument can also be designed, fabricated or used that the influences of all these uncontrollable circumstances are negligible. Using expression (9.3), this means that it is designed and constructed such that $F_{OC} \approx 0$. In other words, a measuring device should be constructed and used such that it is sensitive to changes in Y and at the same time insensitive to changes in the other circumstances (OC), which is therefore called here the ceteris neglectis condition. In economics, the environment often cannot be furnished for measurement purposes, so, a 'natural' nomological machine A have to be looked for satisfying ceteris neglectis requirements. If we have a system fulfilling the ceteris neglectis condition, we do not have to worry about the extent to which the other conditions are changing. They do not have to be controlled as is assumed by the conventional ceteris paribus requirements. Whenever we cannot control the phenomenon's environment, we have to look for a 'natural' system that can function as a measuring instrument. Therefore it is only required that it obeys ceteris neglectis requirements.

Observation with a natural system A that we cannot control – so-called passive observation – does not, however, solve the problem of achieving accuracy. The remaining problem is that it is not possible to identify the reason for a disturbing influence, say Z, being negligible, $F_Z \cdot \Delta Z \approx 0$. We cannot distinguish, 'identify', whether its potential influence is very small, $F_Z \approx 0$, or whether the factual variation of this quantity over the period under consideration is too small, $\Delta Z \approx 0$. The variation of Z is determined by other relationships within the economic system. In some cases, a virtually dormant quantity may become active because of changes in the economic system elsewhere. Each found empirical relationship is a representation of a specific data set. So, for each data set it is not clear whether potential influences are negligible or only dormant.

In practice, the difficulty in economic research does not lie in establishing simple relations, but rather in the fact that the empirically found relations, derived from observations over certain time periods, are still simpler than we expect them to be from theory, so that we are thereby led to throw away elements of a theory that would be sufficient to explain apparent 'breaks in structure' later. This is what Haavelmo (1944) called the problem of autonomy. Some of the empirical found relations have very little 'autonomy' because their existence depends upon the simultaneous fulfillment of a great many other relations. Autonomous relations are those relations that could be expected to have a great degree of invariance with respect to various changes in the economic system.

Confronted with the inability of control, social scientists deal with the problem of invariance and accuracy by using models as virtual laboratories. Morgan (2003) discusses the differences between 'material experiments' and 'mathematical models as experiments'. In a mathematical model, control is not materialized but assumed. As a result, accuracy has to be obtained in a different way. Accuracy is dealt with by the strategy of comprehensiveness and it works as follows (see Sutton, 2000): when a relationship appears to be inaccurate, this is an indication that a potential factor is omitted. As long as the resulting relationship is inaccurate, potential relevant factors should be added. The expectation is that this strategy will result in the fulfillment of two requirements:

(1) the resulting model captures a complete list of factors that exert large and systematic influences;
(2) all remaining influences can be treated as a small noise component.

The problem of passive observations is solved by accumulation of data sets: the expectation is that we converge bit by bit to a closer approximation to the complete model, as all the most important factors reveal their influence. This strategy however is not applicable in cases when there are influences that we cannot measure, proxy, or control for, but which exert a large and systematic influence on the outcomes.

To connect this strategy with measurement theory, let us assume a set of observations

$$x_i = f(y) + \varepsilon_i \quad (i = 1, \ldots, k) \tag{9.6}$$

where f is a representation of the correlation F and ε_i is a symbolic representation of the observational errors E_i. To transform the set of observations into a measurement result the specification of a model is needed. So, to measure Y a model M has to be specified of which the values of the observations x_i functions as input and the output estimate $\hat{y}$ as measurement result. If – and in economics this is often the case – data indicate that M does not model the measurand to

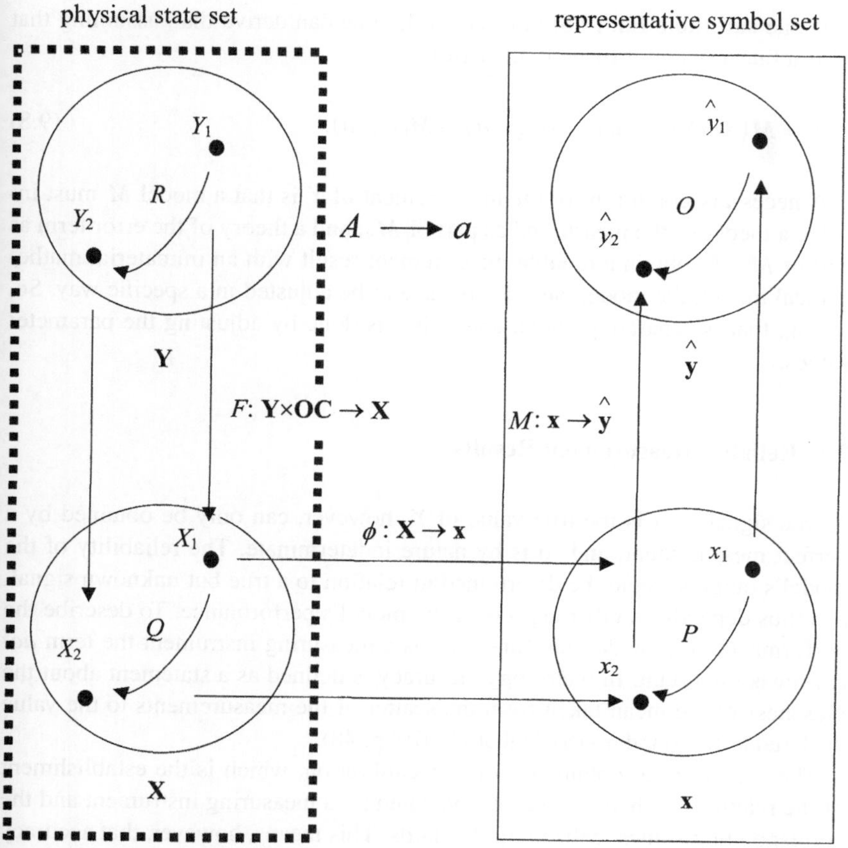

Fig. 9.4: Model measurement.

the degree imposed by the required accuracy of the measurement result, additional input quantities must be included in M to eliminate this inaccuracy. This may require introducing input quantities to reflect incomplete knowledge of a phenomenon that affects the measurand. This means that the model has to incorporate a representation of the full nomological machine A, denoted by a, that is should represent both properties of the phenomenon to be measured as well as the background conditions influencing the observations. To take account of this aspect of measurement, Fig. 9.3 has to be further expanded as shown in Fig. 9.4.

When one has to deal with a natural measuring system A that can only be observed passively, the measurement procedure is first to infer from the observations X_i nature's design of this system to determine next the value of the measurand Y. So, first an adequate representation a of system A has to be specified before we can estimate the value of Y. A measurement result is thus given by

$$\hat{y} = M(x_i; a). \tag{9.7}$$

If one substitute Eq. (9.6) into model M, one can derive that, assuming that M is a linear operator (usually the case):

$$\hat{y} = M\big(f(y) + \varepsilon_i; a\big) = M_y(y; a) + M_\varepsilon(\varepsilon_i; a). \tag{9.8}$$

A necessary condition for the measurement of Y is that a model M must involve a theory of the measurand as part of M_y, and a theory of the error term as part of M_ε. To obtain a reliable measurement result with an immaterial mathematical model, the model parameters have to be adjusted in a specific way. So, tuning, that is separating signal and noise, is done by adjusting the parameter values.

9.4. Reliable Measurement Results

A true signal, that is the true value of Y, however, can only be obtained by a perfect measurement, and so is by nature indeterminate. The reliability of the model's outputs cannot be determined in relation to a true but unknown signal, and thus depends on other aspects of the model's performance. To describe the performance of a model that functions as a measuring instrument the term *accuracy* is important. In metrology, accuracy is defined as a statement about the closeness of the mean taken from the scatter of the measurements to the value declared as the standard (Sydenham, 1979, p. 48).

The procedure to obtain accuracy is calibration, which is the establishment of the relationship between values indicated by a measuring instrument and the corresponding values realized by standards. This means, however, that accuracy can only be assessed in terms of a standard. In this context, a standard is a representation (model) of the properties of the phenomenon as they appear under well-defined conditions.

To discuss this problem in more detail, we split the measurement error in three parts:

$$\hat{\varepsilon} = \hat{y} - y = M_\varepsilon + (M_y - S) + (S - y) \tag{9.9}$$

where S represents the standard. The error term M_ε is reduced as much as possible by reducing the spread of the error terms, in other words by aiming at precision. $(M_x - S)$ is the part of the error term that is reduced by calibration. So, both errors terms can be dealt with by mechanical procedures. However, the reduction of the last term $(S - y)$ can only dealt with by involving theoretical assumptions about the phenomenon and independent empirical studies. Note that the value y is not known. Often the term $(S - y)$ is reduced by building as accurate representations a of the economic system as possible. This third step is called standardization.

9.5. Economic Modeling

An often-used method of evaluation in economics to verify whether the model of the economic system is accurate is to test it on its predictive performance. The modeling procedure is to add to the model a variable, suggested by theory, each time the model predictions can be improved. So, in this above-mentioned strategy of comprehensiveness, two models, I and II, are compared with each other, and the one that provides the best predictions is chosen.

In economics, these representations are often assumed to be linear operators. From now on, therefore, a denotes a matrix: $a = (\alpha_{ij})$, where α_{ij} are the matrix parameters, and x and y denote vectors. The subscript t denotes time:

$$\text{Model I:} \quad \hat{x}^{I}_{it+1} = \sum_{j=1}^{k} \alpha^{I}_{ij} x_{jt} \quad (i\colon 1, \ldots, k), \tag{9.10}$$

$$\text{Model II:} \quad \hat{x}^{II}_{it+1} = \sum_{j=1}^{k+1} \alpha^{II}_{ij} x_{jt} \quad (i\colon 1, \ldots, k+1). \tag{9.11}$$

If $\|x_{it+1} - \hat{x}^{II}_{it+1}\| < \|x_{it+1} - \hat{x}^{I}_{it+1}\|$ for the majority of these error terms $(i\colon 1, \ldots, k)$ and where $\|\cdot\|$ is a statistically defined norm, choose model II. Note that for each additional quantity the model is enlarged with an extra (independent) equation. As a result, the prediction errors are assumed to be reduced by taking into account more and more potential influence quantities. As long as all potential influences are indirectly measurable by the observational proxies, there is no problem, in principle. As data sets accumulate, it might reasonably be expected that the model converge bit by bit to a more accurate representation of the economic system, as all the most important x's reveal their potential influence. But what if there are quantities that cannot be (indirectly) measured, and which exert a large and systematic influence on outcomes? Then their presence will induce a bias in the measurement. This doubt about this strategy was enforced by empirical research that showed large-scale models failed to be better predicting devices than very simple low-order autoregressive (AR) models, or simple autoregressive moving average (ARMA) models, which are used to study time series.

In interpreting these results, Milton Friedman (1951) suggested that the programme of building comprehensive large-scale models is probably faulty and needs reformulation. For him, the ability to predict is the quality of a model that should be evaluated not its realisticness. This methodological standpoint is spelled out in the among economists well-known article 'The Methodology of Positive Economics' (Friedman, 1951). The strategy he suggests is to keep the model a as small as possible by avoiding to model the 'other circumstances' OC and instead to search for those systems for which a is an accurate model (tested by its predictive power). In other words, try to decide by empirical research for which systems the other circumstances are negligible ($F_{OC} \approx 0$). Enlargement of the model is only justified if it is required by the phenomenon to be measured. The relevant question to ask about a model is not whether it is descriptively realistic but whether it is a sufficiently good approximation for the purpose at hand. In this kind of empirical research, the strategy is to start with simple models and to investigate for which domain these models are accurate descriptions.

A very influential paper in macroeconomics (Lucas, 1976) showed that the estimated so-called structural parameters (α_{ij}) achieved by the above strategy are not invariant under changes of policy rules. The problem is that the model equations in economics are often representations of behavioral relationships. Lucas has emphasized that economic agents form expectations of the future and that these expectations play a crucial role in the economy because they influence the behavior of economic actors. People's expectations depend on many things, including the economic policies being pursued by governments and central banks. Thus, estimating the effect of a policy change requires knowing how people's expectations will respond to policy changes. Lucas has argued that the above estimation methods do not sufficiently take into account the influence of changing expectations on the estimated parameter values. Lucas assumed that economic agents have 'rational expectations', that is the expectations based on all information available at time t and they know the model, a, which they use to form these expectations.

Policy-invariant parameters should be obtained in an alternative way. Either they could be supplied from micro-econometric studies, accounting identities, or institutional facts, or they are chosen to secure a good match between a selected set of the characteristics of the actual observed time-series and those of the simulated model output. This latter method is a method of estimation which entails simulating a model with ranges of parameters and selecting from these ranges those elements that best match properties of the simulated data with those of the observed time series. An often-used criterion is to measure the difference between some empirical moments computed on the observed variables x_t and its simulated counterpart $\hat{x}_t$. Let $m(x)$ be the vector of various sample moments, and $m(x)$ could include the sample means and variances of a selected set of observable variables. $m(\hat{x})$ is the vector of simulated moments, that is, the moments of the simulations $\hat{x}(a)$. Then the estimation of the parameters is based on:

$$a_{MSM} = \arg\min_{a} \left\| m(x) - m\big(\hat{x}(a)\big) \right\|. \tag{9.12}$$

These alternative ways of obtaining parameter values is in economics labeled as calibration. Important is that whatever the source is, the facts being used for calibration should be as stable as possible. However, one should note that in social science, standards or constants do not exist in the sense as they do in natural science: lesser universal, more local and of shorter duration. In general, calibration in economics works as follows: use stable facts about a phenomenon to adjust the model parameters.

As a result of Lucas' critique on structural-equations estimations, he introduced a new program for economics, labeled as 'general-equilibrium economics', in which it is no longer required for representations being homomorphic to an empirical relational structure. One should not aim at models as 'accurate descriptive representations of reality':

> A 'theory' is not a collection of assertions about the behavior of the actual economy but rather an explicit set of instructions for building a parallel or analogue system – a mechanical, imitation economy. A 'good' model, from this point of view, will not be exactly more 'real' than a poor one, but will provide better imitations. Of course, what one means by a 'better imitation' will depend on the particular questions to which one wishes answers (Lucas, 1980, pp. 696–697).

This approach was based on Simon's (1969) account of artifacts, which he defines as

> a meeting point – an 'interface' in today's terms – between an 'inner' environment, the substance and organization of the artifact itself, and an 'outer' environment, the surroundings in which it operates. If the inner environment is appropriate to the outer environment, or vice versa, the artifact will serve its intended purpose (Simon, 1969, p. 7).

The advantage of factoring an artificial system into goals, outer environment, and inner environment is that we can predict behavior from knowledge of the system's goals and its outer environment, with only minimal assumptions about the inner environment. It appears that different inner environments accomplish identical goals in similar outer environments, such as weight-driven clocks and spring-driven clocks. A second advantage is that, in many cases, whether a particular system will achieve a particular goal depends on only a few characteristics of the outer environment, and not on the detail of that environment, which might lead to simple models. A model is useful only if it foregoes descriptive realism and selects limited features of reality to reproduce.

Lucas' program was most explicitly implemented by Kydland and Prescott (1996). According to them, any economic 'computational experiment' involves five major steps:

1. *Pose a question*: The purpose of a computational experiment is to derive a quantitative answer to some well-posed question.
2. *Use well-tested theory*: Needed is a theory that has been tested through use and found to provide reliable answers to a class of questions. A theory is not a set of assertions about the actual economy, rather, following Lucas (1980), defined to be an explicit set of instructions for building a mechanical imitation system to answer a question.
3. *Construct a model economy*: An abstraction can be judged only relative to some given question. The features of a given model may be appropriate for some question (or class of questions) but not for others.
4. *Calibrate the model economy*: In a sense, model economies, like thermometers, are measuring devices. Generally, some economic questions have known answers, and the model should give an approximately correct answer to them if we are to have any confidence in the answer given to the question with unknown answer. Thus, data are used to calibrate the model economy so that it

mimics the world as closely as possible along a limited but clearly specified, number of dimensions.

5. *Run the experiment.*

Kydland and Prescott's specific kind of assessment is similar to Lucas' idea of testing, although Lucas didn't call it calibration. To test models as 'useful imitations of reality' we should subject them to shocks 'for which we are fairly certain how actual economies, or parts of economies, would react. The more dimensions on which the model mimics the answer actual economies give to simple questions, the more we trust its answer to harder questions' (Lucas, 1980, pp. 696–697). This kind of testing is similar to calibration as defined by Franklin (1997, p. 31): 'the use of a surrogate signal to standardize an instrument. If an apparatus reproduces known phenomena, then we legitimately strengthen our belief that the apparatus is working properly and that the experimental results produced with that apparatus are reliable'.

The economic questions, for which we have known answers, or, the standard facts with which the model is calibrated, were most explicitly given by Cooley and Prescott (1995). They describe calibration as a selection of the parameters values for the model economy so that it mimics the actual economy on dimensions associated with long-term growth by setting these values equal to certain 'more or less constant' ratios. These ratios were the so-called 'stylized facts' of economic growth, 'striking empirical regularities both over time and across countries', the 'benchmarks of the theory of economic growth'.

What we have seen above is that in modern macroeconomics, the assessment of models as measuring instruments is not based on the evaluation of the homomorphic correspondence between the empirical relational structure and the numerical relational structure. The assessment of these models is more like what is called *validation* in systems engineering. Validity of a model is seen as 'usefulness with respect to some purpose'. Barlas (1996) notes that for an exploration of the notion validation it is crucial to make a distinction between white-box models and black-box models. In black-box models, what matters is the output behavior of the model. The model is assessed to be valid if its output matches the 'real' output within some specified range of accuracy, without any questioning of the validity of the individual relationships that exists in the model. White-box models, on the contrary, are statements as to how real systems actually operate in some aspects. Generating an accurate output behavior is not sufficient for model validity; the validity of the internal structure of the model is crucial too. A white-box model must not only reproduce the behavior of a real system, but also explain how the behavior is generated.

Barlas (1996) discusses three stages of model validation: 'direct structural tests', 'structure-oriented behavior tests' and 'behavior pattern tests'. For white models, all three stages are equally important, for black box models only the last stage matters. Barlas emphasizes the special importance of structure-oriented behavior tests: these are strong behavior tests that can provide information on potential structure flaws. The information, however, provided by these tests does not give any direct access to the structure, in contrast to the direct structure tests.

Though Barlas emphasizes that structure-oriented behavior tests are designed to evaluate the validity of the model structure, his usage of the notion of structure needs some further qualification. The way in which he describes and discusses these tests show that his notion of structure is not limited to homomorphic representations of real system's structures; it also includes other kinds of arrangements. Structure-oriented behavior tests are also 'strong' for the validation of modular-designed models, and for these models the term structure refers to the way the modules are assembled. A module is a self-contained component with a standard interface to their components within a system. Modular design simplifies final assembly because there are fewer modules than subcomponents and because standard interfaces typically are designed for ease of fit (see also den Butter's discussion of flexibility in Chapter 8). Each module can be tested prior to assembly and, in the field, repairs can be made by replacing defective modules. Custom systems can be realized by different combinations of standard components; existing systems can be upgraded with improved modules; and new systems can be realized by new combinations of existing and improved modules (White, 1999, p. 475). These models – in line with the labeling of the other two types of models – could be called gray-box models and should pass the structure-oriented behavior tests and behavior pattern tests. Gray-box models are validated by the kinds of tests that in the general-equilibrium literature all fall under the general heading of 'calibration', where it is defined generally enough to cover all tests which Barlas (1996) called structure-oriented behavior tests. To achieve accurate measurement results, the models that are used should be calibrated and need not to be accurate representations of the relevant economic systems.

References

Barlas, Y. (1996). Formal aspects of model validity and validation in system dynamics. *System Dynamics Review* **12** (3), 183–210.

Campbell, N.R. (1928). *Account of the Principles of Measurement and Calculation*. Longmans, Green, London.

Cartwright, N. (1999). *The Dappled World. A Study of the Boundaries of Science*. Cambridge Univ. Press, Cambridge.

Cooley, T.F., Prescott, E.C. (1995). Economic growth and business cycles. In: Cooley, T.F. (Ed.), *Frontiers of Business Cycle Research*. Princeton Univ. Press, Princeton, pp. 1–38.

Ellis, B. (1968). *Basic Concepts of Measurement*. Cambridge Univ. Press, Cambridge.

Finkelstein, L. (1975). Fundamental concepts of measurement: Definition and scales. *Measurement and Control* **8**, 105–110.

Franklin, A. (1997). Calibration. *Perspectives on Science* **5**, 31–80.

Friedman, M. (1951). The methodology of positive economics. In: *Essays in Positive Economics*. Univ. of Chicago Press, Chicago, pp. 3–43.

Haavelmo, T. (1944). The probability approach in econometrics. *Econometrica* **12**. Supplement.

Heidelberger, M. (1993). Fechner's impact for measurement theory. *Behavioral and Brain Sciences* **16** (1), 146–148.

Heidelberger, M. (1994a). Alternative Interpretationen der Repräsentationstheorie der Messung. In: Meggle, G., Wessels, U. (Eds.), *Proceedings of the 1st Conference "Perspectives in Analytical Philosophy"*. Walter de Gruyter, Berlin and New York, pp. 310–323.

Heidelberger, M. (1994b). Three strands in the history of the representational theory of measurement. Working paper. Humboldt University, Berlin.
IVM (1993). International Vocabulary of Basic and General Terms in Metrology, second ed. International Organization for Standardization, Geneva.
Kydland, F.E., Prescott, E.C. (1996). The computational experiment: An econometric tool. *Journal of Economic Perspectives* **10** (1), 69–85.
Lucas, R.E. (1976). Econometric policy evaluation: A critique. In: Brunner, K., Meltzer, A.H. (Eds.), *The Phillips Curve and Labor Markets*. North-Holland, Amsterdam, pp. 19–46.
Lucas, R.E. (1980). Methods and problems in business cycle theory. *Journal of Money, Credit, and Banking* **12**, 696–715.
Mach, E. [1896] (1968). Critique of the concept of temperature. In: Ellis, B. (Ed.), *Basic Concepts of Measurement*. Cambridge Univ. Press, Cambridge, pp. 183–196 (translated by M.J. Scott-Taggart and B. Ellis).
Morgan, M.S. (2003). Experiments without material intervention: Model experiments, virtual experiments, and virtually experiments. In: Radder, H. (Ed.), *The Philosophy of Scientific Experimentation*. Univ. of Pittsburgh Press, Pittsburgh, pp. 216–235.
Simon, H.A. (1969). *The Sciences of the Artificial*. MIT Press, Cambridge.
Stevens, S.S. (1959). Measurement, psychophysics, and utility. In: Churchman, C.W., Ratoosh, P. (Eds.), *Measurement. Definitions and Theories*. Wiley, New York, pp. 18–63.
Suppes, P., Zinnes, J.L. (1963). Basic measurement theory. In: Luce, R.D., Bush, R.R., Galanter, E. (Eds.), Handbook of Mathematical Psychology. Wiley, New York, London and Sydney, pp. 1–76.
Sutton, J. (2000). *Marshall's Tendencies: What Can Economists Know*? Leuven Univ. Press, Leuven and The MIT Press, Cambridge and London.
Sydenham, P.H. (1979). *Measuring Instruments: Tools of Knowledge and Control*. Peter Peregrinus, London.
White, K.P. (1999). System Design. In: Sage, A.P., Rouse, W.B. (Eds.), *Handbook of Systems Engineering and Management*. Wiley, New York, pp. 455–481.
Woodward, J. (1989). Data and phenomena. *Synthese* **79**, 393–472.

PART III

Representation in Econometrics

CHAPTER 10

Representation in Econometrics: A Historical Perspective

Christopher L. Gilbert[a] and Duo Qin[b]

[a] *Dipartimento di Economia, Università degli Studi di Trento, Italy*
E-mail address: cgilbert@economia.unitn.it

[b] *Department of Economics, Queen Mary, University of London, UK*
E-mail address: d.qin@qmul.ac.uk

Abstract

Measurement forms the substance of econometrics. This chapter outlines the history of econometrics from a measurement perspective – how have measurement errors been dealt with and how, from a methodological standpoint, did econometrics evolve so as to represent theory more adequately in relation to data? The evolution is organised in terms of four phases: 'theory and measurement', 'measurement and theory', 'measurement with theory' and 'measurement without theory'. The question of how measurement research has helped in the advancement of knowledge advance is discussed in the light of this history.

10.1. Prologue

Frisch (1933) defined econometrics as 'a unification of the theoretical-quantitative and the empirical-quantitative approach to economic problems ... by constructive and rigorous thinking similar to that which has come to dominate in the natural sciences'. Measurement has occupied a central place in econometrics and the econometric approach to measurement attempted to emulate that of physics.[1] However, the road to achieving adequate econometric measurements has been bumpy and tortuous, as economics, obliged in the main to rely in non-controllable data, is distinctly different from physics (see e.g. Boumans, 2005). Questions and problems include: What to measure? By what instruments? How to evaluate the measured products, particularly against observed data as well as available theories?

We chart the evolution of econometrics to demonstrate how the above questions have been tackled by econometricians. In other words, we offer a brief

---

[1] There was a strong sense to make 'modern economics' 'scientific', as apposed to humanity, e.g. see Schumpeter (1933) and Mirowski (1989).

historical narrative organised with respect to a measurement perspective. It is not our intention to provide a comprehensive history of econometrics. Rather, our objective is to develop an account of the way in which measurement research in econometrics has helped knowledge advancement. As such, the account is presented from a largely retrospective angle.

There is no unanimous approach to measurement and representation in econometrics. From the measurement viewpoint, we can categorise the evolution of econometrics into three approaches:

- the orthodox structural approach which closely follows the measurement approach of hard science;
- the reformist approach which places measurement in a soft system but does not diverge methodologically from the scientific approach; and
- the heterodox approach which we discuss as 'measurement without theory'.

An initial distinction is between data measurement and theory measurement. The fundamental difference between data measurement and theory measurement is that the former purports to make fact-like statements as to how the world is while the latter is concerned with the quantification of counterfactual statements about how the world might otherwise be. Although we acknowledge that data are always measured relative to and within a theoretical framework, data measurement takes these theoretical constructs as given while theory measurement moves those issues to the foreground and takes the data measurement instruments as being both reliable and neutral with respect to competing theories. This allows us to rely on the modern distinction between economic statistics (data measurement) and econometrics (theory measurement) and focus only on the latter. Within an econometric context, measurement theory focuses on the identification of those measurable attributes of the observed phenomena which reflect economically interesting (in the sense of lawful and invariant) properties of the phenomena (e.g. see Luce et al., 1990) and also Chapter 6 by Backhouse and Chapter 9 by Boumans in this volume. Data measurement is the subject of Chapter 8.

Both econometric theory and practice have adapted over time in the face of problems with earlier theory and practice (such as residual serial correlation and poor forecasting performance), new questions (for example, those generated by the Rational Expectations hypothesis) and fresh challenges (such as the availability of large data sets and fast computers). Some of these demands forced econometricians to re-hone their tools to be able to respond in the new situations – tool adaptation. In other instances, it was not the tools that needed to be adapted but rather the models on which the tools were employed. It was model adaptation which forced the most dramatic changes in the econometric approach to measurement.

10.2. Economic Theory and Measurement[2]

Economists have been concerned with quantification from at least the nineteenth century. Morgan's (1990) history of econometrics starts with W.S. Jevons' attempts to relate business cycles to sunspots (Jevons, 1884). Jevons (1871) was also the first economist to 'fit' a demand equation although Morgan (1990) attributes the first empirical demand function to C. Davenant (1699) at the end of the seventeenth century. Klein (2001) documents measurement of cyclical phenomena commencing with W. Playfair's studies of the rise and decline of nations published during the Napoleonic War (Playfair, 1801, 1805). Hoover and Dowell (2001) discuss the history of measurement of the general price level starting from a digression in Adam Smith's *Wealth of Nations* (Smith, 1776).

More focused empirical studies occurred during the first three decades of the twentieth century. These studies explored various ways of characterising certain economic phenomena, e.g. the demand for a certain product, or its price movement, or the cyclical movement of a composite price index by means of mathematical/statistical measures which would represent certain regular attribute of the phenomena concerned, e.g. see Morgan (1990), Gilbert and Qin (2006) and the Chapter by Chao in this volume. These studies demonstrate a concerted endeavour to transform economics into a scientific discipline through the development of precise and quantifiable measures for the loose and unquantified concepts and ideas widely used in traditional economic discussions.

This broad conception of the role of econometrics continued to be reflected in textbooks written in the first two post-war decades in which econometrics was equated to empirical economics, with emphasis on the measurability in economic relationships. Klein (1974, p. 1) commences the second edition of his 1952 textbook by stating 'Measurement in economics is the subject matter of this volume'. In Klein (1962, p. 1) he says 'The main objective of econometrics is to give empirical content to a priori reasoning in econometrics'. This view of econometrics, which encompassed specification issues and issues of measurement as well as statistical estimation, lagged formal developments in the statistical theory of econometrics.

The formalisation of econometrics was rooted directly in the 'structural method' proposed by Frisch in the late 1930s (1937, 1938). Much of the formalisation was stimulated by the famous Keynes–Tinbergen debate, see Hendry and Morgan (1995, Part VI), and resulted in econometrics becoming a distinct sub-discipline of economics. The essential groundwork of the formalisation comprised the detailed theoretical scheme laid out by Haavelmo (1944) on the basis of probability theory and the work of the Cowles Commission (CC) which elaborated technical aspects of Haavelmo's scheme, see Koopmans (1950) and Hood and Koopmans (1953).[3]

---

[2] This is from the title of the Cowles Commission twenty year research report, see Christ (1952).
[3] For more detailed historical description, see Qin (1993) and Gilbert and Qin (2006).

The Haavelmo-CC edifice defines the core of orthodox econometrics. It is often referred to as the structural approach and may be summarised from several perspectives. At a broad methodological level, it attempted to systematically bridge theory and empirical research in a logically rigorous manner. Specifically, the CC research principle was to make all assumptions explicit in order to facilitate discovery of problems and revision of the assumptions in the light of problems that might subsequently emerge. The assumptions should be as consistent as possible with knowledge of human behaviour and are classified into two types: the first are those assumptions which are statistically testable and the second are provisional working hypotheses (see Marschak, 1946).

At the level of the economics discipline, demarcation between the economists and the econometricians assigned the job of formulating theoretical models to the economists while the econometricians were to specify and estimate structural models deriving from the economists' theoretical models. This demarcation is explicit, for example, in Malinvaud (1964) who states (p. vii) 'Econometrics may be broadly interpreted to include every application of mathematics or of statistical methods to the study of economic phenomena. ... we shall adopt a narrower interpretation and define the aim of econometrics to be the empirical determination of economic laws'. Johnston (1963, p. 3) offers an even clearer distinction: 'Economic theory consists of the study of ... relations which are supposed to describe the functioning of ... an economic system. The task of econometric work is to estimate these relationships statistically ...'. For both Malinvaud and Johnston, the measurement problem in econometrics was equated with the statistical estimation of parameters of law-like relationships.

At the technical level, the CC researchers formalised econometric procedure on the assumption that they were starting from known and accepted theoretical models relayed to them by economists. The modelling procedure was formulated in terms of a simultaneous-equations model (SEM), which was regarded as the most general (linear) theoretical model form since it encompasses a dynamically extended Walrasian system:

$$A_0 x_t = \sum_{i=1}^{p} A_i x_{t-i} + \varepsilon_t. \tag{10.2.1}$$

The econometric procedure comprised model specification, identification and estimation. Specification amounted to adoption of the normal distribution for ε_t following the forceful arguments given by Haavelmo (1944). Identification amounted to formalisation of the conditions under which the structural parameters of interest, crucially those found in the (generally) non-diagonal matrix A_0, are uniquely estimable.[4] The issue was analysed via a transformation of the

[4] Note that 'identification' carried far wider connotation prior to this formalisation, e.g. see Hendry and Morgan (1989) and Qin (1989).

structural model (10.2.1) into what is now known as the 'reduced-form':

$$x_t = \sum_{i=1}^{p} A_0^{-1} A_i x_{t-i} + A_0^{-1} \varepsilon_t = \sum_{i=1}^{p} \Pi_i x_{t-i} + u_t. \tag{10.2.2}$$

Identification requires that structural parameters A_i should be implied uniquely once the non-structural parameters, Π_i, are estimated from data. The role of structural estimation was to deal with the nonlinear nature of the transformation of $\Pi_i \to A_i$. The principle method adopted was maximum likelihood (ML) estimation. Ideally, the full-information maximum likelihood (FIML) estimator was to be used but a computationally more convenient method, known as limited-information maximum likelihood (LIML) estimator, was developed.

From the viewpoint of measurement research, the Haavelmo-CC formalisation standardised econometrics by firmly accepting the probabilistic model formulation and the application of statistical theory in relation to these probabilistic models as the instruments both for measuring parameters defined in terms of economic relationships which had been postulated a priori and also as the criteria for assessing such measurements. The normality assumption for ε_t was the crucial link in this process since the statistically optimal properties of the ML estimators relies on this assumption. This formalisation was believed to guarantee delivery of the most reliable estimates of structural parameters of interest, in a manner comparable to that which natural scientists, in particular physicists, would aim to attain.

The identification issue occupied a central position in the research agenda of structural econometrics. The research touched, and even went beyond, the demarcation boundary dividing economics and econometrics. The CC formulation of the identification problem categorised econometric models into two types – structural and non-structural (reduced-form) models – and similarly parameters were either structural parameters, which quantify causal behavioural relations, or non-structural parameters, which describe the statistical features of data samples. This demarcation implicitly established the evaluation criterion which came to underlie standard econometrics: optimal statistical measurement of structural models. However, the very fact that the most popular type of economic model, the SEM, is in general unidentifiable forced structural econometricians to deal with an additional model specification issue: 'when is an equation system complete for statistical purposes?' (in Koopmans, 1950; see also Koopmans and Reiersøl, 1950), which essentially makes the starting point of the structural approach untenable from a practical standpoint.[5] Moreover, identification is conditioned upon the causal formulation of the model, specifically the 'causal ordering' of the variables in the SEM. Consequently, research in identification inevitably led the CC group into the territory of structural model

[5] The CC group was conscious of the problem and ascribed it to the lack of good theoretical models, see Koopmans (1957) and also Gilbert and Qin (2006).

formulation, which they had initially wished to take as given (see e.g. Simon, 1953).

10.3. Measurement and Economic Theory

The CC's work set the scientific standard for econometric research. Their work was both further developed (tool adaptation) and subjected to criticism in the decades that followed.

The controversy between maximum likelihood (ML) and least squares (LS) estimation methods illustrates the limits of tool adaptation. The argument is related primarily to the validity of the simultaneous representation of economic interdependence, a model formulation issue (e.g. see Wold, 1954, 1960, 1964). The judgement or evaluation related to actual model performance, e.g. measured accuracy of modelled variables against actual values. The reversal out of ML estimation methods back to LS estimation methods provided a clear illustration of the practical limits of tools rather than model adaptation. The Klein-Goldberger model (1955) provided the test-bed (see Christ, 1960 with Waugh, 1961), offering the final judgement in favour of LS methods.

This was one of a number of debates which suggested that there was relatively little to be gained from more sophisticated estimation methods. An overriding concern which came to be felt among researchers was the need for statistical assessment of model validity. This amounted to a shift in focus from the measurement of structural parameters within a given model to examination of the validity if the model itself. It led to the development of a variety of specification methods and test statistics for empirical models.

One important area of research related to the examination of the classical assumptions with regard to the error term, as these sustain statistical optimality of the chosen estimators.[6] Applied research, in particular consumer demand studies, exposed a common problem: residual serial correlation (e.g. see Orcutt, 1948). From that starting point, subsequent research took two different directions. The first was to search for more sophisticated estimators on the basis of an acceptance of a more complicated error structure but remaining within the originally postulated structural model. Thus in the case of residual serial correlation, we have the Cochrane–Orcutt procedure (1949) while in the case of residual heteroscedasticity, we have feasible general least squares (FGLS) both of which involve two stage estimation procedures. These were instances of tool adaptation. The other direction was to modify the model in such a way as to permit estimation on the basis of the classical assumptions (e.g. Brown's 1952 introduction of partial adjustment model into the consumption function, an early instance of model adaptation).

In later decades, it was model adaptation which came to dominate, especially in the field of time-series econometrics. Statistically, this was facilitated by the

---

[6] For a historical account of the error term in econometrics, see Qin and Gilbert (2001).

ease of transition between model-based tool adaptation and tool-based model adaptation. Methodologically, it was due to a lack of theoretical models which clearly met identification criteria as well as to the increasing dissatisfaction with the performance of estimated structural models, despite the improved statistical rigour of the estimators of the supposedly structural parameters.

The accumulating scepticism about, and distrust of, the CC structural approach stimulated a move towards data-instigated model search. Liu (1960) advocated the use of reduced-form models for forecasting. Nelson (1972) used simple autoregressive-integrated-moving average (ARIMA) models of the Box–Jenkins (1970) type to compare the forecasting performance of the structural model jointly developed by the Federal Reserve Board, MIT and the University of Pennsylvania. He found that the ARIMA time-series models enjoyed a superior forecasting performance. Reviews of the then existing structural macroeconometric models threw up evidence of unsatisfactory forecasts and these were taken as a strong indicator of internal model weakness (see e.g. Evans, 1966; Griliches, 1968; Gordon, 1970).

In terms of tool making, the changed focus on model modification led to development of statistical measures for the evaluation of model performance, rather than directly for parameter measurement. Examples are diagnostic tests, such as the DW test (Durbin and Watson, 1950, 1951) and the Chow test (Chow, 1960). In acknowledgement of the recurrent need for model re-specification, Theil (1957, 1958) incorporated the then available test measures into a step-by-step model misspecification analysis procedure, further loosening the grip of economic theory over the measurement procedures. This movement was later reinforced by the Granger causality (Granger, 1969) and the Hausman misspecification tests (Hausman, 1978), both of which allowed model specification to be determined by statistical fit instead of conformity with theory.

The traffic was two-way and developments in macroeconomics were in part a response to the erosion of the foundations of macroeconometrics in economic theory. Theorists devoted substantial effort to the development of models which would combine a firm basis in individual optimising behaviour with the flexibility of the data-instigated macroeconometric models. This culminated in the rational expectations (RE) movement of the 1970s. At this point, it became apparent that it was no longer practically tenable to carry out econometric modelling under the strict CC assumption of a known structural model. The practical problem centred on finding the best possible model rather than on measuring the parameters of a pre-acknowledged model.

10.4. Measurement with Economic Theory

This section sets out how the second generation of econometricians put model search as the focus of their research.

The RE movement, and especially the component associated with the Lucas' (1976) critique, posed a profound methodological challenge to then current approaches to macroeconometrics. Because expectations of endogenous variables are not directly observed by the econometrician but must be inferred from forecasts generated from the solved model, RE forced econometric researchers to abandon the pretence that true models were known up to the values of the structural parameters. The focus became that of dealing squarely and systematically with the issue of 'model choice'. 'Test, test, test' became the golden rule of macroeconometric research (Hendry, 1980). Three prominent schools of methodology emerged from this trend: the Bayesian approach, the VAR (vector autoregression) approach and the so-called LSE (London School of Economics) approach.

Despite some vocal disagreements, the three approaches shared considerable common ground: in particular the perception that there are serious limitations on the extent to which a priori knowledge is useful in assisting model search. In the macroeconomic context, no matter what level of generality claimed by the theory, this is seldom sufficient to provide econometrician with adequate guidance to fit actual data. Hence, a combination of judgement and computer-based statistical tools tend to play the decisive role during model search at the expense of theory.

The Bayesian approach to econometrics was initially elaborated to enhance the internal consistency of the CC paradigm (see Qin, 1996). The focus was on the treatment of unknown parameters, which the Bayesians believed should be regarded as random rather than deterministic. However, early results showed that 'for many (perhaps most) statistical problems which arise in practice the difference between Bayesian methods and traditional methods is too small to worry about and that when the two methods differ it is usually a result of making strongly different assumptions about the problem' (Rothenberg, 1971, p. 195). This may be crudely parsed as 'economic specification is more important than statistical estimation'. Over time, these disappointments induced a change in direction on the part of the Bayesian camp culminating in Leamer's influential book *Specification Searches* (1978). The book opened up a new direction for Bayesian econometrics and gained it the reputation of being an independent approach to econometric methodology rivalling the CC paradigm – see Pagan (1987).

From the measurement standpoint, Leamer's manifesto may be seen as an attempt to use Bayesian priors as the means to explicitly express the uncertainty involved in apparently arbitrary 'data mining' practice, i.e. the ad hoc and seemingly personal methods for dealing with the 'model choice' issue in applied contexts. Leamer offered a broad four-way classification of model specification search activities – interpretation search, hypothesis testing search, simplification search and post-data model construction (i.e. hypothesis-seeking search). The classification and the Bayesian representation of these searches helped expose and alert modellers to the pitfalls and arbitrariness in these practices. But Leamer was unable to offer a systematic alternative strategy for model specification search. Instead, he developed the quasi-Bayesian method of 'extreme-bounds analysis' as a measure of model and/or parameter fragility resulting from specification uncertainty.

Extreme bounds analysis was a retreat from the model specification issue back into parameter measurement, an admission that specification uncertainty severely limits the precision to which economists can measure structural parameters together with a claim that traditional approaches exaggerate the precision they obtain, see also Chapter 12 by Magnus in this volume. The Bayesian approach was unable to offer a systematic solution to specification uncertainty because, in the absence of theoretically given structural parameters, the Bayesian lacked a well-defined domain over which to define the prior distribution.

The VAR approach was the outcome of fusion of the CC tradition and time series statistical methods developed during the 1960s and 1970s, with the RE movement acting as midwife (see Qin, 2006). In spite of the provocative statements made in Sims' (1980) paper, now commonly regarded as the methodological manifesto of the VAR approach, the approach essentially offered the first systematic solution to the issue of 'model choice' which had become endemic in macroeconometrics. The result, contrary to Sims' declared objectives, was to restore the credibility of structural models.

The VAR approach consisted of four steps. The initial step was to set up an unrestricted (reduced-form) VAR model which could adequately characterise the dynamic features of the data. The second step was to simplify the model (by reducing lag lengths, where possible) while the third was to structure the original VAR through the imposition of a causal ordering. In both cases, the objective was identification of a data-coherent structural VAR (SVAR). The second and third steps were preconditions for the final step – transformation of the simplified VAR model into the moving average (MA) representation since, with this ordering in place, the model could then be used for policy simulations (see Sargent and Sims, 1977; Sims, 1980; Sargent, 1981).

The second and third of these steps are those to which VAR econometricians have devoted most of their efforts, placing the issue of structural identification at the top of their research agenda. This reflects maintenance of the CC tradition of developing structural models for policy analysis while the dynamic simplification component was inherited from the time series focus on forecasting.

Relative to the CC tradition, the connotation of identification was enhanced in the VAR approach to include the notion of identification taken from Box and Jenkins (1970), see Section 10.5. It indicates a partial shift of methodological focus towards data and away from theory. However, VAR theorists continued to maintain faith in structural models, as best seen from Sims' view of 'ideal model', which is one which 'contains a fully explicit formal behavioural interpretation of all parameters', 'connects to the data in detail', 'takes account of the range of uncertainty about the behavioural hypotheses invoked' and 'includes a believable probability model that can be used to evaluate the plausibility, given the data, of various behavioural interpretations' (1989). Moreover, the model remains within the SEM framework, virtually the same as in the CC tradition (see Qin, 2006).

In retrospect, the so-called LSE approach to macroeconometrics may be seen as a pragmatic variant of VAR modelling. That claim may seem odd in view of the LSE focus on single equation models whereas the VAR approach is to model the entire closed system. However, a single equation can always be thought of as simply the first equation of a system, and often modellers in the LSE tradition embedded equations of interest in just such a system. Further, because VAR modellers impose a diagonal A_0 matrix on the SEM and LSE modellers have typically opted for conditional representations, the choice of single equation versus system modelling does not have any implications for estimation. Both approaches make heavy use of simplification searches, but these are more structured in the VAR context. Both rely on post-estimation diagnostic testing to gauge model validity. From a practical standpoint, LSE modellers have often regarded VAR models as over-parameterised and likely to be vulnerable to structural breaks, while VAR modellers have questioned the LSE type of models as what they see to be arbitrary (i.e. completely data-based) specification simplifications.

Following Sargan (1964), LSE theorists have often adopted so-called error correction specifications, on the intuition that any well-behaved system would require either or both level and integral controls – see Phillips (1954, 1957), Gilbert (1989) and Hendry (1995). That belief was reinforced by practical experience of use of macroeconometric models in forecasting and policy simulation but lacked any clear theoretical underpinning. This was to come from the 'discovery' of cointegration which rationalised error correction through the Granger Representation Theorem (Engle and Granger, 1987). Johansen (1988) was responsible for the system analysis of cointegration which turned out to fit naturally into a VAR framework. This opened the door to the development of structural VARs involving cointegrated variables. Both LSE and VAR modellers agreed that equilibrium structure is embodied in Johansens's $\alpha\beta'$ matrix. At this point, the differences between the LSE and VAR modellers were reduced to one of style and not substance.

10.5. Measurement without Theory[7]

Data exploration has always been a strong objective in econometric research. It has never been the case that research has been constrained to areas where economic theories are established already waiting for conformational measurement.

Most of the early atheoretical econometric modelling activities were clustered in empirical business cycle studies. The Harvard barometer was one of the earliest leading indicators of this type of data-instigated research, see Persons (1916, 1919).[8] Persons' approach was greatly enhanced in the voluminous business cycle studies carried out by Burns and Mitchell (1946) of the National

[7] This is the title of Koopmans (1947).

[8] See also Gilbert and Qin (2006) for a summary of the data-instigated researches in the 1930s.

Bureau of Economic Research (NBER). However, their work induced strong methodological criticisms from the CC group as 'measurement without theory', see Koopmans (1947) and also Vining (1949). The CC structural approach became dominant among newly trained modellers from the 1950s, following the example of the Klein–Goldberger model (1955).

Despite this, exploratory econometric studies have by no means receded, albeit away from the mainstream. The lack of adequate economic theory provided modellers with the incentive to look for parametric measures of statistical models and attempt, where possible, to provide an interpretable justification of these in terms of 'common sense' economics. Structural models based on the economic optimisation rationale were never regarded as a prerequisite for modelling, nor as delivering the final judgement on model validity. Research in this tradition has been fostered by steady advances in statistics, increasing data availability and the rapid progress of computing technology. In much applied work in government, finance and industry, it was also driven by the requirement for usable results, see also Chapter 13 by Mayer in this volume.

Time-series analysis is the area in which so-called data-mining activities have been most contentious. An interesting example is the use of spectral analysis. This could be traced back to the uses of periodograms and Fourier frequency analysis for the business cycle studies in the early 1900s, e.g. Moore (1914) and Beveridge (1921). However, the frequency approach soon fell from favour and was widely seen as not useful for the analysis of economic time series, e.g. see Greenstein (1935), before econometrics settled on the time-domain representation models in the 1940s. However, the approach was revitalised by Morgenstern (1961), who delegated the research to Granger, see Phillips (1997). Thanks to J.W. Tukey's work on cross-spectral analysis to enable frequency analysis to multivariate cases, see Brillinger (2002), spectral analysis was re-established as a powerful device for economic time-series analysis by Granger and Hatanaka (1964). Notably, the spectral perspective assisted Granger in the derivation of his well-known causality test (1969), which not only relies totally on posterior data information but also abandons the simultaneity connotation of causality which has been a cornerstone of the CC structural model approach. The Granger-causality test was used as a key tool in the simplification process of RE models in the form of VARs (see e.g. Sent, 1998, Chapter 3).

As discussed in Sections 10.3 and 10.4, the time-series approach made a comeback into applied macroeconometric modelling during the 1970s under the impact of the Box–Jenkins' methodology (1970). A striking feature of the Box–Jenkins' approach is their concept of identification, which differs significantly from the concept of the CC's paradigm described in Section 10.2. Instead of seeking unique estimates of theoretical parameters, identification in the Box–Jenkins' framework filters out data features to assist model reduction, a process which aims to obtain a parsimonious model through iterative use of identification, estimation and diagnostic testing. As the final model is for forecasting, data coherence becomes the primary criterion for model acceptance, rather than theory confirmation. The impact of this methodology is clearly discernible in the development of the VAR and the LSE schools described in the previous section.

The increasing appreciation of data-coherent modelling approaches is also embodied in the revival of Burns–Mitchell empiricist pursuit of business cycles since the late 1980s. The revival was mainly boosted by the use of dynamic factor models (DFM) pioneered by Stock and Watson (1989, 1991, 1993), although the idea of applying dynamic factor analysis to macroeconometric models had been put forward by Sargent and Sims (1977) over a decade earlier (see also Diebond and Rudebusch, 1996).[9] The powerful device of DFMs has helped revitalise Persons' leading indicator models for forecasting over recent years, e.g. see Banerjee et al. (2003), Camba-Mendez and Kapetanios (2004) and Forni et al. (2005).

The area where measurement without theory has been most prominent is time-series finance, e.g. see Bollerslev et al. (1992). Two prominent devices developed are the generalised autoregressive conditional heteroscedasticity (GARCH) models, initiated by Engle (1982), and the stochastic regime-switching threshold models, developed originally by Hamilton (1989, 1990). Interestingly, both were initially devised for charactering macroeconomic data. Engle's original application was to a relatively low frequency macroeconomic process (UK inflation), whereas Hamilton proposed the regime-switching model in the context of business cycle research. The GARCH class of models, and its many variants, has been most widely applied to high-frequency financial time series to capture their volatility movement, i.e. the skedastic (or second moment) process. Regime-switching models are used to handle asymmetric conditional states of modelled variables. Typically, they depend on different sets of conditional variables which determine 'good' and 'bad' states of the system (boom versus recession, bull versus bear markets).

Both the GARCH and regime-switching devices were primarily data-instigated and have encouraged econometricians to move further away from the CC's paradigm by referring as 'structural' what the parameters of these time-series models measure, in spite of the considerable gap in the behavioural connotation between these models and underlying theory. The GARCH class of models has always been open to the objection that, by contrast with stochastic volatility (SV) models, the GARCH skedastic process lacks an independent stochastic specification. The preference for GARCH over SV derived from its greater tractability and was despite the fact that SV models are more directly compatible with finance theory – see Hull and White (1987).[10] Switching models are one instance of a much wider class of models which respond in a data-instigated manner to nonlinearities in economic responses – see Granger and Teräsvirta (1993). So long as econometricians restricted attention to linear models, slope parameters

---

[9] The method of factor analysis in a cross-sectional setting was employed in economics as early as the 1940s (see e.g. Waugh, 1942 and Stone, 1947).

[10] Shephard (2006) provides a history of SV models.

could be interpreted as (or in terms of) the first order derivatives of the supposedly underlying theoretical models. By contrast, parameters often lack clear interpretation in nonlinear models and the model must be interpreted through simulation.

10.6. Epilogue: Measurement and Knowledge Advance

The status of models, and hence structure, in philosophy of science, and specifically in the methodology of economics, remains controversial. Even if in some of the natural sciences, parameters may be seen as natural constants relating to universal regularities, it makes more sense in economics to see parameters as objects defined in relation to models, and not in relation either to theories or to the world itself. Econometric measurement becomes co-extensive with model specification and estimation.

The standard view is that models provide a means of interpreting theory into the world. Cartwright (1983) regards models as explications of theories. For Hausman (1992), models are definitional – they say nothing directly about the world, but may have reference to the world. Further, a theory may assert that a particular model does make such reference. These views are broadly in line with the CC conception of econometrics in which models were taken as given by the theorists.

Taking models as given proved unproductive in practice. Estimated models often performed poorly, and more sophisticated estimation (measurement) methods failed to give much improvement; identification problems were often acute; and the availability of richer data sets produced increasing evidence of misspecification in 'off the shelf' economic models. The econometrician's task shifted from model estimation to adaptation. This view was captured by Morgan (1988) who saw empirical models as intermediating theory and the world. For her, the task facing the economist was to find a satisfactory empirical model from the large number of possible models each of which would be more or less closely related to economic theory.

The alternative view of the relationship between theory and models is less linear, even messier. Morrison (1999) asserts that models are autonomous, and may draw from more than one theory or even from observed regularities rather than theories. Boumans (1999), who discusses business cycle theory, also views models as eclectic, 'integrating' (Boumans' term) elements from different theories. In terms of our earlier discussion, this view is more in line with the data-instigated approach to economic modelling which derives from the traditions of time series statistics. In this tradition, economic theory is often loosely related to the estimated statistical model, and provides a guide for interpretation of the estimates rather than a basis for the specification itself.

Wherein lies the measurement problem in econometrics? Econometricians in the CC tradition saw themselves as estimating parameters of well-defined structural models. These structural parameters were often required to be invariant to changes in other parts of the system, such as those induced by policy change. Many of these parameters were first order partial derivatives. But the interpretation of any partial derivative depends on the *ceteris paribus* condition – what is being held constant? The answer depends on the entire model specification. If we follow Boumans (1999) and Morrison (1999) in regarding models as being theoretically eclectic, parameters must relate to models and not theories. The same conclusion follows from Morgan's views of the multiplicity of possible empirical models.

Subsequently, with the fading faith in the existence of a unique correct model for any specific economic structure, measurement shifted away from parameters, which are accidental to model specification, and towards responses, and in particular in time series contexts, to dynamic responses. The VAR emphasis, for example, is often on estimated impulse response functions, rather than the parameters of a particular VAR specification. Similarly, the main interest in error correction specifications is often in the characterisation of the system equilibrium which will be a function of several parameters.

Models may be more or less firmly grounded in theory. The evolution of econometrics may be seen as a continuous effort to pursue best possible statistical measurements for both 'principle models' and 'phenomenological models', to use the model classification suggested by Boniolo (2004).[11] The former are assiduously sought by the orthodox structural econometricians. This probably results from four major attractions of a 'principle' model, see De Leeuw (1990), namely it serves as an efficient medium of cumulative knowledge; it facilitates interpolation, extrapolation and prediction; it allows for deductive reasoning to derive not so apparent consequence; it enables the distilling out of stable and regular information.

Many classes of models in economic theory are deliberately and profoundly unrealistic. This is true, for example, of general equilibrium theory and much of growth theory. Such models make possible 'conceptual, logical and mathematical exploration' of the model premises. These models are useful in so far as they 'increase our conceptual resources' (Hausman, 1992, p. 77) and, we would add, that they allow us to recognise similar aspects of the model behaviour which correspond to real world economic phenomena. In a sense, these models substitute for experiments which are seldom possible for entire economies.

Econometrics claims to be solely occupied with models which are realistic in the sense that they account statistically for behaviour as represented by data sets. For econometricians, the data are the world. Following Haavelmo's (1944) manifesto, Neyman–Pearson testing methodology became the established procedure for establishing congruency of models with data. But the claim to realism is problematic in that models can at best offer partial accounts of any set of phenomena. 'The striving for too much realism in a model may be an obstacle

---

[11] The third model category in Boniolo (2004) is 'object models', which correspond essentially to computable general equilibrium (CGE) type models in econometrics.

to explain the relevant phenomena' (Boumans, 1999, p. 92). During the initial decades of modern econometrics, data sets were limited and sometimes relatively uninformative. Over more recent decades, econometricians have benefited both from larger and more informative data sets and from the computing power to analyse these data. As Leamer anticipated, these rich data would oblige a thorough-going classical econometrician to reject almost any model: '... since a large sample is presumably more informative than a small sample, and since it is apparently the case that we will reject the null hypothesis in a large sample, we might as well begin by rejecting the hypothesis and not sample at all' (Leamer, 1978, p. 89). So either by the force of circumstance in the case of inadequate data, by design in the face of rich and informative data, or through the imposition of strong Bayesian priors, econometricians have abandoned realism in favour of simplicity. The situation is not very different from that of the deliberately unrealistic theory models. Econometricians measure, but measurements are model-specific and are informative about the world only in so far as the models themselves are congruent with the world.

History reflects a gradual 'externalisation' of measurement in terms of Carnap's terminology (1950): the development of measurement instruments is initially for '*internal questions*' and moves gradually towards '*external questions*'. For example, parameters are internal within models, whereas the existence of models is external with respect to the parameters. Econometric research has moved from the issue of how to optimally estimate parameters to the harder issue of how to measure and hence evaluate the efficiency, fruitfulness and simplicity of the models, i.e. the relevance of models as measuring instruments.

Acknowledgements

Thanks are due to O. Bjerkholt, M. Boumans, R. Farebrother and the participants of the workshop 'Measurement in Economics' at the Tinbergen Institute, University of Amsterdam, April 21–22 2006 for their valuable comments and suggestions on the earlier drafts.

References

Banerjee, A., Marcellino, M., Masten, I. (2003). Leading indicators for Euro area inflation and GDP growth. Working paper No. 3893. IGIR.

Beveridge, W.H. (1921). Weather and harvest cycles. *Economic Journal* **31**, 429–452.

Bollerslev, T., Chou, R.Y., Kroner, K.F. (1992). ARCH modelling in finance. *Journal of Econometrics* **52**, 5–59.

Boniolo, G. (2004). Theories and models: Really old hat? In: *Yearbook of the Artificial, vol. II*. Peter Lang Academic Publishing Company, Bern, pp. 61–86.

Boumans, M. (1999). Built-in justification. In: Morgan, M.S., Morrison, M. (Eds.), *Models as Mediators*. Cambridge Univ. Press, Cambridge, pp. 66–96.

Boumans, M. (2005). Measurement in economic systems. *Measurement* **38**, 275–284.

Box, G.E.P., Jenkins, G.M. (1970). *Time Series Analysis, Forecasting and Control*. Holden-Day, San Francisco.

Brillinger, D.R. (2002). John W. Tukey's work on time series and spectrum analysis. *Annals of Statistics* **30**, 1595–1618.

Brown, T.M. (1952). Habit persistence and lags in consumer behaviour. *Econometrica* **20**, 361–383.

Burns, A.F., Mitchell, W.C. (1946). Measuring business cycles. National Bureau of Economic Research, New York.

Camba-Mendez, G., Kapetanios, G. (2004). Forecasting Euro area inflation using dynamic factor measures of underlying inflation. Working paper No. 402. ECB.

Carnap, R. (1950). Empiricism, semantics, and ontology. *Revue Internationale de Philosophie* **4**, 20–40.

Cartwright, N. (1983). *How the Laws of Physics Lie*. Clarendon Press, Oxford.

Christ, C.F. (1952). History of the Cowles Commission, 1932–1952. In: *Economic Theory and Measurement: A Twenty-Year Research Report 1932–1952*. Cowles Commission for Research in Economics, Chicago, pp. 3–65.

Christ, C.F. (1960). Simultaneous equations estimation: Any verdict yet? *Econometrica* **28**, 835–845.

Chow, G.C. (1960). Tests of equality between sets of coefficients in two linear regressions. *Econometrica* **28**, 591–605.

Cochrane, D., Orcutt, G. (1949). Application of least squares regression to relationships containing autocorrelated error terms. *Journal of the American Statistical Association* **44**, 32–61.

Davenant, C. (1699). *An Essay upon the Probable Methods of Making a People Gainers in the Balance of Trade*. R. Horsfield, London.

De Leeuw, J. (1990). Data modelling and theory construction. Chapter 13 in: Hox, J.J., Jon-Gierveld, J.D. (Eds.), *Operationalization and Research Strategy*. Swets & Zeitlinger, Amsterdam.

Diebond, F.X., Rudebusch, G.D. (1996). Measuring business cycles: A modern perspective. *Review of Economics and Statistics* **78**, 67–77.

Durbin, J., Watson, G.S. (1950). Testing for serial correlation in least squares regression, I. *Biometrica* **37**, 409–428.

Durbin, J., Watson, G.S. (1951). Testing for serial correlation in least squares regression, II. *Biometrica* **38**, 159–178.

Engle, R.F. (1982). Autoregressive conditional heteroskedasticity with estimates of the variance of United Kingdom inflation. *Econometrica* **50**, 987–1008.

Engle, R.F., Granger, C.W.J. (1987). Cointegration and error correction: representation, estimation and testing. *Econometrica* **55**, 251–276.

Evans, M. (1966). Multiplier analysis of a post-War quarterly US model and a comparison with several other models. *Review of Economic Studies* **33**, 337–360.

Forni, M., Mallin, M., Lippi, F., Reichlin, L. (2005). The generalised dynamic factor model: One-sided estimation and forecasting. *Journal of the American Statistical Association* **100**, 830–840.

Frisch, R. (1933). Editorial. *Econometrica* **1**, 1–4.

Frisch, R. (1937). An ideal programme for macrodynamic studies. *Econometrica* **5**, 365–366.

Frisch, R. (1938). Autonomy of economic relations, unpublished until inclusion. In: Hendry, D.F., Morgan, M.S. (Eds.) (1995), *The Foundations of Econometric Analysis*. Cambridge Univ. Press, Cambridge, pp. 407–419.

Gilbert, C.L. (1989). LSE and the British approach to time series econometrics. *Oxford Economic Papers* **41**, 108–128.

Gilbert, C.L., Qin, D. (2006). The first fifty years of modern econometrics. In: Patterson, K., Mills, T.C. (Eds.), *Palgrave Handbook of Econometrics*. Palgrave MacMillan, Houndmills, pp. 117–155.

Gordon, R.J. (1970). The Brookings model in action: A review article. *Journal of Political Economy* **78**, 489–525.

Granger, C.W.J. (1969). Investigating causal relations by econometric models and cross-spectral methods. *Econometrica* **37**, 424–438.

Granger, C.W.J., Hatanaka, M. (1964). *Spectral Analysis of Economic Time Series*. Princeton Univ. Press, Princeton.

Granger, C.W.J., Teräsvirta, T. (1993). *Modelling Nonlinear Time Series*. Oxford Univ. Press, Oxford.

Greenstein, B. (1935). Periodogram analysis with special application to business failures in the United States, 1867–1932. *Econometrica* **3**, 170–198.

Griliches, Z. (1968). The Brookings model volume: A review article. *Review of Economics and Statistics* **50**, 215–234.

Haavelmo, T. (1944, mimeograph 1941), The probability approach in econometrics. *Econometrica* **12**, supplement.

Hamilton, J.D. (1989). A new approach to the economic analysis of nonstationary time series and the business cycle. *Econometrica* **57**, 357–384.

Hamilton, J.D. (1990). Analysis of time series subject to changes in regime. *Journal of Econometrics* **45**, 39–70.

Hausman, D.M. (1992). *The Inexact and Separate Science of Economics*. Cambridge Univ. Press, Cambridge.

Hausman, J.A. (1978). Specification tests in econometrics. *Econometrica* **46**, 1251–1271.

Hendry, D.F. (1980). Econometrics – alchemy or science? *Economica* **47**, 387–406.

Hendry, D.F. (1995). *Dynamic Econometrics*. Oxford Univ. Press, Oxford.

Hendry, D.F., Morgan, M.S. (1989). A re-analysis of confluence analysis. *Oxford Economic Papers* **41**, 35–52.

Hendry, D.F., Morgan, M.S. (Eds.) (1995). *The Foundations of Econometric Analysis*. Cambridge Univ. Press, Cambridge.

Hood, W., Koopmans, T.C. (Eds.) (1953). *Studies in Econometric Method*. Cowles Commission Monograph 14. New York.

Hoover, K.D., Dowell, M.E. (2001). Measuring causes: Episodes in the quantitative assessment of the value of money. In: Klein, J.L., Morgan, M.S. (Eds.), *The Age of Economic Measurement*. Duke Univ. Press, Durham (NC), pp. 137–161.

Hull, J., White, A. (1987). The pricing of options on assets with stochastic volatilities. *Journal of Finance* **42**, 28–300.

Jevons, W.S. (1871). *The Theory of Political Economy*. Macmillan, London.

Jevons, W.S. (1884). *Investigations in Currency and Finance*. Macmillan, London.

Johansen, S. (1988). Statistical analysis of cointegration vectors. *Journal of Economic Dynamics and Control* **12**, 231–254.

Johnston, J. (1963). *Econometric Methods*. McGraw-Hill, New York.

Klein, J.L. (2001). Reflections from the age of economic measurement. In: Klein, J.L., Morgan, M.S. (Eds.), *The Age of Economic Measurement*. Duke Univ. Press, Durham (NC), pp. 111–136.

Klein, L.R. (1952, 2nd ed., 1974). *A Textbook in Econometrics*. Prentice Hall, Englewood Cliffs (NJ).

Klein, L.R. (1962). *An Introduction to Econometrics*. Prentice Hall, Englewood Cliffs (NJ).

Klein, L.R., Goldberger, A.S. (1955). *An Econometric Model of the United States 1929–1952*. North-Holland, Amsterdam.

Koopmans, T.C. (1947). Measurement without theory. *Review of Economics and Statistics* **29**, 161–179.

Koopmans, T.C. (Ed.) (1950). *Statistical Inference in Dynamic Economic Models*. Cowles Commission Monograph 10. Wiley, New York.

Koopmans, T.C. (1957). *Three Essays on the State of Economic Science*. McGraw-Hill, New York.

Koopmans, T.C., Reiersøl, O. (1950). The identification of structural characteristics. *Annals of Mathematical Statistics* **21**, 165–181.

Leamer, E.E. (1978). *Specification Searches*. Wiley, New York.

Liu, T.-C. (1960). Underidentification, structural estimation, and forecasting. *Econometrica* **28**, 855–865.

Lucas, R.E. (1976). Econometric policy evaluation: A critique. In: Brunner, K., Meltzer, A.H. (Eds.), *The Phillips Curve and Labor Markets*. Carnegie-Rochester Conference Series on Public Policy, vol. 1. North-Holland, Amsterdam.

Luce, R.D., Krantz, D.H., Suppes, P., Tversky, A. (1990). *Foundations of Measurement, vol. 3: Representation, Axiomatisation and Invariance*. Academic Press, New York.

Malinvaud, E. (1964, English ed. 1968). *Statistical Methods in Econometrics*. North-Holland, Amsterdam.

Marschak, J. (1946). Quantitative studies in economic behaviour (Foundations of rational economic policy). Report to the Rockefeller Foundation, Rockefeller Archive Centre.

Mirowski, P. (1989). *More Heat than Light*. Cambridge Univ. Press, Cambridge.

Moore, H.L. (1914). *Economic Cycles – Their Law and Cause*. MacMillan, New York.

Morgan, M.S. (1988). Finding a satisfactory empirical model. In: de Marchi, N. (Ed.), *The Popperian Legacy in Economics*. Cambridge Univ. Press, Cambridge, pp. 199–211.

Morgan, M.S. (1990). *The History of Econometric Ideas*. Cambridge Univ. Press, Cambridge.

Morgenstern, O. (1961). A new look at economic time series analysis. In: Hegeland, H. (Ed.), *Money, Growth, and Methodology and other Essays in Economics: In Honor of Johan Akerman*. CWK Gleerup Publishers, Lund, pp. 261–272.

Morrison, M. (1999). Models as autonomous agents. In: Morgan, M.S., Morrison, M. (Eds.), *Models as Mediators*. Cambridge Univ. Press, Cambridge, pp. 38–65.

Nelson, C.R. (1972). The prediction performance of the FRB-MIT-PENN model of the US economy. *American Economic Review* **62**, 902–917.

Orcutt, G. (1948). A study of the autoregressive nature of the time series used for Tinbergen's model of the economic system of the United States 1919–1932. *Journal of the Royal Statistical Society, Series B* **10**, 1–45.

Pagan, A. (1987). Three econometric methodologies: A critical appraisal. *Journal of Economic Surveys* **1**, 3–24.

Persons, W.M. (1916). Construction of a business barometer based upon annual data. *American Economic Review* **6**, 739–769.

Persons, W.M. (1919). Indices of business condition. *Review of Economic Studies* **1**, 5–110.

Phillips, A.W. (1954). Stabilisation policy in a closed economy. *Economic Journal* **64**, 290–323.

Phillips, A.W. (1957). Stabilisation policy and the time form of lagged responses. *Economic Journal* **67**, 256–277.

Phillips, P.C.B. (1997). The ET interview: Professor Clive Granger. *Econometric Theory* **13**, 253–303.

Playfair, W. (1801). *The Statistical Breviary*. Bensley, London.

Playfair, W. (1805). *An Inquiry into the Permanent Causes of the Decline and Fall of Wealthy and Powerful Nations*. Greenland and Norris, London.

Qin, D. (1989). Formalisation of identification theory. *Oxford Economic Papers* **41**, 73–93.

Qin, D. (1993). *The Formation of Econometrics: A Historical Perspective*. Oxford Univ. Press, Oxford.

Qin, D. (1996). Bayesian econometrics: The first twenty years. *Econometric Theory* **12**, 500–516.

Qin, D. (2006). VAR modelling approach and Cowles Commission heritage. Economics Department Discussion Paper Series QMUL No. 557.

Qin, D., Gilbert, C.L. (2001). The error term in the history of time series econometrics. *Econometric Theory* **17**, 424–450.

Rothenberg, T.J. (1971). The Bayesian approach and alternatives in econometrics. In: Intriligator, M.D. (Ed.), *Frontiers of Quantitative Economics*. North-Holland, Amsterdam, pp. 194–207.

Sargan, J.D. (1964). Wages and prices in the United Kingdom: A study in econometric methodology. In: Hart, R.E., Mills, G., Whittaker, J.K. (Eds.), *Econometric Analysis for National Economic Planning*. Butterworth, London, pp. 25–63.

Sargent, T.J. (1981). Interpreting economic time series. *Journal of Political Economy* **89**, 213–247.

Sargent, T.J., Sims, C.A. (1977). Business cycle modelling without pretending to have too much a priori economic theory. In: *New Methods in Business Cycle Research: Proceedings from a Conference*. Federal Reserve Bank of Minneapolis, pp. 45–109.

Schumpeter, J. (1933). The common sense of econometrics. *Econometrica* **1**, 5–12.

Sent, E.-M. (1998). *The Evolving Rationality of Rational Expectations: An Assessment of Thomas Sargent's Achievements*. Cambridge Univ. Press, Cambridge.

Shephard, N. (2006). Stochastic volatility. In: Durlauf, S., Blume, L. (Eds.), *New Palgrave Dictionary of Economics, 2nd ed.* Nuffield College, Oxford University. Draft version: Working paper 17.

Simon, H.A. (1953). Causal ordering and identifiability. In: Hood, W., Koopmans, T. (Eds.), *Studies in Econometric Method.* In: *Cowles Commission Monograph 14*, pp. 49–74.

Sims, C.A. (1980). Macroeconomics and reality. *Econometrica* **48**, 1–48.

Sims, C.A. (1989). Models and their uses. *American Journal of Agricultural Economics* **71**, 489–494.

Smith, A. (1904). *An Inquiry into the Causes and Consequences of the Wealth of Nations.* Methuen, London. (E. Cannan's edition first published in 1776.)

Stock, J.H., Watson, M.W. (1989). New indexes and coincident and leading economic indicators. In: Blanchard, O., Fischer, S. (Eds.), *NBER Macroeconomic Annual.* MIT Press, Cambridge, MA, pp. 351–394.

Stock, J.H., Watson, M.W. (1991). A probability model of the coincident economic indicators. In: Lahiri, K., Moore, G.H. (Eds.), *Leading Economic Indicators: New Approaches and Forecasting Records.* Cambridge Univ. Press, Cambridge, pp. 63–89.

Stock, J.H., Watson, M.W. (1993). A procedure for predicting recessions with leading indicators: Econometric issues and recent experience. In: Stock, J.H., Watson, M.W. (Eds.), *Business Cycles, Indicators and Forecasting.* Univ. of Chicago Press for NBER, Chicago, pp. 255–284.

Stone, R. (1947). On the interdependence of blocks of transactions. *Journal of the Royal Statistical Society (suppl.)* **9**, 1–45.

Theil, H. (1957). Specification errors and the estimation of economic relationships. *Review of International Statistical Institute* **25**, 41–51.

Theil, H. (1958). *Economic Forecasts and Policy.* North-Holland, Amsterdam.

Vining, R. (1949). Koopmans on the choice of variables to be studied and of methods of measurement: A rejoinder. *Review of Economics and Statistics* **31**, 77–86, 91–94.

Waugh, F.V. (1942). Regression between two sets of variables. *Econometrica* **10**, 290–310.

Waugh, F.V. (1961). The place of least squares in econometrics. *Econometrica* **29**, 386–396.

Wold, H. (1954). Causality and econometrics. *Econometrica* **22**, 162–177.

Wold, H. (1960). A generalization of causal chain models. *Econometrica* **28**, 443–463.

Wold, H. (Ed.), (1964). *Econometric Model Building: Essays on the Causal Chain Approach.* North-Holland, Amsterdam.

CHAPTER 11

Structure

Hsiang-Ke Chao

Department of Economics, National Tsing Hua University, 101, Section 2, Kuang Fu Road, Hsinchu 300, Taiwan
E-mail address: hkchao@mx.nthu.edu.tw

11.1. Introduction

Structure is an ill-defined term in both economics and econometrics, and usually it is conceived by analogy with the distinct term physical structure (for example, Morgan, 1995, p. 60). Many definitions of it are loosely related to the framework of a system in which many relations between objects involved can be identified. A typical one in economics is similar to the definition proposed by the philosopher of science, Tian Yu Cao (2003, p. 6): "A structure is a stable system of relations among a set of constituents." This definition reveals two characteristics of structure: a system of relations and invariance. As seen in the work of the history of econometrics (for example, Epstein, 1987; Morgan, 1990; Qin, 1993; Hendry and Morgan, 1995, and Gilbert and Qin, Chapter 11, this volume), the evolution of the methods of measuring structure is central on the early stage of the development of econometrics. The notion of structure still remains as one of the most important issues in contemporary econometrics. Measuring structure, with the task including setting up a measurable model and estimating its parameters, provides useful knowledge of structure.

In philosophy of science, structure can serve as a heuristic device. Instead of being an object of measurement, structure is considered as the main concept in constructing a measurement theory. This doctrine can be referred to as the *structural* approach to measurement, for which the dominating representational theory of measurement is a paradigm example. Its philosophical root, the *semantic view* on the structure of scientific theory, has itself become increasingly a popular and convincing account for the role that models play in science and economics.[1]

In this chapter we investigate these two topics: measurement of structure in econometric methodology and a structural approach to measurement in the philosophy of science. We hope to show that these two topics are related not just

[1] Also see Michell (Chapter 2, this volume) for a historical account for the philosophical origin of the representational theory of measurement.

Measurement in Economics: A Handbook
Marcel Boumans (Editor)

because of the similarity in name, but because of their concern of fundamental philosophical issues with respect to structure and measurement.

11.2. Measuring Structure

There are generally two meanings of structure in econometrics. One refers to the understanding that the relationships among variables are specified by theory or a priori information. The other refers to the notion of invariance. In this chapter the former is called the "theory view" while the latter is referred to as the "invariance view". Both the theory view and the invariance view are direct outgrowths of the Cowles Commission approach to econometric modeling. They are compatible rather than conflicting with each other. Each meaning leads to a different model specification and a measurement strategy.

Structure and its measurement are discussed by considering four approaches towards econometric models. They are: the Cowles Commission structural approach, the new classical macroeconomics, the vector autoregressive models, and the London School of Economics (LSE) approach (Gilbert and Qin, Chapter 10, this volume, also discuss the similar issues).[2]

11.2.1. The Cowles Commission approach[3]

Although the methodology of econometric modeling that the Cowles Commission and its predecessors, notably Ragnar Frisch and Jan Tinbergen, proposed has in some sense been regarded as outdated, the definitions and notions of structure we nowadays accept are still due to them. Various ways to measure the structural parameters in a simultaneous system can be seen in contemporary econometrics textbooks (for example, Hamilton, 1994). Historically, it is first shown in Haavelmo (1944) that if we use the ordinary least squares (OLS) method to measure an equation, which is in fact a part of a simultaneous equations model, there would be a positive bias between the true value and the OLS estimate. This bias is known as the Haavelmo bias or simultaneous equations bias (Hamilton, 1994, p. 234). To solve the problem, Haavelmo suggests using the indirect least squares method in Haavelmo (1947).[4] But for Haavelmo, a more appropriate way to measure the structure is to consider estimate the system as a whole and use the maximum likelihood estimators. The idea is to

---

[2] Kevin Hoover has explored extensively on the same issue in a series of his works, but his main concern is the issue of causality. Structure is regarded as causal. Hoover's account can be regarded as a structural approach to causality. See Hoover (2001), Hoover and Jordá (2001), and Demiralp and Hoover (2003).

[3] For more detailed historical accounts, see Epstein (1987), Morgan (1990), Qin (1993), and especially Hendry and Morgan (1995, pp. 60–76).

[4] Qin (1993, p. 68) states that the indirect least square method was first developed by Jan Tinbergen in 1930.

maximize the joint likelihood function of endogenous variables conditional on predetermined variables. However, due to the computing capacity at that time, the full information maximum likelihood (FIML) estimator became too complicated. The limited information maximum likelihood (LIML) method, in that a priori identifying restrictions are imposed on the equations to be estimated, was then invented as a workable alternative for the FIML method. Girshick and Haavelmo (1947) provide the first application of the LIML method on measuring US food consumption at the average per capita level over the period 1922–1941.

All these methods of estimating the simultaneous equations model explicitly or implicitly treat structure as existing, and sometimes it can be known so that a priori restrictions are legitimate. Measurement is thus a means to provide the knowledge of structure. As Girshick and Haavelmo put it: "Knowing the structural parameters, all the relations implied by the model can be derived. In a sense these structural parameters play a role similar to that of the elements in chemistry." (Girshick and Haavelmo, 1947, p. 93). The viewpoint that the Cowles Commission econometricians takes on identifying structures with the help from economic theories is well addressed in Koopmans's (1947) "Measurement without Theory" paper, in which he stresses that in the empirical business cycles research, "Fuller utilization of the concepts and hypotheses of economic theory *as a part of the processes of observation and measurement* promises to be a shorter road, perhaps even the only possible road, to the understanding of cyclical fluctuations." (Koopmans, 1947, p. 162, original emphasis). This is realism about theories: economic theory is true to the world; econometric models, whose structures are specified with the help from economic theory, are thus also true to the world.

In the work of the Cowles Commission econometrics, structure is also understood in terms of the notion of invariance. The origin of the invariance view can be traced to Frisch's distinction between autonomous and confluent relations in economics. In Haavelmo (1944), an autonomous relation is an invariant relation to the changes in the structure. A confluent relation, which has a lower degree of autonomy, is derived from more autonomous relations. Autonomy is a matter of degree (Haavelmo, 1944, p. 29):

> It is obvious that the autonomy of a relation is a highly relative concept, in the sense that any system of hypothetical relations between real phenomena might itself be deducible from another, still more basic system, i.e., a system with still higher degree of autonomy with respect to structural changes.

Marschak (1953) and Hurwicz (1962) are particularly concerned with the issue of invariance under policy intervention. They can be seen as a precedent for the Lucas critique (Lucas, 1976; see below). Hurwicz, for example, along the same line with Haavelmo's view, argues that if the original model and the one modified after some policies are implemented are both unique up to a admissible transformation, then this model can be regarded as containing a structure *with respect to* this policy intervention. Thus, structure is a relative concept:

"the concept of structure is relative to the domain of modifications anticipated" (Hurwicz, 1962, p. 238).[5]

If structure is understood in terms of the theory view, there are some issues pertaining to identifying the structure in the Cowles Commission econometric models. They are usually known as the identification problem. At the formal level, identification requires the rank and order conditions to reduce to a unique representation. Practically, it is achieved by imposing on the model the identifying restrictions chosen with the help from a priori information or theory. However, one problem is to ask whether the structural models represent the true structure - that is, whether the identifying restrictions are "credible". If it is not the case, then we cannot say that these methods provide faithful measures for the structure.

On the other hand, if structure is understood as invariance, then invariance is usually taken as a necessary and sufficient condition for structure. Whether or not an econometric model is invariant under policy intervention seems to be an empirical question. To answer the question, two approaches have been developed (see Hoover, 1988, 1994). One abandons the concept of structure all together and uses a non-structural, atheoretical vector autoregressive method in econometrics to represent the data (Sims and the VAR approach). The other approach has a much stronger belief in economic theory, and accordingly derives from a well-defined representative-agent model, in which some behavioral parameters such as taste and technology are assumed to be constant (Lucas and the real business cycle theory).

11.2.2. The Lucas critique

Even though the Cowles Commission scholars have considered the theme of invariance, their simultaneous equations models have become the targets of the Lucas critique. Lucas (1976) challenges the standard econometric models which do not exhibit invariant relationships as they should be, because they do not properly deal with expectations. Macroeconomists' reaction to the Lucas critique is to construct models based on the *microfoundation* that employs the representative agent assumption and derives a well-articulated optimization model. What is invariant in this model can thus be regarded as structure. For instance, *deep parameters*, indicating the policy-invariant parameters describing taste and technology, are regarded as structural in the real business cycle research. In consumption studies, the Euler equation, denoting the first-order condition of the consumer's intertemporal choices, represents the structure for the new classical aggregate consumption function (Hall, 1978).[6]

---

[5] Woodward's recent work (2000, 2003) discusses extensively the degrees of autonomy and invariance in the context of scientific explanation.

[6] Hall (1990, p. 135): "For consumption, the structural relation, invariant to policy interventions and other shifts elsewhere in the economy, is the intertemporal preference ordering."

When the consumption function is a random-walk model described in Hall (1978), a first-order autoregressive process (AR(1)) of consumption indicates that when the consumption in this period is only the function of the consumption in the previous period plus an innovation (i.e., consumption is a random walk), its structural parameters can be measured directly (Attanasio, 1998, p. 21). The standard procedure is to log-linearize the Euler equation given that the utility function is constant-relative-risk-averse (Hansen and Singleton, 1983) and estimate the consumer's elasticity of intertemporal substitution. Although the deep parameters can be directly measured, the empirical justification of whether the structure is described as the Euler equation is indirect rather than direct. As observed in the literature (e.g., Flavin, 1981), consumption theorists are usually concerned with the final model – whether the consumption function is a random walk. They test whether current consumption, or the change in consumption, is orthogonal to lagged income. Even though sometimes economists conjecture the Euler equation (the "structure") is responsible for some empirical facts, they can neither test such a conjecture alone by ruling out other auxiliary assumptions.

In the real business cycle research, the measuring strategy is *calibration.* Boumans (2002 and Chapter 9 of this volume) understands the method of calibration in three different ways. The conventional thinking is to regard calibration as a simulation-based *estimation* method for obtaining parameters that generate the data whose properties best match with the observed data. Calibration can also be understood as *testing* in the sense that it can be thought of as a "weak test" (Hartley et al., 1998, p. 16) to check whether the simulating model mimics the observed data. However, this is the fallacy of affirming the consequent, because there might be other incompatible theories that are also capable of simulating the same observed data (Hartley et al., ibid). This argument is the same as the problem of *underdetermination of theory by evidence* (see below), hence the identification problem may be regarded as unsolved. The third meaning of calibration in the real business cycle theory is interpreted closely with the meaning understood in metrology. A measuring device requires to be "calibrated" by way of correlating the reading of a device with those of an invariant standard in order to check the accuracy of the measuring device. Similarly, calibration in the real business cycle research can be thought of as making measuring devices for the economy, according to the chosen standards – deep parameters.

11.2.3. Vector autoregressions: non-structural and structural

Sims's vector autoregressive (VAR) (Sims, 1980) approach was inspired by Ta-Chung Liu's critique on the Cowles Commission method. Liu (1960, 1963) asserts that the identifying restrictions exclude many variables that should be included.[7] One of the reasons is that in reality "very few variables can really be legitimately considered as exogenous to economic system" (Liu, 1963, p. 162).

---

[7] In this sense the identifying restrictions are sometimes called "exclusion restrictions".

This is referred by Maddala (2001, p. 375) as the "Liu critique". Therefore, the nature of the models is underidentified rather than overidentified. Sims wants to abandon these "incredible restrictions" altogether and proposes an unrestricted reduced-form model, in which all variables are regarded as endogenous.[8]

The simplest form of the VAR model is reduced-form VAR models. In a reduced-form VAR model each variable is a linear function of the past value of itself and all other variables. Each equation can be estimated by the OLS method. However, it is assumed in reduced-form VARs that error terms, usually denoting shocks in macroeconomic theory, are usually correlated. A problem is caused by interpreting these error terms as particular economic shocks that are normally regarded as uncorrelated. To solve the problem, econometricians can orthogonalize the shocks by using a Choleski factorization to decompose the covariance matrix (Sims, 1980). The Choleski decomposition implies a Wold causal chain on the contemporaneous variables – we have a specific hierarchical causal ordering among the contemporaneous variables. However, the order of the variables is arbitrarily chosen. This means there is a unique Choleski decomposition for each possible order – changing the order of the contemporary variables changes the VAR representation. Therefore, we have a class of observational equivalent VAR representations.

In order to identify a VAR, additional a priori information is in need to choose between many possible links among contemporaneous variables. A VAR that requires these identifying restrictions is known as a *structural VAR*, where the term "structural" is the same as the theory view that we can find in the Cowles Commission models. See Bernanke (1985), Blanchard and Watson (1986), Sims (1986) for some early papers on structural VARs.[9]

11.2.4. The LSE approach

The LSE school of econometrics, led by David Hendry and his collaborators, offers a methodologically promising approach to economic modeling (see Hendry, 1995, 2000). At the outset it is assumed that there exists an unobservable data-generating process (DGP), represented by a conditional joint density function of all the sample data, that is responsible for producing the data we observe. While to uncover the real DGP seems impossible, the best thing that econometricians can do is to build a model which characterizes all types of information at hand. In this sense a model can be said to be *congruent* with the information sets. To achieve a congruent econometric model, the LSE approach provides the *theory of reduction*, claiming that to obtain an empirical econometric model is to impose a sequence of reductions on a hypothetical local DGP (LDGP), a data-generating mechanism of variables under analysis. The purpose is to

---

[8] Some think that Liu first refers such an identification as "incredible". But in fact it is Sims (1980) who originally coins the term.

[9] See also Stock and Watson (2001) for a recent review of the VAR approach.

ensure that the features of the data obtained are not lost in the derived empirical model. The practical implementation of the theory of reduction is the *general-to-specific* methodology. It directs econometricians to start with a general unrestricted model containing all available information that the DGP or the LDGP is supposed to have. They then use econometric concepts to impose various types of tests on the general model so that there is no loss of information when deriving a specified final model.

In the LSE methodology, the notion of structure is equally important to econometric models as in the Cowles Commission methodology. Structure can be represented as (Hendry, 1995, p. 33):

$$E_{t-1}y_t = \rho E_{t-1}z_t, \quad \text{for } \rho \in R,$$

where y_t is the output variable, z_t is the input variable for an agent's decision, and E_{t-1} is the conditional expectations given all available information at $t-1$. When ρ is invariant, the above equation can be said to define a structure. It shows that the LSE methodology subscribes to the invariance view of structure. Economic theory is not much help to determine the invariance. To see whether the model represents an invariant relation, the Chow test for structural change is performed on ρ. Hendry (1997, p. 166) claims, "Succinctly, 'LSE' focuses on structure as invariance under extensions of the information set over time, across regimes, and for new sources of information." Hence structure is embedded in the congruence test which checks for whether parameters are invariant under the extensions of the information sets.

The views on structure in the above-discussed four approaches to macroeconometric modeling can be summarized as follows. The simultaneous equations models that the Cowles Commission proposes involve both the theory view and the invariance view. The new classical and the RBC schools subscribe to the invariance view, but also hold the belief that economic theory is capable of specifying the structure of the model. Both the VAR approach and the LSE approach construe structure as invariance. What contrasts between the VAR and the LSE approaches is that in the VAR approach economic theory is regarded as incapable of imposing credible restrictions on the structure, while in the LSE approach economic theory and other types of measurable information are treated on an equal footing. Yet the distinctions between these competing approaches are rather subtler than this classification suggests. The controversy over structure between the post-Cowles econometric approaches results from their attitudes towards the Lucas critique.

11.2.5. Discussion

Although Sims's VAR modeling is of great contrast with the Cowles Commission simultaneous equations models, he does not see the simultaneous equations models as misrepresenting the structure. Sims's favorite definition of structure comes from Hurwicz (1962) as mentioned above. Sims (1980, 1982) accepts

Hurwicz's idea that invariance is only a matter of degree. Hence, Sims's view is no different from Frisch's and Haavelmo's views on the autonomy and confluence of econometric models. Sims also finds Lucas's assumption of a once-and-for-all policy choice as too strong. A permanent policy action is rare to non-existent. The public would act (rationally) to implement useful information provided by history to take up proper responses to policy interventions (Sims, 1982, 1998).[10]

The meaningfulness of the Lucas critique can be empirically evaluated by checking whether policies have permanent effects on switching the regimes. A recent empirical study by Leeper and Zha (2003) shows that actual monetary policy interventions may not be subject to the Lucas critique. Leeper and Zha distinguish a policy intervention's direct effect from the expectation-formation effect that is induced by the change in people's expectations about a policy regime. They find that many monetary policies are in fact "modest" relative to the Lucas critique in the sense that the policies that the Federal Reserve considers do not have expectation-formation effects. This empirical finding on the one hand demurs the Lucas critique which specifies the fact that a lack of invariance may be due to the effect of changing expectations formation on structure, while on the other hand supports Sims's view that the permanent policy regime changes are only rare events. The Cowles Commission simultaneous equations models remain structural in the sense of Hurwicz and still have the merit of being used in policy analysis. The Lucas critique is merely a "cautionary footnote" (Sims, 1982, p. 108).[11]

Structural VARs, a mixture of the VARs and the Cowles structural models, seem to diverge from the VARs and converge to the new classical macroeconomics. Koopmans's analogy of the Kepler's and the Newton's stages of science to the NBER's and the Cowles Commission's methodologies in his Measurement without Theory paper strikes a chord with the new classical economists. Cooley and LeRoy (1985) argue against the VARs as a retreat to the Kepler stage since theory plays no role in scientific investigation They also point out the identification problem in the non-structural VARs that has to be dealt with. They claim that in order for policy analysis, the VARs must be interpreted as structural in terms of the theory view.

Structural VARs are not without criticism. The most appealing one is that it seems a retreat to what Sims has forcefully argued against the Cowls Commis-

---

10 See Sims (1998) for his reevaluation for the Lucas critique.

11 Sims's view can be envisaged in an analogy to the structures in civil engineering. In analyzing the seismic resistance of a building structure, it is usually required for those "essential structures" (e.g., hospitals, power plants) that must remain operational all the time to resist a much larger seismic force than other structures. Structure thus is also a relative concept: it is defined by its resistance to a certain assigned degree of the strength of earthquakes. It would be implausible to define structure by its capacity of resisting one determining seismic activity that destroys all constructed buildings, because an earthquake this strong has not happened in the past, and it perhaps would never happen in the future.

sion: incredible identifying restrictions. No clue is shown whereby the identifying assumptions applied to the structural VAR models are more credible than that to the simultaneous equations models. Stock and Watson (2001) suggest that credible identifying assumptions can be reached if we "exploit detailed institutional knowledge". However, "institutional knowledge" is itself too vague a concept to be defined. The examples Stock and Watson had in mind range from tax code, spending rules, models of the reserve market, and long-run money neutrality (Stock and Watson, 2001, p. 112). However, it basically is nothing different from Koopmans's (1957, p. 140) appeal to "exploit all the evidence we can secure, directly or indirectly" to help to know the simultaneously interdependently influenced economic system, and for identifying restrictions. Nor does Stock and Watson's claim seem to differ from Hendry's LSE approach in this respect, which utilizes all available information including "institutional knowledge" (Hendry, 1997, p. 165). There is still no proof for these assumptions to be credible.

The debate over the structural VAR highlights the conflation of the concept of structure between invariance version and theory version. One might argue that the VAR approach has the same identification problem to the Cowles structural model, because, as been discussed above, a Choleski-decomposed VAR has many observationally equivalent representations, each is regarded as a different Wold-causal-chain model and is subject to a different theoretical interpretation. A structural VAR needs to be identified among these many possible ones. This is exactly the reason for which Wold's causal-chain model, which is offered as an alternative to Haavelmo's simultaneous equations model, is criticized as being confluent rather than autonomous, in terms of Frisch's terminology (Hendry and Morgan, 1995, p. 65). Hence this type of VARs is not structural in the sense of autonomy or invariance. However, when, as Bernanke (1985) makes it clear that the term "structural" for his structural VAR model refers to the theory version only, this implies the true structure of a VAR model cannot be specified without economic theories. In addition, though VARs are usually not subject to the Lucas critique, one might still ask whether the relationships measured in a structural VAR model satisfy the invariance view of structure in the sense of Lucas.[12]

The LSE approach sides with the VAR approach treating the Lucas critique as an empirical question. Hendry and Mizon (2000) find that in a forecasting model, errors usually result from factors unrelated to the policy change under study. Therefore, the model can be still used for policy analysis despite it yielding inaccurate forecasts. The LSE approach, indicated by the dictum, "to break out of the straightjacket of received theory" (Hendry and Mizon, 1990, p. 121), also rejects the view of starting an econometric model with a well-articulated economic theory that the RBC school proposes. According to the theory of reduction, the new model needs to explain the facts that have been explained by

12 A study by Keating (1990) also shows that standard structural VAR models under rational expectations may yield inconsistent parameter estimates.

the previous theories and also explain the novel facts unexplained by the previous theories. In this sense we say that the new model *encompasses* the models built according to existing theories. Take one of the benchmark models in the LSE approach as an example: the DHSY (an acronym for Davidson et al., 1978) model of consumption. When the LSE practitioners built the DHSY model, they considered the existing theories reflected in the permanent income and the life-cycle hypotheses, and they aimed to encompass both of them. This indicates that economic theories are not superior to other sorts of information.

11.2.6. Conclusion

The views of structure can be distinguished between the theory view and the invariance view. The theory view believes that economic theory is capable of specifying the relationships between variables. The invariance view defines structure as a set of invariant relationships under intervention. The structural VAR approach aligns itself with the Cowles Commission on the theory view. The identifying restrictions are based on a priori information or theory. The new classical school goes further to argue that a macroeconomic model needs to be derived from the representative agent's optimizing behavior. The VAR and the LSE approaches are of empiricism. Theory alone does not define structure.

All approaches generally agree to the invariance view, because it would be strange if there are unstable relationships in their models, yet for the VAR and structural VAR approaches the Lucas critique does not apply. Sims's argument is that the radical policy change is rare to non-existent. For the VAR and the LSE approaches, the invariance is an empirical question. They agree that invariance is a matter of degree. This marks the great legacy of Frisch and Haavelmo.[13]

11.3. The Structural Approach to Measurement

The structural approach to measurement denotes the theories of measurement that are influenced by the semantic view of the structure of scientific theory in the philosophy of science. The semantic view refers commonly to the approach led by Patrick Suppes in identifying the structure of scientific theory with set-theoretical structure. Its application to measurement is used extensively in utility theory in economics. However, in economic methodology, the application of the semantic view is mainly due to the "structuralist" tradition of Joseph Sneed and Wolfgang Stegmüller (see Stegmüller et al., 1982; Balzer and Hamminga, 1989). Consequently, the "structuralist" view of measurement (Balzer, 1992; Díez Calzada, 2000) usually represents the view influenced by the Sneed–Stegmüller structuralism.

---

[13] Lucas might also agree to the idea of degree of invariance. See his (1973) work on cross-country comparisons of the slope of the Phillips curve. (I thank Kevin Hoover for pointing this out to me.)

In the following sessions the discussion will be concentrated on the semantic view of Suppes's and two other developments by Bas van Fraassen and Ronald Giere. For the application of the Sneed–Stegmüller structuralism to economics, see Hands (1985) for a detailed discussion. The accounts of Giere, Suppes and van Fraassen are the most accepted versions of the semantic view and have been zealously debated in the philosophy of science. To understand the semantic view, it is first helpful to know the approach that the semantic philosophers object: the received view.

11.3.1. The received view

The "received view", the name coined by philosopher of science Hilary Putnam, stands for the view of the constitution of scientific theories in the eyes of logical positivists. According to the received view of scientific theories, a theory consists of a set of theoretical axioms on the one hand, and a set of *correspondence rules* on the other. Theoretical axioms are constituted by "theoretical terms" which only exist in the context of theory. The correspondence rules then relate the axioms to the phenomena expressed in "observational terms". The correspondence rules play the central role in the received view. As a part of the theory, the correspondence rules contain both theoretical and observational terms, and offer the theory an interpretation by giving the theory proper empirical meanings.[14] Logical positivist Rudolf Carnap gave an example of the correspondence rules as follows: "The (measured) temperature of a gas is proportional to the mean kinetic energy of its molecules." This correspondence rule links the kinetic energy of molecules (a theoretical term in molecular theory) with the temperature of the gas (an observational terms). If such rules exist, then philosophers are confident in deriving empirical laws about observable entities from theoretical laws (Carnap, 1966, p. 233).

The received view also recommends a deductive method of theorizing, in which logical analysis is applied to deduce consequences from the statements that axioms posit. Since the received view puts great emphasis on the theorization from axioms, it is also known as the *axiomatic approach* (cf. van Fraassen, 1980). However, this type of axiomatization only refers to the theories axiomatized in first-order logic. The received view is also called as the *syntactic view*, because axioms are statements of language and have no direct connection to the world.

The received view may have been dismissed in the methodology of economics (see Blaug, 1992), yet one can still observe theories and practices that follow such a tradition. In addition to the similarities between various economic methodologies and logical positivism (see Caldwell, 1994), Koopmans's (1957) methodological approach is particularly regarded as similar to the received view

[14] In the sense that the theoretical axioms are interpreted by the empirical world, the correspondence rules can be referred to as "rules of interpretation" or "dictionaries". See Suppe (1977).

(see Morgan and Morrison, 1999). Koopmans's (1957, pp. 132–135) proposition to the structure of economic theory starts with "postulates" that consist of logical relations between symbols that he calls "terms". Terms are interpreted if they are connected with the observable phenomena. A set of postulates then are regarded as a theory and can be verified or refuted by observation. Milton Friedman's (1957) permanent income hypothesis may be considered as an example of the application of the syntactic view. The theoretical term "permanent income" is linked with the empirical world by the correspondence rule: "the permanent income is estimated by a weighted pattern of past income" in which "a weighted pattern of past income" is an observational term. Whereas it is questionable that we can derive an empirical law about observable entities (i.e., measured consumption and income) from the permanent income hypothesis in a logical positivistic way, the theory is confirmed as an empirical claim when the deduced consequences are tested against both cross-sectional and time-series data in various respects.[15]

The received view has been criticized for many reasons, two of which are particularly salient, and both regard the correspondence rules.[16] First, there is no sharp distinction between theory and observation. Thomas Kuhn (1962) has pointed out to us that observations are possibly theory-laden. Therefore, correspondence rules do not obtain. Second, the correspondence rules are too naïve to describe the complex interactions between theory and the world. This point has motivated many philosophers to reconsider the structure of theory, particularly the fact that models are used extensively to bridge theory and data in science. One alternative to the syntactic approach is to develop an account that is inspired by model theory in mathematics and scientific practices. The semantic view or model-theoretical approach provides such an alternative.

11.3.2. The semantic view

In contrast with the deductivist axiomatization process suggested in the syntactic view, the semantic view focuses on "satisfactions" or "realizations" of the axioms. This naturally switches the focus to scientific models. Models not only bear such meanings of satisfaction and realization based on the model theory in mathematics, but they also serve as an important means to mediate between theory and the world. Moreover, studying models, non-linguistic entities, might help to avoid the problem of theory-observation distinction that the syntactic view faces.

Patrick Suppes, who is inspired by Alfred Tarski's model theory, is definitely the pioneer of the semantic view. In Suppes's work (1960, 1967, 2002),

---

[15] This kind of test can be regarded as what Kim et al. (1995) call "characteristic tests", that aim to confirm specific characteristics of empirical models. See Mayer's (1972) classic book for an extensive study on testing Friedman's permanent income hypothesis, and Chao (2003, pp. 87–89) for interpreting Friedman's theory in terms of the notion of the characteristic tests.

[16] See Suppe (1977, 1989, 2000) for the criticisms of the received view.

a structure of the theory is usually defined set-theoretically.[17] A set-theoretical structure is presented as an ordered n-tuple containing a set of elements and a set of n-ary relations. In the case of ordered couple,[18] a structure can be denoted as $\langle A, R\rangle$, where A is a set of elements and R is a binary relation. If this structure satisfies a set of axioms of a certain theory, then it can be thought of as a particular type of structure or a model for a theory. Conversely, we can say that a theory is axiomatized set-theoretically when its models can be represented as $\langle A, R\rangle$. To illustrate, consider a case of weak ordering. Let $\mathfrak{A} = \langle A, R\rangle$, where A is a non-empty set, and R be a binary relation defined on A. A structure $\mathfrak{A}$ is then a weak ordering if and only if the following axioms hold for every a, b, and c, in A (adopted from Suppes, 2002, p. 56):

(Axiom 1, Transitive). If aRb and bRc, then aRc.

(Axiom 2, Complete). aRb or bRa.

Similarly, the weak preference in economics can be represented in the following set-theoretical way (Varian, 1992, pp. 94–95): a structure $\mathfrak{B} = \langle A, \succeq\rangle$ is a weak preference, where A is a non-empty set of commodities, $\succeq$ is a binary "at least as good as" relation, if and only if the following axioms hold for every x, y, and z in A.

(Axiom 1, Complete). Either $x \succeq y$ or $y \succeq x$ or both.

(Axiom 2, Reflexive). $x \succeq x$.

(Axiom 3, Transitive). If $x \succeq y$ and $y \succeq z$, then $x \succeq z$.

An entity that has a structure can be thought of as a *model* for the theory, which is a realization of all axioms. There can be many models for the theory if these models all satisfy the axioms. However, since these models have the same structure, an *isomorphism* (one-one mapping) can be constructed between them.

Suppes believes that the notions of models and structure in mathematical logic can also be applied to understand models used in the daily scientific practices. To put models at the center stage of science marks a significant contrast to the received view. As Suppes puts it: "A central topic in the philosophy of science is the analysis of the structure of scientific theories.... The fundamental approach I advocated for a good many years is the analysis of the structure of a theory in terms of the models of the theory" (Suppes, 2002, p. 51).

11.3.3. Models of data

In considering the roles and functions of models, Suppes's seminal article "Models of Data" (Suppes, 1962) pioneered the attempt to explicate the role models

---

[17] "Theory" here means mathematical theory, like theory of group or theory of ordering.

[18] Suppes (1957) shows that ordered n-ary tuples can be reduced to ordered couples.

play in representing the world. Suppes introduces a hierarchy of empirical models. The model builders deal with the related problems for specifying the model. There are particular "theories" associated at different levels. Suppes's example of learning theory in experimental psychology consists of a hierarchy in five levels. In a top-down order, they are:

(1) linear response models that are concerned with the problems of estimating parameters, and checking goodness of fit;
(2) models of experiment that are concerned with the numbers of trials and choices of experimental parameters;
(3) models of data that consider homogeneity, stationarity, and fit of experimental parameters;
(4) experimental design that requires theories for randomization and assignment of subjects;
(5) *ceteris paribus* conditions that deal with the control of extraneous factors.

"Models of Data" is an important landmark in the development of the semantic view.[19] Not only does Suppes shift the focus from the correspondence rules to models, including the functions of and the relations between models, but also does he successfully argue that in the empirical science, it is the models of data, rather than the raw data, that confront the theory.

11.3.4. Two versions of the semantic view: Van Fraassen and Giere

Two of the most discussed versions of the semantic view are offered by van Fraassen (1980, 1989) and Giere (1988), who differ from each other in ontology. Van Fraassen's picture of scientific theories can be depicted as follows. At the outset, there are structures and models that present the theory. Models include a subset called empirical substructures that correspond to the actual phenomena.[20] The type of correspondence that van Fraassen prefers is isomorphism. In his account of *constructive empiricism*, van Fraassen draws a distinction between acceptance of a theory and belief in the truth of a theory. An empiricist does not believe that theory explains the unobservable parts, but only accepts a theory because its *empirical adequacy* – that is, those parts of the models of the theory called *empirical substructures* – are isomorphic to the observational parts of the object investigated.

Giere's *constructive realism* contrasts with van Fraassen's empirical account on two aspects. First, Giere holds a realist position that models can represent the underlying causal structure which may be unobservable. Second, he regards isomorphic mappings as rare in science and suggests *similarity* relations instead. Models for Giere, such as Watson and Crick's scale model of DNA and geographical maps, exhibit a particular *similarity of structure* between models and

---

19 This paper influenced Suppe's version of the semantic view (see Suppe, 1989).
20 Teller (2001) distinguishes many versions of empirical substructures in van Fraassen's work.

the real system (Giere, 1997, pp. 21–24). In Giere's account a theoretical hypothesis is a statement asserting the relationships between a model and a real world. Models that satisfy the axioms are the means to represent the real world up to similarity. There is no truth relationship of correspondence between theoretical hypothesis and the real world, as the received view claims. For Giere, a theoretical hypothesis has the general form as: "Such-and-such identifiable real system is similar to a designated model in indicated respects and degrees." (Giere, 1988, p. 81). What is the concern is the similarity relationship between models and the real world that requires a "redundancy theory" of truth only (Giere, 1988, pp. 78–82).

Similarity propose a weaker interpretation of the relationship between a model and a designated real system than isomorphism, in the sense that isomorphism requires models being "perfect" to exhibit all the details and information contained in the object, but only selected features.[21] Similarity account seems similar to Mary Hesse's (1966) analogy account in that there are positive analogies between the model and the object, yet Giere has been cautious in realizing the problem of a vacuous claim in similarity since anything is similar to anything else. He then introduces the role of scientists who are able to specify the relevant degrees and respects of similarity between model and the world. As Giere (2004, pp. 747–748) once put it,

> Note that I am not saying that the model itself represents an aspect of the world because it is similar to that aspect. There is no such representational relationship. Anything is similar to anything else in countless respects, but not anything represents anything else. It is not the model that is doing the representing; it is the scientist using the model who is doing the representing. One way scientists do this is by picking out some specific features of the model that are then claimed to be similar to features of the designated real system to some (perhaps fairly loosely indicated) degree of fit. It is the existence of the specified similarities that makes possible the use of the model to represent the real system in this way.

In comparison between these two accounts of the semantic view, it can be seen that van Fraassen's empiricist perspective for the semantic view can be incorporated with Suppes's account of the models of data. Consider two types of models: model of theory and model of data. The former represents the theory and the latter represent the real world. Van Fraassen's empirical adequacy can be interpreted as an isomorphic mapping from the empirical substructure of a model of the theory to a corresponding part in the model of data. Thus, the structure of theories is the mapping between two types of models.

The above statement contrasts the received view on two respects. First, the relation between theoretical and empirical aspects is not by deduction, but also by mapping between two models. Second, unlike the correspondence rules in the received view that aim to interpret the theory, mapping requires constructing models representing the theory and the world respectively. These not only put models as the major interest of the study, but also accentuates that the representation is proceeded by structure. This means that models are manipulated as

---

[21] Also see Teller (2001).

relational structures that Suppes proposes in his methodology. A model is about representation; representation is about structure.

Giere's view forcibly highlights the view of model as structural representation. He regards models as the primary representational tools in science. Even though his similarity account does not utilize the set-theoretical relational structure for models, it is suggested in his account that the relationships between models and reality are *similarity of structure* with reality, like a map and the area mapped, and Watson and Crick's scale model and the double helical structure of DNA. Hence, models are able to represent the reality structurally.

11.3.5. Representational theory of measurement: representation theorems and uniqueness theorems

Perhaps the most well-known, most well-established application of the semantic view is representational theory of measurement. Modern representational theory was greatly influenced by S.S. Steven's account, which is regarded as a sharp response to the classical view of measurement that all measurement should be able to be reduced to fundamental measurement that involves the axiom of additivity. Stevens claims that those rules of assigning numerals, which are invariant to the mathematical transformation, are of the same scale type. Since measurement is not merely according to an additive rule, Stevens concludes that measurement is defined as "the assignment of numerals to objects or events according to rule – any rule" (Stevens, 1959, p. 19).

The representational theory later developed into a formal account by Scott and Suppes (1958), Suppes and Zinnes (1963) and by the three-volume set of *Foundations of Measurement* by Krantz, Luce, Suppes, and Tversky (Krantz et al., 1971; Suppes et al., 1989; Luce et al., 1990). (Boumans's and Michell's chapters in this volume offer extensive discussions on the representational theory of measurement.) It appears that the concept of structure, defined set-theoretically as suggested by the semantic view, emerges as a crucial component of distinguishing between various types of scale. For a certain type of scale, there is a unique kind of relational structure to be formulated. In order to ensure that the measurement is a satisfactory numerical measurement, two types of theorems that appear to be the core of representational theory of measurement are needed to be fulfill: *representation theorems* and *uniqueness theorems* (or *invariance theorems* in Suppes, 2002).

Briefly, representation theorems indicate an isomorphism between the object and the model representing it. For measurement, it initially requires a representation theorem in order to secure a quantitative scale on the basis of qualitative empirical observations for a particular type of measurement in the way suggested in the semantic view. The measurement is suggested to proceed as follows. First, the object, its properties and relations, and the empirical operations are characterized set-theoretically as an empirical relational structure. A representation theorem then offers an isomorphic mapping between the empirical relational structure and a selected mathematical structure, call it a numerical relational structure. In this way we say that measurement is a *representation* of the empirical relational structure by the numerical relational structure. The isomorphism is established according to a certain type of scale. Take the above-mentioned cases of weak orderings and weak preferences as examples. A legitimate measure or representation for a weak order or a weak preference is to establish an ordinal scale and no other types of scale. To use a utility function to measure a weak order or a weak preference, we want this utility function to satisfies the listed axiom, meaning that we prove a representation theorem for the utility measurement, so that the numbers that the utility function yields can be regarded as a measure of the case of weak order or weak preference under study.

Uniqueness theorems state that when there is more than one representing model, a reduction to a unique representation can be accomplished by a possible admissible transformation for a scale. Suppose there is an original scale ϕ, the admissible transformation produces a new scale ϕ' whose relations are the same as the original ϕ. Thus, a specific scale type allows a specific admissible transformation so that the measurement is unique up to the corresponding admissible transformation. Formally put, suppose there are two scales ϕ and ϕ', an admissible transformation is such that $\phi \rightarrow f(\phi) = \phi'$. Only a measurement which is unique to an admissible transformation is "meaningful".[22]

As mentioned above, measurement is typically regarded as a scientific task of assigning numbers to the objects to be measured. Whereas the assignment can go by any rule, in the representational theory, to measure an object is to find a numerical system that has the same scale – and the same relational structure – as that of the measured objects, and use the former to represent the latter. Thus, representation between "same structure" utilizes Suppes's idea of isomorphism, which is central to representation theorems.

11.4. Discussion: Structure, Representation, and Invariance

The message that the semantic view delivers is models' structural representation to the theory and to the world. Different versions of the semantic view may shed some interesting light on the methodology of econometric models. Giere's picture of the relations between theory, model, and data is useful to understanding the methodology and practices of economics (see Morgan, 1998). Van Fraassen's constructive empiricism is compatible with the LSE approach. Hendry's empiricist position can be described by his statement: "the proof of empirical puddings lies in their eating, not *a priori* views" (Hendry, 1997, p. 168).[23] Unobservable entities (e.g., the DGP for the LSE approach) exist,

[22] The contribution to the issue of meaningfulness in the theory of measurement is mainly due to Louis Narens. See Falmange and Narens (1983), Narens (1985), and Luce and Narens (1987).

[23] This is a paraphrase of Tinbergen's famous quote in his reply to Keynes (Tinbergen, 1940, p. 154).

explaining that the existence of the unobservables is not the purpose; rather it is to construct a model to match the observed data. This matches Hendry's concept of congruence.

The representational theory of measurement asserts that quantitative representations (i.e., measurement) are required to satisfy both representation and uniqueness theorems. In measuring utility, proving the existence of the representation theorem is essential in building utility functions, even though the axiomatization does not proceed in an explicit set-theoretical way. In econometrics, a discipline of measurement, can this structural approach of measurement shed some light on the measurement of structure? In other words, can we apply the structural approach to measurement to understand the measurement of structure in econometrics?

At the outset, econometricians do regard their models as representation. We see econometricians not only customarily call the VAR models the "VAR representation", but also go further to prove theorems for securing models' representation, even though such representation theorem in econometrics are not presented in terms of relational structures. Perhaps the most famous one is the *Granger representation theorem* by Engle and Granger (1987), in which they prove that co-integrated variables can be represented as an error correction model.

Furthermore, the issue concerning uniqueness theorems consists apparently with (a certain type of) the identification problem – the central topic in the above discussion on measuring structure in econometrics. The basic idea of identification is based on the observational equivalence problem. Observational equivalent structures generate the same data or have the same probability density function. Cooley and LeRoy (1985) argue that Sims's VARs are not identified, because we can easily find several observationally equivalent VARs that generate the same probability distribution for the data. Observationally equivalent structures can be related by what Hsiao (1983, p. 231) calls "admissible transformation", which is equivalent to that we understand in unique theorems. Hence, to find the admissible transformation is to prove the uniqueness theorem for a class of observational equivalent structures. The rank and order conditions for simultaneous equations models are thus considered as a type of uniqueness theorem.

To solve the identification or uniqueness problem, as described in the previous part in this chapter, econometricians usually employ the theory view of structure. Different sets of identifying restrictions imply different theoretical interpretations. Christ (1966, p. 298) describes the identification problem in the following way:

> It is a truism that any given observed fact, or any set of observed facts, can be explained in many ways. That is, a large number of hypotheses can be framed, each of which if true would account for the observance of the given fact or facts.

This interpretation of the problem of observational equivalence is a variant of the philosophical problem of *underdetermination of theory by evidence*:

because there can be many theories capable of interpreting the world, we cannot determine the true theory of data by appealing to the data alone. Theory is thus underdetermined by data. When the theory view is applied to identify the structure, it implies that econometricians hold strong priors (Hoover, 1988; Sutton, 2000) on the theory in the face of the underdetermination problem: identification primarily depends on economic theory, other information such as the pragmatic factors for choosing between models (e.g., mathematical elegance or simplicity) are only secondary in importance. A particular economic theory and its suggested identifying restrictions are true, and therefore other theories and their restrictions can be ruled out. Again Christ (1966, p. 299) claims:

> The purpose of a model, embodying *a priori* information (sometimes called the maintained hypothesis), is to rule out most of the hypotheses that are consistent with the observed facts. The ideal situation is one in which, after appeal has been made both to the facts and to the model, only one hypothesis remains acceptable (i.e., is consistent with both). If the "facts" have been correctly observed and the model is correct, the single hypothesis that is consistent with both facts and model must be correct; .... In a typical econometrics problem the hypothesis we accept or reject is a statement about the relevant structure or a part of it or a transformation of it.

Yet to rule out many other hypotheses according to the theory regarded as real does not suggest that others are false. Uniqueness theorems merely imply that the accepted theory is more fundamental so that other theories can be reduced to this fundamental theory (see Suppes, 2002). The transformation (or reduction) to a unique structure (or models representing theoretical structures) indicates *invariance under transformation*. In the measurement theory, since a uniqueness theorem for a scale asserts transformation among the relational structures up to an isomorphism, the existence of the same structure is a prerequisite for invariance under transformation.

If the purpose of econometric models is to represent something, be it theory or data, then representation theorems are thus required to determine which model is an acceptable representation. We seldom see econometricians write down specific representation theorems of the sort, but they are implicitly stated. As seen already, the notion of structure is usually defined in a set-theoretical way. So a representation theorem for econometric models may be (loosely) stated as:

> If S is a structure, then there exists a (structural) model M representing S if and only if M is identifiable,

or

> If S is a structure, then there exists a (structural) model M representing S if and only if M satisfies (a list of identification conditions).

If structure is defined as the invariance view, then there is a hierarchy of invariance: invariance of intervention defines structures, and representation theorems are required to represent the structure. Invariance under transformation secures a unique representation for the structure.

11.5. Conclusion

One of the major themes in econometrics is the definition and the measurement of the notion of structure. We have distinguished between two definitions of structure: the theory view and the invariance view. The theory view is to consider whether the particular chosen theory is true. But if the theory view is accepted, we can equally say that the theory view provides a "realism-about-structure" attitude towards the relationships between theory and data: economic theory is true to the invariant relations that we call structure.

It is more widely accepted (for both realists and empiricists) that structure is understood in terms of invariance under intervention. Invariance is a matter of degree. It provides a good arguable definition of structure, not only in economics and econometrics, but also in other subjects for which the notion of structure is an essential prerequisite.

The semantic view is a more appropriate approach to understanding and interpreting econometrics than the received view. It is particularly because the semantic view stresses the importance of the function and the role of models, and because models are crucial devices for the aim of econometrics - bridging theory and data. There are several studies that have attempted to apply the semantic view to econometrics, for example, Davis (2000), Chao (2002), and Stigum (1990, 2003).[24] Their views are similar to the idea presented in Morgan and Morrison's (1999) edited volume. The Morgan–Morrison volume provides a broader interpretation of models than the semantic view. For them models are "autonomous agents" in the sense that they have the merit of being not entirely dependent on theory or data. Representation is one of models' functions to mediate between theory and data. Nonetheless, as long as structure is concerned, econometric models can involve representation and uniqueness theorems, as the structural approach to measurement suggests, for representing the structure.

Acknowledgements

I am grateful for the suggestions from Kevin Hoover, Chao-Hsi Huang, Mary Morgan and the participants of the Handbook's review workshop held at the Tinbergen Institute Amsterdam on April 21–22, 2006. I particularly thank Marcel Boumans, the editor, for his invitation, and detail comments and suggestions on an early draft of this chapter. Financial supports from the Department of Economics, National Tsing Hua University and the Taiwan National Science Council under grant 95-2415-H-007-006 are gratefully acknowledged.

---

[24] The origin of Stigum's work is regarded as connected with Haavelmo's econometric methodology. See Hendry and Morgan (1995, p. 68), and Moene and Rødesth (1991, p. 179n).

References

Attanasio, O.P. (1998). Consumption demand. Working paper No. 6466. NBER.

Balzer, W. (1992). The structuralist view of measurement: An extension of received measurement theories. In: Savage, C.W., Ehrlich, P. (Eds.), *Philosophical and Foundational Issues in Measurement Theory*. Lawrence Erlbaum Associates, Hillsdale, NJ, pp. 93–117.

Balzer, W., Hamminga, B. (Eds.) (1989). *Philosophy of Economics*. Kluwer, Amsterdam.

Blaug, M. (1992). *The Methodology of Economics. Or How Economists Explain*. second ed. Cambridge Univ. Press, Cambridge.

Bernanke, B.S. (1985). Alternative explanations of the money-income correlation. In: Brunner, K., Meltzer, A.H. (Eds.), *Real Business Cycles, Real Exchange Rates and Actual Policies*. Carnegie-Rochester Conference Series on Public Policy **25**, pp. 49–100.

Blanchard, O.J., Watson, M.W. (1986). Are business cycles all alike? In: Gordon, R. (Ed.), *The American Business Cycle: Continuity and Change*. Univ. of Chicago Press, Chicago, pp. 123–179.

Boumans, M. (2002). Calibration. In: Snowdon, B., Vane, H.R. (Eds.), *An Encyclopedia of Macroeconomics*. Edward, Elgar, Cheltenham, pp. 105–109.

Caldwell, B.J. (1994). *Beyond Positivism, revised ed*. Routledge, London.

Cao, T.Y. (2003). Structural realism and the interpretation of quantum field theory. *Synthese* **136**, 3–24.

Carnap, R. (1966). *Philosophical Foundations of Physics*. Basic Books, New York.

Chao, H.-K. (2002). Representation and structure: The methodology of econometric models of consumption. PhD dissertation. Faculty of Economics and Econometrics, University of Amsterdam.

Chao, H.-K. (2003). Milton Friedman and the emergence of the permanent income hypothesis. *History of Political Economy* **35**, 77–104.

Christ, C.F. (1966). *Econometric Models and Methods*. Wiley, New York.

Cooley, T.F., LeRoy, S.F. (1985). A theoretical macroeconometrics: A critique. *Journal of Monetary Economics* **16**, 283–308.

Davidson, J.E.H., Hendry, D.F., Srba, F., Yeo, S. (1978). Econometric modelling of the aggregate time-series relationship between consumers' expenditure and income in the United Kingdom. *Economic Journal* **88**, 661–692.

Davis, G.C. (2000). A semantic conception of Haavelmo's structure of econometrics. *Economics and Philosophy* **16**, 205–228.

Demiralp, S., Hoover, K.D. (2003). Searching for causal structure of a vector autoregression. *Oxford Bulletin of Economics and Statistics* **65**, 745–767.

Díez Calzada, J.A. (2000). Structuralist analysis of theories of fundamental measurement. In: Balzer, W., Sneed, J.D., Moulines, C.U. (Eds.), *Structuralist Knowledge Representation: Paradigmatic Examples*. Poznan Studies in the Philosophy of the Sciences and Humanities. **75**, pp. 19–49.

Engle, R.F., Granger, C.W.J. (1987). Co-integration and error correction: Representation, estimation, and testing. *Econometrica* **55**, 251–276.

Epstein, R.J. (1987). *A History of Econometrics*. Elsevier, Amsterdam.

Falmange, J.-C., Narens, L. (1983). Scales and meaningfulness of quantitative laws. *Synthese* **55**, 287–325.

Flavin, M.A. (1981). The adjustment of consumption to changing expectations about future income. *Journal of Political Economy* **89**, 974–1009.

Friedman, M. (1957). *A Theory of the Consumption Function*. Princeton Univ. Press, Princeton.

Haavelmo, T. (1944). The probability approach in econometrics. *Econometrica* **12**, 1–118 (Supplement).

Haavelmo, T. (1947). Methods of measuring the marginal propensity to consume. *Journal of American Statistical Association* **42**, 105–122.

Hall, R.E. (1978). Stochastic implications of the life cycle-permanent income hypothesis: Theory and evidence. *Journal of Political Economy* **86**, 971–987.

Hall, R.E. (1990). Survey of research on the random walk of consumption. In: *The Rational Consumer*. MIT Press, Cambridge, MA, pp. 131–157.

Hamilton, J.D. (1994). *Time Series Analysis*. Princeton Univ. Press, Princeton.

Hands, D.W. (1985). The structuralist view of economic theories: A review essay. *Economics and Philosophy* **1**, 303–335.

Hansen, L.P., Singleton, K.J. (1983). Stochastic consumption, risk aversion and the temporal behavior of asset returns. *Journal of Political Economy* **91**, 249–265.

Hartley, J.E., Hoover, K.D., Salyer, K.D. (1998). The limits of business cycle research. In: *Real Business Cycles: A Reader*. Routledge, London, pp. 3–42.

Hendry, D.F. (1995). *Dynamic Econometrics*. Oxford Univ. Press, Oxford.

Hendry, D.F. (1997). On congruent econometric relations: A comment. *Carnegie-Rochester Conference Series on Public Policy* **47**, 163–190.

Hendry, D.F. (2000). *Econometrics: Alchemy or Science? New ed.* Oxford Univ. Press, Oxford.

Hendry, D.F., Mizon, G.E. (1990). Procrustean econometrics: Or stretching and squeezing data. In: Granger, C.W.J. (Ed.), *Modelling Economic Series*. Oxford Univ. Press, Oxford.

Hendry, D.F., Mizon, G.E. (2000). On selecting policy analysis models by forecast accuracy. In: Atkinson, A.B., Glennester, H., Stern, N.H. (Eds.), *Putting Economics to Work. Volume in Honor of Michio Morishima*. London School of Economics, London, pp. 71–119.

Hendry, D.F., Morgan, M.S. (1995). Introduction. In: Hendry, D.F., Morgan, M.S. (Eds.), *The Foundations of Econometric Analysis*. Cambridge Univ. Press, Cambridge, pp. 1–82.

Hesse, M.B. (1966). *Models and Analogies in Science*. Notre Dame Univ. Press, Notre Dame.

Hoover, K.D. (1988). *The New Classical Macroeconomics: A Skeptical Inquiry*. Basil Blackwell, Oxford.

Hoover, K.D. (1994). Econometrics as observation: The Lucas critique and the nature of econometric inference. *Journal of Economic Methodology* **1**, 65–80.

Hoover, K.D. (2001). *Causality in Macroeconomics*. Cambridge Univ. Press, Cambridge.

Hoover, K.D., Jordá, O. (2001). Measuring systematic monetary policy. *Federal Reserve Bank of St. Louis Review* 113–137.

Hsiao, C. (1983). Identification. In: Griliches, Z., Intriligator, M.D. (Eds.), *Handbook of Econometrics, vol. 1*. Elsevier, Amsterdam, pp. 223–283.

Hurwicz, L. (1962). On the structural form of interdependent systems. In: Nagel, E., Suppes, P., Tarski, A. (Eds.), *Logic, Methodology and Philosophy of Science: Proceedings of the 1960 International Congress*. Stanford Univ. Press, Stanford, pp. 232–239.

Giere, R.N. (1988). *Explaining Science: A Cognitive Approach*. Univ. of Chicago Press, Chicago.

Giere, R.N. (1997). *Understanding Scientific Research, fourth ed.* Holt, Rinehart and Winston, New York.

Giere, R.N. (2004). How models are used to represent reality. *Philosophy of Science* **71**, 742–752.

Girshick, M.A., Haavelmo, T. (1947). Statistical analysis of the demand for food: Examples of simultaneous estimation of structural equations. *Econometrica* **15**, 79–110.

Keating, J. (1990). Identifying VAR models under rational expectations. *Journal of Monetary Economics* **25**, 453–476.

Kim, J., de Marchi, N., Morgan, M.S. (1995). Empirical model particularities and belief in the natural rate hypothesis. *Journal of Econometrics* **67**, 81–102.

Koopmans, T.C. (1947). Measurement without theory. *Review of Economics and Statistics* **29**, 161–172.

Koopmans, T.C. (1957). *Three Essays on the State of Economic Science*. McGraw-Hill, New York.

Krantz, D.H., Luce, R.D., Suppes, P., Tversky, A. (1971). *Foundations of Measurement, vol. 1: Additive and Polynomial Representations*. Academic Press, New York.

Kuhn, T.S. (1962). *The Structure of Scientific Revolutions*. Univ. of Chicago Press, Chicago.

Leeper, E.M., Zha, T. (2003). Modest policy interventions. *Journal of Monetary Economics* **50**, 1673–1700.

Liu, T.-C. (1960). Underidentification, structural estimation and forecasting. *Econometrica* **28**, 855–865.

Liu, T.-C. (1963). Structural estimation and forecasting: A critique of the Cowles Commission method. *Tsing-Hua Journal* **3–4**, 152–171.

Lucas, R.E. (1973). Some international evidence on output–inflation tradeoffs. *American Economic Review* **63**, 326–334.

Lucas, R.E. (1976). Econometric policy evaluation: A critique. In: Brunner, K., Meltzer, A.H. (Eds.), *The Phillips Curve and Labor Markets*. Carnegie-Rochester Conference Series on Public Policy **1**, pp. 19–46.

Luce, R.D., Krantz, D.H., Suppes, P., Tversky, A. (1990). *Foundations of Measurement, vol. 3: Representation, Axiomatization, and Invariance*. Academic Press, San Diego.

Maddala, G.S. (2001). *Introduction to econometrics, third ed.* Wiley, New York.

Marschak, J. (1953). Economic measurement for policy and prediction. In: Hood, W.C., Koopmans, T.C. (Eds.), *Studies in Econometric Method*. Cowles Commission Monograph 14. Wiley, New York, pp. 1–26.

Mayer, T. (1972). *Permanent Income, Wealth, and Consumption: A Critique of the Permanent Income Theory, the Life-Cycle Hypothesis and Related Theories*. Univ. of California Press, Berkeley.

Moene, K.O., Rødseth, A. (1991). Nobel laureate Trygve Haavelmo. *Journal of Economic Perspectives* **5**, 175–92.

Morgan, M.S. (1990). *The History of Econometric Ideas*. Cambridge Univ. Press, Cambridge.

Morgan, M.S. (1998). Models. In: Davis, J.B., Hands, D.W., Mäki, U. (Eds.), *The Handbook of Economic Methodology*. Edward Elgar, Cheltenham, pp. 316–321.

Morgan, M.S., Morrison, M. (1999). *Models as Mediators: Perspectives on Natural and Social Science*. Cambridge Univ. Press, Cambridge.

Narens, L. (1985). *Abstract Measurement Theory*. MIT Press, Cambridge, MA.

Narens, L., Luce, R.D. (1987). Meaningfulness and invariance. In: Eatwell, J., Milgate, M., Newman, P. (Eds.), *The New Palgrave: A Dictionary of Economics, vol. 3*. Macmillan Reference Limited, London, pp. 417–21.

Qin, D. (1993). *The Formation of Econometrics: A Historical Perspective*. Oxford Univ. Press, Oxford.

Scott, D., Suppes, P. (1958). Foundational aspects of theories of measurement. *Journal of Symbolic Logic* **23**, 113–128.

Sims, C.A. (1980). Macroeconomics and reality. *Econometrica* **48**, 1–48.

Sims, C.A. (1982). Policy analysis with econometric models. *Brooking Papers on Economic Activity* 107–152.

Sims, C.A. (1986). Are forecasting models usable for policy analysis? *Federal Reserve Bank of Minneapolis Quarterly Review* **10**, 2–16.

Sims, C.A. (1998). The role of interest rate policy in the generation and propagation of business cycles: What has changed since the '30s? In: Fuhrer, J.C., Schuh, S. (Eds.), *Beyond Shocks: What Causes Business Cycles*? Federal Reserve Bank of Boston, Boston, pp. 121–175.

Stegmüller, W., Balzer, W., Spohn, W. (Eds.) (1982). *Philosophy of Economics*. Springer-Verlag, Berlin.

Stevens, S.S. (1959). Measurement, psychophysics and utility. In: Churchman, C.W., Ratoosh, P. (Eds.), *Measurement: Definitions and Theories*. Wiley, New York, pp. 18–63.

Stigum, B.P. (1990). *Toward a Formal Science of Economics*. MIT Press, Cambridge, MA.

Stigum, B.P. (2003). *Econometrics and the Philosophy of Economics: Theory-Data Confrontations in Economics*. Princeton Univ. Press, Princeton.

Stock, J.H., Watson, M.W. (2001). Vector autoregressions. *Journal of Economic Perspectives* **15**, 101–116.

Suppe, F. (Ed.) (1977). *The Structure of Scientific Theories, second ed.* Univ. of Illinois Press, Urbana.

Suppe, F. (1989). *The Semantic Conception of Theories and Scientific Realism*. Univ. of Illinois Press, Urbana.

Suppe, F. (2000). Understanding scientific theories: an assessment of developments, 1969–1988. *Philosophy of Science* **67**, S102–S115.

Suppes, P. (1957). *Introduction to Logic*. D. Van Nostrand, New Jersey.
Suppes, P. (1960). A comparison of the meaning and uses of models in mathematics and the empirical sciences. *Synthese* **12**, 287–301.
Suppes, P. (1962). Models of data. In: Nagel, E., Suppes, P., Tarski, A. (Eds.), *Logic, Methodology and Philosophy of Science: Proceedings of the 1960 International Congress*. Stanford Univ. Press, Stanford, pp. 252–261.
Suppes, P. (1967). What is a scientific theory? In: Morgenbesser, S. (Ed.), *Philosophy of Science Today*. Basic Book, New York, pp. 55–67.
Suppes, P. (2002). *Representation and Invariance of Scientific Structures*. CSLI Publications, Stanford.
Suppes, P., Zinnes, J.L. (1963). Basic measurement theory. In: Luce, R.D., Bush, R.R., Galanter, E. (Eds.), *Handbook of Mathematical Psychology*. Wiley, New York, pp. 3–76.
Suppes, P., Krantz, D.H., Luce, R.D., Tversky, A. (1989). *Foundations of Measurement, vol. 2: Geometrical, Threshold, and Probabilistic Representations*. Academic Press, San Diego.
Sutton, J. (2000). *Marshall's Tendency: What Can Economists Know*? The MIT Press, Cambridge, MA.
Teller, P. (2001). Twilight of the perfect model model. *Erkenntnis* **55**, 393–415.
Tinbergen, J. (1940). On a method of statistical business-cycle research, a reply. *Economic Journal* **50**, 141–154.
Van Fraassen, B. (1980). *The Scientific Image*. Oxford Univ. Press, Oxford.
Van Fraassen, B. (1989). *Law and Symmetry*. Oxford Univ. Press, Oxford.
Varian, H.R. (1992). *Microeconomic Analysis, third ed.* Norton, New York.
Woodward, J. (2000). Explanation and invariance in the special sciences. *British Journal for the Philosophy of Science* **51**, 197–254.
Woodward, J. (2003). *Making Things Happen*. Oxford Univ. Press, Oxford.

CHAPTER 12

Local Sensitivity in Econometrics

Jan R. Magnus

Department of Econometrics and Operations Research, Tilburg University, The Netherlands
E-mail address: magnus@uvt.nl

Abstract

We investigate a phenomenon which is well known in applied econometrics and statistics: an auxiliary parameter (say θ) is significant in a diagnostic test, but ignoring it (setting $\theta = 0$) makes very little difference for the parameter of interest (say β). In other words, the estimator for β is not sensitive to variations in θ. We shall argue that sensitivity analysis is often more relevant than diagnostic testing, and we shall review some of the sensitivity results that are currently available. In fact, sensitivity analysis and diagnostic testing are both important in econometrics. They play different and, as we shall see, orthogonal roles.

12.1. Motivation

Suppose we are given a cloud of points, as in Fig. 12.1, and assume that these points are generated by a linear relationship

$$y_t = \beta_0 + \beta_1 x_t + \varepsilon_t \quad (t = 1, \dots, n),$$

which we write more compactly as $y = X\beta + \varepsilon$. Assume further that the expectation of the error is $\mathrm{E}(\varepsilon) = 0$ and that its variance is $\mathrm{var}(\varepsilon) = \sigma^2\Omega$. There are three levels of knowledge on Ω. Firstly, we may know Ω completely. This does not happen often, but if it does we would estimate β by generalized least squares (GLS):

$$\tilde{\beta} = \left(X'\Omega^{-1}X\right)^{-1}X'\Omega^{-1}y,$$

and this estimator would be best linear unbiased. Secondly, and more realistically, we might know the *structure* of Ω (for example, an AR(1) process) but not the values of the parameters. Thus we would know that $\Omega = \Omega(\theta)$ where θ is a finite-dimensional parameter vector. Since θ is unknown it needs to be estimated, say by $\tilde{\theta}$. If $\tilde{\theta}$ is a consistent estimator (not necessarily efficient), and writing $\widetilde{\Omega} := \Omega(\tilde{\theta})$, we obtain the *feasible* GLS estimator

$$\tilde{\beta}^* = \left(X'\widetilde{\Omega}^{-1}X\right)^{-1}X'\widetilde{\Omega}^{-1}y.$$

Measurement in Economics: A Handbook
Marcel Boumans (Editor)

In most cases, however, not even the structure of Ω is known. We could then sequentially test, thereby adding more and more noise to our estimator for β, or we might simply set $\Omega = I$. In the latter case, we obtain the ordinary least squares (OLS) estimator for β:

$$\hat{\beta} = (X'X)^{-1}X'y.$$

One question is how good or bad this OLS estimator is, in other words: how sensitive it is to variations in Ω. Let us consider the data plotted in Fig. 12.1. If we estimate the relationship by OLS we obtain the solid line, labeled "OLS regression". In fact, the data have been generated by some ARMA process, and therefore the OLS estimator is not the "right" estimator. Consider the hypothesis that the $\{\varepsilon_t\}$ form an AR(1) process, so that the elements of Ω depend on just one parameter, say θ. We don't know whether this hypothesis is true (in fact, it is not), but we can test the hypothesis using a *diagnostic*, such as the Durbin–Watson statistic. In the present case, the diagnostic is statistically very significant, so that we must reject the null hypothesis (no autocorrelation) in favor of the alternative hypothesis (positive autocorrelation). Given the outcome of the diagnostic test, we estimate the AR(1) parameter θ from the OLS residuals, and estimate β again, this time by feasible GLS. This yields the broken line, labeled "GLS regression".

The broken line is hardly visible in Fig. 12.1, because the OLS and GLS estimates coincide almost exactly. Hence, the OLS estimates are not *sensitive* to

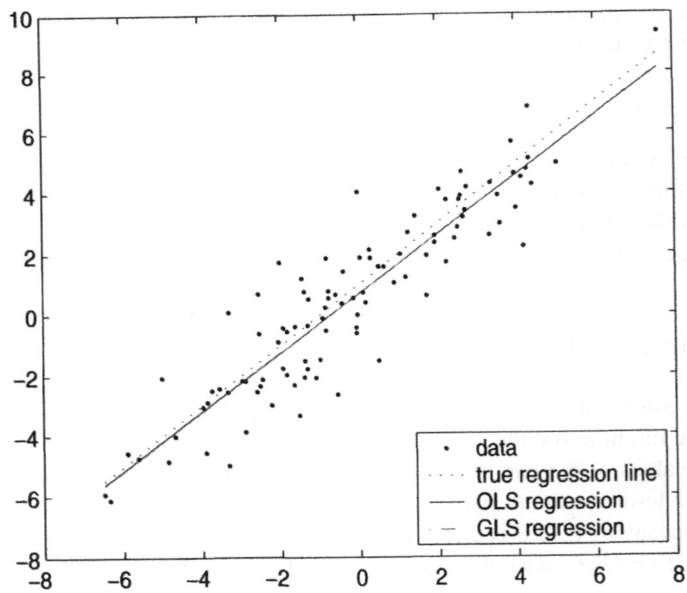

Fig. 12.1: Sensitivity to AR(1) misspecification: simulated example.

whether θ is zero or not, even though the diagnostic test has informed us that θ is significantly different from zero. One may argue that although $\hat{\beta}$ is not affected by the presence θ, the variance of $\hat{\beta}$ will be affected. This is true. In fact, the variance will be quite sensitive to variance misspecification for reasons that will become clear in Section 12.3. This is precisely the reason why in current-day econometrics we usually estimate the variance by some "robust" method such as the one proposed by Newey and West (1987).

This simple example illustrates a phenomenon which is well known in applied econometrics and statistics. An auxiliary parameter (like θ) may show up in a diagnostic test as significant, but ignoring it (setting $\theta = 0$) makes very little difference for the parameter of interest (here β). In other words, the estimator for β is not sensitive to variations in θ. We shall argue that sensitivity analysis is often more relevant than diagnostic testing, and we shall review some of the sensitivity results that are currently available. In fact, sensitivity analysis and diagnostic testing are both important in econometrics. They play different and, as we shall see, orthogonal roles.

We shall thus be concerned with models containing two sets of parameters: focus parameters (β) and nuisance parameters (θ). In such models one often has a choice between the unrestricted estimator $\tilde{\beta}$ (based on the full model) and the restricted estimator $\hat{\beta}$, estimated under the restriction $\theta = 0$. Let us introduce the function $\hat{\beta}(\theta)$, which estimates β for each fixed value of θ. The unrestricted and restricted estimators can then be expressed as $\tilde{\beta} = \hat{\beta}(\tilde{\theta})$ and $\hat{\beta} = \hat{\beta}(0)$, respectively.

A Taylor expansion gives

$$\tilde{\beta} - \hat{\beta} = \hat{\beta}(\tilde{\theta}) - \hat{\beta}(0) = \left.\frac{\partial \hat{\beta}(\theta)}{\partial \theta'}\right|_{\theta=0} \tilde{\theta} + O_p(1/n),$$

which shows that the difference between $\tilde{\beta}$ and $\hat{\beta}$ factorizes as $\tilde{\beta} - \hat{\beta} = S\tilde{\theta}$, where S denotes the *sensitivity*,

$$S := \left.\frac{\partial \hat{\beta}(\theta)}{\partial \theta'}\right|_{\theta=0}.$$

We may think of $\tilde{\theta}$ as the "magnitude" and of S as the "direction" of the impact of the misspecification on $\hat{\beta}$. In applied econometrics the choice between $\tilde{\beta}$ and $\hat{\beta}$ is almost always based exclusively on a t- or F-statistic, or a simple transformation thereof. In other words, the choice is based on a *diagnostic*, answering the question whether $\tilde{\theta}$ is "large" or "small". Since θ is a nuisance parameter, we are not primarily interested in whether $\tilde{\theta}$ is large or small; our interest is in β. It may very well be that $\tilde{\theta}$ is large, but that nevertheless the difference between $\tilde{\beta}$ and $\hat{\beta}$ is small, a frequent observation in econometric practice, which occurs if the sensitivity is small. A proper choice between the estimators should therefore be based on both factors: the diagnostic *and* the sensitivity. The literature on diagnostic testing is huge; the literature on sensitivity analysis is relatively small.

There are two branches of sensitivity analysis: data perturbation and model perturbation. In data perturbation one may perturb the location of the regressors, or the location or the scale of the dependent variable in a regression context. This branch is associated mainly with the work of Huber (2004, first edition 1980) and Cook (1979, 1986). In contrast, model perturbation considers the effects on the parameter of interest (or any other focus) of small deviations from the hypothesized model, such as the deletion of relevant regressors, the misspecification of the variance matrix, or deviations from normality. This branch plays a role in Bayesian statistics, in particular the effect of misspecifying the prior distribution (Leamer, 1978, 1984; Polasek, 1984), but also in classical econometrics (Banerjee and Magnus, 1999, 2000). Our interest lies in the perturbation of models, and "sensitivity analysis" will be understood to mean the study of the effect of small changes in model assumptions on an estimator or test statistic of a parameter of interest. Sensitivity issues are also important in an experimental context; see Harrison et al. (this volume).

Sensitivity analysis and the relationship between sensitivity and diagnostic testing are closely linked to what a model is and what its function should be. Basic to the understanding of sensitivity is the idea that the correctness of a model is neither necessary *nor even desirable*. What matters is that the model fulfills the task for which it has been built, an idea which relates closely to Giere's (1999) constructive realism and his concept of similarity; see also Chao (this volume).

This chapter surveys some recent developments in sensitivity analysis, and relies heavily on three papers: Banerjee and Magnus (1999, 2000) and Magnus and Vasnev (2007). Sections 12.2–12.4 are based on Banerjee and Magnus (1999), and discuss the sensitivity of the OLS predictor (Section 12.2) and the OLS variance estimator (Section 12.3). Two sensitivity statistics are proposed: $B1$ and $D1$, and their behavior is discussed in Section 12.4. Sections 12.5 and 12.6 are based on Banerjee and Magnus (2000), and discuss the sensitivity of the F-test and, more in particular, the t-test. The behavior of the appropriate statistic φ is investigated. Section 12.7 relates to some findings in Magnus and Vasnev (2007), and concerns the relationship between sensitivity and diagnostic tests and in particular the asymptotic independence of sensitivity and the diagnostic. Some concluding remarks for the practitioner are offered in Section 12.8.

12.2. Sensitivity of the OLS Predictor

Let us begin by considering the standard linear regression model

$$y = X\beta + u, \tag{12.1}$$

where y is an $n \times 1$ vector of observations, X is an $n \times k$ matrix of explanatory variables, β is a $k \times 1$ vector of unknown parameters, and u is an $n \times 1$ vector of unobservable disturbances. We assume that all standard assumptions hold, except one. Thus we assume that X is nonrandom with full column-rank k, and that u is normally distributed with mean 0. The disturbance variance matrix, however, is not given by $\sigma^2 I_n$, but by $\sigma^2 \Omega(\theta)$, where σ^2 and the $m \times 1$ vector θ are unknown. Our parameters of interest are $\mathrm{E}(y) = X\beta$ or, which amounts to the same, β. The variance parameters σ^2 and θ are nuisance parameters.

Without any loss of generality we may assume that $\Omega(0) = I_n$. Then, at $\theta = 0$, the ordinary least squares (OLS) estimator and predictor,

$$\hat{\beta} = (X'X)^{-1}X'y \quad \text{and} \quad \hat{y} = X(X'X)^{-1}X'y,$$

are unbiased and efficient. If $\theta \neq 0$, then $\hat{\beta}$ and $\hat{y}$ are, in general, no longer efficient. If we know the structure of Ω and the values of the m elements of θ, then generalized least squares (GLS) is more efficient. If we know the structure Ω but not the value of θ, then estimated GLS is not necessarily more efficient than OLS. But in the most common case, where we don't even know the structure Ω, we have to determine Ω *and* estimate θ. The question then is whether the resulting estimator for β (or $X\beta$) is "better" than the OLS estimator $\hat{\beta}$. In sensitivity analysis we don't ask whether the nuisance parameters (here the θ-parameters) are significantly different from 0 or not. Instead we ask directly whether the GLS estimators $\hat{\beta}(\theta)$ and $\hat{y}(\theta)$ are sensitive to deviations from the white noise assumption.

If θ is known, then the parameters β and σ^2 can be estimated by generalized least squares. Thus,

$$\hat{\beta}(\theta) = \left(X'\Omega^{-1}(\theta)X\right)^{-1} X'\Omega^{-1}(\theta)y \tag{12.2}$$

and

$$\hat{\sigma}^2(\theta) = \frac{(y - \hat{y}(\theta))'\Omega^{-1}(\theta)(y - \hat{y}(\theta))}{n-k}, \tag{12.3}$$

where $\hat{y}(\theta)$ denotes the predictor for y, that is,

$$\hat{y}(\theta) = X\hat{\beta}(\theta). \tag{12.4}$$

The OLS estimators are then given by $\hat{\beta} := \hat{\beta}(0)$, $\hat{\sigma}^2 := \hat{\sigma}^2(0)$, and $\hat{y} := \hat{y}(0)$. We wish to assess how sensitive (linear combinations of) $\hat{\beta}(\theta)$ is with respect to small changes in θ, when θ is close to 0. The predictor is the linear combination most suitable for our analysis. Since any estimable linear combination of $\hat{\beta}(\theta)$ is a linear combination of $\hat{y}(\theta)$, and vice versa, this constitutes no loss of generality.

We now define the *sensitivity* of the predictor $\hat{y}(\theta)$ (with respect to θ_s) as

$$z_s := \left.\frac{\partial \hat{y}(\theta)}{\partial \theta_s}\right|_{\theta=0} \quad (s = 1, \ldots, m), \tag{12.5}$$

which is related to the "impact factor" considered by Omtzigt and Paruolo (2005). The sensitivity of $\hat{\beta}(\theta)$ (with respect to θ_s) is then

$$\left.\frac{\partial\hat{\beta}(\theta)}{\partial\theta_s}\right|_{\theta=0} = (X'X)^{-1}X'z_s.$$

In order to use the (normally distributed) $n \times 1$ vector z_s as a sensitivity statistic, we transform it into a χ^2-variable in the usual way. Defining

$$M := I_n - X(X'X)^{-1}X', \qquad A_s := \left.\frac{\partial\Omega(\theta)}{\partial\theta_s}\right|_{\theta=0}, \qquad C_s := (I_n - M)A_s M,$$

we thus propose

$$B_s := \frac{z_s'(C_s C_s')^- z_s}{(n-k)\hat{\sigma}^2} \tag{12.6}$$

as a statistic to measure the sensitivity of the predictor $\hat{y}(\theta)$ with respect to θ_s. (The notation A^- denotes a generalized inverse of A.) Large values of B_s indicate that $\hat{y}(\theta)$ is sensitive to small changes in θ_s when θ is close to 0, and therefore that setting $\theta_s = 0$ is not justified. The statistic B_s depends only on y and X and can therefore be observed. Since the distribution of y depends on θ, so does the distribution of B_s.

Using standard results of differential calculus (see Magnus and Neudecker, 1988) we obtain the differential of $\hat{y}(\theta)$ from (12.2) and (12.4),

$$\mathrm{d}\hat{y}(\theta) = X\big(X'\Omega^{-1}(\theta)X\big)^{-1}X'\big(\mathrm{d}\Omega^{-1}(\theta)\big)\big(y - X\hat{\beta}(\theta)\big)$$

so that, at $\theta = 0$,

$$z_s = -X(X'X)^{-1}X'A_s My = -C_s y.$$

Hence, using (12.6) and the fact that $\hat{\sigma}^2 = y'My/(n-k)$, we obtain

$$B_s := \frac{z_s'(C_s C_s')^- z_s}{(n-k)\hat{\sigma}^2} = \frac{y'C_s'(C_s C_s')^- C_s y}{y'My}.$$

Next consider the distribution of B_s. We notice that $C_s X = 0$ and $MX = 0$. Evaluating the distribution of y at $\theta = 0$ we then find

$$B_s = \frac{u'W_s u}{u'Mu} = \frac{u'W_s u}{u'W_s u + u'(M - W_s)u}.$$

Now, W_s is idempotent with $\mathrm{rk}(W_s) = \mathrm{rk}(C_s) = r_s$. Also, since $MC_s' = C_s'$, we have $MW_s = W_s$. Hence $M - W_s$ is idempotent as well and its rank is $n - k - r_s$.

The condition $0 < r_s < n-k$ implies that both W_s and $M-W_s$ have rank $\geqslant 1$. It follows that $u'W_s u \sim \sigma^2\chi^2(r_s)$, $u'(M-W_s)u \sim \sigma^2\chi^2(n-k-r_s)$, and the two quadratic forms are independent, because $(M-W_s)W_s = 0$. Therefore, B_s follows a Beta-distribution. Summarizing, we have found

THEOREM 1. *We have*

$$z_s = -C_s y \quad \text{and} \quad B_s = \frac{y'W_s y}{y'My},$$

where $W_s := C_s'(C_s C_s')^- C_s$. *Furthermore, if* $r_s := \mathrm{rk}(C_s)$ *satisfies* $0 < r_s < n-k$, *and the distribution of* y *is evaluated at* $\theta = 0$, *then*

$$B_s \sim \mathrm{Beta}\left(\frac{r_s}{2}, \frac{n-k-r_s}{2}\right),$$

or, what amounts to the same,

$$\frac{n-k-r_s}{r_s} \cdot \frac{B_s}{1-B_s} \sim \mathrm{F}(r_s, n-k-r_s).$$

We shall be primarily interested in the case where A_s is a Toeplitz matrix, so that $A_s = T^{(h)}$ for some $0 \leqslant h \leqslant n-1$, where

$$T^{(h)}(i,j) = \begin{cases} 1 & \text{if } |i-j| = h, \\ 0 & \text{otherwise.} \end{cases}$$

This is a common situation for stationary processes and the matrix C_s then becomes $C_s = (I_n - M)T^{(h)}M$. Our particular focus – and the most important special case in practice – is $A_s = T^{(1)}$, where

$$T^{(1)} = \begin{pmatrix} 0 & 1 & 0 & \dots & 0 & 0 \\ 1 & 0 & 1 & \dots & 0 & 0 \\ 0 & 1 & 0 & \dots & 0 & 0 \\ \vdots & \vdots & \vdots & & \vdots & \vdots \\ 0 & 0 & 0 & \dots & 0 & 1 \\ 0 & 0 & 0 & \dots & 1 & 0 \end{pmatrix}. \tag{12.7}$$

We shall denote the corresponding B_1-statistic as $B1$. We know that $B1$ measures the sensitivity of $\hat{y}(\theta)$ with respect to the AR(1) (or MA(1) or ARMA(1, 1)) parameter. The statistic $B1$ should be seen as an alternative to the Durbin–Watson (DW) statistic. But where the DW-statistic answers the question "Is the AR(1) parameter θ equal to 0?" our $B1$ statistic answers the question "Are $\hat{y}$ and $\hat{\beta}$ sensitive to the fact that θ may not be 0?" In most practical situations the latter question seems more appropriate. In the next section we shall see that DW is essentially the sensitivity of $\hat{\sigma}^2(\theta)$. Hence we can interpret DW as answering the question "Is $\hat{\sigma}^2$ sensitive to θ?" Thus, DW turns out to be measuring the sensitivity of the estimator for the variance of y, while $B1$ measures the sensitivity of the estimator for its mean. Again, in most practical situations our primary interest lies in the mean of y. The statistic $B1$ provides a direct measure for this sensitivity.

12.3. Sensitivity of the OLS Variance Estimator

In the standard linear model we have two parameters of interest: the mean parameters β and the variance parameter σ^2. Having studied the sensitivity of the mean parameter in the previous section, we now turn our attention to the sensitivity of the variance estimator $\hat{\sigma}^2(\theta)$ with respect to small changes in θ.

It is more convenient to consider $\log\hat{\sigma}^2$ instead of $\hat{\sigma}^2$. Thus we define

$$D_s := \left.\frac{\partial \log\hat{\sigma}^2(\theta)}{\partial\theta_s}\right|_{\theta=0} \tag{12.8}$$

as the statistic to measure the sensitivity of the $\hat{\sigma}^2(\theta)$ with respect to θ_s, the counterpart to B_s defined in (12.6). Differentiating $\hat{\sigma}^2(\theta)$ in (12.3) gives

$$\begin{aligned}&(n-k)\mathrm{d}\big(\hat{\sigma}^2(\theta)\big)\\ &\quad= -2\big(y-\hat{y}(\theta)\big)'\Omega^{-1}(\theta)\mathrm{d}\big(\hat{y}(\theta)\big) + \big(y-\hat{y}(\theta)\big)'\big(\mathrm{d}\Omega^{-1}(\theta)\big)\big(y-\hat{y}(\theta)\big),\end{aligned}$$

and hence, at $\theta = 0$,

$$(n-k)\frac{\partial\hat{\sigma}^2(\theta)}{\partial\theta_s} = 2y'MC_s y - y'MA_sMy = -y'MA_sMy,$$

since $MC_s = 0$. Thus we obtain the following counterpart to Theorem 1.

THEOREM 2. *We have*

$$D_s = -\frac{y'MA_sMy}{y'My} = -\frac{v'P'A_sPv}{v'v},$$

where P is an $n\times(n-k)$ matrix containing the $n-k$ eigenvectors of M associated with the eigenvalue 1, that is, $M = PP'$, $P'P = I_{n-k}$, and $v := P'y/\sigma \sim \mathrm{N}(0, P'\Omega(\theta)P)$. Furthermore, if the distribution of y is evaluated at $\theta = 0$, then $v \sim \mathrm{N}(0, I_{n-k})$.

Theorem 2 shows that D_s has the same form as the DW-statistic. The most important special case occurs again when $A_s = T^{(1)}$ (that is, AR(1) or MA(1) or ARMA(1, 1)). The corresponding D_s-statistic will be denoted by $D1$. This case was considered by Dufour and King (1991, Theorem 1) as a locally best invariant test of $\theta = 0$ against $\theta > 0$, where θ denotes the AR(1) parameter. Not surprisingly, $D1$ is closely related to the DW-statistic, a fact first observed by King (1981).

An immediate consequence of Theorems 1 and 2 and the fact that

$$\hat{u}'T^{(1)}\hat{u} = 2\sum_{t=2}^{n}\hat{u}_t\hat{u}_{t-1} = -\sum_{t=2}^{n}(\hat{u}_t - \hat{u}_{t-1})^2 + \sum_{t=2}^{n}\hat{u}_t^2 + \sum_{t=2}^{n}\hat{u}_{t-1}^2$$

is the following important and illuminating special case.

THEOREM 3 (Special Case). *In the special case $A_s = T^{(1)}$, we have*

$$B_s := B1 = \frac{\hat{u}'W^{(1)}\hat{u}}{\hat{u}'\hat{u}}, \qquad D_s := D1 = -\frac{\hat{u}'T^{(1)}\hat{u}}{\hat{u}'\hat{u}} = \mathrm{DW} - 2 + R/n,$$

where

$$W^{(1)} := C^{(1)\prime}\big(C^{(1)}C^{(1)\prime}\big)^{-}C^{(1)}, \quad C^{(1)} := (I - M)T^{(1)}M,$$

and $\hat{u} = My$ is the vector of OLS-residuals, DW denotes the Durbin–Watson statistic,

$$\mathrm{DW} = \sum_{t=2}^{n}(\hat{u}_t - \hat{u}_{t-1})^2 \Big/ \sum_{t=1}^{n}\hat{u}_t^2,$$

and $R = (\hat{u}_1^2 + \hat{u}_n^2)/(\sum\hat{u}_t^2/n)$ is a remainder term.

The matrix $T^{(1)}$ is equally relevant in the AR(1) and MA(1) case (and indeed, the ARMA(1, 1) case). From Theorem 3 we see that $B1$ and $D1$ depend on $T^{(1)}$, and hence are identical for AR(1) and MA(1). This explains, inter alia, the conclusion of Griffiths and Beesley (1984) that a pretest estimator based on an AR and an MA pretest performs essentially the same as a pretest estimator based on only an AR pretest. Any likelihood-based test (such as the Lagrange multiplier test) uses the derivatives of the log-likelihood, in particular $\partial\Omega(\theta)/\partial\theta_s$. Under the null hypothesis that $\theta = 0$ the test thus depends on A_s, which explains why A_s plays such an important role in many test statistics. Any pretest which depends on $A_s = T^{(1)}$ will not be appropriate to distinguish between AR(1) and MA(1). A survey of the DW and $D1$ statistics is given in King (1987).

12.4. Behavior of $B1$ and $D1$

We know from Theorem 1 that $B1$ follows a Beta-distribution when the disturbances are white noise. Our next step is to ask how $B1$ behaves when the disturbances follow some more general stationary process. In this section we answer this question for the case where the disturbances follow a stationary AR(1) process. The variance matrix then has one parameter (apart from σ^2): θ. The correct procedure for measuring the sensitivity of $\hat{y}$ (and $\hat{\beta}$) is to use $B1$. Similarly, the correct procedure for measuring the sensitivity of $\hat{\sigma}^2$ is to use $D1$, which is essentially the DW-statistic.

We perform a little simulation. First we generate five regressors:

x_1	constant	$1, 1, 1, \ldots$
x_2	time trend	$1, 2, 3, \ldots$
x_3	normal distribution	$\mathrm{E}(x_3) = 0$, $\mathrm{var}(x_3) = 9$
x_4	lognormal distribution	$\mathrm{E}(\log x_4) = 0$, $\mathrm{var}(\log x_4) = 9$
x_5	uniform distribution	$-2 \leqslant x_5 \leqslant 2$

These regressors can be combined in various data sets. We consider five data sets with two regressors and five with three regressors, as follows:

	$k = 2$		$k = 3$
1	constant, time trend	6	constant, time trend, normal
2	constant, normal	7	constant, time trend, lognormal
3	constant, lognormal	8	constant, uniform, lognormal
4	uniform, normal	9	uniform, normal, lognormal
5	time trend, normal	10	time trend, normal, uniform

For each of the ten data sets we calculate $B1^*$ and $D1^*$ such that

$$\Pr(B1 > B1^*) = \alpha \quad \text{and} \quad \Pr(D1 \leqslant D1^*) = \alpha,$$

where $\alpha = 0.05$ and the disturbances are assumed to be white noise. In Fig. 12.2 we calculate

$$\Pr(B1 > B1^*) \quad \text{and} \quad \Pr(D1 \leqslant D1^*)$$

under the assumption that the disturbances are AR(1) for values of θ between 0 and 1. Each line in the figure corresponds to one of the ten different data sets. As noted before, the $D1$-statistic is essentially the DW-statistic. As a result, $\Pr(D1 \leqslant D1^*)$ can be interpreted as the power of $D1$ in testing $\theta = 0$ against $\theta > 0$. Alternatively we can interpret $\Pr(D1 \leqslant D1^*)$ as the sensitivity of $\hat{\sigma}^2$ with respect to θ. In the same way, $B1$ measures the sensitivity of $\hat{y}$ (and $\hat{\beta}$) with respect to θ. One glance at Fig. 12.2 shows that $B1$ is quite insensitive, hence robust, with respect to θ, even for values of θ close to 1. The figure

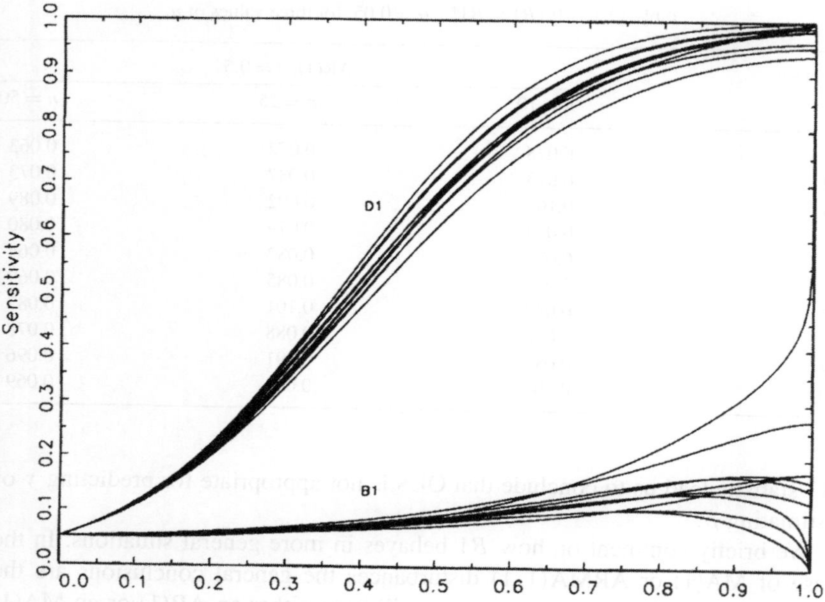

Fig. 12.2: $B1$ and $D1$: AR(1) disturbances as a function of θ ($\alpha = 0.05$).

shows the probabilities $\Pr(B1 > B1^*)$ and $\Pr(D1 \leqslant D1^*)$ for $n = 25$. The main conclusion is that $D1$ is quite sensitive to θ but $B1$ is not. Hence, the $D1$ or DW-statistic may indicate the OLS is not appropriate since θ is "significantly" different from 0, but the $B1$ statistic shows that the estimates $\hat{y}$ and $\hat{\beta}$ are little effected. This explains and illustrates a phenomenon well known to all applied econometricians, namely that OLS estimates are "robust" to variance misspecification (although their distribution may be less robust).

If θ is close to 1, then the limit (or the limiting distribution) can be calculated from Banerjee and Magnus (1999, Appendix 2). The flatness of the $B1$-curves suggests that $B1$ and $D1$ are near-independent. This "near-independence" is based on asymptotic independence, a fact proved in Section 12.8. For $n = 25$ and $\theta = 0.5$ we would decide in only about 7–10% of the cases that $\hat{y}$ is sensitive with respect to θ.

Figure 12.2 gives the sensitivities for one value of n, namely $n = 25$. To see how $B1$ depends on n we calculate for each of our ten data sets $\Pr(B1 > B1^*)$ for three values of n ($n = 10, 25, 50$) and one variance specification: AR(1). The results are given in Table 12.1. Table 12.1 confirms our earlier statements. In only 5–10% of the cases would we conclude that $\hat{y}$ and $\hat{\beta}$ are sensitive to AR(1) disturbances. High values of n are needed to get close to the probability limit and the higher is $\theta > 0$, the higher should be n.

Our calculations thus indicate that OLS is very robust against AR(1) (in fact, ARMA(1, 1)) disturbances. In only about 5–10% of the cases does the

Table 12.1: $\Pr(B1 > B1^*)$, $\alpha = 0.05$, for three values of n.

Data set	AR(1), $\theta = 0.5$		
	$n = 10$	$n = 25$	$n = 50$
1	0.078	0.072	0.063
2	0.073	0.087	0.073
3	0.101	0.092	0.089
4	0.073	0.079	0.080
5	0.077	0.082	0.064
6	0.093	0.085	0.069
7	0.092	0.101	0.087
8	0.096	0.088	0.078
9	0.081	0.091	0.096
10	0.104	0.087	0.069

$B1$ statistic lead us to conclude that OLS is not appropriate for predicting y or estimating β.

We briefly comment on how $B1$ behaves in more general situations. In the case of MA(1) or ARMA(1, 1) disturbances the general conclusions are the same. Almost all stationary processes will have either an AR(1) or an MA(1) component, so that the $B1$ statistic has a justification. We now consider the AR(2) process with parameters θ_1 and θ_2 where $\theta_1 = 0$. In this situation $B1$ is *not* the correct sensitivity statistic, the correct one being

$$B2 := \frac{\hat{u}'C^{(2)\prime}(C^{(2)}C^{(2)\prime})^{-}C^{(2)}\hat{u}}{\hat{u}'\hat{u}},$$

where $\hat{u}$ denotes the vector of OLS residuals and

$$C^{(2)} = (I - M)T^{(2)}M.$$

If we know that AR(2) with $\theta_1 = 0$ is the only alternative to white noise, we would use $B2$ to find out whether OLS is still reasonable or not. In most practical situations, however, we do not know this. If we calculate the probabilities $\Pr(B1 > B1^*)$ and $\Pr(B2 > B2^*)$ for $0 < \theta_2 < 1$ we find that $B1$ is more sensitive than $B2$ with respect to θ_2, even though $B2$ is the correct statistic. This is true for nine of the ten data sets. For $D1$ compared with $D2$ the opposite is the case. $D1$ is less sensitive than $D2$, or, put differently, the DW-test is less powerful than the appropriate AR(2) test, which is what we would expect.

Under the current specification of AR(2) with $\theta_1 = 0$ the correct $B2$ statistic will show sensitivity about 7% of the time, depending of course on the value of θ_2 and the data set. The incorrect $B1$ statistic will show sensitivity about 12% of the time. Thus, using $B1$ in this case will lead us to conclude that OLS is sensitive slightly more often than is justified.

We conclude that $B1$ can be usefully employed even in cases for which it was not designed. With 25 observations we will reject OLS slightly more frequently than is necessary, but of course much less frequently than if we were using the DW-test.

12.5. Sensitivity of the F-test

Suppose now that we are interested, not in estimation, but in testing, in particular testing linear restrictions while we are uncertain about the distribution of the disturbances. The set-up is the same as in Sections 12.3 and 12.4. We have a linear regression model $y = X\beta + u$, where u follows a normal distribution with mean zero and variance $\sigma^2\Omega(\theta)$. In this section, to simplify notation, we assume that θ consists of a single parameter; hence $m = 1$.

If there are restrictions on β, say $R\beta = r_0$, where R is a $q \times k$ matrix of rank $q \geqslant 1$, then the restricted GLS estimator for β is given by

$$\tilde{\beta}(\theta) = \hat{\beta}(\theta) - \left(X'\Omega^{-1}(\theta)X\right)^{-1} R'\left(R\left(X'\Omega^{-1}(\theta)X\right)^{-1} R'\right)^{-1}\left(R\hat{\beta}(\theta) - r_0\right),$$

where

$$\hat{\beta}(\theta) = \left(X'\Omega^{-1}(\theta)X\right)^{-1} X'\Omega^{-1}(\theta)y.$$

If we assume that θ is known, then the usual F-statistic for testing the hypothesis $R\beta = r_0$ can be written as

$$F(\theta) = \frac{(R\hat{\beta} - r_0)'(R(X'\Omega^{-1}(\theta)X)^{-1}R')^{-1}(R\hat{\beta} - r_0)}{\hat{u}'(\theta)\Omega^{-1}(\theta)\hat{u}(\theta)} \cdot \frac{n-k}{q} \tag{12.9}$$

or alternatively as

$$F(\theta) = \frac{\tilde{u}'(\theta)\Omega^{-1}(\theta)\tilde{u}(\theta) - \hat{u}'(\theta)\Omega^{-1}(\theta)\hat{u}(\theta)}{\hat{u}'(\theta)\Omega^{-1}(\theta)\hat{u}(\theta)} \cdot \frac{n-k}{q}, \tag{12.10}$$

where

$$\hat{u}(\theta) = y - X\hat{\beta}(\theta), \qquad \tilde{u}(\theta) = y - X\tilde{\beta}(\theta).$$

Notice that the equality of (12.9) and (12.10) holds whether or not the restriction $R\beta = r_0$ is satisfied. Of course, under the null hypothesis H_0: $R\beta = r_0$, $F(\theta)$ is distributed as $\mathrm{F}(q, n-k)$.

Suppose we believe that $\theta = 0$, which may or may not be the case. Then we would use the OLS estimator $\hat{\beta}(0)$ or the restricted OLS estimator $\tilde{\beta}(0)$. We now define the symmetric idempotent $n \times n$ matrix

$$B := X(X'X)^{-1}R'\left(R(X'X)^{-1}R'\right)^{-1}R(X'X)^{-1}X', \tag{12.11}$$

where we recall that $M = I_n - X(X'X)^{-1}X'$, and we notice that

$$MB = 0, \qquad \mathrm{rk}(M) = n - k, \quad \mathrm{rk}(B) = q.$$

We then have $\hat{u} := \hat{u}(0) = Mu$, and, if the restriction $R\beta = r_0$ is satisfied, $\tilde{u} := \tilde{u}(0) = (M + B)u$.

We want to find out how sensitive the F-statistic is with respect to small changes in θ when θ is close to 0. As in Sections 12.3 and 12.4, we do *not* ask the question whether θ is 0 or not, using for example a Durbin–Watson test. Instead, we think of θ as a nuisance parameter whose estimate may or may not be "significantly" different from 0. But even when θ is "far" from 0, this does not imply that $F(\theta)$ is "far" from $F(0)$. And this is what interests us: Is it legitimate to use $F(0)$ – based on OLS residuals – instead of $F(\theta)$?

We define the sensitivity of the F-statistic $F(\theta)$ as

$$\varphi := \left.\frac{\mathrm{d}F(\theta)}{\mathrm{d}\theta}\right|_{\theta=0}, \tag{12.12}$$

where $F(\theta)$ is given in (12.9) or (12.10). Large values of φ indicate that $F(\theta)$ is sensitive to small changes in θ when θ is close to 0 and hence that setting $\theta = 0$ is not justified. The statistic φ depends only on y and X (and, of course, on R and r_0) and can therefore be observed. The *distribution* of φ does, however, depend on θ (and, if the restriction $R\beta = r_0$ is not satisfied, on σ^2 as well). The following result is proved in Banerjee and Magnus (2000, pp. 170–171).

THEOREM 4. *We have*

$$\varphi = 2\left(F(0) + \frac{n-k}{q}\right)(\hat{\theta} - \tilde{\theta}), \tag{12.13}$$

where

$$\hat{\theta} = \frac{1}{2}\frac{\hat{u}'A\hat{u}}{\hat{u}'\hat{u}}, \qquad \tilde{\theta} = \frac{1}{2}\frac{\tilde{u}'A\tilde{u}}{\tilde{u}'\tilde{u}}, \tag{12.14}$$

and

$$F(0) = \frac{\tilde{u}'\tilde{u} - \hat{u}'\hat{u}}{\hat{u}'\hat{u}} \cdot \frac{n-k}{q}, \tag{12.15}$$

$\hat{u}$ and $\tilde{u}$ denote the unrestricted and restricted OLS residuals, and A is again defined as $\mathrm{d}\Omega(\theta)/\mathrm{d}\theta$ at $\theta = 0$.

We notice that Theorem 4 is valid whether or not the restriction $R\beta = r_0$ is satisfied, and also whether or not the distribution of y is evaluated at $\theta = 0$. We see from Theorem 4 that φ is a function of quadratic forms in normal variables, but, since these quadratic forms are not independent, it does not appear feasible to obtain the density of φ in closed form. We shall obtain certain limiting results in Section 12.6, and also the first two moments of φ exactly.

The notation $\hat{\theta}$ and $\tilde{\theta}$ in (12.13) and (12.14) suggests that these statistics can be interpreted as estimators of θ. This suggestion is based on the following argument. We expand $\Omega(\theta)$ as

$$\Omega(\theta) = I_n + \theta A + \frac{1}{2}\theta^2 H + O(\theta^3),$$

where A is the first derivative of Ω, and H is the second derivative, both at $\theta = 0$. Then,

$$\Omega^{-1}(\theta) = I_n - \theta A + \frac{1}{2}\theta^2(2A^2 - H) + O(\theta^3).$$

If the y-process is covariance stationary, we may assume that the diagonal elements of Ω are all ones. Then, $\operatorname{tr} A = \operatorname{tr} H = 0$ and

$$\operatorname{tr}\left(\frac{\mathrm{d}\Omega^{-1}(\theta)}{\mathrm{d}\theta} \cdot \Omega(\theta)\right) = \theta \operatorname{tr} A^2 + O(\theta^2). \tag{12.16}$$

We next expand $\hat{u}(\theta)$ as

$$\hat{u}(\theta) = \hat{u}(0) + \theta X(X'X)^{-1}X'A\hat{u}(0) + O(\theta^2),$$

so that, writing $\hat{u}$ instead of $\hat{u}(0)$,

$$\hat{u}'(\theta)\frac{\mathrm{d}\Omega^{-1}(\theta)}{\mathrm{d}\theta}\hat{u}(\theta) = -\hat{u}'A\hat{u} + \theta(2\hat{u}'\mathrm{AMA}\hat{u} - \hat{u}'H\hat{u}) + O(\theta^2). \tag{12.17}$$

The maximum likelihood estimator for θ is obtained by equating (12.16) and (12.17); see Magnus (1978). This gives

$$\hat{\theta}_{ML} \approx \frac{\hat{u}'A\hat{u}}{2\hat{u}'AMA\hat{u} - \hat{u}'H\hat{u} - \operatorname{tr} A^2} = \frac{1}{2}\frac{\hat{u}'A\hat{u}}{\hat{u}'\hat{u}}\left(1 + n^{-\frac{1}{2}}\delta\right),$$

where δ will be bounded in probability if $(1/n)\operatorname{tr} A^2 \to 2$. This will usually be the case, certainly for low-order ARMA processes. In essence, therefore, all properties of the distribution of φ are determined by the behavior of $n(\hat{\theta} - \tilde{\theta})$, the difference between the unrestricted and the restricted "estimator" of θ.

12.6. Behavior of φ when $q = 1$

In order to gain further insight into the behavior of φ, we concentrate on the special case $q = 1$, that is, we shall consider the t-test rather than the F-test.

The general results for the F-test can be found in Banerjee and Magnus (2000, Section 4). If $q = 1$ then the null hypothesis is written as H_0: $r'\beta = r_0$, where r is a given $k \times 1$ vector. The matrix B has rank one and can be written as $B = bb'$, where

$$b = \frac{X(X'X)^{-1}r}{\sqrt{r'(X'X)^{-1}r}}$$

and $b'b = 1$. Since φ does not depend on σ^2, we shall set $\sigma^2 = 1$ in this section.

We first recall the following result from Pitman (1937); see also Laha (1954).

PITMAN'S LEMMA. *Let $x_1, x_2, \ldots, x_n$ be identically and independently distributed random variables with a finite second moment. Then,*

$$\frac{\sum_{i=1}^n a_i x_i}{\sum_{i=1}^n x_i} \quad \text{and} \quad \sum_{i=1}^n x_i$$

are independent if and only if each x_i follows a gamma distribution.

Using Pitman's lemma we obtain the exact first two moments of φ. At $\theta = 0$ and assuming $r'\beta = r_0$ we can write

$$\varphi = \frac{u'MAMu \cdot u'bb'u - u'Mu \cdot u'(bb'Abb' + bb'AM + MAbb')u}{(u'Mu)^2/(n-k)},$$

using (12.13)–(12.15) and the facts that $\hat{u} = Mu$ and $\tilde{u} = (M + bb')u$. Let $M = SS'$, $S'S = I_{n-k}$, so that $S'b = 0$. Define the vector $v := S'u$ and the scalar $\eta_1 := b'u$, so that v and η_1 are independent. Then,

$$\varphi = \frac{(v'S'ASv)\eta_1^2 - (b'Ab)(v'v)\eta_1^2 - 2(v'v)(b'ASv)\eta_1}{(v'v)^2/(n-k)}, \tag{12.18}$$

and hence

$$\mathrm{E}(\varphi \mid v) = \frac{R_1 - b'Ab}{w}$$

and

$$\mathrm{E}(\varphi^2 \mid v) = \frac{3R_1^2 + 3(b'Ab)^2 - 6(b'Ab)R_1 + 4(n-k)wR_2^2}{w^2},$$

where

$$R_1 := \frac{v'S'ASv}{v'v}, \quad R_2 := \frac{b'ASv}{\sqrt{v'v}}, \quad w := \frac{v'v}{n-k}.$$

We now use Pitman's lemma, recognizing the fact that R_1 and w are independent, and, similarly, that R_2 and w are independent. Since

$$\mathrm{E}\left(\frac{1}{w}\right)=\frac{n-k}{n-k-2}, \qquad \mathrm{E}\left(\frac{1}{w^2}\right)=\frac{(n-k)^2}{(n-k-2)(n-k-4)},$$

we obtain

THEOREM 5. *Assume that the distribution of y is evaluated at* $\theta=0$ *and that the restriction* $r'\beta=r_0$ *is satisfied. Then,*

$$\mathrm{E}(\varphi)=\frac{n-k}{n-k-2}\left(-b'Ab+\frac{\operatorname{tr}AM}{n-k}\right)$$

and

$$\mathrm{E}(\varphi^2)=\frac{n-k}{n-k-2}\left(\frac{3(n-k)(b'Ab)^2}{n-k-4}+4b'AMAb\right.$$
$$\left.+\frac{6\operatorname{tr}(AM)^2+2(\operatorname{tr}AM)^2}{(n-k+2)(n-k-4)}-\frac{6(b'Ab)(\operatorname{tr}AM)}{n-k-4}\right).$$

Let us next consider the large sample behavior of φ. Let

$$\eta_2:=(b'Ab)\eta_1+2b'ASv=b'A(2SS'+bb')u\sim \mathrm{N}(0,c^2),$$

where

$$c^2:=(b'Ab)^2+4b'AMAb. \tag{12.19}$$

Starting from (12.18), we can then rewrite φ as

$$\varphi=\frac{(v'S'ASv)\eta_1^2-(v'v)\eta_1\eta_2}{(v'v)^2/(n-k)}=-\eta_1\eta_2+\frac{R_1\eta_1^2+(w-1)\eta_1\eta_2}{w}.$$

We shall assume that the distribution of y is evaluated at $\theta=0$ and that the restriction $r'\beta=r_0$ is satisfied, and also that

(i) $\Omega(\theta)$ is normalized such that $\operatorname{tr}\Omega(\theta)=n$ for all θ, and
(ii) the eigenvalues of A are bounded.

Notice that condition (i) can always be achieved by redefining σ^2. The condition implies that $\operatorname{tr}A=0$. Notice also that $\eta_1=O_p(1)$ and $w=1+O_p(n^{-1/2})$. Hence, if we can show that c^2 remains bounded as $n\to\infty$ and that $R_1=O_p(n^{-1/2})$, then φ will behave asymptotically as $-\eta_1\eta_2$.

Let μ_1 denote the largest eigenvalue (in absolute value) of A. Then condition (ii) guarantees that μ_1 remains bounded for all n. As a result,

$$(b'Ab)^2 = \left(\frac{b'Ab}{b'b}\right)^2 \leqslant \mu_1^2,$$

$$b'AMAb = \frac{(Ab)'M(Ab)}{(Ab)'(Ab)} \cdot \frac{b'A^2b}{b'b} \cdot b'b \leqslant \mu_1^2,$$

$$|\operatorname{tr} AM| = \left|\operatorname{tr} A(I_n - M)\right| \leqslant \mu_1 \operatorname{tr}(I_n - M) = k\mu_1,$$

and

$$\operatorname{tr}(AM)^2 \leqslant (\operatorname{tr} M)\, \mu_1(AMA) \leqslant (n-k)\mu_1^2.$$

Therefore c^2 remains finite, and since

$$\mathrm{E}(R_1) = \frac{\operatorname{tr} AM}{n-k} \to 0, \qquad \mathrm{E}\big(R_1^2\big) = \frac{\operatorname{tr}(AM)^2}{(n-k)(n-k+2)} \to 0,$$

we see that $R_1 = O_p(n^{-1/2})$. Since also $w = 1 + O_p(n^{-1/2})$, we obtain

THEOREM 6. *Assume that the distribution of y is evaluated at $\theta = 0$ and that the restriction $r'\beta = r_0$ is satisfied. Assume further that* (i) *$\Omega(\theta)$ is normalized such that* $\operatorname{tr} \Omega(\theta) = n$ *for all θ, and* (ii) *the eigenvalues of A are bounded. Then, for large n,*

$$\varphi = -\eta_1\eta_2 + O_p(1/\sqrt{n}).$$

We notice that $\eta_1\eta_2$ can be expressed as

$$\begin{aligned}\eta_1\eta_2 &= (b'u)\big(2b'AM + (b'Ab)b'\big)u \\ &= u'\big((M + bb')A(M + bb') - MAM\big)u = \tilde{u}'A\tilde{u} - \hat{u}'A\hat{u},\end{aligned}$$

and also as $\eta_1\eta_2 = c \cdot z$, where z follows a "product-normal" distribution with parameter $\rho := b'Ab/c$, that is, z can be expressed as $z = z_1z_2$, where z_1 and z_2 are both standard-normal with $\mathrm{E}(z_1z_2) = \rho$.

Theorem 6 is useful because the distribution of φ at $\theta = 0$ is intractable, but the distribution of $\eta_1\eta_2$ is known. To assess the sensitivity of the t-test, we consider the equation

$$\Pr\big(|\varphi| > \varphi^*\big) = \alpha.$$

According to Theorem 6 this is approximately equal to $\Pr(|z| > \varphi^*/c) = \alpha$. We thus obtain an *asymptotic* sensitivity statistic z whose distribution is simple and

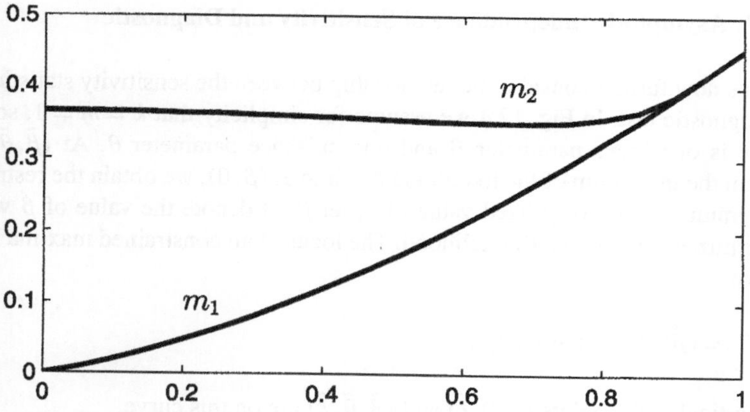

Fig. 12.3: Median m_1 of z and m_2 of $|z|$ as a function of ρ.

depends only on one parameter ρ. We stated – after defining φ in (12.12) – that large values of φ indicate that $F(\theta)$ is sensitive to small changes in θ when θ is close to 0. We did not discuss what we mean by "large." We can now discuss this matter in the context of Theorem 6.

For a given data set we know c and ρ. Hence, given α, φ^* can be obtained from published tables of the product-normal distribution. If $|\varphi| > \varphi^*$, we say that the t-test is sensitive to variance misspecification; if $|\varphi| \leqslant \varphi^*$ we say it is insensitive or robust. There is, of course, some arbitrariness in the choice of α. The most common choice would be $\alpha = 0.05$ or $\alpha = 0.01$, in which case we would (too) frequently conclude that the t-test is robust. In our view the most sensible choice is $\alpha = 0.50$, in which case φ^*/c is the median of $|z|$. We see from Fig. 12.3 that the median of $|z|$ does not depend much on ρ. In fact, $0.35 \leqslant \text{median}(|z|) \leqslant 0.45$. Hence, at $\alpha = 0.50$ we obtain the following "rule of thumb" based on the above asymptotic sensitivity argument.

Rule of thumb: The t-statistic is sensitive (at the 50% level) to variance misspecification if and only if $|\varphi|/c > 0.40$.

In practice, we may compute φ from (12.13) and c from (12.19) and check whether $|\varphi| > 0.40c$. If we know the type of variance misspecification which could occur, we use the A-matrix corresponding to this type of misspecification. In most situations we would not know this. Then we use the Toeplitz matrix $T^{(1)}$, defined in (12.7), as our A-matrix. We know from Sections 12.2–12.4 that this is the appropriate matrix for AR(1), MA(1) and ARMA(1, 1) misspecification. There is evidence that the probability that $|\varphi| > 0.40c$ is extremely close to 0.50. In other words, $0.40c$ is an excellent approximation to the exact (finite sample) median of $|\varphi|$. Park et al. (2002) use the fact that serial correlation has little bearing on the robustness of t- and F-tests in a study on the effects of temperature anomalies and air pressure/wind fluctuations of the sea surface on the supplies of selected vegetables and melons.

12.7. Asymptotic Independence of Sensitivity and Diagnostic

Let us now further consider the relationship between the sensitivity statistic and a diagnostic test. In Fig. 12.4 we assume for simplicity that $k = m = 1$, so that there is one focus parameter β and one nuisance parameter θ. At $(\tilde{\beta}, \tilde{\theta})$ we obtain the maximum of the likelihood $\tilde{\ell}$, while at $(\hat{\beta}, 0)$, we obtain the restricted maximum $\hat{\ell}$. For every fixed value of θ, let $\hat{\beta}(\theta)$ denote the value of β which maximizes the (restricted) likelihood. The locus of all constrained maxima is the curve

$$C := \big(\hat{\beta}(\theta), \theta, \ell(\hat{\beta}(\theta), \theta)\big).$$

In particular, the points $(\hat{\beta}, 0, \hat{\ell})$ and $(\tilde{\beta}, \tilde{\theta}, \tilde{\ell})$ are on this curve.

The $\hat{\beta}(\theta)$-curve is thus the projection of the curve C onto the (β, θ)-plane; we shall call this projection the *sensitivity curve*. In contrast, if we project C onto the (θ, ℓ)-plane, we obtain the curve $\hat{\ell}$ defined as

$$\hat{\ell}(\theta) := \ell\big(\hat{\beta}(\theta), \theta\big),$$

which we shall call the *diagnostic curve*. The diagnostic curve $\hat{\ell}$ in the (θ, ℓ)-plane contains all relevant information needed to perform the usual diagnostic tests. In particular, the LR test is based on $\hat{\ell}(\tilde{\theta}) - \hat{\ell}(\hat{\theta})$, the Wald test is based on $\tilde{\theta}$, and the LM test is based on the derivative of $\hat{\ell}(\theta)$ at $\theta = 0$.

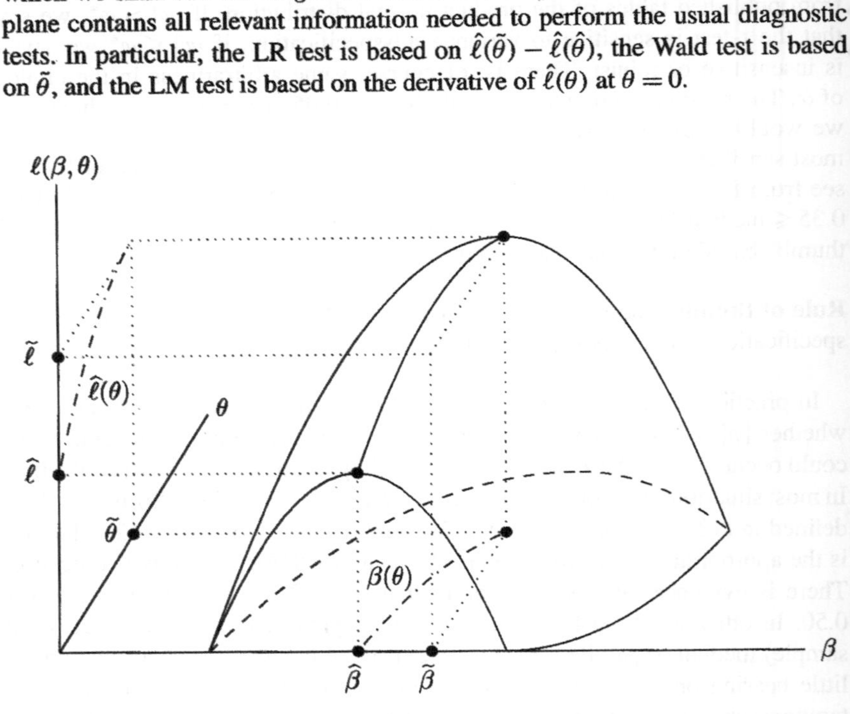

Fig. 12.4: Diagnostic test and sensitivity.

Analogous to the LM test in the (θ, ℓ)-plane, the (local) sensitivity of $\hat{\beta}$ is the derivative of $\hat{\beta}(\theta)$ at $\theta = 0$ in the (β, θ)-plane,

$$S_{\hat{\beta}} := \left.\frac{\partial \hat{\beta}(\theta)}{\partial \theta'}\right|_{\theta=0}.$$

The sensitivity thus measures the effect of small changes in θ on the restricted ML estimator $\hat{\beta}$ and the sensitivity curve contains all restricted ML estimators $\hat{\beta}(\theta)$ as a function of θ.

One might think that sensitivity and diagnostic – although obviously not the same – are nevertheless highly correlated. We shall now argue that this is not the case. In fact, they are asymptotically independent, as demonstrated by Magnus and Vasnev (2007). The fact that the sensitivity curve and the diagnostic curve in Fig. 12.4 live in different planes suggests this orthogonality result, but constitutes no proof.

Since this independence result is a crucial aspect of the importance if sensitivity analysis, let us consider first the simplest example, namely the linear regression model

$$y = X\beta + Z\theta + \varepsilon, \quad \varepsilon \mid (X, Z) \sim \mathrm{N}\left(0, \sigma^2 I_n\right),$$

where (β, σ^2) is the focus parameter and θ is the nuisance parameter. We are interested in the sensitivity of β with respect to θ. The restricted estimator is $\hat{\beta} = (X'X)^{-1}X'y$ and the Lagrange multiplier (LM) test takes the form

$$\mathrm{LM} = \frac{y'MZ(Z'MZ)^{-1}Z'My}{y'My/n}.$$

The sensitivity in this example is

$$S_{\hat{\beta}} := \left.\frac{\partial \hat{\beta}(\theta)}{\partial \theta'}\right|_{\theta=0} = -(X'X)^{-1}X'Z,$$

because $\hat{\beta}(\theta) = (X'X)^{-1}X'(y - Z\theta)$.

The sensitivity $S_{\hat{\beta}}$ and the diagnostic LM are independent, because of the fact that the Wald test in this case is proportional to an F-distribution. As shown by Godfrey (1988, p. 51), the LM and LR tests are related to the Wald test by

$$\mathrm{LM} = \frac{\mathrm{W}}{1 + \mathrm{W}/n}, \qquad \mathrm{LR} = n \log(1 + \mathrm{W}/n),$$

and hence the distribution of LM (and W and LR) does not depend on (X, Z). Thus, for any two measurable functions ϕ and ψ,

$$\begin{aligned} \mathrm{E}\left(\phi(\mathrm{LM})\psi(X, Z)\right) &= \mathrm{E}\left(\mathrm{E}\left(\phi(\mathrm{LM}) \mid X, Z\right)\psi(X, Z)\right) \\ &= \mathrm{E}\left(\phi(\mathrm{LM})\right)\mathrm{E}\left(\psi(X, Z)\right). \end{aligned}$$

Not only are LM and $S_{\hat{\beta}}$ uncorrelated, but any two measurable functions of LM and $S_{\hat{\beta}}$ are uncorrelated as well. Then, by Doob (1953, p. 92), LM and $S_{\hat{\beta}}$ are independent, and the same holds for the Wald and LR tests.

In this simple example, the sensitivity and the diagnostic are not only asymptotically independent, but even independent in finite samples. In the next example – which is more typical – we only find asymptotic independence.

Consider again the linear regression model

$$y = X\beta + u, \quad u \mid X \sim \mathrm{N}\big(0, \sigma^2 \Omega(\theta)\big),$$

where $\Omega(0) = I_n$. We regard (β, σ^2) as the focus parameter and θ as a single nuisance parameter. We are interested in the sensitivity of β to θ.

Letting $M := I_n - X(X'X)^{-1}X'$ and $A := \mathrm{d}\Omega(\theta)/\mathrm{d}\theta$ at $\theta = 0$, the restricted estimator and the sensitivity are

$$\hat{\beta} = (X'X)^{-1}X'y, \qquad S_{\hat{\beta}} = (X'X)^{-1}X'AMy,$$

while the LM test takes the form

$$\mathrm{LM} = \frac{n}{2\,\mathrm{tr}\,A^2/n}\left(\frac{y'MAMy}{y'My} - \frac{\mathrm{tr}\,A}{n}\right)^2,$$

from which we see that the LM test is a quadratic function of u, while the sensitivity is a linear function of u. Hence they are asymptotically independent since both have finite limiting variances.

A limiting result does not, however, inform us how fast the convergence takes place. Thus, we perform a Monte Carlo experiment, based on the same set-up as in Section 12.4. Our assumed alternative is the AR(1) model with parameter θ. Assuming that the null hypothesis that $\theta = 0$ is true, we calculate critical values SS* and LM* such that

$$\Pr(\mathrm{SS} > \mathrm{SS}^*) = \Pr(\mathrm{LM} > \mathrm{LM}^*) = 0.05,$$

where SS refers to the (one-dimensional) "scaled" sensitivity rather than the multi-dimensional sensitivity statistic S. If SS and LM are independent, then the conditional probability $\Pr(\mathrm{SS} < \mathrm{SS}^* \mid \mathrm{LM} \geqslant \mathrm{LM}^*)$ will be equal to 0.95. If, on the other hand, SS and LM are perfectly dependent, then the conditional probability will be zero.

We performed 100,000 Monte Carlo simulations for each of the ten models and for each of $n = 25$, 50, 100, 250, 500, and 1000. Figure 12.5 demonstrates that the convergence to independence is fast, and that the behavior for each of the ten data sets is similar. Interestingly, the LM test and the scaled sensitivity are *negatively* correlated in this case.

We have chosen the LM test as our diagnostic test. The LR test and the Wald tests are asymptotically the same as the LM test, but not in finite samples. Hence,

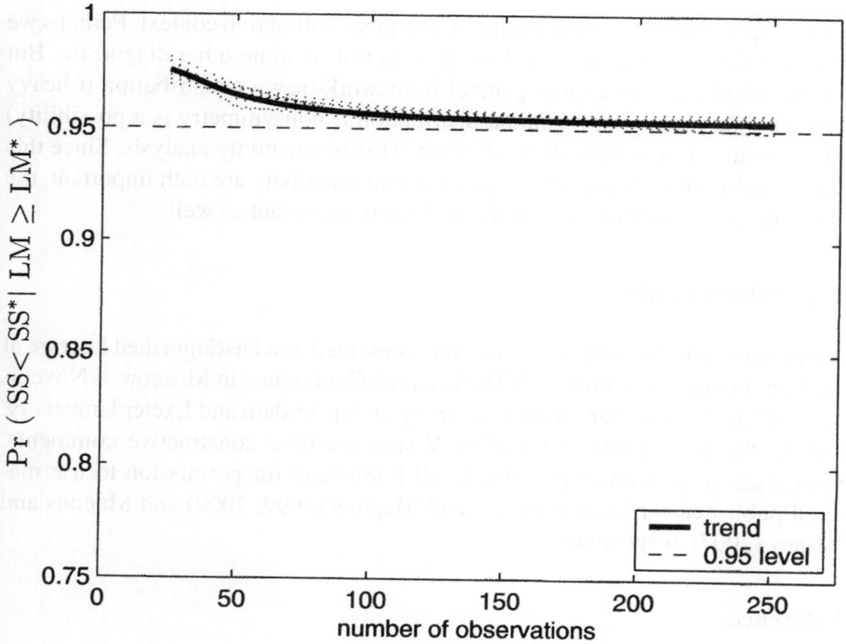

Fig. 12.5: **Nonscalar variance: independence of LM test and sensitivity.**

the LR and Wald tests will also be asymptotically independent of the scaled sensitivity, but the speed of convergence could be different. All three tests converge quickly to the 95% line; the Wald test is the slowest. The Wald test and the LR test are both positively correlated with the scaled sensitivity.

12.8. Conclusions for the Practitioner

Sensitivity analysis matters. The usual diagnostic test provides only half the information required to decide whether a restricted estimator suffices to learn about the focus parameters in the model; the other half is provided by the sensitivity.

What are the implications for the practitioner? If the practical model and estimation environment is covered by the theory and examples in this chapter, then the sensitivity can be computed and its distribution derived. This will provide useful additional information. In many cases encountered in practice, however, the current state of sensitivity analysis does not yet allow formal testing. In those cases ad hoc methods can be fruitfully employed to assess the sensitivity of estimates, forecasts, or policy recommendations. After all, sensitivity analysis simply asks whether the results obtained change "significantly" when one or more of the underlying assumptions is violated. Each time we perform a diagnostic test, we should also ask the corresponding sensitivity question. Suppose, for example, that we assume normality in a given estimation context. Perhaps we even test for normality using a Jarque–Bera test or some other diagnostic. But we should also ask in a more general framework (say a t-distribution if heavy tails are a possibility, or a gamma-distribution if nonsymmetry is a possibility) whether our estimates are affected or not. This is sensitivity analysis. Since this chapter has demonstrated that diagnostics and sensitivity are both important, the inclusion of such ad hoc sensitivity analysis is important as well.

Acknowledgements

Preliminary versions of this chapter were presented as a Distinguished Lecture at the New Economic School's XVIII Research Conference in Moscow, 4 November 2005, and at seminars at the University of Amsterdam and Exeter University. I thank the participants and Andrey Vasnev for their constructive comments. I am grateful to Elsevier and Blackwell Publishing for permission to use material published earlier in Banerjee and Magnus (1999, 2000) and Magnus and Vasnev (2007), respectively.

References

Banerjee, A.N., Magnus, J.R. (1999). The sensitivity of OLS when the variance matrix is (partially) unknown. *Journal of Econometrics* **92**, 295–323.

Banerjee, A.N., Magnus, J.R. (2000). On the sensitivity of the usual t- and F-tests to covariance misspecification. *Journal of Econometrics* **95**, 157–176.

Chao, H.-K. (2007). Structure. In: *this volume*, Chapter 12.

Cook, R.D. (1979). Influential observations in linear regression. *Journal of the American Statistical Association* **74**, 169–174.

Cook, R.D. (1986). Assessment of local influence (with discussion). *Journal of the Royal Statistical Society, Series B* **48**, 133–169.

Doob, J.L. (1953). *Stochastic Processes*. John Wiley, New York.

Dufour, J.-M., King, M.L. (1991). Optimal invariant tests for the autocorrelation coefficient in linear regressions with stationary or nonstationary AR(1) errors, *Journal of Econometrics* **47**, 115–143.

Giere, R.N. (1999). Using models to represent reality. In: Magnani, L., Nersessian, N.J., Thagard, P. (Eds.), *Model-Based Reasoning in Scientific Discovery*. Kluwer Academic/Plenum Publishers, New York.

Godfrey, L.G. (1988). *Misspecification Tests in Econometrics*. Cambridge Univ. Press, Cambridge.

Griffiths, W.E., Beesley, P.A.A. (1984). The small-sample properties of some preliminary test estimators in a linear model with autocorrelated errors, *Journal of Econometrics* **25**, 49–61.

Harrison, G.W., Johnson, E., McInnes, M.M., Rutström, E.E. (2007). Measurement with experimental controls. In: *this volume*, Chapter 4.

Huber, P.J. (2004). *Robust Statistics*. In: *Wiley Series in Probability and Statistics*. John Wiley, Hoboken, NJ.

King M.L. (1981). The alternative Durbin–Watson test. *Journal of Econometrics* **17**, 51–66.

King, M.L. (1987). Testing for autocorrelation in linear regression models: A survey. In: King, M.L., Giles, D.E.A. (Eds.), *Specification analysis in the linear model, Essays in honour of Donald Cochrane*. Routledge & Kegan Paul, London.

Laha, R.G. (1954). On a characterization of the gamma distribution. *The Annals of Mathematical Statistics* **25**, 784–787.

Leamer, E.E. (1978). *Specification Searches*. John Wiley, New York.

Leamer, E. E. (1984). Global sensitivity results for generalized least squares estimates. *Journal of the American Statistical Association* **79**, 867–870.

Magnus, J.R. (1978). Maximum likelihood estimation of the GLS model with unknown parameters in the disturbance covariance matrix. *Journal of Econometrics* **7**, 281–312.

Magnus, J.R., Neudecker, H. (1988). *Matrix Differential Calculus with Applications in Statistics and Econometrics*. Revised Edition 1999. John Wiley, Chichester/New York.

Magnus, J.R., Vasnev, A. (2007). Local sensitivity and diagnostic tests. *Econometrics Journal* **10**, 166–192.

Newey, W.K., West, K.D. (1987). A simple, positive semi-definite, heteroskedasticity and autocorrelation consistent covariance matrix. *Econometrica* **55**, 703–708.

Omtzigt, P., Paruolo, P. (2005). Impact factors. *Journal of Econometrics* **128**, 31–68.

Park, J., Mjelde, J.W., Fuller, S.W., Malaga, J.E., Rosson, C.P. (2002). An assessment of the effects of ENSO events on fresh vegetable and melon supplies. *HortScience* **37**, 287–291.

Pitman, E.J.G. (1937). The "closest" estimates of statistical parameters. *Proceedings of the Cambridge Philosophical Society* **33**, 212–222.

Polasek, W. (1984). Regression diagnostics for general linear regression models. *Journal of the American Statistical Association* **79**, 336–340.

CHAPTER 13

The Empirical Significance of Econometric Models

Thomas Mayer

University of California, Davis, CA 94708, USA

E-mail address: tommayer@lmi.net

Most of the papers in this volume analyze in detail some narrowly specified problem of economic measurement. This paper takes a more general approach and surveys a number of problems that limit the empirical evaluations of economic models. It takes as given that economic models should have empirical relevance, so that they need to be empirically tested.

I therefore focus on some difficulties in testing economic models. The problems being numerous and space being limited, I take up just a few of them, concentrating on those that are at least to some extent remediable, and ignore others, such as the problem of inferring causality, the Lucas critique and some limitations of the available data. This means omitting some important fundamental problems in relating data to theory, such as those discussed in the last chapter of Spanos (1986). Nor do I discuss the problems created by ideological commitments, loyalty to schools of thought, or to the reluctance to admit error.[1] At the same time I have not been reluctant to discuss issues that are already well known – but ignored in practice.

13.1. The Aim of Empirical Models: Understanding or Prediction?

Although this essay focuses on models that make quantitative predictions let us first look at models that are intended in the first instance to provide qualitative understanding. They, too, are empirical since they aim to enhance our understanding of observed phenomena.

One type of such models is what Allen Gibbard and Hal Varian (1978) call "caricature models," that is models that purposely deal with an extreme case because that clarifies the operation of a particular factor that in the real world

[1] Elsewhere (Mayer, 2001b) I have argued that ideological differences do not explain very much of the disagreement among economists. (For a contrary conclusion see Fuchs et al., 1998.) In Mayer (1998) I have presented a case study of how adherence to schools of thought and other personal obstacles have inhibited the debate about a fixed monetary growth rate rule.

Measurement in Economics: A Handbook
Marcel Boumans (Editor)

takes a less extreme form. For example, a model may explain price dispersion by hypothesizing that there are only two types of consumers, those who search until they find the lowest price for a specific item regardless of the time it takes, and those who buy from the first seller they encounter. Such a model can teach us about the importance of search effort. Since that is an empirical issue, it is an empirical model, even though standing on its own, it is only loosely related to empirical prediction. Suppose, for example, that we would find that while the model predicts that the variance of prices is high for a commodity for which there is much consumer search, the data show the opposite. We would not treat this as a contradiction of the model's claim that consumer search lowers the variance of prices, but would attribute it to some disturbing factor, such as reverse causation. Such a caricature model can serve as an input into a more general model that has less restrictive ceteris paribus clauses. It also provides understanding in an informal sense, understanding that Fritz Machlup (1950) has characterized as a sense of "Ahaness." This does not mean that the credibility of a caricature model is entirely independent of its predictive performance. If the larger model in which it is used fails to predict correctly, and if no convenient disturbing factors can be found, then the alleged insight of the model is dubious.

Caricature models carry a potential danger. Particularly if the model is elegant it may be applied over-enthusiastically by ignoring its ceteris paribus conditions, as was done, for example, when Ricardian rent theory was used to predict that rents would absorb a rising share of income. Schumpeter called this type of error the "Ricardian Vice."

Another type of qualitative model, qualitative in the broad sense that it does not require the microscope of econometric analysis, is one that derives its appeal from readily observed experience. In some cases the facts stand out starkly. Thus, the Great Depression showed that prices are not flexible enough to quickly restore equilibrium given a massive negative demand shock. And the Great Inflation showed that a Phillips curve that does not allow for the adjustment of expectations is not a good policy guide. In microeconomics a model that explains why some used goods whose quality is hard to ascertain sell at a greater discount than do others, is empirically validated by ordinary experience without the aid of econometrics. This does not mean that narrower subsidiary hypotheses of these models are not tested, and that these tests are not informative. But our willingness to accept the broad messages of these models does not depend on *t* values, etc. (See Summers, 1991.)

Both of these types of quantitative models raise different issues from qualitative models. For the first type it is whether the feature of reality that the caricature model has pounced on teaches us enough about the real world, or whether it distorts our understanding by focusing our attention on something that may be technically "sweet," but of little actual relevance.[2] That cannot be

[2] For example, take the following model: A government can finance its expenditures only by taxing, borrowing or money creation. Therefore, holding tax receipts and borrowing constant, money

decided by appeal to a methodological rule. One has to rely on one's intuition and on the success of the testable hypotheses that are derived from the insight of the caricature model. For the second type the question is whether such casual empiricism can be trusted. That, too, must be decided by experience.

13.2. Three Basic Problems in Testing Economic Theories

Let us now look at three of the many serious problems that arise in testing economic theories.

13.2.1. Relating theories and data

The traditional procedure is to select as the regressors the major variables implied by the model, run the regression, and then, if necessary add, or perhaps eliminate, some regressors until the diagnostics look good. An alternative procedure coming from LSE econometricians is to use a large number of regressors, some of which may not be closely tied to the hypothesis being tested, and then narrow the analysis by dropping those with insignificant coefficients. Such a search for the data generating process (DGP) usually puts more stress on meeting the assumptions of the underlying statistical model, emphasizes misspecification tests, and rejects quick fixes, such as adding an AR term, than does the traditional procedure, though it does not reject the criteria used in the traditional approach. Thus Spanos (1986, pp. 669–670) cites the following criteria: "theory consistency, goodness of fit, predictive ability, robustness (including nearly orthogonal explanatory variables), encompassing [the results of previous work and] parsimony."

What is at stake here is a more fundamental disagreement than merely a preference for either starting with a simple model and then adding additional variables until the fit becomes satisfactory. or else starting with a general model and then dropping regressors that are not statistically significant. Nobody can start with a truly general model (see Keuzenkamp and McAleer, 1995), and if the reduction does not provide a satisfactory solution a LSE econometrician, too, is likely to add additional regressors at that stage.

The more fundamental disagreement can be viewed in two ways. The first is as emphasizing economic theory versus emphasizing statistical theory. In the former case one may approach a data set with strong priors based on the theory's previous performance on other test. One then sees whether the new data set is also consistent with that theory rather than asking which hypothesized DGP gives the most satisfactory diagnostics, Suppose that the quantity theory

---

creation depends on government expenditures. We can therefore explain the inflation rate by the growth rate of government expenditures. This last statement holds *if* tax receipts and borrowing are constant, but not if – as seems at least as, if not more, likely – the government finances changes in its expenditures by changing tax receipts or borrowing.

gives a good fit for the inflation rates of twenty countries . However, for each of these countries one can estimate a DGP that gives a better fit, but contains an extra variable that differs from country to country. One may then still prefer the quantity theory. LSE econometricians would probably agree, but in practice their method tends to stress econometric criteria rather than the other criteria relevant to theory selection. This issue is well stated by Friedman and Schwartz (1991, pp. 39, 49) who wrote in their debate with Hendry and Ericsson (1991) that one should:

> [E]xamine a wide variety of evidence quantitative and nonquantitative...; test results from one body of evidence on the other bodies, using econometric techniques as one tool in this process, and build up a collection of simple hypotheses. ... [R]egression analysis is a good tool for deriving hypotheses. But any hypothesis must be tested with data or nonquantitative evidence other than that used in deriving the regression, or available when the regression was derived. Low standard errors of estimate, high t values and the like are often tributes to the ingenuity and tenacity of the statistician rather than reliable evidence....

A good illustration of this approach is a paper in which Friedman (2005) tried to confirm the quantity theory of money by comparing changes in the growth rate of money and subsequent recessions in the US in the 1920s and 1990s and in Japan in the 1980s. He has only three observations, so obviously he uses no econometrics. Nonetheless, I found it persuasive – not as conclusive evidence, but as circumstantial evidence, because his findings fit in with much other evidence. By contrast, an adherent of the LSE approach would presumably find it unconvincing.

The second, and deeper way of viewing the disagreement is to treat it as a dispute about the criterion to be applied to economics. Should one require of economics rigor close to that of mathematics and of physics, with the latter's (alleged) reliance on crucial experiments, and hence be hard nosed about meeting econometric criteria, or should one consider this as a generally unattainable goal, and settle for more amorphous extensive circumstantial evidence? (Thus in an unjustly neglected book Benjamin Ward, 1972, argued that economics should model itself more on law, with its emphasis on circumstantial evidence, than on physics.) There are problems with both extremes. The rigorous approach requires us to abandon suggestive evidence even when nothing better is available. The other may degenerate into journalism.

A related issue in the interaction of theory and data is whether data are to be used only to test models, or also to inspire them. Thus Arnold Zellner (1992) advocates searching for "ugly facts," that is puzzling phenomena that cry out for explanation. This fits in with Friedman and Schwartz's just-cited suggestion of looking at many different types of observations rather than analyzing just one particular data set. And it seems to have played an important role in Friedman's own work on the permanent income theory and on the quantity theory, thus demonstrating its fruitfulness.

A third issue is the choice between simple, or more precisely what Zellner (1992) calls "sophisticatedly simple" models and complex models. Although economists in evaluating their own and their colleague's work seem to adhere to a labor theory of value, several econometricians have warned against automatically assuming that a complex model is more useful and predicts better than a simple model. (See Keuzenkamp and McAleer, 1995; Kennedy, 2002; Makridakis and Bibon, 2000; Zellner, 1992.)

13.2.2. Ceteris paribus conditions and testability

Another serious problem both in testing and in applying a model is that the ceteris paribus conditions that define its domain are often insufficiently specified. If we are not told what they are, and the extent to which they can be relaxed without significant damage to the model's applicability, then data cannot be said to refute it, but only to constrain its domain. In day-to-day work this shows up as the question of what variables have to be included among the auxiliary regressors. A dramatic illustration is Edward Leamer's (1978) tabulation of the results obtained when one includes various plausible auxiliary regressors in equations intended to measure the effect of capital punishment on the homicide rate. The results are all over the map. And the same is true in a recent follow-up study (Donohue and Wolfers, 2006). Similarly, as Thomas Cooley and Stephen LeRoy (1981) have shown, in demand functions for money the negative interest elasticity predicted by theory does not emerge clearly from the data, but depends on what other regressors are used.

The ideal solution would be to specify the ceteris paribus conditions of the theoretical model so precisely that it would not leave any choice about what auxiliary regressors to include. But we cannot list *all* the ceteris paribus conditions. New classical theorists claim to have a solution: the selection of auxiliary regressors must be founded on rational-choice theory. But that is unpersuasive. In their empirical work the new classicals substitute for utility either income, or both income and leisure variables, plus perhaps a risk-aversion variable. But behavioral and experimental economics, as well as neuroscience, provide much evidence that there is more to utility than that. And the well documented bounds on rationality open the door to all sorts of additional variables that are not in the new classicals' utility function. Similarly, market imperfections complicate a firms' decisions.

If theory cannot constrain sufficiently the variables that have to be held paribus by the inclusion of regressors for them one possible solution could be: open the floodgates, allow all sorts of plausible variables in, and call the model confirmed only if it works regardless of which auxiliary regressors are included. In this spirit Edward Leamer (1978, 1983) has advocated "extreme bounds analysis," that is, deciding what regressors are plausible, running regressions with various combinations of them, and then treating as confirmed only those hypotheses that survive all of these tests. This procedure has been criticized on technical grounds (see McAleer et al., 1983; Hoover and Perez, 2000). It also has the practical disadvantage that it allows very few hypotheses to survive. Since if economists refuse to answer policy questions they leave more space for the answers of those who know even less, it is doubtful that they should become the Trappist monks that extreme bounds analysis would require of them. However, it *may* be possible to ameliorate this problem by adopting a, say 15 percent significance level instead of the 5 percent level.

Full-scale extreme bounds analysis has found few adherents. Instead, economists now often employ an informal and limited version by reporting as robustness tests, in addition to their preferred regressions, also the results of several alternative regressions that use different auxiliary regressors or empirical definitions of the theoretical variables.[3] This can be interpreted along Duhem–Quinian lines as showing that the validity of the maintained hypothesis does not depend on the validity of certain specific auxiliary hypotheses. While this is a great improvement over reporting just the results of the favored regression it is not clear that economists test – and report on – a sufficient number of regressors and definitions. Indeed, that is not likely because data mining creates an incentives-incompatibility problem between authors (agents) and readers (principals).

13.2.3. Data mining

By the time she runs her regressions a researcher has usually already spent much effort on the project. Hence, if her initial regressions fail to confirm her hypothesis she has a strong incentive to try other regressions, perhaps with differently defined variables, different functional forms, a different sample periods, different auxiliary variables, or different techniques, and to do so until she obtains favorable results. Such pre-testing makes the t values of the final regression worthless.[4] Just as bad, if not worse, such biased data mining also means that the final results "confirm" the hypothesis only in the sense of showing that it is not *necessarily* inconsistent with the data, that there are some decisions about auxiliary regressors, etc., that could save the hypothesis. Suppose a researcher has run, say ten alternative regressions, three of which support his hypothesis and seven that do not. He will be tempted to present one of his successful regressions as his main one and mention the other two successful ones as robustness tests, while ignoring the seven regressions that did not support his hypothesis.[5]

---

[3] I have the impression that this has become much more common in recent years.

[4] There is no way of correctly adjusting t values for pre-testing. (See Greene, 2000; Hoover and Perez, 2000; Spanos, 2000.)

[5] It is often far from obvious whether the results of additional regressions confirm or disconfirm the maintained hypothesis. Suppose, that this hypothesis implies that the coefficient of x is positive. Suppose further that it is positive and significant in the main regression. But in additional regressions that include certain other auxiliary regressors, though again positive, it is significant only at the 20 percent level. Although taken in isolation these additional regressions would usually be read as failures to confirm, they should perhaps be read as enhancing the credibility of the maintained hypothesis, because they suggest that even if the auxiliary hypothesis that these regressors do not belong in the regression is invalid, there is still only a relatively small likelihood that the observed results are due merely to sampling error. Good theory choice takes more than attention to t values.

And that deprives readers of information they need to evaluate the hypothesis.

Data mining can occur not only in conventional econometric tests, but also in calibrations, where there may be many diverse microeconomic estimates among which the calibrator can pick and choose. (Cf. Hansen and Heckman, 1996.) To be convincing a calibration test requires making a compelling case for the particular estimates of the coefficient that has been picked out of the often quite diverse ones in the literature, not just giving a reference to the coefficient found in some particular paper.

Though much practiced (see Backhouse and Morgan, 2000) data mining is widely deplored (see for instance Leamer, 1983; Cooley and LeRoy, 1981). But it has its defenders. Thus Adrian Pagan and Michael Veall (2000) argue that since economists seem willing to accept the output of data miners they cannot be all that concerned about it. But what choice do they have? They do no know what papers have been hyped by biased data mining, and being academic economists they have to read the journals and refer to them. Pagan and Veall also argue that data mining does little damage because if a paper seems important but is not robust, it will be replicated and its fragility will be exposed. But while path breaking papers are likely to be replicated, by no means all unreplicated papers are unimportant; much scientific progress results from normal science. And even when papers are replicated time passes until the erroneous ones are spotted, and in the meantime they shunt researchers onto the wrong track.

A much more persuasive defense of data mining is that it is needed to obtain as much information as we can from the data, so that the learning that results from trying many regressions and testing need to coexist (see Greene, 2000; Spanos, 2000). Thus Hoover and Perez (2000), who focus on generating accurate values for the coefficients of a hypothesis rather than on testing it, argue (mainly in the context of general-to-specific modeling) that we need to try many specifications to find the best one, while Keuzenkamp and McAleer (1995, p. 20) write: "specification freedom is a nuisance to purists, but is an indispensable aid to practical econometricians." (See also Backhouse and Morgan, 2000; Kennedy, 2002.) Testing, Hoover and Perez argue, should then be done in some other way, thus separating the task of exploring a data set from the task of drawing inferences from it. That would be the ideal solution, but in macroeconomics such, multiple independent data sets are generally not available, or if they are they relate to different countries which may complicate research. In much microeconomic work with sample surveys or experimental data, it is, in principle, possible to gather two samples or to divide the sample into two, and to use one to formulate and the other to test the hypothesis. But in practice, funds are often too limited for that. Suppose, for example, that your budget allows you to draw a sample of a 1000 responses. Would you feel comfortable using only 500 responses to estimate the coefficients when another 500 are sitting on your desk? Moreover, a researcher who has two samples can mine surreptitious by peeking at the second sample when estimating the coefficients from the first sample.[6] (See Inoue and Killian, 2002.)

The other polar position on data mining – one usually not stated so starkly but implicit in much criticism of data mining – is to limit each researcher to testing only a single variant of her model. But that is a bad rule, not only for the reasons just mentioned, but also because it leaves too much to luck. A researcher might just happen on the first try to pick the one variant of twenty equally plausible ones that provides a good fit. (See Bronfenbrenner, 1972.) Moreover, even if all data mining by individual researchers were eliminated, it would not put a stop to the harmful effects of data mining because of a publication bias. Only those papers that come up with acceptable t values and other regression diagnostics tend to be printed, so that, at least in the short run, there would still be a bias in favor of the hypothesis.[7] Moreover, it is hard to imagine such a rule of one regression per researcher being effectively enforced.

A more feasible solution that avoids both extremes, is to permit data mining but only as long as it is done transparently. A basic idea underlying the organization of research is the division of labor; instead of having every scientist investigate a particular problem, one scientist does so, and her discoveries become known to all others. This works best if she holds nothing important back, and not well if she withholds information that detracts from the validity of her work, for example, that her results require the assumption that the lag is six months rather than three, nine or twelve months. Hence, a data miner should let readers know if plausible assumptions other than the ones she used yield results that are meaningfully different. The reader can then decide whether to accept the proffered conclusions.

Though I think this is the best of all available alternatives, it, too, has its problems. One is the difficulty (impossibility?) of ensuring that researchers mention *all* their alternative regressions that significantly reduce the credibility of the maintained hypothesis. Your conscience may urge you to do so, but fear that your rivals do not, urges you to override your conscience. A second is that a researcher is likely to run some regressions that she does not take seriously, just to see what would happen if.... Do they have to be reported? And if not, where does one draw the line? Another problem is that a researcher who intends to run, say twelve variants of the maintained hypothesis, and happens to get a good result in say the first two, has a strong incentive to quit while he is ahead, so that potential knowledge is lost.

---

6 This is not necessarily dishonest. If a macroeconomist sets a few year's data aside as a second sample, she knows something about what the data are likely to show simply by having lived through this period, And someone working with survey data may have inadvertently learned something about the second sample in the process of splitting the data or in talking to his research assistant.

7 I say the short run because, as Robert Goldfarb (1995) has shown, once a hypothesis is widely accepted only those papers that test it and disconfirm it tend to be published, because only they provide "new" information.

In macroeconomics another way of ameliorating the effects of data mining would be to require an author to publish, perhaps three to five years after the appearance of his paper, a follow-up note on how well his model fits the subsequent data. (See Greene, 2000.) This is preferable to asking him to hold out the last few year's data when fitting his model, because of the danger that he may be influenced, either consciously or unconsciously, by what he knows happened in these last few years. Moreover, it would provide only a small sample. Besides, policymakers may want to know how well the model performed during the last five years. All in all, there is no perfect solution to the problem of biased data mining, but requiring transparency seems a reasonable compromise.

13.2.4. Significance tests

Most economists seem to view significance tests as a standard accoutrement of a "scientific" paper. They might be surprised that in psychology their use has come in for much criticism, and that there was even an (unsuccessful) attempt to ban them in journals published by the American Psychological Association.[8] Within economics D. McCloskey (1985, Chapter 9) has argued that significance tests are useless because what matters is the magnitude of a coefficient, its "policy oomph" as she calls it, and not its t value, which depends on sample size. Given a large sample even a trivial coefficient can be statistically significant without being substantively significant. McCloskey is right in stressing that one should usually look at the size of a coefficient. But that does not mean that significance tests are unimportant. A researcher usually has to clear two hurdles. She must show that her results are large enough to be interesting, *and* that they are unlikely to be just due to sampling error. And in some special cases even a statistically significant but substantively trivial coefficient may be highly relevant if we are choosing between two theories that have sharply different and tight implications on this point; for example the slight bending of light that supports relativity theory against Newtonian theory (Elliot and Granger, 2004; Horowitz, 2004).[9]

Although the distinction between substantive and statistical significance seems obvious Steven Ziliak and Deidre McCloskey (2004) claim that it is widely ignored. But while it is confused in many cases (see Elliot and Granger, 2004 and Thorbecke, 2004), their claim that this is the common practice is

[8] See for instance, Bruce Thompson (2004), Open Peer Comments (1996). Sui Chow (1996, p. 11), who even though he defends the use of significance tests, writes: "the overall assessment of the ... [null-hypotheses significance test procedure] in psychology is not encouraging. The puzzle is why so many social scientists persist in using the process." He argued persuasively that these criticisms of significance tests are largely due to researchers trying to read too much into them.

[9] McCloskey (1985) also argued that in many cases the sample is, in effect, the whole universe, so that tests for sampling error are meaningless. Hoover and Perez (2000) respond that the hypothesis being tested is intended to be general and thus cover actual or potential observations outside the sample period.

questionable.[10] Kevin Hoover and Mark Siegler (unpublished) have reexamined some of Ziliak and McCloskey's data, and concluded that this confusion is *not* widespread. But even if it occurs only some of the time, that is too much.

A problem may also arise from the interaction of statistical and substantive significance. An economist may first check for statistical significance, and having reassured himself about that, check for substantive significance, and make a confident statement that the coefficient – by which he means its point estimate – is substantively as well as statistically significant. But the confidence intervals should also be checked for substantive significance. If a test of the law of one price finds that the difference between two prices is both statistically significant and substantively large, there is still not a strong case against the law of one price if the lower confidence interval, though it does not include zero, does include a substantively insignificant value.

I now turn to a problem that is less known, and therefore needs more discussion. This is the confusion of "not confirmed" with "disconfirmed," a confusion that sometimes shows up in econometric practice, even though the distinction is well known in the abstract.[11] Imagine first an ideal world in which the dependent variable is explained entirely by a few independent variables, and all data are measured without error, so that using the correct model the standard error of a regression is zero. In this world if a hypothesis implies that the regression coefficient of x is zero, and it is not so in the data, we can say that the hypothesis has been disconfirmed. But what happens in a stochastic world? Suppose the estimated coefficient is 1.0 with a standard error of 0.25, so that its t value is 4 and the hypothesis is rejected. So far no problem. But suppose the standard error is greater, so that the hypothesis that the true value of the coefficient is zero is rejected only at the 20 percent level. Then, the usual procedure is to say that the hypothesis has not been disconfirmed. And while this may be stated cautiously as "the data do not reject the hypothesis," the clear implication is that the test confirmed the hypothesis in the following way: The data were given a chance to reject it, but did not do so. And the more often a hypothesis survives a potentially disconfirming test, the more credible it is. But in the case just described does this make sense? In repeated sampling in only one fifth of the runs would random errors generate that large a discrepancy between the actual and predicted values. And that should count as potential evidence *against*, not for, the hypothesis.[12]

---

[10] In his survey of papers published in the *Journal of Economic History* and in *Explorations in Economic History* Anthony O'Brien (2004) found that of the 185 papers that used regression analysis, 12 percent did so incorrectly, and that in 7 percent of these papers this did matter for the main conclusions of the paper. The confusion of statistical and substantive significance has also been a problem in biology (see Phannkuch and Wild, 2000).

[11] For some specific instances see Robertson (2000), Viscusi and Hamilton (1999), Loeb and Page (2000), McConnell and Perez-Quiros (2000), Papell et al. (2000), Wei (2000). For a further discussion of this problem see Mayer (2001a).

[12] Nothing said above conflicts with the philosophy-of-science proposition that failure to be disconfirmed on a hard test raises the credibility of a hypothesis, because the term "not disconfirmed" is

A related problem arises if a hypothesis is tested more than once. Suppose that on the first test an estimated coefficient that according to the hypothesis should be zero is positive with a t value of 1.7. Suppose further that on a second test using an independent data set it is again positive with a t value of 1.6, and on a third test it is positive with a t value of 1.5. If failure to reject at the 5 percent level is interpreted as confirmation, then the second and third tests must be treated as strengthening the plausibility of the hypothesis, since three tests have now failed to reject it. But the correct message of the second and third tests is just the opposite. The probability of three successive sampling errors that large and with the same sign is so low that the hypothesis should be rejected.

These problems arise from our unsurprising eagerness to have significance tests do more than they are actually capable of. We want them to classify hypotheses as either confirmed or disconfirmed. But all they can do is tell us the probability that the observed result is just due to sampling error or other noise in the data. We then add the rule of thumb that when the probability is less than 5 percent that the observed error is just a sampling or noise error, we refuse to accept the hypothesis. But there is a wide gap between refusing to accept the hypothesis, and believing that it is actually false. In many cases the correct conclusion is neither to accept nor to reject it, but to suspend judgment. Yet this point is sometimes missed in the literature. For example, if the cross-equation restrictions of a model cannot be rejected at the 5 percent level, we act as though they have been satisfied, even if they can be rejected at, at say the 12 percent level. The 5 percent criterion was intended to be a tough taskmaster, but all too often has become a progressive educator.

This raises a difficult problem. Suppose we subject a hypothesis to a tough test, tough in the sense that it tests an implication that is rigorously derived from the hypothesis, and as far as we can tell cannot also be deduced from some other reasonable hypothesis (see Kim, de Marchi and Morgan, 1995). Suppose that on this test the t value of the difference between the predicted and the estimated coefficient is less than, say 0.1. Since it seems unlikely that we got such a small t just by chance, it is reasonable to say that the data support the hypothesis. On the other hand, if the t value is 1.5, then the probability that the difference is due to sampling error is low. If we do not have a null hypothesis that would tell us what t value to expect if the hypothesis is false, we cannot tell whether to treat the 1.5 t value as enhancing or as reducing the credibility of the hypothesis. We have to rely on our subjective judgment – precisely the situation that we, though not the originators of significance tests (see Gigerenzer, 2004), sought to avoid.

Another criticism of significance tests is that despite their prevalence they have had little influence. Keuzenkamp and Magnus (1995) offered a prize to

---

used in two different senses. In the context of significance testing it means that – using a rigorous standard for saying that the hypothesis has been rejected – there is not sufficient evidence to say that it has. In the context of philosophy-of-science failure to be disconfirmed means that the probability that the proposition is false is less than 50 percent.

anyone finding an example of a significance test that changed economist's thinking about some proposition. So far at least, this prize has not been successful claimed. However, the many papers that have sunk some propositions, such as the total interest inelasticity of the demand for money, would probably not have been taken seriously, or even been published, if the relevant coefficients had not been statistically significant. But since statistical significance was just a supportive point in their argument they do not qualify as examples with which to claim the Keuzenkamp–Magnus prize. Moreover, the requirements for the prize are also hard to meet because one of them is that "the particular test has been persuasive to others" (Keuzenkamp and Magnus, 1995, p. 21). But while we can readily observe changes in the opinions of our colleagues, it is harder to determine why they changed their minds. Moreover, important propositions are often sunk not on by a single hit, but by an unrelenting bombardment. (Cf. Hoover and Siegler, unpublished.)

13.2.5. Reliability of the data and of their processing

As several economists have pointed out (see for instance Leontief, 1971) most economists show little concern about the quality of their data.[13] To be sure, they make allowance for sampling error, but that's about it. The standard justifications for this unconcern are first that the obvious need to quantify and test our hypotheses forces us to use whatever data we can find, and as long as they are the best available data, well, that's all we can be expected to do. Second, previous researchers have already decided what the best data sets are, so we can just use these.

Sounds compelling – but isn't. Yes, empirical testing is important, but in some cases even the best available data may not be reliable enough to test the model, and then we should either develop a better data set on our own, or else admit that our model cannot, at least at present, be adequately tested. Or if the available data are neither wholly reliable nor totally inadequate you may use them to test the hypothesis, but inform the reader about the problem, and perhaps do some robustness testing. That others have used a data set is not an adequate justification for your using it, not only because of uncertainty about whether the previous use was successful, but also because, while for some purposes crude estimates suffice, for others they do not. Don't assume that the sophistication of

---

[13] Previously Oskar Morgenstern (1950) had provided a long list of errors that resulted from economists not knowing enough about their data, and Andrew Kamarck (1983) has presented more recent examples. The appearance of downloadable databases probably exacerbated this problem. In the old days when economists had to take the data from the original sources they were more likely to read the accompanying description of the data. Another exacerbating factor is the much greater use of research assistants. A researcher who has to work with data herself is more likely to notice anomalies in the data than are assistants who tend to follow instructions rather than "waste" time by thinking about the data.

your econometrics can compensate for the inadequacy of your data. (Cf. Chatfield, 1991.) Time spent on cleaning up the data, or looking for a data set that provides a better measure of your model's variables, may not impress a referee, but it may improve the results more than the same time spent in learning the latest technique. As Daniel Hamermesh (2000, p. 365) has remarked: "data may be dirty, but in many cases the dirt is more like mud than Original Sin."

In more concrete terms suppose the data seem to disconfirm the hypothesis because the t value of the critical coefficient is low, or because other regression diagnostics look poor. Both of these may be due to data errors and not an error in the hypothesis. To illustrate with an extreme case, albeit one involving an identity rather than a hypothesis, few would deny that for a particular commodity total exports equal total imports, even though the data show them not to. Conversely, data errors may sometimes favor the hypotheses. For example, because of a lack of better data the compilers of a series may have estimated an important component as a simple trend. If the model contains a regressor dominated by a similar trend this data error could provide spurious support for the model.

Because of the reluctance of economists to get involved in the messy details of how their data were derived certain standard conventions are used without question. To illustrate the type of problem frequently swept under the rug consider the savings ratio. How many economists who build models to explain this ratio discuss whether they should use the savings data given in the National Income and Product Accounts (NIPA), or else the very different savings data that can be derived from the flow-of-funds accounts? The former are generally used even though they derive saving by subtracting consumption from income, and are therefore at least potentially subject to large percentage errors.[14] (The flow-of-funds estimates also have their problems.) Moreover, as Reinsdorf (2004) has pointed out, there are some specific problems with the NIPA savings data. One is that the personal income data include income received on behalf of households by pension funds and nonprofit organizations that serve households, that is income that households may not be aware of and take into consideration when deciding on their consumption. Data on the difference between the NIPA personal savings rate and the savings rate of households that exclude these receipts are available since 1992, and while the difference is trivial in 1992–1994, it amounts to 0.7 percentage points – that is about 30 percent of the savings ratio

[14] More precisely, "personal outlays for personal consumption expenditures (PCS), for interest payments on consumer debt, and for current transfer payments are subtracted from disposable personal income" (Reinsdorf, 2004, p. 18). The extent to which errors in estimating either income or consumption affect estimates of the savings ratio depends not only on the size of these errors, but also on their covariance. Suppose income is actually 100, but is estimated to be 101, while consumption is estimated correctly at 95. Then, saving is estimated to be 6 rather than 5, a 20 percent error. But if income has been overestimated by 1 because consumption was overestimated by 1, then these errors lower the estimated savings ratio only by 0.05 percent of income, that is by 1 percent of its actual value.

in 1999 and 2000. Another problem is that the NIPA data treat as interest income (and as also as interest payments on consumer debt, and hence as a component of consumption) nominal instead of real interest payments. Using real instead of nominal interest payments reduces the personal savings rate by 1.5 to 2.4 percentage points during 1980–1992, but only by 0.5 to 1.2 percentage points in 1993–2000.

Another problem is the treatment of capital gains and losses. The NIPA data exclude capital gains from income, and hence from saving, but they deduct the taxes paid on realized capital gains from disposable personal income, and thus indirectly from personal saving. Using an alternative measure that includes in disposable personal income federal taxes on capital gains changes the recorded savings rate by only 0.5 percentage points in 1991–1992 but by 1.65 percentage points in the unusual year, 2000. And then there is the important question whether at least some of the unrealized capital gains and losses shouldn't be counted as saving, since over the long run capital gains are a major component of the yield on stocks.

Other data sets have other problems. For instance the difficulties of measuring the inflation rate are well known, and since real GDP is derived by deflating nominal GDP, errors in estimating the inflation rate generate corresponding errors with the opposite sign in estimated real GDP. Moreover, real GDP estimates are downward biased because of an underground economy that might account for 10 percent or more of total output. Furthermore, GDP revisions are by no means trivial, which raises the question of how reliable the final estimates are. Balance of payments statistics, too, are notoriously bad. The difficult of defining money operationally has led to the quip that the demand for money is stable; it is just the definition of money that keeps changing. And even if one agrees on the appropriate concept of money, real time estimates of quarterly growth rates of money are unreliable. The problems besetting survey data, such as misunderstood questions and biased answers are also large. Moreover, in using survey data it has become a convention in economics not to worry about a possible bias due to non-response, even when the non-response rate is, say 65 percent.

My point here is not that the available data are too poor to test our models. That I believe would be an overstatement. It is also not that economists use wrong data sets, but rather that they tend to select their data sets in a mechanical way without considering alternatives, or asking whether the data are sufficiently accurate for the purpose at hand.

There is also a serious danger of errors in data entry, in calculations, and in the transcription of regression results. Dewald, Thursby and Anderson (1986), show that such errors were frequent and substantial. *Perhaps* as a result of this paper they are now much less common, but perhaps not.[15] Downloading data from a standard database is not a complete safeguard against errors. Without

---

[15] Over many years of working first with desk calculators and then with PCs I have found that even if one checks the data carefully, in any large project mechanical errors do creep in. Calculation errors may be as common, or even more common, now than they were in the days of desk calculators. One

even looking for them I have twice found a substantial error in a widely used database.

Moreover, since various popular software packages can yield sharply different results, regression programs, too, can generate substantial errors. (See Lovell 1994; McCullough and Vinod, 1999; McCullough, 2000.) In particular, McCullough and Vinod speak of:

> the failure of many statistical packages to pass even rudimentary benchmarks for numerical accuracy. ... [E]ven simple linear procedures, such as calculation of the correlation coefficient can be horrendously inaccurate. ... While all [three popular] packages tested did well on linear regression benchmarks – gross errors were uncovered in analyses of variance routines. ... [There are] many procedures for which we were unable to find a benchmark and for which we found discrepancies between packages: linear estimation with AR(1) errors, estimation of an ARMA model, Kalman filtering, ... and so on (pp. 633, 635, 650, 655).

Because this paper appeared in the *Journal of Economic Literature* many economists were surely aware of it. One might therefore have expected them to have recalculated computations in their previously published papers using alternative software packages, and the journals to be full of errata notices. This did not happen. (Mea culpa.) In checking Google for references to the McCullough and Vinod paper for such corrections I did not find a single one.[16]

Even allowing for the natural reluctance to retract one's results, and a tendency for herding (and hence for thinking that if nobody else worries, why should I?) this nonchalant attitude is not so easy to reconcile with the claim that economics is a "science," or even that it is a serious discipline. And yet this "who cares?" attitude should not be surprising to someone who takes our portrayal of "economic man" seriously, because there is only a small chance that an error will be caught. But while we therefore need a system of routinely checking at least some published results (say 5 percent) to discourage both carelessness and occasionally even fraud, we are not likely to get one.

In the natural sciences, too, mechanical checking of other people's results is rare. (See Mirowski and Skilivas, 1991.) But instead of checking the mechanics, such as the correctness of calculations, natural scientists try to "replicate" the results, that is they look for similar results in similar circumstances. (See Backhouse, 1992.) For example, they may repeat an experiment at a different

is more likely to be dividing when one should be multiplying, if one can do so with a single key stroke, than in the old days when in the tedious hours of using a desk calculator one had plenty of time to think about what one was doing.

[16] I did the search on November 4, 2005 using the Google "scholar" option. It is, of course, possible, though unlikely, that some errata were published that did not cite the McCullough–Vinod paper but cited one of the other papers that made a similar point. It is also possible that in their subsequent papers some economists did check whether other programs gave results similar to the one they used, though I do not recall ever seeing any indication of this. Also, some economists may have tried several programs and abandoned their projects when they found that these programs gave substantially different results. It would be interesting to know whether economists in government or business, whose errors could result in large losses, recalculated some of their regressions using different programs.

temperature. If they get similar results then that confirms the original findings, and if they do no]t, that can be read either as a limitation of the domain of the model or as casting doubt on it. If many replications fail to confirm the original findings these are then treated as, at best, a special case. Such replication is not common in economics.

13.3. In Conclusion: All is Not Bleak

This discussion may seem to have struck an unrelieved pessimistic note. But all attempts to advance knowledge, not just economic measurements, face obstacles. For example, economic theory has its unrealistic assumption (and implication) of rational income maximization. All the same, it has greatly advanced our understanding. Moreover, the large volume of economic modeling over the last few decades *has* improved our understanding of the economy and our predictive ability, think, for example, of asymmetric information theory, modern finance theory and behavioral economics. And other fields have their problems too. In medicine a study found that: "16 percent of the top cited clinical research articles on postulated effective medical interventions that have been published within the last 15 years have been contradicted by subsequent clinical studies, and another 16 percent have been found to have initially stronger effects than subsequent research" (Ioannides, 2005, p. 223).

The preceding tale of woe is therefore not a plea for giving up, but instead an argument for modesty in the claims we make. Our papers seem to suggest that there is at least a 95 percent probability that our conclusions are correct. Such a claim is both indefensible and unneeded. If an economist takes a proposition for which the previous evidence suggested a 50:50 probability and shows that it has a 55:45 probability of being right, she has done a useful job. It is also a plea to improve our work by paying more attention to such mundane matters as the quality and meaning of our data, potential computing errors, and the need to at least mention unfavorable as well as favorable results of robustness tests. To be sure, that would still leave some very serious problems, such as the transition from correlation to causation, the Lucas critique, and the limited availability of reliable data, but that there is some opportunity for improvement is a hopeful message. Moreover, that some problems we face are insoluble should make us economists feel good about ourselves, since it suggests that our failure to match the achievements of most natural sciences is not an indication of intellectual inferiority.[17]

None of this would carry much weight if the pessimists are right in saying that in economics empirical evidence is not taken seriously when it conflicts with

---

[17] Alexander Rosenberg, a philosopher of science who specializes in the philosophies of economics and biology, described economics as "a subject on which at least as much sheer *genius* has been lavished as on most natural sciences." (Rosenberg, 1978, p. 685, italics in original.) That is flattering, but not entirely convincing.

an appealing theoretical model. For example McCloskey (1985, p. 182) wrote: "[N]o proposition about economic behavior has yet been overturned by econometrics, at any rate not to the standard that the hypothetico-deductive model of science would demand[.]", and Aris Spanos (1986, p. 660) stated "... to my knowledge no economic theory was ever abandoned because it was rejected by some empirical econometric test, nor was a clear-cut decision between competing theories made on the basis of such a test." Such statements are hard to evaluate because they are vague. Do they include only major, generally accepted propositions or also claims made in a specific paper that has not been widely cited? Moreover, what does "overturned" mean? Suppose a paper states a claim that is then rejected by an econometric test in another paper, and neither paper is cited thereafter. Does that count? Or suppose a model that implies that raw prices of exhaustible resources rise over time at a rate equal to the interest rate, is rejected not only by econometric tests, but also by informal observation. Does that count? If it does it is an obvious counterexample. Besides, well-entrenched propositions – in the physical sciences as well as in economics – seldom fall as a result of a single piece of evidence. And that is more a sign of common sense and good judgment than of a faulty methodology.

Let's therefore turn to a broader issue. Have economists stuck with irrational stubbornness to a model of rational, maximizing behavior, despite extensive empirical evidence to the contrary? (Cf. Hausman, 1992.) In an important way they have, but with two substantial qualifications. First, even within mainstream economics this theory is now being challenged by behavioral economics. Second, much of economic theory, for example, Keynesian theory, monetarism, and comparative-cost theory, require only weak versions of rational maximizing theory, versions that are much less challenged by the empirical evidence cited against the much stronger versions. Empirical evidence has much more influence on what economists actually do when dealing with practical problems than it has on what is emblazoned on their banner. Hard-core versions of new classical theory, Ricardian equivalence, efficient markets theory, etc., that require a rigorous rational, maximizing model cater primarily to niche markets. Perhaps economists should be blamed, not for sticking to disconfirmed hypotheses, but for fooling others (in particular philosophers) by proclaiming what they do not really believe or practice. The reason is that the weakened version of the rational-maximizing principle that economists use in practice is hard to formulate, particularly since it depends on the specific issue being addressed.

But that may be letting economists off too easily. *Some* of their beliefs seem invulnerable to empirical evidence. Macro-economists widely accept rational-expectations theory despite the empirical evidence against it. (See Goldfarb and Stekler, 2000.) I conjecture that no economist ever accepted this theory because he or she found its empirical evidence convincing. Rather, it is widely accepted because it seems to be a necessary implication of rational behavior, and must therefore be defended to the death. But even here ongoing research on how agents learn, and the introduction of such learning models into macro models – a move that does not bring the assumption of rational behavior into question – is now taming rational-expectations theory. *Sometimes* economists do stick stubbornly to their models for a long time in the face of contrary empirical evidence, but eventually reason wins out – even in academia.

References

Backhouse, R.E. (1992). The significance of replication in econometrics. Discussion paper 92-25. Economics Department, University of Birmingham.

Backhouse, R.E., Morgan, M.S. (2000). Introduction: Is data mining a methodological problem? *Journal of Economic Methodology* **7**, June, 173–182.

Bronfenbrenner, M. (1972). Sensitivity analysis for econometricians. *Nebraska Journal of Economics* **2**, 57–66, Autumn.

Chatfield, C. (1991). Avoiding statistical pitfalls. *Statistical Science* **6**, 240–252, August.

Chow, S. (1996). *Statistical Significance*. Sage Publishing, London.

Cooley, T.F., LeRoy, S.F. (1981). Identification and estimation of money demand. *American Economic Review* **71**, 825–843, December.

Dewald, W., Thursby, J., Anderson, R. (1986). Replication in economics: The Journal of Money, Credit and Banking Project. *American Economic Review* **76**, 587–603, September.

Donohue, J., III, Wolfers, J. (2006). Uses and abuses of empirical evidence in the death penalty debate. Working paper 11982. NBER.

Elliot, G., Granger, C.W.J. (2004). Evaluating significance: Comment on 'size matters'. *Journal of Socio-Economics* **33**, 547–550.

Fuchs, V., Kruger, A., Poterba, J. (1998). Economists' views about parameters, values and policies: Survey results in labor and public economics. *Journal of Economic Literature* **36**, 1387–1425, September.

Friedman, M. (2005). A natural experiment in monetary policy covering three periods of growth and decline in the economy and the stock market. *Journal of Economic Perspectives* **19**, 145–150, Fall.

Friedman, M., Schwartz, A. (1991). Alternative approaches to analyzing economic data. *American Economic Review* **81**, 39–49, March.

Gibbard, A., Varian, H. (1978). Economic models. *Journal of Philosophy* **1975**, 665–677, November.

Gigerenzer, G. (2004). Mindless statistics. *Journal of Socio-Economics* **33**, 587–606.

Goldfarb, R. (1995). The economist-as-audience needs a plausible model of inference. *Journal of Economic Methodology* **2**, 201–222, February.

Goldfarb, R., Stekler, H.O. (2000). Why do empirical results change? Forecasts as tests of rational expectations. *History of Political Economy (Annual Supplement)*, 95–116.

Greene, C. (2000). I am not, nor have I have been a member of the data-mining discipline. *Journal of Economic Methodology* **7**, 217–239, June.

Hansen, L.P., Heckman, J. (1996). The empirical foundations of calibration. *Journal of Economic Perspectives* **10**, 87–104, Winter.

Hamermesh, D. (2000). The craft of labrometrics. *Industrial and Labor Relations Review* **53**, 363–380, April.

Hausman, D.M. (1992). *The Inexact and Separate Science of Economics*. Cambridge Univ. Press, Cambridge.

Hendry, D.F., Ericsson, N. (1991). An econometric analysis of UK money demand, in Friedman, M., Schwartz, A.J. (Eds.), Monetary Trends in the United States and the United Kingdom. *American Economic Review* **81**, 8–39, March.

Hoover, K.D., Perez, S. (2000). Three attitudes towards data mining. *Journal of Economic Methodology* **7**, 195–210, June.

Hoover, K.D., Siegler, M. (unpublished). Sound and fury: McCloskey and significance testing in economics.

Horowitz, J. (2004). Comment on size matters. *Journal of Socio-Economics* **33**, 571–575.

Inoue, A., Killian, L. (2002). In-sample or out-of-sample tests of predictability: Which should we use? Working paper No. 195. European Central Bank.

Ioannides, J. (2005). Contradicted and initially stronger effects in highly cited clinical research. *Journal of the American Medical Association* **294**, 219–227, July.

Kamarck, A. (1983). *Economics and the Real World.* Blackwell, Oxford.

Kennedy, P. (2002). Sinning in the basement: What are the rules? The ten commandments of applied econometrics. *Journal of Economic Surveys* **16** (4), 569–585.

Keuzenkamp, H.A., Magnus, J.R. (1995). On tests and significance in econometrics. *Journal of Econometrics* **67**, 5–24.

Keuzenkamp, H.A., McAleer, M. (1995). Simplicity, scientific inference and econometric modelling. *Economic Journal*, January, 1–21.

Kim, J., de Marchi, N., Morgan, M.S. (1995). Empirical model peculiarities and belief in the natural rate hypothesis. *Journal of Econometrics* **67**, 81–102.

Leamer, E.E. (1978). *Specification Searches: Ad Hoc Inference with Nonexperimental Data.* John Wiley, New York.

Leamer, E. (1983). Let's take the con out of econometrics. *American Economic Review* **73**, 31–43, March.

Leontief, W. (1971). Theoretical assumptions and nonobervable facts. *American Economic Review* **61**, 1–7, March.

Loeb, S., Page, M. (2000). Examining of the link between teacher wages and student outcome. *Review of Economics and Statistics* **82**, 393–408, August.

Lovell, M. (1994). Software reviews. *Economic Journal* **104**, 713–726, May.

Machlup, F. (1950). *Methodology of Economics and Other Social Sciences.* Academic Press, New York.

Makridakis, S., Bibon, M. (2000). The M-3 competition: Results, conclusions and implications. *International Journal of Forecasting* **16**, 451–476,

Mayer, T. (1998). Monetarists versus Keynesians on central banking. In: Backhouse, R., Hausman, R., Mäki, D.U., Salanti, A. (Eds.), *Economics and Methodology.* MacMillan, London.

Mayer, T. (2001a). Misinterpreting a failure to disconfirm as a confirmation. http://www.econ.ucdavis.edu/working.

Mayer, T. (2001b). The role of ideology in disagreements among economists: A quantities analysis. *Journal of Economic Methodology* **8**, 253–274, June.

McAleer, M., Pagan, A., Volcker, P. (1983). What will take the con out of econometrics? *American Economic Review* **73**, 293–307, June.

McCloskey, D.N. (1985). *The Rhetoric of Economics.* Univ. of Wisconsin Press, Madison.

McConnell, M., Perez-Quiros, G. (2000). Output fluctuations in the United States: What has changed since the early 1980s? *American Economic Review* **90**, 1464–1476, December.

McCullough, B.D. (2000). Is it safe to assume that software is accurate? *International Journal of Forecasting* **16**, 349–357.

McCullough, B.D., Vinod, H.D. (1999). The numerical reliability of econometric software. *Journal of Economic Literature* **37**, 633–665, June.

Mirowski, P., Skilivas, S. (1991). Why econometricians don't replicate although they do reproduce. *Review of Political Economy* **3** (2), 146–163.

Morgenstern, O. (1950). *On the Accuracy of Economic Observations.* Princeton Univ. Press, Princeton.

O'Brien, A. (2004). Why is the standard error of regression so low using historical data? *Journal of Socio-Economics* **33**, 565–570, November.

Open Peer Comments (1996). *Brain and Behavioral Research.* **19**, 188–228, June.

Pagan, A., Veall, M. (2000). Data mining and the econometrics industry: Comments on the papers by Mayer and of Hoover and Perez. *Journal of Economic Methodology* **7**, 211–216, June.

Papell, D., Murray, C., Ghiblawi, H. (2000). The structure of unemployment. *Review of Economics and Statistics* **82**, 309–315, May.

Phannkuch, M., Wild, C. (2000). Statistical thinking and statistical practice: Themes gleaned from professional statisticians. *Statistical Science* **15** (2), 132–152.

Reinsdorf, M. (2004). Alternative measures of personal saving. *Survey of Current Business* **84**, 17–27, September.

Robertson, R. (2000). Wage shocks and North American labor-market integration. *American Economic Review* **9**, 742–764, September.

Rosenberg, A. (1978). The puzzle of economic modeling. *Journal of Philosophy* **75**, 679–683, November.

Spanos, A. (1986). *Statistical Foundations of Econometric Modeling*. Cambridge Univ. Press, Cambridge.

Spanos, A. (2000). Revisiting data mining: 'Hunting' with or without a license. *Journal of Economic Methodology* **7**, 231–264, June.

Summers, L. (1991). The scientific illusion in empirical macroeconomics. *Swedish Journal of Economics* **93**, 129–148, March.

Thompson, B. (2004). The 'significance' crisis in psychology and education. *Journal of Socio-Economics* **33**, 607–613.

Thorbecke, E. (2004). Economic and statistical significance. Comments on 'size matters'. *Journal of Socio-Economics* **33**, 571–575.

Viscusi, W.K., Hamilton, J.T. (1999). Are risk regulators rational? Evidence from hazardous waste cleanup decisions. *American Economic Review* **89**, 210–227, September.

Ward, B. (1972). *What's Wrong with Economics*. Basic Books, New York.

Wei, S.-J. (2000). How taxing is corruption on international investment? *Review of Economics and Statistics* **82**, 1–11, February.

Zellner, A. (1992). Statistics, science and public policy. *Journal of the American Statistical Association* **87**, 1–6, March.

Ziliak, S., McCloskey, D.N. (2004). Size matters: The standard error of regressions in the "*American Economic Review*." *Journal of Socio-Economics* **33** (5), 527–546.

PART IV

Precision

CHAPTER 14

Precision

Theodore M. Porter

Department of History, UCLA, Los Angeles, CA, USA
E-mail address: tporter@history.ucla.edu

Precision – to be precise – is the quality of being definite and unambiguous, and need not signify correctness. We might for example be given very precise directions, with distances to the nearest centimeter, specifying street names and compass directions including minute descriptions of elevators, halls, and doors, for traveling from our hotel to the university room where a conference on measurement is to begin at 9:00 a.m., and yet, on account of the malign wit of the organizing powers, be led not to the Tinbergen Institute but to the maritime museum, the central railway station, or worse, occasioning who knows what misadventures. In science and technology, where precision has primarily a quantitative meaning, it has come to be distinguished from *accuracy*, which implies the validity of a number in regard to the location, quantity, or magnitude of a thing. *Precision* requires nothing more than a tight clustering of the measurements which, like the bullet holes in a target made by a marksman with a bias, may be very near to each other but some distance from the bull's eye. The densest concentration of shot in the body of the vice president's hunting partner will yet bring down no quail. The quest for greater precision is, nevertheless, a pervasive theme in the history of the sciences since the end of the eighteenth century, of particular significance for those material and social technologies that embody the modern role of science in economies, governments, and societies.

14.1. Measuring Precision

While quantitative precision is not sufficient to assure accuracy, it is in general necessary. A measurement might of course just happen to be very close to the true value, but it would be impossible to know unless that value is somehow given independently. Precision, according to its operational definition, can be characterized statistically in terms of a standard deviation or related measure of dispersion, while accuracy, like the Kantian noumenon, is perhaps unknowable because inaccessible to experience. As Dennis Fixler points out in this volume with respect to quantities in economics, the objects to be measured are often defined by models, and the models are often subject to revision. The same point holds, though not always to the same degree, in the natural sciences, and few if

Measurement in Economics: A Handbook
Marcel Boumans (Editor)

any quantities of interest even in physics can be said to be directly knowable. Still, systematic errors can often be recognized even at the time the measures are taken, and they may also become evident in retrospect when a new method of measurement gives discrepant results. There are, we may suppose, always systematic errors, linked to particular observers and to particular techniques. In 1972, W.J. Youden gathered up the results of fifteen separate measures of the mean distance from the Earth to the Sun (the Astronomical Unit) taken from 1895 to 1961, and showed that each new value lay outside the limits of probable error given by the previous one (Youden, 1972; Gigerenzer et al., 1989, pp. 82–83).

Accurate measurement was intermittently a concern of science, or natural philosophy, from ancient times. For the Greeks, astronomy, mechanics, and geometrical optics were all mathematical fields. This did not necessarily imply any need for precise measurement, since the match between mathematics and observation might be purely qualitative. Plato was a famous believer in mathematical reality, but the cave in his *Republic* did not allow this empyrean domain to be experienced by the empirical observer. Precise measurement was more important to Babylonian astrology, and to the modest Greek ambition to "save the phenomena" (to predict or retrodict) than to a causal and geometrical science of the planets. In Christian Europe, calculating the dates of movable feasts such as Easter gave added incentive for accurate measurement and prediction, which remained essential to astrology (Heilbron, 1999; Porter, 2001). Kepler's reluctant abandonment of perfect spheres in favor of the ellipse as the appropriate geometrical template for the orbit of Mars, and then of all the planets, attests to a new esteem for precision in the natural philosophy of the heavens. This was preserved by Newton, whose most famous title, the *Mathematical Principles of Natural Philosophy*, advertised his belief that natural philosophy should be mathematical. The problem of precision was not always so easy in practice, not even in astronomy, and his need to reconcile, in detail and through calculation, ever more refined measurements with the geometry of an inverse-square force in the case of the moon, a three-body problem, gave him, he said, a headache.

By the late seventeenth century, the role of exact measurement in astronomy was secure. In their drive for ever greater precision, astronomers began working out systematic methods for managing error and minimizing its consequences, a line of developments that would lead by the early nineteenth century to the method of least squares (Stigler, 1986). This effort had several motivations. One was to test predictions derived from Newton's laws, which bore on geodetic measures such as the shape of the Earth as well as the motions of planets, moons, and comets. Often the confrontation of theory and measurement had stakes much lower than validity of the inverse-square law of gravitation or of circular orbits, involving instead minute approximations, as for example in the landmark computational effort to predict the return of Halley's comet in 1758–1759 (Grier, 2005). Increasingly, precision was accepted as important for its own sake, part of the ethics of scientific practice, independently of any bearing on theoretical issues. Greenwich astronomer John Flamsteed's desperate effort to keep his data from Newton (who wanted them for his study of the chronology of ancient kingdoms) until they were perfect shows how obsessive the drive for precision could be. His amendments to Newton's edition, copies of which he hunted down and burned, were few and minor. In the 1790s, Pierre-André Méchain was driven to distraction by an error of a few seconds of arc (implying a discrepancy of about a hundred meters) in his survey of a line of meridian from France through the Pyrenees to Barcelona (Alder, 2002; Gillispie, 2004). These three or four seconds poisoned the remainder of this life, which he spent desperately trying to correct the inconsistency and covering it up, until his more level-headed collaborator Jean-Baptiste Delambre discovered it in his papers after he died.

The role of the metric system in the history of precision goes beyond Méchain's measurement-induced madness. The aspiration to universal measures, based on a meter that would be one ten-millionth part of a quarter meridian, the distance from the equator to the North Pole, was part of a revolutionary ambition to remake the world. The tangle of locally variable units of length, weight, area, and volume given by history was to be replaced by a simple and rational system, removing also those ambiguities that were so often exploited by the powerful and promoting free commerce among the nations of the world (Kula, 1986). A culture of precise, standardized measures would be more open and legible than one based on locality, tacit understanding, and social power. It would facilitate the free movement of knowledge as well as of merchandise.

The late eighteenth century, when the Enlightenment came to fruition, initiated the heyday of precision in the sciences, which has gained momentum in the succeeding centuries. The antique sciences of astronomy, mechanics, and geometrical optics, known to the early modern period as natural philosophy, had long traditions of mathematical precision. Now, chemistry, meteorology, geodesy, and the study of heat, light, electricity, and magnetism, were made experimental and subjected to precise measurement, in most cases before there was much in the way of mathematical theory. The rising standard of precision was made possible by new instruments and the experimental practices that went with them, but the impulse behind it all was not simply a matter of scientific goals. Rather, it grew from a new alliance of scientific study with the forces of state-building, technological improvement, and global commerce and industrial expansion. The metric system, linked as it was to measurements of the earth, depended on techniques of land surveying now deployed on a large scale. The French state, for example, undertook in the early eighteenth century to map the kingdom, the better to administer it, while the British surveyed North America in an effort to regulate settlement and to allow clearer property holdings (Linklater, 2002). The scientific controversy over the shape of the Earth, often explained in terms of Cartesian opposition to Newtonian mechanics, arose in fact from the empirical findings of a French land survey which seemed to show that the Earth was narrower at the equator than a perfect sphere would be (Terrall, 2002). The systematic pursuit of precision extended to many technological domains, including mining and metallurgy, agriculture, forestry, and power production by water wheels as well as steam engines (Frängsmyr et al., 1990). Precise measurement became important also in the human sciences, such as medical studies of smallpox inoculation, In the early 1790s, savants and administrators led by Lavoisier and Lagrange undertook to demonstrate the successes of the Revolution and mobilize the nation for war with a systematic accounting of the French economy. The drive for improved population statistics was stimulated in equal measure by scientific, administrative, and ideological ambitions, to the extent that these can even be distinguished (Rusnock, 2002; Brian, 1994).

Kathryn Olesko argues that the proliferation of instruments of exactitude in the late eighteenth century did not suffice to support a shared understanding of what "precise" measurement must mean (Olesko, 1995, p. 104). The looseness of this concept may be illustrated by Lavoisier's notorious practice of giving many superfluous decimal places, as for example in a paper of 1784 where 0.86866273 pounds of vital air are combined with 0.13133727 pounds of inflammable gas to give 1.00000000 pounds of water (Golinski, 1995, p. 78). Olesko suggests, very reasonably, that the idea of probability, as incorporated into the method of least squares early in the new century, supported a novel concept of precision as the tightness of a cluster of measurements, one that indicates the reliability of the measuring system in the inverse form of the magnitude of expected error. Significantly, the method of least squares was first published in 1805 by Adrien-Marie Legendre with specific reference to the metric surveys. Carl Friedrich Gauss, however, had already incorporated this method of minimizing the squares of errors into his work on planetary astronomy, where the notion of error to be expected with a given measuring apparatus was already familiar. The method of least squares was first applied routinely in these two allied fields, astronomy and geodesy. It was subsequently taken up in experimental physics, first of all in Germany, and much more slowly than in astronomy.

Yet precision as a concept, if not necessarily as a word, was reasonably familiar in the late eighteenth century, before the systematization of least squares for reducing data and fitting curves. Laplace deployed the paired concepts of precision and probability in the 1780s to estimate population. He inferred a measure of population from the number of births – these were systematically recorded and gathered up nationally – using a multiplier, the number of inhabitants per birth. He made an estimate of the multiplier based on samples involving complete population tallies is a few selected towns. He was aware that the individuals sampled could not be independent and random, as if drawn with equal probability from the whole of France, yet proceeded as if they were. He then explained just how many individuals must be counted for the determination of the multiplier, 771,649, in order to have sufficiently high odds – a thousand to one – that the error of the population estimate for the kingdom would be less than half a million. The dubious exactitude of the proposed sample size then vanished as he moved on to a recommendation that the *précision* demanded by the importance of the subject calls for a census of 1,000,000 to 1,200,000. Using similar mathematics he calculated the probability (very low) that the difference between the ratio of male to female births in London compared to Paris could be due merely to chance. He could not replicate the data or the measures, but implicitly he was comparing the actual results with others that might be anticipated based on his customary probability model of drawing balls from an urn, supposing the underlying chances to be the same as those given by the statistics (Bru, 1988; Gillispie, 1997).

The earliest effort to create a system of mass production and interchangeable parts, undertaken in France in the last decades before the French Revolution, also involved a sense of precision as something measurable, though this was not necessarily given an explicitly probabilistic form. In contrast to the American system of mass production, achieved by entrepreneurs and practical engineers, savants had a large role in the early French version. Ken Alder (1997) shows what fundamental changes in systems of manufacture and the organization of labor would have followed from this initiative, had it succeeded. Quantitative standards were to provide the discipline according to which the workmen labored, and the skilled craftsman who worked according to his own, possibly high, individualized standards could not survive. There was no immediate prospect in 1780 of manufacturing weapons more cheaply with interchangeable parts, since the precision required took much labor. The advantage, rather, was a work force under tighter control and a manufacturing process less dependent on special skills monopolized and kept secret by guildsmen. There was also the potential, with standardization, to repair weapons more easily in the field. Precision here took the form of "tolerance," and could be gauged either with a measuring stick or by comparing the piece with a standard. And this effort to create interchangeability provides a standard for us with which to think about the meaning of precision.

Already in this eighteenth-century initiative, precision was about interchangeability and standardization. On one of Janus's faces we see scientific accuracy based on technical knowledge and methods, and on the other, a cultural and economic system of highly disciplined work. Precision instruments by themselves achieve rather little, for the system depends on skilled or highly standardized operation of them, and also on the reliability, hence uniformity, of their construction. A work force of technicians and savants that can produce and operate such instruments presupposes a well-organized system of training and apprenticeship. If the validity of science is to be independent of place, as scientists (and the rest of us) commonly suppose, some of those instruments, and with them the work practices and the institutions that make them possible, must be replicated in new locations. Precision cannot be merely technical, but depends on and helps to create a suitable culture. Such a culture is not indissolubly bound to capitalism or socialism, democracy or oligarchy, yet forms of state and of economy are part of this system as well.

14.2. How Knowledge Travels: Precision, Locality, and Trust

In *Trust in Numbers* (1995), I described objectivity as a "technology of distance." The same year, in *The Values of Precision*, Norton Wise spoke of precision as, among other things, a means by which knowledge can more readily travel. He explains (p. 6): "While qualities do not travel well beyond the local communities where they are culturally valued, quantities seem to be more easily transportable, and the more precise the better." To be sure, a system of precision and objectivity would not survive in an alien world. Its life under such conditions would resemble that of the Connecticut Yankee who tries to raise King Arthur's Court up to the technological standard of nineteenth-century New England, and is defeated by cultural backwardness and superstition. Precision necessarily includes a capacity to replicate itself, to recreate, within a certain tolerance, the social and economic conditions through which it was formed. The universal validity of knowledge is the precondition as well as the outcome of modern science, which manages somehow to transform local knowledge and personal skill, passed on in specific locations from master to apprentice, into truths that are recognized all over the world, if not quite everywhere. Michael Polanyi (1958), who famously emphasized "personal knowledge" and the "tacit dimension" of science, also compared science to a liberal economy of free enterprise. Far from being machinelike and impersonal, socialism incarnate, science for Polanyi was necessarily a spontaneous and highly decentralized cultural form. Against J.D. Bernal and the British enthusiasts for Soviet-style scientific planning, Polanyi insisted that scientists must be left free to follow their intuitions in choosing research problems and methods of solution.

Polanyi's vision depended on a highly idealized version of capitalism as well as of science. One might just as well say that effective (humane, tolerant) socialism depends or would depend on a capacity to nurture rather than to squash or rationalize away local initiative and the expert knowledge of small communities. The question of the *scale* of quantitative precision has no simple answer. Polanyi's insights regarding skill and locality are as valid for the pursuit of precision as for other aspects of science. The last decimal place of precision in a measurement is often purchased at very high cost, and the laboratory that can achieve it may have to be correspondingly large. But such a laboratory will be permeated by non-replicable skills of many sorts, joining forces to combat the sources of error that multiply relentlessly as the scale of the variability at issue becomes ever smaller. Often a program of precision measurement will incorporate also the power of numerous repetitions, thus joining brute force to exquisite craft in the clocklike regularity of the statistical recorder. Finally, the statistical design itself may be, in a subtle way, unique, fitted to the special circumstances of the observations, and it may have to be adapted when things don't work out quite the way they were planned. All of this applies a fortiori to therapeutic experiments, measuring the medical effectiveness of pharmaceuticals, where tightly-organized large-scale experiments are necessary even to detect the effect of a valuable new treatment, and where measurement to two significant figures would be a miracle.

A many-layered precision measurement in a physics or engineering laboratory does not travel easily or carry conviction from the sheer force of the evidence it supplies, but depends for its credibility on trust. Although much of the work may be shielded from the vision of those who are interested in the result, their trust need not be blind. Specialists in the same field will be familiar with the instruments and their limits, and perhaps also with the particular scientists and technicians who carried out the work. Published papers include a description of experimental methods, enough to be illuminating to cognoscenti from the same area of science if not to just any technically-literate person. The data, even as filtered for publication, give indications of the limits of the procedures and of things that might have gone wrong. Also, scientists often have other indications of what the result ought to be, based on a model or on measurements carried out in a somewhat different way, which can be compared with the new one. And they may well try to incorporate some aspects of a new procedure into their own work, and in this limited sense to replicate it.

Moreover, the last word is scarcely ever spoken in science. Brilliantly original but quirky and unreliable techniques get their rough spots sanded down and the conditions within which they work more closely defined. Skilled practices become routine or are automated, and may in effect be incorporated into a manufactured instrument. The cutting-edge precision to which scientists of one generation devote every waking moment will often, in the next, be purchased off the shelf from a supply house and incorporated unthinkingly into work in quite different disciplines. In this way, the most glorious triumphs of precision, pursued often for their own sake, are transformed into instruments and procedures to simplify tasks or improve reliability in the achievement of some other task. Scientific precision, especially in the form that can most easily travel, thus contributes to and depends on that other basic form of precision, manufacturing with standardized, interchangeable parts. Precision machinery forms the nucleus of a system of standardization that has spread over much of the world, an artificial world within which travel is relatively unproblematical. As with Anne Tyler's *Accidental Tourist*, who leaves home with reluctance and would like every foreign location to be as much like his neighborhood in Baltimore as possible, you can eat a *salade niçoise*, replace the battery in your watch, and pick up email on your Blackberry almost anywhere you go.

In a similar fashion, precision and standardization help to make the world administrable, especially by creating the conditions for information to travel. *Information*, as Yaron Ezrahi points out, is knowledge "flattened and simplified." It should require little or no interpretation, and thus presume no deep intellectual preparation, but be immediately available to almost anyone for do-it-yourself use (Ezrahi, 2004). The existence of such information presumes much about the world, which should contain an abundance of self-similar objects, and about its inhabitants, who should be familiar with them: in short, a world of standardized objects and, to a degree, standardized subjects as well. Such a world was not made in a day, and while precision has greatly assisted the Weberian project of rational bureaucracy, it cannot figure in this great drama as the *deus ex machina*. As Wise (1995, p. 93) sagely puts it, "precision comes no more easily than centralized government." The pursuit of precision cannot, unassisted, created a system of legibility and control that makes bureaucracy possible. Rather, systems of precision and of administration have grown up and continue to develop in tandem, each tugging at the bootstraps of the other. Each displays features characteristic of the alliance, which cannot be regarded as intrinsic to bureaucracy or to precision "as such." For example, the intense demands on intimate understanding and trust characteristic of scientific precision as craft are hard to reconcile with the pervasive distrust that structures bureaucracy in its most impersonal form. There, it may be most important to have rules to rein in subjectivity. The prototype of this form of precision is the accounting statement, which may be denominated in terms of quantities of production (this one is especially typical of socialist economies and of economic planning), human individuals, or money.

14.3. Technologies of Distance: Precision and Impersonality

Although this essay emphasizes the dependence of precision in science on skill, locality, and intense interactions among specialists, this is not the only form of precision measurement in science, and perhaps not the most important one. Communities of specialists certify numbers for use by others. So authorized, a technique of quantification can perform as a "technology of distance," a role played by numbers in the most detached scientific endeavors as well as in those linked to technology and to policy. The process may be summed up as the reduction of knowledge to information. Users of information do not customarily ask how the knowledge was produced or what it means, but simply incorporate it into solutions to their own problems. Numbers exemplify this aspect of information because they can be incorporated readily into a mode of analysis governed by formal principles of arithmetic or of statistics. Often it does not even matter whether the units in question are atoms or humans, meters, money, or mental test results.

In public and administrative uses, the role of numbers as a technology of distance becomes all the more dominant. The transformation of knowledge into information, with the attendant obscuring of subtleties that demand interpretation, makes objective numbers suitable for widespread diffusion. "Objectivity," as used here, has a sense like that of precision, implying not truth but constraint, the minimization of subjectivity. Tallying a population, for example, depends on many fussy details of definition such as what counts as a place of residence and how it matters whether one is a citizen and whether one is present legally. It depends also on how the count is administered, including what efforts are made to identify those who do not send in their forms or cannot be found at home. Although census officials recognize that such indeterminacies can mount into the millions, they give population figures to the last unit, and the expectation of random errors of a much smaller order is among the factors that have been invoked against use of probability sampling in place of a complete count.

Similarly, in accounting, a company's balance sheet will change whenever a stock of inventory is determined to unsaleable, or in any "restructuring," which in some cases involves a shift of billions of dollars. Yet such ambiguities do not prevent the accountants from trying to deal properly with much smaller figures, and failure to do so could send them to prison. *Accuracy* can be elusive in relation to quantities like these, but the rules and conventions governing them do produce a kind of precision. Indeed, the pursuit of precision can appear almost obsessive. When, in its infancy, Microsoft's Windows 95 turned up with a bug that would, in extremely rare circumstances, produce an infinitesimal error, this was troubling not to experimental physicists but to accountants. Their precision is, in one sense, of the highest order, since their books must balance to the penny. (Even so, at least one ingenious programmer managed briefly to enrich himself by diverting fractions of cents from bank interest payments into his own account.) Charles Sanders Peirce once remarked that the vaunted precision of physics was on the order of that of upholsterers' measurements, leaving little corners of uncertainty where the effects of pure chance might be tucked away (Porter, 1986).

Index numbers, such as the cost of living or inflation and deflation of the currency, involve sampling and so cannot attain to absolute precision. Yet the numbers are always much more precise and determinate that the concepts (or even the entities) they purport to measure. This imprecision, as Fixler explains in his contribution to this volume, is manifested by regular changes in the models that underlie the measures. Their preciseness follows from the rules and practices of measurement, and depends on the credibility of the agencies that gather up and process the data. For cost of living, assessing the effects of technological change has been particularly thorny. As the experience of the Boskin Commission in the United States in 1996 indicates, the uncertainties could very plausibly involve an alteration of the index on the order of a percentage point per year. Protests by pensioners, who receive annual adjustments based on these numbers, assured that no such recalibration would be put into effect, and the existence of indeterminacy on this scale has not prevented experts in economic measurement from attending assiduously to much smaller errors. A measure so important cannot, after all, be left to amendment by personal judgment or arbitrary whim.

Other economic indicators, those without any direct statutory role, are routinely manipulated rhetorically, and sometimes even redefined, for political advantage. Is the average citizen becoming more prosperous? It makes a great deal of difference whether a mean or a median is presented, and inequalities in the distribution of wealth are quite different from those of income. Personal income and income per household have often moved in opposite directions as households have, in recent years, become smaller. Either number can be calculated with some precision from publicly available data (which may, however, omit the untaxed "unofficial" economy), yet the availability of these superficially similar but quantitatively very different indicators of prosperity allow sharply divergent assessments of the effects of a government's tax and budgetary policies.

The emergence of decision technologies such as cost–benefit analysis illustrates the complex dynamic of precision and accuracy in relation to objectivity and discernment, or information and wisdom. Here, once again, are numbers performing a legal or bureaucratic function. However it often is not within the capacity of a particular agency to pronounce authoritatively on what these numbers should be. In the United States, for example, they have been subject to challenge in Congressional committee hearings and sometimes in the courts. At times the numbers are transparently corrupt, but good intentions provide no guarantee that they will hold up as valid or even that they should. Cost–benefit analysis is often defended as bringing the methods and hence the efficiencies of business to government, but it was from its beginning a technology for public decisions, involving the quantification of effects that would never appear on a balance sheet of a private business. This mighty project of commensuration, which began as a somewhat loose and informal method for analyzing public construction projects, was more and more strictly codified beginning in the 1930s. By 1965 it had emerged as an ideal for the analysis of government expenditures and regulatory actions of all kinds, a way of purging (or pretending to purge) the corrupt play of interests from the decisions of government, which should instead be objective and rational. That is, they should be turned into a problem of measurement and calculation.

Precision in these cost–benefit studies never pretended to absolute exactitude. The engineers who, through the 1950s, normally performed them for such agencies as the Army Corps of Engineers and the Bureau of Reclamation were not always consistent in their use of rounding, but they would rarely claim more than two significant figures, and when the politics shifted or matured, it was quite possible for a dismal benefit–cost ratio of 0.37 to 1 to rise above 1.0 by adding, say, hydroelectric generation facilities that, despite these dazzling economic advantages, had somehow not at first been inserted into the plans (Porter, 1995, p. 160). Only the pressure of powerful opponents, some of them from private industry such as electric utilities and railroads but the most effective ones from rival agencies, caused the rules of measurement to be spelled out more clearly. Even after this, the decision process continued to depend as much on forming an alliance of supporters as on the "objective" economic considerations. Still, when in the 1940s the Bureau of Reclamation and the Corps of Engineers found themselves embattled over projects on the Missouri River or in the epic contest to build the Pine Flat Dam on the Kings River in California, the issue of objectivity in the calculations rose to the surface and had to be defended in a battle of experts.

At times these collisions inspired challenges directed specifically to questions of accuracy. Was the increased revenue to movie theaters in areas where agriculture was promoted by new cheap supplies of irrigation water properly included among the benefits of a dam built by the Bureau of Reclamation? Often, however, precision was the great desideratum. Were the methods devised by the Corps in the 1950s for assigning a value to recreation on reservoirs sufficiently strict so as to exclude manipulation of the calculation and to avoid decisions made for corrupt political reasons instead of rational bureaucratic ones? And the issue of special preferences was, after all, the crucial concern that had stimulated the development of such calculative technologies in the first place. Economic rationality was of interest, but that would be impossible until one could gain control of the pork-barrel impulse, of Congressmen funding projects to win support in their districts and to enrich their key supporters or even themselves. A choice based on criteria that were somewhat arbitrary but rigorous might be preferable to one aiming to advance rational goals that could not easily be measured.

This last point can be illustrated by the rules for measuring the value of human life. This has always been a somewhat sensitive issue, because even economists might be uncomfortable setting a price on a life, and in other walks of life most people find the whole matter loathsome and heartless. One thinks of Jonathan Swift's bitterly ironical *Modest Proposal*, which pretends to demonstrate the economic advantages of bringing starving Irish children to England and serving them up for dinner in prosperous households. Yet, in a system where a dam, a highway, or a hospital is required by law to get over a benefit–cost hurdle by showing a ratio above 1.0, to fail to put a value on life is in effect to assign it a value of zero. Since the eighteenth century, certain institutions had found reason to place a value on human life. These were life insurance companies, and the point was to provide widows and orphans of professionals such as ministers with the capacity to make up the financial loss they would suffer from the death of the father and breadwinner. If his future income and his annual expenses were known, along with rates of return on a safe investment, an actuary could calculate the sum desired. By the twentieth century, determinations of this kind were made routinely. Since they involved the future, they could not be extremely precise, but the uncertainties were reduced by probability: in a cost–benefit analysis, it was an average life rather than some particular ones that the calculation required. There might be more uncertainty in estimating the number of lives saved or lost as a result of constructing a levee or regulating a toxic substance than in the value to be assigned to each.

This monetary sum, the discounted present value of future income, was sufficiently precise and objective for purposes of a cost–benefit analysis. The only problem was that economists, who took these calculations more seriously than engineers, regarded it as the wrong quantity. The value of a life is measured not by income but by welfare or utility, something along the lines of what people on average would be willing to pay to save their lives, or what they would have to be paid to sacrifice them. By this definition, we have a very unpromising object of quantification. There is somewhat more hope in a more nuanced version of the task: how much in increased wages do people require in order to assume certain measurable risks, for example by working in a relatively dangerous job. Even this formulation involves a host of problems, of which the most obvious is separating the effects of risk from other factors that may affect pay in various occupations. Studies of risk and behavior, at least through the 1980s, produced hugely discrepant figures for the value of human life, from negative values into the billions and beyond. Thus, though economists agreed that, conceptually, it was far superior to the alternatives as a way to figure human life into the grand project of commensuration that is cost–benefit analysis, it remained unworkable from the standpoint of precision. The insurance calculation thus remained in use by social scientists, who regarded it as incoherent from the standpoint of the basic assumptions of economics, because it was the only definition of the value of life that admitted a decent level of precision (Porter, 1992). Subsequently, through the miracle of averaging, a value of life in terms of individual preferences was made available for bureaucratic use (Ackerman and Hamerling, 2004).

14.4. Precision and World-Making

As science merges more and more with technology, there is a tendency for accuracy to give way to precision. In a way, this can already be seen in the early history of the metric system. The savants of the 1790s hoped to create a natural unit of measurement, based on the circumference of the Earth. In more recent times, scientists and historians have thought the choice of unit arbitrary, a mere convention, but they forget the ties that bound systems of measurement with the administration of the land and the rationalization of the economy. The makers of the metric system envisioned, as Gillispie (1997, p. 152) points out,

> a universal decimal system, embracing not only ordinary weights and measures but also money, navigation, cartography, and land registry.... In such a system, it would be possible to move from the angular observations of astronomy to linear measurements of the earth's surface by a simple interchange of units involving no numerical conversions; from these linear units to units of area and capacity by squaring and cubing; from these to units of weight by taking advantage of the specific gravity of water taken as unity; and finally from weight to price by virtue of the value of gold and silver in alloys held invariant in composition through a rigorous fiscal policy.

Inevitably there were errors; the meter was not, and of course could not possibly have been, exactly one forty-millionth part of the longitudinal circumference of the Earth. The Euro-doubting *Guardian* newspaper, inspired by Méchain's concealment and by a title advertising a "secret error" in the founding of the metric system, reviewed Alder's book on the topic as evidence of corruption at its very foundation. To modern users of the system, the inaccuracy scarcely matters. Metric measurements are a system of precision, justified by their internal coherence, widespread adoption, and ease of use rather than by any relationship to quantities in nature.

Absolute quantities, of course, still matter to science, and it is difficult not to believe that accuracy is advancing along with precision in the measurement of nature. By now the meter is again defined in terms of a natural quantity, though as an unnatural multiple with many decimal places. Precision is of fundamental economic importance, crucial for the standardization that makes possible not only mass production, but also the interconnection of vast grids of power, transportation, and communication. The field of metrology is presided over by bureaus of standards, of which the prototype was founded in newly-unified Germany in 1871 (Cahan, 1989). Metrology is an engineering science that serves as infrastructure for all the sciences and an indispensable aid to scientific communication. It is concerned less directly with accurate measures of nature than with the coordination of technical activities through the standardization of precision, which, much more than serving as handmaid to the triumphant career of accuracy, helps to constitute it.

Acknowledgements

This paper draws extensively from my essay "Speaking Precision to Power: The Modern Political Role of Social Science," Social Research 73 (4) (2006) 1273–1294.

References

Ackerman, F., Hamerling, L. (2004). *Priceless: On Knowing the Price of Everything and the Value of Nothing*. The New Press, New York.

Alder, K. (1997). *Engineering the Revolution: Arms and Enlightenment in France*. Princeton Univ. Press, Princeton, NJ.

Alder, K. (2002). *The Measure of All Things: The Seven-Year Odyssey and Hidden Error that Transformed the World*. Free Press, New York.

Brian, E. (1994). *La mésure de l'État: Administrateurs et géomètres au XVIIIe siècle*. Albin Michel, Paris.

Bru, B. (1988). Estimations laplaciennes. In: Mairesse, J. (Ed.), *Estimations et sondages*. Editions Albatross, Paris, pp. 7–46.

Cahan, D. (1989). *An Institute for an Empire: The Physikalische-Technische Reichsanstalt, 1871–1918*. Cambridge Univ. Press, Cambridge, UK.

Ezrahi, Y. (2004). Science and the political imagination in contemporary democracies. In: Jasanoff, S. (Ed.), *States of Knowledge*. Routledge, New York, pp. 254–273.

Frängsmyr, T., Heilbron, J.L., Rider, R. (Eds.) (1990). *The Quantifying Spirit in the Enlightenment*. Univ. of California Press, Berkeley.

Gigerenzer, G., Swijtink, Z., Porter, T.M., Daston, L., Beatty, J., Krüger, L. (1989). *The Empire of Chance: How Probability Changed Science and Everyday Life*. Cambridge Univ. Press, New York.

Gillispie, C.C. (1997). *Pierre Simon de Laplace, 1749–1827: A Life in Exact Science*. Princeton Univ. Press, Princeton, NJ.

Gillispie, C.C. (2004). *Science and Polity in France: The Revolutionary and Napoleonic Years*. Princeton Univ. Press, Princeton.

Golinski, J. (1995). The nicety of experiment: Precision of measurement and precision of reasoning in late eighteenth-century chemistry. In: Wise, M.N. (Ed.), *The Values of Precision*. Princeton Univ. Press, Princeton, NJ, pp. 72–91.

Grier, D. (2005). *When Computers Were Human*. Princeton Univ. Press, Princeton, NJ.

Heilbron, J.L. (1999). *The Sun in the Church: Cathedrals as Solar Observatories*. Harvard Univ. Press, Cambridge, MA.

Kula, W. (1986). *Measures and Men*. Princeton Univ. Press, Princeton, NJ (translated by Richard Szreter).

Linklater, A. (2002). *Measuring America: How an Untamed Wilderness Shaped the United States and Fulfilled the Promise of Democracy*. Walker & Company, New York.

Olesko, K.M. (1995). The meaning of precision: The exact sensibility in early nineteenth-century Germany. In: Wise, M.N. (Ed.), *The Values of Precision*. Princeton Univ. Press, Princeton, NJ, pp. 103–134.

Polanyi, M. (1958). *Personal Knowledge: Towards a Post-Critical Philosophy*. Univ. of Chicago Press, Chicago.

Porter, T.M. (1986). *The Rise of Statistical Thinking, 1820–1900*. Princeton Univ. Press, Princeton, NJ.

Porter, T.M. (1992). Objectivity as standardization: The rhetoric of impersonality in measurement, statistics, and cost–benefit analysis. In: Megill, A. (Ed.), *Rethinking Objectivity, Annals of Scholarship* **9**, 19–59.

Porter, T.M. (1995). *Trust in Numbers: The Pursuit of Objectivity in Science and Public Life*. Princeton Univ. Press, Princeton, NJ.

Porter, T.M. (2001). Economics and the history of measurement. In: Klein, J.L., Morgan, M.S. (Eds.), *The Age of Economic Measurement*. Annual supplement to *History of Political Economy*. Duke Univ. Press, Durham, NC, pp. 4–22.

Rusnock, A. (2002). *Vital Accounts: Quantifying Health and Population in Eighteenth-Century England and France*. Cambridge Univ. Press, Cambridge.

Stigler, S.M. (1986). *The History of Statistics: The Measurement of Uncertainty before 1900*. Harvard Univ. Press, Cambridge, MA.

Terrall, M. (2002). *The Man Who Flattened the Earth: Maupertuis and the Sciences in the Enlightenment*. Univ. of Chicago Press, Chicago.

Wise, M.N. (Ed.) (1995). *The Values of Precision*. Princeton Univ. Press, Princeton, NJ.

Youden, W.J. (1972). Enduring values. *Technometrics* **14**, 1–11.

CHAPTER 15

Optimal Experimental Design in Models of Decision and Choice

Peter G. Moffatt

School of Economics, University of East Anglia, Norwich NR4 7TJ, United Kingdom
E-mail address: p.moffatt@uea.ac.uk

Abstract

When dichotomous choice problems are used as a means of eliciting individual preferences, an important issue is how the choice problems should be chosen in order to allow maximal precision in the estimation of the parameters of interest. This issue is addressed by appealing to the theory of optimal experimental design which is well-established in the statistical literature, but has yet to break into most areas of economics. Two examples are provided of situations in which such techniques are applicable: Willingness To Pay (WTP) for an environmental good; and degree of risk aversion. The determinant of Fisher's information matrix is chosen as the criterion for optimal design.

15.1. Introduction

The concept of optimal design of experiments is widespread in many different fields including the physical, biological and behavioural sciences, as well as engineering and marketing. In contrast, it is an unfamiliar concept to the majority of Economists. The reason for this is that traditionally economists have resigned themselves to being passive observers of data generating processes. In fact, when the subject of Econometrics emerged as a separate discipline in the middle of the 20th century, one key feature that distinguished it from orthodox statistical analysis was precisely that it deals with the issues that arise when the investigator has no control over the generation of the data under analysis. Of course, this position changed in the later part of the 20th century, with the explosion of interest in Experimental Economics, in which the investigator clearly does have a significant degree of control. However, it is fair to say that the majority of the first generation of experimental economists are economic theorists who are keen to test theories that would be untestable without the laboratory. Few of this first generation came from the area of statistics or econometrics, although we should be prepared for rapid change here as well. The term "Experimetrics" was coined recently by Camerer (2003) to represent the econometric analysis of data from economic experiments – another research area that is attracting considerable interest at the present time.

Despite these recent changes within the discipline, it is still the case that experimental design theory, that is, the use of a rigorous statistical framework as a means of designing experiments in order for the resulting data sets to be optimally suited to addressing the research questions of interest, has yet to break into the Economics literature. There is, in fact, one notable exception. As we shall witness later in this Chapter, environmental economists who perform Contingent Valuation (CV) studies have already been exposed to experimental design theory (see, for example, Hanemann and Kanninen, 1998). However, in Experimental Economics, perhaps the area in which we would most expect to see such techniques being exploited, there is a strong sense that investigators are, sometimes by their own admission (Hey and di Cagno, 1990), tending to "grope in the dark" when it comes to the design of experiments.

One area not too distant from Economics in which design theory has been usefully applied is marketing research (see, for example, Louviere et al., 2000). In this area, the most common problems involve "stated choice" experiments, in which subjects are asked to make hypothetical choices between alternatives with different combinations of attributes. Many attributes (for example, Airbag or Satellite Navigation in motor vehicles) have just two "levels": present and absent. The experimental design problem then boils down to which combinations of attributes should be present in the choices offered. If all possible combinations are offered, the design is said to be a "full factorial". In practice, it is usually the case that the number of different attributes is such that a full factorial design is impractical. The question then is which of the many possible "fractional factorial designs" is optimal for meeting the objectives of the study.

In this Chapter, we are more concerned with the situation more familiar to Economists that arises when there is a continuous explanatory variable, x_i, which systematically affects the value taken by some other variable, y_i (the dependent variable). The simplest setting that we shall consider is the homoscedastic linear regression model:

$$\begin{aligned} y_i &= \theta_1 + \theta_2 x_i + \varepsilon_i, \quad i = 1, \ldots, n, \\ \varepsilon_i &\sim N\left(0, \sigma^2\right). \end{aligned} \tag{15.1}$$

Here, we imagine that we are in a position to choose the values taken by the explanatory variable x_i in the sample. We set out to make this choice in a way that maximises the *precision* with which the unknown parameters θ_1 and θ_2 can be estimated. "Precision" is a subject that is discussed in more detail and in a more general context in Chapter 14 of this volume (Porter, this volume).

Here, we refer to precision in terms of the variation of an estimator around the true value of the parameter being estimated. Precision in this sense is conventionally measured by the standard error of an estimate. For example, it is well known to anyone who has taken an introductory course in Econometrics that the standard error of the ordinary least squares estimator of the slope parameter θ_2 in (15.1) is:

$$se(\hat{\theta}_2) = \sqrt{\frac{\sigma^2}{\sum_i (x_i - \bar{x})^2}} \approx \sqrt{\frac{\text{Var}(\varepsilon_i)}{n \times \text{Var}(x_i)}}. \tag{15.2}$$

From (15.2), we clearly see that the standard error of the slope estimator, and therefore the precision with which the slope parameter is being estimated, depends on three separate factors: the variance of the equation error, the variance of the explanatory variable, and the sample size. The first of these factors is always outside of our control. The other two are within our control, and both can therefore be used to improve precision. These two factors appear to be equally important: a doubling of the variance of x would appear to have the same effect on precision as a doubling of the sample size. It therefore appears that a design that is optimal for a given sample size is one that maximises the variance in the explanatory variable x. For obvious reasons, this is a sensible optimisation problem only if bounds on x are determined at the outset. Such bounds might be determined by the range of values taken by an analogous variable in a real setting. It is often assumed without loss of generality that x can only take values between -1 and $+1$. Given such an assumption, the optimal design becomes one in which half of the observations in the sample are allocated to the design point $x = -1$, and the other half are allocated to $x = +1$, since this is the combination of x values that maximises the variance of x given the constraint on the range of the variable. In the jargon of experimental design, we are allocating all observations to the "corners of the design space". This simple example illustrates the selection of an optimal design in a highly intuitive way.

A more general approach is to consider all of the model's parameters simultaneously. The *information matrix* is a square symmetric matrix representing the potency of the data in respect of estimating the model's parameters. The most popular criterion of experimental design is D-optimality, in which a design is sought to maximise the determinant of this information matrix. Since the variance of the estimated vector is the inverse of the information matrix, D-optimality is seen to be equivalent to minimising the volume of the "confidence sphere" surrounding the parameter estimates, and the D-optimal design can hence be interpreted as one that maximises the precision with which the parameters (taken together) are estimated.

A feature of linear models such as (15.1) is that the information matrix only involves the values of x appearing in the sample, and does not involve the parameters. In this situation, finding the D-optimal design is easy. In this Chapter, we are more interested in non-linear models, and for these, the information matrix depends on the parameter values. Hence, knowledge of the parameter values is necessary in order to design an optimal experiment. This is sometimes referred to as the "chicken and egg" problem. At first sight this problem appears quite damning: the experiment cannot be designed without knowledge of the parameters whose values the experiment's purpose is to find! However, there are ways of circumventing this problem, as we shall see later.

The type of non-linear models in which we are interested are binary data models. This interest is motivated as follows. There are situations in Economic research in which a certain continuously measurable quantity representing individual preferences is of interest, but the preferred way of eliciting this quantity for a given individual is to present them with a dichotomous choice problem, rather than directly to ask them to state the quantity. Two important examples are contingent valuation studies (e.g. Green et al., 1998), in which Willingness To Pay (WTP) for a public good is elicited by means of a hypothetical referendum, and studies of risk attitude (e.g. Holt and Laury, 2002), in which subjects are asked to choose between pairs of lotteries. In each case, there are reasons, some more convincing than others, for preferring this elicitation method. When dichotomous choice is used to elicit preferences, the resulting variable is binary, calling for non-linear models such as logistic regression or probit in its analysis.

Given the wide acceptance of dichotomous choice as a means of eliciting preferences, it is important for researchers to have guidance on appropriate design. In particular, it is desirable to have a clear framework for choosing the payment levels in referendum questions, and for choosing the parameters of the lottery pairs. Such a framework comes from the statistical literature on optimal experimental design.

While a vast literature exists on the problem of optimal experimental design, most of this work has been applied to linear models (Silvey, 1980; Fedorov, 1972) and most of the seminal papers were highly theoretical. Atkinson (1996) provides a useful review of developments in optimal experimental designs, including more recent, non-linear designs, with particular reference to their practicality. Ford et al. (1992) summarise developments in non-linear experimental design.

A problem that has already been raised is the "chicken and egg" problem: in non-linear settings, the parameters need to be known in advance in order to find the D-optimal design. A possible solution to the problem is to design an "interactive" experiment, in which subjects' choices are continually monitored, and all choices made up to a particular stage in the experiment are used in constructing a design which is locally optimal for the next stage of the experiment. This approach was adopted by Chaudhuri and Mykland (1993, 1995). There is a problem with this approach: it violates the requirements of incentive compatibility. Intelligent subjects have a tendency to alter their behaviour if they believe that their choices may have an influence the future course of an experiment. For this reason, we restrict our attention to the search for a design which can be completely determined before the start of the experiment, although we acknowledge that interactive experiments have recently been performed in ways that avoid the incentive compatibility problem (e.g. Eckel et al., 2005). Such methods are described in Section 15.5.

In theory, the problem of unknown parameter values could be approached by taking expectations of the determinant of the information matrix over a prior distribution for the parameters. However, the algebra involved can be problematic and such a technique would normally rely heavily on numerical routines.

Ponce de Leon (1993) adopted a Bayesian approach for generalised linear models. The approach was then adapted by Müller and Ponce de Leon (1996) to discriminate between two competing pairwise choice models. Although the problem they analysed is similar in spirit to ours, our models are somewhat more complex, with potentially more parameters, which tend to make the Bayesian approach seem less attractive.

Instead we adopt an approach which takes parameter estimates from a past study (or possibly a pilot study), and treats these estimates as is they were true parameter values in the computation of the D-optimal design criterion.

Section 15.2 describes situations in which the dichotomous choice elicitation methods have become popular, and attempts to justify the use of the method in these contexts. Section 15.3 presents a brief introduction to experimental design theory, covering first linear models and then the more relevant non-linear binary data models. Section 15.4 applies the optimal design results introduced in Section 15.3 to the economic models of Section 15.2. Section 15.5 contains discussion of a number of issues relating to the framework developed in the chapter. Section 15.6 concludes.

15.2. Use of Dichotomous Choice in Economics

15.2.1. Valuation of environmental goods

There is a large literature on how best to elicit individuals' valuations of environmental goods (such as air quality or city parks) in ways that are incentive compatible, that is, that avoid, for example, under-valuation caused by a desire to free-ride. Single referendum contingent valuation is one protocol for eliciting Willingness-to-Pay (WTP) for such goods. It was first introduced by Bishop and Heberlein (1979). Subjects are each presented with a hypothetical referendum that specifies a good to be supplied and an amount payable, and asked to vote on this referendum. The decision made by a subject clearly allows us to deduce either an upper bound (if they say "no") or a lower bound (if they say "yes") to their own WTP for the good in question. It is important to recognise that this manner of eliciting valuations is statistically inferior to a scheme in which subjects are simply asked to state their WTP directly (known as an "open-ended" protocol). In terms of information extracted, the latter method is preferable. Also, from the point of view of analysing the results, the latter method is again preferred, because it requires simpler statistical techniques. A question that arises, then, is what accounts for the widespread acceptance of a method that is statistically inefficient and requires analysis that is more complex than is necessary. One important answer appears to be that the two methods give very different results. Other answers summarised by Green et al. (1998) are that the referendum format reduces non-response and avoids zero valuations and implausibly high valuations. A common counter-argument, also developed by Green et al., is that the referendum method induces "anchoring bias".

However one views the validity of reasons given for preferring the referendum format, it must be accepted that this is currently the most popular method for eliciting WTP, and therefore it is important to devote effort to analysing the theoretical underpinnings of the technique.

Let y_i be the true WTP of respondent i. It is natural to allow WTP to depend on characteristics of the respondent (age, gender, income and years of education, say) in a linear fashion:

$$\begin{aligned} y_i &= \beta_0 + \beta_1 age_i + \beta_2 gender_i + \beta_3 income_i + \beta_4 educ_i + \varepsilon_i \\ &= x_i'\beta + \varepsilon_i. \end{aligned} \tag{15.3}$$

The error term, ε_i, is assumed to follow a normal distribution:

$$\varepsilon_i \sim N(0, \sigma^2). \tag{15.4}$$

It follows that:

$$y_i \sim N(x_i'\beta, \sigma^2). \tag{15.5}$$

If the referendum method is used, each respondent is simply asked whether or not they would be willing to pay a suggested amount s_i for the good. Note that the suggested amount varies over the sample.

Let d_i be a binary variable taking the value 1 if respondent i reveals that they are willing to pay s_i, and -1 otherwise. The relationship between d_i and y_i is as follows: $d_i = 1$ if $y_i > s_i$; otherwise $d_i = -1$. The probability of respondent i saying "yes" is therefore:

$$P(d_i = 1) = P(y_i > s_i) = \Phi\left[x_i'\left(\frac{\beta}{\sigma}\right) + s_i\left(-\frac{1}{\sigma}\right)\right] \tag{15.6}$$

where $\Phi(\cdot)$ is the standard normal c.d.f. Equation (15.6) is the definition of a binary probit model, with the suggested amount s_i included as an explanatory variable along with the variables contained in the vector x_i. Note that the coefficient of s_i is necessarily negative, and an estimate of the parameter σ can be deduced from knowledge of it. In turn, an estimate of the vector β could then be deduced from the coefficient of x_i. A further technical issue is that since the structural parameters, β and σ, are non-linear functions of the reduced form parameters estimated using the probit model, the delta-method (Greene, 2003, p. 913) is required in order to compute standard errors.

In the present chapter, we mainly restrict attention to situations in which there are no explanatory variables; all respondents have the same expected WTP, μ. So, instead of (15.3) we have simply:

$$y_i = \mu + \varepsilon_i \tag{15.7}$$

and the probit model is of the simpler form:

$$P(d_i = 1) = P(y_i > s_i) = \Phi\left[\frac{\mu}{\sigma} + \left(-\frac{1}{\sigma}\right)s_i\right]. \tag{15.8}$$

Our ultimate objective will be to choose values of the explanatory variable s_i that will allow the two structural parameters μ and σ to be estimated with greatest precision.

15.2.2. Measuring risk aversion

Asking a subject to report their valuation (or "certainty equivalent") of a lottery enables us to deduce that subject's attitude to risk. For example, if a subject is asked to value a 50:50 gamble with outcomes \$10 and zero, and reports a valuation of \$4, and if we assume that the subject has a Constant Relative Risk Aversion (CRRA) utility function:

$$U(x) = \frac{x^{1-r}}{1-r}, \quad r \neq 1 \tag{15.9}$$

then we can deduce that the subject's coefficient of relative risk aversion is $r = 0.186$. If we are interested in measuring attitudes to risk over the population, this might therefore seem an obvious way to proceed.

It is not obvious how to elicit a subject's certainty equivalent in a way that is incentive compatible. One popular method is the Becker–DeGroot–Marschak (BDM, Becker et al., 1964) mechanism, which operates as follows. It is explained to the subject that when they have reported their valuation of a given lottery, a random price will be drawn from a uniform distribution. If the random price is less than the subject's reported valuation, the subject will play the lottery; if the random price exceeds the valuation, the subject receives that price instead of playing the lottery. It is easily verified that this mechanism has the virtue of incentive compatibility. However, a common criticism of it is that it is hard for subjects to comprehend sufficiently for the incentive compatibility to take hold.

An alternative to BDM which also claims to be Incentive Compatible is the ordinal pay-off scheme (Tversky et al., 1990; Cubitt et al., 2004). In this scheme, subjects are presented with a sequence of lotteries, for each of which they are asked to state a certainty equivalent. They are informed that when they have completed the experiment, *two* of the lotteries will be chosen at random from the sequence, and the subject will play out the one to which they assigned a higher value. Like the BDM scheme, this scheme claims to be incentive compatible.

A commonly reported problem with obtaining certainty equivalents, whichever of the above schemes is used, is that subjects have a tendency to report the expected value of a lottery, that is, they tend to report a risk-neutral certainty equivalent.

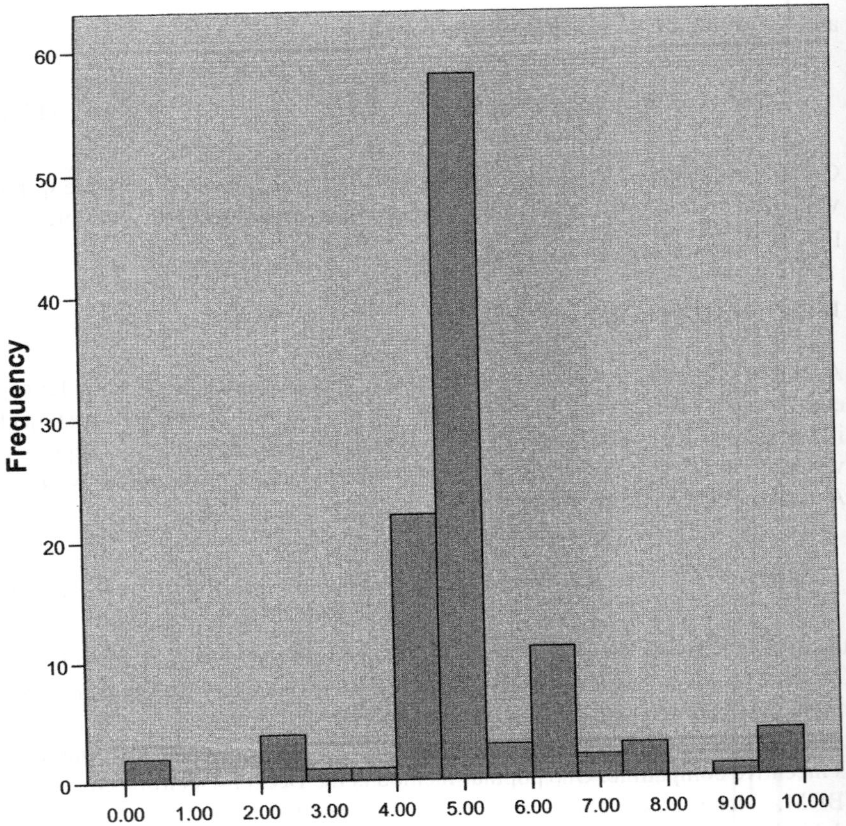

Fig. 15.1: A histogram of the monetary valuations of 112 subjects of the lottery (0.50, £10). *Source*: Cubitt et al. (2004).

To verify this, in Fig. 15.1 we show data from Cubitt et al. (2004), who, as previously noted, use the ordinal pay-off scheme. Shown in Fig. 15.1 is the distribution over the sample of 112 subjects of the certainty equivalents of the lottery (0.50, £10). By this notation, we mean a 50% chance of £10 and a 50% chance of nothing. We see that more than half (58) of the 112 subjects report a valuation of exactly £5.00, which is, of course, the expected value of this lottery. Furthermore, the mean over the sample is 5.07, which is certainly not significantly different from 5.00 ($p = 0.63$). This goes against the widely-accepted belief that the vast majority of people are risk averse.

The important point here is that there are strong reasons for believing that choices between lotteries are a more reliable source of information on risk attitudes than reported valuations of lotteries. In fact, the tendency to use expected values for certainty equivalents is an obvious explanation for the reversal phenomenon (Grether and Plott, 1979) – the tendency to value the riskier lottery more highly but to choose the safer lottery when asked to choose between them.

We therefore have a similar situation to that encountered in Section 15.2.1. Instead of extracting a precise measure of risk attitude for a given subject, we use their choice to deduce either an upper bound (if they choose the riskier alternative) or a lower bound (if they choose safe) to their risk aversion parameter. The estimation of risk attitudes using lottery choice data is pursued in Chapter 4 of this Volume (Harrison et al., this volume).

Let us assume, as do Harrison et al., that all individuals have the CRRA utility function (15.9) and that the coefficient of relative risk aversion varies over the population according to:

$$r \sim N(\mu, \sigma^2). \tag{15.10}$$

Assume that the subject is asked to choose between two lotteries. Numerical techniques can be used to compute the value of r for which a subject is indifferent between the two lotteries in question. We shall refer to this as the threshold risk aversion parameter for the choice problem, and denote it as r^*.

Assume that subject i is presented with a choice problem with threshold risk level r_i^*. Let $y_i = 1$ if the safer of the two lotteries is chosen, and $y_i = -1$ if the riskier is chosen. The probability of the safe choice is:

$$P(y_i = 1) = P(r_i > r_i^*) = \Phi\left(\frac{\mu}{\sigma} + \left(-\frac{1}{\sigma}\right) r_i^*\right). \tag{15.11}$$

Once again we have a probit model, identical in form to that developed in the context of referendum contingent valuation in Section 15.2.1. Once again we are interested in choosing values of the explanatory variable, this time r^*, that allow us to estimate the two structural parameters μ and σ as precisely as possible.

15.3. Rudiments of Experimental Design Theory

15.3.1. The principle of D-optimal design

Consider a model in which the scalar dependent variable is y, the single explanatory variable is x, and the probability, or probability density, associated with a particular observation (y_i, x_i) is $f(y_i \mid x_i; \boldsymbol{\theta})$, where $\boldsymbol{\theta}$ is a $k \times 1$ vector of parameters. Assume that there are a total of n independent observations. The log-likelihood function for this model is:

$$\operatorname{Log} L = \sum_{i=1}^{n} \ln f(y_i \mid x_i; \boldsymbol{\theta}). \tag{15.12}$$

The maximum likelihood estimate (MLE) of the parameter vector $\boldsymbol{\theta}$ is the value that maximises $\operatorname{Log} L$. The information matrix is given by:

$$I = E\left(-\frac{\partial^2 \operatorname{Log} L}{\partial \boldsymbol{\theta} \partial \boldsymbol{\theta}'}\right) = E\left(\frac{\partial \operatorname{Log} L}{\partial \boldsymbol{\theta}} \frac{\partial \operatorname{Log} L}{\partial \boldsymbol{\theta}'}\right). \tag{15.13}$$

The variance of the MLE is given by the inverse of the Information matrix. Hence standard errors of individual estimates are obtained from the square roots of the diagonal elements of I^{-1}.

The principle of D-optimal design is simply to select values of x_i, subject to the specified constraints, that maximise the determinant of the information matrix. This is equivalent to minimising the volume of the "confidence ellipsoid" of the parameters contained in θ, that is, estimating the entire set of parameters with maximal overall precision.

Clearly, the information matrix and its determinant increase with the sample size n. Often, when we are comparing designs, we need to adjust for the number of observations, so we divide the information matrix by n to obtain the per observation information matrix.

15.3.2. Simple linear regression

Consider the simple (normal) regression model:

$$\begin{aligned} &y_i = \theta_1 + \theta_2 x_i + \varepsilon_i, \quad i = 1, \ldots, n, \\ &\varepsilon_i \sim N(0, 1), \\ &-1 \leqslant x_i \leqslant +1 \quad \forall i. \end{aligned} \tag{15.14}$$

Assume that the investigator has control over the values taken by the explanatory variable x_i, subject only to a lower and an upper bound, which we assume without loss of generality to be -1 and 1. Note that the error term is assumed to be normally distributed, and, for the sake of further simplicity, to have unit variance. Given these assumptions concerning the error term, we may construct the log-likelihood function for this model as:

$$\log L = \sum_{i=1}^{n} \left[k - (y_i - \theta_1 - \theta_2 x_i)^2\right] \tag{15.15}$$

where k is a constant. It is easily verified that in this model the MLEs of the two parameters are the same as the estimates from a least squares regression of y on x. Differentiating twice with respect to the two parameters θ_1 and θ_2 we find the information matrix to be:

$$I = \begin{pmatrix} n & \sum x_i \\ \sum x_i & \sum x_i^2 \end{pmatrix}. \tag{15.16}$$

So the variance of the MLE vector is:

$$V\begin{pmatrix} \hat{\theta}_1 \\ \hat{\theta}_2 \end{pmatrix} = I^{-1} = \begin{pmatrix} n & \sum x_i \\ \sum x_i & \sum x_i^2 \end{pmatrix}^{-1}. \tag{15.17}$$

Standard errors are obtained as the square roots of diagonal elements of V.

To obtain the D-optimal design, we need to choose values of x_i that maximise the determinant of I. It may easily be verified that this determinant may be written as:

$$|I| = \sum_{i=1}^{n} \sum_{j=i+1}^{n} (x_i - x_j)^2. \tag{15.18}$$

From (15.18) it is clear that the differences between different x-values must be as great as possible. For this, half of the values must be set to the maximum allowed, and the other half to the minimum. In experimental design jargon, we are choosing all design points from the "corners of the design space".

15.3.3. Simple probit and simple logit

Now consider a binary data setting, in which an underlying continuous variable y^* depends on x according to:

$$y_i^* = \theta_1 + \theta_2 x_i + \varepsilon_i, \quad i = 1, \ldots, n,$$
$$\varepsilon_i \sim N(0, 1) \tag{15.19}$$

but all that is observed is whether y^* is positive or negative. That is, we observe y where:

$$y_i = \begin{cases} 1 & \text{if } y_i^* > 0, \\ -1 & \text{if } y_i^* \leqslant 0. \end{cases} \tag{15.20}$$

This is the well known probit model, with log-likelihood function:

$$\operatorname{Log} L = \sum_{i=1}^{n} \ln \Phi\left[y_i \times (\theta_1 + \theta_2 x_i)\right]. \tag{15.21}$$

The information matrix for this model may be derived as:

$$I = \begin{pmatrix} \sum w_i & \sum w_i x_i \\ \sum w_i x_i & \sum w_i x_i^2 \end{pmatrix} \tag{15.22}$$

where

$$w_i = \frac{[\phi(\theta_1 + \theta_2 x_i)]^2}{\Phi(\theta_1 + \theta_2 x_i)[1 - \Phi(\theta_1 + \theta_2 x_i)]}.$$

The determinant of the information matrix may be written as:

$$|I| = \sum_{i=1}^{n} \sum_{j=i+1}^{n} w_i w_j (x_i - x_j)^2. \tag{15.23}$$

Again, $|I|$ is maximised with just 2 design points. However, $|I|$ is weighted by the w_i's. These weights are maximised when $\Phi(\theta_1 + \theta_2 x_i) = 0.5$, that is, when the probabilities of the two outcomes are equalised. So, the desire to have design points as far from each other as possible, occupying the "corners of the design space," is countered by the desire to have design points giving rise to perfect indifference – the requirement of "utility balance" (Huber and Zwerina, 1996).

In Fig. 15.2, the solid curve shows $|I|$ against the percentile of the upper design point. The design is symmetric, so the lower design point is an equal distance from the centre. We see, as expected, that when both design points are in the centre (percentile = 0.50) the information is zero. The intuition here is that if all design points are in the centre of the distribution, all that can be observed is which side of the centre each observation lies, and the spread of the distribution cannot be identified. We also see that when both design points are the maximum distance from the centre (percentile = 1.0), the information is zero again. Again this is intuitive, if all individuals are given such extreme problems that their choice can be predicted with certainty, the choice data will be of no value. The most important feature of the solid line in Fig. 15.2 is the maximum at 0.87. This implies that the design points that maximise $|I|$ are the 13th and 87th percentiles of the underlying response function. This is the D-optimal design for the probit model.

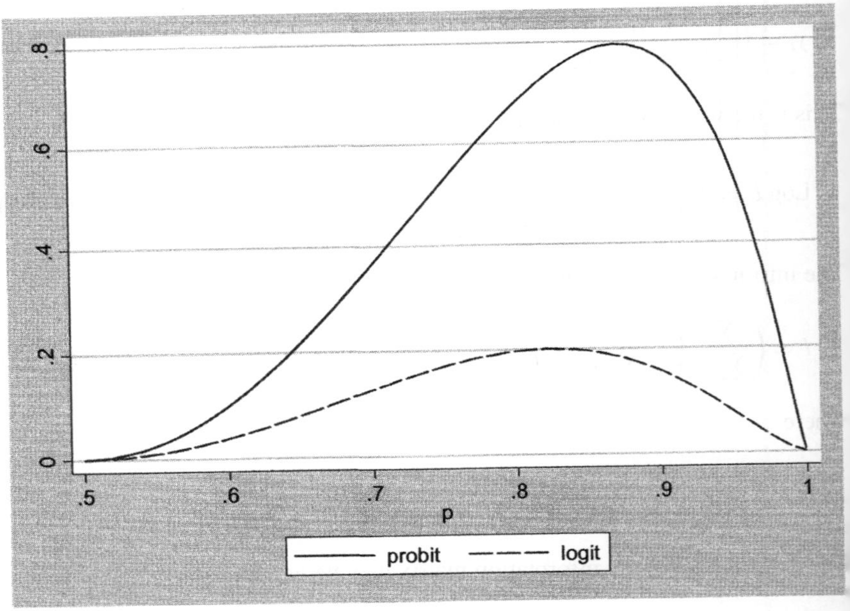

Fig. 15.2: Determinant of information matrix against percentile of larger design point; probit and logit.

If the required number of design points is odd, the optimal design is to place one design point exactly in the centre, and to divide the remaining points equally between the 13th and 87th percentiles.

A well-known alternative to probit for the modelling of binary data is the logit model, defined by:

$$P(y_i = 1) = \frac{\exp(\theta_1 + \theta_2 x_i)}{1 + \exp(\theta_1 + \theta_2 x_i)} \equiv P_i. \tag{15.24}$$

The information matrix has the same form as (15.22) above, with weights given by:

$$w_i = P_i(1 - P_i). \tag{15.25}$$

With (15.25) in (15.23), it is found, again numerically, that the design points that maximise $|I|$ are the 18th and 82nd percentiles of the underlying response function. The broken line in Fig. 15.2 shows $|I|$ against the percentile of the upper design point for the logit model.

We are often led to believe there are no major differences between probit and logit. For example, according to Greene (2003, p. 667), "in most applications, the choice between these two seems not to make much difference". It therefore seems surprising that the optimal design points under probit are five percentiles further into the tails than under logit.

Note that in order to find these optimal design points, the parameters of the underlying distribution (i.e. θ_1 and θ_2) must be known in advance, since obviously these are needed in order to recover a point on the distribution from knowledge of its percentile. This is a manifestation of the "chicken and egg" problem referred to in Section 15.1.

15.4. Optimal Design in Economics

The issues surrounding Optimal Design in Referendum Contingent Valuation studies have already been addressed by Kanninen (1993a, 1993b), Alberini (1995) and Hanemann and Kanninen (1998).

In risk studies, as in experimental economics generally, noticeably less work has been done on Optimal Design. The following quote from Hey and di Cagno (1990) is typical of the attitude to the design problem held by most researchers in the area:

> The choice of questions was not so easy... We tried to get a mixture so that the slope of the line joining the pair of gambles varied considerably: from 1/7 to 7. The idea behind this was that we would then be able to distinguish between very risk-averse people and not-very-risk averse people, but we were rather groping in the dark.

The "slope" referred to in this quote is that of the line connecting two lotteries in the Marschak–Machina triangle, and is analogous to our "threshold risk aversion" measure, r^*, introduced in Section 15.2. This chapter may serve to introduce the notion of optimal experimental design to researchers who have concerns of this nature.

We assume that a choice problem involves four non-negative outcomes $x_1 < x_2 < x_3 < x_4$. The problem requires a choice between two lotteries. The "safe" lottery (S) involves the outcomes x_2 and x_3, with probabilities p_2 and p_3 respectively; the "risky" lottery (R) involves the outcomes x_1 and x_4, with probabilities p_1 and p_4.

We assume the Constant Relative Risk Aversion utility function:

$$U(x) = \begin{cases} \frac{x^{1-r}}{1-r} & r \neq 1, \\ \ln(x) & r = 1. \end{cases} \tag{15.26}$$

The parameter r in (15.26) is the coefficient of relative risk aversion.

Given (15.26), the expected utilities of the two lotteries are:

$$EU(S) = p_2 \frac{x_2^{1-r}}{1-r} + p_3 \frac{x_3^{1-r}}{1-r},$$
$$EU(R) = p_1 \frac{x_1^{1-r}}{1-r} + p_4 \frac{x_4^{1-r}}{1-r}. \tag{15.27}$$

Assuming that individuals obey Expected Utility (EU) Theory, choice S is made if and only if:

$$r > r^*(p_1, p_2, p_3, p_4, x_1, x_2, x_3, x_4). \tag{15.28}$$

That is, the Safer choice is made if the individual's risk aversion parameter exceeds a "threshold" level of risk aversion, r^*, this being a function of all four outcomes and all four probabilities. r^* can be computed numerically for a given choice problem.

Let r have the following distribution over the population:

$$r \sim N(\mu, \eta^2). \tag{15.29}$$

First let us assume that each subject (i) solves only one choice problem with threshold r_i^*. Let $y_i = 1(-1)$ if subject i chooses $S(R)$. The log-likelihood contribution for subject i is:

$$\text{Log}\, L_i = \ln \Phi \left[y_i \times \left(\frac{\mu}{\eta} + \left(-\frac{1}{\eta} \right) r_i^* \right) \right] \tag{15.30}$$

which is a standard probit model as analysed in Sections 15.2 and 15.3.

The optimal design problem here amounts to choosing a set of values of r^* that will give maximal precision in the estimation of the two parameters of the

Table 15.1: The Holt and Laury design, with threshold risk aversion parameter for each choice problem.

Problem	Safe	Risky	r^*	Proportion choosing S
1	(0.1, \$2.00; 0.9, \$1.60)	(0.1, \$3.85; 0.9, \$0.10)	−1.72	1.00
2	(0.2, \$2.00; 0.8, \$1.60)	(0.2, \$3.85; 0.8, \$0.10)	−0.95	0.99
3	(0.3, \$2.00; 0.7, \$1.60)	(0.3, \$3.85; 0.7, \$0.10)	−0.49	0.98
4	(0.4, \$2.00; 0.6, \$1.60)	(0.4, \$3.85; 0.6, \$0.10)	−0.15	0.92
5	(0.5, \$2.00; 0.5, \$1.60)	(0.5, \$3.85; 0.5, \$0.10)	0.15	0.66
6	(0.6, \$2.00; 0.4, \$1.60)	(0.6, \$3.85; 0.4, \$0.10)	0.41	0.40
7	(0.7, \$2.00; 0.3, \$1.60)	(0.7, \$3.85; 0.3, \$0.10)	0.68	0.17
8	(0.8, \$2.00; 0.2, \$1.60)	(0.8, \$3.85; 0.2, \$0.10)	0.97	0.04
9	(0.9, \$2.00; 0.1, \$1.60)	(0.9, \$3.85; 0.1, \$0.10)	1.37	0.01
10	(1.0, \$2.00; 0.0, \$1.60)	(1.0, \$3.85; 0.0, \$0.10)	∞	0.00

model. As explained in Section 15.3, in order to apply the rules of optimal design, prior knowledge concerning the distribution of risk aversion must be available. For this, we appeal to the results of Holt and Laury (2002). Their basic design consists of the ten choice problems shown in Table 15.1. The threshold risk aversion parameter for each choice problem is shown in the final column. The ten problems are ordered: problem 1 is such that nearly everyone chooses the Safe alternative; problem 10 is such that everyone is expected to choose Risky (in fact, for problem 10 the right-hand lottery stochastically dominates).

Each subject was asked to solve the ten problems in order. At some stage in the sequence all subjects are expected to switch from the Safe column to the risky column, and it is of interest at which precise stage they switch, since this sets a lower and an upper bound on their risk aversion parameter.

Figure 15.3 shows an imputed distribution of implied risk attitudes (r), based on the results provided by Holt and Laury. The mean and standard deviation of the imputed distribution are 0.3335 and 0.3892 respectively. From the results of Section 15.3, we may deduce that if an experiment were planned in which only one choice problem would be solved by each subject, and we continued to assume normality of r over the population, the optimal design would consist of one problem with $r^* = 0.33$, and the remainder being divided equally between $r^* = -0.11$ and 0.77. More informatively, we would set one subject the problem:

(0.57, \$2.00; 0.43, \$1.60) (0.57, \$3.85; 0.43, \$0.10)

and we would divide the remaining subjects equally between the two problems:

(0.41, \$2.00; 0.59, \$1.60) (0.41, \$3.85; 0.59, \$0.10)

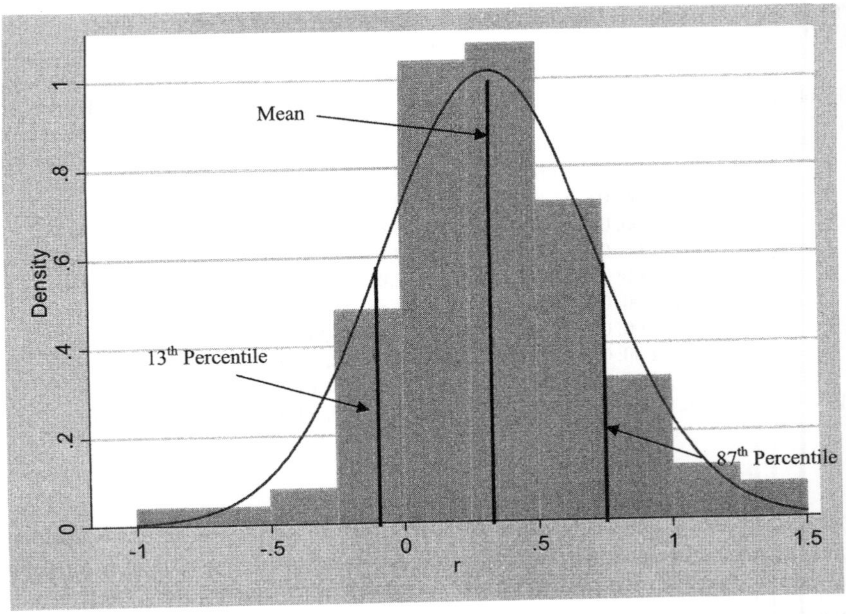

Fig. 15.3: The (imputed) distribution of risk aversion parameters from the Holt Laury experiment. Normal density super-imposed.

and:

(0.73, \$2.00; 0.27, \$1.60) (0.73, \$3.85; 0.27, \$0.10).

15.5. Further Issues

15.5.1. Multiple observations per subject

The optimal design problem solved in Section 15.4 was built on the assumption that only one choice problem would be solved by each subject. It is more usual in experiments of this type for each subject to solve a sequence of choice problems. The Random Lottery Incentive (RLI) system is commonly implemented: at the end of the sequence, *one* of the chosen lotteries is selected at random and played for real. Under reasonable assumptions, this guarantees that subjects treat each lottery as if it were the *only* lottery.

The resulting data set is a panel, containing a set of T choices for each of n subjects. To accommodate the multiple observations per subject, within-subject variation needs to be incorporated into the model. One approach to follow Loomes et al. (2002) and apply the Random Preference assumption, namely that an individual i's risk aversion parameter varies randomly between the T problems according to:

$$r_{it} \sim N(m_i, \sigma^2) \quad t = 1, \ldots, T \tag{15.31}$$

and the mean risk aversion of each subject varies across the population according to:

$$m_i \sim N(\mu, \eta^2). \tag{15.32}$$

This leads to the random effects probit model (Avery et al., 1983). The log-likelihood contribution for a single subject is given by:

$$\text{Log}\, L_i = \ln\left[\int_{-\infty}^{\infty} \left\{\prod_{t=1}^{T} \Phi\left(y_{it} \times \frac{m - r_t^*}{\sigma}\right)\right\} \frac{1}{\eta} \phi\left(\frac{m - \mu}{\eta}\right) dm\right]. \tag{15.33}$$

The random effects model defined in (15.33) has three parameters: the "between" parameters, μ and η; and the "within" parameter, σ.

To obtain the information matrix requires differentiation that is quite demanding, and it is not expressible in closed form, as it was in the examples in Section 15.3. Maximising the determinant of the information matrix is therefore an awkward problem. It is also intuitively obvious that the optimal design will have a more complicated structure than the designs of Section 15.3. Given that there are two sources of randomness, two distinct design points would not be sufficient to identify the parameters separately, and it is not clear what the D-optimal number of design points would be. These are matters for future research.

15.5.2. Sequential designs

Each subject has a different risk attitude so a choice problem which induces indifference for one subject may induce a clear preference for another. A useful approach is therefore to "tailor" problems to individual subjects, using their choices in early problems to identify their risk attitude, and then set later problems that apply an optimal design rule for that subject.

As mentioned in Section 15.1, the obvious criticism of this approach is the potential violation of incentive compatibility: subjects may manipulate the experiment by deliberately making false responses in an effort to "steer" the problem sequence in the direction of the most desirable problem types.

The problem has been addressed by Eckel et al. (2005) who apply a modified version of RLI. A universal set of choice problems is determined at the outset. Then a non-random sequence of problems is drawn from the universal set, with each one chosen in the light of previous responses in order to locate indifference. But, it is made clear at the outset that the problem that is played for real is drawn randomly from the universal set, and not just from the subset of problems solved. If one of the solved problems is drawn, the chosen lottery is played; if one of the unsolved problems is drawn, the subject is asked to solve that problem as an additional task, and then it is immediately played for real.

The crucial feature of this modified RLI system is that the choices made by the subject have no effect whatsoever on the set of problems over which the randomisation is performed, or on the probabilities of each problem being drawn. It is this feature that guarantees incentive compatibility.

15.6. Conclusion

The use of dichotomous choice problems in economic research calls for a thorough analysis of the issue of optimal design of such experiments. The main objective of this chapter has been to bring some well-developed ideas concerning optimal design into the mainstream of economic research. The chosen criterion has been the popular D-optimal design criterion, under which the determinant of the model's information matrix is maximised. The key ideas are that when the model is linear, the design points should be as far apart as possible, at the "corners of the design space", but for binary data models, this requirement is countered by the requirement of "utility balance" – that the design points are in the middle of the underlying distribution. The net effect of these counteracting requirements is, somewhat intriguingly, that the optimal design points in binary data models are at identifiable percentiles of the distribution, fairly near to the tails. The optimal percentiles depend on which model is assumed.

Another issue is that, while in linear models, the optimal design points can be found, in non-linear models such as the binary data models considered in this Chapter, the parameters of the underlying distribution need to be known in order for the optimal design points to be found. This is a problem that can be addressed by using results from a previous study in designing an optimal experiment. It was in this spirit that the example on estimating the distribution of risk attitudes over the population in Section 15.4 was presented.

References

Alberini, A. (1995). Optimal designs for discrete choice contingent valuation surveys: Single-bound, double-bound and bivariate models. *Journal of Environmental Economics and Management* **28**, 287–306.

Atkinson, A.C. (1996). The usefulness of optimum experimental designs. *Journal of the Royal Statistical Society, Series B* **58**, 59–76.

Avery, R.B., Hansen, L.P., Hotz, V.J. (1983). Multiperiod probit models and orthogonality condition estimation. *International Economic Review* **24**, 21–35.

Becker G., DeGroot, M., Marschak, J. (1964). Measuring utility by a single-response sequential method. *Behavioural Science* **9**, 226–236.

Bishop, R.C., Heberlein, T.A. (1979). Measuring values of extra-market goods: Are indirect measures biased? *American Journal of Agricultural Economics* **61**, 926–930.

Camerer, C.F. (2003). *Behavioral Game Theory*. Princeton Univ. Press, Princeton, NJ.

Chaudhuri, P., Mykland, P.A. (1993). Non-linear experiments: Optimal design and inference based on likelihood. *Journal of the American Statistical Association* **88**, 538–546.

Chaudhuri, P., Mykland, P.A. (1995). On efficient designing of non-linear experiments. *Statistica Sinica* **5**, 421–440.

Cubitt, R.P., Munro, A.A., Starmer, C.V. (2004). Testing explanations of preference reversal. *Economic Journal* **114**, 709–726.

Eckel, C., Engle-Warnick, J., Johnson, C. (2005). Adaptive elicitation of risk preferences. Mimeo. CIRANO.

Fedorov, V.V. (1972). *Theory of Optimum Experiments*. Academic Press, New York.

Ford I., Torsney, B. Wu, C.F.J. (1992). The use of a canonical form in the construction of locally optimal designs for non-linear problems. *Journal of the Royal Statistical Society, Series B* **54**, 569–583.

Green D., Jacowitz, K.E., Kahneman, D., McFadden, D. (1998). Referendum contingent valuation, anchoring, and willingness to pay for public goods. *Resource and Energy Economics* **20**, 85–116.

Greene, W.H. (2003). *Econometric Analysis*, fifth ed. Prentice Hall, New York.

Grether, D.M., Plott, C.R. (1979). Economic theory of choice and the preference reversal phenomenon. *American Economic Review* **69**, 623–638.

Hanemann, M., Kanninen, B.J. (1998). The statistical analysis of discrete-response CV data. In: Bateman, I.J., Willis, K.G. (Eds.), *Valuing Environmental Preferences: Theory and Practice of the Contingent Valuation Method in the US, EU and Developing Countries*. OUP, Oxford.

Hey, J.D., di Cagno, D. (1990). Circles and triangles: An experimental estimation of indifference lines in the Marschak–Machina triangle. *Journal of Behavioural Decision Making* **3**, 279–306.

Holt, C.A., Laury, S.K. (2002). Risk aversion and incentive effects. *American Economic Review* **92**, 1644–1655.

Huber, J., Zwerina, K. (1996). The importance of utility balance in efficient choice designs. *Journal of Marketing Research* **23**, 307–317.

Kanninen, B.J. (1993a). Design of sequential experiments for contingent valuation studies. *Journal of Environmental Economics and Management* **25**, S1–S11.

Kanninen, B.J. (1993b). Optimal experimental design for double-bounded dichotomous choice contingent valuation. *Land Economics* **69**, 138–146.

Loomes, G., Moffatt, P.G., Sugden, R. (2002). A microeconometric test of alternative stochastic theories of risky choice. *Journal of Risk and Uncertainty* **24**, 103–130.

Louviere, J.J., Hensher, D.A., Swait, J.D. (2000). *Stated Choice Methods: Analysis and Application*. Cambridge Univ. Press, Cambridge.

Müller, W.G., Ponce de Leon, A.C.M. (1996). Optimal design of an experiment in economics. *Economic Journal* **106**, 122–127.

Ponce de Leon, A.C.M. (1993). Optimum experimental design for model discrimination and generalized linear models. PhD thesis. London School of Economics and Political Sciences, Department of Mathematical and Statistical Sciences, London.

Silvey, S.D. (1980). *Optimum Design*. Chapman and Hall, London.

Tversky, A., Slovic, P., Kahneman, D. (1990). The causes of preference reversal. *American Economic Review* **80**, 204–217.

CHAPTER 16

Least Squares Regression: Graduation and Filters

Tommaso Proietti[a] and Alessandra Luati[b]

[a]*S.E.F. e ME. Q., University of Rome "Tor Vergata", Italy*
E-mail address: Tommaso.proietti@uniroma2.it
[b]*Dipartimento di Scienze Statistiche, University of Bologna, Italy*
E-mail address: luati@stat.unibo.it

Abstract

This chapter provides an introduction to smoothing methods in time series analysis, namely local polynomial regression and polynomial splines, that developed as an extension of least squares regression and result in signal estimates that are linear combinations of the available information. We set off exposing the local polynomial approach and the class of Henderson filters. Very important issues are the treatment of the extremes of the series and real time estimation, as well as the choice of the order of the polynomial and of the bandwidth. The inferential aspects concerning the choice of the bandwidth and the order of the approximating polynomial are also discussed. We next move to semiparametric smoothing using polynomial splines. Our treatment stresses their relationship with popular stochastic trend models proposed in economics, which yield exponential smoothing filters and the Leser or Hodrick–Prescott filter. We deal with signal extraction filters that arise from applying best linear unbiased estimation principles to the the linear mixed model representation of spline models and establish the connection with penalised least squares. After considering several ways of assessing the properties of a linear filter both in time and frequency domain, the chapter concludes with a discussion of the main measurement issues raised by signal extraction in economics and the accuracy in the estimation of the latent signals.

Measurement in Economics: A Handbook
Marcel Boumans (Editor)

Every valley shall be exalted, and every mountain and hill made low,
and the crooked shall be made straight, and the rough places plain.
And the glory of the Lord shall be revealed, and all flesh shall see it together
for the mouth of the Lord hath spoken it.

Isaiah 40:4-5

16.1. Introduction

The smoothing problem has a long and well established tradition in statistics and has a wide range of applications in economics. In its simplest form it aims at providing a measure of the underlying tendency from noisy observations, and takes the name of signal extraction in engineering, trend estimation in econometrics, and graduation in actuarial sciences. This chapter provides an introduction to smoothing methods, namely local polynomial regression and spline smoothing, that developed as an extension of least squares regression and result in signal estimates that are linear combinations of the available information. These linear combinations are often termed filters and the analysis of the filter weights provides useful insight into what the method does.

Although the methods can be applied to cross-sectional data, we shall deal with time series applications. In particular, for a time series y_t we assume an additive model of the form:

$$y_t = \mu_t + \epsilon_t, \quad t = 1, \ldots, n, \tag{16.1}$$

where μ_t is the trend component, also termed the signal, and ϵ_t is the noise, or irregular, component. We assume throughout that $\mathrm{E}(\epsilon_t) = 0$, whereas μ_t can be a random or deterministic function of time. If the observations are not equally spaced, or the model is defined in continuous time, then we shall change our notation to $y(t) = \mu(t) + \epsilon(t)$.

The smoothing problem deals with the estimation of μ_t. If μ_t is random, the minimum mean square estimator of the signal is $\mathrm{E}(\mu_t|Y_n)$, where $Y_t = \{y_1, \ldots, y_t\}$ denotes the information set at time t. Estimation is said to be carried out in real time if it concerns $\mathrm{E}(\mu_t|Y_t)$, using the available information up to and including time t. If the model (16.1) is Gaussian, these inferences are linear in the observations. Why is such set of problems relevant? Essentially, in economics we seek to separate the permanent movements in the series from the transitory ones. A related objective is forecasting future values.

The simplest and historically oldest approach to signal extraction is using a global polynomial model for μ_t, which amounts to regressing y_t on a polynomial of time, where global means that the coefficients of the polynomial are constant across the sample span and it is not possible to control the influence of the individual observations on the fit. In fact, it turns out that global polynomials are amenable to mathematical treatment, but are not very flexible: they can provide bad local approximations and behave rather weirdly at the beginning and at the end of the sample period, which is inconvenient for forecasting

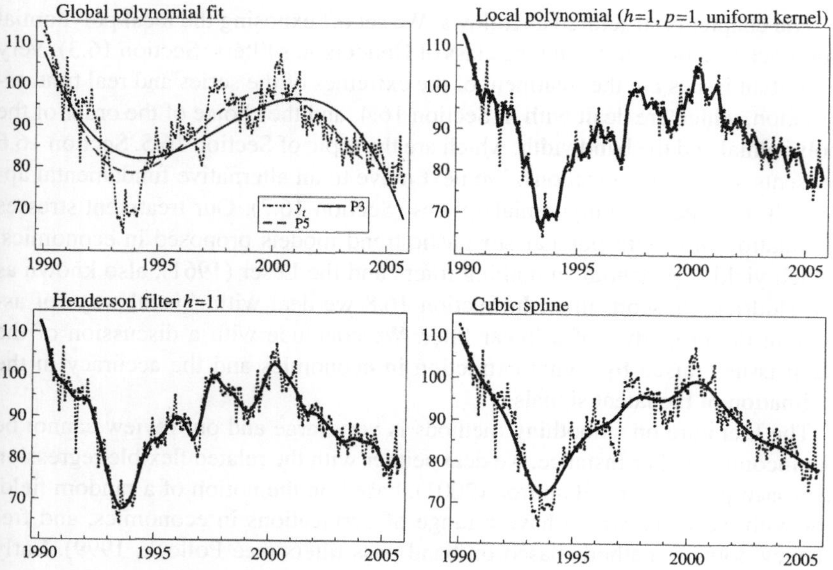

Fig. 16.1: Industrial Production Index, Manufacture and Assembly of Motor Vehicles, seasonally adjusted, Italy, January 1990–October 2005.

purposes. This point is illustrated by the first panel of Fig. 16.1, which plots the original series, representing the industrial production index for the Italian *Automotive* sector (monthly data, 1990.1–2005.10; source: Istat), and the estimate of the trend arising from fitting cubic (P3) and quintic (P5) polynomials of time. In particular, it can be seen that a high order is needed to provide a reasonable fit (the cubic fit being very poor), and that extrapolations would be troublesome at the very least.

The subsequent panels illustrate the smoothed estimates of the trend arising from methods that aim at overcoming the limitations of the global approach, while still retaining its simplicity (due to the linearity). The top right picture plots the smoothed estimates of the trend resulting from the unweighted moving average of three consecutive observations, $(y_{t-1} + y_t + y_{t+1})/3$, which arises from fitting a local linear trend to three consecutive observations, using a uniform kernel (this is also known as a Macaulay's moving average). Little smoothing has taken place.

The bottom left panel plots the estimates resulting from the Henderson filter, which results from fitting a cubic polynomial to 23 consecutive observations centred at t (11 on each side). The plot illustrates the advantages of *local* polynomial fitting over the traditional global polynomial approach: the degree of the approximating polynomials can be chosen of low order to produce a reasonable fit. Finally, the last panel displays the estimates of the smoothing cubic spline trend with smoothness parameter 1600, which yields results indistinguishable from the popular Hodrick–Prescott filter (Hodrick and Prescott, 1997).

The chapter is structured as follows. We set off exposing the local polynomial approach (Section 16.2), and the class of Henderson's filters (Section 16.3). Very important issues are the treatment of the extremes of the series and real time estimation, which are dealt with in Section 16.4, and the choice of the order of the polynomial and the bandwidth, which are the topic of Section 16.5. Section 16.6 presents some generalisations. We next move to an alternative fundamental approach, provided by polynomial splines (Section 16.7). Our treatment stresses its relationships with popular stochastic trend models proposed in economics, which yield exponential smoothing filters and the Leser (1961), also known as the Hodrick–Prescott, filter. In Section 16.8 we deal with several ways of assessing the properties of a linear filter. We conclude with a discussion of the main issues raised by signal extraction in economics and the accuracy in the estimation of the latent signals.

The literature on smoothing methods is very large and our review cannot be but incomplete. For instance, we deal neither with the related flexible regression approach proposed by Hamilton (2001), based on the notion of a random field, nor with wavelets, which have a range of applications in economics, and frequency domain methods based on band-pass filters (see Pollock, 1999). Early references on moving average filters and (local) polynomial time series regression are Kendall et al. (1983) and Anderson (1971). For local polynomial regression essential references are Loader (1999) and Fan and Gjibels (1996). A book on spline smoothing is Green and Silverman (1994), whereas Hastie and Tibshirani (1990), Farhmeir and Tutz (1994) and Ruppert et al. (1989) are excellent references on semiparametric regression. Polynomial spline models are related to the time series literature on unobserved components models, trend estimation, and state space methods, exposed in Harvey (1989) and Durbin and Koopman (2001). An excellent review of graduation is Boumans (2004, Section 3).

16.2. Local Polynomial Regression

Let us assume that in (16.1) μ_t is an unknown deterministic function of time, so that $E(y_t) = \mu_t$, and that equally spaced observations y_{t+j}, $j = 0, \pm 1, 2, \ldots, h$, are available in a neighbourhood of time t. Our interest lies in estimating the level of the trend at time t, μ_t, using the available observations.

If μ_t is differentiable, using the Taylor-series expansion it can be locally approximated by a polynomial of degree p of the time distance, j, between y_t and the neighbouring observations y_{t+j}. Hence, $\mu_{t+j} \approx m_{t+j}$, with

$$m_{t+j} = \beta_0 + \beta_1 j + \cdots + \beta_p j^p, \quad j = 0, \pm 1, \ldots, \pm h.$$

The degree of the polynomial is crucial in determining the accuracy of the approximation. Another essential quantity is the size h of the neighbourhood around time t; in our particular setup the neighbourhood consist of $H = 2h + 1$ consecutive and regularly spaced time points at which observations y_{t+j} are made. The parameter h is the *bandwidth*, for which we assume $p \leqslant 2h$ throughout.

Replacing μ_{t+j} by its approximation gives the local polynomial model:

$$y_{t+j} = \sum_{k=0}^{p} \beta_k j^k + \epsilon_{t+j}, \quad j = 0, \pm 1, \ldots, \pm h. \tag{16.2}$$

If we assume that $\epsilon_{t+j} \sim \mathrm{NID}(0, \sigma^2)$, then (16.2) is a linear Gaussian regression model with explanatory variables given by the powers of the time distance j^k, $k = 0, \ldots, p$ and unknown coefficients β_k, which are proportional to the kth order derivatives of μ_t. Working with the linear Gaussian approximating model, we are faced with the problem of estimating $m_t = \beta_0$, i.e. the value of the approximating polynomial for $j = 0$, which is intercept β_0 of the approximating polynomial.

The model (16.2) can be rewritten in matrix notation as follows:

$$\mathbf{y} = \mathbf{X}\boldsymbol{\beta} + \boldsymbol{\epsilon}, \quad \boldsymbol{\epsilon} \sim \mathrm{N}(\mathbf{0}, \sigma^2\mathbf{I})$$

where $\mathbf{y} = [y_{t-h}, \ldots, y_t, \ldots, y_{t+h}]'$, $\boldsymbol{\epsilon} = [\epsilon_{t-h}, \ldots, \epsilon_t, \ldots, \epsilon_{t+h}]'$,

$$\mathbf{X} = \begin{bmatrix} 1 & -h & \cdots & (-h)^p \\ 1 & -(h-1) & \cdots & [-(h-1)]^p \\ \vdots & \vdots & \cdots & \vdots \\ 1 & 0 & \cdots & 0 \\ \vdots & \vdots & \cdots & \vdots \\ 1 & h-1 & \cdots & (h-1)^p \\ 1 & h & \cdots & h^p \end{bmatrix}, \quad \boldsymbol{\beta} = \begin{bmatrix} \beta_0 \\ \beta_1 \\ \vdots \\ \beta_p \end{bmatrix}.$$

In the estimation of the unknown level, we would like to weight the observations differently according to their distance from time t. In particular, we may want to assign larger weight to the observations that are closer to t. For this purpose we introduce a kernel function κ_j, $j = 0, \pm 1, \ldots, \pm h$, which we assume known, such that $\kappa_j \geqslant 0$, and $\kappa_j = \kappa_{-j}$. Hence, the κ_j's are non-negative and symmetric with respect to j. As a result, the influence of each individual observation is controlled not only by the bandwidth h but also by the kernel.

Provided that $p \leqslant 2h$, the $p+1$ unknown coefficients β_k, $k = 0, \ldots, p$, can be estimated by the method of weighted least squares (WLS), which consists of minimising with respect to the β_k's the objective function:

$$S(\hat{\beta}_0, \ldots, \hat{\beta}_p) = \sum_{j=-h}^{h} \kappa_j \left(y_{t+j} - \hat{\beta}_0 - \hat{\beta}_1 j - \cdots - \hat{\beta}_p j^p\right)^2. \tag{16.3}$$

Defining $\mathbf{K} = \mathrm{diag}(\kappa_h, \ldots, \kappa_1, \kappa_0, \kappa_1, \ldots, \kappa_h)$, the WLS estimate of the coefficients is $\hat{\boldsymbol{\beta}} = (\mathbf{X}'\mathbf{K}\mathbf{X})^{-1}\mathbf{X}'\mathbf{K}\mathbf{y}$. In order to obtain $\hat{m}_t = \hat{\beta}_0$, we need to select the first element of the vector $\hat{\boldsymbol{\beta}}$. Hence, denoting by $\mathbf{e}_1$ the $p+1$ vector

$\mathbf{e}_1' = [1, 0, \ldots, 0]$,

$$\hat{m}_t = \mathbf{e}_1'\hat{\boldsymbol{\beta}} = \mathbf{e}_1'(\mathbf{X}'\mathbf{K}\mathbf{X})^{-1}\mathbf{X}'\mathbf{K}\mathbf{y} = \mathbf{w}'\mathbf{y} = \sum_{j=-h}^{h} \mathrm{w}_j y_{t-j},$$

which expresses the estimate of the trend as a linear combination of the observations with coefficients

$$\mathbf{w}' = \mathbf{e}_1'(\mathbf{X}'\mathbf{K}\mathbf{X})^{-1}\mathbf{X}'\mathbf{K}. \tag{16.4}$$

The trend estimate is local since it depends only on the subset of the observations that belong to the neighbourhood of time t. The linear combination yielding our trend estimate is often termed a (linear) *filter*, and the weights w_j constitute its impulse responses. The latter are time invariant and carry essential information on the nature of the estimated signal; their properties will be discussed in Section 16.8. For the time being we state two important ones: symmetry and reproduction of pth degree polynomials.

Symmetry ($\mathrm{w}_j = \mathrm{w}_{-j}$) follows from the symmetry of the kernel weights κ_j and the assumption that the available observations are equally spaced. Concerning the second, from (16.4) we have that $\mathbf{X}'\mathbf{w} = \mathbf{e}_1$, or equivalently,

$$\sum_{j=-h}^{h} \mathrm{w}_j = 1, \qquad \sum_{j=-h}^{h} j^l \mathrm{w}_j = 0, \quad l = 1, \ldots, p.$$

As a consequence, the filter $\mathbf{w}$ is said to preserve a deterministic polynomial of order p, which means that if the series is $\mathbf{y} = \mathbf{X}\boldsymbol{\beta}$ then the filter will reproduce it exactly, i.e. $\hat{m}_t = \beta_0 = y_t$.

The central weight w_0 measures the *leverage*, that is the contribution of y_t on the estimate of the signal at time t. It is also known as the *influence* of y_t. Defining $\mathbf{e}_{h+1} = [0, \ldots, 0, 1, 0, \ldots, 0]'$ (a $H \times 1$ vector with 1 in the middle position), such that $\mathbf{X}'\mathbf{e}_{h+1} = \mathbf{e}_1$,

$$\mathrm{w}_0 = \mathbf{w}'\mathbf{e}_{h+1} = \mathbf{e}_1'(\mathbf{X}'\mathbf{K}\mathbf{X})^{-1}\mathbf{X}'\mathbf{K}\mathbf{e}_{h+1} = \kappa_0\mathbf{e}_1'(\mathbf{X}'\mathbf{K}\mathbf{X})^{-1}\mathbf{e}_1. \tag{16.5}$$

The filter arising for $\mathbf{K} = \mathbf{I}$ (uniform kernel) has $\mathbf{w} = \mathbf{X}(\mathbf{X}'\mathbf{X})^{-1}\mathbf{e}_1$ and it is known as a *Macaulay's filter*. In the case of a local constant polynomial, that is $p = 0$ and $\kappa_j = 1, \forall j$, the signal extraction filter is the arithmetic moving average: $\mathrm{w}_j = \mathrm{w} = 1/(2h+1)$, $j = 0, \pm 1, \ldots, \pm h$. The same weights arise in the case $p = 1$ i.e. for a local linear fit, but this is true only of the central weights for equally spaced observations.

16.3. Henderson Filters

An important class of local polynomial filters, proposed by Henderson (1916), arises as a particular case of the local cubic fit, $p = 3$ in (16.3). The relevance of Henderson's contribution to modern local regression is stressed in the first chapter of Loader (1999). Still nowadays the Henderson filters are employed for trend estimation in the X-11 nonparametric seasonal adjustment procedure. See Findley et al. (1998) for more details.

The problem faced by Henderson is to determine the weighting function (16.4) which, for a given bandwidth h and $p = 3$ provides the *smoothest* estimates of the trend. The smoothness criterion adopted by Henderson is based on the variance of the third differences of the estimates of the trend, in that the smaller the variance the greater the extent of smoothness, as the trend acceleration is subject to the least variation. Hence, the objective is that of choosing $\{w_j\}$ so as to minimise $\text{Var}(\Delta^3\hat{m}_t)$, where Δ is the difference operator, such that $\Delta\hat{m}_t = \hat{m}_t - \hat{m}_{t-1}$, and $\Delta^3\hat{m}_t = \Delta^2(\hat{m}_t - \hat{m}_{t-1}) = \hat{m}_t - 3\hat{m}_{t-1} + 3\hat{m}_{t-2} - \hat{m}_{t-3}$. At the same time, the weights have to satisfy the cubic polynomial reproduction property: $\sum_j w_j = 1, \sum_j w_j j^k = 0, k = 1, 2, 3$.

Now, since

$$\text{Var}(\Delta^3\hat{m}_t) = \text{Var}\left(\sum_{j=-h}^{h} w_j \Delta^3 \epsilon_{t-j}\right) = \sigma^2 \sum_{j=-h+3}^{h} (\Delta^3 w_j)^2,$$

as it is implied by the assumption that $\epsilon_{t+j} \sim \text{NID}(0, \sigma^2)$, the above constrained minimisation problem is equivalent to determining the weights $\{w_j\}$ that minimise the sum of squared third differences of the weights, $\sum_{j=-h+3}^{h}(\Delta^3 w_j)^2$, subject to the constraints $\sum_j w_j = 1, \sum_j w_j j^k = 0, k = 1, 2, 3$.

It can be shown (Kenny and Durbin, 1982) that the solution is

$$w_j = \kappa_j \frac{(S_4 - S_2 j^2)}{S_0 S_4 - S_2^2},$$
$$\kappa_j = [(h+1)^2 - j^2][(h+2)^2 - j^2][(h+3)^2 - j^2],$$

$j = 0, \pm 1, \ldots, \pm h$, where $S_k = \sum_{j=-h}^{h} \kappa_j j^k$. Therefore, the Henderson filters emerge from WLS estimation of a local cubic polynomial using the particular kernel given above. Table 16.1 reports the filter weights for different values of the bandwidth parameter.

16.4. The Treatment of the Extremes of the Series – Real Time Estimation

Up to now we have assumed the availability of $2h + 1$ observations centred at t and have derived symmetric two sided filters. Obviously, it is not possible to obtain the estimates of the signal for (the first and) last h time points, which is inconvenient, since we are typically most interested at the most recent estimates.

We can envisage two fundamental approaches to the estimation of the signal at the extremes of the sample period:

Table 16.1: Weights w_j of the Henderson filters with $H = 9, 13, 17$, and 23 terms.

j	Weights w_j			
	$h=4$	$h=6$	$h=8$	$h=11$
0	.33114	.24006	.18923	.14406
±1	.26656	.21434	.17639	.13832
±2	.11847	.14736	.14111	.12195
±3	−.00987	.06549	.09229	.09740
±4	−.04072	.00000	.04209	.06830
±5		−.02786	.00247	.03893
±6		−.01935	−.01864	.01343
±7			−.02037	−.00495
±8			−.00996	−.01453
±9				−.01569
±10				−.01092
±11				−.00428

1. the construction of asymmetric filters that result from fitting a local polynomial to the available observations y_t, $t = n - h + 1, n - h + 2, \ldots, n$. The approximate model $y_{t+j} = m_{t+j} + \epsilon_{t+j}$ is assumed to hold for $j = -h, -h+1, \ldots, n-t$, and the estimators of the coefficients $\hat{\beta}_k, k = 0, \ldots, p$, minimise

$$S(\hat{\beta}_0, \ldots, \hat{\beta}_p) = \sum_{j=-h}^{n-t} \kappa_j \left(y_{t+j} - \hat{\beta}_0 - \hat{\beta}_1 j - \cdots - \hat{\beta}_p j^p\right)^2.$$

Hence, the trend estimates for the last h data points, $\hat{m}_{n-h+1}, \ldots, \hat{m}_n$, use respectively $2h, 2h-1, \ldots, h+1$ observations.
2. Apply the symmetric two sided filter to the series extended by h forecasts $\hat{y}_{n+l|n}$, $l = 1, \ldots, h$, (and backcasts $\hat{y}_{1-l|n}$).

In the sequel we shall denote by $\hat{m}_{t|t+r}$ the estimate of the signal at time t using the information available up to time $t + r$, with $0 \leqslant r \leqslant h$; $\hat{m}_{t|t}$ is usually known as the real time estimate since it uses only the past and current information. Figure 16.2 displays the central and asymmetric filters for computing $\hat{m}_{t|t+r}$ of the Henderson filter with $h = 8$.

Both strategies imply that the final h estimates of the trend will be subject to revision as new observations become available. An intuitive and easily established fact is that if the forecasts $\hat{y}_{n+l|n}$ are optimal in the mean square error sense, then the variance of the revision is a minimum. The two strategies coincide only when the future observations are generated according to a polynomial function of time of degree p, so that the optimal forecasts are generated by the same polynomial model.

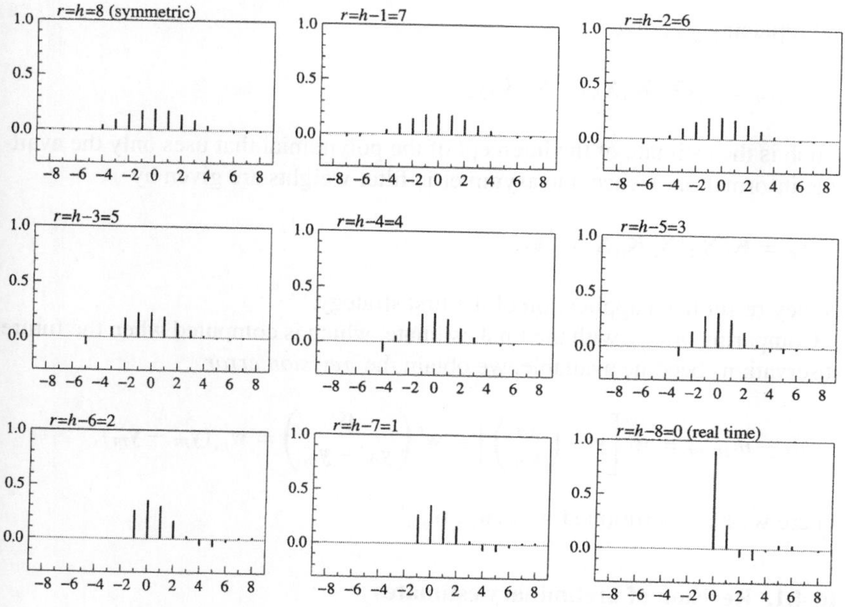

Fig. 16.2: Henderson filter: central and asymmetric weights.

To prove this result let us start by partitioning the matrices $\mathbf{X}$, $\mathbf{K}$ and the vector $\mathbf{y}$ as follows:

$$\mathbf{X} = \begin{bmatrix} \mathbf{X}_a \\ \mathbf{X}_m \end{bmatrix}, \qquad \mathbf{y} = \begin{bmatrix} \mathbf{y}_a \\ \mathbf{y}_m \end{bmatrix}, \qquad \mathbf{K} = \begin{bmatrix} \mathbf{K}_a & \mathbf{0} \\ \mathbf{0} & \mathbf{K}_m \end{bmatrix}$$

where $\mathbf{y}_a$ denotes the set of available observations, whereas $\mathbf{y}_m$ is missing. Under the local polynomial model the forecasted values of $\mathbf{y}_m$ is

$$\hat{\mathbf{y}}_m = \mathbf{X}_m(\mathbf{X}_a'\mathbf{K}_a\mathbf{X}_a)^{-1}\mathbf{X}_a'\mathbf{K}_a\mathbf{y}_a.$$

Applying the two-sided filter $\mathbf{w}$ to the observations extended by the forecasts yields:

$$\hat{m}_{t|t+r} = \mathbf{w}' \begin{bmatrix} \mathbf{y}_a \\ \hat{\mathbf{y}}_m \end{bmatrix} = \mathbf{e}_1'(\mathbf{X}'\mathbf{K}\mathbf{X})^{-1}\mathbf{X}'\mathbf{K} \begin{bmatrix} \mathbf{y}_a \\ \hat{\mathbf{y}}_m \end{bmatrix};$$

using $\mathbf{X}'\mathbf{K} = [\mathbf{X}_a'\mathbf{K}_a, \ \mathbf{X}_m'\mathbf{K}_m]$,

$$\begin{aligned}(\mathbf{X}'\mathbf{K}\mathbf{X})^{-1} &= (\mathbf{X}_a'\mathbf{K}_a\mathbf{X}_a + \mathbf{X}_m'\mathbf{K}_m\mathbf{X}_m)^{-1} \\ &= (\mathbf{X}_a'\mathbf{K}_a\mathbf{X}_a)^{-1}[\mathbf{I} + \mathbf{X}_m'\mathbf{K}_m\mathbf{X}_m(\mathbf{X}_a'\mathbf{K}_a\mathbf{X}_a)^{-1}]^{-1}\end{aligned}$$

and replacing $\hat{\mathbf{y}}_m$, gives

$$\hat{m}_{t|t+r} = \mathbf{e}_1'(\mathbf{X}_a'\mathbf{K}_a\mathbf{X}_a)^{-1}\mathbf{X}_a'\mathbf{K}_a\mathbf{y}_a,$$

which is the estimate of the intercept of the polynomial that uses only the available information. Hence, the asymmetric filter weights are given by

$$\mathbf{w}_a = \mathbf{K}_a\mathbf{X}_a(\mathbf{X}_a'\mathbf{K}_a\mathbf{X}_a)^{-1}\mathbf{e}_1,$$

as they result from application of the first strategy.

Comparing $\hat{m}_{t|t+r}$ with the final estimate, which is computed when the future observations become available, we obtain the *revision error*

$$\hat{m}_t - \hat{m}_{t|t+r} = \mathbf{w}'\left[\mathbf{y} - \begin{pmatrix}\mathbf{y}_a \\ \hat{\mathbf{y}}_m\end{pmatrix}\right] = \mathbf{w}'\begin{pmatrix}\mathbf{0} \\ \mathbf{y}_m - \hat{\mathbf{y}}_m\end{pmatrix} = \mathbf{w}_m'(\mathbf{y}_m - \hat{\mathbf{y}}_m),$$

where we have partitioned $\mathbf{w} = [\mathbf{w}_a', \mathbf{w}_m']'$.

16.4.1. Revision of preliminary estimates

Suppose that we add an observation to the current set $\mathbf{y}_a$, y_{t+r+1}, and denote by $\mathbf{x}_{t+r+1}' = [1, (r+1), (r+1)^2, \ldots, (r+1)^p]$ the $(r+1)$st row of the matrix $\mathbf{X}$. If the first strategy is adopted, then we can express the estimate $\hat{m}_{t|t+r+1}$, which uses the newly available observation, in terms of the previous estimate, plus a revision term which depends on a fraction of the one-step-ahead forecast error:

$$\hat{m}_{t|t+r+1} = \hat{m}_{t|t+r} + \frac{\kappa_{r+1}\mathbf{e}_1'(\mathbf{X}_a'\mathbf{K}_a\mathbf{X}_a)^{-1}\mathbf{x}_{t+r+1}}{1 + \kappa_{r+1}\mathbf{x}_{t+r+1}'(\mathbf{X}_a'\mathbf{K}_a\mathbf{X}_a)^{-1}\mathbf{x}_{t+r+1}} \times (y_{t+r+1} - \hat{y}_{t+r+1|t+r})$$

where $\hat{y}_{t+r+1|t+r} = \mathbf{x}_{t+r+1}'\hat{\boldsymbol{\beta}}_a = \mathbf{x}_{t+r+1}'(\mathbf{X}_a'\mathbf{K}_a\mathbf{X}_a)^{-1}\mathbf{X}_a'\mathbf{K}_a\mathbf{y}_a$ is the one-step-ahead forecast of y_{t+r+1}.

The proof uses the following matrix inversion result (see e.g. Henderson and Searle, 1981): if $\mathbf{A}$ is invertible and b is a scalar,

$$(\mathbf{A} \pm b\mathbf{u}\mathbf{v}')^{-1} = \mathbf{A}^{-1} \mp \frac{b}{1 \pm b\mathbf{v}'\mathbf{A}^{-1}\mathbf{u}}\mathbf{A}^{-1}\mathbf{u}\mathbf{v}'\mathbf{A}^{-1}. \tag{16.6}$$

16.4.2. The use of exogenous forecasts

As illustrated by Fig. 16.2 the asymmetric filter weights of the Henderson filter change rapidly, as new observations are added. This adds to the variability of the estimates of the trend, and is detrimental to their reliability, as they are subject to large revisions. The second strategy (using forecast extensions) is safer if it is thought that the series is not generated by a local polynomial model, provided that we are able to produce optimal forecasts according to some parametric or non parametric device, e.g. fitting a time series model of the ARIMA class. This idea is embodied in the X-11-ARIMA seasonal adjustment procedure (Dagum, 1982). In applied economic time series analysis most often extrapolations have a local linear nature, such as those obtained from ARIMA models with integration order equal to 1 or 2 (provided there is no constant term in the latter case).

When the forecast extensions are exogenous the filter weights are adapted to the property of the series, so that the weights w_j are not fixed, but depend also on y_t. An intermediate strategy, which avoids this dependence, is to assume that outside the sample period the trend is a linear, rather than cubic, function of time. A similar idea is exploited in Musgrave's adaptation of the Henderson filters at the extremes of the series (Musgrave, 1964).

16.5. Inference

The filter (16.4) depends on three characteristics: the degree of the approximating polynomial, the shape of the kernel function and the bandwidth h (or, equivalently, the length of the filter H). All these factors jointly contribute to balance the trade-off between variance and bias, that will be discussed in the following subsection.

16.5.1. Bias–variance trade-off

Recalling that $\hat{m}_t = \hat{\beta}_0 = \sum_j \mathrm{w}_j y_{t-j}$ is the estimate of the level m_t which approximates the "true" underlying signal μ_t,

$$\mathrm{E}(\hat{m}_t) = \mathrm{E}\Big(\sum_j \mathrm{w}_j y_{t-j}\Big) = \mathrm{E}\Big[\sum_j \mathrm{w}_j(\mu_{t-j} + \epsilon_{t-j})\Big] = \sum_j \mathrm{w}_j \mu_{t-j}.$$

Thus $\hat{m}_t$ is biased, unless $\mu_{t+j} = m_{t+j}$, $j = 0, \pm, 1, \ldots, \pm h$, i.e. the true signal is a polynomial of order p. The bias arises from neglecting higher order terms in the Taylor expansion:

$$\mu_t - \mathrm{E}(\hat{m}_t) = \mu_t - \sum_j \mathrm{w}_j \mu_{t-j} = d_t - \sum_j \mathrm{w}_j d_{t-j}$$

where $d_{t-j} = \mu_{t-j} - m_{t-j} = \sum_{k=p+1}^{\infty} \frac{1}{k!}\mu_{t-j}^{(k)} j^k$, is the remainder of the Taylor's approximation, $\mu_{t-j}^{(k)}$ being the kth derivative of the trend at $t - j$.

The bias is inversely related to p and is positively related with h. As a matter of fact, the higher is p, the more reliable is the polynomial approximation (i.e. the size of d_t is lower); also, the suitability of the local polynomial approximation is higher the smaller the neighbourhood of time t that is considered. Hence, in order to minimise the bias we ought to take p high and h low. On the other hand, higher degree polynomials also have more coefficients to estimate, resulting in higher variability. Also, if h is small the estimates use few observations, so that by increasing h we decrease their variance.

As far as the *variance* is concerned,

$$\begin{aligned}\mathrm{Var}(\hat{m}_t) &= \mathrm{E}\big[\hat{m}_t - \mathrm{E}(\hat{m}_t)\big]^2 = \mathrm{E}\Big[\sum_j \mathrm{w}_j(y_{t-j} - \mu_{t-j})\Big]^2 \\ &= \sigma^2 \sum_j \mathrm{w}_j^2 \\ &= \sigma^2 \mathbf{e}_1'(\mathbf{X}'\mathbf{K}\mathbf{X})^{-1}\mathbf{X}'\mathbf{K}^2\mathbf{X}(\mathbf{X}'\mathbf{K}\mathbf{X})^{-1}\mathbf{e}_1.\end{aligned}$$

The factor $\sum_{j=-h}^{h} \mathrm{w}_j^2$ is often termed the variance inflation factor (VIF), as it represents the proportionate increase (reduction if lower than 1, as is the case for the methods considered thus far) in the variance of a filtered white noise sequence due to the smoothing operation. The VIF is one when all the weight is concentrated on the observation to be estimated, say $\hat{m}_t = y_t$.

For a given p, $\mathrm{Var}(\hat{m}_t)$ decreases as h increases. For instance, if $p = 0, 1$ and the kernel is uniform (Macaulay's moving averages), then the VIF is equal to the leverage $\mathrm{w}_0 = (2h+1)^{-1}$; for $p = (2, 3)$, the VIF is 1, 0.49, 0.33, 0.26, 0.21, respectively for $h = 1, 2, 3, 4, 5$. On the contrary, for h given, VIF increases with the even values of p. For instance, for $h = 5$ the VIF is 0.09, 0.21, 0.33, respectively for per $p = (0, 1)$, $p = (2, 3)$, and $p = (4, 5)$.

The shape of the kernel has much less impact on the bias–variance trade-off. The optimal choice of the pair of parameters (p, h) should minimise the mean square estimation error,

$$\mathrm{MSE}(\hat{m}_t) = \mathrm{Var}(\hat{m}_t) + \big[\mu_t - \mathrm{E}(\hat{m}_t)\big]^2,$$

which can be estimated using a variety of methods (see e.g. Fan and Gjibels, 1996).

Usually, $p = 1, 2$ are adequate choices for the degree of the fitting polynomial, although the Henderson filter ($p = 3$) is fairly popular in time series applications.

16.5.2. Cross-validation

It is usually most effective to choose a low degree polynomial and concentrate instead on the selection of the bandwidth. Here we discuss and illustrate with reference to the Henderson filter the choice of the bandwidth according to the cross-validation score. The latter assesses the performance of the fit by comparing each observation with the local regression estimate computed from the remaining $n-1$ data points.

Let $\hat{m}_{t\backslash t}$ denote the two-sided estimate of the signal at time t which does not use y_t. Using (16.5) and the matrix inversion lemma (16.6),

$$\begin{aligned}
\hat{m}_{t\backslash t} &= \mathbf{e}_1'(\mathbf{X}'\mathbf{K}\mathbf{X} - \kappa_0\mathbf{e}_1\mathbf{e}_1')^{-1}(\mathbf{X}'\mathbf{K}\mathbf{y} - \kappa_0 y_t\mathbf{e}_1) \\
&= \mathbf{e}_1'\left[(\mathbf{X}'\mathbf{K}\mathbf{X})^{-1} + \frac{\kappa_0}{1-\kappa_0\mathbf{e}_1'(\mathbf{X}'\mathbf{K}\mathbf{X})^{-1}\mathbf{e}_1}(\mathbf{X}'\mathbf{K}\mathbf{X})^{-1}\mathbf{e}_1\mathbf{e}_1'(\mathbf{X}'\mathbf{K}\mathbf{X})^{-1}\right] \\
&\quad \times (\mathbf{X}'\mathbf{K}\mathbf{y} - \kappa_0 y_t\mathbf{e}_1) \\
&= \frac{1}{1-\mathrm{w}_0}\mathbf{e}_1'(\mathbf{X}'\mathbf{K}\mathbf{X})^{-1}(\mathbf{X}'\mathbf{K}\mathbf{y} - \kappa_0 y_t\mathbf{e}_1) \\
&= \frac{1}{1-\mathrm{w}_0}\hat{m}_t - \frac{\mathrm{w}_0}{1-\mathrm{w}_0}y_t.
\end{aligned}$$

The leave-one-out, or deletion, residual can be expressed in terms of the trend estimate using all the observations:

$$y_t - \hat{m}_{t\backslash t} = \frac{1}{1-\mathrm{w}_0}(y_t - \hat{m}_t).$$

The cross-validation score is the sum of the squared deletion residuals:

$$CV = \sum_{t=1}^{n}(y_t - \hat{m}_{t\backslash t})^2 = \sum_t \frac{(y_t - \hat{m}_t)^2}{(1-\mathrm{w}_{0t})^2},$$

where the subscript t in w_{0t} signifies that the filter weights are different at the extremes of the sample, so that the leverage varies with t.

Figure 16.3 plots CV for different values of the bandwidth parameter and the trend estimates corresponding to the $h = 9$ for which the cross-validation score is a minimum, along with its 95% confidence bounds computed using the standard error estimates obtained as indicated in the next section.

16.5.3. Error variance and interval estimates

The estimation of σ^2 can be done using the residuals from the local polynomial fit: $y_t - \hat{m}_t = y_t - \sum_j \mathrm{w}_{jt}y_{t-j}$, where again we append a subscript t since the filter differs at the extremes.

Assuming $y_t = m_t + \epsilon_t$, i.e. $\mu_t = m_t$, a polynomial of degree p (and thus $\sum_j \mathrm{w}_{jt}m_{t-j} = m_t$ by the polynomial preservation property), the expectation of the residual sum of squares (RSS) is

$$\begin{aligned}
\mathrm{E}(RSS) &= \mathrm{E}\left[\sum_{t=1}^{n}\left(y_t - \sum_j \mathrm{w}_{jt}y_{t-j}\right)^2\right] \\
&= \mathrm{E}\left[\sum_{t=1}^{n}\left(y_t - m_t - \sum_j \mathrm{w}_{jt}(y_{t-j} - m_t)\right)^2\right]
\end{aligned}$$

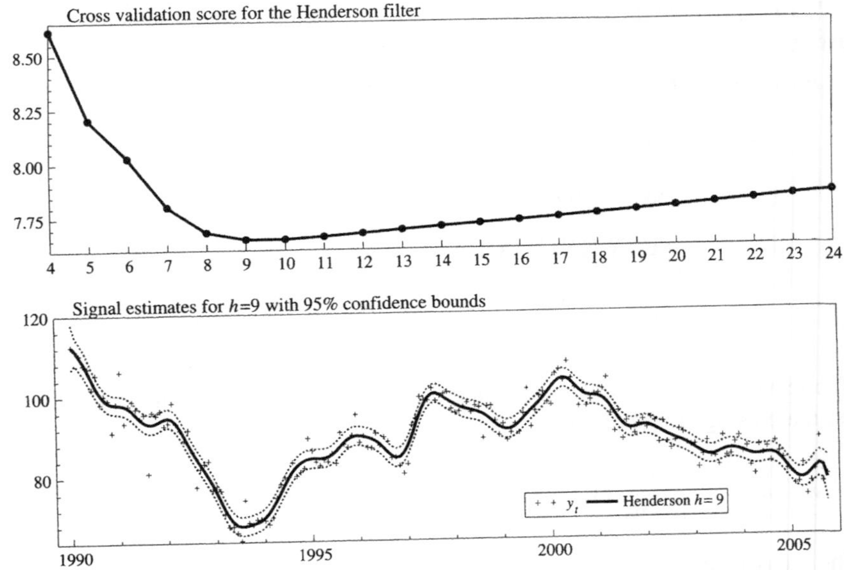

Fig. 16.3: Henderson filter: cross-validation scores and interval estimates of the signal.

$$= \mathrm{E}\left[\sum_{t=1}^{n}\left(\epsilon_t - \sum_j \mathrm{w}_{jt}\epsilon_{t-j}\right)^2\right]$$

$$= \mathrm{E}\left[\sum_{t=1}^{n}\left(\epsilon_t^2 - 2\sum_j \mathrm{w}_{jt}\epsilon_t\epsilon_{t-j} + \left(\sum_j \mathrm{w}_{jt}\epsilon_{t-j}\right)^2\right)\right]$$

$$= \sigma^2\left[n - 2\sum_{t=1}^{n}\mathrm{w}_{0t} + \sum_{t=1}^{n}\left(\sum_j \mathrm{w}_{jt}^2\right)\right].$$

This suggests that we can estimate the error variance by correcting the RSS:

$$\hat{\sigma}^2 = \frac{RSS}{n - 2\sum_{t=1}^{n}\mathrm{w}_{0t} + \sum_{t=1}^{n}(\sum_j \mathrm{w}_{jt}^2)}.$$

This estimate can be used in turn to compute interval estimates of the signal; e.g. an approximate 95% confidence interval for μ_t is

$$\hat{m}_t \pm 2\left(\hat{\sigma}^2\sum_j \mathrm{w}_{jt}^2\right)^{\frac{1}{2}}.$$

16.6. Other Approaches and Generalisations

In the previous sections we have focussed on the simplified case when equally spaced observations are available, the bandwidth is fixed and the support of the kernel is discrete. The generalisation to unequally spaced observations and continuous kernels proceeds as follows. Assuming that n observations $y(t_i)$ are made at the at time points t_i, $i = 1, \ldots, n$, the estimate of the signal at time $t \in (t_1, t_n)$ is computed by minimising the WLS criterion function:

$$S(\hat{\beta}_0, \ldots, \hat{\beta}_p)$$
$$= \sum_{i=1}^{n} \kappa\left(\frac{t_i - t}{b}\right)\left[y(t_i) - \hat{\beta}_0 - \hat{\beta}_1(t_i - t) - \cdots - \hat{\beta}_p(t_i - t)^p\right]^2$$

where $\kappa(z)$ is the kernel function, which is symmetric and non-negative. The smoothing parameter $b > 0$ determines the bandwidth of the kernel, since $\kappa(z) = 0$ for $|z| > 1$. If b tends to zero then $\hat{m}(t_i) = y(t_i)$. On the other hand, if b tends to infinity, then all the observations will receive weight equal to $1/n$ and the estimation gives the ordinary least squares solution.

The estimate of the trend is $\hat{m}(t) = \hat{\beta}_0 = \mathbf{w}_t'\mathbf{y}$, where $\mathbf{y} = [y(t_1), \ldots, y(t_n)]'$, and $\mathbf{w}_t = \mathbf{e}_1'(\mathbf{X}_t'\mathbf{K}_t\mathbf{X}_t)^{-1}\mathbf{X}_t'\mathbf{K}_t$ where $\mathbf{X}_t$ is an $n \times (p+1)$ matrix with ith row $[1, (t_i - t), \ldots, (t_i - t)^p]$, and $\mathbf{K}_t = \text{diag}[\kappa(\frac{t_1 - t}{b}), \ldots, \kappa(\frac{t_n - t}{b})]$ is $n \times n$.

The case $p = 0$ (local constant fit) yields the well-known Nadaraya–Watson estimator (Nadaraya, 1964; Watson, 1964):

$$\hat{m}(t) = \frac{1}{\sum_{i=1}^{n} \kappa(\frac{t_i - t}{b})} \sum_{i=1}^{n} \kappa\left(\frac{t_i - t}{b}\right) y(t_i),$$

where the weights for signal extraction are provided by the normalised kernel coefficients.

There is a large literature on kernels and their properties. An important class, embedding several widely used kernels, is the class of Beta kernels:

$$\kappa(z) = k_{rs}\left(1 - |z|^r\right)^s I\left(|z| \leqslant 1\right), \quad k_{rs} = \frac{r}{2B(s+1, \frac{1}{r})}$$

with $r > 0$, $s \geqslant 0$, and

$$B(a, b) = \int_0^1 z^{a-1}(1 - z)^{b-1}\, dz$$

with $a, b > 0$ is the Beta distribution function. The pair ($r = 1$, $s = 0$) gives the uniform kernel (yielding the Macaulay filters in the discrete case), $r = s = 1$

gives the triangle kernel, ($r = 2$, $s = 1$) the Epanechnikov kernel, $r = s = 2$ the biweight kernel, ($r = 2$, $s = 3$) the triweight kernel, $r = s = 3$ the tricube kernel. The kernel of the Henderson filter can be viewed as discrete version of the triweight kernel. Other kernels are defined from parametric density functions, as in the case of the Gaussian kernel. For a comparative assessment of the various kernels see Wand and Jones (1995). The overall conclusion is that their choice is not very relevant in terms of efficiency.

There are several variations of local polynomial regression. Most of them involve different ways of selecting the bandwidth parameters. One of the most popular locally weighted regression scatterplot smoother is *Loess*, due to Cleveland (1979). The distinctive features is that each $m(t)$ is estimated using a fixed number of points, regardless of the time location t, rather than using a fixed bandwidth. Finally, the choice of the bandwidth parameter can be made local. For instance, the *supersmoother*, proposed by Friedman (1984), selects the bandwidth for each target point using local cross-validation. In regions where the curvature-to-variance ratio is high, a small span is chosen. On the other hand, if the curvature-to-variance ratio is low, then a large span will be preferred.

16.7. Splines and Trend Models

An alternative way of overcoming the limitations of the global polynomial model is to add polynomial pieces at given points, called knots, so that the polynomial sections are joined together ensuring that certain continuity properties are fulfilled. Given the set of points $t_1 < \cdots < t_i < \cdots < t_k$, a polynomial spline function of degree p with k knots $t_1, \ldots, t_k$ is a polynomial of degree p in each of the $k+1$ intervals $[t_i, t_{i+1})$, with $p-2$ continuous derivatives, whereas the $(p-1)$st derivative has jumps at the knots. It can be represented as follows:

$$\mu(t) = \beta_0 + \beta_1(t - t_1) + \cdots + \beta_p(t - t_1)^p + \sum_{i=1}^{k} \eta_i (t - t_i)_+^p, \tag{16.7}$$

where the set of functions

$$(t - t_i)_+^p = \begin{cases} (t - t_i)^p, & t - t_i \geqslant 0, \\ 0, & t - t_i < 0 \end{cases}$$

defines what is usually called the truncated power basis of degree p.

According to (16.7) the spline is a linear combination of polynomial pieces; at each knot a new polynomial piece, starting off at zero, is added so that the derivatives at that point are continuous up to the order $p-2$. There are several equivalent ways of representing a spline function, some of which are more amenable from the computational standpoint. The truncated power representation has the advantage of representing the spline as a multivariate regression model.

An important class of semiparametric and parametric time series models are encompassed by (16.7). The piecewise nature of the spline "reflects the occurrence of structural change" (Poirier, 1973). The knot t_i is the timing of a structural break. The change is "smooth", since certain continuity conditions are ensured. The coefficients η_i, which regulate the size of the break, may be considered as fixed or random. In the latter case $\mu(t)$ is a stochastic process, η_i is interpreted as a *random shock* that drives the evolution of $\mu(t)$, whereas the truncated power function $(t - t_i)_+^p$ describes its *impulse response function*, that is the impact on the future values of the trend.

If the η_i's are considered as random, the spline model can be formulated as a linear mixed model, which is a traditional regression model extended so as to incorporate random effects. Denoting $\mathbf{y} = [y(t_1), \ldots, y(t_n)]'$, $\boldsymbol{\eta} = [\eta_1, \ldots, \eta_n]'$, $\boldsymbol{\epsilon} = [\epsilon(t_1), \ldots, \epsilon(t_n)]'$, $\boldsymbol{\mu} = \mathbf{X}\boldsymbol{\beta} + \mathbf{Z}\boldsymbol{\eta}$,

$$\mathbf{y} = \boldsymbol{\mu} + \boldsymbol{\epsilon} = \mathbf{X}\boldsymbol{\beta} + \mathbf{Z}\boldsymbol{\eta} + \boldsymbol{\epsilon}, \tag{16.8}$$

where the tth row of $\mathbf{X}$ is $[1, (t-1), \ldots, (t-1)^p]$, and $\mathbf{Z}$ is a known matrix whose ith column contains the impulse response signature of the shock η_i, $(t - t_i)_+^p$.

In the sequel we shall assume that observations are available at discrete times, $y(t_i) = y_i$, $i = 1, \ldots, n$, and that the knots are placed at the times at which observations are made ($t_i = i$). Hence, each new observation carries "news", which produce the structural change.

16.7.1. The local level model

The simplest truncated power basis arises for $p = 0$ and consists of step functions with jumps of size 1 at the knots. The corresponding zero degree spline is

$$\mu(t) = \beta_0 + \sum_{i=1}^{n-1} \eta_i (t - i)_+^0 = \beta_0 + \sum_{i=1}^{t-1} \eta_i, \quad t = 1, \ldots, n, \tag{16.9}$$

where $\eta_t \sim \mathrm{NID}(0, \sigma_\eta^2)$ and $(t - i)_+^0 = 1$ for $t > i$, and zero otherwise. Equation (16.9) defines a random walk and can be reformulated as a stochastic difference equation: $\mu_{t+1} = \mu_t + \eta_t, t = 1, \ldots, n-1$, with starting value $\mu_1 = \beta_0$. Thus, a shock η_t occurring at time t is accumulated into the future values of the level and has unit long run impact. The shock signature is constant and is displayed in the upper left panel of Fig. 16.4.

The model $y_t = \mu_t + \epsilon_t$, with μ_t given above and $\epsilon_t \sim \mathrm{NID}(0, \sigma_\epsilon^2)$, is known as the local level model and plays an important role in the time series literature, since the forecasts are an exponentially weighted moving average (EWMA) of the current and past observations, and the smoothed estimates of μ_t are given by a two-sided EWMA.

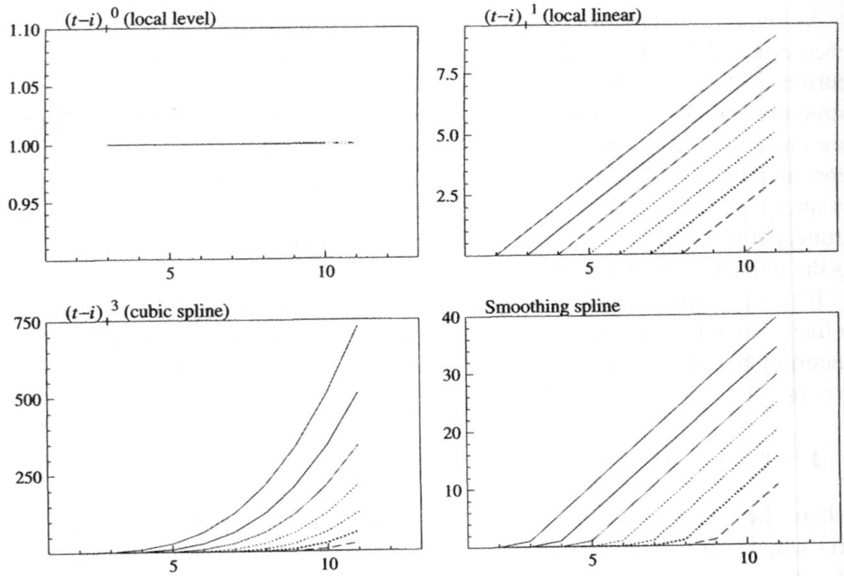

Fig. 16.4: Shock signature for polynomial spline trend models.

If (16.9) is modified as follows:

$$\mu(t) = \beta_0 + \beta_1(t-1) + \sum_{i=2}^{n-1} \eta_i (t-i)_+^0$$

$$= \beta_0 + \beta_1(t-1) + \sum_{i=2}^{t-1} \eta_i, \quad t = 1, \ldots, n,$$

the trend becomes a random walk with drift and can be represented by the stochastic difference equation $\mu_{t+1} = \mu_t + \beta_1 + \eta_t$, $t = 2, \ldots, n-1$, with starting values $\mu_1 = \beta_0$, $\mu_2 = \mu_1 + \beta_1$.

16.7.2. The local linear model

Another important trend model, known as the local linear trend model, arises for $p = 1$:

$$\mu(t) = \beta_0 + \beta_1(t-1) + \sum_{i=2}^{n-1} \eta_i (t-i)_+^1$$

$$= \beta_0 + \beta_1(t-1) + \sum_{i=2}^{t-1} (t-i)\eta_i, \quad t = 1, \ldots, n. \tag{16.10}$$

Notice that, in order to enhance the identifiability of the parameters, the equally spaced knots range from time 2 to $n-1$. Equation (16.10) defines an integrated random walk (IRW) and can be reformulated as a stochastic difference equation: $\mu_{t+1} - 2\mu_t + \mu_{t-1} = \eta_t$, $t = 2, \ldots, n$, with starting values $\mu_1 = \beta_0$, $\mu_2 = \beta_0 + \beta_1$. The impulse response function is linear and a shock is doubly accumulated (integrated) in the future values of the level (see the upper right panel of Fig. 16.4).

It should be noticed that μ_t is continuous at each time point t (whereas the first derivative, $\beta_1 + \sum \eta_i (t-i)^0_+$, is discontinuous at $t = i$). To allow for a discontinuity at each $t = i$ we introduce a linear combination of $(t-i)^0_+$:

$$\begin{aligned}\mu(t) &= \beta_0 + \beta_1(t-1) + \sum_{i=2}^{n-1} \eta_i (t-i)^1_+ + \sum_{i=1}^{n-1} \omega_i (t-i)^0_+ \\ &= \beta_0 + \beta_1(t-1) + \sum_{i=2}^{t-1} (t-i)\eta_i + \sum_{i=2}^{t-1} \omega_i, \end{aligned} \tag{16.11}$$

where we take $\omega_i \sim \mathrm{NID}(0, \sigma^2_\omega)$, uncorrelated with η_i. The trend model (16.11) can be rewritten as a random walk with stochastic drift, δ_t, evolving as a random walk: $\mu_{t+1} = \mu_t + \delta_t + \eta_t$, $\delta_{t+1} = \delta_t + \omega_t$. See Harvey (1989) for more details. Obviously, if $\sigma^2_\omega = 0$, then the model reduces to (16.9).

16.7.3. Cubic splines

Consider the cubic spline model, which arises from setting $p = 3$ in (16.7):

$$\mu(t) = \sum_{j=0}^{3} \beta_j (t-1)^j + \sum_{i=1}^{n} \eta_i (t-i)^3_+. \tag{16.12}$$

The response signature of a shock is a cubic function of time (see the bottom-left panel of Fig. 16.4) and the signal follows a third degree polynomial outside the observations interval. This trend model displays too much flexibility for economic time series, that is paid for with excess variability, especially at the beginning and at the end of the sample period. Out of sample forecasts tend to be not very reliable, as they are subject to high revisions as new observations become available. This is the reason why it is preferable to impose the so called *natural boundary conditions*, which constrain the spline to be linear outside the boundary knots. Similar considerations were made for local polynomial smoothing, see Section 16.4.2.

The original cubic spline model (16.12) has $4 + n$ parameters. The natural boundary conditions require that the second and the third derivatives are zero for $t \leqslant 1$ and $t \geqslant n$. As we shall see shortly they impose 4 restrictions (2 zero restrictions and 2 linear restrictions) on the parameters of the cubic spline. The second and third derivatives are respectively $\mu''(t) = 2\beta_2 + 6\beta_3(t-1) + 6\sum_i \eta_i (t-i)_+$ and $\mu'''(t) = 6\beta_3 + 6\sum_i \eta_i (t-i)_+^0$. For $\mu'''(t)$ to be equal to zero for $t \leqslant 1$ and $t \geqslant n$ we need $\beta_3 = 0$ and $\sum_i i\eta_i = 0$; moreover, $\mu''(t) = 0$ for $t \leqslant 1$ and $t \geqslant n$ requires also $\beta_2 = 0$ and $\sum_i \eta_i = 0$.

Defining $\mathbf{x}(t) = [1, (t-1)]'$, $\boldsymbol{\beta} = [\beta_0, \beta_1]'$, $\mathbf{z}(t) = [(t-1)_+^3, \ldots, (t-n)_+^3]'$, and $\boldsymbol{\eta} = [\eta_1, \ldots, \eta_n]'$, the natural cubic spline can be represented as $\mu(t) = \mathbf{x}(t)'\boldsymbol{\beta} + \mathbf{z}'(t)\boldsymbol{\eta}$. If we further collect in the vector $\boldsymbol{\mu}$ the values of the spline at the data points $i = 1, \ldots, n$, $\boldsymbol{\mu} = [\mu_1, \ldots, \mu_n]'$, and define $\mathbf{X}' = [\mathbf{x}_1, \ldots, \mathbf{x}_n]$, with $\mathbf{x}_i = [1, (i-1)]'$, $\mathbf{Z}' = [\mathbf{z}_1, \ldots, \mathbf{z}_n]$, with $\mathbf{z}_i = [(i-1)_+^3, \ldots, (i-n)_+^3]'$ we can write $\boldsymbol{\mu} = \mathbf{X}\boldsymbol{\beta} + \mathbf{Z}\boldsymbol{\eta}$, where $\boldsymbol{\eta}$ satisfies the constraints $\mathbf{X}'\boldsymbol{\eta} = \mathbf{0}$.

Also, the second derivative can be written as a linear combination of the elements of $\boldsymbol{\eta}$, $\mu''(t) = \mathbf{v}(t)'\boldsymbol{\eta}$, where $\mathbf{v}(t) = 6[(t-1)_+, \ldots, (t-n)_+]'$. Denoting $\gamma_i = \mu_i''$ the value of the second derivative at the ith data point $i = 2, \ldots, n-1$ ($\gamma_1 = \gamma_n = 0$ for a natural spline), and defining the vector $\boldsymbol{\gamma} = [\gamma_2, \ldots, \gamma_{n-1}]'$, the boundary conditions $\mathbf{X}'\boldsymbol{\eta} = \mathbf{0}$ imply that we can write $\boldsymbol{\eta} = \mathbf{D}\boldsymbol{\gamma}$, $\boldsymbol{\gamma} = (\mathbf{D}'\mathbf{D})^{-1}\mathbf{D}'\boldsymbol{\eta}$, where $\mathbf{D}$ is the $n \times (n-2)$ matrix

$$\mathbf{D} = \begin{bmatrix} 1 & 0 & \cdots & \cdots & 0 \\ -2 & 1 & \ddots & \ddots & \vdots \\ 1 & -2 & \ddots & \ddots & \vdots \\ 0 & 1 & \ddots & \ddots & 0 \\ \vdots & 0 & \ddots & \ddots & 1 \\ \vdots & \vdots & \ddots & \ddots & -2 \\ 0 & 0 & \ldots & 0 & 1 \end{bmatrix}. \tag{16.13}$$

Replacing into the expressions for the spline and the second derivative gives:

$$\mu(t) = \mathbf{x}(t)'\boldsymbol{\beta} + \mathbf{z}(t)'\mathbf{D}\boldsymbol{\gamma}, \quad \boldsymbol{\mu} = \mathbf{X}\boldsymbol{\beta} + \mathbf{Z}\mathbf{D}\boldsymbol{\gamma},$$
$$\mu''(t) = \mathbf{v}(t)'\mathbf{D}\boldsymbol{\gamma} = \mathbf{r}(t)'\boldsymbol{\gamma},$$

where we have set $\mathbf{r}(t) = \mathbf{D}'\mathbf{v}(t)$. The generic element of the vector $\mathbf{r}(t)$ is $6[(t-i)_+ - 2(t-i-1)_+ + (t-i-2)_+]$, a triangular function which is nonzero in the interval $(i, i+2)$ and peaking at $i+1$, where it takes the value 6.

The integral of the squared second derivative between $t = 1$ and $t = n$ is

$$\int_1^n [\mu''(t)]^2 dt = \int [\boldsymbol{\eta}'\mathbf{v}(t)\mathbf{v}(t)'\boldsymbol{\eta}] dt = \boldsymbol{\gamma}'\left[\int \mathbf{r}(t)\mathbf{r}(t)' dt\right]\boldsymbol{\gamma} = 6\boldsymbol{\gamma}'\mathbf{R}\boldsymbol{\gamma}$$

where $\mathbf{R}$ is the $(n-2) \times (n-2)$ tridiagonal matrix

$$\mathbf{R} = \begin{bmatrix} 4 & 1 & 0 & \cdots & 0 \\ 1 & 4 & \ddots & \ddots & \vdots \\ 0 & 1 & \ddots & \ddots & 0 \\ \vdots & \ddots & \ddots & \ddots & 1 \\ 0 & \ldots & 0 & 1 & 4 \end{bmatrix}.$$

The matrix $\mathbf{D}$ is such that $\mathbf{D}'\mathbf{X} = \mathbf{0}$, $\mathbf{D}'\mathbf{Z}\mathbf{D} = \frac{1}{6}\mathbf{R}$, which gives the following key relationship between the second differences of the spline and the values of the second derivative at the knots: $\mathbf{D}'\boldsymbol{\mu} = \frac{1}{6}\mathbf{R}\boldsymbol{\gamma}$, or equivalently $\mu_{t+1} - 2\mu_t - \mu_{t-1} = \frac{1}{6}\gamma_{t+1} + \frac{2}{3}\gamma_t + \frac{1}{6}\gamma_{t-1}$ (see e.g. Green and Silverman, 1994, Theorem 2.1).

A smoothing spline is a natural cubic spline which solves the following penalised least squares (PLS) problem:

$$\min\left\{(\mathbf{y} - \boldsymbol{\mu})'(\mathbf{y} - \boldsymbol{\mu}) + \lambda \int \left[\mu''(t)\right]^2 dt\right\}, \tag{16.14}$$

where $\lambda \geqslant 0$ is the smoothness parameter, $\int [\mu''(t)]^2\, dt = 6\boldsymbol{\gamma}'\mathbf{R}\boldsymbol{\gamma}$, and $\mathbf{D}'\boldsymbol{\mu} = \mathbf{R}\boldsymbol{\gamma}$. In the next section we argue that minimising the PLS objective function with respect to $\boldsymbol{\mu}$ is equivalent to maximising the posterior density $f(\boldsymbol{\mu}|\mathbf{y})$, assuming the prior density $\boldsymbol{\gamma} \sim \mathrm{N}(\mathbf{0}, \sigma_\gamma^2\mathbf{R}^{-1})$, for a given scalar σ_γ^2.

The shock signature of the smoothing spline can be obtained as $\mathbf{ZDR}^{-1/2}$, where $\mathbf{R}^{1/2}$ is the Choleski factor of $\mathbf{R}$. The bottom right panel of Fig. 16.4 shows that this is cubic between knot i and knot $i+2$, after which reverts to a linear function of time.

16.7.4. Inference

Writing the polynomial spline model as (16.8) with $\boldsymbol{\eta} \sim \mathrm{N}(\mathbf{0}, \boldsymbol{\Sigma}_\eta)$ and $\boldsymbol{\epsilon} \sim \mathrm{N}(\mathbf{0}, \boldsymbol{\Sigma}_\epsilon)$, we will now determine the values of $\boldsymbol{\beta}$ and $\boldsymbol{\eta}$ that maximise the posterior density $f(\boldsymbol{\eta}|\mathbf{y}) \propto f(\mathbf{y}|\boldsymbol{\eta})f(\boldsymbol{\eta})$, or equivalently the joint density $f(\mathbf{y}, \boldsymbol{\eta})$; see Robinson (1991) for various approaches to the estimation of fixed and random effects in a mixed model. The mode of the posterior density can be found by minimising

$$(\mathbf{y} - \mathbf{X}\boldsymbol{\beta} - \mathbf{Z}\boldsymbol{\eta})'\boldsymbol{\Sigma}_\epsilon^{-1}(\mathbf{y} - \mathbf{X}\boldsymbol{\beta} - \mathbf{Z}\boldsymbol{\eta}) + \boldsymbol{\eta}'\boldsymbol{\Sigma}_\eta^{-1}\boldsymbol{\eta} \tag{16.15}$$

with respect to $\boldsymbol{\beta}$ and $\boldsymbol{\eta}$. The first term measures the fit and the second can be seen as a penalisation term. It is perhaps worthwhile to stress that here $\boldsymbol{\beta}$ is fixed but unknown.

Differentiating (16.15) with respect to $\boldsymbol{\beta}$ and $\boldsymbol{\eta}$ yields the first-order conditions

$$(\boldsymbol{\Sigma}_\eta^{-1} + \mathbf{Z}'\boldsymbol{\Sigma}_\epsilon^{-1}\mathbf{Z})\boldsymbol{\eta} - \mathbf{Z}'\boldsymbol{\Sigma}_\epsilon^{-1}(\mathbf{y} - \mathbf{X}\boldsymbol{\beta}) = \mathbf{0},$$
$$\mathbf{X}'\left[\boldsymbol{\Sigma}_\epsilon^{-1} - \boldsymbol{\Sigma}_\epsilon^{-1}\mathbf{Z}\left(\boldsymbol{\Sigma}_\eta^{-1} + \mathbf{Z}'\boldsymbol{\Sigma}_\epsilon^{-1}\mathbf{Z}\right)^{-1}\mathbf{Z}\boldsymbol{\Sigma}_\epsilon^{-1}\right](\mathbf{y} - \mathbf{X}\boldsymbol{\beta}) = \mathbf{0}.$$

Resolving the second equation with respect to $\boldsymbol{\beta}$ and noticing[1]

$$\left[\boldsymbol{\Sigma}_\epsilon^{-1} - \boldsymbol{\Sigma}_\epsilon^{-1}\mathbf{Z}\left(\boldsymbol{\Sigma}_\eta^{-1} + \mathbf{Z}'\boldsymbol{\Sigma}_\epsilon^{-1}\mathbf{Z}\right)^{-1}\mathbf{Z}\boldsymbol{\Sigma}_\epsilon^{-1}\right] = (\boldsymbol{\Sigma}_\epsilon + \mathbf{Z}\boldsymbol{\Sigma}_\eta\mathbf{Z}')^{-1} = \boldsymbol{\Sigma}_y^{-1}$$

we obtain:

$$\hat{\boldsymbol{\beta}} = \left(\mathbf{X}'\boldsymbol{\Sigma}_y^{-1}\mathbf{X}\right)^{-1}\mathbf{X}'\boldsymbol{\Sigma}_y^{-1}\mathbf{y}, \qquad \hat{\boldsymbol{\eta}} = \left(\boldsymbol{\Sigma}_\eta^{-1} + \mathbf{Z}'\boldsymbol{\Sigma}_\epsilon^{-1}\mathbf{Z}\right)^{-1}\mathbf{Z}'\boldsymbol{\Sigma}_\epsilon^{-1}(\mathbf{y} - \mathbf{X}\hat{\boldsymbol{\beta}}).$$

The latter can be rewritten:

$$\begin{aligned}\hat{\boldsymbol{\eta}} &= \boldsymbol{\Sigma}_\eta\mathbf{Z}'\boldsymbol{\Sigma}_y^{-1}(\mathbf{y} - \mathbf{X}\hat{\boldsymbol{\beta}}) \\ &= \mathrm{E}(\boldsymbol{\eta}) + \mathrm{Cov}(\boldsymbol{\eta}, \mathbf{y})\left[\mathrm{Var}(\mathbf{y})\right]^{-1}\left(\mathbf{y} - \mathrm{E}(\mathbf{y})\right).\end{aligned} \tag{16.16}$$

Hence, denoting $\boldsymbol{\Sigma}_\mu = \mathbf{Z}\boldsymbol{\Sigma}_\eta\mathbf{Z}' = \mathrm{Cov}(\boldsymbol{\mu}, \mathbf{y})$,

$$\begin{aligned}\hat{\boldsymbol{\mu}} &= \mathbf{X}\hat{\boldsymbol{\beta}} + \boldsymbol{\Sigma}_\mu\boldsymbol{\Sigma}_y^{-1}(\mathbf{y} - \mathbf{X}\hat{\boldsymbol{\beta}}) \\ &= \mathrm{E}(\boldsymbol{\mu}) + \mathrm{Cov}(\boldsymbol{\mu}, \mathbf{y})\left[\mathrm{Var}(\mathbf{y})\right]^{-1}\left(\mathbf{y} - \mathrm{E}(\mathbf{y})\right).\end{aligned} \tag{16.17}$$

Posterior mode estimation yields the optimal estimator of the trend in the sense that $\mathrm{MSE}(\hat{\boldsymbol{\mu}})$ is a minimum. In particular, for a Gaussian model the mode is coincident with the mean, and thus $\hat{\boldsymbol{\mu}} = \mathrm{E}(\boldsymbol{\mu}|\mathbf{y})$, the estimation error has zero mean, $\mathrm{E}(\hat{\boldsymbol{\mu}} - \boldsymbol{\mu}|\mathbf{y}) = \mathbf{0}$, and $\mathrm{E}[(\boldsymbol{\mu} - \hat{\boldsymbol{\mu}})(\boldsymbol{\mu} - \hat{\boldsymbol{\mu}})'|\mathbf{y}] = \boldsymbol{\Sigma}_\mu\boldsymbol{\Sigma}_y^{-1}\boldsymbol{\Sigma}_\epsilon + \boldsymbol{\Sigma}_\epsilon\boldsymbol{\Sigma}_y^{-1}\mathbf{X}(\mathbf{X}'\boldsymbol{\Sigma}_y^{-1}\mathbf{X})^{-1}\mathbf{X}'\boldsymbol{\Sigma}_y^{-1}\boldsymbol{\Sigma}_\epsilon$ is a minimum. If gaussianity is not assumed the previous expressions provide the best linear unbiased estimators of the fixed and random effects.

If $\boldsymbol{\beta}$ is taken as a diffuse vector, $\boldsymbol{\beta} \sim \mathrm{N}(\mathbf{0}, \boldsymbol{\Sigma}_\beta)$, $\boldsymbol{\Sigma}_\beta^{-1} \to 0$, the solution is unchanged. As a matter of fact, posterior mode estimation entails the maximisation of the joint density $f(\boldsymbol{\beta}, \boldsymbol{\eta}|\mathbf{y}) \propto f(\boldsymbol{\eta})f(\boldsymbol{\beta})f(\mathbf{y}|\boldsymbol{\eta}, \boldsymbol{\beta})$, but the prior $f(\boldsymbol{\beta})$ does not depend on $\boldsymbol{\beta}$ ($\boldsymbol{\beta}'\boldsymbol{\Sigma}_\beta^{-1}\boldsymbol{\beta} \to 0$).

An alternative equivalent characterisation of the trend estimates proceeds from the following argument. Let $\boldsymbol{\Delta}$ be a matrix which spans the nullity of $\mathbf{X}$, so that $\boldsymbol{\Delta}'\mathbf{X} = \mathbf{0}$. If the columns of $\mathbf{X}$ span a polynomial of degree k, $\boldsymbol{\Delta}'$ is a matrix performing $(k + 1)$st order differences. Then, premultiplying both sides of the trend equation by $\boldsymbol{\Delta}$ yields $\boldsymbol{\Delta}'\boldsymbol{\mu} = \boldsymbol{\Delta}'\mathbf{Z}\boldsymbol{\eta}$. A rank $n - k - 1$ linear transformation is performed to annihilate the regression effects, and thus

---

[1] This result generalises the matrix inversion lemma (16.6), see Henderson and Searle (1981).

$\mathbf{\Delta}'\boldsymbol{\mu} \sim \mathrm{N}(\mathbf{0}, \mathbf{\Delta}'\mathbf{Z}\mathbf{\Sigma}_\eta\mathbf{Z}'\mathbf{\Delta})$. The prior distribution of $\boldsymbol{\mu}$ can be singular, as it occurs for all the spline models discussed in the previous section, for which the rank of $\mathbf{Z}\mathbf{\Sigma}_\eta\mathbf{Z}'$ is n minus the column rank of the $\mathbf{X}$ matrix, but $\mathbf{\Delta}'\boldsymbol{\mu}$ has a nonsingular normal distribution.

Let us consider the problem of choosing $\boldsymbol{\mu}$ so as to maximise

$$(\mathbf{y}-\boldsymbol{\mu})'\mathbf{\Sigma}_\epsilon^{-1}(\mathbf{y}-\boldsymbol{\mu})+\boldsymbol{\mu}'\mathbf{\Delta}(\mathbf{\Delta}'\mathbf{Z}\mathbf{\Sigma}_\eta\mathbf{Z}'\mathbf{\Delta})^{-1}\mathbf{\Delta}'\boldsymbol{\mu}. \tag{16.18}$$

The above objective function is a penalised least squares criterion. The optimal estimate of a signal arises from maximising a composite criterion function which has two components, the first measuring the closeness to the data, and the second the departure from zero of the differences $\mathbf{\Delta}'\boldsymbol{\mu}$ (i.e. a measure of roughness). Penalised least squares is among the most popular criteria for designing filters that has a long and well established tradition in actuarial sciences and economics (see Whittaker, 1923; Henderson, 1916; Leser, 1961, and, more recently, Hodrick and Prescott, 1997).

Differentiating with respect to $\boldsymbol{\mu}$ and equating to zero, we obtain

$$\begin{aligned}\hat{\boldsymbol{\mu}} &= \left[\mathbf{\Sigma}_\epsilon^{-1}+\mathbf{\Delta}(\mathbf{\Delta}'\mathbf{Z}\mathbf{\Sigma}_\eta\mathbf{Z}'\mathbf{\Delta})^{-1}\mathbf{\Delta}'\right]^{-1}\mathbf{\Sigma}_\epsilon^{-1}\mathbf{y}\\ &= \left[\mathbf{I}-\mathbf{\Sigma}_\epsilon\mathbf{\Delta}(\mathbf{\Delta}'\mathbf{Z}\mathbf{\Sigma}_\eta\mathbf{Z}'\mathbf{\Delta}+\mathbf{\Delta}'\mathbf{\Sigma}_\epsilon\mathbf{\Delta})^{-1}\mathbf{\Delta}'\right]\mathbf{y}\\ &= \left[\mathbf{I}-\mathbf{\Sigma}_\epsilon\mathbf{\Delta}\mathbf{\Sigma}_{\Delta y}^{-1}\mathbf{\Delta}'\right]\mathbf{y}\\ &= \mathbf{y}-\hat{\boldsymbol{\epsilon}},\end{aligned}$$

with $\mathbf{\Sigma}_{\Delta y}=\mathbf{\Delta}'(\mathbf{Z}\mathbf{\Sigma}_\eta\mathbf{Z}'+\mathbf{\Sigma}_\epsilon)\mathbf{\Delta}$, and $\hat{\boldsymbol{\epsilon}}=\mathbf{\Sigma}_\epsilon\mathbf{\Delta}\mathbf{\Sigma}_{\Delta y}^{-1}\mathbf{\Delta}'\mathbf{y}=\mathrm{Cov}(\boldsymbol{\epsilon},\Delta'\mathbf{y})\times[\mathrm{Var}(\mathbf{\Delta}'\mathbf{y})]^{-1}\mathbf{\Delta}\mathbf{y}$.

The equivalence with the expression (16.17) is demonstrated as follows. We start defining the projection matrices

$$\mathbf{Q}_X=\mathbf{X}(\mathbf{X}'\mathbf{\Sigma}_y^{-1}\mathbf{X}')^{-1}\mathbf{X}'\mathbf{\Sigma}_y^{-1},\qquad \mathbf{Q}_\Delta=\mathbf{\Sigma}_y\mathbf{\Delta}(\mathbf{\Delta}'\mathbf{\Sigma}_y\mathbf{\Delta})^{-1}\mathbf{\Delta}', \tag{16.19}$$

such that $\mathbf{Q}_X\mathbf{Q}_\Delta=\mathbf{Q}_\Delta\mathbf{Q}_X=\mathbf{0}$, $\mathbf{Q}_\Delta=\mathbf{I}-\mathbf{Q}_X$. Then (16.17) can be rewritten as

$$\begin{aligned}\hat{\boldsymbol{\mu}} &= \mathbf{Q}_X\mathbf{y}+\mathbf{\Sigma}_\mu\mathbf{\Sigma}_y^{-1}\mathbf{Q}_\Delta\mathbf{y}\\ &= \left[\mathbf{I}-(\mathbf{I}-\mathbf{\Sigma}_\mu\mathbf{\Sigma}_y^{-1})\mathbf{Q}_\Delta\right]\mathbf{y}\\ &= (\mathbf{I}-\mathbf{\Sigma}_\epsilon\mathbf{\Sigma}_y^{-1}\mathbf{Q}_\Delta)\mathbf{y}\\ &= \left[\mathbf{I}-\mathbf{\Sigma}_\epsilon\mathbf{\Delta}(\mathbf{\Delta}'\mathbf{\Sigma}_y\mathbf{\Delta})^{-1}\mathbf{\Delta}'\right]\mathbf{y}\\ &= \left[\mathbf{I}-\mathbf{\Sigma}_\epsilon\mathbf{\Delta}\mathbf{\Sigma}_{\Delta y}^{-1}\mathbf{\Delta}'\right]\mathbf{y}\end{aligned}$$

which coincides with the above expression.

Often, the polynomial spline model is formulated so that $\mathbf{\Delta}'\mathbf{Z} = \mathbf{I}$, $\mathbf{\Sigma}_\epsilon = \sigma_\epsilon^2\mathbf{I}$, $\mathbf{\Sigma}_\eta = \sigma_\eta^2\mathbf{I}$, and thus minimising (16.18) is equivalent to find the minimum of the penalised least squares criterion:

$$(\mathbf{y} - \boldsymbol{\mu})'(\mathbf{y} - \boldsymbol{\mu}) + \lambda\boldsymbol{\mu}'\mathbf{\Delta}\mathbf{\Delta}'\boldsymbol{\mu},$$

where $\lambda = \sigma_\epsilon^2/\sigma_\eta^2$ is the reciprocal of the signal–noise ratio and provides a measure of the smoothness of the fit. The solution simplifies to $\hat{\boldsymbol{\mu}} = (\mathbf{I} + \lambda\mathbf{\Delta}\mathbf{\Delta}')^{-1}\mathbf{y}$. If $\lambda = 0$, the smoothing matrix is the identity matrix, $\hat{\boldsymbol{\mu}} = \mathbf{y}$, and no smoothing occurs. On the contrary, when $\lambda \to \infty$, $\hat{\boldsymbol{\mu}} = \mathbf{X}\boldsymbol{\beta}$, a polynomial trend.

For the local level model $\mathbf{\Delta}'\boldsymbol{\mu}$ yields the first differences $\mu_{t+1} - \mu_t$ and it can be shown (Harvey and Koopman, 2000) that if a doubly infinite sample is available, the estimate of the trend in the middle of the sample is $\hat{\mu}_t = \frac{1-\theta}{1+\theta}\sum_j(\theta)^j y_{t-j}$, where $\theta = (\lambda^{-1} + 2 - \sqrt{\lambda^{-2} + 4\lambda^{-1}})/2$, and the real time estimate is an exponentially weighted moving average of the available observations, $\hat{\mu}_{t|t} = \sum_{j=0}^{\infty}\theta^j y_{t-j}$. The corresponding filter is known as an *exponential smoothing* (ES) filter. See Gardner (1985) for a review.

The Leser (1961) and Hodrick–Prescott (Hodrick and Prescott, 1997, HP) filter arises in the special case $\mathbf{\Sigma}_\epsilon = \sigma_\epsilon^2\mathbf{I}$, $\mathbf{\Sigma}_\eta = \sigma_\eta^2\mathbf{I}$, $\lambda = \sigma_\epsilon^2/\sigma_\eta^2$, and $\mathbf{\Delta}$ is equal to the matrix $\mathbf{D}$ given in (16.13). Figure 16.5 displays the middle and the last row of the smoothing matrices $(\mathbf{I} + \lambda\mathbf{\Delta}\mathbf{\Delta}')^{-1}$ and $(\mathbf{I} + \lambda\mathbf{D}\mathbf{D}')^{-1}$ for the ES and the Leser-HP filter with different smoothness parameters and $n = 101$.

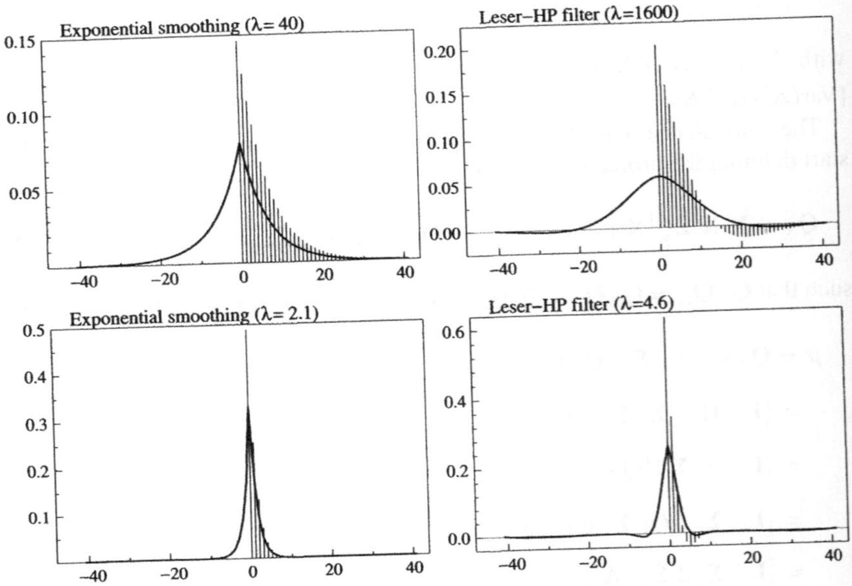

Fig. 16.5: Two-sided and one-sided filter weights for the ES and Leser–HP filters for different values of the smoothness parameter λ.

For the cubic smoothing spline, recalling $\mathbf{D}'\boldsymbol{\mu} = \mathbf{R}\boldsymbol{\gamma}$, and assuming $\boldsymbol{\gamma} \sim \mathrm{N}(\mathbf{0}, \sigma_\gamma^2\mathbf{R}^{-1})$ solving (16.18) amounts to solving the PLS problem (16.14) where $\lambda = \sigma_\epsilon^2/\sigma_\gamma^2$, i.e. to minimising:

$$(\mathbf{y}-\boldsymbol{\mu})'(\mathbf{y}-\boldsymbol{\mu}) + \lambda\boldsymbol{\mu}'\mathbf{D}\mathbf{R}^{-1}\mathbf{D}'\boldsymbol{\mu}.$$

The solution yields $\hat{\boldsymbol{\mu}} = (\mathbf{I}+\lambda\mathbf{D}\mathbf{R}^{-1}\mathbf{D}')^{-1}\mathbf{y} = [\mathbf{I} - \lambda\mathbf{D}(\mathbf{R}+\lambda\mathbf{D}'\mathbf{D})^{-1}\mathbf{D}']\mathbf{y}$. Notice that $\mathbf{D}'\boldsymbol{\mu} \sim \mathrm{N}(\mathbf{0}, \sigma_\gamma^2\mathbf{R})$ is the matrix formulation of an ARIMA(0,2,1) model for the trend, $\Delta\mu_{t+1} = \xi_t + \vartheta\xi_{t-1}$, where $\vartheta/(1+\vartheta^2) = 1/4$.

Suitable algorithms are available for the efficient computation of $\hat{\boldsymbol{\mu}}$; for smoothing splines, the Reinsch algorithm (Green and Silverman, 1994) exploits the banded structure of $\mathbf{R}$ and $\mathbf{D}\mathbf{D}'$. If the polynomial spline models are cast in the state space form, the computations can be carried out efficiently via the Kalman filter and smoother (KFS, see Harvey, 1989, and Durbin and Koopman, 2001). The cross-validation residuals are also computed by KFS (de Jong, 1988). The use of state space methods is advantageous also because the evaluation of the likelihood, the computation of forecasts and the time series innovations, along with other diagnostic quantities, are produced as a by-product of the KFS calculations.

The smoothness parameter λ, and more generally the covariance matrices $\boldsymbol{\Sigma}_\eta$ and $\boldsymbol{\Sigma}_\epsilon$, play an essential role in the estimation of $\boldsymbol{\mu}$, determining the bandwidth of the smoothing filter. As Fig. 16.5 illustrates, when λ increases the weights pattern becomes more smeared across adjacent time points. The estimation of the variance parameters can be performed by cross-validation or by maximum likelihood estimation (MLE), where the log-likelihood is given by

$$\ell(\mathbf{y}; \boldsymbol{\Sigma}_\eta, \boldsymbol{\Sigma}_\epsilon, \boldsymbol{\beta}) = -\frac{1}{2}\{\ln|\mathbf{Z}\boldsymbol{\Sigma}_\eta\mathbf{Z}' + \boldsymbol{\Sigma}_\epsilon| + (\mathbf{y}-\mathbf{X}\boldsymbol{\beta})'(\mathbf{Z}\boldsymbol{\Sigma}_\eta\mathbf{Z}' + \boldsymbol{\Sigma}_\epsilon)^{-1}(\mathbf{y}-\mathbf{X}\boldsymbol{\beta})\};$$

obviously, the parameter vector $\boldsymbol{\beta}$ can be concentrated out of the likelihood, and replacing $\hat{\boldsymbol{\beta}} = (\mathbf{X}'\boldsymbol{\Sigma}_y^{-1}\mathbf{X})^{-1}\mathbf{X}'\boldsymbol{\Sigma}_y^{-1}\mathbf{y}$ into $\ell(\mathbf{y}; \boldsymbol{\Sigma}_\eta, \boldsymbol{\Sigma}_\epsilon, \boldsymbol{\beta})$ yields the profile likelihood $\ell_\beta(\mathbf{y}; \boldsymbol{\Sigma}_\eta, \boldsymbol{\Sigma}_\epsilon)$.

Alternatively, the restricted or marginal log-likelihood can be maximised (Patterson and Thompson, 1971; Harville, 1977):

$$\ell_R(\mathbf{y}; \boldsymbol{\Sigma}_\eta, \boldsymbol{\Sigma}_\epsilon) = \ell_\beta(\mathbf{y}; \boldsymbol{\Sigma}_\eta, \boldsymbol{\Sigma}_\epsilon) - \frac{1}{2}\ln\left|\mathbf{X}'(\mathbf{Z}\boldsymbol{\Sigma}_\eta\mathbf{Z}' + \boldsymbol{\Sigma}_\epsilon)^{-1}\mathbf{X}\right|.$$

The restricted likelihood is the likelihood of a non-invertible linear transformation of the data, $\boldsymbol{\Delta}'\mathbf{y}$, which eliminates the dependence on $\boldsymbol{\beta}$, the transformation being such that $\boldsymbol{\Delta}'\mathbf{X} = \mathbf{0}$. Using $\ell_R(\mathbf{y}; \boldsymbol{\Sigma}_\eta, \boldsymbol{\Sigma}_\epsilon)$ is preferable when n is small and the variance of η_t is small compared to σ_ϵ^2. The marginal likelihood arises if it is assumed that the vector $\boldsymbol{\beta}$ is a diffuse random vector, i.e. it has an improper distribution with a mean of zero and an arbitrarily large variance matrix. This is suitable if the stochastic process for the trend has started in the indefinite past; then the diffuse assumption is a reflection of the nonstationarity of μ_t.

16.8. The Properties of the Filters

Local polynomial smoothing and polynomial splines yield estimates that can be written $\hat{\boldsymbol{\mu}} = \mathbf{W}\mathbf{y}$, where $\mathbf{W}$ is the smoothing matrix. The plot of the (reversed) rows of $\mathbf{W}$ provides useful information; Fig. 16.2 plots the central and the final h rows of the Henderson smoothing matrix with $h = 8$, whereas Fig. 16.5 displays the central and real time weights of the ES and Leser–HP filters.

Let us denote the spectral decomposition of the smoothing matrix $\mathbf{W} = \sum_{i=1}^{n} \rho_i \mathbf{v}_i \mathbf{v}_i'$, where $\mathbf{v}_i$ denotes the eigenvector corresponding to the ith eigenvalue ρ_i, so that $\mathbf{W}\mathbf{v}_i = \rho_i \mathbf{v}_i$, $\rho_1 \geqslant \cdots \geqslant \rho_n$, and $\mathbf{v}_i'\mathbf{v}_j = I(i = j)$. The decomposition can be used to characterise the nature of the filter, as the eigenvectors illustrate what sequences are preserved or compressed via a scalar multiplication. If $\rho_i = 1$ then the sequence $\mathbf{v}_i$ is preserved with no modification, if $\rho_i > 1$ then it is amplified, otherwise it is damped. If $\rho_i = 0$ then it is annihilated.

The rank of $\mathbf{W}$ quantifies the computational complexity of the smoother, in the sense that low rank smoothers use considerably less than n basis components (eigenvectors) whereas full-rank smoothers uses approximately the same number of basis components as the sample size. A related measure is the number of equivalent the degrees of freedom, which is often used for measuring the smoothness (on an inverted scale) of the filter. Developing a notion first introduced by Cleveland (1979), Hastie and Tibshirani (1990) define $df = \mathrm{tr}(\mathbf{W})$ as the degrees of freedom of a smoother, which corresponds to total influence of the observations. In local polynomial smoothing df increases with the order of the polynomial and decreases as the bandwidth increases; for polynomial spline models, it is inversely related to the smoothness parameter. The maximum value is $df = n$, which occurs for $\mathbf{W} = \mathbf{I}$.

The residual degrees of freedom of a smoother are defined as $df_{\mathrm{res}} = n - 2\,\mathrm{tr}(\mathbf{W}) + \mathrm{tr}(\mathbf{W}\mathbf{W}')$. This measure has been already used when we corrected the residual sum of squares in polynomial regression to produce an estimate of the error variance (see Section 16.5.3).

A different and perhaps more informative approach in a time series setting is the analysis of the filter in the frequency domain. A comprehensive treatment of filtering in the frequency domain is provided by Pollock (1999). Given a filter, e.g. any one of the rows of the matrix $\mathbf{W}$, we can investigate the effect of the filter by measuring the effects induced on particular sequences, $y_t = \cos(\omega t)$, where ω is the frequency in radians, that describe a regular periodic pattern with unit amplitude and periodicity equal to $2\pi/\omega$. As the frequency ω increases, the period reduces and for $\omega = \pi$, $\cos(\pi t) = (-1)^t$ describes a cycle with a period of two observations.

Applying standard trigonometric identities, the filtered series is:

$$\begin{aligned}\sum_j w_j y_{t-j} &= \sum_j w_j \cos\big(\omega(t-j)\big)\\ &= \sum_j w_j \cos(\omega t)\cos(\omega j) + \sum_j w_j \sin(\omega t)\sin(\omega j)\\ &= \alpha(\omega)\cos(\omega t) + \alpha^*(\omega)\sin(\omega t)\\ &= G(\omega)\cos\big(\omega t - \theta(\omega)\big)\end{aligned}$$

where $\alpha(\omega) = \sum_j w_j \cos(\omega j)$, $\alpha^*(\omega) = \sum_j w_j \sin(\omega j)$.

The function

$$G(\omega) = \sqrt{\alpha^2(\omega) + \alpha^{2*}(\omega)}$$

is the gain of the filter and measures how the amplitude of the periodic components that make up a signal are modified by the filter. If the gain is 1 at a particular frequency, this implies that the periodic component defined at that frequency is preserved; vice versa, fluctuations with periodicity at which the gain is less than one are compressed. The function $\theta(\omega) = \arctan[\alpha^*(\omega)/\alpha(\omega)]$ is the phase function and measures the displacement of the periodic function along the time axis. For symmetric filters the phase function is zero, since $\sum_j w_j \sin(\omega j) = 0$.

Figure 16.6 plots the gain $G(\omega)$ versus the frequency ω for the central weights of local polynomial and spline filters. The top panels refer to the local cubic fit

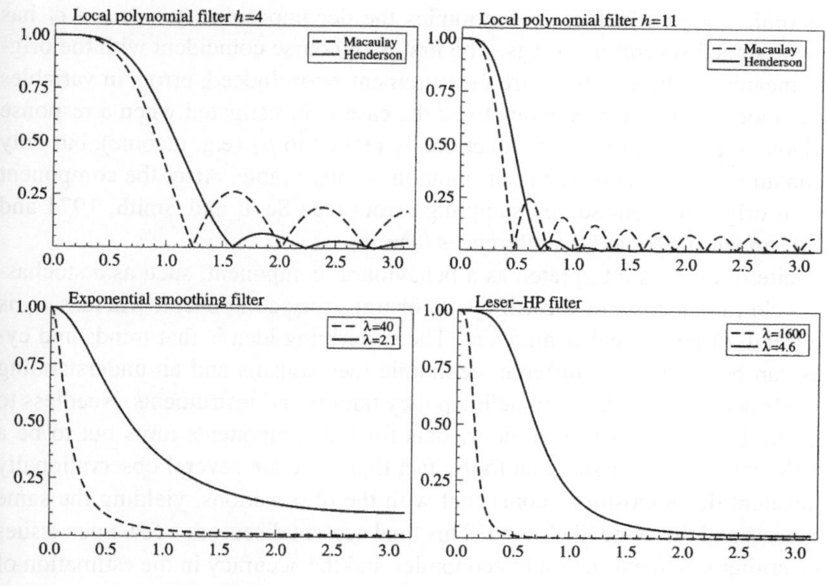

Fig. 16.6: Gain of local polynomial and spline filters.

using a uniform kernel (Macaulay) and the Henderson filters for two values of the bandwidth parameter. The filters preserve the low frequency components in the original series to a different extent. In particular, increasing h, yields smoother estimates, as the amplitude of the high frequency components is further reduced. The zeros in the gain imply that certain cycles are annihilated. The example also illustrates that the choice of the kernel does matter when one considers the effects on the amplitude of periodic components. The bottom panels exemplify the role of the smoothness parameter on the properties of the ES and Leser–HP filters. In particular, increasing λ enhances the smoothness of the filtered estimates as the filter retains to a greater extent the low frequency components, corresponding to fluctuations with a long period. Also, it can be anticipated that the Henderson filter with $h = 11$ will produce a rougher estimate of the signal compared to Leser–HP with $\lambda = 1600$.

16.9. Discussion

This chapter has dealt with signal extraction methods which originate from different approaches and which yield linear filters, that is linear combinations or moving averages of the observations, to extract the feature of interest. Filtering has a long tradition is economics and actuarial sciences (Anderson, 1971, Chapter 3). Some methods (e.g. smoothing by polynomial splines) originated in other fields and were later imported into economics, were data are observational rather than experimental (see Spanos, 1999). In this process the components of the measurement model were somewhat *reified*, by attaching to them peculiar economic content. In fact, in economics the decomposition $y_t = \mu_t + \epsilon_t$ has been assigned several meanings. The first is of course coincident with the original meaning, where ϵ_t is a pure measurement error. Indeed, errors in variables have a long tradition in econometrics: the case is investigated when a response variable (e.g. consumption) is functionally related to μ_t (e.g. income), but only a contaminated version, y_t in our notation, is observable. Also, the component ϵ_t can originate from survey sampling errors (see Scott and Smith, 1974 and Pfeffermann, 1991, and the references therein).

Quite often ϵ_t is interpreted as a behavioural component, such as a stochastic cycle (a deviation or growth cycle) or transitory component, whereas μ_t is the trend, or permanent component. The underlying idea is that trends and cycles can be ascribed to different economic mechanisms and an understanding of their determinants helps to define policy targets and instruments. Needless to say, the formulation of dynamic models for the components turns out to be a highly controversial issue, due to the fact that there are several observationally equivalent decompositions consistent with the observations, yielding the same forecasts and the same likelihood. This final section discusses a few open issues concerning signal extraction in economics and the accuracy in the estimation of the latent signals.

16.9.1. Accuracy

Key estimation problems in macroeconomics concern latent variables, or unobserved components of a time series, such as potential output and the complementary notion of an output gap, the non-accelerating-inflation rate of unemployment (NAIRU), core inflation, and so forth. The underlying "true value", μ_t, is a deterministic function of time in the nonparametric local polynomial regression or a random process (e.g. a random walk) in the stochastic approach. In other approaches, such as band-pass filtering, which are fairly popular in economics, see for instance Baxter and King (1999), the notion of a "true value" is more blurred and has significance in the frequency domain rather than in the time domain.

The previous sections have presented different smoothing methods that can be used to measure the underlying signals. Let $\hat{\mu}_t$ denote the estimator of μ_t based on the representation (model) μ_t^* used for it, $\hat{\mu}_t = \sum_j w_{jt} y_{t-j}$. We assume that $\hat{\mu}_t$ is the optimal signal extraction method for μ_t^*. How do we judge the *accuracy* of the method? Following Boumans (2005, and Chapter 1 of this Volume) accuracy is a statement concerning the closeness of $\hat{\mu}_t$ and μ_t. The discrepancy $\hat{\mu}_t - \mu_t$ can be broken down into two components: $(\hat{\mu}_t - \mu_t^*) + (\mu_t^* - \mu_t)$, which are associated to the *reliability*, or precision, of the method, and to the *validity*, or bias, of the representation chosen. The components are uncorrelated, and thus independent under normality, given the observations, if and only if $\hat{\mu}_t = \mathrm{E}(\mu_t^* | \mathbf{y})$. Precision is measured by (the inverse of) $V(\hat{\mu}_t) = \mathrm{E}[(\hat{\mu}_t - \mu_t^*)^2 | \mathbf{y}]$, whereas $B(\hat{\mu}_t) = \mathrm{E}[(\mu_t^* - \mu_t)^2 | \mathbf{y}]$ represents the bias.

16.9.1.1. Validity

The validity (bias) of a smoother is usually difficult to ascertain, as it is related to the appropriateness μ_t^* as a model for the signal. This is a complex assessment, involving many subjective elements, such as any a priori available information and the original motivation for signal extraction. Goodness of fit measures can be used along with cross-validation, but one needs to take into consideration the well-known risk of overfitting, which takes place when too much variation of the observed data is explained by the model.

In local polynomial and spline smoothing $B(\hat{\mu}_t)$ arises from misspecifying the degree of the polynomial. Increasing the degree is beneficial for the bias at the cost of an inflated variance (less precision). This issue is related to overdifferencing and to that of spuriousness, which shall be considered shortly. In the analysis of economic time series a great deal of research has been attracted by making inference on the order of integration. The trade-offs arising when high order trends are entertained, e.g. $\Delta^d \mu_t^* = \eta_t$, where η_t is a purely random disturbance and $d \geqslant 2$, are discussed in Proietti (2007).

Recently, there has been a surge of interest in model uncertainty and in model averaging. Typically, several methods $\hat{\mu}_{it}$ are compared (e.g. for measuring the trend in output we may compare structural vector autoregressive models, calibrated filtering techniques, such as Hodrick–Prescott with a fixed λ, the Beveridge–Nelson decomposition, etc.). Very often the conclusions from these exercises are rather pessimistic, as different methods may produce incompatible answers; see, for instance, Canova (1998), for detrending techniques, Orphanides and Van Norden (2002), who consider the estimation of the output gap. The individual estimates may be combined linearly, giving $\hat{\hat{\mu}}_t = \sum_i c_i \hat{\mu}_{it}$, where the coefficients c_i depend on the mean square errors of the methods.

It is more viable to assess two other aspects of validity, namely concurrent and predictive validity. The first is concerned with the contemporaneous relationship between the measure $\hat{\mu}_t$ and a related alternative measure of the same phenomenon; for instance we may compute the correlation between the output gap and another indicator of the same domain produced independently, such as a measure of capacity utilisation or an index of consumer and producer sentiment.

Predictive validity relates to the ability to forecast future realisation of y_t or related variables; evaluating the mean forecast error yields useful insight on its predictive validity, as possible bias would emerge. This criterion is adopted by a number of authors; for instance, Camba-Mendez and Rodriguez-Palenzuela (2003) and Proietti et al. (2007) assess the accuracy of alternative output gap estimates through their capability to predict future inflation.

16.9.1.2. Reliability

A measurement method is reliable (precise) if repeated measurements of the same quantity are in close agreement. Loosely speaking, reliability and precision are inversely related to the uncertainty of an estimates. In the measurement of immaterial constructs the sources of reliability would include:

(i) *parameter uncertainty*, due to the fact that the core parameters of the representation μ_t^*, such as the variance of the disturbances driving the components, are unknown and have to be estimated;
(ii) *estimation error*, the latent components are estimated with a positive variance even if a doubly infinite sample on y_t is available;
(iii) *statistical revision*, as new observations become available, the estimate of a signal are updated so as to incorporate the new information.

The first source can be assessed by various methods both in the classical (Ansley and Kohn, 1986) and the Bayesian approach (Hamilton, 1986; Quenneville and Singh, 2000). In an unobserved component framework the Kalman filter and smoother provide all the relevant information for assessing (ii) and (iii); for nonparametric filters such as X-11 sliding span diagnostics and revision histories have been proposed (Findley et al., 1990).

Staiger et al. (1997) and Laubach (2001) find that estimates of the NAIRU, obtained from a variety of methods, are highly imprecise, in that if one attempted to construct confidence intervals around the point estimates, he/she would realise that they are too wide to be of any practical use for policy purposes; similar findings are documented in Smets (2002) Orphanides and van Norden (2002).

Somewhat different conclusions are reached by Planas and Rossi (2004) and Proietti, Musso and Westermann (2007). The implications of the uncertainty surrounding the output gap estimates for monetary policy are considered in Smets (2002).

The sources (ii) and (iii) typically arise due to the fact that the individual components are unobserved and they have a dynamic representation. The availability of additional time series observations helps to improve the estimation of an unobserved component, apart from degenerate cases, such as the Beveridge–Nelson (1981) decomposition and those arising from structural vector autoregressions, for which the latent variable is actually measurable with respect to past and current information.

Recently, large dimensional dynamic factor models have become increasingly popular in empirical macroeconomics. The essential idea is that the precision by which the common components are estimated can be increased by bringing in more information from related series: suppose for simplicity that $y_{it} = \theta_i \mu_t + \epsilon_{it}$, where the ith series, $i = 1, \ldots, N$, depends on the same common factor, which is responsible for the observed comovements of economic time series, plus an idiosyncratic component, which includes measurement error and local shocks. Generally, multivariate methods provide more reliable measurements provided that a set of related series can be viewed as repeated measures of the same underlying latent variable. Stock and Watson (2002a and 2002b) and Forni et al. (2000) discuss the conditions on μ_t and ϵ_{it} under which dynamic or static principal components yield consistent estimates of the underlying factor μ_t as both N and n tend to infinity.

An additional source of uncertainty is data revision, which concerns y_t. Timely economic data are only provisional and are revised subsequently with the accrual of more complete information. Data revision is particularly relevant for national accounts aggregates, which require integrating statistical information from different sources and balancing it so as to produce internally consistent estimates (see Chapter 8 of this volume).

16.9.2. Trends and cycles in economic time series

The characterisation of trends and cycles has always been at the core of the econometric analysis of time series, since it involves an assessment of the role of supply and demand shock. A first issue is whether the kind of nonstationary behaviour displayed by economic time series is best captured by deterministic or stochastic trends. In the former case it is also said that the series is trend-stationary, implying that it can be decomposed into a deterministic function of time (possibly subject to few large breaks) and a stationary cycle; in the second the series can be made stationary after suitable differencing and so it is said to be difference-stationary or integrated order of order d (or I(d)), where d denotes the power of the stationary inducing transformation, $(1 - L)^d$.

The characterisation of the nature of the series was addressed in a very influential paper by Nelson and Plosser (1982), who adopted the (augmented)

Dickey–Fuller test for testing the hypothesis that the series is I(1) versus the alternative that it is trend-stationary. Using a set of annual US macroeconomic time series they are unable to reject the null for most series and discuss the implications for economic interpretation. Another approach is to test stationarity against a unit root alternative; see Kwiatkowski et al. (1992).

A second issue deals with the specification of a time series model for the trend component for difference-stationary processes and the correlation between the components μ_t and ϵ_t. References on this issue are Watson (1986), Morley et al. (2002) and Proietti (2006).

Another view is that any decomposition $y_t = \mu_t + \epsilon_t$ is just an approximation to a true trend cycle decomposition, but still it may yield sound inferences for a given purpose, such as forecasting more than one step ahead, provided that the parameters are estimated according to a criterion that is consistent with that purpose (e.g. multistep or adaptive estimation. See Cox, 1961, and Tiao and Xu, 1993, for the local level model).

16.9.3. Spurious cycles and the Sluztky–Yule effect

According to Klein (1997) one of the first uses of moving averages was to disguise statistical information, rather than to unveil a hidden signal. The smoothing properties of arithmetic moving averages would have been exploited by the Bank of England in order to conceal the true level of gold reserves, which was falling steeply, whereas the filtered series gave a much more optimistic view. However, this episode just illustrates a bad practice in data publication rather than the inherent limitations of filters: it is the data supplier that has to be blamed and not the instrument. The latter has well known properties, which can be bent to particular needs, but are independent of their uses. Indeed the publication and availability of filtered series is a service to the scientific community provided that the raw observations are also made available and the methods employed are made transparent. Economic analysts, policy makers and the general public do make widespread use of filtered information: the availability and the resources devoted to seasonal adjustment testify this. The same considerations apply: the original unadjusted data should be available along with the adjusted series.

In the analysis of economic time series, there is great concern about the statistical "artifacts" about the economy that could emerge from the application of ad hoc filters (i.e. filters applied regardless of the properties of the series under investigation), such as the Hodrick–Prescott filter (King and Rebelo, 1993; Harvey and Jaeger, 1993; Cogley and Nason, 1995). This issue has particular relevance with respect to the measurement of the business cycle.

The Slutzky–Yule effect is concerned with the fact that a moving average repeatedly applied to a purely random series can introduce artificial cycles (Slutsky, 1937). As such it is a rather natural phenomenon; as a matter of fact, the squared gain $|G(\omega)|^2$ of a filter $w(L)$ (see Section 16.8) can be viewed as the spectral density of the series resulting from the application of the filter $w(L)$ to a white noise sequence. Nevertheless, the application to nonstationary series can create pseudo-cyclical behaviour due to the substantial leakage of power from the long run components. Harvey and Jaeger (1993) show that if the true series is generated by the model $\Delta^d y_t = \xi_t \sim \mathrm{WN}(0, \sigma^2)$, so that it has no cycles, the HP smoothed series will display a periodicity which depends on the value of the smoothness parameter. Filtering will also affect the measurement of comovements between independent time series.

The last phenomenon has many contact points with the problem of spuriousness in correlation and regression considered in Yule (1926) and Granger and Newbold (1974), where two independent white noise series are transformed using an integration filter (i.e. the values are cumulated). Finally, when model-based filters are interpreted, with less *reification*, as devices for extracting components at given frequencies (band-pass filters) as in Gómez (2001), Kaiser and Maravall (2005) and Proietti (2007), the issue of spuriousness is not cogent.

References

Anderson, T.W. (1971). *The Statistical Analysis of Time Series*. Wiley, New York.

Ansley, C., Kohn, R. (1986). Prediction mean square error for state space models with estimated parameters. *Biometrika* **73**, 467–473.

Baxter, M., King, R.G. (1999). Measuring business cycles: Approximate band-pass filters for economic time series. *Review of Economics and Statistics* **81**, 575–593.

Beveridge, S., Nelson, C.R. (1981). A new approach to decomposition of economic time series into permanent and transitory components with particular attention to measurement of the 'business cycle'. *Journal of Monetary Economics* **7**, 151–174.

Boumans, M. (2004). The reliability of an instrument. *Social Epistemology* **18**, 215–246.

Boumans, M. (2005). Economics, strategies in social sciences. In: *Encyclopedia of Social Measurement, vol. 1*. Elsevier, pp. 751–760.

Camba-Mendez, G., Rodriguez-Palenzuela, D. (2003). Assessment criteria for output gap estimates. *Economic Modelling* **20**, 529–562.

Canova, F. (1998). Detrending and business cycle facts. *Journal of Monetary Economics* **41**, 475–512.

Cleveland, W.S. (1979). Robust locally weighted regression and smoothing scatterplots. *Journal of the American Statistical Association* **74**, 829–836.

Cogley, T., Nason, J.M. (1995). Effects of the Hodrick–Prescott filter on trend and difference stationary time series: Implications for business cycle research. *Journal of Economic Dynamics and Control* **19**, 253–278.

Cox, D.R. (1961). Prediction by exponentially weighted moving averages and related methods. *Journal of the Royal Statistical Society, Series B* **23**, 414–422.

Dagum, E.B. (1982). The effects of asymmetric filters of seasonal factor revisions. *Journal of the American Statistical Association* **77**, 732–738.

de Jong, P. (1988). A cross-validation filter for time series models. *Biometrika* **75**, 594–600.

Durbin, J., Koopman, S.J. (2001). *Time Series Analysis by State Space Methods*. Oxford Univ. Press, New York.

Farhmeir, L., Tutz, G. (1994). *Multivariate Statistical Modelling Based Generalized Linear Models*. Springer-Verlag, New-York.

Fan, J., Gjibels, I. (1996). *Local Polynomial Modelling and its Applications*. Chapman and Hall, New York.

Findley, D.F., Monsell, B.C., Shulman, H.B., Pugh, M.G. (1990). Sliding spans diagnostic for seasonal and related adjustments. *Journal of the American Statistical Association* **85**, 345–355.

Findley, D.F., Monsell, B.C., Bell, W.R., Otto, M.C., Chen, B. (1998). New capabilities and methods of the X12-ARIMA seasonal adjustment program. *Journal of Business and Economic Statistics* **16**, 2.

Forni, M., Hallin, M., Lippi, F., Reichlin, L. (2000). The generalized dynamic factor model: Identification and estimation. *Review of Economics and Statistics* **82**, 540–554.

Friedman, J.H. (1984). A variable span smoother. Technical report LCS 05. Department of Statistics, Stanford University, USA.

Gardner, E.S. (1985). Exponential smoothing: The state of the art. *Journal of Forecasting* **4**, 1–28.

Granger, C.W.J., Newbold, P. (1974). Spurious regressions in econometrics. *Journal of Econometrics* **2**, 111–120.

Green, P.J., Silverman, B.V. (1994). *Nonparametric Regression and Generalized Linear Models: A Roughness Penalty Approach*. Chapman & Hall, London.

Gómez, V. (2001). The use of Butterworth filters for trend and cycles estimation in economic time series. *Journal of Business and Economic Statistics* **19**, 365–373.

Hamilton, J.D. (1986). A standard error for the estimated state vector of a state space model. *Journal of Econometrics* **33**, 387–397.

Hamilton, J.D. (2001). A parametric approach to flexible nonlinear inference. *Econometrica* **69**, 537–573.

Harvey, A.C. (1989). *Forecasting, Structural Time Series and the Kalman Filter*. Cambridge Univ. Press, Cambridge, UK.

Harvey, A.C., Jaeger, A. (1993). Detrending, stylised facts and the business cycle. *Journal of Applied Econometric* **8**, 231–247.

Harvey, A.C., Koopman, S.J. (2000). Signal extraction and the formulation of unobserved components. *Econometrics Journal* **3**, 84–107.

Harville, D. (1977). Maximum likelihood approaches to variance components and related problems. *Journal of the American Statistical Association* **72**, 320–340.

Hastie, T.J., Tibshirani, R.J. (1990). *Generalized Additive Models*. Chapman and Hall, London.

Henderson, R. (1916). Note on graduation by adjusted average. *Transaction of the Actuarial Society of America* **17**, 43–48.

Henderson, H.V., Searle, S.R. (1981). On deriving the inverse of a sum of matrices. *SIAM Review* **23**, 53–60.

Hodrick, R., Prescott, E.C. (1997). Postwar US business cycle: An empirical investigation. *Journal of Money, Credit and Banking* **29** (1), 1–16.

Kaiser, R., Maravall, A. (2005). Combining filter design with model-based filtering (with an application to business-cycle estimation). *International Journal of Forecasting* **21**, 691–710.

Kendall, M., Stuart, A., Ord, J.K. (1983). *The Advanced Theory of Statistics, vol. 3*. C. Griffin.

Kenny, P.B., Durbin, J. (1982). Local trend estimation and seasonal adjustment of economic and social time series. *Journal of the Royal Statistical Society, Series A* **145** (I), 1–41.

King, R.G., Rebelo, S. (1993). Low frequency filtering and real business cycles. *Journal of Economic Dynamics and Control* **17**, 251–231.

Klein, J.L. (1997). *Statistical Visions in Time: A History of Time Series Analysis, 1662–1938*. Cambridge Univ. Press. Cambridge, UK.

Kwiatkowski, D., Phillips, P.C.B., Schmidt P., Shin, Y. (1992). Testing the null hypothesis of stationarity against the alternative of a unit root: How sure are we that economic time series have a unit root? *Journal of Econometrics* **44**, 159–178.

Leser, C.E.V. (1961). A simple method of trend construction. *Journal of the Royal Statistical Society, Series B* **23**, 91–107.

Laubach, T. (2001). Measuring the NAIRU: Evidence from seven economies. *Review of Economics and Statistics* **83**, 218–231.

Loader, C. (1999). *Local regression and likelihood*. Springer-Verlag, New York.

Morley, J.C., Nelson, C.R., Zivot, E. (2002). Why are Beveridge–Nelson and unobserved-component decompositions of GDP so different? *Review of Economics and Statistics* **85**, 235–243.

Musgrave, J. (1964). A set of end weights to end all end weights. Working paper. Census Bureau, Washington.

Nadaraya, E.A. (1964). On estimating regression. *Theory of Probability and its Applications* **10**, 186–190.

Nelson, C.R., Plosser, C.I. (1982). Trends and random walks in macroeconomic time series: Some evidence and implications. *Journal of Monetary Economics* **10**, 139–162.

Orphanides, A., van Norden, S. (2002). The unreliability of output gap estimates in real time. *Review of Economics and Statistics* **84**, 569–583.

Patterson, H.D., Thompson, R. (1971). Recovery of inter-block information when block sizes are unequal. *Biometrika* **58**, 545–554.

Pfeffermann, D. (1991). Estimation and seasonal adjustment of population means using data from repeated surveys. *Journal of Business and Economic Statistics* **9**, 163–177. Reprinted in: Harvey, A.C., Proietti, T. (Eds.), *Readings in Unobserved Components Models*. Oxford Univ. Press, Oxford, UK, 2005.

Poirier, D.J. (1973). Piecewise regression using cubic splines, *Journal of the American Statistical Association* **68**, 515–524.

Pollock, D.S.G. (1999). *Handbook of Time Series Analysis, Signal Processing and Dynamics*. Academic Press.

Proietti, T. (2006). Trend-cycle decompositions with correlated components. *Econometric Reviews* **25**, 61–84.

Proietti, T. (2007). On the model based interpretation of filters and the reliability of trend-cycle estimates. *Econometric Reviews*. In press.

Proietti, T., Musso, A., Westermann, T. (2007). Estimating potential output and the output gap for the euro area: A model-based production function approach. *Empirical Economics*. In press.

Quenneville, B., Singh, A.C. (2000). Bayesian prediction mean squared error for state space models with estimated parameters. *Journal of Time Series Analysis* **21**, 219–236.

Robinson, G.K. (1991). That BLUP is a good thing: The estimation of random effects. *Statistical Science* **6** (1), 15–32.

Rossi, A., Planas, C. (2004). Can inflation data improve the real-time reliability of output gap estimates? *Journal of Applied Econometrics* **19**, 121–133.

Ruppert, D., Wand, M.P., Carroll, R.J. (1989). *Semiparametric Regression*. Cambridge Univ. Press.

Scott, A.J., Smith, T.M.F. (1974). Analysis of repeated surveys using time series methods. *Journal of the American Statistical Association* **69**, 647–678.

Slutsky, E. (1937). The summation of random causes at the source of cyclic processes. *Econometrica* **5**, 105.

Smets, F.R. (2002). Output gap uncertainty: Does it matter for the Taylor rule? *Empirical Economics* **27**, 113–129.

Spanos, A. (1999). *Probability Theory And Statistical Inference: Econometric Modeling With Observational Data*. Cambridge Univ. Press, Cambridge, UK.

Staiger, D., Stock, J.H., Watson, M.W. (1997). The NAIRU, unemployment and monetary policy. *Journal of Economic Perspectives* **11**, 33–50.

Stock, J.H., Watson, M.W. (2002a). Macroeconomic forecasting using diffusion indexes. *Journal of Business and Economic Statistics* **20**, 147–162.

Stock, J.H., Watson, M.W. (2002b). Forecasting using principal components from a large number of predictors. *Journal of the American Statistical Association* **97**, 1167–1179.

Tiao, G.C., Xu, D. (1993). Robustness of maximum likelihood estimates for multi-step predictions: The exponential smoothing case. *Biometrika* **80**, 623–641.

Wand, M.P., Jones, M.C. (1995). *Kernel Smoothing*. In: *Monographs on Statistics and Applied Probability 60*. Chapman & Hall.

Watson, G.S. (1964). Smooth regression analysis. *Shankya Series A* **26**, 359–372.

Watson, M.W. (1986). Univariate detrending methods with stochastic trends. *Journal of Monetary Economics* **18**, 49–75. Reprinted in: Harvey, A.C., Proietti, T. (Eds.). *Readings in Unobserved Components Models*. Oxford Univ. Press, Oxford, UK, 2005.

Whittaker, E. (1923). On new method of graduation. *Proceedings of the Edinburgh Mathematical Society* **41**, 63–75.

Yule, G.U. (1926). Why do we sometimese get nonsense-correlations between time series? *Journal of the Royal Statistical Society* **89**, 1

CHAPTER 17

Timeliness and Accuracy

Dennis Fixler

Bureau of Economic Analysis, 1441 L Street NW, Washington, DC 20230, USA
E-mail address: dennis.fixler@bea.gov

Abstract

Government, business and households require timely information to make current period decisions and to cast future plans. Producers of national economic statistics seek to provide their users with timely and accurate estimates of economic activity where the former refers to the release of estimates "close" to the end of the reference period and the latter refers both to the validity of the measure and its reliability. Their ability to do so is constrained by the flow of data and thereby necessitates a flow of vintage estimates that encompass revisions. Though a trade-off between accuracy and timeliness is somewhat intuitive, the paper explains that care should be taken in assessing the impact of the trade-off. In the US, there does not seem be a trade-off between timeliness and accuracy save perhaps between the first and second current quarterly vintages of GDP estimates for the reference period. This finding does not negate the usefulness of having a sequence of revisions because the sequence of revisions incorporates new information which enables users to view the later estimates as closer approximations of the truth, with the latest as being the closest.

17.1. Introduction

Timely information about the economy is used by government, business and households to make current period decisions and to formulate future plans. The value of such information is contingent on its accuracy. If the information turns out to be systematically incorrect or if there is a stream of unscheduled updates then the usefulness of the information is low. It is often perceived that satisfying the timeliness goal comes at the expense of accuracy. Before addressing this issue it is important to examine each aspect.

Timeliness is usually taken to mean the issuance of data at a frequency that users find relevant to their decision making. For example, central bankers, who generally meet at least once a quarter to set monetary policy, desire at least a quarterly frequency. More frequent estimates are useful in that they shed light on recent activities. Businessman continually make decisions about investments, marketing plans and the like but because of the custom of releasing performance estimates on a quarterly basis, they too are interested in at least quarterly frequencies. Households' demand for timely data is more difficult to assess because decisions are on-going. Investors would like daily information if it were possible.

From the perspective of the producers of economic statistics, timeliness requires the ability to collect, edit, process, analyze and publish data at a time period "close" to the reference period. In other words, they are interested in minimizing the time between the end of the reference period and the publishing of statistics describing the economic activity in the reference period. Thus the chief metric for measuring timeliness is the number of days between the end of the reference period and the release of statistics. The determination of the optimal number of days should take into account the needs of both suppliers and demanders of the estimates, including the demanders' need for accuracy of the estimates. The demand for quarterly data would disappear if it were impossible to produce accurate quarterly estimates.

The availability of data on aggregate economic activity can affect the nature of decision-making. Monetary policy-makers often debate the merits of adopting policy rules in lieu of discretionary policy. This debate has been ongoing since Milton Friedman (1968) advocated a non-discretionary monetary policy rule and continues today in regard to the merits of inflation targeting. Because the purpose of policy rules is to reduce the uncertainty of future policy actions, reliance on a rule requires a high degree of accuracy for the measures of economic performance. In the US, monetary policy is decided at the meetings of the Federal Open Market Committee that occur about every 6 weeks, with daily intervention in the money markets to assure that the policy is carried out. Thus if the rule were that some money aggregate should increase at some multiple of Gross Domestic Product (GDP) growth then volatile estimates of GDP growth would produce volatility in the growth in the money aggregate. In contrast, a discretionary policy implicitly assumes that the estimates are "nearly" accurate and allows for corrections or anticipations of corrections. In principle the implementation of rules could also anticipate revisions and accordingly adjust a point of time estimate. Alan Greenspan (2003) expressed the idea succinctly "Rules by their nature are simple, and when significant and shifting uncertainties exist in the economic environment, they cannot substitute for risk-management paradigms, which are far better suited to policymaking."[1]

Paradigms of the economy are not only useful to policy-making, they are also the basis for formulating measures of economic activity. That is to say, national income accountants must first define an interesting and useful measure of aggregate economic activity, and second, they must design methods for estimating the value of that measure, taking the definition as fixed. One cannot address the accuracy of those measures without first establishing their conceptual foundations.

---

[1] Greenspan (2003, p. 6).

In the case of GDP, the most widely used measure of economic activity, the conceptual foundation began to be formed in the in the 17th century, as described in Stone (1986) and in den Butter (this volume), and has undergone changes as economies have changed.

The existence of a trade-off between timeliness and accuracy is somewhat intuitive and has been recognized for quite awhile. If one desires to provide estimates of economic activity near the end of the reference period (or even before) then the amount and quality of the available of the data are going to be less than would be the case if the estimates were to released later. In the first issue of the *Survey of Current Business*, in July 1921, the introduction stated[2]:

> "In preparing these figures every effort is made to secure accuracy and completeness. On the other hand, it is realized that timeliness is often of more value then extreme accuracy. In certain cases it is necessary to use preliminary figures or advance estimates in order to avoid too great delay in publication after the end of each month."

The magnitude of the trade-off, however, has a subjective component.[3] Different users have different preferences for timeliness and, most important, they have different preferences for the optimal combination of accuracy and timeliness. The needs of a central bank policy staff are different from those of business decision-makers. Statistical agencies must balance the preferences of all of their data users.

After discussing some aspects of timeliness and the production of estimates of economic activity, this analysis will turn to the concept of accuracy and the trade-off between the two.[4]

17.2. Timeliness and the Production Process

The production of estimates of economic activity, like any production process, is constrained by labor, capital, and technology. That process concerns the collection of data from different actors in the economy, which is in some sense a separate production process, the review and edit of those data and then the aggregation of them to the level of the desired estimate. All of the necessary data cannot be collected at one time and so statistical agencies experience a flow of data. As a result, economic estimates are produced in vintages, with later vintages incorporating source data that were not previously available. The problem for a statistical agency is to determine the most practical and useful set of release dates; that is, it must set the release dates for the sequence of vintages so that they are "close" to the end of the reference period and progressively incorporate more source data so as to increase their usefulness. For the US, the Bureau of

---

[2] The *Survey of Current Business* is the journal of record for the US estimates of national output and income.

[3] See Rytan (1997).

[4] The analysis will not address price indexes because they are typically provided on a monthly basis and are not the subject of the discussions about the trade-off between timeliness and accuracy.

Economic Analysis has set the following sequence of vintages: the initial current quarterly estimate of GDP is made about 30 days after the reference period, two more estimates are made about 30 and 60 days later and then follow annual and comprehensive revisions that take place even later.[5] The estimates that are released in the first 90 days after the end of the reference period receive most of the attention of policy-makers and decision-makers.

There have been considerable efforts by other countries to produce more timely data as well. Several studies have compared the differences between the US and other countries regarding the timeliness of the data.[6] The general finding was that the US was able to provide estimates relatively sooner after the end of the reference period for a variety of economic measures. A topic of concern in these studies was the need for decision makers to have timely data, with the caveat the data be useful to the decision process – thus release dates cannot be independent of the attending accuracy of the estimates.

17.3. Accuracy

Accuracy is a complex concept that may be thought of as having two aspects, validity and reliability.[7] To illustrate, suppose one is interested in attribute A of the economy and further suppose that one has a measure of A and a process for producing that measure. With respect to validity, one is interested in knowing whether the measure of A yields systematically distorted information. In other words, validity concerns the ability of the measurement procedure to measure what we want it to measure. With respect to reliability, one is interested in knowing whether the measurement process underlying A yields randomly inaccurate results. That is, the notion of reliability concerns the differences between results from successive multiple measurements of A.

To assess the first aspect of accuracy, one generally refers to the difference between an estimate of a measure and its true value. In the natural sciences, the true value is well defined and the assessment of accuracy usually involves the construction of measuring instruments to compare an estimate with the true value. For example, there is a true value of the distance between the earth and the sun, and though there were many estimates of that distance it was not until Michelson and Morely in 1887 developed the interferometer and measured the speed of light that an accurate estimate of the true value was obtained. In the case of a measure of economic activity, the notion of the true value is more subjective and therefore more difficult to define and quantify. Consequently it is more challenging to measure deviations from the true value. For economic statistics, measuring the deviations from the true value includes the application of

[5] See Grimm and Weadock (2006) for a discussion of the flow of data into the early estimates of US GDP.

[6] See, for example, Richard McKenzie (2005).

[7] Hand (2004, p. 129).

statistical theory and an assessment of the source data – the respondents to surveys, regulatory forms (administrative data) and so on – as well as an assessment of the methodologies used to produce the estimates. In the case of survey-based data collections, the attention is on the total survey error, which is comprised of both sampling and non-sampling error. Examples of the evaluations for total survey error include examining how respondents interpret the questions, errors in reviewing and editing response, and errors in imputing missing data.

17.3.1. Accuracy and economic activity

In this paper, the focus will be on the attribute "aggregate economic activity," though the discussion could apply to any economic measure. The notion of measuring economic activity requires the use of economic theories to form the conceptual foundation for the measurement concept and the production boundary for the economy. Both provide the context for defining the "true" value of economic activity that serves as the basis for gaging accuracy. The production boundary limits the set of activities that are deemed admissible to the measure. For example, though household production is clearly an important economic activity, it is treated as outside the boundary of aggregate economic activity measures such as Gross Domestic Product (GDP). Such exclusions apply to a host of non-market transactions.

A prerequisite for a measure of economic activity to achieve the first aspect of accuracy, validity, is the use of classification system grounded in economic principles. For example, to measure the output of all industries in the economy one needs a classification system that organizes firms into industries according to an economics based guideline. The Industrial Standard Industrial Classification of All Economic Activities (ISIC) organizes industries according to similarity in the firm activities while the North American Industrial Classification System (NAICS) organizes industries according to similarity in the firm's production process.

In addition, national economic accounts are designed to provide a system yielding a measure of aggregate production or aggregate economic activity, as well as ways of measuring the component parts. The acceptance of these measures, which is based on a perception of their accuracy, relies in turn on the acceptance of the system.[8] If decision makers had no confidence in the conceptual foundations of the system upon which the estimates are based then it would be meaningless to talk of accuracy – regardless of the statistical properties of the estimates. Manuals such as the one for the United Nations System of National Accounts and other standardizations of techniques provide imprimaturs of general acceptance that in turn provide the aura of objectivity necessary to perceptions of accuracy and confidence in the estimates. In addition, they are

[8] Porter (1995) similarly maintains that it is the creation of rules and their adoption that give rise to the confidence in the quantification of economic activity.

crucial to making the measures replicable, which as in the natural sciences, is a means of verification.

The role of conceptual models in developing economic measures has received much attention in economics. In a broad sense, as noted by Katzner (1991), there must be "reasonable agreement between the relevant measures on the one hand and theories on the other."[9] Or in the words of Koopmans (1947), "Fuller utilization of the concepts and hypotheses of economic theory *as a part of the processes of observation and measurement* promises to be a shorter road, perhaps even the only possible road, to the understanding of economic fluctuations" (emphasis in the original).[10] Increasingly the conceptual foundations of the estimates are driving improvements in the measures. For example, recent methodological innovations in the US national accounts, such as the incorporation of software in investment instead of current expenditure or the implementation of the user cost approach to measuring implicit financial services of banks, were respectively due to the application of notions of capital theory and the theory of financial intermediation. Sometimes there has been tension between the desire to incorporate sophisticated economic theory and the computational techniques available, though the rapid and substantial advancement in computer technology and software capabilities has greatly expanded the capacity of economists to estimate complex economic phenomena.

Defining the conceptual foundation for the measure does not necessarily make it measurable. Morgan (2001) describes measurement strategies as consisting of three elements: principles, judgments and techniques.[11] In particular the notion of aggregate economy activity has largely been viewed as being measured by GDP and its computation incorporates all 3 of these strategies. To illustrate, consider the three common methods of computing GDP. First, one could sum all of the expenditures on final goods and services – that is, the summation is over goods and services produced as final product. Another approach focuses on incomes. The intuition is that expenditures on goods and services result in income for the attending producers and so tallying the income provides another method of computation. A third, production approach says that GDP equals the contribution of each industry to GDP – this is taken as the sum of value added – the difference between revenue and intermediate consumption. In theory all three approaches should provide the same estimate. In practice they do not. One reason is that, depending on the vintage, each method uses different judgments and techniques to fill in missing data. If the 3 methods are thought to provide true measure of aggregate economic activity, then the differences between them can serve as indicators of measurement error. Indeed, in the US, the difference

---

[9] Katzner (1991).

[10] Koopmans (1947, p. 162).

[11] Morgan (2001).

between the income and expenditure measure of GDP is labeled the statistical discrepancy and is often cited as such an indicator.[12]

The measurement of the second aspect of accuracy, reliability, focuses on the revisions to the vintages of estimates that arise from the flow of source data. It is this dimension of accuracy that is tied to timeliness.

17.4. Timeliness and Accuracy

The relationship between timeliness and accuracy partly depends on the production process for the estimates. Estimates compiled from survey-based data have a number of sources of errors; inadequate sampling, concealment and falsification by respondents, inadequately trained collectors and a host of other sources that are broadly classified into the category of total survey error. For all estimates there is also potential error in the reconciliation of the available data and the measurement objective. In other words, how are the requirements of the measure satisfied when there are gaps in the underlying data? The uncertainty surrounding the production of information and the validity of the measures bears on the usefulness of the data released at any period of time. The intuition underlying the trade-off between timeliness and uncertainty is that the longer one waits the error in the data arising from these sources is reduced. As stated in Bier and Ahert (2001):

> "The main reason is that improving timeliness forces the producers to compile the indicators from incomplete source data. As more data become available afterwards, a so called recompilation process produced different results and so revisions. The ECB (European Central Bank) considers it necessary to balance timeliness and accuracy. To determine the optimal balance is not straightforward."[13]

Rytan (1997) suggested that the balance between timeliness and accuracy can be conceptualized by adhering to the intuition of optimization theory: consumers of data choose the combination of timeliness and accuracy according to their preference structure, thereby balancing the benefits and costs of different combinations while producers of data choose the combination of timeliness and accuracy subject to a budget constraint. Oberg (2002) postulated that there can be improvements to timeliness without any cost in accuracy when the organization is operating inefficiently.[14] For example, if the process yields a first estimate 60 days after the end of the reference period, it may be possible to reduce the lag to 30 days without any erosion in accuracy. Indeed such has been the discussion within the OECD about the production of "flash" estimates of GDP as discussed in Shearing (2003).[15] The point is that the trade-off may not be continuous and depends on the efficiency of the production process.

---

[12] Many countries allocate the difference across the sectors of the economy and do not publish the difference. In the US accounts, the sum of industry value added is constrained to equal GDP.

[13] Bier and Ahert (2001, p. 4).

[14] Oberg (2002).

[15] Shearing (2003).

17.4.1. Revision magnitudes as indicators of accuracy

As Bowman (1964) put it: "Revisions in the data reflect the needs for timeliness, frequency of reporting and accuracy. Timeliness can only be obtained by using partial information."[16] Here, revision patterns are used to discuss the timeliness and accuracy dimensions for US GDP estimates for which the latest estimates are treated as the most accurate – the latest estimates are viewed as closest to the true measure. Thus it is the second aspect of accuracy, reliability, that is the focus of concern when evaluating revision magnitudes.[17]

The study of revision patterns in US GDP estimates has a long history – starting with Jaszi (1965). Revisions primarily come from 5 sources: (1) Replacement of early source data with later, more comprehensive data; (2) Replacement of judgmental estimates with estimates based on source data; (3) Introductions of changes in definitions and estimating procedures; (4) Updating of seasonal adjustment factors; and (5) Corrections of errors in source data or computations. Aside from examining the statistical properties of revisions such as mean revision, mean absolute revision and standard deviation of revision, one can use the revisions to assess the quality of the GDP estimates in the context of how well those estimates perform with respect to four basic questions:[18]

1. Do the estimates provide a reliable indication of the direction in which real aggregate economic activity is moving?
2. Do they provide a reliable indication of whether the change in real aggregate economic activity is accelerating or decelerating?
3. Do they provide a reliable indication of whether the change in real aggregate economic activity differs significantly from the longer run?
4. Do they provide a reliable indication of cyclical turning points?

To answer theses questions one must pick the standard of measure and, as mentioned, that is usually chosen to be the latest estimates. The latest estimates provide the most informed picture of aggregate economic activity for the time period of the current quarterly estimates. In the US, the latest estimates embody additions to the source data that were unavailable when the current quarterly estimates were made and have also undergone some comprehensive revisions – in these revisions the US not only incorporates improved source data – typically data from the Economic Censuses, but also the definitions of the measures. Changes in definitions are made to adapt the measures to a changing economy. Comprehensive revisions are performed about every 5 years and historical series are revised as far back as possible. For example, the 1996 comprehensive revision changed the name of the government component of GDP

---

[16] Bowman (1964).

[17] A caveat should be kept in mind when evaluating revisions to aggregate statistics: a zero revision does not imply the absence of error. One way of thinking about this is to consider that an aggregate estimate can have a zero revision while the components can have large but offsetting revisions.

[18] See Grimm and Parker (1998).

from "government expenditures" to "government consumption expenditures and gross investment" to reflect the idea that some expenditures were more accurately treated as investment than as expenditures and this change was carried as far back as 1929. This is another example of the point made earlier that the underlying measurement concept plays a role in the measurement of the "true" value and that this concept can evolve as knowledge and measurement techniques improve.

17.4.2. The case of the GDP flash estimate and the perceived trade-off

To satisfy the needs of policy makers an estimate of the Gross National Product (the preferred measure of aggregate measure of US economic activity before 1992) was made 15 days *before* the end of the reference period and provided to policy makers – the Council of Economic Advisors, the Office of Management and Budget, the Federal Reserve Board, and the Treasury and Commerce Departments – and was not publicly released.[19] The estimates were first produced in the mid 1960s and the confidentiality of the estimates did not become an issue until the early 1980s when these estimates somehow leaked into the public domain. Widespread interest in these early estimates resulted in BEA deciding, in September 1983, to release them to the public as the minus 15-day estimate – the moniker "flash" became attached afterward. The remaining vintages of the estimates were released about 15 days, 45 days, and 75 days after the end of the reference period.[20] There was considerable discussion about the public release of the flash estimate – in particular whether the subsequent revisions would be confusing to the public. In an attempt to minimize such confusion, the flash estimates were characterized as projections because they were being formed on partial data. Nevertheless, the concern persisted and it was reinforced when revisions to the flash received much attention. Characteristic of these concerns is the following excerpt from a New York Times editorial on September 9, 1985[21]:

> According to the Commerce Department's "flash" report, the economy grew at an annual rate of 2.8 percent in the third quarter. Don't bet your savings on it. For the last 3 years, this quarterly report has been at least one-half point off the mark every time; once it was three points off. A statistic so dependently wrong is one to do without.

---

[19] More specifically these agencies were provided with estimates of current and constant dollar GNP as well as the related measures of price change, and charges against GNP and its components. These estimates were produced by the Department of Commerce first in the Office of Business Economics and then the Bureau of Economic Analysis as a result of a re-organization.

[20] The estimates that were released as part of the flash were: GNP in current and constant dollars, GNP fixed weight price index and GNP implicit price deflator – not exactly the full set that was provided under limited distribution.

[21] Note that the quote focuses on the magnitude of specific revisions and not on statistical measures of reliability such as mean and standard deviation.

Such reviews prompted much discussion about whether the flash should continue.

Given the fact that revisions are a necessary part of the process of providing timely estimates, the central issue concerned the performance of the flash estimate with respect to the 15-day estimate. In other words, as the quote from the New York Times suggests, would users be better off if the flash estimate were dropped and the first estimate was released 15 days after the end of the quarter?

The validity of the flash estimate was first assessed on three non-statistical metrics: accuracy as an indicator of whether GNP is increasing or decreasing, by approximately how much, and whether the change is larger or smaller than the change in the previous quarter. These metrics convey the idea that although the flash estimate was expressed in terms of a point estimate it was not intended to provide such an estimate of GNP growth but rather to provide – on the basis of incomplete data – a perception of how the economy was performing relative to the estimates of the previous quarter. An internal BEA study found that the revisions to the flash estimate relative to the later vintage estimates, especially the 15-day estimate, performed with respect to the 3 metrics in a way that was not significantly different from those of the 15-day estimate. Despite this evidence, the perception that the flash estimate was providing policy makers and decision makers with erroneous information about the economy persisted and in January 1986 the flash estimate was discontinued by BEA at the direction of the Commerce Department.

In an unrelated study, Mankiw and Shapiro (1966) examined the revision pattern of BEA estimates including the flash estimate for the period 1976, Quarter 1 to 1982, Quarter 4. Their central emphasis was whether the revisions were due to the availability of new information or due to measurement error. If the flash estimate of GNP was an efficient estimate, in the sense that it incorporated all available information, then the standard deviation of the 15-day estimate should be higher. In addition the correlation between the revision from the flash to the 15-day estimate and the 15-day estimate should be significant. Table 17.1 is part of their findings.

Note that the standard deviation of the 15-day estimate is higher than that of the flash. They also found that the standard deviation in the revision of the growth rates from the flash estimate to the 15-day estimate was 1.2 percentage

Table 17.1: Summary Statistics GNP Growth Rates, 1976 Q1 to 1982 Q4, Percent at annual rate

	Mean	St. Dev.	Revision correlation
Nominal GNP			
Flash (15 day)	9.0	4.0	
15-Day	9.0	4.6	0.57 (significant at 1% level)
Constant Dollar GNP			
Flash	1.7	3.8	
15-Day	2.0	4.0	0.35 (not significant)

points at an annual rate, for nominal GNP, and 1.0 percentage point for constant dollar GNP. This revision was significantly correlated with the 15-day estimate in the case of nominal GNP and not significantly correlated in the case of constant dollar GNP (the third column in the table above).[22] These findings suggest that the accuracy of the flash estimates was about the same as the 15-day estimates and that the revision was due to the availability of new information and not measurement error – that is to say, the flash estimates were efficient estimates.

The case of the flash estimate illustrates that the presumption of a trade-off between timeliness and accuracy in conjunction with routine revisions can lead to an inaccurate assessment of an estimate's performance. In this case the misperception of inaccuracy undermined its usefulness and led to its discontinuance.

17.4.3. The current picture

In turns out that even with BEA's current estimates and procedures, there does not seem be a trade-off between timeliness and accuracy save perhaps between the first and second current quarterly vintages of the estimates. Table 17.2 illustrates the mean revisions for different vintages of GDP growth in the period 1983–2002. The current quarterly vintages are now labeled Advance, Preliminary and Final estimates, which are respectively released about 30, 60 and 90 days after the end of the reference period. Note that if the Advance estimate were to be eliminated so that the first estimate would be the Preliminary estimate then there would be a modest drop in the average revision. Instead of observing a 0.09 percentage point revision from the Advance to the Final, users would see a –0.01 percentage point revision in the Preliminary estimate.[23] It thus appears that new information is received in the time between the Advance and Preliminary estimate and that for these two vintages there is a trade-off between timeliness and accuracy.[24] This result also holds when one looks at the revision to the current quarterly estimates using the 1st annual revision as the standard – the magnitude of the revision is greatest for the Advance estimate. The revisions with respect to the Latest estimates are large because these estimates contain all available information – this includes new source data and changes in methodology and definitions occurring with comprehensive revisions. None of the mean revisions, however, are statistically significantly different from zero. This result does not negate the usefulness of having a sequence of revisions. Because the sequence of revisions incorporates new information, mostly new data but also, especially for the later revisions, new estimation techniques and new definitions,

---

[22] The revision is not correlated with the flash estimate in either case.

[23] The magnitudes of the revision with respect to the latest estimates reflect the definitional changes that occur in comprehensive revisions. These changes have often increased the level and rate of increase of GDP. See for example Fixler and Grimm (2005).

[24] More than half of the advance estimates are based at least in part on trend-based estimates. A large majority of these are replaced with annual frequency data in the first annual estimates. See Grimm and Weadock (2006, p. 12).

Table 17.2: Mean Revisions to Successive Vintages of Estimates of Quarterly Changes in Real GDP to Later Vintages of Estimates, 1983–2002/1/
[Percentage points]

Vintage of estimate	Vintage of revision used as standard			
	Preliminary	Final	1st annual	Latest/2
Advance	0.09	0.09	0.06	0.42
Preliminary		−0.01	−0.03	0.32
Final			−0.02	0.33
1st annual				0.35

Notes: 1. 2001 for 1st annual.
2. The magnitudes of revision using the latest estimate reflect the definitional changes that occur in comprehensive revisions. These changes have often increased the level and rate of increase of GDP.

Table 17.3: Mean Absolute Revisions to Successive Vintages of Estimates of Quarterly Changes in Real GDP to Later Vintages of Estimates, 1983–2002/1/
[Percentage points]

Vintage of estimate	Vintage of revision used as standard			
	Preliminary	Final	1st annual	Latest
Advance	0.51	0.59	1.12	1.29
Preliminary		0.26	0.94	1.26
Final			0.94	1.32
1st annual				1.14

Note: 2001 for 3rd annual.

users can view the later estimates as closer approximations of the truth, with the latest as being the closest.

Similar findings hold true for the mean absolute revisions, as can be seen in Table 17.3. These revisions are computed without regard to sign and they provide an idea of the dispersion of the revision. Note that once again elimination of the Advance estimate – in other words, not releasing the Advance estimate and waiting until all of the data used in the Preliminary estimate are available – would result in substantially lower mean absolute revisions; with the Final as the standard the revision would fall to 0.26 percentage points, and with the first annual estimate the reduction is from 1.12 percentage points to 0.94 percentage points. Note that with the latest estimates as the standard there is very little difference in the revision between the Advance, Preliminary and Final estimates.

As mentioned, the revisions to the vintages of the estimates can also be evaluated in terms of the four questions listed earlier. For the period 1983–2002, the quarterly estimates of constant dollar GDP: successfully indicated the direction of change in real GDP 98 percent of the time; correctly indicated whether real GDP was accelerating or decelerating 74 percent of the time; indicated whether real GDP growth was high relative to trend about two-thirds of the time and whether it was low relative to the trend about three-fifths of the time; and successfully indicated the 2 cyclical troughs in the period but only one of the cyclical peaks.[25]

17.5. Summary and Conclusion

Producers of national economic statistics seek to provide their users with timely and accurate estimates of economic activity, especially aggregate economic activity. Their ability to do so is constrained by the flow of data. Thus the problem for national statistic offices is to determine how close the release dates for estimates can be to the end of the reference period and at the same time provide accurate estimates. Because the data come from a variety of sources, many of which are not based on probabilistic samples, it is not possible to determine how close the estimates are to the true value in a statistical sense. Furthermore, the concept of the true value depends on a host of definitions of economic activity as well as the underlying conceptual framework of the economy.

Intuitively, there should be a trade-off between timeliness and accuracy because early estimates are based on less data than later estimates. Yet if the methods used to project the missing data are efficient so that the projections have small error, then it need not be true that there is a meaningful trade-off. This inference follows from the BEA experience with the flash estimates. However, this is not say that the early estimates are forecasts, although the distinction between forecasts and early actual values is not sharp because each is simply an estimate based on partial incomplete information.[26] If forecasts are admitted into the competition for accurate estimates of the "true" nature of economic activity, then an assessment of the trade-off ought to include the benefits to users of having information *before* the reference period ends.

An analysis of data on revisions to US GDP estimates yields the following conclusions about the trade-off between timeliness and accuracy. First, there are modest average revisions from the advance to the two later current quarterly estimates. Second, revisions to the latest estimates largely reflect definitional revisions that adapt the US National Income and Product Accounts to a changing economy. Third, relative to the latest estimates the three current quarterly vintages of GDP estimates have about the same average revision without regard to sign. One can therefore conclude that there is little cost, in accuracy, of making advance estimates containing relatively a large number of trend-based projections. Waiting a year to publish estimates of GDP would reduce the average revision without regard to sign of real GDP by only 0.1 to 0.2 percentage points.

Research is continuing on how to improve the efficiency of the estimates. Recently, in the US the use of real time data (original and unrevised data that are available at the time the estimates are made) has been examined to see if they

---

[25] The last recession in the period occurred from March 2001 (peak) to November 2001 (trough) and the short duration probably played a role in the mis-estimation of the peak.

[26] McNees (1986).

can predict revisions or provide better estimates. This research focuses on data that are available at the time that the estimate is being made but not included in the set of data upon which the estimates are based. In effect, such studies seek to examine whether the estimates can be considered as rational – in the sense that all of the available information is used to formulate the estimate.[27] Fixler and Grimm (2006) examined whether the revisions to GDP estimates are rational with respect to real time data and found that while such data can somewhat predict revisions, thereby making the GDP estimates irrational, there may not be much advantage in incorporating the additional data. Relatedly, Fixler and Nalewaik (2006) use the difference between the income and expenditure approaches to GDP measurement as measure of differences in available data, along with the attending to revisions to the estimates, to provide a better estimate of the "true" GDP.

Acknowledgements

I would like to thank Adam Copeland, Bruce Grimm, Steve Landefeld, and Marshall Reinsdorf for their valuable comments. The views expressed do not represent those of the Bureau of Economic Analysis or the Department of Commerce.

References

Bier, W., Ahert, H. (2001). Trade-off between timeliness and accuracy. ECB Requirements for General Economic Statistics. Article published in Dutch in *Economisch Statistische Berichten (ESB)* 15 March, 4299.

Bowman, R. (1964). Comments on Qui Numerare Incipit Errare Incipit by Oskar Morgenstern. *American Statistician*, June, 10–20.

Fixler, D., Grimm, B. (2006). GDP estimates: Rationality tests and turning point performance. *Journal of Productivity Analysis* **25**, 213–229.

Fixler, D., Nalewaik, J. (2006). News, Noise and Estimates of the "True" Unobserved State of the Economy, unpublished paper, February.

Fixler, D., Grimm, B. (2005). Reliability of the NIPA estimates of US economic activity. *Survey of Current Business*, February, 8–19.

Friedman, M. (1968). The role of monetary policy. *The American Economic Review* **58** (1), 1–17.

Greenspan, A. (2003). Opening remarks in *Monetary Policy and Uncertainty: Adapting to a Changing Economy*. Federal Reserve Bank of Kansas City Symposium, Jackson Hole, Wyoming, August.

Grimm, B., Parker, R. (1998). Reliability of the quarterly and annual estimates of GDP and gross domestic income. *Survey of Current Business*, Decemver, 12–21.

Grimm, B., Weadock, T. (2006). Gross domestic product: Revisions and source data. *Survey of Current Business*, February, 11–15.

Hand, D. (2004). *Measurement Theory and Practice*. Arnold, London.

---

27 The notion comes from the rational expectations literature. Expectations are rationally formed if an economic agent uses all of the available information.

Jaszi, G. (1965). The Quarterly Income and Product Accounts of the United States: 1942–1962. In: *Short-Term National Accounts and Long-Term Economic Growth.* Studies in Income and Wealth, edited by Simon Goldberg and Phyllis Deane, 100-187. London: Bowes & Bowes, for the International Association for Research in Income and Wealth.

Katzner, D. (1991). Our mad rush to measure how did we get into this mess? *Methodus*, December.

Koopmans, T.C. (1947). Measurement without theory. *The Review of Economic Statistics* **29** (3), August, 161–172.

Mankiw, G., Shapiro, M. (1966). News or noise: An analysis of GDP revisions. *Survey of Current Business*, May, 20–25.

McKenzie, R. (2005). Improving the timeliness of short-term economic statistics. Working paper No 5. OECD Statistics.

McNees, S. (1986). Estimating GNP: The trade-off between timeliness and accuracy, January, 3–10.

Morgan, M.S. (2001). Making measurement instruments. In: Klein, Morgan (Eds.), *The Age of Economic Measurement, Annual Supplement to Volume 23, History of Political Economy*. Duke Univ. Press, pp. 235–251.

Oberg, S. (2002). Quality and timeliness of statistics: Is it really a trade-off? Paper presented at 88th DGINS Conference Palermo, 19 and 20 September.

Porter, T.M. (1995). *Trust in Numbers*. Princeton Univ. Press, Princeton, NJ.

Rytan, J. (1997). Timeliness and reliability: A necessary trade-off. *Economic Statistics, Accuracy, Timeliness and Relevance*. Kenesy, Z. (Ed.), US Department of Commerce, Bureau of Economic Analysis, Washington, DC, June.

Shearing, M. (2003). Producing flash estimates of GDP. Recent Developments and the Experiences of Selected OECD countries. Paper prepared for UN Economic Commission of Europe for discussion at OECD Meeting of National Accounts Experts, Paris, 10 October.

Stone, R. (1986). Nobel memorial lecture 1984: The accounts of society. *Journal of Applied Econometrics* 1, 5–28.

Author Index

Numbers in *italics* indicate page numbers when the names appear in the reference list.

Ackerman, F., 354, *355*
Ackland, R., 109, *131*
Adams, E.W., 31, *36*
Afriat, S.N., 172, *185*
Ahert, H., see Bier, W., *426*
Alberini, A., 369, *374*
Alder, K., 345, 347, *355*
Allen, R.G.D., 162, *185*
Anderson, R., see Dewald, W., *338*
Anderson, T.W., 380, 404, *409*
Ansley, C., 406, *409*
Armstrong, D.M., 24, 34, *37*
Armstrong, K., 166, *185*
Asheim, G.B., 218, *227*
Atkinson, A.C., 360, *374*
Attanasio, O.P., 275, *291*
Avery, R.B., 373, *374*
Axilrod, S.H., 125, *131*

Backhouse, R.E., 5, 8, 11, 127, 135, 140, 145–151, *151*, *152*, 207, 252, 327, 335, *338*
Balk, B.M., 165–167, 173, 175, 178, 182, *186*
Ballinger, T.P., 85, *103*
Balzer, W., 280, *291*
Balzer, W., see Stegmüller, W., *293*
Banerjee, A., 262, *265*
Banerjee, A.N., 298, 305, 308, 310, 318, *318*
Banerjee, K.S., 164, *186*
Banister, H., see Ferguson, A., *37*
Bank of England, 148, 151, *152*
Banzhaf, S., 109, *131*
Barlas, Y., 246, 247, *247*
Barnett, W., 127, *131*
Bartlett, F.C., see Ferguson, A., *37*
Bartlett, R.J., see Ferguson, A., *37*
Baxter, M., 405, *409*
Beatty, J., see Gigerenzer, G., *355*
Becker, G., 363, *374*
Beesley, P.A.A., see Griffiths, W.E., *318*
Bell, W.R., see Findley, D.F., *409*
Benoit, E., 69, *76*
Bernanke, B.S., 276, 279, *291*
Beveridge, S., 407, *409*
Beveridge, W.H., 261, *265*
Bibon, M., see Makridakis, S., *339*
Bier, W., 419, *426*
Bishop, R.C., 361, *374*
Bjerkholt, O., 207, *227*
Blackorby, C., 164, *186*
Blades, D., 215, *227*
Blanchard, O.J., 276, *291*
Blaug, M., 135, *152*, 281, *291*
Bleichrodt, H., 102, *103*
Bloem, A.M., 216, *228*
Blow, L., 172, *186*
Board of Governors of the Federal Reserve System, 111, 112, *131*
Bollerslev, T., 262, *265*
Boniolo, G., 264, *265*
Bordo, M.D., 121, 127, *131*
Bos, F., 193, 195, 196, 216, 217, *228*
Bos, F., see Bloem, A.M., *228*
Bosch, P.R., see Hueting, R., *228*
Bosch, P.R., see de Boo, A.J., *228*
Botelho, A., 80, *103*
Boumans, M., 8, 11, 12, *17*, 31, 35, *37*, 54, *76*, 105, 107, 108, 116, 122, *131*, 137, 151, *152*, 165, *186*, 194, *228* 251, 252, 263–265, *265*, 275, 286, *291*, 380, 405, *409*
Bowley, A.L., 162, *186*
Bowman, R., 420, *426*
Box, G.E.P., 257, 259, 261, *265*
Bradley, F.H., 34, *37*
Brian, E., 346, *355*
Bridgman, P.W., 25, *37*, 47, *76*
Brillinger, D.R., 261, *266*
Bronfenbrenner, M., 328, *338*
Brown, T.M., 256, *266*
Brown, W., see Ferguson, A., *37*
Bru, B., 347, *355*
Buchholz, W., see Asheim, G.B., *227*
Buglione, L., see Carbone, P., *77*
Burns, A.F., 260, *266*

Cahan, D., 354, *355*
Caldwell, B.J., 281, *291*
Camba-Mendez, G., 262, *266*, 406, *409*

Camerer, C.F., 357, *374*
Camerer, C.F., see Harless, D.W., *103*
Campbell, N.R., 22, *37*, 232, *247*
Campbell, N.R., see Ferguson, A., *37*
Canova, F., 406, *409*
Cao, T.Y., 271, *291*
Carbone, E., 85, *103*
Carbone, P., 41, *77*
Carnap, R., 25, *37*, 265, *266*, 281, *291*
Carroll, R.J., see Ruppert, D., *411*
Cartwright, N., 145, *152*, 238, *247*, 263, *266*
Catton, P., 32, *37*
Chang, H., 120, *131*
Chao, H.-K., 7, 11, 13, 23, *37*, 107, 127, *131*, 194, 253, 282, 290, *291*, 298, *318*
Charness, G., 82, *103*
Chatfield, C., 333, *338*
Chaudhuri, P., 360, *375*
Chen, B., see Findley, D.F., *409*
Chou, R.Y., see Bollerslev, T., *265*
Chow, G.C., 257, *266*
Chow, S., 329, *338*
Christ, C.F., 253, 256, *266*, 288, 289, *291*
Clark, C., 222, *228*
Cleveland, W.S., 392, 402, *409*
Cochrane, D., 256, *266*
Cogley, T., 408, *409*
Cohen, M.R., 23, 25, 34, *37*
Cohen, R.S., *37*, 39
Coller, M., 80, *103*
Comim, F., 213, 214, *228*
Cook, R.D., 298, *318*
Cooley, T.F., 246, *247*, 278, 288, *291*, 325, 327, *338*
Cox, D.R., 408, *409*
Cox, J.C., 80, 82, 102, *103*
Craik, K.J.W., see Ferguson, A., *37*
Cramer, J.S., 128, *131*
Crawford, I., see Blow, L., *186*
Cubitt, R.P., 363, 364, *375*

D'Agostini, G., 63, *77*
Dagum, E.B., 387, *409*
Daston, L., see Gigerenzer, G., *355*
Davenant, C., 253, *266*
Davidson, J.E.H., 280, *291*
Davis, G.C., 290, *291*
Davis, H., see Stevens, S.S., *38*
Davison, M.L., 30, *37*
de Boer, B., see Hueting, R., *228*
de Boo, A.J., 223, *228*
de Haan, M., 223, *228*
de Jong, P., 401, *409*
De Leeuw, J., 264, *266*
de Marchi, N., see Kim, J., *292*, *339*
De Morgan, A., 20, *37*
de Ruijter, W.A., see Keuning, S.J., *229*
de Vos, A.F., see Magnus, J.R., *229*
Deaton, A., 179, *186*
DeGroot, M., see Becker, G., *374*
Dellink, R., see Gerlagh, R., *228*
Demiralp, S., 272, *291*
den Bakker, G.P., 196, *228*
den Butter, F.A.G., 8, 11, 17, 110, 126, 136, 141, 148, *152*, 158, 199, 203, 204, 218, 222, 223, *228*, 247, 415
Deneffe, E., see Wakker, P.P., *104*
Dewald, W., 334, *338*
di Cagno, D., see Hey, J.D., *375*
Diamond, P., 149, *152*
Diebond, F.X., 262, *266*
Diewert, W.E., 155, 164, 166, 167, 170, 172, 174, 178, *186*, 220, *228*
Diewert, W.E., see Reinsdorf, M.B., *188*
Díez Calzada, J.A., 280, *291*
Dingle, H., 19, *37*
Don, F.J.H., 194, 204, *228*
Donohue, J., III, 325, *338*
Doob, J.L., 316, *318*
Dorfman, A., see Reinsdorf, M.B., *188*
Dowell, M.E., see Hoover, K.D., *267*
Downward, P., 148, *152*
Dowrick, S., 172, *186*
Dowrick, S., see Ackland, R., *131*
Drever, J., see Ferguson, A., *37*
Dufour, J.-M., 302, *318*
Durbin, J., 257, *266*, 380, 401, *409*
Durbin, J., see Kenny, P.B., *410*

Eckel, C., 360, 373, *375*
Ehemann, C., 178, *186*
Ehemann, C., see Reinsdorf, M.B., *188*
Eichhorn, W., 162, 165, 175, 177, *186*
Elkana, Y., see Cohen, R.S., *37*
Elliot, G., 329, *338*
Ellis, B., 235, *247*
Eltetö, Ö., 166, *187*
Engle, R.F., 260, 262, *266*, 288, *291*
Engle-Warnick, J., 80, *103*
Engle-Warnick, J., see Eckel, C., *375*
Epstein, R.J., 271, 272, *291*
Ericsson, N., see Hendry, D.F., *338*
Ernst, C., see Michell, J., *38*
Evans, M., 257, *266*
Ezrahi, Y., 349, *355*

Falmange, J.-C., 287, *291*

Fan, J., 380, 388, *409*
Farhmeir, L., 380, *409*
Fechner, G.T., 35, *37*
Federal Open Market Committee, 123, 124, *131*
Fedorov, V.V., 360, *375*
Ferger, W.F., 154, *187*
Ferguson, A., 23, 25, *37*
Findley, D.F., 383, 406, *409*
Finkelstein, L., 7, *17*, 60, *77*, 106, 130, *131*, 238, *247*
Fisher, I., 115–119, *131*, 158, 161, 167, 176, 177, *187*
Fisher, W., 113, *131*
Fisher, W.C., 154, *187*
Fixler, D., 11, 16, 17, 126, 215, 343, 351, 423, 426, *426*
Flavin, M.A., 275, *291*
Ford, I., 360, *375*
Forni, M., 262, *266*, 407, *410*
Foulloy, L., see Benoit, E., *76*
Frängsmyr, T., 345, *355*
Franklin, A., 246, *247*
Frege, G., 21, *37*
Freyens, B., see Ackland, R., *131*
Friedman, B.M., 123, 124, 126, *131*
Friedman, J.H., 392, *410*
Friedman, M., 144, 150, 151, *152*, 243, *247*, 282, *291*, 324, *338*, 414, *426*
Frisch, R., 155, 162, *187*, 251, 253, *266*
Fuchs, V., 321, *338*
Fudenberg, D., 82, *103*
Fuller, S.W., see Park, J., *319*
Funke, H., 165, *187*

Gardner, E.S., 400, *410*
Garter, C.N., see de Boo, A.J., *228*
Geary, R.C., 166, *187*
Georgeseu-Roegen, N., 144, *152*
Gerlagh, R., 223, *228*
Ghiblawi, H., see Papell, D., *339*
Gibbard, A., 150, *152*, 321, *338*
Giere, R.N., 284, 285, *292*, 298, *318*
Gigerenzer, G., 331, *338*, 344, *355*
Gilbert, C.L., 12, 145, 253, 255, 260, *266*, 271, 272
Gilbert, C.L., see Qin, D., *268*
Gillispie, C.C., 345, 347, 354, *355*
Gini, C., 162, *187*
Girshick, M.A., 273, *292*
Gjibels, I., see Fan, J., *409*
Godfrey, L.G., 315, *318*
Goldberger, A.S., see Klein, L.R., *267*
Goldfarb, R., 147, *152*, 328, 337, *338*
Golinski, J., 346, *355*
Gómez, V., 409, *410*
Gordon, R.J., 257, *266*
Gorter, C.N., see Bloem, A.M., *228*
Gould, J.P., 127, *131*
Granger, C.W.J., 257, 261, 262, *266*, *267*, 409, *410*
Granger, C.W.J., see Elliot, G., *338*
Granger, C.W.J., see Engle, R.F., *266*, *291*
Green, D., 360, 361, *375*
Green, P.J., 380, 397, 401, *410*
Greene, C., 326, 327, 329, *338*
Greene, W.H., 362, 369, *375*
Greenspan, A., 414, *426*
Greenstein, B., 261, *267*
Grether, D.M., 85, 86, *103*, 364, *375*
Grier, D., 344, *355*
Griffiths, W.E., 303, *318*
Griliches, Z., 257, *267*
Grimm, B., 416, 420, 423, *426*
Grimm, B., see Fixler, D., *426*
Guild, J., see Ferguson, A., *37*
GUM, 4, 15, *17*

Haavelmo, T., 9, 17, *18*, 234, 240, *247*, 253, 254, 264, *267*, 272, 273, *291*
Haavelmo, T., see Girshick, M.A., *292*
Haberler, G., 162, *187*
Hacker, G., see Funke, H., *187*
Hall, R.E., 274, 275, *291*, *292*
Hallin, M., see Forni, M., *410*
Hamerling, L., see Ackerman, F., *355*
Hamermesh, D., 333, *338*
Hamilton, J.D., 262, *267*, 272, *292*, 380, 406, *410*
Hamilton, J.T., see Viscusi, W.K., *340*
Hamminga, B., see Balzer, W., *291*
Hand, D., 416, *426*
Hands, D.W., 281, *292*
Hanemann, M., 358, 369, *375*
Hansen, A., 123, *131*
Hansen, L.P., 275, *292*, 327, *338*
Hansen, L.P., see Avery, R.B., *374*
Harbaugh, W.T., 82, *103*
Harless, D.W., 85, *103*
Harrison, G.W., 10, *18*, 80, 83, 85, 86, 88, 90, 96, 101, 102, *103*, *104*, 298, *318*, 365
Harrison, G.W., see Botelho, A., *103*
Harrison, G.W., see Coller, M., *103*
Hartley, J.E., 275, *292*
Harvey, A.C., 380, 395, 400, 401, 408, 409, *410*
Harville, D., 401, *410*

Hastie, T.J., 380, 402, *410*
Hatanaka, M., see Granger, C.W.J., *266*
Hausman, D.M., 135, 137, 142, 145, *152*, 263, 264, *267*, 337, *338*
Hausman, J.A., 257, *267*
Heath, T.L., 20, *37*
Heberlein, T.A., see Bishop, R.C., *374*
Heckman, J., see Hansen, L.P., *338*
Heidelberger, M., 35, *37*, 234, 235, *247*, *248*
Heilbron, J.L., 344, *355*
Heilbron, J.L., see Frängsmyr, T., *355*
Helliwell, J.F., 222, *228*
Henderson, H.V., 386, 398, *410*
Henderson, R., 382, 399, *410*
Hendry, D.F., 253, 254, 258, 260, *267*, 271, 272, 276, 277, 279, 287, 290, *292*, 324, *338*
Hendry, D.F., see Davidson, J.E.H., *291*
Hensher, D.A., see Louviere, J.J., *375*
Hesse, M.B., 285, *292*
Heston, A., see Summers, R., *229*
Hey, J.D., 85, *104*, 358, 369, *375*
Hill, R.J., 167, 168, *187*
Hodrick, R., 379, 399, 400, *410*
Hofkes, M.W., see Gerlagh, R., *228*
Hölder, O., 19, 20, 35, *37*, 38
Holt, C.A., 82, 88, 90, *104*, 360, 371, *375*
Holtrop, M.W., 120, *131*
Hood, W., 253, *267*
Hoover, K.D., 12, *18*, 141, 145, 147, *152*, 253, *267*, 272, 274, 289, *292*, 325–327, 329, 330, 332, *338*
Hoover, K.D., see Demiralp, S., *291*
Hoover, K.D., see Hartley, J.E., *292*
Hope, C., 223, *228*
Horowitz, J., 329, *338*
Hotz, V.J., see Avery, R.B., *374*
Houstoun, R.A., see Ferguson, A., *37*
Hsiao, C., 288, *292*
Huber, J., 368, *375*
Huber, P.J., 298, *318*
Hueting, R., 223, *228*
Hull, J., 262, *267*
Hulten, C.R., 182, *187*
Humphrey, T.M., 126, *131*
Hurwicz, L., 182, *187*, 273, 274, 277, *292*

Inoue, A., 328, *339*
International Labor Organization, 167, *187*
International Organization for Standardization (ISO), 46, 56, 59, 62, 64, 65, 67, 69, 73, *77*
Ioannides, J., 336, *339*
Irwin, J.C., see Ferguson, A., *37*
IVM, 236, *248*
IVM, see VIM

Jacowitz, K.E., see Green, D., *375*
Jaeger, A., see Harvey, A.C., *410*
Jaszi, G., 420, *427*
Jenkins, G.M., see Box, G.E.P., *265*
Jevons, W.S., 111, 116, *131*, 253, *267*
Jick, T.D., 14, *18*
Johansen, S., 260, *267*
Johnson, C., see Eckel, C., *375*
Johnson, E., see Harrison, G.W., 10, *103*, *104*, 298, *318*, 365
Johnson, H.M., 23, *37*
Johnston, J., 254, *267*
Jones, M.C., see Wand, M.P., *411*
Jonung, L., see Bordo, M.D., *131*
Jordá, O., see Hoover, K.D., *292*

Kahneman, D., see Green, D., *375*
Kahneman, D., see Tversky, A., *375*
Kaiser, R., 409, *410*
Kamarck, A., 332, *339*
Kanninen, B.J., 369, *375*
Kanninen, B.J., see Hanemann, M., *375*
Kapetanios, G., see Camba-Mendez, G., *266*
Karlan, D., 80, *104*
Katzner, D., 418, *427*
Kaye, G.W.C., see Ferguson, A., *37*
Keating, J., 279, *292*
Kemmerer, E.W., 114, *131*
Kendall, M., 380, *410*
Kendrick, J.W., 195, *228*
Kenessey, Z., 199, *228*
Kennedy, P., 325, 327, *339*
Kenny, P.B., 383, *410*
Keuning, S.J., 217, 223, *229*
Keuning, S.J., see Bloem, A.M., *228*
Keuning, S.J., see de Boo, A.J., *228*
Keuning, S.J., see de Haan, M., *228*
Keuzenkamp, H.A., 150, *152*, 323, 325, 327, 331, 332, *339*
Keynes, J.M., 154, *187*
Khamis, S.H., 166, *187*
Killian, L., see Inoue, A., *339*
Kim, J., 282, *292*, 331, *339*
King, M.L., 303, *318*
King, M.L., see Dufour, J.-M., *318*
King, R.G., 408, *410*
King, R.G., see Baxter, M., *409*
Kinley, D., 114, 118, *132*

Klein, J.L., 114, 131, 132, *132*, 253, *267*, 408, *410*
Klein, L.R., 253, 256, 261, *267*
Klep, P.M.M., 199, 200, *229*
Kline, P., 26, *37*
Kocher, M., 80, *104*
Kohn, R., see Ansley, C., *409*
Konus, A.A., 162, *187*
Koopman, S.J., see Durbin, J., *409*
Koopman, S.J., see Harvey, A.C., *410*
Koopmans, T.C., 253, 255, 260, 261, *267*, 273, 279, 281, 282, *292*, 418, *427*
Koopmans, T.C., see Hood, W., *267*
Köves, P., see Eltetö, Ö., *187*
Krantz, D.H., 6, 7, 11, *18*, 26, 27, 29–31, 35, *37*, 106, *132*, 286, *292*
Krantz, D.H., see Luce, R.D., *38*, *268*, *293*
Krantz, D.H., see Suppes, P., *38*, *294*
Krause, K., see Harbaugh, W.T., *103*
Kroner, K.F., see Bollerslev, T., *265*
Krtscha, M., 165, *187*
Krueger, A., see Fuchs, V., *338*
Krüger, L., see Gigerenzer, G., *355*
Kuhn, T.S., 64, *77*, 282, *292*
Kula, W., 345, *355*
Kuyatt, C.E., see Taylor, B.N., *77*
Kwiatkowski, D., 408, *410*
Kydland, F.E., 245, *248*

Laha, R.G., 310, *318*
Lau, M.I., see Harrison, G.W., *104*
Laubach, T., 406, *410*
Laury, S.K., see Holt, C.A., *104*, *375*
Layard, R., 222, *229*
Lazear, E.P., 80, *104*
Leamer, E.E., 82, *104*, 258, 265, *267*, 298, *318*, *319*, 325, 327, *339*
Leaning, M., see Finkelstein, L., *77*
Leeper, E.M., 278, *292*
Leontief, W., 332, *339*
Lerner, A.P., 162, *187*
LeRoy, S.F., see Cooley, T.F., *291*, *338*
Leser, C.E.V., 380, 399, 400, *410*
Levine, D.K., see Fudenberg, D., *103*
Linklater, A., 345, *355*
Lippi, F., see Forni, M., *266*, *410*
Lipsey, R.G., 135, 138, 144, *152*
Lira, I., 72, *77*
List, J.A., see Harrison, G.W., *18*, *103*
Liu, T.-C., 257, *267*, 275, *292*, *293*
Loader, C., 380, 383, *410*
Locke, J., 24, *37*
Loeb, S., 330, *339*
Loomes, G., 85, *104*, 372, *375*
Louviere, J.J., 358, *375*
Lovell, M., 335, *339*
Luati, A., see Proietti, T., 6, 16
Lucas, R.E., 149, *152*, 244–246, *248*, 257, *267*, 273, 274, 280, *293*
Luce, R.D., 26, 30–32, *37*, *38*, 252, *268*, 286, *293*
Luce, R.D., see Krantz, D.H., *18*, *37*, *132*, *292*
Luce, R.D., see Narens, L., *38*, *293*
Luce, R.D., see Suppes, P., *38*, *294*

Maas, H., 115, *132*
Mach, E., 235, *248*
Machlup, F., 322, *339*
Maddala, G.S., 276, *293*
Magnus, J.R., 13, 82, *104*, 215, *229*, 259, 298, 300, 309, 315, 318, *319*
Magnus, J.R., see Banerjee, A.N., *318*
Magnus, J.R., see Keuzenkamp, H.A., *152*, *339*
Makridakis, S., 325, *339*
Malaga, J.E., see Park, J., *319*
Mäler, K.-G., 222, *229*
Malinvaud, E., 254, *268*
Mallin, M., see Forni, M., *266*
Malmendier, U., see Lazear, E.P., *104*
Mankiw, G., 422, *427*
Manser, M., 172, *187*
Maravall, A., see Kaiser, R., *410*
Marcellino, M., see Banerjee, A., *265*
Marget, A.W., 121, *132*
Mari, L., 4, 8, 12, 14, 33, *38*, 48, 49, 60, 61, 67, 68, *77*, 107
Mari, L., see Carbone, P., *77*
Marschak, J., 254, *268*, 273, *293*
Marschak, J., see Becker, G., *374*
Marshall, A., 127, *132*
Masten, I., see Banerjee, A., *265*
Mauris, G., see Benoit, E., *76*
Mauris, G., see Mari, L., *77*
Mayer, T., 13, 17, *18*, 82, *104*, 140, 145, 146, 217, 261, 282, *293*, 321, 330, *339*
McAleer, M., 325, *339*
McAleer, M., see Keuzenkamp, H.A., *339*
McCloskey, D.N., 140, *152*, 329, 337, *339*
McCloskey, D.N., see Ziliak, S., *340*
McConnell, M., 330, *339*
McCullough, B.D., 335, *339*
McDonald, R., see Manser, M., *187*
McFadden, D., see Green, D., *375*
McInnes, M.M., see Harrison, G.W., 10, *103*, *104*, 298, *318*, 365

McKenzie, R., 416, *427*
McNees, S., 425, *427*
Mearman, A., see Downward, P., *152*
Mellens, M., 192, *229*
Michell, J., 7, 8, 20, 21, 23, 26, 30, 34, 37, *38*, 48, 53, *77*, 103, 135, 271, 286
Mirowski, P., 251, *268*, 335, *339*
Mitchell, W.C., 114, *132*
Mitchell, W.C., see Burns, A.F., *266*
Mizon, G.E., see Hendry, D.F., 292
Mjelde, J.W., see Park, J., *319*
Moene, K.O., 290, *293*
Moffatt, P.G., 5, 15, 81, 86, *104*
Moffatt, P.G., see Loomes, G., *104*, *375*
Monsell, B.C., see Findley, D.F., *409*
Montgomery, J.K., 164, *187*
Mooij, J., 201, *229*
Moore, H.L., 261, *268*
Morgan, M.S., 7, 8, 10, 11, 13, *18*, 41, *77*, 109, 110, 115, 130, *132*, 162, 200, *229*, 240, *248*, 253, 263, *268*, 271, 272, 282, 287, 290, *293*, 418, *427*
Morgan, M.S., see Backhouse, R.E., *152*, *338*
Morgan, M.S., see Boumans, M., *17*
Morgan, M.S., see den Butter, F.A.G., *152*, *228*
Morgan, M.S., see Hendry, D.F., *267*, 292
Morgan, M.S., see Kim, J., *292*, *339*
Morgan, M.S., see Klein, J.L., *132*
Morgan, M.S., see Morrison, M., *18*
Morgenstern, O., 261, *268*, 332, *339*
Morgenstern, O., see Von Neumann, J., *18*
Morley, J.C., 408, *410*
Morrison, M., 7, *18*, 263, 264, *268*
Morrison, M., see Morgan, M.S., *293*
Mosch, R.H.J., see den Butter, F.A.G., *228*
Müller, W.G., 361, *375*
Mundy, B., 19, 33, *38*
Munro, A.A., see Cubitt, R.P., *375*
Murray, C., see Papell, D., *339*
Musgrave, J., 387, *410*
Musso, A., see Proietti, T., *411*
Myers, C.S., see Ferguson, A., *37*
Mykland, P.A., see Chaudhuri, P., *375*

Nadaraya, E.A., 391, *410*
Nagel, E., 34, *38*
Nagel, E., see Cohen, M.R., *37*
Nalewaik, J., see Fixler, D., *426*
Narens, L., 30, 34, *38*, 287, *293*
Narens, L., see Falmange, J.-C., *291*
Nason, J.M., see Cogley, T., *409*
National Research Council, 179, *187*
Nelson, C.R., 257, *268*, 407, *411*
Nelson, C.R., see Beveridge, S., *409*
Nelson, C.R., see Gould, J.P., *131*
Nelson, C.R., see Morley, J.C., *410*
Neudecker, H., see Magnus, J.R., *319*
Newbold, P., see Granger, C.W.J., *410*
Newey, W.K., 297, *319*
Newton, I., 20, *38*
Nickell, S.J., 141, *152*

Oberg, S., 419, *427*
O'Brien, A., 330, *339*
Olesko, K.M., 346, *355*
Omtzigt, P., 300, *319*
Open Peer Comments, 329, *339*
Orcutt, G., 256, *268*
Orcutt, G., see Cochrane, D., *266*
Ord, J.K., see Kendall, M., *410*
Orme, C., see Hey, J.D., *104*
Orphanides, A., 127, *132*, 406, *411*
Otto, M.C., see Findley, D.F., *409*

Pagan, A., 258, *268*, 327, *339*
Pagan, A., see McAleer, M., *339*
Page, M., see Loeb, S., *339*
Pannekoek, J., 224, *229*
Papell, D., 330, *339*
Park, J., 313, *319*
Parker, J., see Hope, C., *228*
Parker, R., see Grimm, B., *426*
Paruolo, P., see Omtzigt, P., *319*
Patterson, H.D., 401, *411*
Peake, S., see Hope, C., *228*
Peart, S.J., 115, *132*
Perez, S., see Hoover, K.D., *338*
Perez-Quiros, G., see McConnell, M., *339*
Persons, W.M., 260, *268*
Petri, D., see Carbone, P., *77*
Petty, W., 112, *132*
Pfeffermann, D., 404, *411*
Phannkuch, M., 330, *339*
Phillips, A., 150, *152*
Phillips, A.W., 260, *268*
Phillips, P.C.B., 261, *268*
Phillips, P.C.B., see Kwiatkowski, D., *410*
Philpott, S.J.F., see Ferguson, A., *37*
Pierson, N.G., 157, *187*
Pigou, A.C., 161, *187*
Pinto, J.L., see Bleichrodt, H., *103*
Pinto, L.M.C., see Botelho, A., *103*
Pitman, E.J.G., 310, *319*
Planas, C., see Rossi, A., *411*
Playfair, W., 253, *268*

Plosser, C.I., see Nelson, C.R., *411*
Plott, C.R., see Grether, D.M., *103*, *375*
Poirier, D.J., 393, *411*
Polanyi, M., 348, *355*
Polasek, W., 298, *319*
Pollak, R., 170, *188*
Pollock, D.S.G., 380, 402, *411*
Ponce de Leon, A.C.M., 361, *375*
Ponce de Leon, A.C.M., see Müller, W.G., *375*
Porter, R., see Orphanides, A., *132*
Porter, T.M., 15, 17, *18*, 107, 108, *132*, 344, 347, 351, 352, 354, *356*, 358, 417, *427*
Porter, T.M., see Gigerenzer, G., *355*
Poterba, J., see Fuchs, V., *338*
Prelec, D., 82, *104*
Prescott, E.C., see Cooley, T.F., *247*
Prescott, E.C., see Hodrick, R., *410*
Prescott, E.C., see Kydland, F.E., *248*
Primont, D., see Blackorby, C., *186*
Proietti, T., 6, 16, 405–409, *411*
Pugh, M.G., see Findley, D.F., *409*

Qin, D., 253, 254, 256, 258, 259, *268*, 271, 272, *293*
Qin, D., see Gilbert, C.L., 12, 145, *266*, 271, 272
Quenneville, B., 406, *411*
Quiggin, J., see Dowrick, S., *186*
Quine, W.V.O., 62, *77*

Rabin, M., 81, 82, *104*
Rabin, M., see Charness, G., *103*
Ramsay, J.O., 32, *38*
Rebelo, S., see King, R.G., *410*
Reichlin, L., see Forni, M., *266*, *410*
Reiersøl, O., see Koopmans, T.C., *267*
Reinsdorf, M.B., 11, 27, *38*, 109, 110, 136, 164, 167, 179, *188*, 219, 333, *340*
Richardson, L.F., see Ferguson, A., *37*
Richter, M., see Hurwicz, L., *187*
Rider, R., see Frängsmyr, T., *355*
Robbins, L.C., 144, *152*
Robertson, R., 330, *340*
Robinson, G.K., 397, *411*
Rodenburg, P., 10, *18*, 106, 130, *132*
Rodriguez-Palenzuela, D., see Camba-Mendez, G., *409*
Rødseth, A., see Moene, K.O., *293*
Rosenberg, A., 336, *340*
Rossi, A., 407, *411*
Rossi, G.B., 65, *77*
Rosson, C.P., see Park, J., *319*
Rothbarth, E., 162, *188*
Rothenberg, T.J., 258, *268*
Rubinstein, A., 82, *104*
Rudebusch, G.D., see Diebond, F.X., *266*
Ruppert, D., 380, *411*
Rusnock, A., 346, *356*
Russell, B., 19, 24, *38*, 69, *77*
Russell, B., see Whitehead, A.N., *39*
Rutström, E.E., see Botelho, A., *103*
Rutström, E.E., see Coller, M., *103*
Rutström, E.E., see Harrison, G.W., 10, *103*, *104*, *318*, 298, 365
Rytan, J., 415, 419, *427*

Sadiraj, V., see Cox, J.C., *103*
Salyer, K.D., see Hartley, J.E., *292*
Samuelson, P.A., 162, *188*
Sargan, J.D., 260, *268*
Sargent, T.J., 259, 262, *268*
Sato, K., 164, *188*
Schlimm, D., 8, *18*
Schmidt, P., see Kwiatkowski, D., *410*
Schumpeter, J., 251, *268*
Schut, C.M., see Pannekoek, J., *229*
Schwartz, A., see Friedman, M., *338*
Scott, A.J., 404, *411*
Scott, D., 286, *293*
Searle, S.R., see Henderson, H.V., *410*
Seater, J., 149, *152*
Selden, R.T., 122, 127, *132*
Sent, E.-M., 261, *268*
Serlitis, A., see Barnett, W., *131*
Shannon, C.E., 46, *77*
Shapiro, M., see Mankiw, G., *427*
Sharma, A.R., see Davison, M.L., *37*
Shaxby, J.H., see Ferguson, A., *37*
Shearing, M., 419, *427*
Shephard, N., 262, *269*
Shin, Y., see Kwiatkowski, D., *410*
Shulman, H.B., see Findley, D.F., *409*
Siegler, M., see Hoover, K.D., *338*
Silverman, B.V., see Green, P.J., *410*
Silvey, S.D., 360, *375*
Simon, H.A., 245, *248*, 256, *269*
Sims, C.A., 259, *269*, 275–278, *293*
Sims, C.A., see Sargent, T.J., *268*
Singh, A.C., see Quenneville, B., *411*
Singleton, K.J., see Hansen, L.P., *292*
Skilivas, S., see Mirowski, P., *339*
Slovic, P., see Tversky, A., *375*
Slutsky, E., 408, *411*
Smets, F.R., 406, 407, *411*
Smith, A., 253, *269*
Smith, T., see Ferguson, A., *37*

Smith, T.M.F., see Scott, A.J., *411*
Smith, V.L., see Cox, J.C., *103*
Spanos, A., 321, 323, 326, 327, 337, *340*, 404, *411*
Spohn, W., see Stegmüller, W., *293*
Srba, F., see Davidson, J.E.H., *291*
Staehle, H., 162, *188*
Staiger, D., 406, *411*
Stamhuis, I.H., 201, *229*
Stamhuis, I.H., see Klep, P.M.M., *229*
Starmer, C.V., see Cubitt, R.P., *375*
Stegmüller, W., 280, *293*
Stekler, H.O., see Goldfarb, R., *338*
Stevens, S.S., 24–26, 30, *38*, 232, *248*, 286, *293*
Stigler, S.M., 344, *356*
Stigum, B.P., 290, *293*
Stock, J.H., 262, *269*, 276, 279, *293*, 407, *411*
Stock, J.H., see Staiger, D., *411*
Stone, R., 262, *269*, 415, *427*
Strauß, S., see Kocher, M., *104*
Stuart, A., see Kendall, M., *410*
Stuvel, G., 164, 174, *188*
Sugden, R., see Loomes, G., *104*, *375*
Sullivan, M.B., see Harrison, G.W., *104*
Summers, L., 147, *152*, 322, *340*
Summers, R., 197, *229*
Suppe, F., 281, 282, 284, *293*
Suppes, P., 26, 28, 30, 31, *38*, 106, *132*, 236, *248*, 282, 283, 286, 289, *294*
Suppes, P., see Krantz, D.H., *18*, *37*, *132*, *292*
Suppes, P., see Luce, R.D., *38*, *268*, *293*
Suppes, P., see Scott, D., *293*
Sutter, M., see Kocher, M., *104*
Sutton, J., 147, *152*, 240, *248*, 289, *294*
Swait, J.D., see Louviere, J.J., *375*
Swamy, S., 163, *188*
Swamy, S., see Samuelson, P.A., *188*
Swijtink, Z., see Gigerenzer, G., *355*
Swoyer, C., 33, *39*
Sydenham, P.H., 106, *132*, 242, *248*
Szulc, B., 166, *188*

Taylor, B.N., 69, *77*
Teller, P., 284, 285, *294*
Teräsvirta, T., see Granger, C.W.J., *267*
Terrall, M., 345, *356*
Theil, H., 257, *269*
Thompson, B., 329, *340*
Thompson, R., see Patterson, H.D., *411*
Thorbecke, E., 329, *340*
Thouless, R.H., see Ferguson, A., *37*
Thursby, J., see Dewald, W., *338*
Tiao, G.C., 408, *411*
Tibshirani, R.J., see Hastie, T.J., *410*
Tinbergen, J., 198, 202, 203, *229*, 287, *294*
Törnqvist, L., 167, *188*
Torsney, B., see Ford, I., *375*
Triplett, J.E., 179, *188*
Trivedi, P.K., 178, *188*
Tucker, W.S., see Ferguson, A., *37*
Tutz, G., see Farhmeir, L., *409*
Tversky, A., 363, *375*
Tversky, A., see Krantz, D.H., *18*, *37*, *132*, *292*
Tversky, A., see Luce, R.D., *38*, *268*, *293*
Tversky, A., see Suppes, P., *38*, *294*

van Ark, B., 219, *229*
van den Bergh, J.C.J.M., 221, *229*
van den Bogaard, A., 202, 203, *229*
van der Eyden, J.A.C., see den Butter, F.A.G., *228*
Van Fraassen, B., 281, 284, *294*
van IJzeren, J., 164, 174, *188*
van Norden, S., see Orphanides, A., *411*
van Tongeren, J.W., see Magnus, J.R., *229*
van Zanden, J.L., 202, *229*
Varian, H.R., 172, *188*, 283, *294*
Varian, H.R., see Gibbard, A., *152*, *338*
Vartia, Y.O., 164, 169, *188*
Vasnev, A., see Magnus, J.R., *319*
Veall, M., see Pagan, A., *339*
Verbruggen, H., see den Butter, F.A.G., *228*
Verbruggen, H., see Gerlagh, R., *228*
Verbruggen, J.P., see Don, F.J.H., *228*
Vesterlund, L., see Harbaugh, W.T., *103*
Ville, J., 172, 182, *188*
VIM, 4, 14, *18*
VIM, see IVM
Vining, R., 261, *269*
Vinod, H.D., see McCullough, B.D., *339*
Viscusi, W.K., 330, *340*
Voeller, J., see Eichhorn, W., *186*
Voeller, J., see Funke, H., *187*
Vogt, A., 165, *188*
Volcker, P., see McAleer, M., *339*
von Helmholtz, H., 22, *39*
Von Neumann, J., 11, *18*

Wakker, P.P., 102, *104*
Walker, J.M., see Cox, J.C., *103*
Walsh, C.M., 157, 161, *188*
Wand, M.P., 392, *411*
Wand, M.P., see Ruppert, D., *411*

Ward, B., 324, *340*
Watson, G.S., 391, *411*
Watson, G.S., see Durbin, J., *266*
Watson, M.W., 408, *411*
Watson, M.W., see Blanchard, O.J., *291*
Watson, M.W., see Staiger, D., *411*
Watson, M.W., see Stock, J.H., *269*, *293*, *411*
Waugh, F.V., 256, 262, *269*
Weadock, T., see Grimm, B., *426*
Weber, R.A., see Lazear, E.P., *104*
Wei, S.-J., 330, *340*
Weitzman, M.L., 218, *229*
West, K.D., see Newey, W.K., *319*
Westermann, T., see Proietti, T., *411*
Wetenschappelijke Raad voor het Regeringsbeleid, 224, *229*
Weymark, J.A., see Vartia, Y.O., *188*
White, A., see Hull, J., *267*
White, K.P., 247, *248*
Whitehead, A.N., 21, *39*
Whittaker, E., 399, *411*
Wilcox, N.T., see Ballinger, T.P., *103*
Wild, C., see Phannkuch, M., *339*
Wise, M.N., 349, *356*
Wold, H., 256, *269*
Wolfers, J., see Donohue, J., III, *338*
Woodward, J., 232, 233, *248*, 274, *294*
Wu, C.F.J., see Ford, I., *375*

Xu, D., see Tiao, G.C., *411*

Yeo, S., see Davidson, J.E.H., *291*
Youden, W.J., 344, *356*
Yule, G.U., 409, *411*

Zellner, A., 324, 325, *340*
Zha, T., see Leeper, E.M., *292*
Ziliak, S., 329, *340*
Zingales, G., see Mari, L., *77*
Zinman, J., see Karlan, D., *104*
Zinnes, J.L., see Suppes, P., *38*, *248*, *294*
Zivot, E., see Morley, J.C., *410*
Zwerina, K., see Huber, J., *375*

Subject Index

accounting 110, 129, 346, 350, 351
macro 109
national 190, 191, 194, 196–199, 202, 207, 208, 212–214, 218, 220–223
expenditure approach 191, 214, 426
income approach 191, 214, 426
output approach 191
national income 110, 218
accounting principle 110
accounting system 11, 17, 110, 130, 192, 194, 207, 208, 216
accuracy 4–6, 8, 11–15, 17, 62, 66, 69, 109, 238–242, 246, 247, 256, 275, 343, 347, 351, 352, 354, 355, 377, 380, 405, 406, 413–417, 419, 420, 422, 423, 425
accuracy of national accounts, *see* national accounts, accuracy
accurate representation, *see* representation, accurate
aggregation problem 227
anchoring bias, *see* bias, anchoring
approximation 65, 68, 154, 178, 240, 244, 344, 380, 408, 413
associative measurement, *see* measurement, associative
astrology 344
astronomy 344–346
autonomy
of an empirical relation 123–125, 240, 273, 274, 278, 279
of a model 263, 290
autoregressive-integrated-moving average (ARIMA) model, *see* model, autoregressive-integrated-moving average
auxiliary parameter, *see* parameter, auxiliary
axiom, *see* index formula, axiom
axiomatic approach 7, 11, 12, 25, 153, 162, 163, 179, 194, 281
axiomatic index number theory, *see* index number theory, axiomatic
axiomatization 7, 8, 281, 282, 288

Bank of England 148, 151, 207
barometer 16, 117, 118, 260
Bayesian approach 80, 258, 259, 298, 361, 406
quasi-Bayesian method 258
Becker–DeGroot–Marschak (BDM) mechanism 363
behavioral economics 11, 144, 336, 337
bias 6, 65, 81, 157, 158, 161, 172, 177, 179, 224, 233, 243, 272, 326–329, 334, 387, 388, 405, 406
anchoring 362
black box model (of measurement) 41, 246
bootstrap 115, 118, 350
Boskin commission 109, 179, 220, 351
Box–Jenkins' methodology 257, 259, 261
Brookings Institution 210
Bundesbank, Germany 211
Bureau of Economic Analysis (BEA), US 209, 421–423, 425
bureaucracy 107, 126, 349, 350
bureau of standards 354
business cycle study 260, 261

calculation error, *see* error, calculation
calibration 8, 12, 49, 54–56, 61, 62, 64, 65, 70, 81, 102, 107, 118, 223, 234, 236, 239, 242, 244–247, 275, 327, 406
capital gain 334
caricature model, *see* model, caricature
causality test, *see* test, causality
census 118, 206, 346, 350, 420
Census Bureau, US 209
Central Bureau of Statistics (CBS), Netherlands 193, 196, 198, 201–203, 205, 215, 217, 223, 224
Central Planning Bureau (CPB), Netherlands 148, 202–204, 207, 210, 212, 225
Central Statistical Office (CSO), UK 206, 218
certainty equivalent 83, 363, 364
ceteris absentibus 8, 239
ceteris neglectis 239
ceteris paribus 5, 8, 238, 239, 264, 284, 322, 325
characteristic test, *see* test, characteristic
characterization for an index, *see* index formula, characterization
checking 14, 32, 335
checking device 114, 115, 119, 121, 123, 129
chemistry 144, 273, 345, 346

"chicken and egg" problem 359, 360, 369
Chow test, *see* test, Chow
circularity test, *see* index formula, test, circularity
classical approach, *see* metrology, classical approach
Cobb–Douglas index, *see* index, Cobb–Douglas
cointegration 260
combined standard uncertainty, *see* uncertainty, combined standard
commensurability axiom, *see* index formula, axiom, commensurability
commensuration 352, 353
common ratio test, *see* test, common ratio
comparability of national accounts, *see* national accounts, comparability
comparative proportionality test, *see* index formula, test, comparative proportionality
compatibility 73
compound property of money 121, 126
computational experiment, *see* experiment, computational
conceptual issue 113, 121
confidence interval 69, 81, 82, 92, 102, 140, 330, 406
conformance 45, 73, 74
Congressional Budget Office, US 210
congruence 276, 277, 288
consensus view 148, 203, 205
consistency 11, 17
consistency in aggregation, *see* index formula, test, consistency in aggregation
consistency of national accounts, *see* national accounts, consistency
constant basket test, *see* index formula, test, constant basket
constant relative risk aversion (CRRA), *see* risk aversion, constant relative
constructive empiricism 284, 287
constructive realism, *see* realism, constructive
consumer price index (CPI), *see* index, consumer price
consumption model, *see* model, consumption
core module system (national accounts) 215, 216
correctness of a model 298
correlative interpretation of measurement, *see* measurement, correlative interpretation
correspondence rule 7, 281, 282, 284, 285
cost of living index, *see* index, cost of living
cost–benefit analysis 108, 351–353
Council of Economic Advisers (CEA), US 209, 210, 421
coverage factor 71
Cowles Commission (CC) 253, 272–274, 277, 280
CPB Netherlands Bureau for Economic Policy Analysis, *see* Central Planning Bureau, Netherlands
cross-spectral analysis, *see also* spectral analysis 261
cubic spline 379, 395–397

D-optimal design, *see* experimental design, D-optimal design
data 9, 11–13, 16, 114, 232–234, 240, 243–245
  before theorizing, *see also* data mining, measurement without theory, statistics 151
  quality of 332–336
data mining 14, 146, 151, 258, 261, 326–329
data perturbation, *see* perturbation
data-generating process (DGP) 80, 276, 277, 287, 323, 324, 357
  local 276, 277
data-instigated model, *see* model, data-instigated
database 332, 334, 335
deep parameter, *see* parameter, deep
derived measurement, *see* measurement, derived
description 140–142
descriptive statistics, *see* statistics, descriptive
design of measuring instrument, *see* measuring instrument, design principle
Deutsches Institut für Wirtschaftsforschung (DIW) 211, 212
DHSY model of consumption, *see* model, consumption
diagnostic 296, 297, 315, 323, 328, 333, 401
diagnostic and sensitivity 297, 298, 314–318
diagnostic curve 314, 315
diagnostic test, *see* test, diagnostic
direct measurement, *see* measurement, direct
direct measurement scale, *see* scale of measurement, direct
Direction de Prévision (DP), France 213
Divisia index, *see* index, Divisia
domestic product 160, 190–193, 216

Durbin and Watson (DW) test, *see* test, Durbin and Watson
dynamic factor model (DFM), *see* model, dynamic factor
dynamic system 12, 44

eco-circ system 207
econometric methodology, *see also* London School of Economics econometric approach 194, 201, 258, 271, 287, 290
econometrics 3, 6, 8, 12, 13, 16, 145–147, 149–151, 233, 234, 271
economic approach to index numbers, *see* index number theory, economic approach
economic theory 142, 143, 150
  versus statistical theory 323
empirical adequacy 284, 285
empirical model, *see* model, empirical
empirical relational structure, *see* relational structure, empirical
empirical sensitivity, *see* sensitivity, empirical
empirical substructure, *see* structure, empirical substructure
empirical system 19, 26, 27, 30–32, 34, 36
Enlightenment 345
environmental degradation 190, 217, 222
error 5, 6, 14–16, 81, 85, 86, 94, 98, 102, 232, 233, 238, 242, 243, 344, 348
  calculation 334, 335
  measurement 6, 60, 178, 234, 242, 404, 407, 418, 422, 423
  observational 232, 233, 238, 240
  prediction 96, 243
  random 63, 64, 330, 350
  sampling 81, 326, 329, 331, 332, 404, 417
  systematic 63, 64, 70, 344
  type 1 vs. type 2 74
error correction 260, 264, 288
error rate 94
error term 5, 6, 16, 127, 238, 242, 243, 256
estimate 113, 122
  flash 215, 419, 421–423, 425
  revision 413, 414, 416, 419–426
estimation 5, 12, 139, 147, 244, 245, 253–256, 258, 260, 261, 263, 275, 378, 380, 381, 383, 389, 401, 405–407
estimator 6, 13, 256, 257, 297, 298, 358
European Union 190, 192, 217
evaluation, measurement as 41, 56
expanded uncertainty, *see* uncertainty, expanded
expected utility theory (EUT) 79, 80–83, 85, 86, 88, 90, 92–94, 96, 98, 101, 102
expected value of a lottery, *see* lottery, expected value
expenditure approach of national accounting, *see* accounting, national, expenditure approach
experience 11, 25, 45, 69, 70, 106, 118, 136–138, 140, 260, 322, 323, 343
experiment 9, 10, 15, 17, 80, 82, 83, 86, 88, 90, 101, 102, 106, 142, 144, 151, 239, 240, 264
  computational 245, 246
  field 10, 79, 83
  laboratory 8, 10, 79, 80, 83
  natural 9, 10
  stated choice 358
  thought 107, 130, 144
experimental design 5, 15, 80, 81, 83, 233, 238, 284, 357–375
  between-subjects 81
  D-optimal design 81, 359–361, 365–368, 373, 374
  factorial
    fractional 358
    full 358
  multiple price list 88
  sequential 373
  within-subjects 79, 81–83
experimental design theory 358, 361, 365
experimental procedure 7, 80, 82, 88, 98, 101
experimetrics 357
extreme bounds analysis 258, 259, 325, 326

factor reversal test, *see* index formula, test, factor reversal
factual influence, *see* influence, factual
falsificationism 135, 137
feasible general least squares method, *see* least squares method, feasible general
Federal Reserve Board (Fed), US 111, 113, 121, 123–125, 209, 210, 257, 278, 421
field experiment, *see* experiment, field
filter 5, 15, 16, 377-411
  Henderson 377, 379, 380, 382–384, 386–388, 392, 404
  Kalman 401, 406
  Hodrick and Prescott 400, 402, 404, 409
filtering 107, 402, 405
Fisher's ideal index, *see* index, Fisher's ideal
flash estimate, *see* estimate, flash
flexibility of national accounts, *see* national accounts, flexibility

formalization 68, 253, 255
fractional factorial design, *see* experimental design, factorial, fractional
full factorial design, *see* experimental design, factorial, full
full-information maximum likelihood (FIML), *see* maximum likelihood, full-information
fundamental measurement, *see* measurement, fundamental

game theory 11
'garbage in, garbage out' principle 45
gross domestic product (GDP) 111, 122, 125, 158, 160, 215, 219, 334, 414–420, 424, 425
  per capita 216, 219
general equilibrium theory 264
generalized autoregressive conditional heteroscedasticity (GARCH) model, *see* model, generalized autoregressive conditional heteroscedasticity
general-to-specific methodology 277, 327
generic measuring instrument, *see* measuring instrument, generic
graduation 16, 378, 380
Granger representation theorem 260, 288
Granger-causality test, *see* test, causality, Granger
'green' GNP, *see* sustainable gross national product
guesstimate 112, 113, 128
guesswork 114

happiness 222
hedonic method 220
Henderson filter, *see* filter, Henderson
history 3, 11, 136, 138, 140, 142, 143
  of economics 107, 109
  of measurement 8, 10, 41, 47, 105, 111, 114, 120, 130, 265, 354
  of national accounting 190, 194, 196, 199
  of science 32, 106, 111, 343
  of the social sciences 107
homomorphism 7, 8, 11, 19, 26, 27, 28, 48, 56–59, 106, 231, 232, 245–247
human development index (HDI), *see* index, human development
hypothetico-deductive method 135, 138, 139, 143, 337

idealized entities 10, 127
idealized model, *see* model, idealized
identifiability 105, 113, 122–126, 128, 129, 395
identification 12, 252, 254, 255, 257, 259, 261, 263, 274–276, 278, 279, 288, 289
ideological commitment 321, 346
implicit price index, *see* index, implicit price
implicit quantity index, *see* index, implicit quantity
impulse response function 264, 382, 393, 395
income approach of national accounting, *see* accounting, national, income approach
independent data set 205, 327, 331
index, *see also* price index
  Cobb–Douglas 163, 176, 179, 184
  consumer price 155, 173, 179, 220, 224
  cost of living 120, 153, 154, 167–170, 172, 177, 181, 184, 351
  Divisia 110, 127, 172, 178, 181, 182, 184, 185
  Fisher's ideal 108, 109, 161, 162, 164–168, 174, 178, 179
  human development 216, 219
  implicit price 159, 174, 184
  implicit quantity 158–160, 167, 169, 170, 176, 177, 182, 183
  Laspeyres 109, 110, 156, 158–161, 164, 168–175, 177, 178, 182–185
  Paasche 110, 156, 158–161, 164, 168–175, 177, 178, 182–185
  Sato–Vartia 165, 167, 168, 176, 178, 185
  Törnqvist 167, 174, 176, 178, 179, 185
index formula 11, 108–110, 153, 154, 156, 157, 159, 161, 162, 165, 166, 177, 184
  axiom 108, 109, 153
    commensurability 155–157, 159–163, 165, 175–177, 179–181, 183
    linear homogeneity in comparison period prices 175–177, 183
    local monotonicity 168, 176
    monotonicity 163, 165–168, 175–177, 179, 183
    ordinal circularity 171
    price dimensionality 165, 175, 177, 183
    proportionality 157, 159–163, 165, 168, 174, 175, 179–181, 183, 184
    weak axiom of revealed preference 169, 171, 184
    weak monotonicity 176, 177
  characterization 163, 165, 167, 173, 179, 185
  test

comparative proportionality 160, 175, 184
consistency in aggregation 164, 173–175, 177, 183
constant basket 157–159, 167
circularity 156, 157, 160–163, 166, 170, 178–183
factor reversal 160–162, 164, 166, 173, 174, 177, 179, 183, 185
homogeneity of degree zero 164, 165, 183
mean value 165, 167, 177, 181, 183
product 158, 159, 171, 174, 177, 184
strong proportionality 157, 184
time reversal 157, 160–162, 164, 168, 174, 177, 184, 185
index number 5, 11, 16, 109, 110, 114, 116, 351
index number theory 3, 11, 116, 220
axiomatic 11, 153–188
economic approach 153, 162, 163, 167, 168, 172, 175, 177–179, 181
stochastic approach 153, 154, 166, 179
indicator 123, 189–229, 260, 262, 351, 419
interpretation 227
indirect least squares method, *see* least squares method, indirect
indirect measurement, *see* measurement, indirect
inference (measurement as a tool for) 43, 49, 50
influence 4, 5, 9, 10, 237–241, 243, 244
factual 9
potential 9, 239, 240, 243
influence quantity 67
information 3, 4, 8, 14, 41–43, 46–48, 50–52, 57, 58, 62, 63, 67, 68, 76, 81, 86, 349, 352
information matrix 359, 360, 365, 366, 373, 374
input/output analysis 109–111, 208
input/output tables 197, 208, 219
Institut National de la Statistique et des Études Économiques (INSEE), France 212, 213
institutional set-up of policy preparation 190, 202–205, 227
instrument measurement, *see* measurement, instrument
interpretation of indicator, *see* indicator, interpretation
intersubjectivity 42, 43, 48, 50, 53, 54, 58, 76
interval regression 92, 96, 98, 101
invariance 4, 5, 9, 11–13, 17, 107, 111, 122, 126, 213, 214, 216, 233, 239, 240, 244, 271, 273, 274, 278, 280, 287
under intervention 273, 289, 290
under transformation 30, 286, 289, 290
invariance view on structure, *see* structure, invariance view
isomorphism 25, 31, 33, 34, 283–287, 289

joint hypothesis about risk attitudes and consistent behavior 86, 88

Klein–Goldberger model, *see* model, Klein–Goldberger
knowledge 135–138, 143, 147, 148, 151

laboratory experiment, *see* experiment, laboratory
land survey 345
Laspeyres index, *see* index, Laspeyres
latent process 80, 82, 98
law of nature 7, 8, 235, 236, 238
leading indicator model, *see* model, leading indicator
League of Nations 199
least squares method 16, 256, 344, 346, 366, 378
feasible general 256
indirect 272
generalized 295, 299
ordinary 272, 296, 299, 359, 391
life insurance 353
limited-information maximum likelihood (LIML), *see* maximum likelihood, limited-information
linear homogeneity in comparison period prices, *see* index formula, axiom, linear homogeneity in comparison period prices
Liu critique 275, 276
local data-generating process (LDGP), *see* data-generating process, local
local monotonicity axiom, *see* index formula, axiom, local monotonicity
local polynomial regression 377, 378, 380, 392, 405
logical positivism 7, 25, 26, 281, 282
logit model, *see* model, logit
London School of Economics (LSE) econometric approach 258, 260, 262, 272, 276, 277, 279, 280, 287, 323, 324
lottery
choice 81, 83, 85, 86, 88, 90, 92–94, 98, 101, 142, 360, 363–365, 370, 372, 374

expected value 86, 88, 364
Lucas critique 149, 244, 245, 257, 273, 274, 277–280, 321, 336

Maastricht criteria 192
macro model, *see* model, macro
macro-accounting, *see* accounting, macro
macro-aggregate 121
magnitude 20–22, 27, 33, 34, 343
Marschak–Machina triangle 369
mathematical statistics, *see* statistics, mathematical
maximum likelihood (ML) 255, 256, 272
full-information 255, 273
limited-information 255, 273
mean value test, *see* index formula, test, mean value
measurability 20, 41, 42, 48, 60, 68, 76, 105, 107, 108, 113, 117, 120, 121, 123, 125, 126, 128, 129, 253
measurand 3–6, 8, 10, 12–15, 17, 46, 48, 50–52, 55, 56, 60–71, 73, 76, 235, 237, 238, 240–242
definition 65
measurement 114, 135, 141, 343, 348
associative 235, 236
correlative interpretation 35, 234–238
derived 22, 23, 45, 51, 71, 114, 121, 130, 235
direct 10, 45, 51, 59, 71, 119, 233, 235, 236
fundamental 22, 23, 235, 286
indirect 4, 10, 45, 51, 59, 235, 243
instrument 235–238
model 8, 10, 241
physical 23, 31, 32, 43
pointer 236
measurement error, *see* error, measurement
measurement method 4, 14, 59, 65, 344, 406
measurement principle 10, 14
measurement result 4, 5, 10, 11, 13–16, 42, 46, 48, 49, 52–55, 60, 61, 63, 67–71, 73–76, 233, 240–242, 247
measurement science, *see also* metrology 50, 61, 64, 65, 68
measurement strategy 4, 6, 8, 10, 272
measurement system 15, 68
measurement theory 33, 34, *see also* representational theory of measurement
measurement without theory 252, 261, 262, 273, 278
measuring formula, *see also* index formula 113, 121, 122
measuring instrument, *see also* barometer, thermometer 10, 14, 15, 56, 105, 107–111, 113, 115, 118–123, 125–130, 140, 233, 234, 236, 238, 239, 242, 246, 265, 416
design principle 108–111, 125, 128
generic 109, 110, 127
mechanical balance 106, 115, 116
medicine 336, 346, 348
meta-analysis 147
metaphysical assumption 11, 136, 137
metric system 345, 354
metrology, *see also* measurement science 4, 8, 12–14, 106, 107, 111, 236, 242, 275, 354
classical approach 4, 14
uncertainty approach 4, 14, 15
microfoundation 274
misspecification test, *see* test, misspecification
mistake 85, 148, 169,
mixture model, *see* model, mixture
model, *see also* representation 5, 7, 10–13, 15, 17, 61, 67, 107, 108, 117, 119, 127, 231–233, 240–247, 282–286, 288, 343, 351
autoregressive-integrated-moving average 257, 387
caricature 150, 321–323
complex vs. simple 324, 325
consumption 280
data-instigated 257, 263
dynamic factor 262, 407
empirical 139, 140, 143, 145–150, 191, 256, 263, 264, 277, 282, 284, 322
generalized autoregressive conditional heteroscedasticity 262
idealized 105, 128, 129
Klein–Goldberger 256, 261
leading indicator 262
logit 141, 369
macro 198, 202, 337
mixture 80
of data 283, 284, 285
of theory 285
probit 360, 362, 363, 365, 367–370, 373
random preference 372
reduced form 255, 257, 276
reduced form vector autoregressive 259, 276
regime-switching 262
simultaneous-equations 254, 255, 259, 260, 272–274, 277–279, 288

structural vector autoregressive 260, 276, 278–280, 405
trend 377, 380, 392, 394
theoretical 12, 137, 139, 141–145, 254, 255, 257, 263, 325, 337
vector autoregressive 272, 288
visual 117, 118
model choice 258, 259
model measurement, *see* measurement, model
model of data, *see* model, of data
model of theory, *see* model, of theory
model perturbation, *see* perturbation
model selection 146
model specification 12, 13, 253–255, 257–259, 264, 272
model theory of measurement, *see also* representational theory of measurement 231
model validity 12, 13, 246, 247, 256, 260, 261
modeling 5, 7–9, 11, 17, 135–141, 144, 147–149, 151, 234, 243
monetary aggregate 121, 141
monotonicity axiom, *see also* index formula, axiom, monotonicity 28, 58
multiple price list, *see* experimental design, multiple price list

national accounting, *see* accounting, national
national accounts 3, 11, 16, 136, 141, 158, 160, 179, 189–199, 202, 203, 206–209, 212–215, 217–219, 221–223, 226, 227, 407, 417, 418
accuracy 214, 215
comparability 193, 195, 197, 199, 216, 217
consistency 11, 17, 192, 213, 214, 219, 227
flexibility 11, 213, 214, 216, 217, 227, 247
revision 214, 215
standardization 11, 214, 417
national bookkeeping, *see also* national accounts 190, 191, 195, 196, 198, 217
National Bureau of Economic Research (NBER), US 151, 210, 260, 278
national income 120–122, 130, 189–192, 194–198, 213, 214, 217, 218, 221–223
national income accounting, *see* accounting, national income
national product 149, 218, 421
national wealth 195
natural constant 122, 263
natural experiment, *see* experiment, natural
natural philosophy 344, 345
Netherlands Central Planning Bureau, *see* Central Planning Bureau, Netherlands
Netherlands Central Bureau of Statistics, *see* Central Bureau of Statistics, Netherlands
new classical economics 272, 277, 278, 280, 325, 337
Neyman–Pearson testing methodology 264
nomological machine 145, 238, 239, 241
non-accelerating inflation rate of unemployment (NAIRU) 140, 405, 406
non-observable, *see also* observable 10, 80, 105, 115, 118, 129, 130, 145, 276, 284, 287, 288
non-structural model, *see* model, reduced form
normality assumption 255, 318, 371
nuisance parameter, *see* parameter, nuisance
numerical relational structure, *see* relational structure, numerical
numerical system 19, 26, 27, 36, 287

objectivity 43, 48, 50, 58, 62, 76, 106, 107, 347, 348, 350–353, 417
observable, *see also* non-observable 7, 10, 17, 33, 36, 60, 80, 105, 130, 173, 233, 237, 244, 281, 282, 404
observation 4, 5, 10, 13, 15, 16, 107, 114, 129, 130, 232, 233, 237–241
passive 9, 239–241, 357
theory-laden 41, 282
observation post 13, 116, 117, 119, 121
observational error, *see* error, observational
Office for National Statistics (ONS), UK 206
operationalism 25, 26, 47, 66, 232, 234
ordinal circularity axiom, *see* index formula, axiom, ordinal circularity
ordinal pay-off scheme 363, 364
ordinary least squares (OLS) method, *see* least squares method, ordinary
output approach of national accounting, *see* accounting, national, output approach
outsourcing 224

Paasche index, *see* index, Paasche
parameter 5, 12, 13, 81, 86, 102, 139, 184, 198, 242–244, 257, 261, 263–265, 274, 359, 360, 361
auxiliary 297

deep 274, 275
nuisance 13, 80, 297, 299, 308, 314–316
of interest 82, 297–299, 302
structural 244, 254–259, 262, 263, 272, 273, 275, 362, 363, 365
parametric characterization 96, 101
passive observation, *see* observation, passive
permanent income hypothesis 280, 282, 324
perturbation 82, 102, 298
philosophy of science 7, 106, 111, 235, 263, 271, 280, 281
physical measurement, *see* measurement, physical
physics 20, 26, 30–32, 43, 68, 251, 324, 344, 346, 351
pillarized society 202, 203
Pitman's lemma 310, 311
pointer measurement, *see* measurement, pointer
policy analysis 189, 190, 192, 194, 199, 202, 203, 205, 207–213, 259, 278, 279
political arithmetik 130
political economy 200
positive economics 144, 148
potential influence, *see* influence, potential
precision 4–6, 8, 12, 14–17, 62, 69, 82, 83, 86, 88, 96, 98, 101, 102, 107, 242, 259, 343–356, 358, 359, 363, 366, 370, 405–407
prediction error, *see* error, prediction
preference 81, 83, 92, 283, 287, 360, 373
revealed 79
preference reversal 85, 86, 94, 142
price dimensionality axiom, *see* index formula, axiom, price dimensionality
price index, *see also* index 109, 146, 153, 155, 219–221, 253
principal–agent relationship 217, 218
prior distribution 259, 298
probit model, *see* model, probit
product test, *see* index formula, test, product
product-normal distribution 312, 313
propagation uncertainty, *see* uncertainty, propagation
proportionality axiom, *see* index formula, axiom, proportionality
prospect theory 80, 82, 86
psychology 8, 11, 19, 20, 23, 26, 106, 284, 329
purchasing power 155, 189, 191, 197, 225, 227

quantitative 19, 20, 23, 25, 31, 33–36
quantity of information 46
quasi-Bayesian method, *see* Bayesian approach, quasi-Bayesian method

random lottery incentive (RLI) system 372–374
random preference model, *see* model, random preference
random-walk consumption function 275
rational expectations 244, 252, 257, 279, 338
rationality 144, 145, 325, 353
realism 24, 245, 264, 265, 273, 290
constructive 284, 298
reality 13, 140, 143, 145, 150, 179, 203, 245, 246, 286, 322
received view, *see also* syntactic view 7, 25, 281–283, 285, 290
reduced-form model, *see* model, reduced form
reduced-form vector autoregressive model, *see* model, reduced form vector autoregressive
reference object 48–53, 55, 58, 59, 61, 62, 65
reference scale 53, 58–60
reference set 51–53
regime-switching model, *see* model, regime-switching
regression equation 127, 146
regression method 110, 129
relational structure 8, 24, 33, 286–289
empirical 7, 11, 19, 26, 27, 30–32, 34, 36, 106, 108, 109, 111, 114, 128, 231, 232, 245, 246, 286, 287
numerical 7, 106, 108, 111, 114, 128, 231, 246, 287
reliability 4, 8, 13, 17, 46, 62, 79, 128, 233, 242, 346, 347, 349, 405, 406, 413, 416, 419–421
repeatability 14, 15, 62, 64, 65, 73
replication 53, 149, 335, 336
representation, *see also* model 5–7, 11, 13, 111, 117, 119, 127, 135, 240–245, 287, 288, 290
accurate 6, 11–13, 17, 242, 243, 245, 247
structural 286, 287
visual 115–117
representation problem 232
representation theorem 7, 26, 31, 286–289
representational definition of measurement, *see also* representational theory of measurement 48, 53, 56, 58, 59
representational theory of measurement 6–8, 11, 19, 20, 36, 106, 108, 109, 114,

126, 135, 151, 162, 194, 231, 232, 234, 235, 271, 286, 288
reproducibility 14
residual heteroscedasticity 256
residual serial correlation 252, 256
resolution 44, 65, 68
revealed preference, *see* preference, revealed
reversal phenomenon 364
revision of estimate, *see* estimate, revision
revision of national accounts, *see* national accounts, revision
risk 80, 353
 attitude 79–83, 86, 90, 92, 96, 98, 101, 102
 aversion 79–83, 85, 86, 88, 90, 93, 94, 96, 98, 101, 102
  constant relative 83, 85, 86, 88, 90, 92, 94, 96, 98, 101, 102, 275, 363, 365, 370
 loving 88, 92
 neutral 86, 88, 92, 101
robustness test, *see* test, robustness
Royal Netherlands Economic Association 201

Sachverständigenrat, Germany 210, 211
sample survey 113, 119–121, 127, 128, 327
sampling error, *see* error, sampling
sampling strategy 119
sampling system 110
Sato–Vartia index, *see* index, Sato–Vartia
savings ratio 333, 334
scale of measurement, *see also* reference scale 25–28, 30, 31, 48, 56–58, 231, 235–237, 286, 287, 289
 direct 235
scale unit 53
scarcity 144
semantic view 7, 271, 280–282, 284–287, 290
sensitivity
 analysis 13, 295–319
 coefficient 13, 72, 298
 curve 314
 definition 297, 299, 302, 308, 315
 empirical 82
 of F-test 307–309
 of OLS predictor 298–302
 of OLS variance estimator 302, 303
 of t-test 309–313
 of t-test rule of thumb 313
 relationship with diagnostic test 314–317
sensor (as input transducer) 55, 56, 61, 62
sequential experimental design, *see* experimental design, sequential
significance test, *see* test, significance
similarity 25, 28, 284–286, 298
simultaneous-equations model (SEM), *see* model, simultaneous-equations
smoothing 378–380, 388, 400
social accounting matrix (SAM) 217
Social Economic Council (SER), Netherlands 204, 205, 225
social studies of science 106, 111
software package 146, 335, 418
specification, *see* model specification
specification search 258
spectral analysis 261
stability 4, 49, 65, 107, 124, 125
Stability and Growth Pact (SGP) of the EU 192
standard 14, 15, 55, 56, 65, 122, 207, 217, 223, 227, 236, 242, 244, 246, 275, 347, 354
standard deviation 70, 72, 343, 421
standard uncertainty, *see* uncertainty, standard
standardization 11, 17, 242, 246, 345, 347, 349, 354, 355, 417
standardization of national accounts, *see* national accounts, standardization
standardized quantitative rule 107–109, 111, 119, 126, 128
stated choice experiment, *see* experiment, stated choice
statistical office 107, 189, 193, 227
statistics 136, 138, 139, 142, 145, 343, 348
 descriptive 200
 mathematical 200
Statistics Norway 207, 209
Statistische Bundesamt, Germany 210
stochastic approach to index numbers, *see* index number theory, stochastic approach
stochastic volatility (SV) 262
strong proportionality test, *see* index formula, test, strong proportionality
structural approach in econometrics 252, 254, 255, 257, 261, 272
structural approach to measurement 271, 272, 280, 288, 290
structural parameter, *see* parameter, structural
structural representation, *see* representation, structural
structural vector autoregressive (SVAR) model, *see* model, structural vector autoregressive

structuralism 280, 281
structuralist view of measurement 280
structure 8, 11–13, 240, 246, 247, 271, 273, 277, 283, 287, 288
empirical substructure 284, 285
invariance view 272, 273, 277, 279, 280, 289, 290
theory view 272, 274, 276–278, 280, 288–290
subcontracting 224
substitutability 44, 46, 47, 50, 51, 73
sustainable gross national product 222
sustainable national income 223
syntactic view, *see also* received view 7, 281, 282

target uncertainty, *see* uncertainty, target
technology of distance 347, 350
test
causality 261
Granger 257, 261
characteristic 282
Chow 257, 277
common ratio 83
diagnostic 12, 13, 257, 260, 261, 296–298, 314, 316–318
Durbin and Watson 257, 296, 301, 303, 308,
misspecification 257, 323
robustness 326, 332, 336
significance 329–332
test of homogeneity of degree zero, *see* index formula, test, homogeneity of degree zero
theoretical model, *see* model, theoretical
theory of reduction 276, 277, 279
theory view on structure, *see* structure, theory view
theory-laden observation, *see* observation, theory-laden
thermometer 107, 120, 122, 126, 233, 234, 236, 245
thought experiment, *see* experiment, thought
time reversal test, *see* index formula, test, time reversal
time series 141, 195, 198, 219, 243, 244, 282, 377, 378, 407, 408
time-series econometrics 194, 243, 256, 259, 261,
timeliness 11, 16, 214, 413–416, 419, 420, 423, 425
tolerance 73, 86, 347, 348
Törnqvist index, *see* index, Törnqvist
traceability 54–56, 61, 65
transaction costs 217, 218, 224, 227
treatment of services 219
trend model, *see* model, trend
triangulation 14, 148
true value 4, 14, 15, 48, 60, 61, 63, 64, 76, 242, 272, 343, 358, 405, 416, 417, 421, 425
trust in numbers 15, 69–71, 107–109, 115, 126, 128, 348–350
type 1 vs. type 2 error, *see* error, type 1 vs. type 2

ugly fact 324
UN Human Development Index, *see* index, human development
uncertainty 4, 13–15, 46, 64, 65, 73–76, 98, 121, 124, 239, 351, 353
combined standard 72
expanded 70, 71
intrinsic 66, 67
propagation 13, 71, 72
standard 70–72
target 75
uncertainty approach, *see* metrology, uncertainty approach
underdetermination of theory by evidence 275, 288, 289
unemployment 10, 106, 107, 130, 141, 142, 149, 209, 211
uniqueness theorem 26, 286–290
unobservable, *see* non-observable

validity of a measure 413, 416, 417, 419, 422
vector autoregression (VAR) approach 258–260, 262, 264, 274–277, 279, 280
vector autoregressive (VAR) model, *see* model, vector autoregressive
visual model, *see* model, visual
visual representation, *see* representation, visual

Walrasian system 254
weak axiom of revealed preference, *see* index formula, axiom, weak axiom of revealed preference
weak monotonicity axiom, *see* index formula, axiom, weak monotonicity
wealth effect 92
weighted average 16, 110, 113, 116
welfare 218, 221
function 202, 203, 218, 222
indicator 190, 221, 222
willingness-to-pay (WTP) 360–362

Printed and bound by CPI Group (UK) Ltd, Croydon, CR0 4YY

16/09/2026

14963399-0002